Principles of International Economics

Principles of International Economics

Miltiades Chacholiades
Research Professor of Economics
Georgia State University

McGraw-Hill Book Company

New York   St. Louis   San Francisco   Auckland   Bogotá   Hamburg
Johannesburg   London   Madrid   Mexico   Montreal   New Delhi
Panama   Paris   São Paulo   Singapore   Sydney   Tokyo   Toronto

This book was set in Times Roman by A Graphic Method Inc.
The editors were Bonnie E. Lieberman and M. Susan Norton;
the production supervisor was Donna Piligra.
The cover was designed by Mark Weiboldt.
The drawings were done by VIP Graphics.
Fairfield Graphics was printer and binder.

PRINCIPLES OF INTERNATIONAL ECONOMICS

234567890 FGFG 8987654321

Library of Congress Cataloging in Publication Data

Chacholiades, Miltiades.
    Principles of international economics.

    Includes bibliographies and index.
    1. International economic relations.
2. Commercial policy. I. Title.
HF1411.C412   337   80-18137
ISBN 0-07-010345-3

To my mother

Contents

1

CAUSES AND EFFECTS OF TRADE

2

COMMERCIAL POLICY

3

THE INTERNATIONAL ADJUSTMENT PROCESS

4

ADJUSTMENT POLICIES

Preface

The main objective of this book is to present those principles of international economics that are necessary for an understanding of the world economy. During the last few years, the international economy has undergone dramatic changes, such as the creation of OPEC and the substitution of flexible exchange rates for the adjustable peg. This book elucidates these changes and provides the necessary tools for the analysis of future changes.

This book is primarily addressed to undergraduate students with a major interest in international relations. However, it is flexible enough to serve the needs of readers with broader interests. Except for the *optional* appendix to Chapter 15, which uses some differential calculus, the exposition relies on simple geometry and high school algebra. The only prerequisites for this book are an introductory course in economics and the desire to learn. Readers with broader interests can safely omit all appendixes and optional sections (which are clearly indicated in the text).

The book is divided into four parts. Parts 1 (Chapters 2–7) and 2 (Chapters 8–11) deal with the microeconomic aspects of international economics (usually referred to as international trade theory and policy). Parts 3 (Chapters 12–17) and 4 (Chapters 18–22) deal with the macroeconomic aspects of international economics (known as international monetary theory and policy, or international finance).

For the benefit of the reader, each chapter concludes with a brief summary plus a short list of suggested additional readings.

Ideally, the book can serve the needs of a two-semester course, with Parts 1 and 2 covered in the first semester and Parts 3 and 4 covered in the second semester. However, the book is quite flexible and can be used in several different ways. For instance, a course in international finance could cover Parts 3 and 4 only (and perhaps Chapter 2, depending on the tastes of the instructor), without prior knowledge of Parts 1 and 2. Similarly, a one-semester course in international economics could cover Chapters 2–5, 8, 12, 13, 15–18, and 20–21, omitting all optional sections and appendixes.

I would like to thank Alan V. Deardorff, Heidemarie Sherman, Martin Bronfenbrenner, Loraine Donaldson, Klaus Friedrich, and Richard Anderson, who read the entire manuscript and offered numerous suggestions for improvement. I also wish to thank my colleague John Klein, who commented on several chapters of Parts 3 and 4; and Wilfred Ethier, Ian Giddy, and Ingo Walter, who reviewed the manuscript in its early stages. Needless to say, any remaining deficiencies are all mine.

I also wish to thank the Economics Editor of the McGraw-Hill Book Company, Bonnie E. Lieberman, for her assistance in preparing the manuscript and for expediting the publication process. Further, I want to thank Tom Marks, who served as my research assistant. In addition, thanks are due to Marilyn King, who typed the entire manuscript; and to Michel Ellen Cook, June Shipley, and George Bechtold, who assisted her. Above all, I wish to thank my wife and my children (Lea, Marina, and Linda) not only for proofreading the entire manuscript but also for their understanding during the time I spent writing the book.

Miltiades Chacholiades

Chapter One

Introduction

This introductory chapter deals briefly with the distinction between microeconomics and macroeconomics, as well as between positive economics and welfare economics; the relationship between international economics and general economic theory; the role of trade in raising the standards of living of all countries of the world; the role of international monetary relations; and the overall organizational structure of the book.

1-1 MICROECONOMICS VERSUS MACROECONOMICS

Economics is a social science. Broadly speaking, it is concerned with the use of scarce resources (for example, different kinds of labor skills, land of various qualities, and the capital goods that modern technology produces) for the satisfaction of human wants.

Like most disciplines, economics is divided into several branches and subbranches. Its two major branches are *microeconomics* and *macroeconomics*. Microeconomics is concerned with the behavior of individuals and well-defined groups of individuals, or microunits, such as households, firms, and industries. Macroeconomics, on the other hand, deals with broad aggregates, such as national income, employment, consumption, and investment.

In a sense, the micro-macro distinction is artificial, because the actual decisions about production, consumption, investment, employment, and so on are made by the microunits of the economy. Therefore, the basic principles of economic theory are those which explain the behavior of the microunits. However, the distinction is justified by the basic differences in the objectives and methods of the two branches.

Microeconomics deals primarily with the analysis of price determination and the allocation of specific resources to particular uses. Macroeconomics, on the other hand, deals with the determination of the levels of national income, aggregate consumption, aggregate investment, and aggregate resource employment.

While microeconomics deals with individual prices (for example, the price of beef, the price of corn, and the price of wine) and their relationship to one another, macroeconomics deals with aggregate price indices (for example, the consumer price index and the wholesale price index). As a result, the relationship between individual units and aggregates is not clear in macroeconomics. Nevertheless, the simplifications introduced by aggregation are helpful.

Despite its great usefulness in explaining how the individual decision-making units of the economy fit together to form a coherent whole, microeconomics is severely limited by its enormous complexity and confusing detail when it comes to explaining aggregate behavior. This problem is very much like the problem experienced by a person driving from Los Angeles to New York using a road map that shows every little street along the way.

Macroeconomics offers a practical approach to aggregate economic behavior; it attempts to describe the behavior of the economic system in terms of a few simple aggregates. Surely it is much easier to study the overall performance of an economic system in such terms as national income, aggregate investment, and aggregate consumption than it is to study the behavior of each individual consumer and producer. To pursue our earlier analogy, the driver from Los Angeles to New York could greatly benefit from a road map that shows only the major highways, not a lot of unnecessary detail.

When properly understood, microeconomics and macroeconomics become complementary, rather than competitive, branches of economic theory. Thus, macroeconomics can enable policymakers to pursue appropriate strategies to ensure an economic environment that validates the verities of microeconomics. Similarly, microeconomics can often be a fruitful source of hypotheses that can be used, with suitable modifications, to explain aggregate behavior.

1-2 POSITIVE ECONOMICS VERSUS WELFARE ECONOMICS

Economics is also divided into *positive economics* and *welfare economics*. Positive economics is concerned with what actually *is*. Welfare economics, on the other hand, deals with what *ought to be*.

In particular, positive economics is concerned with the problem of how the economic system actually functions, why it produces the results it does, and how changes in the fundamental data of the economy (such as factor endowments, factor ownership, tastes, and technology) affect the solution of the economic problem. In principle, positive economics is independent of ethical judgments, and its propositions can be tested against the facts of the real world that they purport to explain.

In contrast, welfare economics deals with propositions that are themselves logical deductions from a set of assumptions which may or may not be ethical in nature. In contrast with those of positive economics, the propositions of welfare economics cannot be tested against the facts of the real world. The reason is simple: Welfare is not an observable quantity. Usually welfare propositions are tested indirectly by testing the assumptions from which they are derived —and this is an extremely delicate task.

The conclusions of welfare economics depend crucially on ethical judgments. Indeed, most disagreements among economists in the area of economic policy can be traced to some difference in ethical beliefs, not positive economics. Unfortunately, in public debate over economic policy, such differences in ethical beliefs are not always made explicit.

1-3 THE SCOPE OF INTERNATIONAL ECONOMICS

While general economic theory deals with the problems of a single closed economy, international economics deals with the problems of two or more open economies. In particular, international economics deals with the same problems as general economic theory, but it deals with them in their international setting. Thus, international economics studies how a number of distinct economies interact with each other in the process of allocating scarce resources to satisfy human wants. (This will be explained in Chapter 2.)

Clearly, international economics is more general than the economics of a closed economy, the latter being a special case of international economics (the number of trading countries reduced from many to one). Further, the study of general economic theory dealing with the problems of a closed economy is only a first (but necessary) step toward the study of the behavior of a real economy. Surely, there is no closed economy in the real world except the world economy.

Parallel to the dividing of economic theory into microeconomics and macroeconomics is the breaking down of international economics into two major branches: (1) international trade theory and policy and (2) international monetary theory and policy. The former is a long-run static-equilibrium theory of barter in which the short-run monetary-adjustment process is assumed completed, with money assuming its true, classical role as a veil. Its approach is basically microeconomic in nature. The latter is centered upon the monetary aspects of international monetary relations. Its approach is mainly macroeconomic in nature, and it deals particularly with the short-run problems of balance-of-payments disequilibrium and adjustment.

1-4 THE ROLE OF TRADE

The importance of trade springs from the extensive degree of specialization that exists in the twentieth-century societies. Indeed, even in the most primitive societies, people cooperate in the use of their scarce resources. The reason is obvious: Through such cooperation more goods are produced.

In other words, the high degree of specialization that exists in our society is due to the fact that specialization increases the standard of living by making more goods and services available for consumption.

Nevertheless, *specialization necessarily implies trade and cannot occur without it*. This follows from the fact that people usually want to have a "balanced diet." The specialized producer uses only a small part—maybe none—of the product for his or her personal consumption and exchanges the surplus for the goods and services of other specialized producers.

For instance, a shoemaker does not, and cannot, consume only shoes; he needs, in addition, many other goods and services, such as food, clothing, shelter, entertainment, and transportation. To obtain these other goods and services, the shoemaker exchanges his surplus production of shoes (which, for practical purposes, may be identified with his total output of shoes) for the specialized outputs of farmers, auto producers, physicians, tailors, builders, and the like. Such an exchange of goods and services among specialized producers is exactly what is meant by trade.

The exchange of goods and services among residents of the same country is usually called *domestic trade*. This book, however, is concerned with *international trade,* that is, the exchange of goods and services among residents of different countries.

For simplicity, in this book we shall speak of countries as economic units. It is important to remember, however, that it is the individuals who carry out the transactions.

Countries cannot live alone any more effectively than individuals can. Thus, each country tends to specialize in the production of those commodities it can produce more cheaply than other countries, and then exchanges its surplus for the surpluses of other countries. This process brings about an international division of labor that makes it possible for all nations to consume more of all goods and services.

Incidentally, the commodities a country imports can be divided into two categories: (1) those commodities which other countries produce more cheaply than the importing country and (2) those commodities which the importing country cannot produce at all. For instance, the United States may import textiles from Taiwan because Taiwan produces textiles more cheaply than the United States, not because the United States cannot produce textiles domestically. On the other hand, Japan may have to import oil from Saudi Arabia simply because Japan does not have any oil fields.

In the same way that the division of labor (specialization) within a single closed economy increases the standard of living of all its residents, the international division of labor (specialization among nations) increases the standard of living of all countries. Further, in the same way that specialization within a single closed economy necessarily implies domestic trade and cannot occur without it, international specialization necessarily implies international trade and cannot occur without it.

Given the preceding discussion on the mutual gains from trade, one would expect the flow of commodity trade across national frontiers to be free from government interference. Yet for hundreds of years the nations of the world have impeded the free flow of international trade by means of tariffs, quotas, technical or administrative rules and procedures, and exchange control. In general, these policies are influenced by political, sociological, and economic considerations, and they reduce world efficiency and welfare. In this book, we shall explore in detail the nature and economic effects of such barriers to free trade as well as the motives behind them.

Being aware of the existence and importance of the gains from trade, nations often move to liberalize international trade. Basically, there are two approaches to international trade liberalization: the international approach and the regional approach. The former involves international conferences under the aegis of the General Agreement on Tariffs and Trade (GATT), such as the Kennedy Round and the Tokyo Round of multilateral trade negotiations, whose purpose is to reduce tariffs and nontariff barriers to international trade. The latter involves agreements among small numbers of nations, such as the European Economic Community, whose purpose is to promote free trade among themselves while maintaining barriers to trade with the rest of the world.

1-5 THE ROLE OF INTERNATIONAL MONETARY RELATIONS

Although in the long run money is a mere veil, its short-run significance is unquestionable. Indeed, economies, including the world economy, live only in the short run. The long run is an ideal that is almost never attained.

International monetary theory and policy (or international finance) deals with the foreign exchange market and the balance of payments. In particular, it deals with the short-run adjustment processes and the difficulties that the world economy faces in attaining international equilibrium. In addition, international finance deals with the economic policies that may be necessary for the achievement of international equilibrium when the automatic processes are too slow or are not working properly.

The importance of a smoothly functioning international monetary system cannot be underestimated. The main function of the international monetary system is to enable the fundamental economic processes of production and distribution to operate as smoothly and efficiently as possible, to maximize, so to speak, the gains from trade by permitting the fullest use of efficient division of labor among the nations of the world.

Adam Smith called the international monetary system the "great wheel."

When the wheel turns effortlessly, international specialization produces a maximum flow of goods and services that go to satisfy human wants in every corner of the globe. But when the wheel turns badly, the international flow of goods and services is interrupted, with serious consequences to the economic welfare of nations.

As it turns out, when the short-run processes work smoothly and the wheel turns effortlessly, international monetary relations do not make the headlines. Rather, they become inconspicuous and are taken for granted. On the other hand, people become aware of the significance of international monetary relations during international monetary crises (that is, when the wheel turns badly).

Indeed, when the short-run processes do not work smoothly, those countries suffering from serious balance-of-payments problems (particularly deficits) often attempt to solve their problems by imposing trade restrictions. Unfortunately, such restrictions on international trade reverse the beneficial division of labor among countries and deny the world the gains from international specialization and exchange.

1-6 THE PLAN OF THE BOOK

This book deals with both branches of international economics, namely, international trade theory and policy and international finance. Its main concern is with the basic theoretical principles of international economics, the available empirical evidence, and, finally, the question of international economic policy. It is divided into four parts: causes and effects of trade (Part 1); commercial policy (Part 2); the international adjustment process (Part 3); and adjustment policies (Part 4).

Causes and Effects of Trade

The first part of the book (Chapters 2 through 7) deals with the causes and effects of trade. In particular, Chapter 2 examines the classical law of comparative advantage in the context of the simple labor theory of value and generalizes the results by introducing the concept of opportunity cost. Although simple and straightforward, this is an important chapter, and the student must study it carefully before proceeding to the rest of the book.

Chapter 3 deals with the fundamental concepts of opportunity cost and social indifference—the twin concepts that form the basis of the neoclassical theory of international values. The reader who is not interested in these tools may omit most of this chapter: Sections 3-2, 3-5, and 3-6, as well as the Appendix to Chapter 3, are all optional, especially for a one-semester course.

The important topic of international equilibrium and its properties is examined in Chapter 4. In a sense, the discussion in this chapter generalizes the results of Chapter 2. This chapter introduces the offer curve, a tool that is extremely important in the demonstration of international equilibrium. The Appendix to Chapter 4, which deals with James Meade's ingenious geometric technique, may be safely omitted.

Chapter 5 deals with the Heckscher-Ohlin model, the gist of which can be summarized by two propositions: (1) the cause of international trade is to be found largely in differences between the factor endowments of different countries (Heckscher-Ohlin theorem), and (2) the effect of international trade is to tend to equalize factor prices between countries, and thus serve to some extent as a substitute for factor mobility (factor-price equalization theorem). The Heckscher-Ohlin model is important not only to international economics but to other fields as well (such as the theory of growth and the theory of distribution). The analysis of Chapter 5 is cast in rather simple terms so that students can easily understand it. The Appendix to Chapter 5 may be omitted.

The empirical verification of international trade models is the subject of Chapter 6. In particular, Part A deals with the empirical testing of the Ricardian model of Chapter 2, and Part B deals with the empirical testing of the Heckscher-Ohlin model, and specifically the Leontief paradox. Part C and the Appendix to Chapter 6 deal with the phenomenon of factor-intensity reversals. The appendix may be omitted.

Finally, Chapter 7 deals with the comparative-static analysis of the effects of factor-endowment growth and technical progress on the growing open economy's production, consumption, terms of trade, and social welfare. Even though the subject matter of this chapter is important, it may be omitted, especially in a one-semester course.

Commercial Policy

The second part of the book (Chapters 8 through 11) deals with commercial policy. In particular, Chapter 8 examines the effects of the most common instrument of commercial policy, the tariff on an imported good. Chapter 9 considers the theory of domestic distortions, the infant-industry argument for protection, and several other arguments for protection.

The effects of other nontariff barriers to international trade are studied in Chapter 10. In particular, after a brief discussion of export taxes as well as export and import subsidies, this chapter discusses the effects of quantitative restrictions (or quotas), international cartels, dumping, and other nontariff barriers. Chapter 10 also provides some highlights of the U.S. tariff history and some discussion of the trade negotiations that have taken place during the postwar era under the aegis of GATT.

Finally, Chapter 11 deals exclusively with the regional approach to international trade liberalization. Specifically, this chapter examines the partial equilibrium approach to preferential trading.

The International Adjustment Process

The third part of the book (Chapters 12 through 17) deals with the international adjustment process.

The foreign exchange market and the balance of payments are examined in Chapters 12 and 13, respectively. These concepts are indispensable for preparing to deal with the great issues of international finance. In particular, Chapter 12 examines the nature, organization, and functions of the foreign exchange market; the forward market and its relationship to the spot market; and finally the Eurodollar market. Chapter 13, on the other hand, deals with the basic principles of balance-of-payments accounting and the concept of balance-of-payments equilibrium, including some discussion of various well-known accounting balances, such as the merchandise balance, the balance on goods and services, the current account balance, the basic balance, the liquidity balance, and the official settlements balance.

Chapter 14 draws on concepts developed in the first part of the book (especially Chapters 2 through 4) to develop a rather simplified model that illustrates well most issues of international finance. In this sense, this chapter serves as a general introduction to the rest of the book.

Chapters 15 and 16 study two important adjustment mechanisms: the price-adjustment mechanism (Chapter 15) and the income-adjustment mechanism (Chapter 16). In particular, Chapter 15 develops the partial-equilibrium model and studies the effects of exchange-rate adjustments on the balance of payments (and the terms of trade). In addition, it considers the special problems of nontraded goods, the price-specie-flow mechanism, and the purchasing-power-parity theory, as well as the econometric difficulties in estimating import-demand elasticities. The Appendix to Chapter 15 may be omitted. Chapter 16, on the other hand, examines the national-income multiplier theory and the balance-of-trade multiplier theory.

Finally, Chapter 17 introduces money systematically into the adjustment process and studies the mutual interaction that exists between money and the balance of payments. This chapter develops the IS-LM model, properly modified to suit the needs of an open economy. (This model is used extensively in Part 4 of the book.) In addition, Chapter 17 provides some insights into the new monetary approach to the balance of payments.

Adjustment Policies

The last part of the book deals with the problem of international economic policy. Chapter 18 considers some general principles that can serve as a guide in the formulation of economic policy; the important distinction between temporary and fundamental balance-of-payments equilibria; the proper meaning of the term *internal balance* in the light of the recent discussions of the Phillips curve; and how expenditure-adjusting policies can be combined with expenditure-switching policies in order to achieve internal and external balance.

Chapter 19 discusses the effects of direct controls (that is, selective expenditure-switching policies whose aim is to control particular elements in the balance of payments) and their desirability. This chapter may be omitted, especially in a one-semester course.

Chapter 20 deals with the Mundellian approach to internal and external balance (that is, the appropriate use of fiscal and monetary policy), the assignment problem, and the drawbacks of the fiscal-monetary mix.

The economics of the flexible-exchange-rate system are examined in Chapter 21. In particular, this chapter deals with the theory of employment under flexible exchange rates and the question of insulation, the difficulties of stabilization policy, the problem of whether the fixed or flexible exchange-rate system shields better the open economy against the vagaries of economic disturbances, and some important arguments in the continuing debate over fixed and flexible exchange rates.

The book concludes with Chapter 22, which considers the special problems that arise in connection with the international monetary system. In particular, Chapter 22 examines the characteristics of a good international monetary system; the important concepts of adjustment, liquidity, and confidence; and the actual systems that have existed over the last century or so, such as the gold standard, the interwar attempts to restore the gold standard, the Bretton Woods system, the present system of managed flexibility, and the new European Monetary System.

Part One

Causes and Effects of Trade

Chapter Two

The Law of Comparative Advantage

Without doubt, the *law of comparative advantage,* or *comparative cost,* must be singled out as one of the greatest achievements of the classical school of economic thought. The message of this fundamental law is very simple: *The countries of the world can benefit from international specialization and free trade.* Equally simple is the model used to obtain this important result.

In addition to being aesthetically pleasing, the closely reasoned doctrine of comparative advantage is so powerful that it quickly exposes the many fallacies that are contained in the propaganda for protection. Any interference with free trade can be shown to be harmful to the welfare of the world. This chapter deals exclusively with the often-misunderstood law of comparative advantage.

2-1 THREE BASIC QUESTIONS

The law of comparative advantage is the central pillar of what Alfred Marshall called the *pure theory of international trade.* Marshall used the adjective "pure" to indicate a theory that deals with "real," as opposed to "monetary," factors. Thus, the pure theory of international trade is a long-run theory that penetrates the "veil of money" and concentrates on the real factors which determine the observed international specialization and trade (such as the availability and quality of resources, production techniques, and tastes) and which enhance the welfare of the world.

The pure theory of international trade, as expounded by the classical economists Robert Torrens (1808, 1815), David Ricardo (1821), and John Stuart Mill (1902), is mainly concerned with the following three important questions:

1 *What are the gains from trade?* In other words, do countries benefit from international trade? Where do the gains from trade come from, and how are they divided among the trading countries? To put it differently, what are the costs of protection? How high is the cost of complete self-sufficiency?

2 *What is the structure (or direction or pattern) of trade?* In other words, which goods are exported, and which are imported, by each trading country? What are the fundamental laws that govern the international allocation of resources and the flow of trade?

3 *What are the terms of trade?* In other words, at what prices are the exported and imported goods exchanged?

The above questions are basic to the theory of international trade and form the foundation for most of the discussion of Part 1 of this book. Before we get down to specifics, it is interesting to see how the classical economists answer these three questions in a rather general fashion.

According to the classical theory, each country specializes in the production of those goods which can be produced *at a lower cost relative to other countries.* For instance, if America can produce food at a lower cost than Britain, whereas Britain can produce clothing at a lower cost than America, then America should (and will) specialize in the production of food, while Britain should (and will) specialize in the production of clothing. Later on, America should export her surplus (that is, the excess of American production over American consumption) of food to Britain in exchange for Britain's surplus of clothing. Such *international division of labor* leads to increased output of both food and clothing, with the result that more is available to each country for consumption than would be the case in an autarkic situation (that is, a situation in which there is no trade among countries, and each country is completely self-sufficient or closed). The gains from trade are reflected in the increased consumption made possible by the preceding pattern of international specialization and exchange. The division of the gains from trade between America and Britain depends on the terms of trade, that is, the number of units of, say, clothing, that exchange in the international market for 1 unit of food. The terms of trade are determined by international supply and demand conditions.

2-2 THE LABOR THEORY OF VALUE: A DIGRESSION

The classical economists adopted the simplifying assumption of the *labor theory of value.* This theory asserts that labor is the only factor of production and that *in a closed economy* the prices of commodities are determined by their labor content. In particular, according to the labor theory of value, goods are exchanged according to the relative amounts of labor they represent.

Adam Smith (1937, p. 47) illustrates the proposition that goods exchange for one another according to the relative amounts of labor they embody by means of the following well-known example of hunting:

> If among a nation of hunters, for example, it usually costs twice the labor to kill a beaver which it does to kill a deer, one beaver should naturally exchange for or be worth two deer.

To see why this should be so, assume that the current market exchange ratio is 1:1, that is, one beaver for one deer. Under these circumstances, the hunting of beaver will cease, since it is cheaper (in terms of hours spent) to first kill deer and then exchange it in the market for beaver. Accordingly, the supply of deer will increase while the supply of beaver will fall, until the equilibrium exchange ratio of 1 beaver:2 deer is established.

It is generally agreed that the labor theory of value is an oversimplification of reality. In particular, for the labor theory of value to hold, labor must be the only factor of production, and it must be homogeneous (that is, all labor must be of the same quality); in addition, every occupation must be open to all, and perfect competition must rule everywhere. However, labor is neither homogeneous nor the sole factor of production. Further, labor mobility is tempered by institutional, sociological, and personal considerations; and elements of monopoly, oligopoly, monopsony, and monopolistic competition are pervasive in modern societies.

Labor consists of numerous qualitatively different subgroups, which John Eliot Cairnes (1874) called "noncompeting groups." At any particular time, these groups are not substitutable, although in the long run substitution is possible. For instance, if the demand for medical services increases while the demand for servicing automobiles decreases, it would hardly be conceivable to expect auto mechanics to assume the role of physicians; the wage rates of the two groups, at least in the short run, would tend to move in opposite directions.

Even if labor were indeed homogeneous and commanded a single wage rate in a perfectly competitive market, there remains the more fundamental objection that labor is not the only factor of production: Goods are usually produced by various combinations of land, labor, and capital. This makes it impossible to use the labor theory of value, however qualified.

Incidentally, the element of time is a difficulty that the labor theory of value cannot surmount. With a positive rate of interest, a commodity's average cost of production, and hence its price, is influenced not only by the amount of labor required for the production of 1 unit of the commodity but also by the length of time during which that labor is embodied (or invested) in production, as in the aging of wine.

Despite the obvious shortcomings of the labor theory of value, we shall adopt it as our point of departure for two reasons. First, it will enable us, with relatively little effort, to bring out quite sharply the nature of the problem of international specialization and the gains from trade. Second, when we later dispense with the simplified world of the labor theory of value, we shall not have to give up the results obtained from it.

2-3 ABSOLUTE ADVANTAGE

Adam Smith (1937) emphasized the importance of free trade in increasing the wealth of all trading nations. He declared that "it is the maxim of every prudent master of a family, never to attempt to make at home what it will cost him more to make than to buy." He later stated (pp. 424–426):

> What is prudence in the conduct of every private family, can scarce be folly in that of a great kingdom. If a foreign country can supply us with a commodity cheaper than we ourselves make it, better buy it of them with some part of the produce of our own industry, employed in a way in which we have some advantage. . . . By means of glasses, hotbeds, and hotwalls, very good grapes can be raised in Scotland, and very good wine too can be made of them at about thirty times the expense for which at least equally good can be bought from foreign countries. Would it be a reasonable law to prohibit the importation of all foreign wines, merely to encourage the making of claret and burgundy in Scotland? . . . As long as the one country has those advantages, and the other wants them, it will always be more advantageous for the latter, rather to buy of the former than to make.

Illustration of Absolute Advantage

Adam Smith's principle of *absolute advantage* can be easily clarified by means of a simple illustration. Consider two countries, America and Britain, endowed with homogeneous labor and producing two commodities, food and clothing. Suppose that in America the production of each unit of food requires 8 units of labor, while the production of each unit of clothing requires 4 units of labor. In Britain each unit of food requires 10 units of labor, while each unit of clothing requires 2 units of labor. All this information is summarized in Table 2-1.

In this illustration, America is more efficient in the production of food, while Britain is more efficient in the production of clothing. In particular, 1 unit of food requires more units of labor in Britain than in America (10 > 8). Similarly, 1 unit of clothing requires more units of labor in America than in Britain (4 > 2). This state of affairs is usually expressed as follows: *America has an absolute advantage in the production of food, and Britain has an absolute advantage in the production of clothing*. We speak of an *absolute* ad-

Table 2-1 Absolute Advantage

	America	Britain
Labor requirements per unit of:		
Food	8	10
Clothing	4	2

vantage because each country can produce one commodity at an absolutely lower cost—measured in labor units—than the other country.

Autarkic Prices

In the absence of international trade, 1 unit of food will exchange for 2 units of clothing in America, since in America the amount of labor needed to produce 1 unit of food is two times as high as the amount of labor needed to produce 1 unit of clothing (that is, 8 is twice as large as 4). Similarly, in Britain, 1 unit of food will exchange for 5 units of clothing, since in Britain the amount of labor needed for the production of 1 unit of food is five times as high as the amount of labor needed to produce 1 unit of clothing (that is, 10 is five times as large as 2).

The Gains from Trade

Is international trade profitable between America and Britain? Adam Smith would answer "yes." Adam Smith would also go on to say that it would be to the advantage of both countries for America to specialize in the production of food and Britain in the production of clothing. How is Adam Smith's proposition proved?

One way to prove it is to consider some arbitrary reallocation of labor in America and Britain. Thus, starting with their autarkic general-equilibrium states, let America transfer 16 units of labor from the production of clothing to the production of food, and let Britain transfer 10 units of labor from the production of food to the production of clothing. Obviously, in America the production of food increases by 2 units (that is, $^{16}/_8$), while the production of clothing falls by 4 units (that is, $^{16}/_4$). Similarly, in Britain the production of food falls by 1 unit (that is, $^{10}/_{10}$), while the production of clothing increases by 5 units (that is, $^{10}/_2$). What is the net effect on the world outputs of food and clothing? They both increase! Specifically, the world output of food increases by 1 unit, since it increases by 2 units in America and falls by only 1 unit in Britain. Similarly, the world output of clothing increases by 1 unit, since it increases by 5 units in Britain and falls by 4 units in America.

There is another illuminating way of proving Adam Smith's proposition. As we have seen, in the autarkic general-equilibrium state, 1 unit of food exchanges for 2 units of clothing in America but for 5 units of clothing in Britain. Now allow America and Britain to trade food and clothing *at terms that lie in between their respective autarkic prices*. In particular, suppose that in the international market 1 unit of food can be traded for 4 units of clothing. Now both countries can benefit from international trade if they specialize according to Adam Smith's advice, that is, if each country specializes in that commodity in whose production she has an absolute advantage.

Consider America first. The production of 1 unit of clothing costs America 4 units of labor. On the other hand, America can obtain clothing by *importing* it from Britain. What is America's cost for importing 1 unit of clothing from Britain? Well, America must *export* to Britain $^1/_4$ of 1 unit of food, since by assumption 1 unit of food exchanges for 4 units of clothing. How much labor does

America need to produce $^1/_4$ of 1 unit of food? Only 2 units of labor (that is, $8 \times {}^1/_4$). We conclude, therefore, that while the *direct* cost of production of 1 unit of clothing in America is 4 units of labor, America can obtain 1 unit of clothing *indirectly* by using only 2 units of labor to produce $^1/_4$ of 1 unit of food and then exchanging it in the international market for 1 unit of clothing. Obviously America benefits from international trade, since now each unit of clothing costs America only 2 units of labor instead of 4. Accordingly, international trade enables America to increase her consumption of all commodities.

Are America's gains from trade Britain's losses? No, they are not. Consider Britain's position. Britain has an absolute advantage in the production of clothing but an absolute disadvantage in the production of food. Hence, Britain can benefit from international trade by specializing in the production of clothing and by importing food from America. In particular, for each unit of food Britain imports from America, Britain must export 4 units of clothing. Since each unit of clothing requires 2 units of labor in Britain, it follows that each unit of imported food costs Britain 8 units of labor (that is, 4×2). Compare this indirect cost of food (that is, 8 units of labor per unit of food) with the direct cost of production of food in Britain, which is 10 units of labor per unit of food. Evidently, Britain benefits from international trade, since she saves 2 units of labor (that is, $10 - 8$) per unit of food that she imports from America. Accordingly, Britain gains from international trade. In particular, international trade enables Britain to consume more of every commodity. To put it another way, Britain can consume as much as she would in autarky but enjoy more leisure; that is, with trade, Britain, and America of course, can consume the same quantities of commodities as in autarky but with a smaller expenditure of resources.

The alert reader will think of the analogy between international trade and technical progress. In the same way that technical progress makes possible the production of commodities using fewer resources, international trade enables countries to obtain commodities at lower prices. The indirect acquisition of commodities through international trade is tantamount to the discovery of more efficient production techniques. For instance, assuming that the terms of trade are 4:1, as before, we could say that trade acts like a new technique, whereby 1 unit of food can be transformed into 4 units of clothing and vice versa.

The present discussion of the gains from trade will be clarified further in the rest of this chapter.

Money Prices and Money-Wage Rates

The preceding analysis shows that if each country specializes in that commodity in whose production she has an absolute advantage, the world output of every commodity will increase. Are there economic forces, however, that can be counted on to bring about this international division of labor? Indeed there are, and we must now show how perfect competition actually leads to the desirable pattern of international specialization. This is easily accomplished by first converting labor costs into money costs.

Suppose that America's currency is the dollar and Britain's the pound. Assume that America's money-wage rate is $10, while Britain's is £5. Combining this information with the labor requirements per unit of food and clothing in America and Britain (see Table 2-1), we can easily determine the cost of production of food and clothing in monetary terms. Thus, the cost of food in America is $80 (that is, 8 × $10); the cost of clothing in America is $40 (that is, 4 × $10); the cost of food in Britain is £50 (that is, 10 × £5); and, finally, the cost of clothing in Britain is £10 (that is, 2 × £5). All this information is summarized in columns (1) and (3) of Table 2-2.

Is food cheaper in America or Britain? Is clothing cheaper in America or Britain? We do not know yet. To answer these questions, we must express all prices in terms of the *same* currency. To do so, we must have an exchange rate between the two currencies. How many dollars exchange for 1 pound? At the moment, we cannot determine precisely what this *rate of exchange* is, although, as we shall see, we can specify certain limits for it. To illustrate how the rate of exchange presently works, assume for the moment that £1 = $2, that is, 1 pound is equivalent to 2 dollars.

Column (2) of Table 2-2 gives the American cost of food and clothing in pounds on the assumption that £1 = $2. Similarly, column (4) of Table 2-2 gives the British cost of food and clothing in dollars, again on the assumption that £1 = $2. Whether we compare prices in dollars or pounds, it is evident from Table 2-2 that food is cheaper in America ($80 < $100, or £40 < £50) and, therefore, that America will stop the production of clothing and specialize in the production of food. Similarly, clothing is cheaper in Britain (£10 < £20, or $20 < $40) and, therefore, Britain will stop the production of food and specialize in the production of clothing. In addition, both in dollars and pounds, the price of food in the international market is four times as high as the price of clothing (that is, $80 = 4 × $20 and £40 = 4 × £10). Therefore, in the final analysis, 1 unit of food exchanges for 4 units of clothing, which is consistent with the assumption we made earlier during the discussion of the gains from trade. Accordingly, our earlier conclusions concerning the gains from trade are now confirmed.

Given that the money-wage rates in America and Britain are $10 and £5, respectively, the preceding pattern of specialization will come about as long as £1 exchanges for something between $1.60 and $4. The reader is urged to try

Table 2-2   Absolute Advantage: Money Prices
(Assumption: £1 = $2)

	America		Britain	
	Dollars (1)	Pounds (2)	Pounds (3)	Dollars (4)
Food	$80	£40	£50	$100
Clothing	$40	£20	£10	$ 20

various rates of exchange between $1.60 and $4 (say, $1.80, $2.50, $3.00, and $3.50) and to show that for all those rates America's cost of food is lower than Britain's and that Britain's cost of clothing is lower than America's.

Observe that in the present case of absolute advantage it is always true that the wage rate may be higher in either country. For instance, in our illustration, at the rate of £1 = $2, the wage rate is the same in America as it is in Britain. When £1 exchanges for less than $2—say, $1.80—the wage rate is higher in America. Finally, when £1 exchanges for more than $2—say, $3—the wage rate is higher in Britain.

When £1 exchanges for more than $4, both commodities are cheaper in America. For instance, at £1 = $5, Britain's costs of food and clothing are, respectively, $250 and $50, which are *higher* than America's corresponding costs of $80 and $40. Similarly, when £1 exchanges for less than $1.60, both commodities are cheaper in Britain. For instance, at £1 = $1, the British costs of food and clothing become, respectively, $40 and $20, which are now *lower* than America's corresponding costs. Thus, unless £1 exchanges for something between $1.60 and $4, one country will undersell the other in every line of production. How, then, can we be absolutely sure that international specialization will actually proceed as proposed by Adam Smith?

While it is possible for the rate of exchange to lie outside the admissible range of between $1.60 and $4, such a state of affairs cannot last for long. It is a short-run disequilibrium situation that will be corrected in one of two ways, depending on the institutional arrangement of the *foreign exchange market.* Thus, either the forces of supply and demand in the foreign exchange market will cause the rate of exchange to change until it is made to lie between $1.60 and $4, or the money-wage rates of America and Britain will be forced to change in such a way as to shift the admissible range of the rate of exchange to accommodate the current rate. For instance, suppose that £1 = $1 and Britain undersells America in both food and clothing. Since America will tend to import both food and clothing from Britain, there will be an excess demand for pounds (since British exporters must be paid in pounds, but American importers have dollars), which, under a flexible exchange-rate system, will cause the pound to become more expensive. Thus, assuming that the rate of foreign exchange is left free to be determined by supply and demand, the pound will soon exchange for more than $1.60.

Alternatively, if America and Britain agree to maintain the rate of exchange constant at, say, £1 = $1, as will be the case, for instance, under an international *gold standard,* America will be paying for its imports of both food and clothing by means of international reserves (in this case, gold). Assuming wage flexibility, this flow of gold will cause America's money supply and money-wage rate to fall and Britain's money supply and money-wage rate to rise. In particular, suppose that America's wage rate falls to $7, while Britain's wage rate rises to £7. America's cost of food falls to $56 (that is, 8 × $7), while Britain's cost of food rises to £70, which, at the rate £1 = $1, is equivalent to $70. Hence, it becomes profitable for America to export food to Britain. However, Britain continues to have a cost advantage in the production of clothing ($2 \times £7 = £14$, or \$14, versus $4 \times \$7 = \$28$).

The short-run adjustment mechanism is discussed more thoroughly later on in Parts 3 and 4 of the book. The purpose of the present discussion, which by necessity is oversimplified, is merely to show that our earlier conclusions based on barter economies are not inconsistent with the functioning of economies using money.

Absolute Advantage Is Not Needed for Profitable Trade

What is the fundamental reason for the existence of profitable trade? In particular, why is it that the world output of commodities increases in our illustration when America specializes in the production of food and Britain in the production of clothing? Adam Smith would hasten to point out that such international division of labor is profitable because America has an *absolute advantage* in the production of food and Britain an *absolute advantage* in the production of clothing. Even today many people fall into the trap of believing that exporters must have an absolute advantage over their foreign rivals. Although Adam Smith's answer does contain some element of truth, it is superficial and misleading, because it does not really go directly to the crux of the matter.

Suppose that America had an absolute advantage in both food and clothing. How should international specialization and trade be organized then? If we adhered strictly to Adam Smith's principle of absolute advantage, we would reach the absurd conclusion that America should produce both food and clothing and Britain nothing. This would make sense only if labor was free to migrate from Britain to America, either because Britain and America happen to be two regions of the same country or because both countries happen to be so liberal that they do not take measures to prevent the influx of foreigners. But what if America and Britain are indeed separate sovereign nations and labor cannot move between them? Is it not then reasonable to conclude that even the more inefficient country, Britain, must produce something?

It appears, then, that the fundamental reason for profitable trade is not to be found in the absolute differences in labor cost between America and Britain. In other words, it appears that *profitable international trade does not necessarily require an exporter to have an absolute advantage over foreign rivals.* But if this is so, what is the raison d'être for profitable international trade? The rest of this chapter is concerned primarily with this important question.

2-4 COMPARATIVE ADVANTAGE

In complete contrast with Adam Smith's world of absolute advantage is David Ricardo's world of comparative advantage. Ricardo considered as typical the case in which one country is more efficient than another in every line of production. Ricardo (as well as Robert Torrens) was able to show that, even under these circumstances, international trade is still profitable. He further explained that *international specialization must be based on comparative advantage.*

Illustration of Comparative Advantage

To gain further insight into Ricardo's world of comparative advantage, which incidentally includes Adam Smith's world of absolute advantage as a special case, return to the illustration of Table 2-1, and assume that America experiences a rapid pace of technical progress with the result that her unit-labor requirements for the production of food and clothing are reduced to 2 and 1, respectively. In other words, assume that both unit-labor requirements (or *labor coefficients of production*, as they are usually called) are reduced to 25 percent of their respective original values. This new state of affairs, which Ricardo considered typical, is summarized in Table 2-3.

In the new illustration of Table 2-3, America can produce both food and clothing with a smaller expenditure (cost) of labor than Britain (that is, 2 < 10 and 1 < 2). In other words, America has an absolute advantage in the production of both commodities. Surely if America and Britain were two regions of the same country, all workers would migrate to the more efficient region, America, and eventually all commodities would end up being produced in America, where costs are lower in an absolute sense. Nevertheless, Ricardo emphasized that the main distinguishing feature of international trade is the international immobility of labor coupled with its perfect mobility within countries. What happens in the presence of labor immobility between America and Britain? Is international trade still profitable?

Autarkic Prices

Before going any further, it is interesting to note that in the absence of international trade (that is, in autarky), 1 unit of food exchanges for 2 units of clothing in America—as in Adam Smith's example of absolute advantage. Of course, in Britain 1 unit of food continues to exchange for 5 units of clothing since, by assumption, Britain's labor coefficients of production are the same as in Table 2-1. The implications of relative prices are brought out in Section 2-5.

Arguments against Free Trade

It is also interesting at this point to note some of the arguments against free trade that could be advanced in both America and Britain.

In Britain some politicians and editorial writers might argue that America's efficiency is so great that she would undersell British producers in every line of production. How could the British producers, who are technologically inferior to their American counterparts, compete? To protect Britain's "honest"

Table 2-3 Comparative Advantage

	America	Britain
Labor requirements per unit of:		
Food	2	10
Clothing	1	2

workers from ruinous foreign competition, import tariffs are needed. It is often suggested that a "scientific" tariff that "equalizes costs of production" be imposed.[1]

On the other hand, American politicians and editorial writers might argue that because the British wage rate is so much lower than the American wage rate, the American real wage rate will be drastically reduced if the American workers are subjected to the competition of the British cheap labor. Accordingly, protective tariffs are needed to protect the American standard of living from the cheap foreign labor.

The greatest contribution of Ricardo and Torrens was to show that both of the preceding arguments are wrong. They are pseudo arguments that do not stand up to scientific scrutiny. Indeed, Ricardo and Torrens showed that the workers of both America and Britain can benefit from free international trade.

Definition of Comparative Advantage

Consider again Table 2-3. America has an absolute advantage in the production of both food and clothing, because $2 < 10$ and $1 < 2$. However, America's absolute advantage is greater in the production of food than in clothing, since $^2/_{10} < ^1/_2$. In other words, America's labor requirements for the production of food and clothing as a percentage of the corresponding British labor requirements are:

Food	Clothing
$^2/_{10}$ or 20 percent	$^1/_2$ or 50 percent

Hence, America's absolute advantage is greater in the production of food, since 20 percent $<$ 50 percent. Ricardo describes this state of affairs by saying that America has a *comparative advantage* (or *relative advantage*) in the production of food and a *comparative disadvantage* (or *relative disadvantage*) in the production of clothing.

Similarly, Britain has an *absolute disadvantage* in the production of both food and clothing, because $10 > 2$ and $2 > 1$. However, Britain's disadvantage is smaller in the production of clothing than in the production of food, since $^2/_1 < ^{10}/_2$. This is expressed by saying that Britain has a *comparative advantage* in the production of clothing and a *comparative disadvantage* in the production of food.

Comparative advantage, as opposed to absolute advantage, is a *relative* term. Essentially the same inequality is used to determine each country's comparative advantage. In other words, the inequality $^2/_{10} < ^1/_2$ (which is used to determine America's comparative advantage) is mathematically equivalent to the inequality $^2/_1 < ^{10}/_2$ (which is used to determine Britain's comparative advantage). Accordingly, when one country's comparative advantage is determined, the other country's comparative advantage is automatically decided

---

[1]The notion of the "scientific" tariff is actually embodied in the Tariff Act of 1922 and is retained in the Smoot-Hawley Act of 1930.

also. In addition, every country, whether technologically advanced or backward, has, by definition, a comparative advantage.

The Law of Comparative Advantage

Can international trade be profitable even when one country has an absolute advantage in the production of every commodity? The great classical achievement was to show that this is actually true. This important result is summarized by the law of comparative advantage.

Law of comparative advantage: When each country specializes in the production of that commodity in which she has a comparative advantage, the total world output of every commodity necessarily increases (potentially) with the result that all countries become better off (save the limiting case of a "large" country).[2]

How can we prove the law of comparative advantage? In exactly the same way that we proved Adam Smith's principle of absolute advantage. Thus, starting again from the isolated general equilibrium states of the two countries, let America transfer 4 units of labor from the production of clothing to the production of food. American food increases by 2 units, and American clothing falls by 4 units. (Incidentally, these are the precise changes in food and clothing that America experienced in our earlier example of absolute advantage! This must be so because America is four times more efficient now than before.) In addition, let Britain transfer, as in the case of absolute advantage, 10 units of labor from the production of food to the production of clothing. British food falls by 1 unit, and British clothing increases by 5 units. Thus both countries experience the same changes in food and clothing as in Adam Smith's case of absolute advantage. Accordingly, the world output of each commodity increases by 1 unit, *as in our earlier example of absolute advantage.*

We can also prove the validity of the law of comparative advantage in another way, as we did in the example of absolute advantage. Thus, before trade, 1 unit of food exchanges for 2 units of clothing in America but for 5 units of clothing in Britain (exactly the same as in our earlier example of absolute advantage). Now we can follow step by step the earlier discussion on absolute advantage to show that if America and Britain are allowed to trade food and clothing at terms which lie in between their respective autarkic prices—say, 1 unit of food for 4 units of clothing—then both countries can benefit by specializing according to the law of comparative advantage. Since this analysis is identical to that given earlier for the case of absolute advantage, the details are left as an exercise for the reader.

[2] When two trading countries are of unequal size, the equilibrium terms of trade could coincide with the large country's autarkic price ratio, since the large country may have to produce both commodities in order to satisfy world demand. For instance, if the world consisted of the United States and Cyprus, it would be impossible for Cyprus, with a presumed comparative advantage in wine, to satisfy the huge U.S. market. In this case, the United States would have to produce some wine; world prices would have to reflect American costs; and all the gains from trade would accrue to Cyprus (small country), with the United States (large country) gaining nothing.

"Equal" Advantage

Free international trade is profitable (that is, it increases potentially the world output of every commodity) if, and only if, there exists a difference in the relative labor requirements between countries. For instance, if America is more efficient than Britain in both food and clothing, but her degree of superiority is the same everywhere, then there is no basis for trade. For instance, return to Table 2-3 and increase America's labor coefficient in the production of food from 2 to 5 while holding all the other coefficients constant. In this case, there is no basis for mutually profitable trade, because America's relative superiority is the same in food as in clothing: $^5/_{10} = {}^1/_2$.

Money Prices and Money Wages

As with absolute advantage, the comparative differences in cost can be easily converted into absolute differences in money prices. Suppose that Britain's money wage rate is £5, as before, and that America's wage rate is $40 (that is, four times as high as before, since America is four times more efficient now). Under these circumstances, the cost of production of food and clothing in America and Britain is still given by Table 2-2; that is, it is the same as in Adam Smith's case of absolute advantage. As before, for any rate of exchange between £1 = $1.60 and £1 = $4, America's cost of food is lower than Britain's, and Britain's cost of clothing is lower than America's. Table 2-2 illustrates the case in which £1 = $2. Note also that the short-run adjustment mechanism which keeps the rate of exchange within its admissible range is exactly the same as before and requires no further discussion at this point.

There is one fundamental difference between absolute advantage and comparative advantage. We saw earlier that in the presence of absolute advantage the wage rate may be higher in either country. This is not the case with comparative advantage, because now we can easily show that *the more efficient country* (that is, the country which has an absolute advantage in every commodity) *must have a higher wage*. This is indeed verified in our example. Thus, while the American wage rate is $40, the upper limit for the British wage rate is only $20 (that is, 4×5, where 5 is the British wage rate and 4 the most favorable rate of exchange from Britain's point of view). This is an important conclusion, which must be kept in mind: *Wages are high where labor productivity is high.*

Concluding Remarks for the Arguments against Free Trade

The reader should reconsider now the earlier pseudo arguments against free trade. The argument that America cannot compete with Britain because of the British cheap labor is fallacious. We have seen that America can benefit from free trade by specializing in food, that is, the commodity in which she has a comparative advantage. The higher American wage rate stands on the firm foundation of higher American labor productivity, and the lower British wage rate is no threat to the American standard of living. In particular, we saw in our example that, provided £1 exchanges for something between $1.60 and $4, food is always cheaper in America even though the American wage is at least twice as high as the British wage rate. Moreover, with specialization and free trade, American workers can consume more of everything.

The other argument, that Britain must protect her "honest" workers from American competition because America is so technologically advanced that she will undersell Britain in every line of production, is equally fallacious. We have seen that *every country has, by definition, a comparative advantage*. Erecting tariff walls, whether "scientific" or otherwise, and interfering with the free flow of international trade, prevents the world from maximizing the fruits of the international division of labor. In particular, a "scientific" tariff to "equalize costs of production" tends to eliminate all trade among nations and with it all those gains which could be achieved.

General Validity of the Law of Comparative Advantage

The law of comparative advantage has general validity: it applies to the division of labor between individual persons. Examples are not difficult to find. A business manager, though a great typist, employs somebody else to do the typing because it pays to concentrate upon those tasks in which the manager's superiority, and thus his or her comparative advantage, is greatest. The same is true of the doctor who employs a gardener or the teacher who employs an assistant to grade the students' papers.

2-5 OPPORTUNITY COST

So far, it has been demonstrated that international trade does not require offsetting absolute advantages but is possible, and indeed profitable to both trading countries, in general, whenever a comparative advantage exists. However, our conclusion seems to depend on the restrictive assumption of the labor theory of value. As noted earlier, the labor theory of value is not valid and must eventually be replaced by a more general theory of production. What happens to the important classical conclusion—namely, that specialization according to comparative advantage increases potentially the total world output of every commodity—after the labor theory of value is discarded? Should the classical conclusion be discarded also? Fortunately, this is not the case. Gottfried Haberler (1936) succeeded in developing the *theory of opportunity costs,* which actually frees the classical theory from the restrictive assumption of the labor theory of value. As Haberler (1936, p. 126) puts it, we can dispense with the labor theory of value "without having to discard the results obtained from it: these will remain, just as a building remains after the scaffolding, having served its purpose, is removed." It is important for us at this stage to take a close look at the theory of opportunity costs.

Definition of Opportunity Cost

Consider again the example summarized in Table 2-3. Recall that the inequality $^2/_{10} < ^1/_2$ was used to determine that America has a comparative advantage in food and Britain a comparative advantage in clothing. Mathematically, the inequality $^2/_{10} < ^1/_2$ is equivalent to $^2/_1 < ^{10}/_2$. As it turns out, the latter inequality is much more interesting and useful.

Consider the ratio $^2/_1$, keeping in mind that 2 and 1 are America's labor coefficients for food and clothing, respectively. What is the meaning of the ratio $^2/_1$? It simply shows the (minimum) amount of clothing that America must give up in order to produce 1 additional unit of food (by freeing sufficient labor from the production of clothing). The amount of clothing that must be sacrificed for each extra unit of food is called the *opportunity cost* of food in terms of clothing (or the *marginal rate of transformation*).

Similarly, the ratio $^{10}/_2$ (where 10 and 2 are Britain's labor coefficients for food and clothing, respectively) shows Britain's opportunity cost of food in terms of clothing, since it shows the number of units of clothing (that is, 5) that Britain must sacrifice in order to free a sufficient amount of labor from the production of clothing (that is, $5 \times 2 = 10$) in order to produce an additional unit of food.

Note that the opportunity cost of clothing in terms of food is simply the reciprocal of the opportunity cost of food in terms of clothing. Thus, the opportunity cost of clothing in terms of food is $^1/_2$ in America and $^2/_{10}$ in Britain.

Comparative Advantage and Opportunity Cost

Given the preceding definition of opportunity cost, it becomes apparent that comparative advantage can be recast in terms of opportunity cost. Thus, America has a comparative advantage in food, because her opportunity cost of food in terms of clothing (that is, 2) is *lower* than Britain's corresponding opportunity cost (that is, $^{10}/_2$, or 5). Similarly, Britain has a comparative advantage in clothing, because her opportunity cost of clothing in terms of food (that is, $^2/_{10}$) is *lower* than America's corresponding opportunity cost (that is, $^1/_2$).

We conclude, therefore, that international specialization takes place according to opportunity costs—not absolute labor costs. A commodity, in other words, is always produced by the low-cost producer. But what the student must clearly understand is that the significant concept of cost which must be used in the present context is that of opportunity cost, *not* labor cost. *Cost is forsaken opportunity*—not the amount of some input.

Significance of the Theory of Opportunity Costs

The student must give careful thought to the implications of the theory of opportunity costs. The crucial point to remember is that once comparative advantage is defined in terms of opportunity cost, which reflects forgone production of other commodities, *it makes no difference whether commodities are actually produced by labor alone.* In other words, given the opportunity costs in America and Britain, our earlier analysis can be used to show that international specialization and exchange increase potentially the output of all commodities, whether the commodities are produced by labor alone or by any number of factors of production. This accounts for the superiority of the theory of opportunity costs, which, like the deus ex machina, saves the classical conclusions. As Haberler repeatedly emphasized, the sole purpose of the labor theory of value is to determine the opportunity cost of one commodity in terms of another in each of the two countries.

Opportunity Costs versus Relative Commodity Prices

Returning to the example of Table 2-3, it becomes apparent that the autarkic relative prices in America and Britain correspond to their respective opportunity costs. For instance, we have seen that in America the opportunity cost of food in terms of clothing is 2, and also that in autarky, 1 unit of food exchanges for 2 units of clothing. Although, later in the book, we shall consider cases in which opportunity costs differ from relative market prices, we shall treat all those cases as exceptional and assume from now on that opportunity costs are in general equal to relative prices. Any exceptional cases will be noted separately. With this convention, we can define comparative advantage in terms of autarkic relative prices. For instance, in our earlier example, America has a comparative advantage in the production of food, because before trade, food is relatively cheaper in America than in Britain.

2-6 GEOMETRICAL ANALYSIS

In this section, we are introduced to the concept of the *production-possibilities frontier* (or *transformation curve*) in an effort to restate the preceding analysis graphically. This step is essential for two reasons. First, it will help us sharpen our understanding of the earlier analysis. Second, it will prepare the ground for the neoclassical and modern theories.

Production-Possibilities Frontier

In general, a country's production-possibilities frontier shows the maximum amount of, say, food, that the economy can produce for any given output of clothing. Return to the information of Table 2-3, and assume that America is endowed with 100 units of labor, while Britain is endowed with 200 units of labor. By arbitrarily allocating labor between food and clothing, we can discover all alternative combinations of food and clothing that can be produced in each of the two countries, as shown in Table 2-4.

Consider initially the first four columns of Table 2-4. The entries in columns (1) and (3) show, respectively, the amounts of labor allocated to food and clothing. Since America is endowed with 100 units of labor, in each of these allocations (that is, A, B, C, D, E, and F) the sum of labor allocated to food and clothing must always equal 100. Thus, when 100 units of labor are allocated to food, zero units of labor are allocated to clothing; when 80 units of labor are allocated to food, 20 units of labor are allocated to clothing; and so on.

Given the allocations of labor in columns (1) and (3), we easily compute the resultant amounts of output from our knowledge of the labor coefficients of

Table 2-4   Alternative Combinations of Food and Clothing

	America					Britain			
	Food		Clothing			Food		Clothing	
	Labor (1)	Output (2)	Labor (3)	Output (4)		Labor (5)	Output (6)	Labor (7)	Output (8)
A	100	50	0	0	A'	200	20	0	0
B	80	40	20	20	B'	160	16	40	20
C	60	30	40	40	C'	120	12	80	40
D	40	20	60	60	D'	80	8	120	60
E	20	10	80	80	E'	40	4	160	80
F	0	0	100	100	F'	0	0	200	100

production. We know from Table 2-3 that in America 2 units of labor are needed to produce 1 unit of food. Hence, we determine the output of the food industry by dividing by 2 the amount of labor allocated to food. For instance, when 80 units of labor are allocated to food, 40 units of food are produced, and so on. In the same way we determine all entries in column (2).

The entries in column (4) are similarly determined. From Table 2-3 we know that 1 unit of labor is needed for the production of 1 unit of clothing. Hence, the number of units of clothing produced are always equal to the number of units of labor allocated to the clothing industry.

The entries in columns (5–8) give Britain's production possibilities and are similarly derived. Keep in mind that Britain is endowed with 200 units of labor and that the British labor coefficients of production are 10 for food and 2 for clothing. To illustrate: When 160 units of labor are allocated to food, and thus 40 units of labor are allocated to clothing, 16 units of food (that is, $^{160}/_{10}$) and 20 units of clothing (that is, $^{40}/_{2}$), are produced.

The production information contained in columns (2), (4), (6), and (8) is used to draw the graphs in Figure 2-1. The top panel shows America's production-possibilities frontier and the bottom panel Britain's. The letters A–E and A'–E' have been placed on the top and bottom panel, respectively, to facilitate the association between points on the frontiers and the entries in Table 2-4. Note carefully that both production-possibilities frontiers are linear. This is an important feature of the classical model and is primarily due to the assumptions that there is only one factor—labor—and that the labor coefficients of production remain constant irrespective of the scale of operations in either industry.

The absolute slope of America's production-possibilities frontier (that is, $^{100}/_{50} = 2$) gives America's opportunity cost of food in terms of clothing. Similarly, the absolute slope of Britain's production-possibilities frontier (that is, $^{100}/_{20} = 5$) gives Britain's opportunity cost of food in terms of clothing. Note that Britain's frontier, which is drawn on the same scale as America's, is much steeper than America's. This confirms graphically our earlier conclusion that America has a comparative advantage in food and Britain one in clothing.

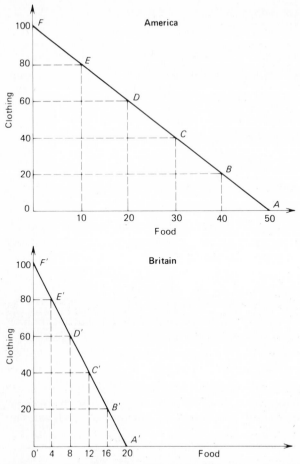

Figure 2-1　*Production-possibilities frontiers of America and Britain.*
The points on America's production frontier correspond to the entries in columns (2) and (4) of Table 2-4. Similarly, the points on Britain's production frontier correspond to the entries of columns (6) and (8) of Table 2-4.

The Gains from Trade Again

The production-possibilities frontiers of Figure 2-1 can be used to illustrate graphically the gains from trade. This is done in Figure 2-2, which is based on the assumption that America specializes completely in the production of food and Britain in clothing. Thus, the total world production is 50 units of food and 100 units of clothing, as shown by the sides of rectangle $OAO'F$. Rectangle $OAO'F$ *is obtained by rotating Britain's production-possibilities frontier by 180° and placing point F' on point A.*

Before trade, America can consume only what she can produce. The same goes for Britain. Therefore, before international specialization and trade, both America and Britain consume *on* their respective production-possibilities

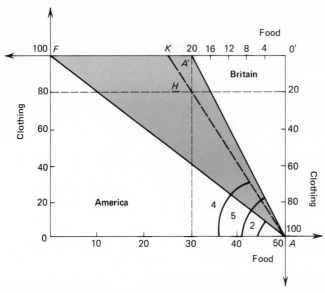

Figure 2-2 *The gains from trade.*
America specializes in food, and Britain in clothing. The shaded triangle *FAA'* shows the gains from trade. Like a blade, the terms-of-trade line *AK* divides the gains from trade into two parts: *KAF* (America's share) and *KAA'* (Britain's share).

frontiers. Measuring American consumption of food and clothing with respect to origin *O*, we see that America can consume only combinations that lie along line *AF*. Similarly, measuring British consumption of food and clothing with respect to origin *O'*, we see that Britain can consume, before trade, only combinations along line *AA'*.

On the other hand, *international specialization according to comparative advantage enhances the consumption possibilities of the two countries by the shaded triangular area FAA'*. This shaded area is indeed the source of the gains from trade. The larger the divergence between the slopes of the two production-possibilities frontiers, the larger the shaded area and the gains from trade. In the limiting case of "equal" advantage, in which the two frontiers have equal slope, the shaded area shrinks to zero and the gains from trade disappear. This confirms our earlier conclusion that in the "equal" advantage case there is no basis for trade.

How are the gains from trade distributed between America and Britain? That depends on the equilibrium terms of trade. We shall study this problem in the future. Nevertheless, we showed earlier in this chapter that when the terms of trade lie between the autarkic price ratios of the two countries, both countries benefit. To illustrate this proposition graphically, assume, as before, that 1 unit of food exchanges for 4 units of clothing. This is shown in Figure 2-2 by *terms-of-trade line AK*. Note carefully that the slope of *AK* gives the assumed terms of trade. Thus, America could, for instance, export to Britain 20 units of food in exchange for 80 units of clothing. This exchange would enable both countries to consume at point *H*, which lies beyond both production-possibilities frontiers, as do all points in the shaded triangle *FAA'*.

Terms-of-trade line *AK* can be viewed as a blade cutting the gains-from-trade area into two parts: *KAF* and *KAA'*. Portion *KAF* goes to America, while portion *KAA'* goes to Britain. Obviously, the closer the terms-of-trade line lies to a country's production-possibilities frontier, the smaller that country's share of the gains. In the limiting case, where the terms-of-trade line coincides with America's frontier, America gains nothing and all the gains go to Britain. Finally, when the terms-of-trade line coincides with Britain's frontier, all the gains go to America and Britain gains nothing.

2-7 LIMITATIONS OF THE CLASSICAL THEORY

The classical theory explains that profitable international trade takes place because of the existence of comparative-cost differences. But, then, why do comparative-cost differences exist? Within the context of the labor theory of value, it appears that a necessary condition for the existence of comparative-cost differences is the existence of different production functions between countries. If production functions were the same between countries, the labor requirements for the production of any commodity would, by necessity, be the same in all countries; that is, all countries would be equally efficient in every line of production. This state of affairs, however, leaves no room for international trade. Therefore, it appears that the sine qua non for the existence of international trade is the disparity of production functions between countries. But if this is so, why do production functions differ between countries? Unfortunately, the classical theory does not offer any answers—although in Ricardo's classic example, the implicit reason is climatic differences. Without a satisfactory answer to this important question, the classical theory loses most of its explanatory usefulness. As we shall see later, the modern theory of trade starts with the assumption that production functions are indeed identical among countries and explains the existence of comparative advantage with differences in factor proportions.

The classical theory offers a clear explanation of the gains from trade and as such has made an important contribution to welfare, as opposed to positive, economics. In addition, it demonstrates convincingly that trade barriers are harmful to the world economy and that free trade is potentially the best policy.

2-8 SUMMARY

1   The classical theory of international trade is mainly concerned with (a) the gains from trade, (b) the structure of trade, and (c) the terms of trade.

2   Although it is generally recognized that the labor theory of value is not valid, its use can elucidate the problem of international specialization and the gains from trade. The major results obtained in this fashion continue to hold even after the labor theory of value is discarded.

3 Absolute advantage is not necessary for profitable international trade. Indeed, a basis for profitable trade exists even when one country is more efficient than another in every line of production, assuming only that the first country's degree of superiority differs from industry to industry. In this case, the "advanced" country should (and will) specialize in the production of those commodities in which its absolute advantage is highest, and import those commodities in which its absolute advantage is lowest.

4 The equilibrium terms of trade necessarily lie between the autarkic price ratios of the trading countries. The division of the gains from trade between countries depends crucially on the equilibrium terms of trade.

5 Comparative differences in cost can be easily converted into absolute differences in money prices.

6 Comparative advantage can be cast in terms of opportunity cost, which reflects foregone production of other commodities. Thus, a country should produce (and export) those goods in which her opportunity cost is lowest, and import those goods in which her opportunity cost is highest. This approach actually frees the classical theory from the restrictive assumption of the labor theory of value.

7 Opportunity costs are given graphically by the absolute slope of the production-possibilities frontier (or transformation curve).

8 Within the context of the labor theory of value, comparative-cost differences exist only when the production functions are different between countries. However, the classical theory does not offer any satisfactory explanation as to why the production functions differ between countries.

SUGGESTED READING

Cairnes, J. E. (1874). *Some Leading Principles of Political Economy.* Macmillan and Company, Ltd., London.

Chacholiades, M. (1978). *International Trade Theory and Policy.* McGraw-Hill Book Company, New York, chaps. 2–3.

Haberler, G. (1936). *The Theory of International Trade.* W. Hodge and Company, London, chaps. 9–11.

Mill, J. S. (1902). *Principles of Political Economy.* Appleton, New York, chaps. 17, 18, and 25.

Ricardo, D. (1821). *The Principles of Political Economy and Taxation.* J. Murray, London, chap. 7.

Smith, A. (1937). *An Inquiry into the Nature and Causes of the Wealth of Nations.* The Modern Library, New York.

Torrens, R. (1808). *The Economists Refuted.* S. A. and H. Oddy, London. Reprinted in R. Torrens, *The Principles and Practical Operation of Sir Robert Peel's Act of 1844 Explained and Defended,* 3d ed., Longmans, London, 1858.

——— (1815). *An Essay on the External Corn Trade.* J. Hatchard, London.

Viner, J. (1937). *Studies in the Theory of International Trade.* Harper and Brothers, New York, chap. 7.

Chapter Three

Opportunity Cost and Community Indifference

Before we proceed any further with the development of the pure theory of international trade, we must pause briefly to consider the fundamental concepts of *opportunity cost* and *social* (or *community*) *indifference*. These twin concepts form the basis for the neoclassical theory of international values, the main architects of which are Edgeworth, Haberler, Leontief, Marshall, and Meade.

The discussion is divided into two parts. Part A deals with the concept of opportunity cost in the context of neoclassical production theory. Part B deals with the useful concept of *social indifference curves* and draws attention to its limitations.

PART A: Opportunity Cost

3-1 INCREASING OPPORTUNITY COSTS

As already indicated in Chapter 2, the theory of opportunity costs frees the classical theory of international values from the restrictive and invalid assumption of the labor theory of value. All we have to do is define comparative advantage in terms of opportunity cost reflecting forgone production of other commodities. Once this is done, it makes no difference whether commodities are produced by labor alone or by labor and other factors.

Opportunity costs are usually illustrated by means of *production-possibilities frontiers,* also known as *transformation curves.* In general, a country's production-possibilities frontier shows the maximum amount of one commodity that the country can produce given (1) its factor endowment, (2) its technology (that is, *production functions*), and (3) the quantities of all other commodities produced. Drawn in commodity space, the production-possibilities frontier shows explicitly the menu of alternative combinations of commodities that the country can produce by means of its given resources, natural and manufactured, and its technical know-how. The concept of the production-possibilities frontier is a constant reminder of the *law of scarcity,* that is, the empirical observation that no country has ever been able to produce as much as it desired of all commodities.

Production-possibilities frontiers were employed in Chapter 2 during our geometrical analysis of the classical theory of international values. Nevertheless, that discussion was rather limited by the assumption of the labor theory of value, which required all production-possibilities frontiers to be *linear,* as shown in Figures 2-1 and 2-2. What is wrong with linear production-possibilities frontiers?

Linear production-possibilities frontiers imply that opportunity costs are *constant*—that the opportunity cost of a commodity remains constant as the output of that commodity increases from zero to its maximum. For instance, in Chapter 2 we saw that America's opportunity cost of food in terms of clothing was 2, that is, for each additional unit of food produced, America had to give up 2 units of clothing. This was true whether America was producing 20, 40, 60, or 80 units of food. Recall that America's opportunity cost of food in terms of clothing was given by the absolute slope of America's production-possibilities frontier; and since the production-possibilities frontier was linear with a unique slope, America's opportunity costs were constant.

Neoclassical economists raised serious objections to the Ricardian assumption of constant opportunity costs. To begin with, constant opportunity costs contradict the empirical observation that many industries operate under conditions of *increasing* costs. What is even worse, constant opportunity costs lead to *complete specialization.* Return to Figure 2-2, and observe carefully that both America and Britain specialize completely: America produces only food, and Britain only clothing. But complete specialization is not consistent with the facts, either. For instance, the United States continues to produce domestically most of the commodities (such as TV sets, automobiles, and textiles) she imports from foreign countries. Finally, as is shown below, there are strong theoretical reasons for rejecting constant opportunity costs and replacing them with *increasing* opportunity costs.

Increasing opportunity costs are illustrated by a production-possibilities frontier that is concave to (or bowed out from) the origin, as shown in Figure

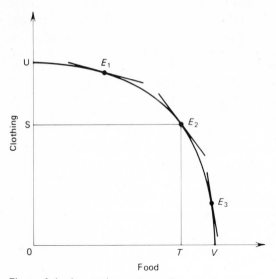

Figure 3-1 *Increasing opportunity costs.*
As the economy moves from E_1 to E_2 and then to E_3 (that is, as the economy increases its
production of food), the absolute slope of the production-possibilities frontier (which shows
food's *marginal* opportunity cost) becomes bigger and bigger.

3-1 by curve UV. What is the opportunity cost of food in terms of clothing? We
can answer this question only when a production point is actually selected on
frontier UV. For even though, in general, the opportunity cost of food continues to be given by the absolute slope of the production-possibilities frontier,
that slope is no longer unique. For instance, suppose the economy produces
currently at E_1 and decides to increase the output of the food industry by one
additional unit. Since, by assumption, all resources are fully employed, the food
industry can increase its output only if a sufficient amount of resources is transferred to it from the clothing industry. What is the minimum amount of clothing
that must be sacrificed in this manner? The (minimum) amount of clothing that
must be sacrificed for the production of one additional unit of food is given by
the absolute slope of curve UV at E_1. This is the opportunity cost of food *at the
margin,* or food's *marginal opportunity cost* at E_1.

As the production of food increases (and that of clothing decreases), the
marginal opportunity cost of food increases. For instance, at E_2 the absolute
slope of curve UV is greater than at E_1, and at E_3 it is greater than at E_2.

(For the rest of our discussion, we shall omit the adjective "marginal" from
the expression "marginal opportunity cost." Since there can hardly be any confusion, the shorter term "opportunity cost" will be used for convenience.)

When the production-possibilities frontier is concave to the origin, *both* industries experience increasing opportunity costs. Recall that the opportunity
cost of clothing in terms of food is merely the reciprocal of the opportunity cost
of food in terms of clothing. Hence, as the economy moves from E_3 to E_1, the
opportunity cost of food falls, while the opportunity cost of clothing rises.

What lies behind the phenomenon of increasing opportunity costs? This is an important question. Sections 3-2 through 3-4 consider this question thoroughly in the context of the *modern theory of international trade,* which is the subject matter of Chapter 5. This is done intentionally in order to allow the student to become familiar with basic concepts. In the meantime, we will consider briefly an alternative explanation that is intuitively obvious.

At the intuitive level, increasing opportunity costs can be explained by the fact that factors of production are *product specific,* that is, specialized in the production of certain commodities and of relatively less use in the production of other commodities. Examples are not hard to find, since more often than not factors are not homogeneous for many purposes but, as we saw in Chapter 2, divide into "noncompeting groups." For instance, while highly skilled labor may be required for the production of clothing, such skills may be totally useless in the production of food. Similarly, the fertility of land differs from acre to acre and from industry to industry: While a piece of land may be good for growing grapes, it may be of much less use, or of no use at all, for raising cattle. Likewise, minerals can only be produced from certain ore-bearing types of land. And so on.

How does the product-specificity of factors explain the phenomenon of increasing opportunity costs? Return to Figure 3-1, and suppose that currently all resources are employed in the production of clothing; that is, the economy produces at U. Imagine now that the economy continually transfers resources from the production of clothing to the production of food. At the beginning, resources that are highly efficient in the production of food (for example, the best grade of fertile land) will be transferred from clothing to food. Thus, while the output of food will be rising fast, the output of clothing will be falling slowly; that is, the opportunity cost of food will be very low. This explains why the production-possibilities frontier is rather flat in region UE_1. As the production of food continues to increase, it becomes necessary to employ less-fertile land and workers who are highly skilled in the production of clothing. Thus, from E_2 to V each additional unit of food causes the output of clothing to fall much faster. The production-possibilities frontier becomes steeper, signifying rising opportunity costs in the production of food. An analogous story can be told when production shifts continuously from V to U.

It is interesting to note that the degree of specificity of a factor may be a function of time. With the passage of time, new skills may be acquired, and one type of machinery may be converted into something else through depreciation and reinvestment. In the very short run, some factors may be totally specific to the production of food and useless to the production of clothing, and the rest of the factors specific to the production of clothing and useless to the production of food. This extreme situation is best illustrated by the case of already-produced outputs—already-harvested crops. The production-possibilities frontier reduces, in this case, to a rectangle, as shown in Figure 3-1 by OTE_2S. In the long run, of course, the economy can move to frontier UV.

The rest of our discussion in this part shows that increasing opportunity costs can prevail even when all factors are homogeneous in the sense that all workers and all acres of land have the same productivity in the production of both food and clothing. As we shall see, increasing opportunity costs result from the fact that different industries use factors in different proportions. This observation becomes important in Chapter 5.

3-2 THE NEOCLASSICAL THEORY OF PRODUCTION: A DIGRESSION[1]

This section provides a brief survey of the neoclassical theory of production, since this theory is of vital importance to our future progress.

The Production Function: A Definition

Consider a firm using two factors of production, homogeneous labor L and homogeneous land T, and producing a single homogeneous output Q. The firm's *production function* is merely a statement of the *maximum* quantity of output that it can produce with any specified quantities of labor and land. The production function is a purely *physical* concept; that is, it is a relationship between the *physical* quantities of output and input—not their values.

Further, the production function incorporates the concept of *engineering efficiency*. That is, the production function is based on the assumption that all inefficient methods of production are disregarded and only the most efficient method is used in each case. In other words, given any combination of inputs, the firm is assumed to choose only that technique which maximizes output and to ignore all other (inefficient) techniques. This is the reason we emphasized in the definition that the production function gives the *maximum* amount of output for any specified amounts of labor and land.

There is a very good reason for assuming engineering efficiency, of course. It is that those firms which do not use the best production techniques will incur higher production costs than other competitors and that they will eventually be driven out of business. Competition, therefore, forces producers to follow the rules of engineering efficiency.

The Isoquant Map

The production function is usually illustrated by means of the *isoquant map,* as shown in Figure 3-2. Each curve, or *isoquant,* or *equal-product curve,* is the locus of alternative combinations of labor and land, all of which yield the same amount of output. For instance, consider curve 1. It shows all combinations of labor and land that can produce 20 units of output. In particular, two such combinations are shown by the coordinates of points A and B.

What are the general properties of isoquants? These are easily summarized as follows:

1   Isoquants are negatively sloped (at least in the economically relevant middle region).

[1] The reader who is already familiar with production functions and cost minimization may omit this section. However, the properties of constant returns to scale (not necessarily their proofs) should be reviewed.

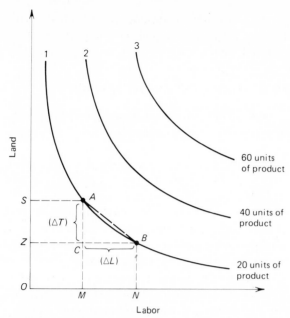

Figure 3-2 *The isoquant map.*
Isoquants 1, 2, and 3 show all combinations of labor and land that yield 20, 40, and 60 units of output, respectively. For instance, points A and B on isoquant 1 give two combinations of labor and land, [that is, (*OM, OS*) and (*ON, OZ*)], that yield 20 units of output. In moving from A to B, the firm substitutes *MN* (or Δ*L*) units of labor for *SZ* (or Δ*T*) units of land.

    2 Isoquants do not intersect each other.
    3 Isoquants lying farther from the origin imply a higher amount of output.
    4 Isoquants are convex to the origin.

    The first property ("negatively sloped") follows from the justifiable assumption that additional units of any factor produce additional *positive* amounts of output—no producer will ever employ a factor up to the point where its *marginal product* becomes negative, or even zero, since factors do cost something. The second property ("do not intersect") follows from the observation that a point of intersection between two isoquants would represent two different levels of maximum output, which is nonsensical. The third property ("farther from the origin . . . higher output") follows from the reasonable assumption that in order to produce more output, it is necessary to use more inputs. Finally, the last property ("convex to the origin") follows from the so-called *law of diminishing marginal rate of substitution*, which is discussed next.

The Marginal Rate of Substitution

As we have seen, isoquants normally have a negative slope—at least within the relevant range. Within this range, factors are substitutable. For instance, in Figure 3-2, assume that 20 units of output are produced by means of OM units of labor and OS units of land. The same amount of output (that is, 20 units) can also be produced by, say, ON units of labor and OZ units of land. In moving from point A to point B along isoquant 1, the firm substitutes MN units of labor for SZ units of land. This factor substitution is an important economic phenomenon.

The *marginal rate of substitution* of labor for land (MRS_{LT}) gives the number of units of land that can be replaced by an extra unit of labor, assuming that production continues at the initial rate. In the above example, the movement from point A to point B along isoquant 1 implies that, *on the average, SZ/MN* units of land are replaced by each additional unit of labor employed. Thus, one could say that the marginal rate of substitution of labor for land is given by the ratio SZ/MN. This ratio gives, of course, the absolute slope of the broken line connecting points A and B. However, this measure of the marginal rate of substitution suffers from one severe drawback: it is indeterminate. Thus, starting at point A, we cannot determine the marginal rate of substitution unless a second point, such as B, is chosen. Since there are many points to choose from, and since each point necessarily generates a different ratio SZ/MN, it appears that an impasse is reached. How do we get out of this impasse?

Imagine that point B travels along isoquant 1 toward A. The slope of the line AB will move closer and closer to the slope of the tangent at A. This limiting value of the slope of the tangent at A, which is uniquely determined, we define as the marginal rate of substitution of labor for land at A. The absolute slope at point A gives the rate at which land has to be given up per additional unit of labor. As soon as the firm moves ever so slightly away from A, the slope of the isoquant changes (and the marginal rate of substitution becomes different). A good analogy is a car that runs at a variable speed at each and every point along a highway. The speed of the car at a point is perfectly determined and corresponds to our concept of the marginal rate of substitution, while the average speed between any two points depends not only on the initial point but also on the final point.

The fourth property of isoquants ("convex to the origin") implies that the marginal rate of substitution diminishes as one factor is substituted for another. This is the law of diminishing marginal rate of substitution. What this law actually asserts is this: As the substitution of one factor for the other proceeds, that substitution becomes progressively more difficult. An additional economic justification for this law is given below. (See the subsection entitled "Cost Minimization.")

Marginal Physical Products and the Marginal Rate of Substitution

There is a close relationship between the *marginal physical products* of labor and land and the marginal rate of substitution. (The marginal physical product of a factor—say, labor—is the extra amount of output that can be secured by increasing labor by one unit while leaving all other factors unchanged.)

Return to Figure 3-2, and assume again that we move from A to B. Divide this movement into two parts: (1) a movement from A to C and (2) a movement from C to B. In the first step, SZ (or ΔT) units of land are given up, and output necessarily falls. By how much? By $\Delta T \cdot MPP_T$, where $MPP_T \equiv$ marginal physical product of land. In the second step, the employment of labor increases by MN (or ΔL) units, and output increases by $\Delta L \cdot MPP_L$, where $MPP_L \equiv$ marginal physical product of labor. What is the overall change in output? Since in the final analysis we move along the same isoquant from A to B, it follows that by definition the overall change in output must be zero; that is, the sum of the two separate changes in output must be zero. Accordingly, we obtain the following equation:

$$\Delta T \cdot MPP_T + \Delta L \cdot MPP_L = 0 \tag{3-1}$$

To bring out the relationship between the marginal rate of substitution of labor for land (MRS_{LT}) and the marginal physical products of labor and land, we rearrange equation (3-1) as follows:

$$MRS_{LT} \equiv -\frac{\Delta T}{\Delta L} = \frac{MPP_L}{MPP_T} \tag{3-2}$$

Consequently, the marginal rate of substitution of labor for land is equal to the ratio of the marginal physical product of labor to the marginal physical product of land.

Returns to Scale

What happens to output when all inputs increase proportionately (that is, by the same percentage)? For instance, what happens to output when all inputs are doubled? The term *returns to scale* refers to the relationship between a change in the physical quantity of output and a proportionate change in the physical quantity of all inputs. There are three possibilities:

   1 *Constant returns to scale* prevail when the physical quantity of output changes in the same proportion as all inputs. For instance, when all inputs are doubled, output doubles.
   2 *Increasing returns to scale* prevail when the physical quantity of output increases faster than all inputs. For instance, when all inputs are doubled, output more than doubles.
   3 *Decreasing returns to scale* prevail when the physical quantity of output increases slower than all inputs. For instance, when all inputs are doubled, output increases but falls short of being doubled.

Whether returns to scale are constant, increasing, or decreasing is an empirical question. Most, but not all, of the pure theory of international trade is based on the assumption that returns to scale are constant. Indeed, this will be our assumption here. Any deviations from constant returns to scale will be treated as exceptions and studied separately.

The reader is no doubt familiar with production functions of firms that are not characterized by constant returns to scale. The production function of the typical firm exhibits increasing returns at the beginning (justified by the familiar fact of "economies of large-scale production"), followed by constant and decreasing returns successively, presumably because of increasing difficulties of supervision. For instance, we usually observe a U-shaped average-cost curve for the firm instead of the horizontal average-cost curve implied by constant returns to scale.

Why then assume that constant returns to scale are the rule? Because in the theory of international trade we bypass the firm and work directly with the *industry*. Now, for the whole industry, constant returns to scale is not an unrealistic assumption. The presumption is that a factory can always be duplicated; and as demand increases, more firms come into the industry, with each new firm doing exactly the same thing as old firms. For instance, since labor and land are homogeneous factors (by assumption), whatever a producer does on one acre of land, a second producer can duplicate on a second acre of land, and so on. Thus, as the acres of land together with their identical crews double, output also doubles; and this is what we mean by constant returns to scale.

Properties of Constant Returns to Scale[2]

When returns to scale are constant, the production function has several notable properties. Because of the importance of constant returns to scale to the theory of international trade, it is useful to summarize these properties.

1 *The average physical product of each factor depends only on the proportion in which labor and land are used.* For instance, the average physical product of land (that is, the ratio total output/total number of acres of land) is given by the amount of output produced on each acre of land since each acre is like all the others! But the amount of output produced on each acre depends on the number of workers employed on each acre.

2 *The marginal physical product of each factor also depends only on the proportion in which labor and land are used.* For instance, the marginal physical product of labor depends on how many workers are already working on each acre of land.

3 *The marginal rate of substiution also depends on the proportion in which factors are used.* This is obvious from the fact that the marginal rate of substitution is given by the ratio of marginal physical products, and these depend on factor proportions. Note that this property implies that any straight line through the origin (implying a fixed labor/land ratio) will intersect all isoquants at points which have the same slope (that is, the same MRS_{LT}).

4 *The whole isoquant map is a blown-up version of the unit isoquant.*

---

[2] The reader who has decided to skip Section 3-2 must at least read this subsection on the properties of constant returns to scale (omitting, if necessary, all proofs).

Thus, when the unit isoquant (or any other isoquant, for that matter) is given, the whole isoquant map can be easily constructed.

   5 *The total output Q is exactly exhausted by the distributive shares of all factors when each factor is paid the amount of its marginal physical product.* This is known as *Euler's theorem.* Sometimes it is also referred to as the *adding-up theorem.*

   For a rigorous proof of Euler's theorem, see Chacholiades (1978, p. 92). For our present purposes the following heuristic proof is sufficient. Suppose that L_0 units of labor and T_0 units of land are currently employed in the production of Q_0 units of output. If labor increases by ΔL units, and land by ΔT units, output will increase by

$$\Delta Q = \Delta L \cdot MPP_L + \Delta T \cdot MPP_T \tag{3-3}$$

Now suppose that the factor increases ΔL and ΔT are indeed proportional to the initial amounts L_0 and T_0, respectively. In particular, assume that $\Delta L = \lambda L_0$, and $\Delta T = \lambda T_0$, where λ is a constant. Because of constant returns to scale, we must also have $\Delta Q = \lambda Q_0$. Substituting the values λL_0, λT_0, and λQ_0 into equation (3-3), we obtain

$$\lambda Q_0 = \lambda L_0 \cdot MPP_L + \lambda T_0 \cdot MPP_T$$

or, by cancelling the common factor λ,

$$Q_0 = L_0 \cdot MPP_L + T_0 \cdot MPP_T \tag{3-4}$$

Equation (3-4) is Euler's theorem.

   6 *When the isoquants are convex to the origin (that is, when the marginal rate of substitution is diminishing), the marginal physical products of labor and land are diminishing (that is, the law of diminishing returns holds).*

   Property 6 is illustrated in Figure 3-3, where three isoquants are drawn for 20, 30, and 40 units of output, respectively. Straight line OK intersects the three isoquants at points A, B, and C, respectively. Because of constant returns to scale, the slopes at A, B, and C are identical, and distance AB is equal to distance BC. Hence, the tangents to the three isoquants at A, B, and C, respectively, are all parallel to each other, and $DB = BF$. Now suppose that production occurs currently at E. We wish to show that, keeping land fixed at OS units, successive increases of labor will cause output to increase by smaller and smaller amounts, or, which is the same thing, successive increases of output by equal amounts, say, 10 units, will require larger and larger additional amounts of labor. Now to increase output from 20 to 30 units, we must increase labor by EB units; and to increase output from 30 to 40 units, we must increase labor by

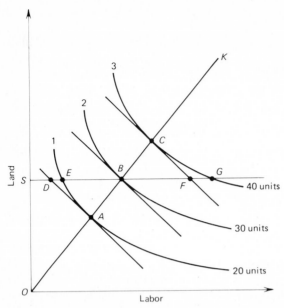

Figure 3-3 *Constant returns to scale and diminishing returns to each factor.*
Keeping land fixed at *OS*, the firm can increase its output from 20 to 30 units by increasing labor by *EB* units. To increase its output from 30 to 40 units, the firm must increase labor by *BG* units. Since *BG* > *EB*, the marginal physical product of labor must be diminishing.

BG units. To prove diminishing returns to labor, we must show that *BG* > *EB*. However, this must be obvious, since *DB* = *BF* and *EB* < *DB* = *BF* < *BG*.

The Isocost Map

Each point on an isoquant corresponds to a different technological method of producing the specified output. Given these alternative technological methods, a real choice remains to be made among them. This choice is an economic one, because it is not determined by wholly technical or engineering considerations. It depends, in addition, on factor prices and the behavioral assumption that firms try to minimize cost, which is part and parcel of the profit-maximization assumption.

Assume that the wage rate *w* for labor services and the rent *r* for land services are constant. This is a perfectly valid assumption, because under perfect competition each producer is a price-taker in the factor markets. Consider Figure 3-4, which, in addition to the two isoquants (1 and 2), shows three *isocost lines: T_1L_1, T_2L_2,* and *T_3L_3.* Each isocost line shows all combinations of labor and land that can be purchased with a fixed sum of money—very much like a budget line of a consumer. For instance, T_1L_1 shows all possible combinations of labor and land that cost exactly $500; T_2L_2 represents a total cost of $600, and T_3L_3, $1,000. Note that as the total cost increases, the firm shifts to an isocost line which lies farther from the origin.

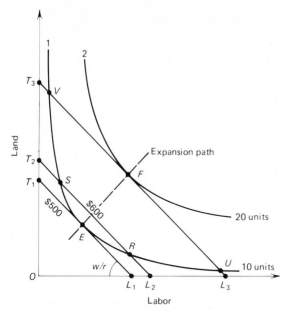

Figure 3-4 *The isocost map, cost minimization, and the expansion path.*
Costs are minimized at points of tangency between isocost lines and convex isoquants, as illustrated by points *E* and *F*. The locus of all such tangencies is the expansion path (see broken curve through *E* and *F*).

Each isocost line is drawn as a straight line, and all are parallel to each other, since the slope of an isocost line gives the constant wage/rent (or w/r) ratio. For instance, since OT_1 units of land cost \$500, and OL_1 units of labor also cost \$500, it follows that $r \cdot OT_1 = w \cdot OL_1$ or $OT_1/OL_1 = w/r$. But the ratio OT_1/OL_1 gives the absolute slope of isocost line T_1L_1.

Cost Minimization

Suppose that the firm wants to produce 10 units of output. For this purpose, the firm must choose a combination of labor and land that coincides with the coordinates of some point on isoquant 1. Which combination will the firm choose? That combination which minimizes cost. Apparently cost is minimized at E, where isocost line T_1L_1 is just tangent to isoquant 1. Anywhere else, cost is higher. Thus, none of the other combinations (such as V, S, R, and U) that lie on isoquant 1 can be attained with a total cost of just \$500—they all require a higher cost.

The above analysis gives the economic reason for assuming that isoquants are convex to the origin. At a point of tangency between an isocost line and an isoquant, such as E, the isoquant must be convex to the origin for that tangency to represent a point of minimum cost. If the isoquant were concave to the origin, such a tangency would represent a point of maximum cost, and the firm would never produce there. Accordingly, when isoquants are concave to the origin, the firm will never produce in the middle area but will move to either axis; that is, the firm will employ one factor only. Since such behavior contradicts the empirical observation that, as a rule, firms use more than one factor, we conclude that isoquants must be convex to the origin—at least in the economically relevant region.

The above argument does not, of course, rule out the possibility that isoquants may have concave parts. Nevertheless, we disregard this possibility because a firm will never choose a factor combination along a concave region of an isoquant.

From the preceding discussion, it follows that a necessary condition for cost minimization is that the slope of the isocost line (which, as we have seen, is equal to the factor-price ratio w/r) be equal to the slope of the isoquant (that is, the marginal rate of substitution of labor for land). In other words, for cost minimization, it is required that

$$\frac{w}{r} = \frac{MPP_L}{MPP_T} \tag{3-5}$$

The above condition can also be written in the following equivalent forms:

$$\frac{w}{MPP_L} = \frac{r}{MPP_T} \tag{3-6}$$

and

$$\frac{MPP_L}{w} = \frac{MPP_T}{r} \tag{3-7}$$

What is the meaning of equations (3-6) and (3-7)?

Consider first the economic interpretation of the ratio w/MPP_L. When the employment of labor increases by one unit, two things happen: (1) The total cost increases by the wage rate w, and (2) the total output increases by the marginal physical product of labor MPP_L. Accordingly, the ratio w/MPP_L shows the cost per additional unit of output at the margin (that is, the marginal cost of output) when the increase in output occurs through an increase in the employment of labor. Similarly, the ratio r/MPP_T gives the marginal cost of output if land were to increase and raise output by one unit. To minimize total cost, the two ratios must be equal, as shown by equation (3-6). Otherwise, total cost can be reduced by transferring expenditure from the factor whose "marginal cost" is high to the other factor whose "marginal cost" is low. The common value of the ratios w/MPP_L and r/MPP_T is none other than the firm's unique *long-run marginal cost.*

Turn now to an interpretation of equation (3-7). The ratio MPP_L/w shows the extra output that is produced by the last dollar spent on labor. Similarly, the ratio MPP_T/r shows the extra output that is produced by the last dollar spent on land. Accordingly, a rational firm will minimize its total cost by hiring factors until their marginal-physical-products-per-last-dollar-spent are equalized.

The Expansion Path

We have just seen how, in an effort to minimize cost, a rational producer will combine the factors labor and land to produce a specified amount of output. The same procedure can be followed, of course, for all levels of output. Thus, returning to Figure 3-4, a rational entrepreneur who wants to produce 20 units of output will produce at F, that is, the tangency between isocost line T_3L_3 and isoquant 2. The locus of all such tangencies (such as E and F) is called the *expansion path*. This is illustrated in Figure 3-4 by the broken curve passing through points E and F.

When a production function is characterized by constant returns to scale, the expansion path is necessarily a straight line through the origin (because of property 3).

Total Cost, Average Cost, and Marginal Cost

The expansion path gives all the information necessary for the derivation of the *long-run total-cost curve*. An isoquant and an isocost line pass through every point along the expansion path. The former gives the amount of output produced, and the latter gives the (lowest) total cost of production. For instance, at E (of Figure 3-4) the firm produces 10 units of output at a total cost of $500. This information enables us to determine a point on the total-cost curve. By repeating the same experiment for all points along the expansion path, we can determine all points along the total-cost curve.

After the total-cost curve is determined, the average-cost and marginal-cost curves are easily determined. The average cost is given by the ratio total cost/total ouput, while the marginal cost is given by the slope of the total-cost curve.

When the production function is characterized by constant returns to scale, the total-cost curve is reduced to a straight line through the origin, and the average-cost curve and the marginal-cost curve are represented by a horizontal line since, in this case, average cost equals marginal cost, and they both remain constant at all levels of output.

3-3 THE BOX DIAGRAM

Consider an economy endowed with fixed quantities of labor and land—say, $L_0 = 200$ and $T_0 = 100$, respectively—and producing two commodities, food and clothing. Each industry's production function is characterized by constant returns to scale. How should the economy allocate its fixed supplies of labor and land? Optimally! Now an allocation of resources can be said to be optimal if, and only if, it puts the economy on its production-possibilities frontier. How is this accomplished? We shall answer this question by employing the so-called

Edgeworth-Bowley box diagram. This is a very useful tool, and we must master it.

Interpreting the Axes of the Box Diagram

The box diagram is illustrated in Figure 3-5. The sides of rectangle O_cMO_fN are determined by the given amounts of labor and land. Thus, horizontal distances O_cM and O_fN each equal 200 units of labor, and vertical distances O_cN and O_fM each equal 100 units of land. Along the lower horizontal axis O_cM, we measure, moving from O_c toward M, the amount of labor allocated to the production of clothing. Along the left-hand vertical axis, we measure, moving from O_c toward N, the amount of land allocated to the production of clothing. The upper horizontal axis indicates, moving from O_f toward N, the amount of labor employed in the production of food. Finally, along the right-hand vertical axis, we measure, moving from O_f toward M, the amount of land used in the production of food.

Given the above interpretation of the axes, it is evident that any point in the box represents four quantities: the amounts of labor and of land allocated to the production of food and to the production of clothing. For instance, at point Z, 50 units of labor are allocated to the production of clothing, and the rest (that is, 150 units of labor) are allocated to the production of food. Similarly, 70 units

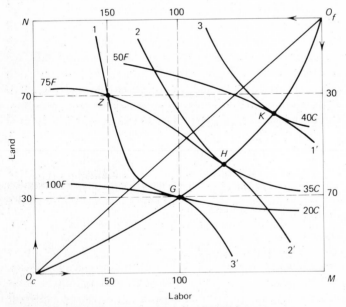

Figure 3-5 *The box diagram and the contract curve.*
The locus of tangencies between the two sets of isoquants defines the contract curve. Resources are allocated optimally along the contract curve only. By moving from Z to some point on the contract curve between G and H, the economy can increase the output of both commodities.

of land are allocated to clothing, and the rest (that is, 30 units of land) are allocated to food.

The Isoquant Maps

Introduce now into the box the isoquant maps of the food and clothing industries. Draw the isoquant map of the clothing industry with respect to the origin O_c, as illustrated by the three isoquants 1, 2, and 3, which represent 20, 35, and 40 units of clothing, respectively. Similarly, draw the isoquant map of the food industry with respect to the origin O_f, as illustrated by the three isoquants 1', 2', and 3', which represent 50, 75, and 100 units of food, respectively.

Now observe carefully that any arbitrary point in the box corresponds to a definite allocation of labor and land between the two industries and gives rise to definite production levels of both commodities. For instance, at Z the economy produces 20 units of clothing and 75 units of food.

The Contract Curve

The economy cannot produce on its production-possibilities frontier by allocating resources arbitrarily. What rules must the economy follow in order to achieve optimality?

Suppose that the economy arbitrarily chooses point Z. Thus, the economy produces 20 units of clothing and 75 units of food. Does this combination of food and clothing determine a point on the economy's production-possibilities frontier? Definitely not, because the economy can reallocate its resources and produce more food without giving up any clothing. Thus, the economy could move from Z to G by transferring 50 units of labor from the food industry to the clothing industry and 40 units of land from the clothing industry to the food industry. At point G the economy is still producing 20 units of clothing, because point G lies on the same isoquant 1 of the clothing industry as point Z. Nevertheless, the economy is now producing (at G) 100 units of food as compared to 75 at Z. This is indeed remarkable, as the economy appears to be producing something out of nothing through a mere reallocation of resources—no worker is working any harder!

Alternatively, the economy could move from Z to H. At H the economy continues to produce 75 units of food but enjoys a much higher level of output of clothing—35 units (versus 20 at Z).

Suppose now that the economy is at a point of tangency between two isoquants (one of each industry), such as G, H, and K. Can the economy, by a mere reallocation of resources, still increase the output of, say, food, without giving up any clothing? The reader should inspect Figure 3-5 and be convinced that this is not possible. Starting at a tangency, any attempt to move to a higher isoquant of one of the industries necessarily brings the economy to a lower isoquant of the other industry. This is important to know, because this is the property we have been looking for: *Resources are allocated optimally only at points where the isoquants of the two industries are tangent to one another.*

The locus of all such tangencies between the two sets of isoquants is known as the *contract curve*. In Figure 3-5, the contract curve is illustrated by curve $O_c GHKO_f$.

In summary, resources are allocated optimally along the contract curve. This means that if the economy is on the contract curve, it is impossible to increase the outputs of both commodities (or increase the output of one without reducing the output of the other) by a mere reallocation of resources. Thus, starting from a point along the contract curve, an increase in the production of food necessarily implies a decrease in the production of clothing and vice versa. On the other hand, if the economy is not on the contract curve, it is possible to increase the outputs of both commodities by a mere reallocation of resources that moves the economy to the contract curve. For instance, if the economy were at Z of Figure 3-5, the output of both commodities could be increased by moving to some point on the contract curve in region GH.

Perfect Competition and the Efficient Allocation of Resources

In a centrally planned economy, a planning bureau could intentionally allocate resources at some point on the contract curve. How is this accomplished in a free enterprise system? It is accomplished by perfect competition. As Adam Smith would say, in a free enterprise system an "invisible hand" guides the efficient allocation of resources.

As we saw earlier, the marginal rate of substitution of labor for land MRS_{LT} in each industry must necessarily be equal to the factor-price ratio w/r in long-run equilibrium. Since factors are homogeneous and *factor prices are uniform throughout the economy,* it follows that in the long run the economy must be allocating resources in a way that equalizes the MRS_{LT} in the two industries. What this means is that in the long run the economy will be allocating resources along the contract curve.

The Contract Curve Never Crosses the Diagonal

Under constant returns to scale, the contract curve never crosses the diagonal—it must lie on one side of the diagonal of the box diagram, as shown in Figure 3-5. The reason is simple. As we have seen, when returns to scale are constant, the marginal rate of substitution MRS_{LT} remains constant along any straight line through the origin. Hence, along the diagonal of the box diagram, the MRS_{LT} of each industry remains constant. If the MRS_{LT} of the food industry and the MRS_{LT} of the clothing industry happen to be equal at some point along the diagonal, they must continue to be equal at all points of the diagonal; and then the contract curve coincides with the diagonal. On the other hand, if the MRS_{LT} of the food industry and the MRS_{LT} of the clothing industry are different at some point along the diagonal, they must be different at all other points along the diagonal; and the contract curve will have no points in common with the diagonal—excluding the origins O_c and O_f. This geometrical property assumes economic importance later on in Chapter 5.

3-4 THE PRODUCTION-POSSIBILITIES FRONTIER

The production-possibilities frontier (or transformation curve) shows the maximum obtainable amount of one commodity for any given amount of the other.
As we saw earlier, it depends on two fundamental data: factor supplies (or endowments) and technology (or production functions).

The discussion of the box-diagram technique in the preceding section leads
to the following important conclusion: When the economy allocates its
resources along the contract curve, it is impossible to increase the output of one
commodity without decreasing the output of the other commodity. Hence, each
point on the contract curve corresponds to a point on the production-possibilities frontier and vice versa. Figure 3-6 shows the production-possibilities frontier that is derived from the box diagram of Figure 3-5. Points *K*, *H*, and *G* in
Figure 3-6 correspond to the synonymous points in Figure 3-5.

The Shape of the Production-Possibilities Frontier

When the contract curve coincides with the diagonal of the box, the production-possibilities frontier is necessarily a straight line, as in the classical theory.
This should not come as a surprise. Along the diagonal, the factors labor and
land are used in a fixed proportion in both industries. Thus, in the example of
Figure 3-5, where the economy is, by assumption, endowed with 200 units of
labor and 100 units of land, each industry will be using 2 units of labor per unit

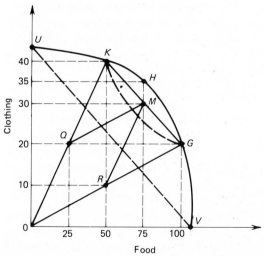

Figure 3-6 *The production-possibilities frontier derived from the box diagram of Figure 3.5.*
Points *K* and *G* correspond to two different techniques. By allocating resources arbitrarily to
these two techniques, we can always reach points along straight line *KMG*. For instance,
when half of all resources are allocated to *K* and the other half to *G*, technique *K* yields combination *Q*, and technique *G* combination *R*. Addition of *Q* and *R* (by means of the parallelogram rule) yields point *M*.

of land (when resources are allocated along the diagonal of the box). But technically we can always consider the mixture of 2 units of labor and 1 unit of land as a unit of a composite factor of production. Hence, the two factors, labor and land, reduce technically to a single factor. From our discussion of the classical theory, we know that the existence of a single factor combined with constant returns to scale generates a linear production-possibilities frontier exhibiting constant opportunity costs.

Normally the contract curve will lie on one side of the diagonal. (For instance, in Figure 3-5 the contract curve lies below the diagonal.) When this happens, the production-possibilities frontier becomes concave to the origin, exhibiting increasing opportunity costs. Why should this be so? While a rigorous proof of this proposition is left to more advanced texts [see, for instance, Chacholiades (1978, pp. 107–109)], we can still make some heuristic comments to make the argument plausible.

First, note that the economy can always reach broken straight line UV in Figure 3-6 by allocating its resources *arbitrarily* along the diagonal of the box in Figure 3-5. Thus, we rule out the possibility that the production-possibilities frontier may be totally convex to the origin.

Second, we can also rule out any convex regions of the production frontier, such as convex broken curve KG in Figure 3-6. Points K and G correspond to two different production techniques. By allocating resources *arbitrarily* to these two techniques, we can always reach points along the straight line that joins points K and G in Figure 3-6. For instance, when half of all resources (that is, 100 units of labor and 50 units of land) are allocated to technique "K," the output of food will be 25 and the output of clothing 20 (that is, half of what the economy produces with *all* resources at K). When the other half of all resources are allocated to technique "G," an additional 50 units of food and 10 units of clothing will be produced (that is, half of what the economy produces with *all* resources at G). With this *arbitrary* allocation of resources, the total amounts of output are: 75 units of food (that is, 25 plus 50), and 30 units of clothing (that is, 20 plus 10). But 75 units of food and 30 units of clothing determine point M, which lies on the straight-line segment KG, halfway between K and G, as shown in Figure 3-6. Therefore, we can rule out the convex region KG because we can always reach points on the straight line KMG.

The Marginal Rate of Transformation and Relative Commodity Prices

As we saw in Chapter 2, relative commodity prices are, in general, equal to their respective opportunity costs (or marginal rates of transformation). This proposition was shown to be true within the context of the labor theory of value. However, as noted then, this equality between opportunity costs and relative prices is true even in the present case.

Actually, the marginal rate of transformation gives the ratio of marginal costs. But under perfect competition, prices are equal to their corresponding marginal costs. Accordingly, the marginal rate of transformation must also be equal to the ratio of commodity prices (that is, relative prices). For a rigorous proof, see Chacholiades (1978), pp. 110–114.

When opportunity costs are constant, as in the classical theory, autarkic relative prices are determined by the unique absolute slope of the production-possibilities frontier, irrespective of demand (assuming only that some positive amounts of both commodities are consumed). In the presence of increasing opportunity costs, however, the pretrade prices are determined by the slope of the production-possibilities frontier at the pretrade equilibrium point, which can only be determined if demand is introduced into the picture. Accordingly, before we go any further, we must discuss demand. This is the subject matter of Part B.

PART B: Community Indifference

The reader may recall from Chapter 2 that the Ricardian theory could not explain how the equilibrium terms of trade were actually determined. To do this it is necessary that demand be introduced into the picture, as John Stuart Mill emphasized. The difficulty is greater, of course, when opportunity costs are increasing—and when they are, even pretrade prices, and thus comparative advantage, cannot be determined without introducing demand. The purpose of this part, then, is to introduce demand.

It is assumed that the reader is already familiar with the concept of indifference curves. However, for the benefit of those who wish to refresh their memories, Section 3-5 summarizes briefly the properties of indifference curves and illustrates the concept of consumer equilibrium. Section 3-6 deals with the useful concept of social indifference curves, which summarize the tastes of a society as opposed to the tastes of a single individual consumer.

3-5 INDIFFERENCE CURVES[3]

Economists usually represent the tastes of a consumer by means of *indifference curves*. As is well known, an indifference curve is the locus of all alternative combinations of, say, food and clothing that enable the consumer to attain a given level of *satisfaction* or *utility*. The collection of all indifference curves forms the *indifference map*. Indifference curves are similar to isoquants, except that utility cannot be measured cardinally, as output is—utility is an ordinal concept.

Indifference curves are illustrated in Figure 3-7. Their general properties are:

1 They slope downward.
2 They never intersect each other.

[3] Readers who are already familiar with indifference curves may omit this section.

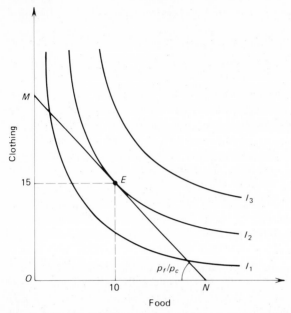

Figure 3-7 *The indifference map and consumer equilibrium.*
The consumer maximizes his or her utility at the point where the budget line (*MN*) becomes
tangent to the highest indifference curve (*I₂*), as illustrated by point *E*.

3 They represent levels of satisfaction or utility; specifically, a movement from a lower to a higher indifference curve (such as from I_1 to I_2) implies an increase in the utility enjoyed by the consumer.
   4 They are convex to the origin.

The marginal rate of substitution of food for clothing shows the number of units of clothing that the consumer could give up for an extra unit of food and still continue to enjoy the same level of satisfaction or utility, that is, continue to consume on the same indifference curve. This marginal rate of substitution is given graphically by the absolute slope of the indifference curve at a specified consumption point. All this is very similar to our earlier discussion of isoquants.

The assumed convexity of indifference curves implies again that the marginal rate of substitution is diminishing. That is, as the substitution of one commodity for another proceeds, that substitution becomes progressively more difficult.

The object of the consumer is to reach the highest possible indifference curve, that is, attain the highest level of satisfaction given a fixed money income and fixed commodity prices. This is accomplished at the point (*E*) where the consumer's budget line (*MN*) becomes just tangent to the highest indifference curve (*I₂*). At consumer equilibrium point *E*, the marginal rate of substitution of food for clothing (MRS_{FC}) equals the relative price of food (p_f/p_c). The equality $MRS_{FC} = \dfrac{p_f}{p_c}$ is a necessary condition for utility maximization and is similar to the condition for cost minimization.

3-6   SOCIAL INDIFFERENCE CURVES[4]

The neoclassical theory of international trade makes two simplifying assumptions: (1) that the tastes of a society—as opposed to the tastes of the individual consumer—can be conveniently summarized by a *social indifference map*, qualitatively similar to the indifference map of an individual consumer; and (2) that the society behaves as if it were trying to attain the highest possible social indifference curve. In this book, we shall adopt these simplifications. This raises several questions, however. For instance, what meaning should be attached to a social indifference curve? Do social indifference curves having the same properties as the indifference curves of an individual consumer exist? If they do exist, how can they be derived? This section deals briefly with these questions.

The Uses of Social Indifference Curves

Why do we need social indifference curves? For the same reasons we need indifference curves for the individual consumer: (1) to describe *positive behavior* and (2) to show how *welfare* changes when a change in consumption occurs.

For instance, given the budget line of the consumer (which depends only on his or her income and on commodity prices), we can determine, as in Figure 3-7, how much food and how much clothing the consumer will buy. Now suppose that the price of food falls while the price of clothing and the income of the consumer stay the same. The consumer will shift to a new equilibrium by determining the point of tangency between the *new* budget line and the highest possible indifference curve. The consumer will change his or her purchases of food and clothing in a certain way. This is what we mean by "positive behavior."

But there is another important question: Is the consumer better off or worse off as a result of the reduction in the price of food? This is a *normative* question. As the reader probably knows already, we can say that the consumer is better off (that is, the consumer experiences an increase in his or her economic welfare, or well-being) since the reduction in the price of food enables consumption on a higher indifference curve. (As we saw earlier, one of the properties of indifference curves is that movement from a lower to a higher indifference curve implies an increase in the satisfaction or utility enjoyed by the consumer.)

Similarly, we need the social indifference curves to determine the aggregate consumption levels of food and clothing given the budget line of the

[4] This section is optional. The reader who decides to omit it may proceed on the assumption that the tastes of a society can be conveniently summarized by a well-behaved indifference map that has the same properties as the indifference map of a typical consumer.

society and—as that budget line shifts (as a result of a change in prices or national income)—to determine how the aggregate consumption levels of food and clothing will change. In addition, we like to be able to say whether social welfare increases or decreases as a result of a structural change (brought about by a government policy, a change in world markets, an invention or some other factor).

Unlike the indifference map of the consumer, a social indifference map need not exist at all. Even if it does, it may describe positive behavior only, remaining totally silent on the question of welfare changes. Therefore, we must be extremely careful in our use of social indifference curves, especially before passing any judgment on whether social welfare increases or decreases as the society moves from one indifference curve to another.

An important justification for the continued use of social indifference curves is, besides their simplicity, the fact that they give rise to results that are qualitatively similar to those derived more laboriously by the use of a totally disaggregated model.

Definition and Difficulties

An individual consumer's indifference curve gives all combinations of food and clothing that yield the same amount of utility to the consumer. In principle, it can be derived by asking the consumer to *reveal* his or her preferences. For instance, given any two combinations of food and clothing, say, A and B, we could ask the consumer whether A is preferred to B, or B to A, or whether the consumer is indifferent between them. If the consumer is indifferent, then we know that A and B lie on the same indifference curve. By giving the consumer more options, we can discover the entire indifference map.

How are we to define a social indifference curve? One might be tempted to say that a social indifference curve is the locus of all combinations of food and clothing that yield the same amount of social welfare. But what is social welfare, and how can it be measured? Further, how can we determine all those combinations that yield the same amount of social welfare? We cannot subject society to the kind of questioning we subjected the individual consumer to, because society is composed of many individuals with divergent views. A majority vote will not do.

Economists today agree that social welfare is a function of the welfare of each and every citizen. Nevertheless, unlike earlier generations of economists, modern economists stop short of suggesting that social welfare is the sum of all individual satisfactions enjoyed by all consumers. For one thing, the utility enjoyed by each consumer is an ordinal concept and cannot be measured cardinally. For another, *interpersonal comparisons* of utility are ruled out as unscientific. For instance, suppose that one individual becomes better off, and at the same time another individual becomes worse off. We cannot say what happens to social welfare unless we find a way to compare the gain of the first individual with the loss of the second individual. Such a comparison, though, requires a judgment of a purely ethical nature and cannot be made objectively. Different ethical observers will pass different judgments.

Modern economists accept the Paretian ethic that when one individual becomes better off without anyone else becoming worse off, social welfare increases. However, when some individuals become better off and others worse off, we are still unable to say whether social welfare increases or decreases, although some progress has been made by means of the so-called *compensation principle*.

It must be clear now why, in general, it is not possible to draw a social indifference curve and pretend it is the locus of all combinations of food and clothing that yield the same amount of social welfare. Points along a social indifference curve represent *aggregate* amounts of food and clothing—they give absolutely no information regarding the distribution of these aggregates among the individual consumers. Hence, even if we were to accept someone's ethical belief of how one individual's welfare is to be added to another's, a given combination of food and clothing (say, 100 units of food and 80 units of clothing) would represent not one level of social welfare but many, each level depending on how the 100 units of food and the 80 units of clothing were distributed among the members of the society. Also, if the supplies of food and clothing were to increase to, say, 120 and 110, respectively (a change which would normally imply a shift to a higher indifference curve and higher welfare), we could not assert that social welfare would increase, because we would have no information on the distribution of income. We must, therefore, conclude that in general social indifference curves do not exist.

3-7 SUMMARY

1 The fundamental concepts of opportunity cost and social indifference form the basis for the neoclassical theory of international values.

2 Linear production-possibilities frontiers imply *constant* opportunity costs. *Increasing* opportunity costs, illustrated by production-possibilities frontiers that are concave to the origin, offer a better description of reality. In addition to the fact that many industries operate under increasing (not constant) costs, increasing opportunity costs do not lead to the unrealistic situation of complete specialization (whereas constant opportunity costs do).

3 Increasing opportunity costs can be explained in one of two ways: (1) by invoking the product specificity of factors or (2) by observing that technology is such that different commodities use homogeneous factors in different proportions.

4 Constant returns to scale have several important properties, as follows: both the average and the marginal physical product of each factor, as well as the marginal rate of substitution, depend only on the proportion in which factors are used; the whole isoquant map is a blown-up version of the unit isoquant; when each factor is paid its marginal product, the total output is exactly exhausted (Euler's theorem); and when the marginal rate of substitution is diminishing (convex isoquants), the law of diminishing returns holds.

5   Resources are allocated optimally only along the contract curve, that is, the locus of tangencies between the two sets of isoquants drawn inside the Edgeworth-Bowley box diagram. Under constant returns to scale, the contract curve never crosses the diagonal but may coincide with it.

6   With homogeneous factors and uniform factor prices throughout the economy, perfect competition leads to an optimal allocation of resources.

7   The production-possibilities frontier shows the maximal combinations of outputs that the economy can produce. It depends on two fundamental data: (1) factor supplies (or endowments) and (2) technology (or production functions). Each point on the production-possibilities frontier corresponds to a point on the contract curve and vice versa.

8   Under constant returns to scale, the production-possibilities frontier is *linear* (*constant* opportunity costs) when the contract curve coincides with the diagonal of the box diagram; it becomes *concave* to the origin (*increasing* opportunity costs) when the contract curve lies on only one side of the diagonal—a situation that arises when different commodities use factors in different proportions.

9   The neoclassical theory of international trade makes two simplifying assumptions: (1) that society's tastes can be summarized by a well-behaved social indifference map and (2) that the society tries to reach the highest social indifference curve.

10   There are only a few special cases in which the use of social indifference curves can be made rigorous. In general, social indifference curves do not exist; and their continued use is justified only by the fact that they give rise to results that are qualitatively similar to those derived by more rigorous methods.

APPENDIX: Some Special Cases of Social Indifference Curves[5]

Even though, in general, social indifference curves do not exist, there are some special cases in the literature where the use of social indifference curves can be justified. These cases are as follows:

1   A Robinson Crusoe Economy

The simplest, and at the same time most trivial, case is a Robinson Crusoe economy, that is, an economy composed of a single individual. Here the problem of aggregation of indifference maps does not arise. There exists only one indifference map, which is also the social indifference map. This case cannot be taken seriously.

2   A Totalitarian Economy

In a totalitarian economy, or even when a planning bureau exists, the indifference map of the dictator, or of the planning bureau, becomes the social indifference map. Here, as in the preceding case, the problem of aggregation does not arise.

---

[5] The reader may omit this appendix.

3　Identical Tastes and Factor Endowments

A more realistic case is that of a country inhabited by individuals having identical tastes and factor endowments. Thus, these individuals must be equally endowed capitalists (or landowners) and also equally productive workers. In the present case, the aggregate consumption of each commodity is always a multiple of the consumption of the *representative citizen*. Therefore, the social indifference map is a blown-up version of the representative citizen's indifference map.

Note that because of the assumed identity of tastes and factor endowments, when one individual becomes better off, all do; and social welfare clearly increases. Hence, a movement from a lower to a higher social indifference curve does imply, in the present case, an increase in social welfare.

The identity of tastes is not very unrealistic, particularly within a single nation and culture. However, the identity of factor endowments is most certainly violated in the real world.

4　Identical and Homothetic Tastes

Another case is that of a country inhabited by individuals having identical indifference maps which are also *homothetic*. Homothetic indifference maps have the property that any straight line through the origin intersects all indifference curves at points of equal slope, as in the case of isoquant maps characterized by constant returns to scale. What this really means is this: Each and every consumer divides his or her income between food and clothing in the same way, irrespective of how high or how low the income happens to be. Accordingly, any redistribution of income leaves the aggregate consumption of food and clothing unchanged: the reduction in the amounts of food and clothing by those whose incomes are reduced is always matched exactly by the increase in the amounts of food and clothing by those whose incomes are increased. Hence, the aggregate amounts of food and clothing depend on relative prices only—*not* the distribution of income. In this case, the social indifference map coincides with the indifference map of any one of the many identical individuals.

Note that because in this case no information is given on the distribution of income, the present indifference map cannot be used to measure changes in welfare. Thus, a movement from a lower to a higher social indifference curve can very well be associated with a reduction in social welfare, provided, of course, that such a movement worsens the distribution of income sufficiently.

5　Optimizing Income-Redistribution Policy

The final case is when a *specific social welfare function* is known and the government always redistributes income in such a way as to maximize social welfare. The social welfare function summarizes the ethical beliefs of some ethical observer and shows systematically how one person's welfare is to be "added" to another's.

To understand how the maximization of a social welfare function can lead to the construction of a social indifference map, recall our earlier observation that a given combination of food and clothing would represent many levels of welfare because there are many possible ways to distribute income. What the present procedure suggests is to remove the indeterminacy by merely choosing the *maximum* amount of social welfare for each combination of food and clothing. Once this is done, we can assign a unique level of welfare to each point in the commodity space. Then we can draw social indifference curves merely by connecting all points that represent the same amount of welfare.

SUGGESTED READING

Chacholiades, M. (1978). *International Trade Theory and Policy*. McGraw-Hill Book Company, New York, chaps. 4–5.

Haberler, G. (1936). *The Theory of International Trade*. W. Hodge and Company, London, chap. 12.

Hirshleifer, J. (1976). *Price Theory and Applications*. Prentice-Hall, Inc., Englewood Cliffs, N.J.

Leontief, W. W. (1933). "The Use of Indifference Curves in the Analysis of Foreign Trade." *Quarterly Journal of Economics*, vol. 47, pp. 493–503. Reprinted in AEA *Readings in the Theory of International Trade*. Richard D. Irwin, Inc., Homewood, Illinois, 1950.

Samuelson, P. A. (1956). "Social Indifference Curves." *Quarterly Journal of Economics*, vol. 70, pp. 1–22.

Savosnik, K. M. (1958). "The Box Diagram and the Production-Possibility Curve." *Ekonomisk Tidskrift*, vol. 60, pp. 183–197.

Viner, J. (1937). *Studies in the Theory of International Trade*. Harper and Brothers, New York, chaps. 7 and 9.

Chapter Four

International Equilibrium

This chapter deals with the important topic of international equilibrium and its properties. It is divided into five sections. Section 4-1 deals with the problem of general equilibrium in a single (closed or open) economy. Section 4-2 provides a brief neoclassical demonstration of comparative advantage. Section 4-3 examines the offer curve and then uses it to demonstrate international equilibrium. Section 4-4 discusses briefly the concept of the terms of trade and considers whether this concept can serve as an index of social welfare. The chapter concludes with a discussion of decreasing opportunity costs. In the appendix to the chapter there is an examination of Meade's ingenious geometric technique for deriving the offer curve and demonstrating international equilibrium by bringing together production, consumption, and trade.

4-1 GENERAL EQUILBRIUM IN A SINGLE ECONOMY

We begin our discussion by demonstrating how the basic tools we studied in Chapter 3 (for example, the production-possibilities frontier and the social indifference map) can be used to portray general equilibrium in a single economy.

General Equilibrium in a Closed Economy

Figure 4-1 shows the general equilibrium of a closed economy. Panel (*a*) illustrates the Ricardian case of *constant* opportunity costs, panel (*b*) the neoclassical case of *increasing* opportunity costs. In both cases, curve UP_0V is the economy's production-possibilities frontier, and curves 1, 2, and 3 are illustrative social indifference curves.

Recall that the production-possibilities frontier depends on two fundamental data: factor endowments and technology. The case of constant opportunity costs of panel (*a*) need not reflect the existence of a single factor, such as labor. It may very well reflect the fact that the factors labor and land are used in exactly the same proportion in the food and clothing industries. In this situation, as we saw in Chapter 3, the contract curve in the box diagram coincides with the diagonal, and the production-possibilities frontier becomes linear, reflecting constant opportunity costs. The case of increasing opportunity costs of panel (*b*) reflects the fact that the factors labor and land are used in different proportions in the food and clothing industries; and as the economy moves along the production-possibilities frontier, these proportions change, bringing into action the famous law of diminishing returns to a variable factor. Further insights into these subtle changes in the production process must wait until the next chapter.

General equilibrium occurs in both panels at point P_0, where the production-possibilities frontier is tangent to the highest possible social indifference curve. The economy acts like a huge consumer, whose budget line is given by the production-possibilities frontier and whose tastes are given by the social indifference map. This remarkable result is not brought about by the deliberate actions of any central authority. This is the outcome of one of the most complex social processes, in which millions of individuals play an important role, acting as individual consumers and producers in the pursuit of their own selfish interests. These divergent interests are guided and coordinated by the forces of competition (Adam Smith's invisible hand) until a general equilibrium, as in Figure 4-1, is reached.

The common absolute slope of the production-possibilities frontier and social indifference curve 1 at P_0 gives the equilibrium relative price of food, that is, p_f/p_c. *Therefore, in general equilibrium, the commodity price ratio is equal to both the marginal rate of transformation (or the opportunity cost of food in terms of clothing) and the marginal rate of substitution in consumption.*

Note, however, the basic difference between the cases of constant cost and increasing opportunity cost. In the former (constant cost), the equilibrium price ratio can be inferred from the unique slope of the production-possibilities frontier without any information about demand—assuming only that both commodities are produced and consumed in equilibrium. Under the neoclassical assumption of increasing opportunity costs, the equilibrium price ratio cannot be inferred from the production-possibilities frontier alone: full information about demand is also necessary. To use Marshall's metaphor, it is both blades of the scissors that do the cutting.

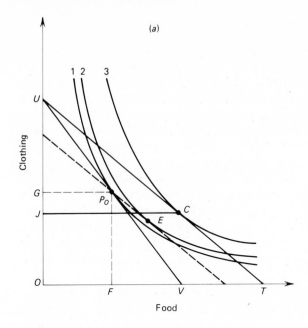

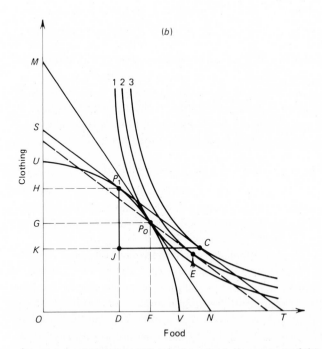

Figure 4-1 *General equilibrium in a single economy and the gains from trade.*
Panel (*a*) illustrates the case of constant opportunity costs and panel (*b*) the case of increasing opportunity costs.

Equilibrium in a Simple Open Economy

Assume now that as a result of some exogenous event, such as a huge reduction of transportation costs or the elimination of prohibitive tariffs, our closed economy is granted the opportunity to trade food and clothing in the international market. For the moment, we shall assume that our country is so small that her sales and purchases (exports and imports) in the world markets do not have any appreciable effect on world prices. In short, our economy is a price taker in international trade. How does our country reach general equilibrium now that trade with the rest of the world is possible?

Perfect competition will force, sooner or later, our domestic price ratio to be the same as the international price ratio. In addition, perfect competition will force our producers to adjust their production plans so that their marginal costs are equal to the given international prices. Similarly, perfect competition will force our consumers to adjust their consumption plans so that their marginal rates of substitution are equal to the given international price ratio. All this is illustrated in Figure 4-1.

Consider panel (b) first. The autarkic price ratio is given by (the absolute slope of) line MN. Food is assumed to be cheaper in the international market. In particular, the international price ratio is assumed to be given by line ST. As our domestic price ratio falls to ST, the food producers find the price of food to be lower than the marginal cost of food; and the motive of profit maximization forces them to release factors and cut output until the marginal cost of food becomes equal to the new, lower price of food.

Similarly, the clothing producers find the increased price of clothing to be higher than the marginal cost of clothing, and they realize that more profits can be reaped by expanding their output. Indeed, to maximize their profits, the clothing producers must continue to increase their output until their marginal cost becomes equal to the new, higher price of clothing. They accomplish this by employing the resources released by the food industry.

As the production of food falls and the production of clothing rises, the economy moves along the production-possibilities frontier from P_0 toward U. In particular, the economy moves to P_1, where the ratio of marginal costs (slope of the production-possibilities frontier) equals the international price ratio (slope of ST). Accordingly, at P_1 prices are indeed equal to marginal costs, and all producers maximize their profits.

It is important to note that national income (that is, the value of output produced) is *maximized* at P_1. This is a fundamental result of perfect competition. For instance, if the society insisted on producing at P_0 (that is, at the autarkic equilibrium point), its "budget line" would be the broken line passing through points P_0 and E. This is definitely inferior to "budget line" ST, which our economy can attain by producing at P_1. In fact, production at any point other than P_1 necessarily gives rise to a "community budget line" that is inferior to ST. Accordingly, national income is maximized at P_1, where the marginal rate of transformation is equal to the international price ratio.

Because of its great significance, community budget line ST is called the *consumption-possibilities frontier*. This means that by producing at P_1, our economy can actually *consume* any combination of food and clothing along line ST. This is accomplished, of course, by trading appropriate amounts of food and clothing in the international market.

What is the relationship between production-possibilities frontier UV and consumption-possibilities frontier ST? They have only one point in common: optimum production point P_1. Everywhere else, the consumption-possibilities frontier lies beyond the production-possibilities frontier. This is a remarkable result. It shows that while our country is *always* constrained by her production-possibilities frontier as far as production is concerned, *free international trade makes it possible for her to consume beyond the boundaries of the production frontier*. Herein lies the essence of the gains from trade.

Where does our economy consume after it is opened up to international trade? This occurs at point C, where the consumption-possibilities frontier touches the highest possible social indifference curve (curve 3). Note that our economy would not have been able to reach social indifference curve 3 had it remained closed—the production-possibilities frontier does not reach social indifference curve 3.

In summary, the opportunity to trade enables our small economy to produce at P_1 (where the marginal rate of transformation is equal to the international price ratio) and consume at C (where consumption-possibilities frontier ST is tangent to social indifference curve 3). Point C lies outside of the production frontier.

What are our country's exports and imports at the free-trade equilibrium? These are determined as the differences between the amounts produced and the amounts consumed. Graphically, they are given by the perpendicular sides of *trade triangle P_1JC*. Thus, our economy exports P_1J units of clothing and imports JC units of food. Observe that $P_1J = P_1D - JD$; that is, the exports of clothing are given by the difference between the domestic production and consumption of clothing. Similarly, $JC = KC - KJ$; that is, the imports of food are equal to the domestic consumption of food minus the domestic production of food.

Turn now briefly to the constant-cost case of panel (a). Before the introduction of international trade, our economy produces and consumes at P_0. When the economy is opened up to international trade, production shifts to U and consumption to C, with line UT being the consumption-possibilities frontier. Again the opportunity to trade enables our economy to separate the domestic consumption from the domestic production, and to increase social welfare by consuming at point C, which is the point of tangency between the consumption-possibilities frontier and social indifference curve 3. Point C lies again beyond the production frontier. The only notable difference between this and the previous case of increasing opportunity costs is the fact that *our economy specializes now completely in the production of clothing*. All food consumed domestically is imported from the rest of the world. Thus, the trade triangle is now given by UCJ; and our economy exports JU units of clothing in exchange for JC units of food.

The Gains from Trade

The total gain from trade is represented in Figure 4-1 by the shift in consumption from point P_0 (autarkic consumption) to C (free-trade consumption). This total gain from trade is usually divided into the following two components:

   1   The *consumption gain* (or the *gain from international exchange*), which accrues to the economy when the same bundle of commodities produced under autarky is produced under free trade. In Figure 4-1, the consumption gain is illustrated by the imaginary movement from P_0 to E in both panels.
   2   The *production gain* (or the *gain from specialization*), which accrues to the economy in addition to the consumption gain as a result of the shift of the production point from autarkic equilibrium point P_0 to the free-trade equilibrium point, that is, U in panel (*a*) or P_1 in panel (*b*). This adjustment in the economy's production results in a higher national income and enables the economy to shift its consumption from E to C, as shown in both panels of Figure 4-1.

   Why is it important to divide the total gain into a consumption gain plus a production gain? Because such a breakdown illuminates the fact that free trade is beneficial to every country; even to a backward country that lacks the capacity to transform its autarkic production bundle into something else, that is, a country whose production-possibilities frontier is given by rectangle OFP_0G. Even in this extreme case, the consumption gain continues to be positive while the production gain is zero.

4-2   A NEOCLASSICAL DEMONSTRATION OF COMPARATIVE ADVANTAGE

Having considered at some length the problem of general equilibrium of a single open economy, the analysis should logically be extended to consider the problem of general equilibrium of a two-country model. This is done in the rest of this chapter. The present section reconsiders the theory of comparative advantage but within the neoclassical world of increasing opportunity costs. Not only does this step prepare the ground for future investigations, it also enables us to keep in touch with the basic questions raised back in Chapter 2.

The Setting

Assume two countries, America and Britain. Each country is endowed with two factors of production—homogeneous labor and homogeneous land—and produces two commodities, food and clothing, under constant returns to scale.

   Figure 4-2 summarizes the autarkic equilibrium positions of the two countries. In the first panel, America produces and consumes at E_a, which is the

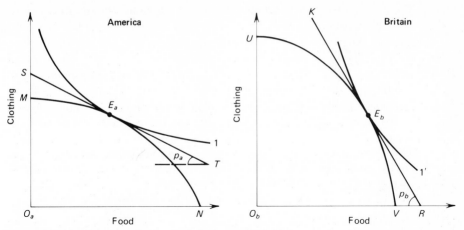

Figure 4-2 *Autarkic equilibrium in America and Britain.*
Before trade, America consumes at E_a (first panel) and Britain at E_b (second panel). Food is
relatively cheaper in America ($p_a < p_b$). Accordingly, America should specialize in food and
Britain in clothing.

tangency between America's production frontier MN and social indifference
curve 1. America's pretrade price ratio p_a is given by the slope of the tangent
ST. Similarly, in the second panel, Britain produces and consumes at E_b, which
is the tangency between Britain's production frontier UV and social indifference curve 1'. Britain's pretrade price ratio p_b is given by the slope of KR. Figure 4-2 is drawn on the assumption that food is cheaper in America in the initial
autarkic equilibrium states.

Is trade between America and Britain possible? Is it profitable? Which
commodity should each country export? At what terms of trade will food and
clothing be traded under a regime of free trade? These are fundamental questions, and our analysis has progressed sufficiently to permit us to venture at
least some tentative answers.

Comparative Advantage and the Gains from Trade

We learned back in Chapter 2 that in the Ricardian world of constant opportunity costs, a country should specialize in the production of that commodity
which, under autarky, it produces relatively more cheaply than the other
country. This fundamental principle continues to hold in the neoclassical world
of increasing opportunity costs. The proof of this proposition is very simple.

Suppose that America's autarkic relative price of food is 2 and Britain's 5.
Since prices are equal to opportunity costs, this means that to *increase* her
production of food by 1 unit, America must sacrifice only 2 units of clothing.
On the other hand, for each unit of food given up, Britain can increase her output of clothing by 5 units. The final outcome of such a reorganization of production is, of course, a net amount of 3 units of clothing (that is, 5 − 2). Such gains

can continue to be reaped by further adjustments in production until the opportunity costs of the two countries are equalized.

Figure 4.3 illustrates graphically the outcome of specialization according to comparative advantage. We derive it from Figure 4-2 through trial and error. In particular, we rotate Britain's diagram by 180°, and then place Britain's production frontier tangent to America's production frontier at a point, such as E. International equilibrium occurs when the common tangent at E (see broken line CE) also happens to pass through a tangency between two social indifference curves, as shown in Figure 4-3 by point C. Thus, in Figure 4-3 both countries produce at E and consume at C. America exports JE units of food to Britain, and in return Britain exports JC units of clothing to America. The equilibrium terms of trade are thus given by the ratio JC/JE, which is the absolute slope of terms-of-trade line EC. Observe how free trade enables America to increase her welfare by moving to social indifference curve 2. Britain also benefits from free trade by moving to social indifference curve 2'. Finally, observe how the equilibrium terms of trade lie between the autarkic price ratios of America and Britain. Something similar to this last result was anticipated in Chapter 2.

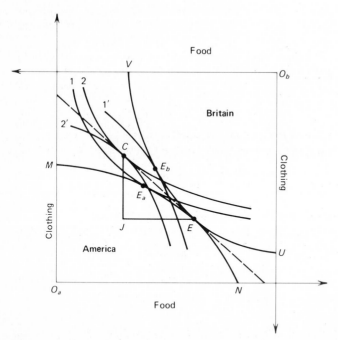

Figure 4-3 *Specialization according to comparative advantage, and the gains from trade.* Through trial and error, we determine international equilibrium by placing Britain's production frontier tangent to America's frontier at E and letting the common tangent (see broken line CE) pass through a point of tangency (see point C) between two social indifference curves. Both countries produce at E and consume at C (which lies beyond both production frontiers).

4-3 OFFER CURVES

International equilibrium occurs when the terms of trade are such that world supply equals world demand in each and every market. At that point, all producers sell all they wish to sell, and all consumers buy all they wish to buy. All are satisfied, and no one has any incentive to change his or her behavior. How is international equilibrium determined? How do we bring world supply and demand together to determine the equilibrium terms of trade?

We have already portrayed international equilibrium in Figure 4-3. The reader should inspect this figure carefully in order to be convinced that world supply equals world demand in both the food market and the clothing market. Unfortunately, Figure 4-3 does not give us a general method of determining international equilibrium. Such a diagram can only be constructed through trial and error.

It is not a simple task to derive world supply and demand curves for all commodities simultaneously and use them to determine the equilibrium terms of trade. For this reason, Alfred Marshall sought an alternative device, the *offer curve*. The nature of Marshall's ingenious device, how it is derived, and how it is used in international economics is studied in this section. It is also studied further in the appendix to this chapter.

Exports and Imports

As we have seen, international equilibrium is attained when the terms of trade are such that world supply equals world demand in each and every market. For instance, equilibrium in the food market occurs when the following equation holds:

America's production of food *plus* Britain's production of food
= America's consumption of food *plus* Britain's consumption of food.

However, this equation is equivalent to the following:

America's production of food *minus* America's consumption of food
= Britain's consumption of food *minus* Britain's production of food

or more simply:

America's exports of food = Britain's imports of food

Similarly, equilibrium in the clothing market is attained when

America's imports of clothing = Britain's exports of clothing

Note that in our present discussion we assume that America has a comparative advantage in the production of food, Britain a comparative advantage in the production of clothing. This is, however, a simplifying assumption. The important point is that international equilibrium can be cast in terms of each country's exports and imports only—not in terms of world supply and demand. In other words, international equilibrium prevails when an equality exists between what the first country is *willing to export* and what the second country is *willing to import*. Such an equality, of course, does imply that world supply equals world demand. Nevertheless, the subtle switch to exports and imports facilitates tremendously the determination of international equilibrium.

Before going any further, there is a methodological point that must be cleared. When we speak of exports and imports in the present context, we do not mean the quantities of food and clothing that are *actually* shipped by one country to another. Rather we mean those quantities of food and clothing that a country is *willing to export or import*, as the case may be. For instance, the amount of food shipped by America to Britain must be precisely equal to the amount of food actually imported by Britain. There can be no difference here between the amount of food actually exported by America and the amount of food actually imported by Britain; and this equality between *actual exports* and *actual imports* holds whether the market for food is in equilibrium or not. Now for a market to be in equilibrium, it is necessary for all buyers to be able to buy all they want at current prices and for all sellers to be able to sell all they want at current prices. Only with the absence of any frustrated buyers or sellers do we have equilibrium. It is for this reason that in the present context, the term "exports" means the quantity that a country is willing to export at the current terms of trade. Similarly, the term "imports" means the quantity that a country is willing to import at the current terms of trade. These two quantities are equal only in equilibrium.

The Derivation of Offer Curves

An offer curve merely shows the *offers* of a country at alternative terms of trade. An offer is represented by two numbers: the amount of, say, food, that the country is willing to export and the amount of clothing that the country is willing to import. The locus of all offers of the country is the country's offer curve.

Because of the long-run equality between the value of exports and the value of imports of a country, there exists a strict relationship among exports, imports, and the terms of trade.[1] For instance, suppose that the price of food is $2 and the price of clothing $5 and that America is willing to export 500 units of food and import 200 units of clothing. Obviously, the value of exports ($2 × 500 = $1,000) is equal to the value of imports ($5 × 200 = $1,000). But we also have:

$$^{\$2}/_{\$5} = {}^{200}/_{500}$$

---

[1] For simplicity, we disregard long-term capital flows that could permit unbalanced trade even in the long run.

or

$$\text{Relative price of food} = \frac{\text{imports of clothing}}{\text{exports of food}}$$

The above equality holds for all offers. Accordingly, when two of the three elements of an offer are given, the third element is easily inferred. As we shall see, an offer curve gives explicitly only the amounts that a country is willing to export and import. The country's terms of trade are then determined by the ratio of imports to exports.

How are offers determined? We already know the answer to this question. Return to Figure 4-1b, and observe that at autarkic price ratio MN the country is content to consume all she produces domestically. Thus, the country's offer is zero units of food and zero units of clothing. At terms of trade ST, the country produces at P_1 and consumes at C. Therefore, the offer of the country is JC units of imports of food and JP_1 units of exports of clothing. As we said earlier, this offer is determined by the perpendicular sides of *trade triangle* P_1JC. To determine other offers at other terms of trade, we follow the same procedure; that is, we draw other price lines, determine tangencies, and complete the corresponding trade triangles.

Each offer determines a point on the offer curve. For instance, Figure 4-4 presents an offer curve that is derived from the information given in Figure 4-1b. Along the horizontal axis, we measure the alternative amounts of food that the country is willing to import. Along the vertical axis, we measure the alternative amounts of clothing that the country is willing to export. For instance, at point P_1 the country is willing to export JP_1 units of clothing in exchange for OJ units of imports of food. Observe that triangle OJP_1 is identical to triangle CJP_1 of Figure 4-1b. The only insignificant difference lies in the fact that triangle OJP_1 is the mirror image of triangle CJP_1. It is as if a page in the "triangular book" CJP_1 has been flipped over to the left. For this reason, the *absolute slope* of *terms-of-trade line* 2 in Figure 4-4 is equal to the *absolute slope* of consumption-possibilities frontier ST in Figure 4-1b. The fact that the slope of line 2 in Figure 4-4 is positive and the slope of ST in Figure 4-1b is negative is a detail of no significance.

Similarly, terms-of-trade line 1 in Figure 4-4 corresponds to line MN in Figure 4-1b. Since at these terms of trade the offer of the country is zero, it is represented in Figure 4-4 by the origin of the diagram. This is the reason terms-of-trade line 1 meets the offer curve at the origin only—in fact, it is tangent to the offer curve at the origin.

For each value of the terms of trade, we can determine first an offer in Figure 4-1. This is done by determining the optimum production and consumption points—a procedure that yields a trade triangle, such as CJP_1. With the trade triangle at hand, we can determine a point on the offer curve in Figure 4-4, as described above. The offer curve is finally obtained by connecting all these points by means of a continuous line, as shown in Figure 4-4 by OP_1QENGF.

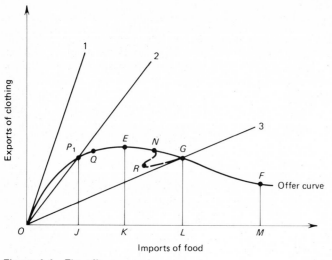

Figure 4-4 *The offer curve.*
The offer curve shows the offers of the country at alternative terms of trade. For instance, at the terms of trade represented by the slope of line 3, the country's offer is given by point G, that is, the country is willing to export LG units of clothing and import OL units of food.

Once the offer curve is determined, we can use it to determine the willingness of the country to trade at alternative terms of trade. Thus, for any given terms of trade, we draw a corresponding terms-of-trade line, such as lines 1, 2, or 3 in Figure 4-4. The intersection between the terms-of-trade line and the offer curve shows the offer of the country. For instance, at the terms of trade represented by the slope of line 3, the country's offer is given by point G; that is, the country is willing to export LG units of clothing and import OL units of food. This procedure is indeed very useful since we no longer have to refer back to Figure 4-1 to determine a country's offer.

The Nature of Offer Curves

An offer curve represents a very complex relationship that we must always keep in mind. Edgeworth (1905, p. 70) summarized the complexity of this relationship in the following well-known statement:

> There is more than meets the eye in Professor Marshall's foreign trade curves. As it has been said by one who used this sort of curve, a movement along a supply-and-demand curve of international trade should be considered as attended with rearrangements of internal trade; as the movement of the hand of a clock corresponds to considerable unseen movements of the machinery.

Edgeworth was actually quoting himself (Edgeworth, 1894, pp. 424–425).
An offer curve is neither a demand curve nor a supply curve but a combination of elements of both. What is more, as Edgeworth so beautifully described, any movement along an offer curve usually implies a movement

along the production-possibilities frontier. We studied in Chapter 3 what a movement along the production frontier actually involves: a shift of resources from one industry to the other; a change in the methods of production; and, as we shall see in the next chapter, a change in factor prices and the distribution of income. On top of all these changes that occur in the production sector of the economy, we must add the changes that occur in consumption as a result of the price and income changes. Accordingly, even a small movement along the offer curve implies a total reorganization of the economy, just "as the hand of a clock corresponds to considerable unseen movements of the machinery."

For our present purposes, we shall be content merely with the use of offer curves in the determination of international equilibrium. Nevertheless, the reader should always keep in mind the considerable unseen movements of the economic machinery. As economists, we must be profoundly concerned with what goes on behind the offer curves. Future chapters will illuminate this complex economic process as much as possible.

The Elasticity of Demand for Imports and the Offer Curve

The reader must be familiar with the concept of the elasticity of demand. It is defined as follows:

$$\text{Elasticity of demand} = \frac{\text{percentage change in quantity demanded}}{\text{percentage change in price}}$$

When the price of a commodity falls, the quantity demanded increases. The elasticity of demand is merely the ratio of the percentage change in the quantity demanded to the percentage change in the price. When these percentage changes are equal (in absolute terms), the elasticity of demand is unity. When the quantity demanded changes faster than the price, the elasticity of demand is higher than unity, and we say that demand is *elastic*. Finally, when the quantity demanded changes more slowly than the price, the elasticity of demand is lower than unity, and we say that demand is *inelastic*.

There is an important relationship between the elasticity of demand and the total expenditure (price × quantity) on the commodity under consideration. Suppose that the price falls by 1 percent. If the quantity demanded increases by more than 1 percent (that is, if demand is elastic), then the total expenditure on the commodity will increase. On the other hand, if the quantity demanded increases by less than 1 percent (that is, if demand is inelastic), then total expenditure will fall. In the limiting case of unit-elastic demand, total expenditure remains the same.

The above ideas are directly applicable to the demand for imports. For instance, the *elasticity of demand for imports* of food is given by the ratio of the percentage change in the quantity of food imported to the percentage change in the relative price of food. The same relationship that exists between the ordinary elasticity of demand and changes in total expenditure also exists between the elasticity of demand for imports and total expenditure on imports. This observation is very important, because we can use it to predict from the mere shape of the offer curve whether the demand for imports is elastic or inelastic at a certain point.

Return to Figure 4-4. What is the total expenditure on the imports of food at point P_1? By definition, we have:

Total expenditure on imports of food
= relative price of food × imports of food
= exports of clothing

Accordingly, the total expenditure on the imports of food at any point is given by the amount of clothing that the country must export to pay for the imports of food. Remember that a country pays for her imports by means of her exports. For instance, at P_1 the total expenditure for the imports of OJ units of food is represented by the amount of JP_1 units of clothing.

Suppose now that the relative price of food is given by the slope of terms-of-trade line 2 in Figure 4-4 and the economy is trading at P_1. Is the demand for imports elastic or inelastic at P_1? Consider a very small reduction in the relative price of food. This price reduction can be represented by a small clockwise rotation of line 2 as implied by line OQ (not drawn). At this lower price, the economy will be willing to trade at Q. What has happened to the total expenditure on imports? Note that point P_1 (and Q) happens to be on an upward-sloping region of the offer curve. Accordingly, as food becomes cheaper and the country moves from P_1 to Q, the total exports of clothing (that is, total expenditure on imports) increase. From this, we immediately infer that the demand for imports is elastic at P_1.

Following this analysis, we can easily conclude that the demand for imports is elastic at all points which lie in upward-sloping region OE of the offer curve, that it is inelastic at all points which lie in forward-falling region EF, and that it is unit elastic at point E.

Substitution, Income, and Production Effects

Return to Figure 4-4, and observe that as the relative price of imports (food) falls from its autarkic level (line 1) toward zero (the horizontal axis), the offer of the country travels along the offer curve from the origin toward F. Because the offer curve does not "bend backwards," as illustrated by dotted region NR, it follows that as food becomes cheaper the demand for imports *increases*. What are the economic reasons for this behavior of imports? As we shall see, more is involved here than the ordinary *law of demand*—the offer curve combines elements of both demand and supply.

By definition, the imports of food are given by the difference between the domestic consumption of food and the domestic production of food. In general, as food becomes cheaper, three effects can be recognized, as follows:

    1 *The production (or output) effect.* As food becomes cheaper, the

domestic production of food falls because of increasing opportunity costs. Other things being equal, this reduction in food production tends to increase the demand for imports by the same amount and is known as the *production effect*, or *output effect*.

2 *The Income Effect.* As food becomes cheaper, the economy's real income increases for two reasons (a) because imports of food can be obtained with fewer exports of, say, clothing (that is, because the terms of trade improve), and (b) because domestic production is readjusted to maximize income—resources are transferred from the food industry to the clothing industry. Unless food is an inferior commodity, the increase in real income causes the domestic consumption of food to increase; and this, in turn, causes the demand for imports to increase *pari passu*. (An *inferior good* is a good whose demand falls as income increases. A *superior*, or *normal*, good is a good whose demand increases as income increases. Finally, a *neutral good* is a good whose demand is not influenced by any income change.)

3 *The Substitution Effect.* We are already familiar with the law of diminishing marginal rate of substitution. As food becomes cheaper, food is substituted for clothing until the marginal rate of substitution of food for clothing is reduced to the lower level of the relative price of food. Thus, the consumption of food increases, causing the demand for imports to increase.

These three effects of a terms-of-trade improvement are illustrated in Figure 4-5. The initial terms of trade are given by line ST. Thus, the economy initially produces at P_0 and consumes at C_0, importing EF units of food. Suppose now that food becomes cheaper, as shown by line MN. The economy's production and consumption points move to P_1 and C_1, respectively, and the imports of food increase to DK. What is the increase in imports made of?

First, the domestic production of food falls by DE, as the production point shifts from P_0 to P_1. Hence, the imports of food must increase by DE to fill up the gap left by the reduction in the domestic production. Accordingly, DE illustrates the production (or output) effect of the terms-of-trade improvement.

Second, the economy's real income increases, as revealed by the shift from social indifference curve 1 to social indifference curve 2. In fact, it must be clear from Figure 4-5 that the economy could move to social indifference curve 2, not by a terms-of-trade improvement but rather by means of an *equivalent increase in income*, as shown by broken line HG, which is parallel to ST and tangent to social indifference curve 2 at Q. Now if this equivalent increase in income had taken place instead, the economy's consumption point would have shifted from C_0 to Q, and both the domestic consumption of food and the imports of food would increase by FJ. The amount FJ is the income effect of the terms-of-trade improvement.

Finally, the economy's consumption point cannot remain at the auxiliary position Q; it must shift to C_1, where the marginal rate of substitution of food for clothing is reduced to the new, lower relative price of food. Thus, both the domestic consumption of food and the demand for imports of food increase by additional amount JK. Since the movement along indifference curve 2 from Q

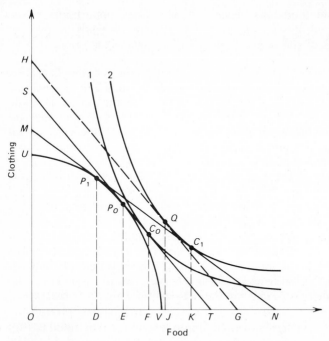

Figure 4-5 *Substitution, income, and production effects.*
At the initial terms of trade given by line *ST*, the economy produces at P_0 and consumes at C_0, importing *EF* units of food. As food becomes cheaper (see line *MN*), the economy shifts its production and consumption to points P_1 and C_1, respectively. The total increase in imports is made up of: (a) a production effect (*DE*), (b) an income effect(*FJ*), and (c) a substitution effect (*JK*)

to C_1 involves merely a substitution of food for clothing, the increase in imports by JK is called the substitution effect.

In summary, then, the reduction in the relative price of food from ST to MN causes imports to increase by: (a) a production effect (DE), (b) an income effect (FJ), and (c) a substitution effect (JK).

It must be clear from Figure 4-5 that both the production effect and the substitution effect cause the demand for imports to increase as imports become cheaper. There is a limit, though, to the production effect: after the country becomes completely specialized, the production effect drops to zero.

As is well known from price theory, the income effect is not so reliable as the production and substitution effects. Thus, when the imported commodity is inferior, the increase in income will cause both the domestic consumption of food and the imports of food to fall. However, such a perverse income effect cannot be expected to occur for the whole class of imported commodities. Even if it did, it could not be very strong; anyway, it cannot be expected to outweigh the favorable production and substitution effects. Therefore, we can safely ignore any backward-bending portion of the offer curve, as illustrated in Figure 4-4 by broken curve NR.

International Equilibrium

We finally proceed to a demonstration of how international equilibrium can be determined by means of offer curves. We again assume two countries, America and Britain. They produce and consume two commodities, food and clothing. To fix ideas, we assume that in the autarkic state food is cheaper in America than in Britain; that is, America has a comparative advantage in the production of food, Britain a comparative advantage in the production of clothing. All this is summarized in Figure 4-6.

Britain's offer curve is very similar to the offer curve we studied earlier in Figure 4-4. Note that Britain's autarkic relative price of food (p_b) is given by (the slope of) line OB, which is tangent to Britain's offer curve at the origin. Note also that Britain's offer curve must necessarily lie between line OB and the horizontal axis, which measures Britain's imports of food. In fact, it seems reasonable to assume that Britain's offer curve becomes asymptotic to the horizontal axis—simply because as food's relative price tends to zero, Britain can theoretically obtain unlimited amounts of food by exporting a negligible amount of clothing—even though exceptions do exist.

America's offer curve has a curvature opposite to that of Britain's offer curve. The reason is simple: American imports of clothing are measured along the vertical axis. Therefore, America's offer curve lies between the vertical axis

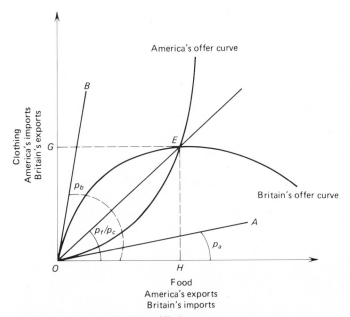

Figure 4-6 *International equilibrium.*
International equilibrium occurs at *E*, where the offer curves intersect. America exports *OH* units of food to Britain and imports *OG* units of clothing from Britain. The slope of terms-of-trade line *OE* gives equilibrium terms of trade *OG/OH*.

and line OA, which is tangent to the offer curve at the origin and which shows America's relative price of food (p_a) in autarky.

International equilibrium occurs at the intersection of the two offer curves, as shown by point E. At E America exports OH units of food to Britain in exchange for OG units of clothing. Point E is the only point in Figure 4-6 at which each country's desired imports are exactly matched by the other country's desired exports.

The equilibrium terms of trade are given by (the slope of) terms-of-trade line OE. Note that these terms of trade (that is, the relative price of food) are given by the ratio OG/OH (that is, American imports of clothing/American exports of food). The ratio OG/OH, which gives the number of units of clothing that exchange for 1 unit of food, lies between the autarkic prices of America and of Britain, as revealed by the fact that terms-of-trade line OE lies between lines OA and OB.

4-4 THE TERMS OF TRADE

The preceding analysis sheds much light on the significance of the concept of the terms of trade in international equilibrium. The domestic employment of factors; the techniques of production; the distribution of income; the production, consumption, exporting and importing of commodities—all depend on the terms of trade. No wonder, then, that economists as well as statisticians, policymakers, and politicians pay so much attention to this concept.

So far we have used the phrase "terms of trade" to mean the relative price of the exported commodity. For instance, in our earlier discussion in which America imported clothing and exported food, America's terms of trade were defined as the relative price of food—that is, the ratio of the price of food to the price of clothing. As we have seen, the relative price of food (or America's terms of trade) shows the number of units of clothing that exchange in the international market for 1 unit of food.

In practice, each country exports many commodities, not just one. For this reason, economists and statisticians define the concept of the terms of trade as an index-number statistical measure given by the ratio of an index of export prices to an index of import prices and expressed as a percentage. Both export price and import price indices must, of course, have the same base year. (Export price and import price indices are regularly reported by the International Monetary Fund in its monthly *International Financial Statistics*.) For instance, take 1979 as the base year and suppose that by the end of 1980 America's export prices increased by 10 percent; that is, suppose that America's export price index rose from 100 in 1979 to 110 in 1980. Suppose further that the import price index rose from 100 in 1979 to 105 in 1980. America's terms of trade increased from 100 in 1979 to 104.76 in 1980: $^{110}/_{105} \times 100 = 104.76$. This is also expressed by saying that America's terms of trade improved by 4.76 percent.

It is often taken for granted that an "improvement" in the statistical measure of the terms of trade of, say, America, is equivalent to an increase in America's real income and social welfare. The idea, of course, is that a rise in America's terms of trade means that more units of imports can be obtained per unit of exports; and for this reason it is thought that America is better off. Such a feeling is usually reinforced by a diagram, such as Figure 4-1b, where an improvement in the terms of trade apparently results in an improvement in social welfare. Unfortunately, the concept of the terms of trade is not a good index of social welfare; and any statements made on the basis of historical changes in a country's terms of trade, if not rejected offhand, must be scrutinized thoroughly before they are actually accepted.

Consider, for instance, America, which exports food and imports clothing. America's terms of trade are said to "improve" (that is, become "favorable") when clothing becomes relatively cheaper. Similarly, America's terms of trade are said to "deteriorate" (that is, become "unfavorable") when food becomes relatively cheaper. A change in a country's terms of trade may reflect a change in either domestic or foreign economic behavior. When the terms of trade change as a result of foreign behavior (that is, a change in foreign tastes, technology, or factor endowments), then we must conclude on the basis of our earlier analysis (Section 4-1) that an improvement in the terms of trade is equivalent to an increase in American welfare and that a deterioration is equivalent to a reduction in social welfare.

Suppose, however, that the change in America's terms of trade is the result of a change in American conditions. In particular, suppose that as a result of tremendous advances in American technology, America can produce large amounts of food very cheaply. As a result, the American production-possibilities frontier shifts outward. Suppose further that this overabundance of food forces a reduction in the relative price of food in world markets. Such a reduction in the relative price of food is not unreasonable but should be expected from the normal operation of the *law of supply and demand*. Nevertheless, the reduction in the relative price of food will be registered by statisticians as an "unfavorable" change in America's terms of trade. Is America worse off because of the mere deterioration of her terms of trade? Such a hasty conclusion is not warranted. The outward shift in the American production-possibilities frontier must also be taken into consideration before a conclusion is reached. The outcome could go either way,[2] as our analysis in Chapter 7 will show.

4-5 DECREASING OPPORTUNITY COSTS

Our analysis so far has been based on the assumption of constant returns to scale, which normally gives rise to increasing opportunity costs. Yet in many countries of the world, such as the United States, Britain, Japan, and Germany, one observes a large number of manufacturing industries that appear to be sub-

---

[2] However, had the technical change *not* been accompanied by a deterioration of America's terms of trade, America would necessarily have been better off.

ject to increasing returns to scale. For this reason, we must study briefly the phenomenon of increasing returns and its significance to the theory of international trade.

Internal and External Economies

Increasing returns are usually attributable to certain "economies"—economies that are reflected in cost reductions. These economies may be internal or external to the firm. Our discussion of constant returns to scale is not inconsistent with the existence of economies internal to the firm. Thus, even though the industry production function may be characterized by constant returns to scale, the production function of the firm may successively exhibit increasing, constant, and decreasing returns to scale, giving rise to the usual U-shaped average-cost curve. The initial phase of increasing returns in the firm's production function is due to *internal economies,* such as division of labor within the firm. Sooner or later, these internal economies come to an end. They are succeeded by constant and decreasing returns to scale, largely because of the difficulties of supervision.

If the internal economies of the firm were to continue indefinitely, perfect competition would break down, because eventually one firm would become so large that it would be able to supply the whole industry output. Recall that the supply curve of a purely competitive firm does not exist in the region of decreasing average cost. When the internal economies of a firm continue indefinitely, and thus the average-cost curve slopes downward throughout, the firm finds it profitable to increase output beyond all bounds, provided that its average-cost curve dips below the average-revenue curve after a certain point. Thus, the firm eventually becomes so large that it is able to affect the price of its product; that is, it stops being a perfect competitor. Accordingly, unlimited increasing returns to scale due to internal economies are incompatible with perfect competition.

To reconcile the phenomenon of increasing returns with perfectly competitive conditions, Marshall introduced in 1890 the concept of *external economies.* This concept was later refined by Edgeworth, Haberler, Knight, Viner, Kemp, Meade, and others. The basic idea behind the concept of external economies is that the cost curves of individual firms *shift downward* as the industry's output expands. The lower costs can be attributed to either lower factor prices or increased efficiency of each firm. Those external economies due to lower factor prices are called *pecuniary,* and those due to increased efficiency are called *technological.* The pecuniary external economies present no new difficulties, whereas the technological external economies do.

Pecuniary external economies cannot be observed in the case of primary factors, such as labor and land. They can only be observed in the case of intermediate goods when the supplying industry is either a monopoly or a decreasing-cost industry subject to technological external economies. In the former case, perfect competition is ruled out; in the latter, the pecuniary economies arise because of the existence of technological external economies.

Increasing Returns and the Production-Possibilities Frontier

The introduction of technological external economies gives rise to several difficulties. First, it can be shown that the economy may not produce on the production frontier even under perfectly competitive conditions. Second, the marginal rate of transformation (that is, the slope of the production frontier) need no longer be equal to the ratio of commodity prices. Finally, the production frontier need not be concave to the origin; it may be totally convex to the origin or it may combine regions of concavity with regions of convexity. For further discussion of these difficulties, the reader is referred to Chacholiades (1978, Chapters 7 and 20).

In the section that follows, we discuss the problem of decreasing opportunity costs only. In order to simplify our exposition, we assume that through an appropriate system of taxes and subsidies on the production of commodities as well as the use of factors, production takes place on the production-possibilities frontier and relative prices are rendered equal to opportunity costs.

Decreasing Opportunity Costs and International Trade

Decreasing opportunity costs are illustrated in Figure 4-7. Production-possibilities frontier UV is convex to the origin. This diagram represents only one of many possible cases. To maintain symmetry with the previous diagrams, we continue to measure food and clothing along the axes, although it would be more appropriate now to use other commodities, such as ships and aircraft.

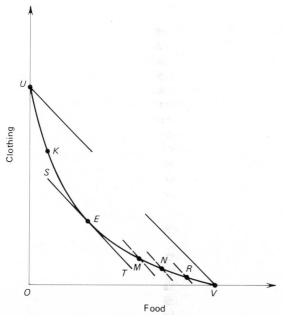

Figure 4-7 *Decreasing opportunity costs and the gains from trade.*

Countries may still benefit from international trade even when opportunity costs are decreasing. But now countries are likely to *specialize completely* under a regime of decreasing costs, as in the Ricardian world of constant costs. Points implying incomplete specialization, such as *E,* are unstable; and in addition the country can be much better off by producing at either *U* or *V,* where national income is maximized.

To understand the problem of instability of point *E,* assume that the economy happens to be in equilibrium at *E.* Note that at *E* the ratio of marginal costs (slope of *UV*) equals the world price ratio (slope of *ST*). If the economy were to move ever so slightly from *E* to another point, such as *M,* economic forces would push the economy to specialize completely in the production of food. Thus, at *M* the marginal cost of food is lower than the price of food, and the marginal cost of clothing is higher than the price of clothing. The motive of profit maximization would force the producers of food to expand, and the producers of clothing to reduce, their respective production. However, the same inequality between marginal costs and prices that exists at point *M* persists until the economy specializes completely in the production of food (see points *N* and *R*). Accordingly, the economy must eventually move all the way to point *V.*

The reader may provide a similar argument for the case in which the economy's initial shift is from *E* to *K* and may argue that the economy must now specialize completely in the production of clothing.

Unfortunately, in the world of decreasing costs a country may become worse off with free international trade. This is indeed a paradoxical phenomenon; the interested reader is referred to Matthews (1950), who first noted this phenomenon, and Chacholiades (1978, Chapter 7) for further discussion.

4-6 SUMMARY

1 In a closed economy, general equilibrium occurs at the point where the production-possibilities frontier becomes tangent to the highest possible social indifference curve. The equilibrium commodity price ratio is equal to both the marginal rate of transformation (that is, the slope of the production frontier) and the marginal rate of substitution in consumption (that is, the slope of the social indifference curve) at the equilibrium point.

2 As in the Ricardian model, comparative advantage is decided on the basis of the opportunity costs that prevail in each trading country before trade. However, with increasing opportunity costs, pretrade costs cannot be inferred from the production-possibilities frontier without full information about demand.

3 The opportunity to trade enables an open economy to separate its domestic consumption from its domestic production. In particular, an open economy (a) maximizes its national income by producing at the point where its marginal rate of transformation equals the international price ratio and (b) maximizes its welfare by consuming at the point of tangency between its con-

sumption-possibilities frontier (that is, the community budget line through the optimal production point) and the highest social indifference curve, a point that normally lies beyond the production frontier.

4   The total gain from trade is divided into a consumption gain (or gain from international exchange), which is normally positive, and a production gain (or gain from specialization), which could be zero (but never negative) in a backward economy that lacks the capacity to transform its autarkic production bundle into a more profitable bundle.

5   The offer curve is an ingenious device (developed by Alfred Marshall) that summarizes the offers of a country at alternative terms of trade. When the offer curve slopes upward, the country's demand for imports is elastic; when it slopes downward [or bends backward (as happens when imports are measured along the vertical axis)], the demand for imports is inelastic. The slope of the offer curve at the origin gives the country's autarkic price ratio.

6   The total effect on imports, following a reduction in their relative price, is divided into three separate effects: (a) the production (or output) effect, (b) the income effect, and (c) the substitution effect. Both the production effect and the substitution effect cause the demand for imports to increase. The income effect could be perverse (when imports are an inferior good). However, a perverse income effect cannot be expected to outweigh the favorable production and substitution effects.

7   International equilibrium occurs when world supply equals world demand in every market, or alternatively when each country's desired imports match exactly the other country's desired exports. Graphically, international equilibrium occurs at the intersection of the offer curves of the trading countries, with the slope of the terms-of-trade line (which connects the origin with the equilibrium point) giving the equilibrium terms of trade.

8   Because countries export and import many commodities, economists and statisticians measure a country's terms of trade by the ratio of an index of the country's export prices to an index of the country's import prices.

9   An improvement (deterioration) in a country's terms of trade is unambiguously equivalent to an increase (decrease) in that country's welfare only when the change in the terms of trade is due to a change in foreign behavior (such as a change in foreign tastes or technology). When the change in the terms of trade is due to a change in domestic conditions, its effect on domestic welfare cannot always be inferred from the direction of change in the terms of trade.

10   Increasing returns due to technological external economies give rise to three complications: (a) They may prevent the economy from producing on its production-possibilities frontier; (b) they may break the equality between relative commodity prices and opportunity costs; and (c) they may give rise to decreasing opportunity costs, that is, cause the production-possibilities frontier to become convex to the origin (either throughout or over certain regions).

11   With decreasing opportunity costs, countries are likely to specialize completely, as in the Ricardian model of constant costs. In addition, in a world of decreasing costs, countries may still benefit from international trade, even though we cannot exclude the paradoxical possibility that now a country may actually become worse off with free trade.

APPENDIX: Meade's Geometric Technique[3]

In the early 1930s, Leontief (1933) and Lerner (1934) provided a geometric technique for obtaining a country's offer curve from its social indifference curves and production-possibilities frontier. Two decades later the Leontief-Lerner technique was finally perfected by James E. Meade in his *Geometry of International Trade* (1952). Meade's ingenious geometric technique is the subject of this appendix.

Trade Indifference Curves

The crucial first step in Meade's approach is the derivation of the *trade indifference map,* as shown in Figure A4-1. Following Meade's notation, measure A-exportables along the horizontal axis, and B-exportables along the vertical axis. Meade's terms "A-exportables" and "B-exportables" correspond to the "food" and "clothing" that we have been using so far. Note that for reasons which will become evident as we proceed, the horizontal axis measures positive quantities from right to left—not from left to right. Accordingly, the economy's (America's) production-possibilities frontier is drawn in the

[3] The reader may omit this appendix.

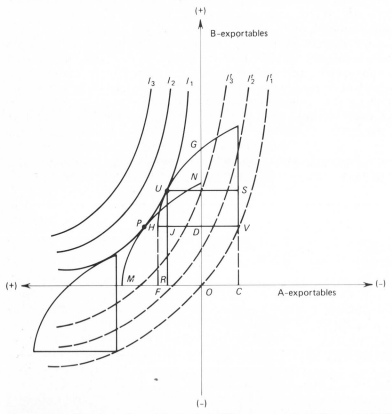

Figure A4-1 The derivation of the trade indifference map from the social indifference map and the production-possibilities frontier.

second (upper-left) quadrant, as shown by MPN. The social indifference map is similarly drawn in the second quadrant, as shown by the curves I_1, I_2, and I_3. Before trade, America produces and consumes at point P, enjoying the level of social welfare implied by the social indifference curve I_1.

Now think of production set $OMPN$ as a block that can be moved anywhere on the diagram. Slide block $OMPN$ along social indifference curve I_1 so that curve MPN remains tangent to I_1 at all times and line MO remains in a horizontal position. During this process, the origin of the block (that is, point O) traces out broken curve I_1', which is known as a *trade indifference curve*.

What is the significance of trade indifference curve I_1'? It merely gives all the alternative export-import combinations that enable America to reach social indifference curve I_1. For instance, consider point V, where America exports $OC(= DV)$ units of A-exportables in exchange for $OD(= CV)$ units of imports of B-exportables. To verify that this export-import combination enables America to reach social indifference curve I_1 (and not a higher one), first let America make the exchange of OC units of A-exportables for OD units of B-exportables. After this exchange, America can consume only along curve $FHUG$, where straight line FH is perpendicular. Accordingly, America will consume at U, where the production block is tangent to I_1. In particular, America will produce VJ units of A-exportables, out of which she will export DV units and consume only JD. Similarly, America will produce $VS(= JU)$ units of B-exportables, which along with the imports of $CV(= RJ)$ units make up the total consumption RU of B-exportables. Similar reasoning applies to all other points lying on I_1'.

In general, a trade indifference curve can be derived for each social indifference curve (or consumption indifference curve, as Meade calls it). Thus, as we slide production block $OMPN$ along social indifference curve I_2, the origin of the block traces a new trade indifference curve, as illustrated by I_2'. Observe that I_2' lies consistently above and to the left of I_1', since I_2 lies consistently above and to the left of I_1. In general, one trade indifference curve corresponds to one social indifference curve; and the higher the social indifference curve, the higher the corresponding trade indifference curve.

Under increasing opportunity costs, the trade indifference curves have the same convexity as the social indifference curves. In addition, the slope of a trade indifference curve at any point is equal to the slope of the corresponding social indifference curve and the slope of the production-possibilities frontier at the corresponding point. For instance, the slope of I_1' at V is equal to the common slope of I_1 and the production block at U.

The Offer Curve

With the trade indifference map at hand, we proceed now with the derivation of the offer curve, which is the locus of tangencies between terms-of-trade lines and trade indifference curves, as shown in Figure A4-2.

Terms-of-trade line TOT_1, which is tangent to the trade indifference curve I_1' at the origin, corresponds to America's pretrade equilibrium price ratio. Imagine that A-exportables become progressively more expensive in the international market, causing the terms-of-trade line to become steeper and steeper, as illustrated by terms-of-trade lines TOT_2 and TOT_3. Trace out the tangencies between the various terms-of-trade lines and the trade indifference curves. The locus of all these tangencies, as illustrated by curve OE_2E_3, is the first part of America's offer curve.

Alternatively, we could allow terms-of-trade line TOT_1 to rotate clockwise (as A-

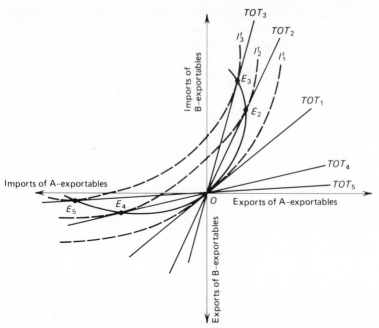

Figure A4-2 The derivation of America's offer curve from the trade indifference map.

exportables become cheaper and cheaper in the international market) and trace out the remaining part of the offer curve in the third quadrant, as illustrated by curve OE_4E_5. Thus, America's full offer curve is given by solid curve $E_5E_4OE_2E_3$.

It must be clear from the construction of Figure A4-2 that the offer curve has two important properties: (1) It passes through the origin and lies totally above and to the left of terms-of-trade line TOT_1 (whose slope gives the pretrade price ratio); and (2) terms-of-trade line TOT_1 is tangent to the offer curve at the origin; that is, the slope of the offer curve at the origin shows the pretrade price ratio.

International Equilibrium

The same procedure can be repeated to derive the offer curve of a second country, say, Britain. International equilibrium can then be shown in terms of the two offer curves by superimposing one diagram on the other, after Britain's diagram has been rotated by 180° to match the axes of America's diagram, as illustrated in Figure A4-3.

International equilibrium occurs at point E in the first quadrant, where the two offer curves intersect each other. America exports OR units of A-exportables to Britain, and Britain exports OS units of B-exportables to America. The equilibrium terms of trade are given by the slope of terms-of-trade line OE, which is equal to the ratio OS/OR. Note that line OE lies in between lines OA and OB, which give, respectively, America's and Britain's autarkic prices. Further, America consumes at C_A in the second quadrant (that is, OV units of A-exportables and VC_A units of B-exportables). Similarly, Britain consumes at C_B in the fourth quadrant (that is, OD units of B-exportables and DC_B units of A-exportables). Finally, America produces EU units of A-exportables and UC_A units of B-exportables, while Britain produces EZ units of B-exportables and ZC_B units of A-exportables. Thus, the total production of A-exportables by both countries

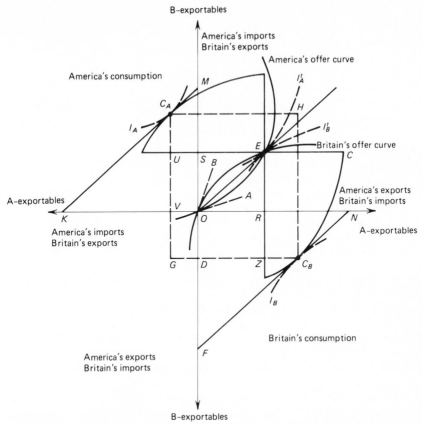

Figure A4-8 Meade's demonstration of international equilibrium. Production, consumption, and trade are brought together.

is given by $EU + ZC_B = GZ + ZC_B = GC_B$, and the total production of B-exportables is given by $EZ + UC_A = GU + UC_A = GC_A$.

The sides of rectangle GC_BHC_A show the world production of A-exportables and B-exportables. But the sides of the same rectangle also show the world consumption of A-exportables and B-exportables, because $SU + DC_B = GD + DC_B = GC_B$ and $VC_A + RZ = VC_A + GV = GC_A$. In other words, rectangle GC_BHC_A can be thought of as a *production box*. The coordinates of point E with respect to corner C_A show America's production (or endowments) of A-exportables and B-exportables, while the coordinates of E with respect to C_B show Britain's production of A-exportables and B-exportables. Similarly, the coordinates of point O with respect to C_A (C_B) show America's (Britain's) consumption of A-exportables and B-exportables, and the coordinates of O with respect to E show America's exports of A-exportables and imports of B-exportables.

Note that terms-of-trade line OE is tangent to both America's and Britain's trade indifference curves at E. Further, America's consumption-possibilities frontier KC_AM is tangent to America's social indifference curve at C_A, and Britain's consumption-possibilities frontier NC_BF is tangent to Britain's social indifference curve at C_B. Therefore, all equilibrium conditions are indeed satisfied.

Figure A4-3 brings together production, consumption, and trade in an ingenious way and illuminates a multitude of relationships. This diagram, which we owe to Meade, is the culmination of the neoclassical model.

SUGGESTED READING

Chacholiades, M. (1978). *International Trade Theory and Policy.* McGraw-Hill Book Company, chaps. 5–7.

Edgeworth, F. Y. (1894). "The Theory of International Values." *Economic Journal,* vol. 4, pp. 35–50, 424–443, and 606–638. Reprinted in F. Y. Edgeworth, *Papers Relating to Political Economy.* Macmillan and Company, London, 1925.

_____(1905). "Review of Henry Cunynghame's *A Geometrical Political Economy.*" *Economic Journal,* vol. 15, pp. 62–71.

Leontief, W. W. (1933). "The Use of Indifference Curves in the Analysis of Foreign Trade." *Quarterly Journal of Economics,* vol. 47, pp. 493–503. Reprinted in AEA *Readings in the Theory of International Trade.* Richard D. Irwin, Inc., Homewood, Ill., 1950.

Lerner, A. P. (1932). "The Diagrammatic Representation of Cost Conditions in International Trade." *Economica,* vol. 12, pp. 346–356. Reprinted in A. P. Lerner, *Essays in Economic Analysis.* Macmillan and Company, London, 1953.

_____(1934). "The Diagrammatic Representation of Demand Condition in International Trade." *Economica,* N.S. 1, pp. 319–334. Reprinted in A. P. Lerner, *Essays in Economic Analysis.* Macmillan and Company, London, 1953.

Marshall, A. (1879). *The Pure Theory of Foreign Trade.* (Printed for private circulation in 1879; reprinted in 1930.) London School of Economics and Political Science, London.

_____(1923). *Money, Credit, and Commerce.* Macmillan and Company, London.

Matthews, R. C. O. (1950). "Reciprocal Demand and Increasing Returns." *Review of Economic Studies,* vol. 17, pp. 149–158.

Meade, J. E. (1952). *A Geometry of International Trade.* George Allen and Unwin, Ltd., London, chaps. 1–4.

Chapter Five

The Heckscher-Ohlin Model

5-1 GENERAL INTRODUCTION

What are the ultimate determinants of comparative advantage? The preceding chapters show that the direction of trade is determined by the pretrade equilibrium price ratios. These pretrade price ratios depend on the production-possibilities frontiers of the trading countries and their respective demand conditions. Since the production-possibilities frontiers depend, in turn, on the fundamental data of technology (production functions) and factor endowments, we conclude that the factors which ultimately determine the structure of trade can be traced back to differences in the three fundamental data of the countries involved:

1 Factor endowments
2 Technology
3 Tastes

This should not come as a surprise, because any general-equilibrium configuration necessarily depends on the exogenous data.

Ricardo did not bother to explain the ultimate determinants of comparative advantage. In his theory, comparative advantage depended on comparative differences in labor productivity (that is, differences in technology), but he did not explain the basis for these differences—even though the implicit reason was climatic differences.

One of the main objectives of the Heckscher-Ohlin theory (also known as the factor-endowment theory) is the prediction of the pattern of trade on the basis of the observable characteristics of the trading countries. In particular, the Heckscher-Ohlin theory assumes that technology and tastes are similar between countries and attributes comparative advantage to differences in factor endowments. The gist of this theory is summarized by the following two propositions:

1   The *cause* of international trade is to be found largely in the *differences between the factor endowments of different countries*. In particular, a country has a comparative advantage in the production of that commodity which uses more intensively the country's more abundant factor. This proposition is known as the *Heckscher-Ohlin theorem*.

2   The *effect* of international trade is to tend to *equalize factor prices* between countries, and thus serve to some extent as a *substitute for factor mobility*. This proposition is known as the *factor-price equalization theorem*.

The validity of the above propositions depends on certain factual assumptions, which we will analyze in this chapter.

The founders of the factor-endowment theory are the two Swedish economists, Heckscher (1919) and his student Ohlin (1933). However, the theory owes much to Stolper and Samuelson (1941) and to Samuelson (1948, 1949).

This chapter deals exclusively with the theoretical aspects of the Heckscher-Ohlin model, leaving to the following chapter the question of empirical testing. After a brief summary of the model (Section 5-2), we take a critical look at two of its basic assumptions: identical production functions between countries (Section 5-3) and the meaning of factor intensity (Section 5-4). We then clarify the concept of factor abundance (Section 5-5) and the basic relationship between factor prices and commodity prices (Section 5-6). The last two sections deal with the proofs of the factor-price equalization theorem (Section 5-7) and the Heckscher-Ohlin theorem (Section 5-8).

5-2   THE BASIC ASSUMPTIONS OF THE HECKSCHER-OHLIN MODEL

The Heckscher-Ohlin model of international trade assumes that each of two countries, say, America and Britain, is endowed with two homogeneous factors of production, say, labor and land, and produces under constant returns to scale two commodities, say, food and clothing. In addition, the two homogeneous factors are indifferent between uses, are of the same quality in all countries, and are supplied inelastically in all countries (that is, the supply curves of labor and land are vertical, which actually means that the available quantities of labor and land are independent of their prices). Further, the output of each commodity depends only on the amounts of labor and land that enter into the production process of that commodity alone—that is, the Heckscher-Ohlin model assumes complete absence of production externalities.

All the preceding assumptions are, of course, familiar to us from Chapter 3. The following two assumptions, however, incorporate some new elements, and for this reason they are singled out for special scrutiny. These assumptions are:

1   Technology is the same in all countries. This means that the production function of food is the same in Britain as in America. The same holds true for the production function of clothing.

2   One commodity, say, clothing, is *always* labor intensive relative to the second commodity (food). This is equivalent to saying that food is land intensive relative to clothing. What this assumption really means is that under all circumstances, *the clothing industry will be using more units of labor per unit of land than the food industry.*

The next two sections take a closer look at these two special assumptions of the Heckscher-Ohlin model.

5-3   THE IDENTITY OF PRODUCTION FUNCTIONS BETWEEN COUNTRIES

One of the crucial assumptions of the Heckscher-Ohlin theorem is that production functions are identical between countries. In fact, Ohlin appears to have taken it for granted that production functions are the same everywhere. He based his assertion on the empirical observation that the laws of physics are everywhere the same. In the words of Ohlin (1933, p. 14), "the physical conditions of production . . . are everywhere the same."

The assumption that production functions are identical between countries raises the fundamental question of the proper definition of two concepts: production functions and factors of production. As we saw in Chapter 3, the production function is a statement of the maximum quantity of output that can be secured with any specified quantities of factors. What must be included in the second concept, "factors of production"?

Broadly speaking, we can distinguish four different categories of factors of production, as follows:

1   Concrete input items (such as raw materials) purchasable in the marketplace

2   Nonappropriable scarce factors [such as weather conditions (humidity, rainfall, sunshine, temperature, etc.)] that have a zero price in the marketplace even though they are not available in unlimited quantities

   3 Free factors (such as air) that are available in unlimited quantities and
bear a zero price in the marketplace
   4 Conditions bearing on production (such as technical knowledge)

When all four categories are included in "factors of production," the production functions become identical between countries by definition. This is, however, a useless tautology.

   There is general agreement that concrete input items purchasable in the
marketplace must be included in "factors of production." Also, we can easily
dispense with the free factors (the third category) without any serious
consequence. By definition, these are not economic factors at all. They are
found in unlimited quantities in all countries—at least for the time being.

   The second category of factors (nonappropriable scarce factors) presents
some difficulties. Ricardo's production functions illustrate the point. He
specifically assumed the following relationships between the input of labor L
and the output of wine Q:

Portugal: $Q = \dfrac{L}{80}$

England: $Q = \dfrac{L}{120}$

If labor, of course, were the only "factor of production," it would be obvious
that England and Portugal would indeed have different production functions.
However, the two countries may be regarded as sharing a common production
function according to which the output of wine depends not only on labor but
also on "the peculiar powers bestowed by nature" (Ricardo's phrase), such as
temperature, humidity, sunshine, and rainfall. The reason the production functions of Portugal and England appear to be different is that "the peculiar
powers bestowed by nature," which assume different values in the two countries, are excluded from consideration.

   Difficulties are also created by the fact that labor and land are not
homogeneous factors. A highly skilled worker is not the same thing as an un-
trained worker, just as an acre of land in oil-rich Saudi Arabia is not the same
thing as an acre of land in Italy or Greece.

   Incidentally, various commodities require for their production certain
types of resources that are only found in some countries. For this reason some
commodity flows in the world economy are not difficult to explain. For instance, Saudi Arabia exports oil, Brazil exports coffee, Bolivia exports tin, and
Greece and Italy "export" tourist services.

   To consider labor and land as the only two homogeneous factors of
production is to ignore the economically relevant, qualitative differences
among various units of each category of factors and at the same time render the
production functions of the various countries different from one another.

   Consider finally the problem of technical knowledge that delimits the *form* of the production function—it should not be properly classified as a factor of production. Production functions incorporate all known efficient techniques, and at any one time such technical know-how cannot be expected to be the same in all countries, especially in a period of incessant inventions.

Because the theory of international trade is a long-run, comparative-statics theory, there are those who argue that the only proper assumption to make is that knowledge available to one country is available also to another—sooner or later new inventions in one country are disseminated throughout the rest of the world. This is a powerful argument. The only trouble is that when technical progress is continuous and systematically concentrated in only a small number of countries, the rest of the world appears to be always technically backward—the other countries never have the time to catch up. To argue that in the long run technical knowledge must be the same in all countries, without even defining how long is "long run," is to ignore an interesting and most important aspect of international economic life. We shall have more to say on this topic in the next chapter.

We conclude that we must reject the notion that production functions are identical between countries on a priori grounds. Whether or not production functions are identical between countries is, at bottom, an empirical question.

It must be emphasized that the identity of production functions between countries is a necessary assumption for the Heckscher-Ohlin theorem. With different production functions, trade can take place between any two countries with similar factor endowments and consumption patterns. Thus, any empirical evidence contrary to that indicated by factor proportions could always be explained by arbitary differences in production functions. But then it is necessary to explain when and how production functions come to differ—a prerequisite to using the theory of comparative advantage to predict ex ante the pattern of trade.

5-4 THE MEANING OF FACTOR INTENSITY

For its logical validity, the Heckscher-Ohlin model requires that one commodity (clothing) is *labor intensive* relative to the other commodity (food). What does the term "labor intensive" (or the term "land intensive") mean?

Consider the simple case of *fixed coefficients of production.* In particular, assume that it takes 6 units of labor and 2 units of land to produce 1 unit of clothing and 8 units of labor and 4 units of land to produce 1 unit of food. Assume that these are the only techniques known. Which is the labor-intensive commodity?

Do *not* fall into the trap of arguing that food is labor intensive relative to clothing because each unit of food requires 8 units of labor to clothing's 6. Such a comparison is meaningless, if only because the units of measurement (yards, bushels, and so on) are arbitrary. What is important is the *proportion* in which labor and land are used.

Evidently clothing is labor intensive relative to food because, *per unit of land,* the production of clothing requires 3 (that is, $^6/_2$) units of labor, while the production of food requires only 2 (that is, $^8/_4$), irrespective of the units in which food and clothing are measured. In other words, clothing is defined to be labor intensive relative to food because $^6/_2 > ^8/_4$.

How do we decide which is the labor-intensive commodity when there are many known techniques for each commodity? Obviously we cannot expect each and every technique for producing clothing to use more units of labor per unit of land than all techniques for producing food. How can we, then, compare clothing's labor intensity with that of food?

Even though there may be many techniques for each commodity, we can rest assured that perfect competition will always force all producers in each industry to use only one technique: that technique which minimizes their cost. It is only these *optimal* techniques that we must compare.

How are the optimal techniques selected? We already know the answer from Chapter 3: For any given factor-price ratio (that is, wage-rent ratio w/r), a commodity's optimal coefficients of production (that is, the number of units of labor and land needed to produce 1 unit of output) are determined by the coordinates of the point on the unit isoquant where the marginal rate of substitution of labor for land is equal to the given factor-price ratio w/r.

The selection of a commodity's optimal coefficients is illustrated in Figure 5-1. Curve FF' is the unit isoquant (of the food industry). When the factor-price ratio is given by ratio OM/ON (which is assumed to be equal to 2), the optimal coefficients of production are given by the coordinates of point E (that is, 1 unit of labor and 2 units of land). As the factor-price ratio falls to $M'N'$ (that is, $^3/_4$), the optimal coefficients shift to point E'. Because of the law of diminishing marginal rate of substitution, the relatively cheaper factor (labor) is substituted for the relatively more expensive factor (land). Thus, at E' the production of 1 unit of output requires 2 units of labor and only 1 unit of land. In moving from E to E', the labor intensity of the commodity increases from $^1/_2$ to $^2/_1$, as the labor coefficient increases absolutely and the land coefficient decreases absolutely.

The relationship between labor intensity and the factor-price ratio is given more clearly in Figure 5-2. Points E and E' along *food's labor-intensity curve* correspond to the synonymous points along food's unit isoquant given in Figure 5-1. In fact, each point on the labor-intensity curve corresponds to a point on the unit isoquant. Note that the labor-intensity curve must slope downward because of the law of diminishing marginal rate of substitution. Thus, as labor becomes cheaper, each industry becomes more labor intensive; that is, it substitutes labor for land along the unit isoquant.

Figure 5-2 gives the labor-intensity curves of both food and clothing. It reveals the same assumption about labor intensity that we made earlier: Clothing is labor intensive relative to food. We do not deny that if techniques were chosen at random, food could be produced with more labor-intensive techniques than clothing—as illustrated, for instance, by points N and E'. Nevertheless, a comparison between points such as N and E' must be ruled out. The clothing industry will operate at N when the wage-rent ratio is 2, and the food industry will operate at E' when the wage-rent ratio is only $^3/_4$. We must

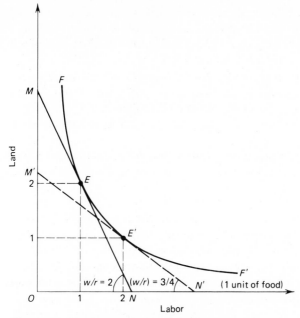

Figure 5-1 *The choice of optimal techniques.*
The optimal coefficients of a commodity coincide with the coordinates of that point on the unit isoquant where the marginal rate of substitution of labor for land equals the given wage-rent ratio, as illustrated by points *E* and *E'*.

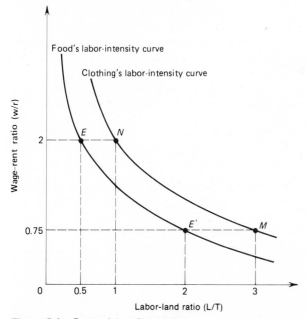

Figure 5-2 *Factor-intensity curves.*
Food's (clothing's) labor-intensity curve shows the optimal labor-land ratio used by the food (clothing) industry at alternative wage-rent ratios. Points *E* and *E'* on food's labor-intensity curve coincide with the synonymous points of the unit isoquant of Figure 5-1.

compare techniques at the *same* wage-rent ratio. Thus, when the wage-rent ratio is 2, the clothing industry will operate at *N* and the food industry at *E*; and when the wage-rent ratio falls to $^3/_4$, the clothing industry will shift to *M* and the food industry to *E'*. Because the labor-intensity curve of the clothing industry has been drawn totally to the right of the labor-intensity curve of the food industry, the clothing industry must be using more labor per unit of land at *all* wage-rent ratios. It is in this sense, then, that we can conclude that clothing is labor intensive relative to food.

Note that "factor intensity" is a relative term. When clothing is found to be labor intensive relative to food, it automatically follows that food is land intensive relative to clothing; that is, food uses more units of land per unit of labor than clothing.

It must be emphasized that we can unequivocally classify clothing as labor intensive relative to food only when clothing's labor-intensity curve lies totally to the right of that of food. *There is no a priori reason that this should be so.* It is only an assumption. In fact, in the next chapter we shall study the implications of *factor-intensity reversals,* which can occur if, and only if, the two labor-intensity curves of Figure 5-2 intersect each other. In the meantime, however, we shall assume that the labor-intensity curves do not cross.

5-5 FACTOR ABUNDANCE

Another concept that needs further clarification is factor abundance. On what basis do we classify countries into labor abundant and capital abundant? Basically there are two (often contradictory) criteria that can be used for this purpose: *physical* abundance and *economic* abundance. These criteria lead to the following two definitions:

Definition 1 (physical definition). Britain is said to be labor abundant relative to America because Britain is endowed with more units of labor per acre of land than America.[1]
Definition 2 (price definition). Britain is said to be labor abundant relative to America because at their respective autarkic equilibrium states labor is relatively cheaper in Britain than in America.

To begin with, observe that factor abundance, like comparative advantage, is a relative concept. When Britain is found to be labor abundant relative to America, it must also be true that America is land abundant relative to Britain. This must be true for both definitions.

Because factor abundance is a relative concept, we cannot decide which country is labor abundant merely by comparing the absolute number of units of labor available. For instance, suppose America is endowed with more units of labor and land than Britain. Can we conclude that America is both labor abun-

---

[1] We use the physical definition only in the appendix to this chapter. Accordingly, the reader may omit any discussion in this section that pertains to the physical definition.

dant and land abundant relative to Britain? Not at all. The important consideration is not whether America is endowed with absolutely more units of labor or land than Britain. Rather, what is significant is the proportion in which labor and land exist in each country. If Britain has more workers *per acre of land* than America, then Britain is the labor-abundant country even though America may have many more workers than Britain.

Alternatively, if the price definition is used, a country is classified as labor abundant only if her pretrade wage-rent ratio is lower than that of the other country—not when her absolute wage rate is lower than that of the other country.

The first definition of relative factor abundance is called the *physical definition* because it bases factor abundance on just the physical quantities of factor endowments. Despite its great simplicity, the physical definition faces serious conceptual difficulties in empirical investigations because of the implied homogeneity of the factors of production. As we stressed earlier, there are important qualitative differences between units of the same "factor." For instance, labor cannot be considered a homogeneous factor in view of differences in the educational background, motivation, health, nutrition, and other qualities of workers. Similarly, two different parcels of land cannot be expected to be identical in view of differences in fertility, sunshine, rainfall, location, and so on. Finally, capital is not a homogeneous factor because it includes all kinds of *produced means of production,* such as buildings, machinery of all sorts, buses, airplanes, and so on.

The price definition of relative factor abundance is concerned with economic rather than physical abundance. Thus, it classifies countries into labor abundant and land abundant on the basis of pretrade relative factor prices (w/r). Equilibrium factor prices, like commodity prices, are determined by both supply and demand. In fact, this is the major difference between the two definitions: The physical definition is based solely on supply, ignoring completely the influence of demand, while the price definition is based on both supply and demand influences.

Demand conditions may outweigh supply conditions with the result that the two definitions of factor abundance may give rise to contradictory classifications of the two countries. For instance, assume that Britain is labor abundant relative to America on the basis of the physical definition. If Britain's consumers have a much stronger bias than America's consumers toward the consumption of labor-intensive commodities, then labor may actually be more expensive in Britain than in America before trade. Accordingly, Britain is land abundant (labor scarce) according to the price definition; and this contradicts the initial assumption that Britain is labor abundant on the basis of the physical definition.

Even though it sounds very simple, the price definition suffers from a severe drawback when it comes to empirical investigations: pretrade prices are in general unknown.

To keep our discussion as simple as possible, we shall judge factor abundance on the basis of the price definition for the rest of this chapter. The complications raised by the physical definition are summarized separately in the appendix to this chapter. The appendix may be omitted.

5-6 FACTOR PRICES AND COMMODITY PRICES

The production functions of the food and clothing industries imply a definite relationship among the optimal labor-land ratios in the two industries, the wage-rent ratio, and the relative costs of production (or relative prices). Section 5-4 has already considered the relationship between the wage-rent ratio and the optimal labor-land ratios. This section explores the relationship between factor prices and commodity prices.

The basic proposition is this: *As labor becomes relatively cheaper (that is, as the wage-rent ratio falls), the labor-intensive commodity becomes cheaper relative to the land-intensive commodity.*[2] In our model it is assumed that clothing is the labor-intensive commodity. Therefore, as the wage-rent ratio w/r falls, clothing becomes cheaper relative to food. This is a crucial relationship, and we should always keep it in mind.

A rigorous proof is beyond the scope of this book. [The interested reader can consult Chacholiades (1978), pp. 244–246.] Nevertheless, the following discussion is very suggestive and will go a long way toward convincing the reader about the general validity of the above proposition.

A Numerical Illustration

Perhaps a numerical example would prove useful at this stage. Suppose that at the current factor prices of $w = \$10$ and $r = \$5$ the optimum coefficients of production are:

> Food: 1 unit of labor plus 4 units of land
> Clothing: 3 units of labor plus 2 units of land

Thus, the costs of production (and thus prices) are:

> Price of food $= \$10 \times 1 + \$5 \times 4 = \$30$
> Price of clothing $= \$10 \times 3 + \$5 \times 2 = \$40$

Accordingly, the initial relative price of food is given by:

$$P_0 \equiv \frac{\text{price of food}}{\text{price of clothing}} = \frac{\$30}{\$40} = 0.75$$

Two important observations must be made at this point. First, clothing is labor intensive relative to food because clothing requires $^3/_2$ units of labor per

---

[2] Readers may wish to accept this proposition without any proof. In that case, they may skip the rest of this section and proceed to Section 5-7.

unit of land and food requires only $1/4$ of 1 unit. Second, the relative price of food does *not* depend on the *absolute* factor prices (that is, $w = \$10$ and $r = \$5$)—it depends on their ratio (that is, $w/r = 10/5 = 2$) only. [The reader is encouraged to use the factor prices $w = \$50$ and $r = \$25$ and verify that the relative price of food continues to be equal to 0.75 (despite the fact that the absolute prices of food and clothing are five times higher than before).]

Suppose now that the wage-rent ratio falls to $1/2$ (that is, labor becomes relatively cheaper). Even though the absolute factor prices are not relevent, assume for the clarity of the exposition that the new factor prices are $w = \$10$ and $r = \$20$. What happens to the relative price of food? According to our fundamental proposition, food must become relatively more expensive, *assuming only that clothing is labor intensive relative to food at all factor-price ratios*.

Assume first that the coefficients of production remain *fixed* at their initial levels—no other techniques are known. Then the new relative price of food is easily calculated as follows:

$$P_1 = \frac{\text{price of food}}{\text{price of clothing}} = \frac{\$10 \times 1 + \$20 \times 4}{\$10 \times 3 + \$20 \times 2} = \frac{\$90}{\$70} = 1.29$$

We therefore conclude that food is relatively more expensive (since $1.29 > 0.75$) or that clothing, the labor-intensive commodity, is relatively cheaper. This result is in agreement, of course, with our proposition.

The above analysis may be objected to since it does not allow any factor substitutability—it might be thought that the result could be reversed if we allowed industries to substitute the cheaper factor (labor) for the more expensive factor (land). What if the food industry were able to substitute labor for land more easily than the clothing industry? Is it not possible then that food, the land-intensive commodity, could become cheaper as the wage-rent ratio falls? The answer is "no!"

Consider the most favorable case. In particular, assume zero factor substitutability in the clothing industry, and allow only the food industry to substitute labor for land, with the proviso that clothing continues to be labor intensive relative to food. For instance, as the wage-rent ratio falls from 2 to 1, let the food industry substitute 1.5 units of labor for 2 units of land. This means that at the new factor prices, the optimal production coefficients of the food industry become 2.5 units of labor plus 2 units of land. Note that the clothing industry continues to be labor intensive relative to the food industry ($3/2 > 2.5/2$). The relative price of food is now given by:

$$P_2 = \frac{\text{price of food}}{\text{price of clothing}} = \frac{\$10 \times 2.5 + \$20 \times 2}{\$10 \times 3 + \$20 \times 2} = \frac{\$65}{\$70} = 0.93$$

Thus, even under the assumed favorable conditions, food continues to remain relatively more expensive ($0.93 > 0.75$) but not *as* expensive as in the preceding case of fixed coefficients ($1.29 > 0.93$).

We therefore conclude that even though factor substitutability may slow down the increase in the relative price of food as labor becomes cheaper relative to land, factor substitutability *cannot* reverse the trend.

We now proceed with a heuristic proof of our basic proposition.

A Heuristic Proof

We established in Chapter 3 that, under the present assumptions of constant returns to scale and differing labor intensities between food and clothing, the production-possibilities frontier is necessarily concave to the origin, exhibiting increasing opportunity costs. We can now use this result to show that as the wage-rent ratio falls, the output of the land-intensive commodity (food) increases, while the output of the labor-intensive commodity (clothing) decreases; and because of increasing opportunity costs, the land-intensive commodity (food) becomes more expensive relative to the labor-intensive commodity (clothing).

It may be easier to follow this argument if we pursue a little further our earlier numerical illustration. Recall that at the initial factor-price ratio $w/r = {}^{10}/_5 = 2$, the production of 1 unit of food employs 1 unit of labor plus 4 units of land and the production of 1 unit of clothing employs 3 units of labor plus 2 units of land. Let us now assume further that the economy is also endowed with 2,800 units of labor and 3,200 units of land. Can we determine, on the basis of this information alone, how much food and how much clothing our economy will produce? We most certainly can. This is because *there is only one combination of food and clothing that is consistent with the assumption of full employment of both labor and land.* That combination happens to be 400 units of food and 800 units of clothing, as shown in Figure 5-3 by point *B* (that is, the intersection between the *labor constraint* and the *land constraint*).

The linear labor constraint (like the production-possibilities frontier of the Ricardian model we studied in Chapter 2) gives all combinations of food and clothing that fully employ the available supply of labor. It is easily drawn by first determining its intercepts with the food and clothing axes. The intercept with the food axis is given by the maximum output of food $(2,800 \div 1)$ that could employ all available labor if no clothing were produced. Similarly, the intercept with the clothing axis is given by the maximum output of clothing $(2,800 \div 3)$ that could employ all available labor if no food were produced.

The interpretation of the land constraint is the same as that of the labor constraint. The food-axis intercept of the land constraint is given by $3,200 \div 4 = 800$; its clothing-axis intercept, by $3,200 \div 2 = 1,600$.

It is important to note that *the land constraint is steeper than the labor constraint.* This is no accident. It merely reflects the fact that *clothing is labor intensive relative to food.* Thus, the slope of the land constraint is ${}^4/_2$, where 4 and 2 are the *land coefficients* of food and clothing, respectively. Similarly, the slope of the labor constraint is given by ${}^1/_3$, where 1 and 3 are the *labor coefficients* of food and clothing, respectively. The inequality ${}^4/_2 > {}^1/_3$ implies, of course, that the land constraint is steeper than the labor constraint. However,

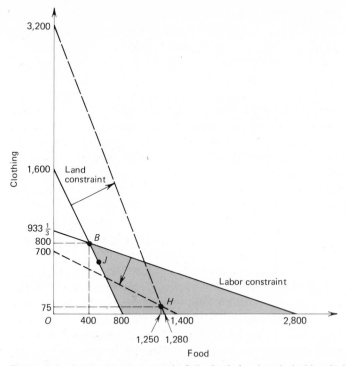

Figure 5-3 As the wage-rent ratio falls, both food and clothing industries substitute labor for land. This substitution causes the labor constraint to shift inward and the land constraint outward. As a result, the full-employment combination of food and clothing shifts from *B* to *H*.

the inequality $^4/_2 > ^1/_3$ is equivalent to the inequality $^3/_2 > ^1/_4$. The latter inequality must be easily recognized: It is the inequality we used earlier to say that clothing is labor intensive relative to food.

Suppose now that labor becomes relatively cheaper. In particular, let the wage-rent ratio fall from 2 to $^1/_2$, as before. As we have seen, the reduction in the wage-rent ratio causes both industries to substitute labor for land; that is, both industries tend to become more labor intensive. This factor substitution is necessary for cost minimization. To fix ideas, assume that the optimal coefficients of production become:

Food: 2 units of labor plus 2.5 units of land
Clothing: 4 units of labor plus 1 unit of land

What combination of food and clothing is now consistent with full employment of both labor and land?

The answer is again given graphically in Figure 5-3. As the labor coefficients of both industries rise, the labor constraint shifts inward—its food-axis intercept falls to $2,800 \div 2 = 1,400$, and its clothing-axis intercept falls to $2,800 \div 4 = 700$. On the other hand, as the land coefficients of both industries fall, the land constraint shifts outward—its food-axis intercept increases to $3,200 \div 2.5 = 1,280$, and its clothing-axis intercept increases to $3,200 \div 1 = 3,200$. The new full-employment combination of food and clothing is now given by H, that is, 1,250 units of food and 75 units of clothing.

Note that point H must necessarily lie in the shaded triangle. This assures that as the wage-rent ratio falls and both commodities become more labor intensive, the output of the labor-intensive commodity (clothing) falls and the output of the land-intensive commodity (food) rises; and because of the underlying increasing opportunity costs, the labor-intensive commodity (clothing) becomes cheaper relative to the land-intensive commodity (food).

The preceding discussion proceeds from factor prices to commodity prices. Perhaps a dynamic sequence of events would proceed along opposite lines. For instance, suppose that a change in tastes in favor of food disturbs the initial equilibrium at B of Figure 5-3. The first impact of the change in tastes is reflected immediately in a higher price of food relative to clothing. The food producers will enjoy positive profits, and the clothing producers will sustain losses. In turn, the profits in the food industry will induce the food producers to increase their output, and the losses in the clothing industry will force the clothing producers to curtail their output. Before factor prices change, the economy will start moving along the land constraint from B to, say, J. However, since J lies inside the labor constraint, labor is no longer fully employed. This unemployment of labor causes the wage-rent ratio to fall. The reduction in the wage-rent ratio causes both industries to substitute labor for land, and this process continues until a new equilibrium is eventually established at H.

5-7 FACTOR-PRICE EQUALIZATION

We are now ready to consider the main propositions of the Heckscher-Ohlin model. In particular, this section deals with the factor-price equalization theorem, and the following section with the Heckscher-Ohlin theorem.

Theorem 5-1 (factor-price equalization theorem) When the assumptions enumerated in Section 5-2 are satisfied, and, in addition, when free commodity trade leads to (a) commodity-price equalization and (b) incomplete specialization in production in both America and Britain, then both relative and absolute factor prices are completely equalized between America and Britain.

It should be emphasized that the term "factor prices" in this context does not mean "asset prices of the factors of production" (that is, the price of a piece of land, a piece of machinery, or a "slave"). It means, rather, the *rentals* for the *services* of these factors, such as the rent for the services of one acre of land and the wage rate for the services of one worker, per unit of time (week, month, or year). The equalization of factor rentals is neither necessary nor sufficient for the equalization of the prices of the factors of production. The relation between a factor's rental and its price is determined by, among other things, the rate of interest, and this is equalized between countries only in special circumstances. Thus, it is entirely possible for, say, one acre of homogeneous land to earn the same real rental in America as in Britain and yet command substantially different "asset" prices in the two countries.

The factor-price equalization theorem is indeed a remarkable result. The theorem asserts that, even in the absence of any factor migration between countries, free commodity trade brings about a situation in which workers earn the same real wage, and land the same real rent, in both America and Britain. In effect, the Heckscher-Ohlin model points to an indirect exchange of factors between countries—an exchange that tends to equalize the proportion in which labor and land services are indirectly consumed (through commodity consumption) in spite of the fact that the overall labor-land ratios differ between countries (that is, one country is labor abundant and the other land abundant). Accordingly, the Heckscher-Ohlin model implies that factors do indeed migrate between countries, not directly but *indirectly* through the commodity flows between countries. If Mohammed cannot go to the mountain, the mountain goes to Mohammed.

Proof of the Factor-Price Equalization Theorem[3]

How can we prove the factor-price equalization theorem? Although a rigorous proof is beyond the scope of this book, we can still sketch a proof on the basis of the relationships that we have developed so far.

To prove the factor-price equalization theorem we must first show that as a result of the assumptions enumerated in Section 5-2, plus the assumption of incomplete specialization, there exists the *same* one-to-one correspondence between the equilibrium commodity-price ratio and the factor-price ratio in both countries. Then we can observe that in the absence of trade impediments (such as tariffs and quotas) and transportation costs, commodity trade equalizes commodity prices between countries. Finally, we can argue that because of the one-to-one correspondence between commodity prices and factor prices, free international trade equalizes factor prices also.

We saw in Section 5-6 that the technical possibilities of production (summarized by the production functions) imply a definite relationship between the wage-rent ratio and the commodity-price ratio, as illustrated in Figure 5-4 by downward-sloping curve PP'. This relationship must be negatively sloped (as shown in Figure 5-4) because as the wage-rent ratio falls, the land-intensive commodity (food) becomes more expensive relative to the labor-intensive commodity (clothing). In addition, this relationship must be the same in both countries, because by assumption the production functions of America are identical to the corresponding production functions of Britain.

What, then, is the difference, if any, between America and Britain? America is endowed with fewer units of labor per acre of land than Britain. In

---

[3] This subsection may be skipped without interrupting the continuity of the book.

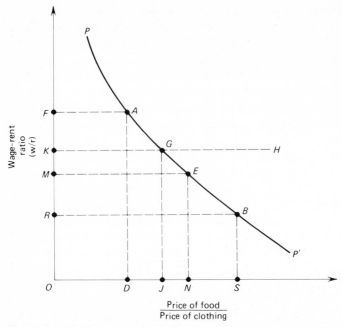

Figure 5-4 *Factor-price equalization.*
Before trade, America operates at *A* and Britain at *B*. America exports food and Britain clothing. Relative commodity prices are equalized by free trade at *ON*. Thus, both countries operate at *E* after trade, enjoying the common wage-rent ratio *OM*.

other words, the only difference between America and Britain lies with their factor endowments.

Now different factor endowments force America and Britain to operate *before trade* at different points along curve *PP'* of Figure 5-4, as illustrated by points *A* and *B*, respectively. Thus, before trade, the relative price of food is given by *OD* in America and by *OS* in Britain, while the wage-rent ratio is given by *OF* in America and by *OR* in Britain. Accordingly, before trade, America produces food more cheaply relative to Britain; that is, America has a comparative advantage in food and Britain a comparative advantage in clothing.

When free commodity trade is allowed between the two countries, America will export food to Britain in exchange for clothing. The relative price of food will rise in America and fall in Britain until a common price ratio, say, *ON*, is established in both countries. What does this commodity-price equalization (which is brought about by free commodity trade) imply for the factor prices in America and Britain?

For any commodity-price ratio at which a country produces positive amounts of both food and clothing, the corresponding wage-rent ratio is always read off curve *PP'* of Figure 5-4, which is common to both countries by assumption. Therefore, in the absence of complete specialization in either country, both America and Britain operate, after trade, at a common point, say, E. Accordingly, the same wage-rent ratio OM will prevail in both countries.

The Significance of Incomplete Specialization

What is the importance of incomplete specialization in the preceding argument? When a country specializes completely in the production of a commodity, say, food, the relationship between the wage-rent ratio and the relative price of food is no longer given by curve PP'. To understand this well, consider America only.

Assume that America is currently producing both food and clothing. Because of, say, a change in world tastes, the relative price of food starts rising in the international market and in America. As this happens, the American producers transfer resources from the clothing industry to the food industry. Assume that when the relative price of food rises to OJ, America becomes completely specialized in food. America's wage-rent ratio is at that moment (when complete specialization first occurs) given by OK—America becomes completely specialized in food at G along curve PP'. What happens to America's wage-rent ratio if the relative price of food continues to rise beyond OJ because of international supply and demand conditions?

The relative price of food must certainly continue to rise in America also, but America's wage-rent ratio must remain at OK. Why? Because America's wage-rent ratio must remain equal to the marginal rate of substitution of labor for land in the food industry. Now the marginal rate of substitution of labor for land in the food industry depends only on that industry's labor intensity. However, as the relative price of food increases beyond OJ, no change can be expected in the labor intensity of the food industry—all available labor and land are already employed by the food industry.

We therefore conclude that, as the relative price of food increases beyond OJ, America will not follow curve PP'. Rather, she will follow broken horizontal line GH.

When one or both countries become completely specialized, they no longer operate along common curve PP'—they move off it. As a result, complete factor-price equalization cannot occur, although the wage-rent ratios of the two countries move closer to each other.

Absolute versus Relative Factor Prices

Does the equalization of the wage-rent *ratio* between countries imply the equalization of the real wage rate and the real rental for land services also? It most certainly does!

The real factor rentals are, of course, given by the marginal physical productivities of the factors. As we saw in Chapter 3, these marginal productivities depend only on the proportion in which labor and land are used in the production of food and clothing—not on the absolute quantities of labor and land employed by each industry. This follows from the assumption of constant returns to scale. Further, each industry's labor-land ratio is perfectly determined when the wage-rent ratio is given.

Since the production functions are by assumption identical between countries, it follows that the equalization of the wage-rent ratio between America and Britain necessarily equalizes America's marginal physical productivities of labor and land to the corresponding marginal productivities of Britain.

The Empirical Relevance of the Assumptions of the Factor-Price Equalization Theorem

It is not difficult to figure out that the prediction of the factor-price equalization theorem is not borne out in the real world. Domestic servants, bricklayers, shoemakers, barbers, and so on do not earn the same wages in India and Pakistan as they do in the United States or Germany.

No logical objections can be raised in regard to the factor-price equalization theorem. If the assumptions enumerated earlier are correct, factor prices must be completely equalized between countries via free trade in commodities. The fact that they are not must then be attributed to the assumptions made. Which assumption, or set of assumptions, is actually responsible for the gap between the model and the real world? Economists are not yet sure about the answer. Each assumption is both crucial to the theory and unrealistic to some degree. But this is to be expected: All models (or theories) are simplifications of complex reality. This does not mean that our models are necessarily bad. A map of New York City drawn on a one-to-one scale is useless. Similarly, a model whose complexity approaches that of the real world offers us absolutely no assistance in our search for the fundamental economic laws that govern the world economy.

To realize how crucial each assumption is to the validity of the factor-price equalization theorem, consider some of them—for instance, the assumption of perfect competition. The introduction of oligopolistic market structures, wage and price rigidities, and so on necessarily impedes the equalization of factor prices via commodity movements. Commodity prices are no longer equal to the costs of production. Therefore, we cannot determine commodity prices, let alone the reverse proposition of going from commodity prices to factor prices, by knowing factor prices, and thus costs of production. In short, in the absence of perfect competition, we can no longer draw curve PP' of Figure 5-4.

Factor-intensity reversals may also interfere with factor-price equalization. This phenomenon will be discussed in the next chapter.

Also the assumption that production functions are identical between countries is crucial. If production functions are different between countries, factor prices cannot be equalized—curve PP' of Figure 5-4 cannot be the same in America as in Britain.

The assumption of constant returns to scale cannot be relaxed, either. With variable returns to scale, the absolute factor prices do not depend only on the labor-land ratios of the two industries; they depend, in addition, on the scales of output. Further, with increasing returns to scale due to economies internal to the firm, perfect competition breaks down.

Trade restrictions and transportation costs do exist in the real world. This means that commodity trade does not even equalize relative commodity prices in the real world. Thus, even if curve PP' of Figure 5-4 were accepted as a valid representation of reality, complete factor-price equalization would still not occur in the real world.

However, even though its basic assumptions are violated and its prediction is not borne out in the real world, the factor-price equalization theorem remains a significant result. The importance of the theorem springs mainly from the fact that it directs our attention toward the examination of the relevant variables that determine the impact of free commodity trade on factor prices. The factor-price equalization theorem emphasizes that free commodity trade is a substitute, albeit imperfect, for factor movements between countries. It can also tell us how far we can hope to go toward world efficiency (while maintaining barriers to factor movements) through free commodity trade plus technical assistance plus, possibly, capital movements (the latter two being "foreign aid").

5-8 THE HECKSCHER-OHLIN THEOREM

We now proceed to the Heckscher-Ohlin theorem. This theorem can be formulated on the basis of either the price definition of factor abundance or the physical definition of factor abundance. In this section, we concentrate on the former formulation (price definition), which is simpler. We discuss the latter formulation (physical definition), which is more difficult, in the appendix to this chapter.

Return again to the scenario of Section 5-2. As we have seen, the Heckscher-Ohlin theorem is the hypothesis that a country has a comparative advantage in the production of that commodity which uses more intensively the country's relatively abundant factor. When the price definition of factor abundance is adopted, the Heckscher-Ohlin theorem takes the following form:

Theorem 5-2 (Heckscher-Ohlin theorem—price definition) When the assumptions enumerated in Section 5-2 are satisfied, then the country with the lowest wage-rent ratio in the autarkic state (that is, the labor-abundant country) has a comparative advantage in the labor-intensive commodity (clothing) and the land-abundant country has a comparative advantage in the land-intensive commodity (food).

Proof To prove theorem (5-2), we must show that the country which has the lowest opportunity cost of clothing in terms of food before trade is also the country with the lowest pretrade wage-rent ratio. But this must be obvious from Figure 5-4. Thus, before trade, America and Britain operate at two (in general, different) points on curve PP' of Figure 5-4, such as A and B, respectively. Since curve PP' slopes downward throughout, it follows that a lower wage-rent ratio implies a higher relative price of food (or a lower relative price of clothing). Accordingly, the labor-intensive commodity (clothing) must be cheaper, before trade, in the labor-abundant country (Britain), that is, the country with the lower wage-rent ratio. This completes the proof.

Note that nowhere in the preceding proof was it assumed that consumption patterns were identical between countries. Consequently, when the price definition of factor abundance is adopted, the Heckscher-Ohlin theorem is necessarily true irrespective of any differences in tastes between America and Britain.

5-9 SUMMARY

1   The Heckscher-Ohlin theory, also known as the factor-endowment theory, can be summarized by two important theorems: the Heckscher-Ohlin theorem and the factor-price equalization theorem.

2   The Heckscher-Ohlin theorem states that a country has a comparative advantage in the production of that commodity which uses more intensively the country's more abundant factor.

3   The factor-price equalization theorem states that free international trade equalizes factor prices between countries, relatively and absolutely, and thus serves as a substitute for international factor mobility.

4   The simplest version of the Heckscher-Ohlin model assumes that each of two countries is endowed with two inelastically supplied homogeneous factors (say, labor and land) and produces under constant returns to scale (and without any production externalities) two commodities. The factors are perfectly mobile within each country but perfectly immobile between countries. Further, the two countries share the same technology; in addition, one commodity is labor intensive relative to the second commodity at all factor prices.

5   Although Ohlin took it for granted that production functions are identical between countries, the issue cannot be settled by a priori arguments—it is an empirical problem.

6   The labor-intensive commodity is that commodity which uses more units of labor per unit of land at all wage-rent ratios. Like comparative advantage, factor intensity is a relative concept.

7   A country is labor abundant when her pretrade wage-rent ratio is lower than the corresponding wage-rent ratio of the second country. Factor abundance is also a relative concept.

8   The production functions imply a fundamental relationship between factor prices and commodity prices (or costs): *As the wage-rent ratio falls, the labor-intensive commodity becomes cheaper relative to the land-intensive commodity.* This fundamental relationship (which is common to both countries because they share the same technology) lies at the very heart of both the factor-price equalization theorem and the Heckscher-Ohlin theorem.

9   Because of the fundamental relationship between factor prices and commodity prices, the labor-intensive commodity is necessarily cheaper before trade in the country with the lowest wage-rent ratio (that is, the labor-abundant

country). In other words, the labor-abundant country necessarily has a comparative advantage in the labor-intensive commodity.

10 When free trade leads to (a) commodity-price equalization between countries and (b) incomplete specialization in each country, factor prices are necessarily equalized, both relatively and absolutely. This must be so because of the existence of a one-to-one correspondence between commodity prices and factor prices.

APPENDIX: The Heckscher-Ohlin Theorem on the Basis of the Physical Definition of Factor Abundance

In this appendix we discuss the Heckscher-Ohlin theorem on the basis of the physical definition of factor abudance. (See Section 5-5.) For this purpose, it is necessary to make the additional assumption that tastes are largely similar betweeen countries. This is usually interpreted to mean that the tastes of each and every country are given by the same homothetic social indifference map. Therefore, before we proceed with the statement and proof of the Heckscher-Ohlin theorem, we must clarify the meaning of identical and homothetic tastes between countries.

A5-1 IDENTICAL AND HOMOTHETIC TASTES BETWEEN COUNTRIES

The Heckscher-Ohlin model assumes that the tastes of all trading nations are given by the same homothetic social indifference map. We are already familiar with the technical term "homotheticity" from our discussion in Chapter 3. A homothetic indifference map is one whose income-consumption curves are straight lines through the origin. It looks very much like a constant-returns-to-scale isoquant map, except that the numbers which indicate levels of welfare have *ordinal* significance only and can be changed at will provided the initial ordering is preserved.

In simple English, "identical and homothetic tastes between countries" means the following: Given the same commodity prices in all countries (a result brought about by free trade), all countries will divide their incomes between food consumption and clothing consumption in exactly the same way, irrespective of how high each nation's national income, or per capita income, is. For instance, if at the current prices America spends 60 percent of its income on food and 40 percent on clothing, Britain must also be spending 60 percent of its income on food and 40 percent on clothing.

It must be clear that homotheticity of tastes is a necessary condition for the above result. Thus, suppose we start at a position where both countries divide their incomes between food and clothing in exactly the same way. The same consumption behavior cannot continue to be observed if either nation's income is allowed to rise, unless the social indifference map is homothetic.

Homotheticity of tastes runs against the famous *Engel's Law*. As the reader will recall, Ernst Engel (not to be confused with Karl Marx's friend Friedrich Engels) was a nineteenth century German statistician who asserted that if demographic factors are held constant, an increase in income will lower the proportion of income spent on food. This proposition, known as Engel's Law, has been tested empirically and found valid. But if Engel's Law is accepted, we must reject the homotheticity of tastes, which actually denies the law.

Nevertheless, as we shall see later, similarity and homotheticity of tastes is a simplifying assumption that does not adversely affect the empirical validity of the Heckscher-Ohlin model. Similarity and homotheticity of tastes is actually a very strong assumption. In technical terms, it is only a sufficient (but not necessary) assumption for the validity of the Heckscher-Ohlin model, which requires only that tastes are largely similar between countries. Empirical studies do suggest that there is considerable similarity in demand functions among countries. Whether such similarity is the result of trade itself and the strong *demonstration effect* that easy communication between countries gives rise to is a question which need not concern us at the moment.

A5-2 THE HECKSCHER-OHLIN THEOREM

Turn now to the validity of the Heckscher-Ohlin theorem when factor abundance is decided on the basis of the physical definition. The theorem takes now the following form:

Theorem A5-1 (Heckscher-Ohlin theorem—physical definition) When the assumptions enumerated in Section 5-2 are satisfied, the country (Britain) that is endowed with more units of labor per unit of land (that is, the labor-abundant country) has a comparative advantage in the labor-intensive commodity (clothing) and the land-abundant country (America) has a comparative advantage in the land-intensive commodity (food).

Proof To prove theorem (A5-1), we must demonstrate that in the autarkic state clothing (that is, the labor-intensive commodity) is relatively cheaper in Britain (that is, the labor-abundant country).

First compare the production frontiers of America and Britain given in Figure A5-1. America's frontier UV lies beyond Britain's frontier MK because we assume that America is endowed with absolutely more units of both labor and land. Nevertheless, *at any common commodity-price ratio, America always produces a greater food-clothing output ratio than Britain* (or, alternatively, Britain produces a greater clothing-food output ratio than America). This is illustrated by points E_a and J, where the two frontiers have the same slope. Taking this property for granted for the moment, the proof of theorem (A5-1) is immediate.

While America reaches autarkic equilibrium at E_a (where America's frontier UV is tangent to the highest *common* social indifference curve, I_3), Britain reaches autarkic equilibrium at E_b. Because the common social indifference map is assumed homothetic, it follows that the marginal rate of substitution of food for clothing (which is equivalent to the relative price of food) is lower at E_a than at E_b. This becomes obvious when we notice that the slope of I_3 at E_a is equal to the slope of I_1 at N, and, in addition, the slope of I_2 at E_b is equal to the slope of I_1 at Q. Because of the law of diminishing marginal rate of substitution, the slope at N is smaller than the slope at Q. Hence, we conclude that in the autarkic state food is relatively cheaper in America.

Note that if it were possible for Britain's equilibrium to occur in region MJ, Brit-

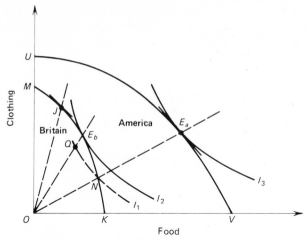

Figure A5-1 *The Heckscher-Ohlin theorem on the basis of the physical definition of factor abundance.*
America is absolutely larger than Britain. Thus, Britain's production frontier *MK* lies inside production frontier *UV* of America. Because she is land abundant relative to Britain, America always produces a greater food-clothing output ratio than Britain at any common commodity price ratio, as illustrated by points E_a and *J*. America reaches autarkic equilibrium at E_a and Britain at E_b. Thus, food is cheaper in America before trade.

ain's opportunity cost of food would be lower than America's (at E_a), and thus Britain (not America) would have a comparative advantage in the production of food. Why, one may ask, is it not possible for Britain's equilibrium to take place somewhere along region *MJ*? The answer must be obvious from what we have said already. In particular, in region *MJ* Britain's marginal rate of substitution of food for clothing is consistently higher than Britain's opportunity cost of food. A quick inspection of Figure A5-1 reveals that the social indifference curves necessarily *intersect* region *MJ* from above. This means that Britain's equilibrium must occur in region *JK*, as is actually illustrated by point E_b.

What remains to be done is to demonstrate that at any common commodity-price ratio America always produces a greater food-clothing output ratio than Britain. This is not difficult to do.

The Factor-price equalization theorem tells us that when the commodity-price ratio is the same in both countries, the wage-rent ratio, and thus the production coefficients, must also be the same. To fix ideas, suppose that at a certain common commodity-price ratio, the common production coefficients are:

	Labor	Land
Food	1	4
Clothing	3	2

Suppose further that Britain is endowed with 2,800 units of labor and 3,200 units of land. This is the same illustration we used in Section 5-6. Thus, Britain's output mix is given by point *B* of Figure 5-3, which for convenience is reproduced in Figure A5-2.

Consider now America's position. If America were endowed with exactly twice as

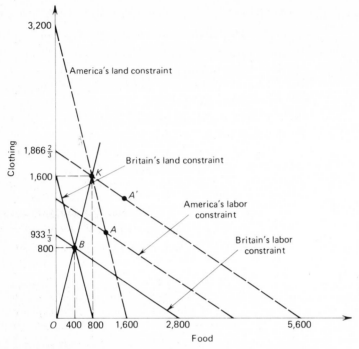

Figure A5-2 At the same factor and commodity prices, the land-abundant country (America) produces a higher food-clothing output ratio (at *A* or *A'*) than the labor-abundant country (Britain), which produces at *B*.

many units of labor and land as Britain (that is, 5,600 units of labor and 6,400 units of land), America would be producing at *K*—that is, twice as many units of food and clothing as Britain. In general, if America's endowments of labor and land were proportional to Britain's, America would be producing food and clothing somewhere along ray *OK*; that is, America's food-clothing output ratio would be equal to Britain's. However, America is land abundant relative to Britain. This means that if America has twice as many units of land as Britain, she must have less than twice as many units of labor; and thus she must actually produce at a point such as *A*. Alternatively, if America has twice as many units of labor as Britain, she must have more than twice as many units of land; and thus she must produce at a point such as *A'*. Since points *A* and *A'* lie below ray *OK*, we must conclude that America produces a greater food-clothing output ratio than Britain, which is exactly what we wished to demonstrate.

SUGGESTED READING

Chacholiades, M. (1978). *International Trade Theory and Policy*. McGraw-Hill Book Company, New York, chaps. 8–10.

Heckscher, E. (1919). "The Effect of Foreign Trade on the Distribution of Income." *Ekonomisk Tidskrift*, vol. 21, pp. 1–32. Reprinted in AEA *Readings in the Theory of International Trade*. Richard D. Irwin, Inc., Homewood, Ill., 1950.

Johnson, H. G. (1957). "Factor Endowments, International Trade and Factor Prices." *Manchester School of Economics and Social Studies,* vol. 25 (September), pp. 270–283. Reprinted in H. G. Johnson, *International Trade and Economic Growth.* George Allen and Unwin, Ltd., London, 1958.

Jones, R. W. (1956). "Factor Proportions and the Heckscher-Ohlin Theorem." *Review of Economic Studies,* vol. 24, pp. 1–10.

Lerner, A. P. (1953). *Essays in Economic Analysis.* Macmillan and Company, Ltd., London.

Ohlin, B. (1933). *Interregional and International Trade.* Harvard University Press, Cambridge, Mass.

Samuelson, P. A. (1948). "International Trade and the Equalization of Factor Prices." *Economic Journal,* vol. 58, pp. 165–184.

——— (1949). "International Factor Price Equalization Once Again." *Economic Journal,* vol. 59, pp. 181–197. Reprinted in AEA *Readings in International Economics.* Richard D. Irwin, Inc., Homewood, Ill., 1968.

Stolper, W. F. and P. A. Samuelson (1941). "Protection and Real Wages." *Review of Economic Studies,* vol. 9, pp. 58–73. Reprinted in AEA *Readings in the Theory of International Trade.* Richard D. Irwin, Inc., Homewood, Ill., 1950.

Chapter Six

Empirical Testing

Having discussed the theoretical foundations of the Ricardian and the Heckscher-Ohlin models of international trade, we now turn to their empirical verification. Our discussion is divided into three parts. Part A deals with the empirical testing of the Ricardian model, Part B with the empirical testing of the Heckscher-Ohlin theorem, and Part C with the implications of factor-intensity reversals.

PART A: Empirical Testing of the Ricardian Model

The first serious attempt to test empirically the predictive capacity of the classical theory was made by MacDougall (1951). Similar studies supporting MacDougall's initial empirical findings were made by Balassa (1963) and Stern (1962). All three studies were carried out on the basis of data for the United States and the United Kingdom for the years 1937 (MacDougall), 1950 (Balassa), and 1950 and 1959 (Stern).

The hypothesis that MacDougall (1951, p. 697) tested is this: Given two countries, say, A and B, "each will export those goods for which the ratio of its output per worker to that of the other exceeds the ratio of its money wage-rate to that of the other."

To test his hypothesis, MacDougall calculated for some 25 industry groups both the ratio of American to British exports and the ratio of American to British output per worker. In calculating the export ratio, MacDougall excluded the mutual trade between the United States and the United Kingdom because (1) as a result of the high American and British tariffs, the bulk (more than 95 percent) of American and British exports in 1937 went to third countries and (2) the height of both the American and the British tariff varied from sector to sector and tended to offset differences in labor productivity. In general, both the American and the British exporters faced the same tariff walls in the rest of the world.

MacDougall found that in 1937 American wages were about double those in Britain. He concluded that American money costs of production are approximately equal to, lower than, or higher than British money costs according to the productivity ratio (output per U.S. worker/output per U.K. worker) being equal to, higher than, or lower than 2. In other words, for productivity ratios lower than 2, Britain had the cost advantage; for productivity ratios higher than 2, America had the cost advantage; and for productivity ratios equal to 2, neither country enjoyed a significant cost advantage. Indeed, MacDougall found that 20 out of his 25 industry groups obeyed this general rule: When the productivity ratio was higher than 2, America had a larger share of the export market; and when the productivity ratio was lower than 2, Britain had a larger share of the export market. MacDougall and other economists took these findings as support for the classical theory.

Figure 6-1 (drawn on a double logarithmic scale) summarizes MacDougall's results and brings out another striking fact: The observed points lie fairly close to a positively sloped straight line (KL). This shows that there is a *tendency for each country to capture an ever-increasing share of the export market as its comparative advantage grows.*

The classical theory, of course, does not imply such a relationship. Indeed, the classical theory suggests that when the productivity ratio exceeds 2, America will capture the entire export market and when the productivity ratio is lower than 2, Britain will capture the entire export market. Only when the productivity ratio is exactly 2, will America and Britain share the export market (although, in this case, in which neither country has a cost advantage, the classical theory predicts nothing about the sharing of an export market).

Why does the country that has the cost advantage not capture the whole export market, as the classical theory would lead us to believe? MacDougall attributes this phenomenon to the existence of imperfect markets (monopolistic and oligopolistic), nonhomogeneous products, transport costs, and the like. For instance, each of the 25 industry groups studied by MacDougall is an aggregate of related but nevertheless different products. Even though Britain may have an overall advantage in a certain industry group, such as footwear, America may

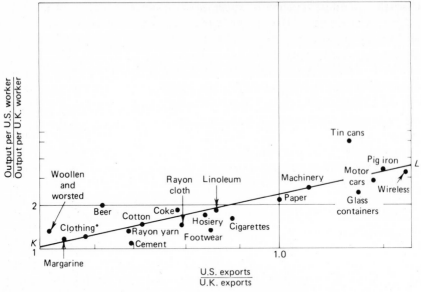

Figure 6-1 MacDougall's findings. (After MacDougall, 1951.)

still have a cost advantage in the production of certain kinds of shoes. Or if foreign buyers perceive British cars to be different from American cars in some crucial respects, some of them may prefer to buy British cars even though America has a cost advantage.

Until future research refutes the important findings of MacDougall (which were confirmed by Balassa and Stern), we must conclude that they provide strong evidence that the classical theory really works. However, the greatest defect of the classical theory remains the fact that it does not shed any light on what determines comparative advantage and on how comparative advantage may be expected to change in the future.

PART B: The Leontief Paradox

6-1 INTRODUCTION

After its reformulation by Bertil Ohlin, the validity of the Heckscher-Ohlin theorem (that is, the proposition that each country exports those commodities which use more intensively its abundant factor) was not questioned. Rather, the theorem was generally accepted on the basis of casual empiricism. The first serious attempt to test the theorem empirically was made by Wassily W. Leontief (1953). Leontief reached the paradoxical conclusion that the United States, the most capital-abundant country in the world by any criterion, exported labor-intensive commodities and imported capital-intensive commodities.[1] This conclusion, which came to be known in the literature as Leontief's paradox, took the profession by surprise and stimulated an enormous amount of empirical and theoretical research.

This part of Chapter 6 summarizes the main empirical findings and then reviews the chief explanations of the Leontief paradox that are found in the literature.

6-2 EMPIRICAL FINDINGS

This section deals with the empirical findings concerning the pattern of trade of the United States and other countries.

The Pattern of U.S. Trade

To perform his test, Leontief (1953) used the 1947 input-output table of the U.S. economy. He aggregated industries into 50 sectors (38 of which traded their products directly on the international market) and factors into two categories—labor and capital. Then he estimated the capital and labor requirements for the production of a representative bundle (1 million dollars' worth) of U.S. exports and a representative bundle (also 1 million dollars' worth) of U.S. import-competing commodities. He surprised himself—and the rest of the profession—with the discovery that U.S. import replacements required 30 percent *more* capital per worker than U.S. exports. This finding was just the opposite of what the Heckscher-Ohlin model predicted.

Note that because he had only U.S. data, Leontief was practically forced to calculate the capital and labor requirements of U.S. import-competing commodities rather than the factor requirements of actual imports. For this reason, he also had to ignore noncompetitive imports, that is, products not produced in the United States, mainly coffee, tea, and jute.

Leontief was criticized on both methodological and statistical grounds. For instance, Ellsworth (1954) argued that it was not appropriate for Leontief to use the U.S. capital-labor ratio for "import" production. Ellsworth claimed that the capital-labor ratio prevailing in the rest of the world for the actual production of such U.S. imports, which, according to Ellsworth, was substantially lower than the corresponding U.S. ratio, is the appropriate figure to compare with the capital-labor ratio for U.S. exports. Ellsworth's argument rests on the existence of either different production functions between countries or factor-intensity reversals (see Part C).

On statistical matters, some economists complained that 1947 was not a typical year: The postwar disorganization of production overseas had not been corrected by that time, and the results were biased both by the capital-labor

---

[1] If Leontief's empirical findings are actually correct, then not only is the Heckscher-Ohlin theorem refuted, but certain important policy implications follow immediately. For instance, U.S. tariff protection would appear to be detrimental rather than beneficial to U.S. labor. See the discussion of the Stolper-Samuelson theorem in Chapter 8.

ratios of a few industries (such as agriculture and fisheries) with significant export or import positions and by the way in which transport, commercial services, and wholesale trade were incorporated into the analysis. In addition, some economists argued that the capital coefficients used by Leontief were essentially "investment-requirements coefficients" and did not really account for the difference in the durability of capital in the various industries.

To quiet his critics, Leontief (1956) repeated the test using the average composition of U.S. exports and imports that prevailed in 1951. In this later study, he retained the 1947 U.S. production structure but disaggregated into 192 sectors of commodity groups. He found that U.S. import replacements were still more capital intensive relative to U.S. exports even though their capital intensity over U.S. exports was reduced to only 6 percent. When Leontief (1956, p. 397, computation A) included capital replacement in the input-output coefficients, he showed that the U.S. import-competing sector was 17.57 percent more capital intensive than the U.S. export sector. More recent studies have confirmed Leontief's findings.

Trade Patterns of Other Countries

Leontief's methodology was used by a number of economists to study the trade patterns of other countries as well. Thus, Tatemoto and Ichimura (1959) studied Japan's trade pattern and discovered another paradox: Japan, a labor-abundant country, exports capital-intensive commodities and imports labor-intensive commodities. Tatemoto and Ichimura attributed this to the fact that Japan's place in the world economy is somewhere between the advanced and the underdeveloped countries. They found that 25 percent of Japanese exports went to advanced countries and 75 percent to underdeveloped countries; and they argued that Japan may be expected to have a comparative advantage in labor-intensive commodities when trading with the advanced countries and a comparative advantage in capital-intensive commodities when trading with the underdeveloped countries.

To substantiate their conjecture, Tatemoto and Ichimura computed the capital-labor ratio of Japanese exports to the United States and found that it was much lower than the capital-labor ratio of Japan's total exports. They also computed the capital-labor ratio of U.S. exports to Japan and found that it was larger than the capital-labor ratio of both the U.S. total exports and U.S. competitive imports. They took these findings to mean two things: (1) that Japan's foreign trade is indeed two-sided, as they had thought, and (2) the Leontief paradox is reversed when the U.S.-Japanese trade is considered.

Stolper and Roskamp (1961) applied Leontief's methods to the trade pattern of East Germany and found that East German exports are capital intensive relative to East German imports. Since about three-quarters of East German trade is with the communist block within which East Germany is considered to be capital abundant, Stolper and Roskamp find their empirical result consistent with the Heckscher-Ohlin theorem.

Wahl (1961) studied Canada's pattern of trade and found that Canadian exports are capital intensive relative to Canadian imports. Since most Canadian trade is with the United States, Wahl's result apparently runs against the Heckscher-Ohlin theorem.

Finally, Bharadwaj (1962a) studied India's trade pattern and found that Indian exports are labor intensive relative to Indian imports. This is apparently consistent with the Heckscher-Ohlin hypothesis. Nevertheless, when Bharadwaj (1962b) considered the Indian trade with the United States, he found that Indian exports to the United States are capital intensive relative to Indian imports from the United States.

Before turning to the various explanations of the Leontief paradox, we should perhaps note that there is no theoretical necessity for the Heckscher-Ohlin relationship to hold bilaterally.

6-3 EXPLANATIONS OF THE LEONTIEF PARADOX

The empirical evidence that has been accumulated so far does not dispel the Leontief paradox. How then are the empirical findings reconciled with the Heckscher-Ohlin theorem? Several economists have tried to explain the paradox. Some of them attempt to bring about a reconciliation within the Heckscher-Ohlin model itself. Others attempt to go beyond the Heckscher-Ohlin model and provide new theories which are basically dynamic in character and which deal with technical progress and the product cycle. These alternative explanations of the Leontief paradox are summarized below.

Effectiveness of U.S. Labor

The first unsuccessful attempt to explain Leontief's paradox was made by Leontief himself. He asserted that the apparent higher abundance of capital per worker in the United States relative to that of other countries is actually an illusion. The United States, Leontief argued, is instead a labor-abundant country, because American workers are much more productive than foreign workers. In particular, he suggested that one worker-year of American labor is equivalent to three worker-years of foreign labor—the number of American workers must be multiplied by 3. Leontief attributed the higher productivity of American labor not to the employment of a larger amount of capital per worker but rather to American entrepreneurship, superior organization, and favorable environment.

Unfortunately, it is very difficult to accept Leontief's explanation. American entrepreneurship, superior organization, and favorable environment may indeed raise the productivity of American labor. Nevertheless, they also raise the productivity of American capital. Leontief's argument may be admissible only to the extent that these factors raise the productivity of U.S. labor much more than they raise the productivity of U.S. capital—for if they raise the productivity of U.S. capital by the same amount by which they raise the productivity of U.S. labor, then the greater abundance of capital in the United States relative to other countries remains intact.

To test empirically Leontief's conjecture, Kreinin (1965) conducted a survey of managers and engineers familiar with production conditions in the United States and abroad. The results of the survey confirmed that U.S. labor is indeed superior to its foreign counterpart, although such superiority amounts perhaps to 20 or 25 percent (not 300 percent, as Leontief claimed) and is not sufficient to convert the United States into a labor-abundant country.

Consumption Patterns

When we judge factor abundance on the basis of the physical definition, the Heckscher-Ohlin theorem is valid only to the extent that tastes are largely similar between countries (see the Appendix to Chapter 5). In particular, if her tastes are strongly biased toward the capital-intensive commodity, the capital-abundant country may actually export the labor-intensive commodity.

Accordingly, Leontief's paradox could be easily explained if it were shown that the United States has a strong consumption bias toward capital-intensive goods. Nevertheless, no economist has argued strongly that consumption bias is the major explanation of the Leontief paradox. For one thing, empirical studies suggest that there is considerable similarity in demand functions among countries. For another, as per capita incomes rise, people tend to spend more on labor-intensive goods (such as services) than on capital-intensive goods. Hence, if there is indeed a consumption bias in the United States, the bias must be toward labor-intensive rather than capital-intensive goods—that is, the opposite of what is actually needed to explain Leontief's paradox.

Factor-Intensity Reversals

Factor-intensity reversals occur when the labor-intensity curves of food and clothing intersect. When, in addition, the overall factor proportions of America and Britain are such that the same commodity, say, food, is land intensive in America but labor intensive in Britain, *one of the two countries must show a Leontief paradox.*

Suppose, as before, that America is land abundant relative to Britain and that America exports food (that is, her land-intensive commodity). Thus, the Heckscher-Ohlin theorem appears to be valid for America. Unfortunately, Britain must exhibit a Leontief paradox—for Britain, the labor-abundant country, must export clothing, which is *her* land-intensive commodity.

During the last two decades, several economists have tried to determine empirically whether factor-intensity reversals do occur extensively in the real world. Unfortunately, their results up to the present time are inconclusive. All one can say at this stage is that the matter of factor-intensity reversals remains unresolved.

Because of its inherent complexity, the phenomenon of factor-intensity reversals, along with its theoretical implications for the Heckscher-Ohlin model, is studied separately in Part C of this chapter.

Tariffs and Other Distortions

In addition to distortions in their domestic markets, virtually all nations interfere with the free flow of their international trade by means of tariffs and nontariff barriers (see Chapters 8–11). Travis (1964) has argued that these tariffs and nontariff barriers to trade may have been responsible for the Leontief paradox in that they restricted U.S. imports of labor-intensive commodities. Baldwin (1971) showed that there is a grain of truth in the Travis thesis in the sense that tariffs and nontariff bariers operate in the direction of, but are not responsible for, the Leontief paradox. According to Baldwin, if all tariffs and nontariff barriers were removed, the capital-labor ratio of U.S. imports would fall by only 5 percent, and this is not enough to explain the Leontief paradox.

In connection with market imperfections, Diab (1956, pp. 53–56) made the interesting suggestion that perhaps production abroad by American corporations or their subsidiaries (aided by American capital, technology, and labor and managerial skills) should be considered an extension of the American economy. Diab argued that once these "American economic colonies" are structurally incorporated in the "mother economy of the United States," their (highly capital-intensive) shipments to the United States would be regarded as part of the U.S. internal trade rather than as U.S. imports. In turn, such a procedure may reverse the capital intensity of the American trade with the rest of the world, and thus explain the Leontief paradox.

Natural Resources

Leontief was criticized by Diab (1956) and Vanek (1959, 1963) for ignoring natural resources. In particular, Diab (1956, pp. 46–56) divided the products traded by the United States on the international market into two groups: manufacturing (that is, those products whose production does not depend crucially on natural resources) and nonmanufacturing (that is, those products whose production depends crucially on natural resources). He then observed that (1) the nonmanufacturing group was more predominant in U.S. competitive imports (where they constituted 65 percent) than in U.S. exports (where they constituted only 15 percent) and (2) the capital-labor ratios of the nonmanufacturing group was higher than the capital-labor ratio of the manufacturing group, while the corresponding capital-labor ratios of the two groups were practically the same in U.S. exports and U.S. competitive imports. Given this information he concluded that the Leontief paradox was due to the fact that "the highly capital-intensive non-manufacturing group of industries enjoys, percentagewise, a higher weighting in import replacements than in exports ..." (p. 50). He attributed the high percentage of nonmanufacturing products in U.S. imports to the relative scarcity and poor quality of U.S. natural resources and also to the fact that because of the sheer size of the country, U.S. producers often import their raw materials from neighboring countries, rather than from other parts of the United States.

Vanek (1963, pp. 132–135) provided additional support to Diab's contention. Specifically, he found that natural resources are relatively scarce in the United States. In addition, Vanek assumed that capital is strongly complementary to natural resources and concluded that although capital may well be a relatively abundant factor in the United States, U.S. imports are capital-intensive relative to U.S. exports because natural resources, the scarce factor, enter efficient production only in conjunction with large amounts of capital.

In his subsequent work, Leontief (1956, p. 398, computation D) made allowance for the natural resource factor. In particular, by eliminating 19 natural resource products from his matrix (that is, by treating them as noncompetitive imports), he succeeded in eliminating the paradox that the United States is exporting labor-intensive commodities. On the other hand, Baldwin (1971) found that when natural resource products are eliminated from the factor-content calculations, the capital intensity of U.S. import replacements drops substantially—but U.S. imports remain more capital intensive than U.S. exports by 4 percent. Thus, the paradox continues. Perhaps it should be pointed out that in all such calculations the precise definition of natural resource industries is both arbitrary and critical to the outcome.

Human Capital

Another important factor that must be taken into account in evaluating the Leontief paradox is *human capital*. The idea is simple: Human capital is created by "investing" in education. Education, like physical capital, requires time and uses resources. The skills and expertise that education and training create last a long time and tend to increase substantially the productivity of the labor force. The view of education as capital creation has assumed a predominant role in the economics of education.

There are two alternative ways in which the concept of human capital may be used to explain the Leontief paradox. One way is to argue that countries which are relatively abundant in highly trained labor, like the United States, will have a comparative advantage in, and will export, skill-intensive commodities. Alternatively, it may be argued that the value of human capital must be added to the value of physical capital, as is done, for example, by Kenen (1965), as explained below.

Leontief (1956, pp. 398–399) did not include the value of human capital in his calculations, although he recognized its significance and stressed that the U.S. export industries employed more skilled labor than U.S. import-competing industries. This conclusion, which was later confirmed by Baldwin (1971), was consistent with the findings of Kravis (1956a), who observed that wages in U.S. export industries tend to be higher than wages in U.S. import-competing industries—a tendency that seems to exist in most countries.

Using a 9 percent rate of discount, Kenen (1965) estimated the value of human capital involved in U.S. exports and import-competing products by capitalizing the excess income of skilled over unskilled workers. He then added the estimates of human capital to Leontief's physical capital estimates and found that the Leontief paradox was reversed. (Kenen also showed that the Leontief paradox is reversed only when the rate of discount used in the capitalization process is less than 12.7 percent). Baldwin (1971), on the other hand, used the costs of education plus forgone earnings to obtain a crude measure of the human capital involved in U.S. export and import-competing production, and concluded that the addition of such a measure of human capital to the estimates of physical capital was not sufficient to reverse the paradox except when the natural resource products were excluded.

Technological Gap and Product Cycle

The Heckscher-Ohlin theory is static. Several distinguished economists have argued recently that perhaps the composition of trade depends on dynamic factors, such as technical change. In particular, it has been argued that what allows the United States to compete successfully in world markets is its ability to supply a steady flow of new products.

The *technological-gap theory* makes use of the sequence of innovation and imitation particularly as it affects exports. As a new product is developed and becomes profitable in the domestic market, the innovating firm, which enjoys a temporary monopoly, initially has an easy access to foreign markets. At first, the country's exports grow. Later on, however, the profits of the innovating firm prompt imitation in other countries, which may actually prove to have a comparative advantage in the production of the new commodity after the innovation is disseminated. But as the innovating country loses, through imitation, its absolute advantage in one commodity, a new cycle of innovation-imitation begins in another commodity. Thus, the innovating country may continue to develop new products and may continue to have a temporary absolute advantage in products that are eventually produced more efficiently in other countries.

Catering for the domestic market first, before expanding into foreign mardets, is an idea which was stressed originally by Linder (1961). He specifically claimed that exports start out as goods produced for the domestic market and that a necessary condition for manufactures to eventually become exports is the existence of sufficient domestic demand for them. Exceptions do exist, as is illustrated by the exports of Christmas trees by Japan and Korea, two non-Christian countries.

Several years ago Kravis (1956b) argued that a country's exports are determined by *availability*. He did not give a precise definition to the term "availability." He used it in the sense that the domestic supply of exports is "elastic" (perhaps relative to the corresponding foreign supply). Kravis claimed that availability is a reflection of a country's relative abundance of natural resources and temporary superiority in *technology* that innovation confers upon the country.

The technological-gap theory fails to explain why the gap is what it is and why it is not larger or smaller. Vernon (1966) generalized the theory into the *product cycle,* which stresses the standardization of products. In particular, Vernon suggested three stages: new product, maturing product, and standardized product. He also suggested that the input requirements change over the life cycle of a new product. For instance, at the new-product stage, production requires much highly skilled labor for the development and improvement of the product. As the product matures, marketing and capital costs become dominant. Finally, at the standardized-product stage, the technology stabilizes and the product enjoys general consumer acceptance. This leads to mass production, which largely requires raw materials, capital, and unskilled labor. Accordingly, as the product matures and becomes standardized, comparative advantage may shift from a country relatively abundant in skilled labor to a country abundant in unskilled labor.

Keesing (1967), Gruber, Mehta, and Vernon (1967), and others have taken research and development (R&D) expenditures as a proxy for temporary, comparative-cost advantages created by the development of new products. They have found a strong correlation between the intensity of R&D activity and export performance. Such evidence tends to support both the technological-gap theory and the product-cycle theory.

Why does the United States have a comparative advantage based on technology and innovation? Several factors are usually cited for this phenomenon. First, the United States has a per capita income that is high by international standards—a fact which creates unique consumption patterns and a favorable market for new or improved products. Second, the development of new or improved products requires much skilled labor, which is relatively abundant in the United States. Third, because of the high U.S. labor costs and the alleged tendency of innovations to be labor saving, there is a greater incentive to innovate in the United States. Finally, the development and marketing of new or improved products may be associated with economies of scale, which tend to be realizable in large, high-income markets like those of the United States. This last point is, of course, closely related to the first.

PART C: Factor-Intensity Reversals

One of the most crucial assumptions of the Heckscher-Ohlin model is that one commodity (clothing) is labor intensive relative to the other (food) at *all* factor prices. As we pointed out in Chapter 5, there is no a priori reason that this should be so. Whether such a strong factor-intensity assumption is justified is an empirical matter that can be resolved only by means of hard, empirical work. Unfortunately, this empirical problem remains unresolved.

This part deals briefly with the theoretical implications of the phenomenon of factor-intensity reversals. The student who is in a hurry may skip this part.

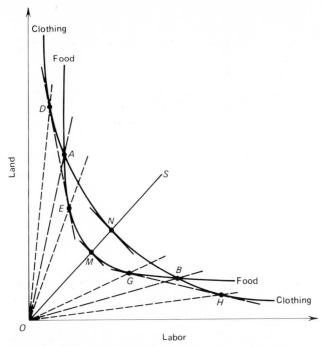

Figure 6-2 *Factor-intensity reversals.*
At the wage-rent ratio (indicated by the absolute slope of) *DE*, food's expansion path is given by broken line *OE* and clothing's by *OD*. Hence, at *DE*, food is labor intensive relative to clothing. On the other hand, at wage-rent ratio *GH*, food is land intensive relative to clothing.

Factor-Intensity Reversals in Terms of Isoquants

The phenomenon of factor-intensity reversals is illustrated in Figure 6-2. At the wage-rent ratio indicated by the absolute slope of *DE*, food's expansion path is given by broken line *OE* and clothing's by *OD*. Since *OE* is flatter than *OD, food is labor intensive relative to clothing.* On the other hand, at wage-rent ratio *GH*, food's expansion path *OG* is steeper than clothing's *OH*, and therefore *food is land intensive relative to clothing.* Because of the assumed smooth substitutability between labor and land, at the intermediate wage-rent ratio shown by the slopes at *M* and *N*, food and clothing display the same labor intensity.

Factor Prices and Commodity Prices

The immediate implication of factor-intensity reversals is the breakdown of the one-to-one correspondence between factor prices and commodity prices. This is shown in Figure 6-3, which is based on Figure 6-2.

Wage-rent ratio *OM* (Figure 6-3) corresponds to the common slope at *M* and *N* in Figure 6-2. For wage-rent ratios *higher* than *OM* (such as *DE* in Figure 6-2), food is *labor intensive* relative to clothing. As labor becomes cheaper

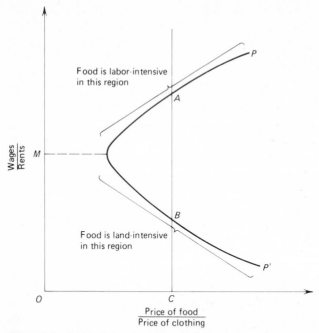

Figure 6-3 Factor-intensity reversals destroy the one-to-one correspondence between factor prices and commodity prices. At wage-rent ratios *higher* than *OM,* food is labor intensive relative to clothing, and the relative price of food *falls* as the wage-rent ratio falls. Curve *PP'* slopes *upward* in this area. At wage-rent ratios *lower* than *OM,* food is land intensive relative to clothing, and curve *PP'* slopes *downward.* The same relative price of food, say, *OC,* corresponds now to two different wage-rent ratios, *CA* and *CB.*

(that is, as the wage-rent ratio falls), food becomes relatively cheaper in accordance with the basic proposition we studied in Section 5-6. This accounts for the *positive* slope of curve *PP'* of Figure 6-3 for all wage-rent ratios higher than *OM.*

For wage-rent ratios *lower* than *OM* (such as *GH* in Figure 6-2), food becomes *land intensive* relative to clothing. Now as labor becomes cheaper, food becomes relatively more expensive. Thus, curve *PP'* has a *negative* slope in this region.

Given curve *PP'* of Figure 6-3, it is no longer possible to associate only one wage-rent ratio to each commodity-price ratio. Thus, food's relative price *OC* is consistent with two wage-rent ratios, *CA* and *CB.* This is the fundamental reason we can no longer be sure that commodity-price equalization (brought about by means of free commodity trade) necessarily leads to factor-price equalization. At common commodity-price ratio *OC,* it is now *possible* for America's wage-rent ratio to be given by *CA,* and Britain's by *CB, even though neither country specializes completely.*

In addition, the validity of the Heckscher-Ohlin theorem is uncertain. When America's posttrade equilibrium wage-rent ratio is given by *CA,* and

Britain's by CB, food is labor intensive in America and land intensive in Britain. With such a contradictory factor-intensity ranking of commodities between countries, one country must exhibit a "Leontief paradox." For instance, assume that America is land abundant relative to Britain. If America exports food, then she must exhibit a Leontief paradox, since food is America's labor-intensive commodity. On the other hand, if America exports clothing, Britain must export food, which is her *land-intensive* commodity. Hence, Britain must exhibit a Leontief paradox in this case.

For further details on the implications of factor-intensity reversals, see the appendix to this chapter.

6-4 SUMMARY

1 Empirical studies by MacDougall and other economists provide strong support for the classical theory of comparative advantage.

2 Leontief tested the hypothesis that U.S. exports are capital intensive relative to U.S. imports. However, he reached the paradoxical conclusion that the United States actually exports labor-intensive commodities and imports capital-intensive commodities. Empirical studies for other countries have often (but not always) generated similar paradoxes.

3 There are several explanations of the Leontief paradox. Some of them attempt to bring about a reconciliation within the Heckscher-Ohlin model itself. Others attempt to go beyond the Heckscher-Ohlin model and provide new dynamic theories dealing with technical progress and the product cycle.

4 Two unacceptable explanations of the Leontief paradox are as follows. (a) U.S. labor is so much more superior to foreign labor that the United States is actually a labor-abundant country. (b) Perhaps the United States has a strong consumption bias toward capital-intensive goods.

5 More serious explanations of the Leontief paradox are as follows. (a) Factor-intensity reversals separate the United States from the rest of the world and invalidate the Heckscher-Ohlin theorem. (b) By protecting U.S. industries, which are relatively intensive in unskilled labor, U.S. tariffs and nontariff barriers to international trade tend to exclude labor-intensive imports. (c) Natural resources are relatively scarce in the United States. As a result, the United States imports natural resource products, which are highly capital intensive. (d) U.S. export industries use intensively highly skilled labor, which is relatively abundant in America. (e) A large portion of wages paid to highly skilled labor is actually a return to human capital. When the human-capital element of skilled labor is properly accounted for, the Leontief paradox is reversed.

6 The technological-gap theory is based on the sequence of innovation and imitation (particularly as they affect exports). The argument is that the United States has a comparative advantage in research and development and tends to export technologically advanced manufactured goods.

7 The product-cycle theory suggests three product stages (new product, maturing product, and standardized product). It then explains the speed of dissemination of innovation on the basis of both the changing input requirements over the life cycle of a new product and the factor endowments of countries.

APPENDIX: Box Diagrams and Factor-Intensity Reversals[2]

This appendix illustrates graphically the breakdown of both the Heckscher-Ohlin theorem and the factor-price equalization theorem in the presence of factor-intensity reversals.

Consider Figure A6-1, which is constructed on the basis of the information given earlier in Figure 6-2. In particular, Figure A6-1 is a combination of three box diagrams: America's $ORA'Q$, Britain's $OKB'M$, and the auxiliary box diagram $ORNM$. The diagonals of these three diagrams—that is, OA', OB', and ON—correspond to the vectors OA, OB, and ON, respectively, of Figure 6-2. Also, clothing's unit isoquant as well as points A, B, and N in Figure A6-1 are exactly the same as those of Figure 6.2.

When the overall labor-land ratio is given by ON (as shown by the box diagram $ORNM$), the marginal rates of substitution of labor for land of the food and clothing industries are necessarily equal along diagonal ON—the unit isoquants are by assumption tangent to each other at N. Hence, the contract curve must coincide with diagonal ON in this case.

On the other hand, when the overall labor-land ratio is given by OA' (that is, America's factor proportions), the contract curve must lie *above* the diagonal, as shown by America's box diagram $ORA'Q$. Nevertheless, when the overall labor-land ratio is given by OB' (that is, Britain's factor proportions), the contract curve must lie *below* the diagonal, as shown by Britain's box diagram $OKB'M$. All this can be easily verified by inspecting Figure A6-1 carefully after recalling an important conclusion reached in Chapter 3, namely, that *the contract curve never crosses the diagonal.*

It must be obvious that under the circumstances of Figure A6-1 food is labor intensive in America, but land intensive in Britain, relative to clothing. Such a contradictory classification of commodities must always be the case when the overall labor-land ratios of America and Britain are separated by vector OS (along which the factor-intensity reversal occurs).

Because of the contradictory ranking of food and clothing between America and Britain, one of the two countries *must* exhibit a Leontief paradox. The reader should verify that the country which exports food must also exhibit the Leontief paradox. Accordingly, the Heckscher-Ohlin theorem breaks down.

Finally, note that factor prices cannot be equalized between America and Britain. Thus, the wage-rent ratios along America's contract curve OJA' are all higher than the wage-rent ratios along Britain's contract curve OGB'. This becomes obvious when we notice that in Figure A6-1 the isoquants of the clothing industry are common to both America's and Britain's box diagrams. Therefore, America and Britain must always operate along different expansion paths of the clothing industry. From this observation we infer that the marginal rate of substitution of labor for land, and thus the wage-rent ratio, must always be different between the two countries. In fact, the reader should verify from Figure A6-1 that the wage-rent ratio must be higher in America than Britain, both before and after trade.

We therefore conclude that when a factor-intensity reversal separates the overall labor-land ratios of the two countries, neither the Heckscher-Ohlin theorem nor the factor-price equalization theorem is valid. Nevertheless, when the labor-land ratios of

---

[2] The reader may skip this appendix without interrupting the continuity of the book.

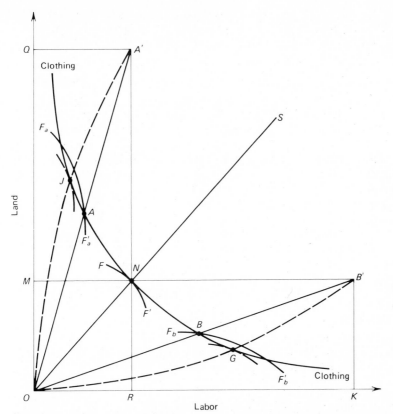

Figure A6-1 America's box diagram is given by *ORA'Q* and Britain's by *OKB'M*. Clothing's isoquant as well as points *A*, *B*, and *N* in Figure A6-1 are the same as those of Figure 6-2. The overall labor-land ratios of America (*OA'*) and Britain (*OB'*) are separated by a factor-intensity reversal (ray *OS*). As a result, food is labor intensive in America but land intensive in Britain; and one of the two countries *must* exhibit a Leontief paradox. Also, the wage-rent ratios along America's contract curve *OJA'* are all higher than all wage-rent ratios along Britain's contract curve *OGB'*. Hence, no factor-price equalization is possible.

America and Britain are *not* separated by a factor-intensity reversal (that is, when the factor proportions of both countries lie either below or above vector *OS*), the factor-intensity reversal is totally harmless.

SUGGESTED READING

Balassa, B. (1963). "An Empirical Demonstration of Comparative Cost." *Review of Economics and Statistics,* vol. 45, pp. 231–238.

Baldwin, R. E. (1971). "Determinants of the Commodity Structure of U.S. Trade." *American Economic Review,* vol. LXI, no. 1 (March), pp. 126–146.

Bharadwaj, R. (1962a). *Structural Basis of India's Foreign Trade.* Series in Monetary and International Economics, no. 6. University of Bombay.

——— (1962b). "Factor Proportions and the Structure of Indo-U.S. Trade." *Indian Economic Journal,* vol. 10 (October).

Diab, M. A. (1956). *The United States Capital Position and the Structure of Its Foreign Trade.* Amsterdam: North-Holland Publishing Company.

Ellsworth, P. T. (1954). "The Structure of American Foreign Trade: A New View Examined." *Review of Economics and Statistics,* vol. 36 (August), pp. 279–285.

Gruber, W., D. Mehta, and R. Vernon (1967). "The R&D Factor in International Trade and Investment of United States Industries." *Journal of Political Economy,* vol. 75 (February), pp. 20–37. Reprinted (with footnotes and references omitted) in R. E. Baldwin and J. D. Richardson (eds.), *International Trade and Finance.* Boston: Little, Brown and Company.

Keesing, D. B. (1967). "The Impact of Research and Development on the United States Trade." *Journal of Political Economy,* vol. 75, no. 1, pp. 38–48. Reprinted in P. B. Kenen and R. Lawrence (eds.), *The Open Economy.* New York: Columbia University Press, 1968.

Kenen, P. B. (1965). "Nature, Capital and Trade." *Journal of Political Economy,* vol. 73 (October), pp. 437–460.

Kravis, I. B. (1956a). "Wages and Foreign Trade." *Review of Economics and Statistics,* vol. 38 (February), pp. 14–30.

————— (1956b). "Availability and Other Influences on the Commodity Composition of Trade." *Journal of Political Economy,* vol. 64 (April).

Kreinin, M. E. (1965). "Comparative Labor Effectiveness and the Leontief Scarce Factor Paradox." *American Economic Review,* vol. 55 (March), pp. 131–140.

Leontief, W. W. (1953). "Domestic Production and Foreign Trade; the American Position Re-examined." *Proceedings of the American Philosophical Society,* vol. 97 (September), pp. 332–349. Reprinted in H. G. Johnson and R. E. Caves (eds.), *Readings in International Economics.* Homewood, Ill.: Richard D. Irwin, Inc., 1968.

————— (1956). "Factor Proportions and the Structure of American Trade: Further Theoretical and Empirical Analysis." *Review of Economics and Statistics,* vol. 38 (November), pp. 386–407.

Linder, S. B. (1961). *An Essay on Trade and Transformation.* Stockholm: Almqvist and Wiksell.

MacDougall, G. D. A. (1951). "British and American Exports: A Study Suggested by the Theory of Comparative Costs, Part I," *Economic Journal,* vol. 61, pp. 697–724. Reprinted in H. G. Johnson and R. E. Caves (eds.), *Readings in International Economics.* Homewood, Ill.: Richard D. Irwin, Inc.

Stern, R. M. (1962). "British and American Productivity and Comparative Costs in International Trade." *Oxford Economic Papers,* vol. 14, pp. 275–296.

Stolper, W. and K. Roskamp (1961). "Input-Output Table for East Germany with Applications to Foreign Trade." *Bulletin of the Oxford University Institute of Statistics,* vol. 23 (November).

Tatemoto, M. and S. Ichimura (1959). "Factor Proportions and Foreign Trade: The Case of Japan." *Review of Economics and Statistics,* vol. 41 (November).

Travis, W. P. (1964). *The Theory of Trade and Protection.* Cambridge, Mass.: Harvard University Press.

Vanek, J. (1959). "The Natural Resource Content of Foreign Trade, 1870–1955, and the Relative Abundance of Natural Resources in the United States." *Review of Economics and Statistics,* vol. 41 (May), pp. 146–153.

——— (1963). *The Natural Resource Content of United States Foreign Trade 1870–1955*. Cambridge, Mass.: The MIT Press.

Vernon, R. (1966). "International Investment and International Trade in the Product Cycle." *Quarterly Journal of Economics*, vol. 80, (May), pp. 190–207.

——— (ed.), (1970). *The Technology Factor in International Trade*. New York: Columbia University Press.

Wahl, D. F. (1961). "Capital and Labour Requirements for Canada's Foreign Trade." *Canadian Journal of Economics and Political Science*, vol. 27 (August).

Chapter Seven

Growth and Trade

This chapter deals with the *comparative-statics analysis* of the effects of *factor-endowment growth* and *technical progress* on the growing economy's production, consumption, terms of trade, and social welfare. The discussion is divided into four parts. Part A deals with the nature of the growth process and the peculiarities of each of the three basic sources of economic growth (labor growth, capital accumulation, and technical progress). Parts B and C deal with the effects of growth on "small" and "large" countries, respectively. Part D deals with the secular behavior of the terms of trade of the less developed countries.

PART A: The Nature of the Growth Process

The preceding chapters are limited by the assumption that the two fundamental data (that is, factor endowments and technology) which delimit the production-possibilities frontier or transformation curve are given. But in our constantly changing world neither factor endowments nor technology remain static. With the passage of time, factor endowments grow, and new and more efficient methods of production replace older, less efficient ones.

Factor-endowment growth and technical progress give rise to some interesting problems. The study of these problems is known as the *theory of the effects of economic growth on trade.*

This part of the chapter provides a general introduction to the nature of the growth process. In particular, it deals with the main sources of economic growth and the classification of technical progress.

7-1   THE SOURCES OF ECONOMIC GROWTH

The three main sources of economic growth are: *labor growth, capital accumulation,* and *technical progress.* Their common characteristic is that *they all cause the growing economy's transformation curve to shift outward over time.* The following discussion deals briefly with some of the peculiarities of each of these three sources of economic growth.

Labor Growth

The reader is no doubt aware of the unprecedented population explosion the world experienced during the last two centuries. During this time more than 3 billion people have been added to the world's population (which currently stands at about 4 billion). Population continues to grow in most countries. It grows faster in the less developed countries of Asia and Latin America (such as China, India, Indonesia, Brazil, Pakistan, and Mexico) than in the advanced countries of North America and Western Europe (such as the United States, West Germany, United Kingdom, Italy, and France).

Population growth leads, of course, to labor growth; and the expansion of the supply of labor causes the production-possibilities frontier to shift outward. Nevertheless, it would be a mistake to conclude, on the basis of the outward shift of the transformation curve alone, that the growing country comes to be better off.

An important yardstick of welfare is provided by the economy's per capita income. Because of the law of diminishing returns, labor growth in itself tends to lower the per capita income and the standard of living. It was particularly for this reason that Malthus, a contemporary of Ricardo, painted a rather gloomy picture of the world—namely, that labor growth would drive wages down to the minimum subsistence level. While wages are above the subsistence level, Malthus argued, population will continue to grow; and when wages fall below the subsistence level, population will die off either through an increase in the death rate (because of disease, famine, and war) or perhaps through a reduction in the birthrate (as a result of birth control). Only at the subsistence level can there be long-run equilibrium. It is no wonder, then, why after he read Malthus, Thomas Carlyle called economics the "dismal science."

Capital Accumulation

One of the basic facts of economic history in Western Europe, North America, Japan, and Australia is that the stock of capital increased much faster than population. Economists refer to this phenomenon as *capital deepening.* Like labor growth, capital accumulation causes the transformation curve to shift outward over time. However, unlike labor growth, capital accumulation leads to higher per capita incomes and standards of living.

The factor capital should be understood to mean "produced means of production"—for example, machines. How does capital come into existence? Through *saving* and *investment*. By abstaining from current consumption (saving), the economy frees factors from the production of consumption goods and diverts them toward the formation of new capital goods (investment).

Unlike the growth of the labor force, which economists consider exogenous (determined by demographic factors), the growth of the capital stock is endogenous. That is, the capital stock is determined by the behavior of the economic system itself—the acts of saving and investment form an integral part of the economic process. This view of capital accumulation leads directly to the construction of a dynamic model of economic growth in which today's production affects tomorrow's capital stock and production. However, this is the domain of the *modern theory of economic growth*, which lies beyond the scope of this book.

Our approach is rather modest: We wish to discuss the effects of labor growth, capital accumulation, and technical progress within a *comparative-statics* framework. In other words, we shall ask questions such as this: How does a *once-and-for-all* increase in our home country's labor force or stock of capital affect our economy's production, consumption, terms of trade, and social welfare? In this discussion, we shall make no attempt to explain where the factor increases come from. We shall only study their long-run, comparative-statics effects.

Technical Progress

Technical progress is an important factor of economic growth. It occurs when increased output can be obtained over time from given resources of capital and labor. The importance of technical progress was overlooked by Malthus.

Even a casual glance at the data reveals that the United States must have experienced remarkable technical progress during the twentieth century. While the capital-output ratio of the United States has remained fairly close to 3 (years)[1], the stock of capital has increased much faster than the supply of labor (capital deepening), and the real rate of interest has shown no long-run trend. It appears, then, that technical progress did occur and actually offset the diminishing returns to capital. Several empirical studies by Abramovitz, Fabricant, Kendrick, Solow, and others seem to confirm this important conclusion. These studies show that by far the larger part of the observed increase in per capita income is the result of technical progress rather than capital deepening.

---

[1]Since capital is a stock (measured at a particular time) and income is a flow (measured over a period of time, such as a year), the capital-output ratio has the same dimensionality as income, that is, time (or years).

Technical progress implies that increased output can be obtained over time from given quantities of labor and capital. Graphically, technical progress can be viewed as an *inward shift of all isoquants* of an industry undergoing technical progress.

7-2 CLASSIFICATION OF TECHNICAL PROGRESS

Technical progress is usually classified into *neutral, labor saving,* and *capital saving.* Unfortunately, there exist several distinct sets of definitions of neutral, labor-saving, and capital-saving technical progress. In general, the different definitions give rise to different classifications of otherwise similar phenomena. The most appropriate for our purposes are the definitions formulated by Sir John Hicks, usually referred to as the Hicksian definitions. These are the only definitions discussed below.

We will assume that constant returns to scale prevail before and after the occurrence of technical progress and that technical progress occurs in a once-and-for-all fashion.

Neutral Technical Progress

Neutral technical progress occurs in an industry when (1) increased output is obtained from given quantities of labor and capital and (2) the same capital-labor ratio is optimal before and after the change for each and every value of the wage-rent ratio. In other words, the isoquants of the industry undergoing neutral technical progress shift inward, and in addition the marginal rate of substitution of labor for capital is the same before and after the technical change for all possible capital-labor ratios.

Graphically, this type of technical progress amounts to a mere renumbering of the isoquants of the industry undergoing change. After the technical change, each isoquant bears a larger number of units of output.

Labor-Saving Technical Progress[2]

Labor-saving technical progress occurs in an industry when (1) increased output is obtained from given quantities of labor and capital and (2) for any wage-rent ratio, fewer units of labor per unit of capital (that is, a larger capital-labor ratio) are optimally employed after the change than before. Thus, *labor is being saved per unit of capital employed.* This does not mean that only labor is saved while capital is not. Whatever combination of labor and capital was originally used to produce a specified amount of output, there is at least one new combination of fewer units of labor and fewer units of capital that yields the same amount of output after the change. Remember that *for all types of technical progress each isoquant shifts totally inward.*

The case of labor-saving technical progress is illustrated in Figure 7-1.

---

[2] This subsection may be skipped without interrupting the continuity of the book.

Curve *bb* is the unit isoquant *before* the change, and curve *aa* is the unit isoquant *after* the change. New isoquant *aa* lies totally inside old isoquant *bb*. In addition, for any wage-rent ratio, the optimal capital-labor ratio is *higher* after the change than before. For instance, at the wage-rent ratio depicted by the slope of the line at *B*, the optimal capital-labor ratios before and after the change are given by the slopes of rays *OB* and *OA*, respectively. Since ray *OA* is steeper than ray *OB*, it follows that more units of capital per unit of labor (or fewer units of labor per unit of capital) are employed after than before the change. This same relationship must hold for all wage-rent ratios.

Labor-saving technical progress in a certain industry tends to make that industry more capital intensive. As a result, the industry will continue to employ capital and labor in the same proportion after as before the change if, and only if, labor becomes, after the change, sufficiently cheaper relative to capital. For instance, in Figure 7-1 the industry will continue to employ capital and labor in the proportion depicted by the slope of ray *OB* if the wage-rent ratio falls from the slope of the line at *B* to the slope of the line at *C*.

Many economists, such as Sir John Hicks and William Fellner, believe that there exists an inherent bias in our capitalistic system toward labor-saving technical progress. This bias is usually attributed to the continuous rise in real wage rates, which allegedly induces businesses to invent labor-saving techniques. This bias toward labor-saving inventions is usually offered as an expla-

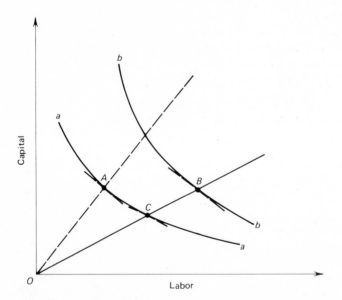

Figure 7-1 *Labor-saving technical progress.*
The unit isoquant is given by curve *bb* before the change and by curve *aa* after the change. Note that new unit isoquant *aa* lies totally inside old isoquant *bb*. In addition, at the wage-rent ratio depicted by the slope of *bb* at *B*, the capital-labor ratio after the change (shown by the slope of ray *OA*) is higher than the capital-labor ratio before the change (shown by the slope of ray *OB*).

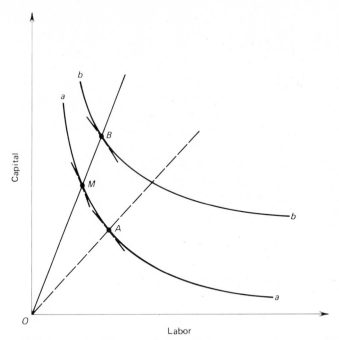

Figure 7-2   *Capital-saving technical progress.*
Curves *bb* and *aa* are the unit isoquants before and after the change, respectively. New isoquant *aa* lies totally inside old isoquant *bb*. In addition, at the wage-rent ratio depicted by the slope of *bb* at *B*, the optimal capital-labor ratio falls from the slope of *OB* (before the change) to the slope of *OA* (after the change).

nation for the observed failure of capital deepening to bring down the rate of return to capital. Incidentally, it is interesting to note that Karl Marx employed a similar reasoning and argued that labor-saving technical progress enables capitalists to maintain a "reserve army of the unemployed" and keep wages at the minimum subsistence level, that is, perpetuate the "misery of the proletariat."

Capital-Saving Technical Progress[3]

Capital-saving technical progress occurs in an industry when (1) increased output is obtained from given quantities of labor and capital and (2) for any wage-rent ratio, fewer units of capital per unit of labor (that is, a smaller capital-labor ratio) are optimally employed after the change than before. Therefore, *capital is being saved per unit of labor employed.* Again, this does not mean that only capital is saved while labor is not.

The case of capital-saving technical progress is illustrated in Figure 7-2. As before, curves *bb* and *aa* are the unit isoquants before and after the change, respectively. Note again that new isoquant *aa* lies totally inside old isoquant *bb*. But now, for any wage-rent ratio, the optimal capital-labor ratio is *lower* after the change than before. For instance, at the wage-rent ratio depicted by

---

[3] This subsection may be skipped without interrupting the continuity of the book.

the slope of the line at B, the optimal capital-labor ratio falls from its initial value indicated by the slope of expansion path OB (before the change) to that shown by the slope of expansion path OA (after the change). Since ray OA is flatter than ray OB, it follows that fewer units of capital per unit of labor are employed after than before the change. This same relationship holds for all wage-rent ratios.

Capital-saving technical progress in a certain industry tends to make that industry more labor intensive. As a result the industry will continue to employ capital and labor in the same proportion after as before the change if, and only if, capital becomes after the change sufficiently cheaper relative to labor. For instance, in Figure 7-2 the industry will continue to employ capital and labor in the proportion depicted by the slope of expansion path OB if the wage-rent ratio increases from the slope of the line at B to the slope of the line at M.

PART B: The Effects of Growth on Small Countries

In this part, we will discuss the effects of economic growth on a small country that is a price taker in the international market. Not only does this analysis shed light on those economies which in the real world are actually small in the sense that their exports and imports have no influence on their terms of trade, it also serves as an important building block in our investigation into the effects of economic growth on large countries (Part C), whose exports and imports do affect their terms of trade.

7-3   THE SCENARIO

Assume that America is endowed with fixed quantities of two homogeneous factors, labor and capital,[4] and produces under constant returns to scale two commodities, food and clothing. Assume further that clothing is labor intensive relative to food at all factor-price ratios. America is a "small" country and trades food and clothing in a huge international market at fixed prices.

In the rest of this part, we will let America experience various types of growth. Our objective is to study how each type of growth affects America's production, consumption, exports, and imports of food and clothing. In addition, we are concerned with the effect of growth on America's social welfare.

To avoid any confusion and muddled thinking insofar as growth's effect on social welfare is concerned, we assume that America is inhabited by a number of citizens who have identical tastes and factor endowments. Accordingly, we can deduce the effect of growth on America's social welfare from the effect of

---

[4] Because capital accumulation is an important source of economic growth, we now use the factors labor and *capital,* instead of labor and *land.*

growth on America's "representative citizen": If growth makes one representative citizen better off, it makes all better off and social welfare improves. On the other hand, if growth makes one representative worse off, it makes all worse off and social welfare deteriorates.

When all citizens are identical with respect to tastes and factor endowments, the production-possibilities frontier can be scaled down in proportion to the representative citizen.[5] All this is made possible by the assumption of constant returns to scale.

Figure 7-3 illustrates America's pregrowth equilibrium position. Curve *UEV* is America's pregrowth production-possibilities frontier. The given international price ratio is depicted by the slope of the production-possibilities frontier at *E*. Accordingly, America produces, before growth, at point *E* on her production-possibilities frontier *UEV*.

7-4 FACTOR ACCUMULATION

Any increase in America's factor endowments necessarily causes her production-possibilities frontier to shift outward. The precise shift of the production-possibilities frontier and the concomitant output changes depend only on how America's factor endowments grow. Fortunately, it can be shown that any arbitrary increase in factor endowments can always be broken down into a combination of two out of three simple cases.

Balanced Growth

Suppose that America's labor and capital grow at the *same* rate (say, 5 percent) so that America's overall capital-labor ratio remains constant. How is America's production-possibilities frontier affected? How do the outputs of the food and clothing industries change? The reader will be happy to know that we already have the answers to these questions from our earlier discussion of the Heckscher-Ohlin model (Chapter 5). In particular, the production-possibilities frontier shifts out evenly in all directions, and the outputs of food and clothing increase at the *same* rate (that is, 5 percent) as labor and capital. This is shown in Figure 7-3. (See broken curve *U'E'V'*.)

This is the case of *balanced growth*. It is also known as *neutral production effect,* since no production bias is revealed toward either food or clothing—both expand at the same rate.

We discovered in the Appendix to Chapter 5 that at constant terms of trade the proportion in which food and clothing are produced depends only on the overall capital-labor ratio of the economy, irrespective of how large or how small the economy happens to be. Thus, when capital and labor grow at the same rate, the overall capital-labor ratio remains constant, and the economy continues to produce food and clothing in the pregrowth ratio. This implies that food and clothing grow at the same rate.

[5] See the Appendix to Chapter 3.

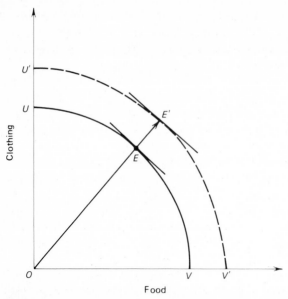

Figure 7-3 *Balanced growth.*
When labor and capital increase at the same rate, production-possibilities frontier *UV* shifts out evenly in all directions, as illustrated by broken curve *U'V'*. The optimum production point shifts from *E* to *E'*, and food and clothing grow at the same rate as labor and capital. The slopes at *E* and *E'* are the same.

At the intuitive level, balanced growth means that the economy's representative citizens increase (by, say, 5 percent). Since each representative citizen does as all others do, it follows that the outputs of food and clothing must increase at the same rate (that is, 5 percent).

How does balanced growth affect America's social welfare? Be careful. Because America's production-possibilities frontier shifts outward and apparently America can move to a "higher" social indifference curve, one might assume that America's social welfare increases. This is illusory, however. The only significant effect of balanced growth is the increase in the number of representative citizens. Each citizen is producing and consuming exactly the same amounts of food and clothing before and after growth. Accordingly, each citizen maintains the status quo, becoming neither better off nor worse off with balanced growth. Unless we pass the ethical judgment that more citizens are better (presumably because of a stronger defense against the enemy), we must conclude that balanced growth leaves America's social welfare intact.

One final note: Since the number of representative citizens increases by, say, 5 percent, the *aggregate* production, consumption, exports, and imports of food and clothing all increase at the same rate (that is, 5 percent). The fact that *America's volume of trade necessarily increases* (at the balanced-growth rate) assumes significance in the next part of this chapter.

The Rybczynski Theorem

Suppose that only one factor grows, either labor or capital but not both. How do the outputs of the food and clothing industries change? Here we have an important theorem, named after its originator, T. M. Rybczynski (1955).

Rybczynski theorem   When the endowment of only one factor of production increases, the output of the commodity that uses intensively the increased factor expands, and the output of the other commodity contracts absolutely.

The proof of the Rybczynski theorem is implicit in our discussion of the Heckscher-Ohlin model (Chapter 5). For instance, suppose that America's labor force increases. *Because America's terms of trade remain constant by assumption,* America's wage-rent ratio as well as the optimal coefficients of production of her food and clothing industries must also remain constant. (This follows from the one-to-one correspondence that necessarily exists between relative commodity prices and factor prices—See Sections 5-6 and 5-7.) In terms of Figure 5-3, the increase in labor causes America's labor constraint to shift outward (in parallel fashion), while the capital constraint[6] remains the same. As a result, the full-employment output of the labor-intensive commodity (clothing) increases, and the output of the capital-intensive commodity (food) decreases.

The reader should be able to verify that as labor grows, the output of the labor-intensive commodity must expand to absorb the excess supply of labor. But since labor must be combined with capital and capital's supply, by assumption, remains fixed, the output of the capital-intensive commodity must decrease absolutely in order to release the necessary amounts of capital. On the other hand, if capital increases, the output of the capital-intensive commodity must increase, and the output of the labor-intensive commodity must decrease absolutely.

The cases of sheer labor and sheer capital growth are illustrated in Figures 7-4 and 7-5, respectively. In each case, as the production-possibilities frontier shifts outward from UV to $U'V'$, the optimum production point shifts from E to E'. Note the production bias in favor of the commodity that uses intensively the expanded factor.

How does sheer labor growth, or sheer capital growth, affect America's social welfare? We must again look at the representative citizen. With sheer labor growth, the representative citizen necessarily becomes *worse off.* The fixed amount of capital is spread more thinly over the expanded population. Therefore, each representative citizen has less capital to work with, and his or her *individual* production-possibilities frontier shifts *inward.* With sheer labor growth, America experiences *negative* capital deepening, and her social wel-

---

[6] The terms "capital constraint" and "capital-intensive commodity" correspond to the earlier terms "land constraint" and "land-intensive commodity," respectively.

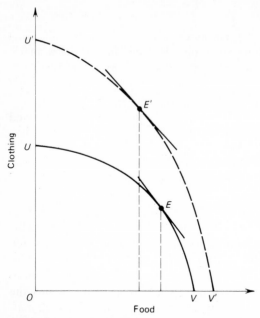

Figure 7-4 *Sheer labor growth.*
When only labor increases, production-possibilities frontier *UV* shifts outward but with a marked bias in favor of the labor-intensive commodity (clothing), as shown by broken curve *U'V'*. The optimum production point shifts from *E* to *E'*, where the output of food is absolutely smaller. The slopes at *E* and *E'* are the same.

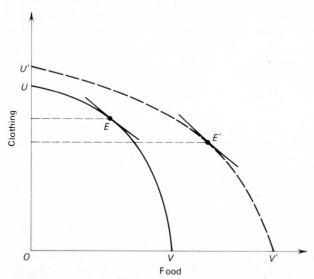

Figure 7-5 *Sheer capital growth.*
When only capital increases, production-possibilities frontier *UV* shifts outward but with a marked bias in favor of the capital-intensive commodity (food), as shown by broken curve *U'V'*. The optimum production point shifts from *E* to *E'*, where the output of clothing is absolutely smaller. The slopes at *E* and *E'* are the same.

fare falls, even though her overall production-possibilities frontier shifts outward.

On the other hand, with sheer capital growth America experiences *positive* capital deepening. Now her representative citizen has more capital to work with, and thus his or her *individual* production-possibilities frontier shifts *outward.* The representative citizen becomes better off, and social welfare improves.

How does sheer labor growth affect America's volume of trade? That depends on America's structure of trade. If America *exports* the *capital-intensive commodity,* food, whose output *falls,* America's volume of trade will *fall,* since America's consumption of food can be expected to increase. (For simplicity, we exclude inferiority in the consumption of either commodity throughout this chapter.) On the other hand, if America *imports* the capital-intensive commodity, her volume of trade will tend to rise.

With sheer capital growth, America's volume of trade will tend to expand when she *exports,* and to contract when she *imports,* the capital-intensive commodity, food.

Other Cases of Factor Accumulation

Any arbitrary increase in the endowments of labor and capital can be broken down into a case of balanced growth plus a case of sheer labor (or capital) growth. However, more definitive results can be obtained if the following case is kept in mind also: *When the additional amounts of labor and capital happen to be in the proportion in which the factors labor and capital are employed by one of the industries, say, the food industry, then the output of that industry (food) increases while the output of the other industry remains the same.*

7-5 TECHNICAL PROGRESS

Like factor accumulation, technical progress causes the growing economy's (America's) production-possibilities frontier to shift outward. But unlike factor accumulation, technical progress also causes the scaled-down production-possibilities frontier of the representative citizen *always* to shift outward. (Recall that the production-possibilities frontier of the representative citizen shifts *outward* when capital-deepening is *positive* and *inward* when it is *negative.*) Accordingly, insofar as the effect of technical progress on the social welfare of a *small* country is concerned, the answer must be very clear: *Technical progress always increases the social welfare of small countries.* This remarkable result is true for all types of technical progress.

Unfortunately, the analysis of the outward shift of the production-possibilities frontier is not as easy in the case of technical progress as it is in the case of factor accumulation. Two reasons account for this.

1   There are three types of technical progress (neutral, labor saving, and capital saving), and they can occur in one or both industries and at different

rates. Accordingly, the approach must be taxonomic, which is very cumbersome.

   2 In general, technical progress alters the basic relationship between factor prices and commodity prices (as illustrated by curve PP' in Figure 5-4).

   The rest of this section clarifies the effect of technical progress on the basic relationship between factor prices and commodity prices and then studies in some detail some cases that illustrate the special problems to which technical progress gives rise.

Technical Progress and the Relationship between Factor Prices and Commodity Prices

Suppose that technical progress occurs in the food industry only. Then, for any *given* factor prices, the relative price of food must be lower after the change than before, irrespective of the type of technical progress. This must be so because the unit isoquant of the food industry necessarily shifts inward with technical progress, and thus a *lower* isocost line is tangent to it after the change than before. Accordingly, the average cost of food, which is equal to the price of food, is necessarily lower after the change *for any given factor prices*. Since the price of clothing remains the same by assumption, the *relative* price of food (that is, price of food/price of clothing) necessarily falls. This can be illustrated in Figure 5-4 by *shifting* curve PP' to the left.

   When both industries experience technical progress, the analysis becomes more complicated. In general, the effect on relative commodity prices depends on the rates, but also the types, of technical progress experienced by the two industries. For instance, if both industries undergo neutral technical progress at precisely the same rate (for example, if the outputs of food and clothing increase by 20 percent at all factor combinations), then the relative price of food remains the same at all factor prices. On the other hand, if the neutral technical progress is more rapid in the food industry than in the clothing industry (for example, if the output of food increases by 30 percent and the output of clothing by 10 percent at all factor combinations), then the relative price of food must be lower after the change at all factor prices; that is, curve PP' of Figure 5-4 must shift to the left.

Balanced Growth with Neutral Technical Progress

Suppose that America's food and clothing industries undergo *neutral* technical progress at the *same* rate, say, 25 percent. How does America's production-possibilities frontier shift? What happens to America's production of food and clothing as well as her volume of trade at the given international terms of trade?

   This case is very similar to the case of balanced factor accumulation that we studied in the preceding section. Thus, America's production-possibilities frontier again shifts out evenly in all directions, and all initial combinations of food and clothing increase by 25 percent, as shown in Figure 7-3. At every commodity-price ratio, America continues, after the technical progress, to produce food and clothing in the same proportion as before the change. This type of balanced growth produces a neutral production effect in the sense that both food and clothing expand at the same rate—no bias is revealed in either direction.

Unlike balanced factor accumulation, balanced neutral technical progress necessarily improves the welfare of America's representative citizen. This must be obvious, because now the scaled-down production-possibilities frontier of America's representative citizen also shifts out evenly in all directions as the aggregate production frontier. Thus, America's social welfare improves.

How does balanced neutral technical progress affect America's volume of trade at the given terms of trade? That depends on how America's consumption of food and clothing behaves. If America's consumption of food and clothing increases at the same rate as production (for example, 25 percent), then obviously America's volume of trade must increase at the same rate also. Otherwise, America's volume of trade may either increase or decrease depending on whether America's consumers have a bias toward the imported or the exported commodity, as the reader should be able to show.

Neutral Technical Progress in the Export Industry (Food)

Suppose that *neutral* technical progress occurs in the export industry (food) only. Recall that food is assumed to be capital-intensive relative to clothing. How does America's production-possibilities frontier shift? How do America's outputs of food and clothing change at the given terms of trade?

As noted earlier, neutral technical progress in any industry results in a mere *renumbering* of that industry's isoquants, with each isoquant corresponding to a higher output after the change than before. From a purely geometrical point of view, as the food industry experiences neutral technical progress, its isoquants (inside the box diagram—recall Figure 3-5) and the contract curve remain the same after the change as before. Does this mean that America's production-possibilities frontier also remains the same? No, for despite the fact that the isoquants and the contract curve continue to remain unchanged, the renumbering of the isoquants of the food industry necessarily causes the production-possibilities frontier to shift outward—after the technical progress, each point on the contract curve corresponds to the same output of clothing but to a higher output of food.

The above conclusion is illustrated in Figure 7-6. The initial production-possibilities frontier is given by curve *UV*. After the neutral technical progress in the food industry, the production-possibilities frontier shifts outward, as shown by broken curve *UV'*, in the direction of food at a uniform percentage that coincides with the rate of technical progress in the food industry (say, 25 percent). For instance, point *E* shifts to *E'*, as the production of food increases by 25 percent (that is, from 300 to 375). Similarly, all other points on initial frontier *UV* shift to the right by 25 percent.

How does the neutral technical progress in the food industry affect America's production of food and clothing at the given terms of trade? Put differently, at what point will America produce on new frontier UV' (Figure 7-6)? Observe that each and every point on the contract curve implies the same marginal rate of substitution of labor for capital in both industries after as before the change. Hence, each and every point on the contract curve implies the same wage-rent ratio before and after the change. Accordingly, if the wage-rent ratio were kept constant at the pregrowth level, America's production point would shift from, say, E to E'. But the tangent to broken frontier UV' at E' is necessarily flatter than the tangent to UV at E—for any given factor prices, food becomes relatively cheaper after the food industry experiences technical progress. Accordingly, at the pregrowth commodity prices indicated by the slope at E, America must be producing somewhere in region $E'V'$, as illustrated by point P.

In summary, *the output of the industry experiencing neutral technical progress (food) increases, while the output of the other industry (clothing) decreases.*

PART C: The Effects of Growth on Large Countries

Our analysis so far has been carried out under the simplifying assumption that the growing country is "small" in the sense that it is a price taker in the international market. The time has now come to drop this simplifying assumption and

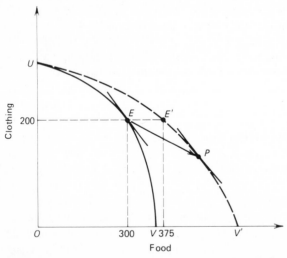

Figure 7-6 *Neutral technical progress in the food industry.*
Production-possibilities frontier UV shifts outward, as illustrated by broken curve UV', in the direction of food. For instance, point E shifts to E'. The production point, however, shifts from E to P because the technical progress tends to make food relatively cheaper. The slopes at E and P are the same.

consider the effects of economic growth on the "large" country whose exports and imports do affect the terms of trade. As we mentioned earlier, the analysis of the small country serves as an important building block in our new investigation.

7-6   THE TERMS-OF-TRADE EFFECT

Before we pass a final judgment on the effect of growth on the social welfare of a growing open economy, we must take into consideration, in addition to the shift of the production-possibilities frontier of the representative citizen, the effect on the terms of trade. Other things being equal, an improvement in the terms of trade tends to enhance, and a deterioration tends to reduce, the social welfare of the growing country. How does growth affect the terms of trade of the growing country?

The New Scenario

Consider again two countries, America and Britain. Each country is endowed with two factors, labor and capital, and produces under constant returns to scale two commodities, food and clothing. We assume throughout that food is capital intensive relative to clothing at all factor prices both before and after technical progress. Each country is inhabited by individuals who have identical tastes and factor endowments. America's representative citizen is distinctly different from Britain's, as America, the capital-abundant country, is endowed with more units of capital per worker than Britain. Thus, America's representative citizen has more capital to work with than Britain's representative citizen.

The pregrowth international equilibrium position can be shown in terms of the familiar offer curves, as illustrated in Figure 7-7. Equilibrium occurs initially at the intersection of the pregrowth offer curves, that is, point E. America exports OF units of food to Britain in exchange for OC units of clothing. This pattern of trade is in line with the Heckscher-Ohlin theorem. The slope of terms-of-trade line TOT (that is, OC/OF) gives the relative price of food in terms of clothing, which is America's terms of trade.

When a country grows, her offer curve necessarily shifts, giving rise to a new international equilibrium. In general, the growing country's terms of trade may either improve or deteriorate during this process depending on just how her offer curve shifts.

In what follows, we assume that only America grows. Thus, only America's offer curve shifts through time. Britain's offer curve remains the same, although the equilibrium point travels along Britain's offer curve as America's offer curve shifts.

The Effect of Growth on the Volume of Trade at Constant Prices

Assuming that international equilibrium is unique and stable before and after growth, we can predict the effect of growth on the terms of trade of the growing

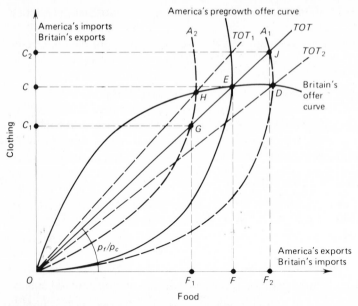

Figure 7-7 *The effect of growth on the terms of trade.*
Equilibrium occurs initially at *E*, where America exports food and Britain clothing. When America's volume of trade tends to expand with growth, as illustrated by broken curve *ODJA*₁, America's terms of trade tend to deteriorate. Thus, at postgrowth equilibrium point *D*, food is cheaper than at the initial point *E*. On the other hand, when America's volume of trade tends to contract with growth, America's terms of trade tend to improve. This is illustrated by the shift of America's offer curve to *OGHA*₂ with postgrowth equilibrium occurring at *H*.

country (America) from the mere knowledge of the effect of growth on America's *desired* volume of trade at *constant prices*. This explains the significance of the analysis in Part B that dealt with the effects of growth on the "small" country.

Consider again Figure 7-7. Assume that at the pregrowth terms of trade America's growth is such that her desired volume of trade *expands* from *OE* to *OJ*. This means that at the pregrowth terms of trade America's demand for imports of clothing increases by *CC*₂. Also, America's supply of exports of food increases by *FF*₂. (Compare points *E* and *J*.) Since Britain's (that is, the rest of the world's) demand for imports of food and supply of exports of clothing remain the same (by assumption), it follows that at the pregrowth terms of trade there emerges in world markets an excess supply of food (*FF*₂) and a shortage of clothing (*CC*₂). As a result, the price of food tends to fall relative to the price of clothing; that is, *America's terms of trade tend to deteriorate*. This is illustrated in Figure 7-7 by the shift of America's offer curve to *ODJA*₁, giving rise to a new international equilibrium at *D*. America's terms of trade after growth are given by the slope of terms-of-trade line *TOT*₂, which is smaller than the slope of *TOT*. Accordingly, *when America's volume of trade tends to expand at constant prices, America's terms of trade tend to deteriorate.*

When America's volume of trade tends to *contract* at constant prices, her terms of trade tend to *improve*. This proposition is also illustrated in Figure 7-7. Assume that growth causes America's offer curve to shift to the left, as shown by broken curve $OGHA_2$. At pregrowth prices, America's desired volume of trade contracts from OE to OG. In particular, America's supply of exports of food decreases by F_1F, while her demand for imports of clothing decreases by C_1C. Accordingly, there emerges in world markets an excess demand for (that is, shortage of) food (F_1F) as well as an excess supply (that is, surplus) of clothing (C_1C). As a result, the relative price of food tends to rise, as illustrated by the slope of terms-of-trade line TOT_1 at new equilibrium point H.

Types of Growth and Terms-of-Trade Effect

The effect of growth on America's volume of trade at constant prices, and thus the terms-of-trade effect, depends on the particular type of growth experienced by America. This must be clear from our earlier discussion in Part B. There, as the reader may recall, we considered various types of growth (generated by either factor accumulation or technical progress), and we saw, among other things, that the effect of growth on the desired volume of trade can be either positive or negative. Can we formulate any general propositions insofar as the effect of growth on the desired volume of trade and terms of trade is concerned?

Other things being equal, the type of growth that expands America's production of food (exportables) more than it expands her production of clothing (importables) causes America's volume of trade (at constant prices) to expand and her terms of trade to worsen. For instance, if America's supply of capital increases, or if technical progress (either neutral or capital saving) takes place in the capital-intensive food industry (export industry), America's volume of trade at constant prices will tend to expand, and her terms of trade will tend to deteriorate.

Note that *balanced growth* tends to expand America's volume of trade at the balanced-growth rate, assuming only that tastes are homothetic so that each commodity's consumption expands at the common rate. This is taken by some economists to mean that growth has a built-in bias toward terms-of-trade deterioration, because balanced growth implies *neutrality* all around. This is, of course, true, but on the assumption that only one country grows. If both America and Britain experience balanced growth at the same rate, the volumes of trade of the two countries will be growing *pari passu*, and there will be no tendency for the terms of trade of either country to deteriorate. Accordingly, we must conclude that, in general, there are no a priori reasons to believe that growth will on balance worsen the terms of trade of a country.

7-7 THE EFFECT OF GROWTH ON SOCIAL WELFARE

How does America's growth affect her social welfare? This is an important question, and our analysis has progressed sufficiently to venture an answer.

As before, we assume that America is inhabited by identical individuals with respect to tastes and factor endowments both before and after growth. Accordingly, we can infer the effect of growth on America's social welfare from the effect of growth on America's representative citizen.

The Two Effects on Welfare

In general, we can distinguish between two effects: a *wealth effect* and a *terms-of-trade effect*. The wealth effect corresponds to the shift of the production-possibilities frontier of America's representative citizen, and it may be either positive or negative. Similarly, the terms-of-trade effect corresponds to the change in the relative price of food (America's exportables), and this too can be either positive or negative.

The total effect on the welfare of America's representative citizen is the sum of the wealth effect plus the terms-of-trade effect. When neither is unfavorable, America's representative citizen definitely becomes better off with growth; and when neither is favorable, he or she definitely becomes worse off. But when one effect is favorable and the other unfavorable, the total effect is indeterminate: the outcome depends on which of the two effects outweighs the other.

Factor Accumulation versus Technical Progress

Technical progress always gives rise to a favorable wealth effect. Thus, technical progress of whatever type and in whichever industry causes America's production-possibilities frontier to shift outward; and because the *number* of representative citizens remains the same, the scaled-down production frontier of America's representative citizen shifts outward also. Thus, *the wealth effect of technical progress is always positive*.

On the other hand, the wealth effect of factor accumulation may be positive, negative, or zero. Thus, when capital increases faster than labor (that is, when the overall capital-labor ratio rises) and America experiences capital deepening, each citizen has more capital to work with, and the production frontier of the representative citizen shifts *outward* (positive wealth effect). When labor increases faster than capital, each citizen has less capital to work with (negative capital deepening), and the production frontier of the representative citizen shifts *inward* (negative wealth effect). Finally, when labor and capital increase at the same rate (balanced growth), the production frontier of the representative citizen remains the same (zero wealth effect).

If growth is the result of technical progress that occurs more predominantly in the import-competing sector (that is, America's clothing industry), then, other things being equal, America's terms of trade will tend to *improve*. Therefore, America's representative citizen will tend to become better off, enjoying both a favorable wealth effect plus a favorable terms-of-trade effect. On the other hand, when the technical progress occurs more predominantly in the export sector (that is, America's food industry), America's terms of trade will tend to deteriorate, and the representative citizen may become either worse off or better off with growth.

Immiserizing Growth

The paradox that a growing country may become worse off with growth was first noted by Edgeworth (1894, pp. 40–42). Bhagwati (1958) rediscovered this phenomenon, which he named "immiserizing growth."

Economists have been aware of the detrimental effects on welfare of rapid labor growth relative to capital since the beginning of economic science. What is surprising here is that even technical progress may reduce social welfare.

The possibility of immiserizing growth is illustrated in Figure 7-8. Before growth America produces at P_0 and consumes at C_0. As a result of technical progress, which is concentrated more predominantly in the export sector (food industry), America's production frontier shifts outward from UV to $U'V'$. Because America's volume of trade expands at the pregrowth terms of trade (given by the slope of MN), America's terms of trade fall to the level indicated by the slope of SP_1T. America's production shifts from P_0 to P_1 and consumption from C_0 to C_1. Thus, economic growth reduces America's welfare, since social indifference curve I_1 lies below social indifference curve I_0.

Note that Figure 7-8 illustrates what happens to America's representative citizen as well. For this purpose, curves UV and $U'V'$ must be interpreted as the scaled-down production frontiers of the representative citizen before and after growth, respectively; curves I_0 and I_1 as the indifference curves; and, fi-

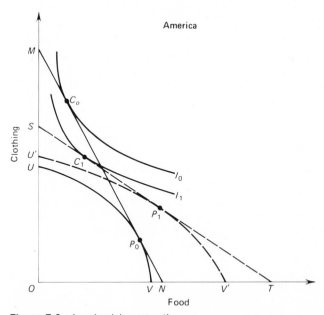

Figure 7-8 *Immiserizing growth.*
Before growth, America produces at P_0 and consumes at C_0. Technical progress (concentrated more predominantly in the export sector) causes America's production-possibilities frontier UV to shift outward, as illustrated by broken curve $U'V'$. America's terms of trade fall to the level indicated by the slope at P_1. America's production shifts from P_0 to P_1 while her consumption shifts from C_0 to C_1. Since C_1 lies on the social indifference curve I_1, which is lower than I_0, it follows that America becomes worse off with growth.

nally, curves *MN* and *ST* as the budget lines before and after growth, respectively.

What conditions are necessary for the occurrence of immiserizing growth? At least six seem crucial:

1   *America's growth must cause her desired volume of trade to increase substantially at constant prices.* This condition ensures that America's supply of exports increases substantially with growth and causes her terms of trade to deteriorate. Although not strictly necessary, export-biased growth (that is, growth which is heavily biased toward the export sector) certainly satisfies this condition.

2   *Britain's (that is, the rest-of-the-world's) import-demand elasticity for food must be very low.* This condition implies that America's terms of trade must fall sharply to restore international equilibrium.

3   *America must be heavily dependent on foreign trade.* In other words, America's exports of food must be a very high percentage of America's domestic production of food. This condition ensures that the terms-of-trade deterioration will be great enough to offset the favorable wealth effect.

4   *America's technical progress must be relatively small.* This condition is most crucial. If technical progress is very large in the sense that it pushes the production-possibilities frontier so far out that it at least touches the social indifference curve attained by America before growth, then technical progress will improve America's welfare irrespective of what happens to the terms of trade.

5   *America must be a "large" country.* Immiserizing growth, under free-trade conditions, can occur only if the growing country is important enough in world markets to affect her terms of trade. If the growing country is small, that is, a price taker, her terms of trade will remain unaltered, and her social welfare will improve because of the favorable wealth effect. This condition is apparently related to condition 2.

A "small" country can also experience immiserizing growth, but only if she is providing tariff protection for her import-competing industry or is suffering from some other distortion. This possibility, which was first noticed by Johnson (1967), is considered in Chapter 9.

6   *America must not pursue an optimal-tariff policy.* The significance of this condition will become clearer in the second part of this book. For the moment, the reader may note that if America pursues an optimal-tariff policy, then technical progress always improves America's social welfare. Put differently, the phenomenon of immiserizing growth occurs in the presence of a *foreign distortion*: Either a growing large country does not impose the optimal tariff or a growing small country (whose optimal tariff is zero) provides tariff protection for her import-competing industry. *Domestic* distortions may also give rise to immiserizing growth. (We return to this topic in Chapter 9.)

Some economists believe that Brazil may have satisfied the conditions for immiserizing growth before the 1930s, when coffee constituted over 70 percent of the Brazilian value of exports and Brazil's share of the world market for coffee was more than 50 percent.

Immiserizing growth is very similar to the problem of agriculture. Increased agricultural output is often an anathema to the farmer, because prices fall sharply as a result of the low elasticity of demand for agricultural products. Thus, increased agricultural output often means lower income for the farmer! The actors of the agricultural drama are indeed the same as those of immiserizing growth—only they wear a different disguise.

PART D: The Terms of Trade of Primary-Product Exporters[7]

7-8 INTRODUCTION

Many economists have emphasized the importance of international trade during the growth process. Trade unleashes several dynamic forces that are conducive to economic growth. As markets expand, competition becomes less personal, and producers tend to encroach upon each other's markets. This increased competition offers all inefficient producers a hard choice: they must either close down or become more efficient. Accordingly, increased competition improves economic efficiency, often through technical progress, and leads to increased investment, which is necessary in order to take advantage of the newly created opportunities.

It is generally agreed that for many countries in North America and Western Europe which developed during the nineteenth century, international trade did serve as an "engine of growth." Unfortunately, this is not the case for the countries of the Third World, which contain over 2 billion people. These less developed countries of Africa, Asia, and Latin America have long been active exporters of primary products (agricultural products and minerals). They account for over half the world population but receive only 14 percent of world product. Most of their inhabitants still live under conditions of extreme poverty, and the future does not look very bright. Their annual per capita income is roughly $350, which is actually less than 8 percent of the annual per capita income in the developed world (Western Europe, North America, Australia, Japan, South Africa, and New Zealand). What is even more disheartening is the fact that these less developed countries have seen the gap between their incomes and those of the developed countries widen tenaciously.

Note that because of the large (absolute) gap which exists between the per capita income of the developed countries and that of the less developed countries, such a (absolute) gap will tend to widen for a long time even if the less developed countries grow at a much faster rate than the developed countries. For instance, an income of $350 growing at 4 percent per annum will become

---

[7] This part may be skipped without interrupting the continuity of the book.

$17,676 in 100 years. Similarly, an income of, say, $4,500 growing at only 2 percent will become $32,600 in the same amount of time. Accordingly, even though the low income of $350 grows at the fast rate of 4 percent, its absolute difference from the high income of $4,500, which grows at the low rate of only 2 percent, will rise from $4,150 (that is, $4,500 − $350) to $14,924 in 100 years. The absolute gap between these two incomes will actually continue to *rise* for a little over 130 years. After that, the gap will start falling sharply. The point is that even if per capita income grows faster in less developed economies, the real-income gap between the two groups of countries will continue to widen for over a century.

Why does the Third World continue to live in poverty? Why is it that the less developed countries cannot ride the "engine of growth," which apparently played a crucial role in the development of North America and Western Europe during the nineteenth century? Are there any critical conditions or elements which existed in the nineteenth century but which are missing in the twentieth century? Are today's less developed countries experiencing immiserizing growth? These are important questions, but economists do not have all the answers yet.

It is not our intention to embark on a long discussion on the general problem of economic development. The reader who wants to learn more about the problems of the less developed countries and what the profession has to offer must consult other books that deal exclusively with this area. Our major concern here is the more narrow issue of whether international trade has inhibited the development of the Third World.

7-9 THE PREBISCH-SINGER THESIS

Statement of the Hypothesis

In the early 1950s several economists, such as Rául Prebisch, Hans Singer, and Gunnar Myrdal, argued that the primary-exporting countries, particularly those of the Third World, had been experiencing a systematic deterioration in their terms of trade, a trend which they expected would continue in the future. The implications of this argument, which is often referred to as the Prebisch-Singer thesis, are clear: The less developed countries had to export increasing amounts of their primary products in exchange for imports of manufactures from the industrially advanced countries. This was naturally considered to be one of the reasons these countries had remained underdeveloped.

Policy Recommendations

Given their dissatisfaction with the performance of the terms of trade of the less developed countries, Prebisch, Singer, Myrdal, and others formulated several policy recommendations. The guiding principle of these recommendations was that the less developed countries should allocate more of their resources to their industrial sector than to their primary sector.

On the one hand, they called for a reduction in the barriers of the developed countries against imports of manufactures from the less developed countries. (In fact, the less developed countries actually demanded that such barriers be removed *preferentially*, so that exports of manufactures by less developed countries would face lower barriers than those exported by developed countries.) On the other hand, they argued for a restriction of imports of manufactures into the less developed countries.

Effective rates of protection[8] of 300 percent or more became widespread, particularly in India and Pakistan and in Argentina and Brazil. The hope was that the less developed countries could take advantage of the already-existing demand for industrial products within their national boundaries. In fact, those manufactures actually imported in relatively large volumes were considered good candidates for protected domestic production.

While such import-substituting industrialization is still the prevailing policy among less developed countries, it is becoming increasingly evident that such schemes are not living up to the expectations of their advocates. This frustrating conclusion has been documented by numerous empirical studies of protected industries in many less developed countries (among them, Argentina, Brazil, India, Mexico, Pakistan, Taiwan, and Turkey). The net national welfare losses are often placed up to almost 10 percent of national income. The reason for such negative results is simple. Import-substituting industrialization gives rise to economic inefficiency—highly inefficient industries come into existence behind high tariff walls, with the result that resources are not allocated optimally. This topic is discussed further in Chapters 9 and 11.

The Two Variants of the Prebisch-Singer Thesis

Two variants of the Prebisch-Singer thesis can be discerned. One has to do with dissatisfaction with the *level* of the terms of trade of the less developed countries, and the other with dissatisfaction with the *secular trend* of these terms of trade over time (that is, the long-run deterioration of these terms of trade). The former (dissatisfaction with the level of the terms of trade) is often attributed by the less developed countries to strong monopoly elements in the advanced countries, such as imperfect markets and high tariffs. The reasons for the latter (the long-run deterioration of the terms of trade of the less developed countries) are discussed below.

Both variants of the Prebisch-Singer thesis incorporate *normative* elements, which are often forgotten in public debate over this highly emotional issue. Specifically, at the bottom of this whole controversy lies a normative question: What should be the international distribution of income between the industrially advanced countries and the less developed nations? Because of the purely ethical character of the problem, no scientifically acceptable answer can be given, and the debate will continue.

The rest of this section deals exclusively with the alleged long-run deterioration of the terms of trade of the less developed countries. Are there any eco-

---

[8] The theory of effective protection is discussed in Section 8-6.

nomic reasons that cause the terms of trade of the primary-exporting countries to deteriorate over time? Do the data actually support the Prebisch-Singer claim? It is to these questions that we now turn.

Theoretical Foundations of the Prebisch-Singer Thesis

What are the theoretical foundations of the presumed secular deterioration of the terms of trade of the less developed countries? Three principal theoretical arguments are usually cited, as follows.

1. Demand Bias   The Prebisch-Singer thesis rests partly on Engel's Law: as income rises, the proportion of income spent on food declines. Even though it is supposed to hold for food only, Engel's Law is invoked in this connection to stress a double demand bias: (a) that the income-elasticity of demand for primary products is less than unity, which actually means that as incomes increase, the demand for primary products increases less than proportionately; and (b) that the income-elasticity of demand for manufactures is higher than unity, which means that as incomes increase, the demand for manufactures increases more than proportionately. Other things remaining equal, such demand bias causes the terms of trade of primary-product exporters to deteriorate over time.

What are the main objections to the demand-bias argument? There are two. (a) The terms "less developed countries" and "primary-product exporters" are not synonymous. For instance, the United States, Canada, and Australia are major exporters of food, while countries like South Korea and Taiwan export low-skill manufactures (for example, transistor radios). To the extent that this is true, the effect of the demand bias is, of course, reversed. (b) More important, the demand-bias argument gives only a partial view. To be able to say anything about relative prices (that is, terms of trade), we must also know what happens to supply—as Marshall put it, it is both blades of the scissors that do the cutting. It is a matter of record that the supply of manufactures has experienced phenomenal growth in the developed countries. Therefore, we cannot argue from the demand bias alone that the less developed countries must have experienced, or will experience, a secular deterioration of their terms of trade.

2. Raw-Materials-Saving Innovations   To the extent that technical progress is raw-materials-saving, the overall demand for primary products tends to fall, causing a deterioration of the terms of trade of the primary-product exporters over time. This seems to have been the reason, for instance, for the dramatic fall in the price of natural rubber due to the development of low-cost synthetic rubber. (However, it is commonly recognized now that the case of natural rubber is unique.) In general, technical progress gives rise to new products and processes that make up for the reduced use of raw materials in the production of other products.

3. Market Imperfections   A final argument rests with market imperfections. It is often contended that the secular deterioration of the terms of trade of the less developed countries is partly due to the higher degree of monopoly power that exists in industry than in agriculture. But while this argument could presumably explain why the terms of trade of the less developed countries are low, *it cannot explain their tendency to fall over time*. A secular deterioration of the terms of trade could only be explained by a *continuously increasing* degree of monopoly in industry versus agriculture assuming *equal* rates of technical progress in industry and agriculture. With faster technical progress in industry than in agriculture, the monopoly degree in industry must be increasing very sharply relative to agriculture in order to produce a secular deterioration of the terms of trade of the less developed economies. Such a claim has never been substantiated.

A more sophisticated version of the market-imperfections argument attributes the secular deterioration of the terms of trade of the less developed countries to the monopoly power of labor unions in the industrial countries. In developed countries where there is labor scarcity, technical progress results in higher wages and constant prices because of the power of the labor unions. On the other hand, in less developed countries where there is labor surplus, technical progress results in lower prices as factor returns hold steady. As a result, the terms of trade of the less developed countries tend to deteriorate over time.

Even though the above argument could be taken as a valid point concerning the internal distribution of income within each set of countries separately, it does not shed any light on the behavior of the terms of trade over time. In the present context, the concept "terms of trade" can only mean *long-run equilibrium-relative* (*not absolute*) *prices*. When the price levels of countries change for any reason, we cannot jump to the conclusion that the terms of trade necessarily change, because of the offsetting changes in exchange rates. Thus, if international equilibrium is unique and independent of the internal distribution of income, any changes in money prices that result from, say, changes in money-wage rates, will be completely offset by changes in exchange rates, leaving the long-run equilibrium terms of trade unchanged. To assert that the power of the labor unions in developed countries causes the terms of trade of the less developed countries to deteriorate over time is to be blindfolded by the "veil of money."

In summary, we find no logical necessity for a secular deterioration of the terms of trade of the less developed countries.

Empirical Foundations of the Prebisch-Singer Thesis

We finally turn to the empirical foundations of the Prebisch-Singer thesis. What do the data actually show?

Because price indices were not available for many less developed countries, Prebisch (1950) used in his original empirical work the terms-of-trade data for the United Kingdom from 1870 to 1938. He found that the British terms of trade improved substantially during this period. He took this to mean that the terms of trade of the less developed countries trading with the United Kingdom deteriorated substantially during the same period.

On the basis of the World Bank index of terms of trade for nonpetroleum primary commodities, Behrman (1978, Chapter 4) provides evidence that during the 1954–1975 period the terms of trade of primary-product exporters declined substantially (about 20 percent). While they do not dispute this finding, Kindleberger and Lindert (1978, pp. 72–76) find only a gentle downward trend in the terms of trade of the primary-product exporters for the last century (that is, from the 1870s to the 1970s). In particular, Kindleberger and Lindert point out that only the price of natural rubber fell sharply, while the price of wheat declined by about 25 percent. Oil and other fossil fuels as well as forest products experienced relative price increases, but other products showed no clear trend.

Three objections have been raised in relation to the empirical evidence, as follows:

1 *Quality changes.* The price indices used to determine the terms of trade over time do not take into consideration quality improvements in manufactures.

It is an undisputed fact that the quality of manufactures has improved over the years. For instance, the automobile of the 1970s is not the same as that of the 1920s or 1930s. Accordingly, the reported deterioration of the terms of trade of the less developed countries is overstated, particularly because the quality of primary products tends to remain relatively constant over time.

2 *New products.* The composition of trade and industrial output changes continuously over time. New products come into existence as old products disappear from the market. In addition to the insurmountable theoretical problems that the analyst faces in constructing a terms-of-trade series to reflect welfare changes, there is also a practical problem: Most new products (for example, radios) were not included in the price indices when they first appeared on the international market and their prices were high—they were included later. Because the prices of these products tend to fall drastically some time after they are first introduced, the reported price indices do not take into account the initial cheapening, and thus the terms-of-trade deterioration is overstated.

3 *Transportation costs.* All price data have been collected in metropolitan countries (Europe and North America), not in the periphery (primary-exporting countries). Because of the persistent reduction in transportation costs over time, such price indices overstate the terms-of-trade deterioration of the primary-product exporters.

By definition, the terms of trade (T) of the less developed countries are given by

$$T = \frac{p_x}{p_m} = \frac{p_x^* - t_x}{p_m^* + t_m}$$

and not by the reported ratio p_x^*/p_m^*,

where $p_m \equiv$ prices of manufactures paid by the less developed countries

$\quad\quad p_x \equiv$ prices of primary products received by less developed countries

$\quad\quad p_m^* \equiv$ prices of manufactures received by the advanced countries

$\quad\quad p_x^* \equiv$ prices of primary products paid by advanced countries

$\quad\quad t_x \equiv$ average transportation costs of primary products

$\quad\quad t_m \equiv$ average transportation costs of manufactures

Accordingly, the reported terms-of-trade deterioration is overstated for two reasons: (1) the prices *received* by the less developed countries (p_x) rose faster than the prices *paid* by the industrial nations (p_x^*) *because the transportation-cost element (t_x) was declining over time;* and (2) the prices of manufactures *paid* by the less developed countries did not rise as fast as the prices received by the industrial nations, again because the transportation-cost element (t_m) was persistently falling over time. This means that while the reported ratio p_x^*/p_m^* may have been declining mildly over time, the crucial ratio p_x/p_m may have been rising mildly over time.

Conclusion

We must conclude that the case has not yet been made for the alleged secular deterioration of the terms of trade of the less developed countries. As we have seen, there are important objections to both the theoretical and the empirical foundations of the Prebisch-Singer thesis. This does not mean, of course, that the less developed countries never experience deteriorating terms of trade, nor that such occasional phenomena do not disrupt their development process. It only means that we must reject the notion that the Prebisch-Singer thesis is an ineluctable phenomenon which must be accepted as an economic law. We found no evidence, either theoretical or empirical, that economic forces conspire in some way to make the rich richer and the poor poorer. The important economic problem of why the less developed countries remain backward cannot be blamed on either the industrially advanced countries or some conspiracy of economic forces. It is a most complex social phenomenon, which must be attacked head on.

7-10 SUMMARY

  1 The three main sources of economic growth are: labor growth, capital accumulation, and technical progress. Their common characteristic is that they all cause the growing economy's production-possibilities frontier to shift outward over time.

  2 When a country grows, her offer curve necessarily shifts, giving rise to a new international equilibrium that, by assumption, is unique and stable. When the growing country's volume of trade expands (contracts) at constant prices, her terms of trade deteriorate (improve).

  3 In judging the effect of growth on social welfare, it is useful to assume that the growing country is made up of "representative citizens" (that is, citizens who have identical tastes and factor endowments). If growth makes one representative citizen better off (worse off), it makes all better off (worse off), and social welfare improves (deteriorates).

4 Because of constant returns to scale, the growing economy's production-possibilities frontier can be scaled down in proportion to the representative citizen.

5 Growth has two effects on the welfare of the representative citizen: (a) a wealth effect, which may be positive or negative depending on whether the production-possibilities frontier of the representative citizen shifts outward or inward, respectively; and (b) a terms-of-trade effect, which may be positive or negative depending on whether the growing country's terms of trade improve or deteriorate, respectively. When both effects are positive (negative), the representative citizen becomes better off (worse off). When one effect is positive and the other negative, the total effect is indeterminate.

6 The wealth effect of factor accumulation may be: (a) positive, when capital grows faster than labor with the result that the representative citizen has more capital to work with and thus his or her individual production-possibilities frontier shifts outward; (b) negative, when labor grows faster than capital and the representative citizen has less capital to work with; or (c) zero, when labor and capital grow at the same rate (balanced growth).

7 When capital and labor grow at the same rate (that is, when the number of representative citizens increases), the capital-labor ratio remains constant; the economy's production-possibilities frontier shifts out evenly in all directions, even though the production-possibilities frontier of the representative citizen stays the same; and at the pregrowth terms of trade, the economy's aggregate production and consumption of all goods as well as its volume of trade increase at the balanced growth rate.

8 The Rybczynski theorem states that when only one factor increases and the terms of trade are fixed, the output of the commodity which uses intensively the increased factor expands, while the output of the other commodity contracts.

9 At fixed terms of trade, the output of the industry that uses the two factors in the proportion in which the additional amounts of labor and capital become available expands, while the output of the other industry remains the same.

10 Technical progress occurs when increased output can be obtained over time from given amounts of capital and labor. It is usually classified into neutral, labor saving, and capital saving. Graphically, technical progress can be viewed as an inward shift of all isoquants of the industry undergoing change. In particular, neutral technical progress amounts to a mere renumbering of the isoquants of the industry undergoing change.

11 Technical progress always gives rise to a positive (favorable) wealth effect. Accordingly, with fixed terms of trade, technical progress always improves social welfare.

12 The commodity of the industry that experiences technical progress becomes cheaper relative to the second commodity at all factor prices. When both industries experience technical progress, the outcome on relative prices depends on circumstances.

13 When the terms of trade are fixed, the output of the industry that experiences neutral technical progress increases, while the output of the other industry decreases.

14 When both industries undergo neutral technical progress at the same rate, the production-possibilities frontier shifts out evenly in all directions, as in the case of balanced factor growth. At fixed terms of trade, production and consumption of each commodity as well as the volume of trade increase at the same rate (assuming homothetic tastes).

15 When technical progress occurs more predominantly in the import-competing sector, the presumption is that the growing country's terms of trade improve (even though exceptions do exist), and its representative citizen becomes better off.

16 When technical progress occurs more predominantly in the export sector, the presumption is that the growing country's terms of trade deteriorate (even though exceptions exist), and its representative citizen may become worse off. A large country that is heavily dependent on foreign trade and does not pursue an optimal tariff policy may experience such immiserizing growth when a strong negative terms-of-trade effect (due to low elasticity of demand for imports by the rest of the world) outweighs a weak wealth effect of a relatively small technical change in the export sector.

17 In the early 1950s several economists, such as Prebisch, Singer, and Myrdal, argued that the less developed countries had been experiencing a systematic deterioration in their terms of trade, a trend which had inhibited their economic development and which was expected to continue in the future. They attributed this secular terms-of-trade deterioration to (a) demand bias, (b) raw-materials-saving innovations, and (c) market imperfections; and they argued that the less developed countries should allocate more of their resources to their industrial sector.

18 There is no logical necessity for the Prebisch-Singer thesis. In addition, the empirical data failed to account properly for (a) quality changes, (b) new products, and (c) transportation costs.

SUGGESTED READING

Behrman, J. R. (1978). *Development, the International Economic Order, and Commodity Agreements.* Addison-Wesley Publishing Company, Reading, Mass.

Bhagwati, J. (1958). "Immiserizing Growth: A Geometrical Note." *Review of Economic Studies,* vol. 25, pp. 201–205. Reprinted in R. E. Caves and H. G. Johnson (eds.), AEA *Readings in International Economics.* Richard D. Irwin, Inc., Homewood, Ill., 1968.

Chacholiades, M. (1978). *International Trade Theory and Policy.* McGraw-Hill Book Company, New York, chaps. 12 and 13.

Edgeworth, F. Y. (1894). "The Theory of International Values." *Economic Journal,* vol. 4, pp. 35–50.

Johnson, H. G. (1962). *Money, Trade and Economic Growth.* Harvard University Press, Cambridge, Mass., chap. 4. Reprinted in R. E. Caves and H. G. Johnson (eds.), AEA *Readings in International Economics.* Richard D. Irwin, Inc., Homewood, Ill., 1968.

——— (1967). "The Possibility of Income Losses from Increased Efficiency or Factor Accumulation in the Presence of Tariffs." *Economic Journal,* vol. 77, pp. 151–154. Reprinted in H. G. Johnson, *Aspects of the Theory of Tariffs.* Harvard University Press, Cambridge, Mass., 1972.

Kindleberger, C. P. and P. H. Lindert (1978). *International Economics,* 6th edition. Richard D. Irwin, Inc., Homewood, Ill., chaps. 4 and 11.

Myrdal, G. (1956). *An International Economy.* Harper and Row, Publishers, New York.

Rybczynski, T. M. (1955). "Factor Endowment and Relative Commodity Prices," *Economica,* vol. 22, pp. 336–341. Reprinted in R. E. Caves and H. G. Johnson (eds.), AEA *Readings in International Economics.* Richard D. Irwin, Inc., Homewood, Ill., 1968.

Singer, H. W. (1950). "The Distribution of Gains between Investing and Borrowing Countries," *American Economic Review,* vol. 40, pp. 473–485. Reprinted in R. E. Caves and H. G. Johnson (eds.), AEA *Readings in International Economics.* Richard D. Irwin, Inc., Homewood, Ill., 1968.

United Nations, Commission for Latin America (1950). *The Economic Development of Latin America and Its Principal Problems.* (Prebisch's views are set out forcefully in this publication.)

Part Two

Commercial Policy

Chapter Eight

The Theory of Tariffs

The first part of this book demonstrated that free trade benefits all trading countries. This thesis has never been refuted, even though most arguments for protection are asserted with great conviction. Given the mutual gains from free trade, one would expect the flow of commodity trade across national borders to be free from government interference. Yet for hundreds of years the nations of the world have impeded the free flow of international trade by means of several devices, such as tariffs, quotas, technical or administrative rules and procedures, and exchange control. Such policies, which are designed to affect a country's trade relations with the rest of the world, are usually known as *commercial policies*. In general, these policies are influenced by political, sociological, and economic considerations. Part 2 of this book explores the nature and economic effects of such barriers to free trade as well as the motives behind them.

This chapter deals primarily with the effects of the most common instrument of commercial policy, the tariff on an imported good. (Similar effects are generated by other forms of trade restriction, as shown in Chapter 10.) Chapter 9 deals with the theory of domestic distortions, the infant-industry argument, and several other noneconomic arguments for protection. Chapter 10 shows how the theory of tariffs is easily extended to export and import taxes and subsidies and, in addition, examines other nontariff barriers. Finally, Chapter 11 deals with the theory of customs unions.

8-1 TYPES OF TARIFF

The tariff is a tax (or duty) levied on a commodity when it crosses a national boundary. The most common tariff is the *import duty*, that is, the tax imposed on an imported commodity. A less common tariff is the *export duty*, that is, the tax levied on an exported commodity. Export duties are often levied by primary-product exporting countries either to raise revenue or to create scarcity in world markets and thus raise world prices. For example, rice exports have been taxed by Thailand and Burma; cocoa exports, by Ghana; and coffee exports, by Brazil.

It is interesting to note that the Constitution of the United States prohibits the imposition of export taxes. Accordingly, the U.S. government resorts to other forms of export restriction (such as export quotas) whenever conditions justify such trade intervention.

Perhaps tariffs originated as a convenient source of government revenue. Even though many less developed countries continue to use the tariff as a main source of revenue, the industrial countries today impose tariffs mainly to protect their domestic industries from foreign competition. Since the end of the nineteenth century, customs receipts in the United States have dwindled from over 50 percent of the total federal revenue to less than 1 percent. Like other advanced countries, the United States relies now more heavily on the income tax.

Ad Valorem, Specific, and Compound Tariffs

In general, taxes (whether on imports or exports) can be imposed in any one of three forms, as follows:

1   *The ad valorem duty.* This tax, or duty, is legally specified as a fixed percentage of the value of the commodity imported or exported, inclusive or exclusive of transport cost. For instance, suppose that an ad valorem import duty of 10 percent is imposed on the value of imports, exclusive of transport cost. An importer of commodities that were valued at $100 would be required to pay $10 import duty to the government.

2   *The specific duty.* This tax is legally specified as a fixed sum of money per physical unit imported or exported. For instance, an American importer of a European car may be required to pay $100 import duty to the American government irrespective of the price paid for the car.

3   *The compound duty.* This is a combination of an ad valorem tax *and* a specific tax. For instance, the American importer of a foreign car may be required to pay $100 plus 1 percent of the value of the car.

The United States uses both ad valorem and specific duties (approximately at the same frequency), but European countries use primarily ad valorem taxes.

Differences between Ad Valorem and Specific Rates

Given the price of the commodity (exported or imported) there exists a one-to-one correspondence between ad valorem rates and specific rates. For instance, the import duty on an imported car whose price is $5,000 may be specified as either $100 (specific duty) or 2 percent of the price of the car (ad valorem duty). Because of this correspondence, one might think it immaterial whether a country specifies her taxes on the specific or the ad valorem basis. Such a conclusion is not warranted, however, as there are some important differences between the two.

The main differences between specific and ad valorem rates are as follows:

  1 Where various qualities of a certain commodity exist and a flat ad valorem rate is used for all qualities, the absolute per unit tax (that is, the equivalent specific tax) is lower for cheaper qualities. On the other hand, if a flat specific rate is used for all qualities, the equivalent ad valorem rate is lower for the more expensive qualities. It appears then that the ad valorem tax is more equitable than the regressive specific tax.

  2 During periods of inflation, the ad valorem incidence of a specific tax tends to fall. Similarly, during deflationary periods, when money prices tend to fall, the ad valorem incidence of a specific tax tends to rise. Now the degree of protection provided by a tariff is best measured by its ad valorem incidence. Accordingly, the ad valorem tariff provides a constant level of protection, while the level of protection provided by a specific tariff varies inversely with the general level of prices. Since the tendency of prices is to rise through time, producers of products subject to specific duties often complain about erosion in the level of their protection because of inflation.

  3 Administratively, the specific duty is very easy to apply. An ad valorem duty, on the other hand, can be calculated only after the value of the commodity is determined.

The calculation of a commodity value for tariff purposes is not always straightforward. It is necessary to decide first what must be included in the commodity value. In general, a country may use either the f.o.b. ("free on board") price or the c.i.f. ("cost, insurance, freight") price. The f.o.b. price coincides with the cost of the commodity on board ship at the port of embarkation. A variant of the f.o.b. price is the f.a.s. ("free along side") price, which is lower than the f.o.b. price by ship-loading costs. The c.i.f. price coincides with the cost of the commodity at the port of entry. Thus, the c.i.f. price is higher than the f.o.b. price by the transport costs, that is, ocean freight, insurance, etc.

8-2 THE EFFECTS OF THE TARIFF ON A SMALL COUNTRY

This section analyzes the various effects of a tariff imposed by a small country, that is, a country which is a price taker in world markets. As we shall see, the tariff affects everything: domestic commodity prices, production, consumption, volume of trade, allocation of resources, distribution of income, and social welfare. Our job is to study all these effects.

The Effect on Domestic Prices

The most obvious and direct effect of the tariff is on domestic prices. A tariff is a discriminatory tax in the sense that it is applied only to commodities imported from the rest of the world—it is not applied to commodities produced domestically. As a result, the tariff drives a wedge between domestic prices and world prices.

For instance, suppose that our small country exports food and imports clothing at the current world prices: $p_f = \$10$ and $p_c = \$50$, respectively. Under free-trade conditions, the prices that prevail in world markets (that is, $p_f = \$10$ and $p_c = \$50$) prevail in the small country also. Assume now that in an effort to protect her clothing industry, the small country imposes a 20 percent tariff on the imports of clothing. Accordingly, the domestic price of clothing rises to $1.20 \times \$50 = \$60$. That is, the domestic buyers of clothing must now pay a tariff of 20 percent of $50, or $10, in addition to the world price of $50. The domestic producers receive the domestic price of $60—not the world price of $50. Accordingly, while in the world markets the relative price of clothing continues to remain 5 (that is, $50/\$10$), in the small country it rises to 6 (that is, $60/\$10$). This change in the domestic relative price of clothing has profound effects on the domestic organization of the economy of the small country.

The Effect on Domestic Production

As we have just seen, a tariff imposed by a small country raises the relative price of the imported commodity (clothing) by the full extent of the tariff. As a result, resources shift from the production of food (export industry) to the production of clothing (import-competing industry), as illustrated in Figure 8-1. Before she imposes the tariff, the small country produces at P_0, where the opportunity cost of food in terms of clothing (given by the absolute slope of production-possibilities frontier UV at P_0) is equal to the given relative price of food in the world markets (shown by the slope of consumption-possibilities frontier MN). After the imposition of the tariff, the relative price of clothing increases (or the relative price of food decreases) in the small country, as shown by the slope of line DF, causing production to shift from P_0 to P_1. Accordingly, the tariff causes resources to shift from the food industry to the *protected* clothing industry. This is known as the *protective effect* of the tariff.

The Effect on the Value of Production and Welfare

An important effect of the tariff that works to the detriment of the welfare of the tariff-imposing country is the reduction in the value of output produced at world prices. Thus, in Figure 8-1 the value of production at world prices is necessarily lower at P_1 than at the free-trade, optimal production point P_0. This is illustrated by the fact that broken line SP_1T, which is parallel to MN, lies inside free-trade consumption-possibilities frontier MN. This should not come as a

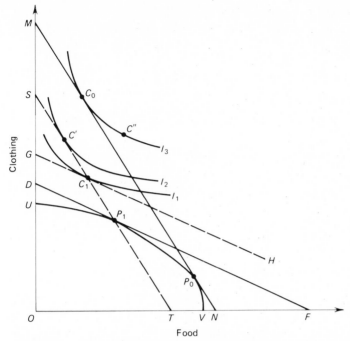

Figure 8-1 *The effects of a tariff on domestic production, consumption, and real income.*
Production occurs initially at P_0, where the domestic opportunity cost of food (shown by the
slope of production-possibilities frontier UV at P_0) is equal to the relative price of food in
world markets (shown by the slope of consumption-possibilities frontier MN). A tariff on imports of clothing raises the domestic relative price of clothing, as shown by line DF.
Resources are transferred from the food industry to the protected clothing industry, as
production shifts from P_0 to P_1. Once production shifts to P_1, the country can consume only
along broken line SP_1T. Thus, the economy's real income and welfare fall with the tariff, as the
consumption point shifts from C_0 to C_1.

surprise. As we saw in Part 1, the value of production at world prices is *maximized* at free-trade production point P_0. Hence, production at any other point
gives rise to a lower real income.

The reduction in the value of production (at world prices) has important
implications for the small country's social welfare. Once the production point
shifts to P_1, the small country can consume only along broken line SP_1T. Social
welfare necessarily declines as the country shifts to a lower social indifference
curve.

The Effect on Domestic Consumption

As we have seen, once production shifts to P_1 the economy will consume along
broken line SP_1T. But where exactly on SP_1T will the economy consume? Certainly *not* at C', that is, the point of tangency between line SP_1T and the highest
social indifference curve.

Recall that the slope of line SP_1T gives the *world* relative prices. The domestic consumers, however, trade at the *domestic* relative prices, as indicated by the slope of DF. Accordingly, consumption occurs along line SP_1T at the point where the marginal rate of substitution in consumption is equal to the domestic price ratio. This is illustrated in Figure 8-1 by point C_1.

The Tariff Revenue

Return to Figure 8-1 and observe carefully that the value of output produced is *lower* than the value of ouput consumed *at domestic prices*. Thus, line DF, which indicates the value of output produced at domestic prices (that is, what is known in national income accounting as *national income at factor cost*), lies inside line GH, which shows the value of consumption at domestic prices (that is, what is known in national income accounting as *aggregate expenditure*). What generates the discrepancy between these two aggregates?

The discrepancy between the value of production and the value of consumption (at domestic prices) is due to the tariff revenue collected by the government. Thus, in the presence of a tariff, the aggregate expenditure on food and clothing must be higher than the income that accrues directly to the factors of production by the precise amount of the tariff revenue. This proposition must be true whether the government spends the tariff revenue directly on food and clothing for public consumption or redistributes it to private consumers in the form of either lump-sum transfers or a general income-tax reduction. In Figure 8-1 the tariff revenue expressed in terms of clothing is given by vertical distance DG.

In this book, we shall always assume that the government redistributes the tariff revenue to private consumers. This is in line with our earlier observation that in today's international economy the role of the tariff as a source of revenue is insignificant. Accordingly, in a study of the effects of a tariff it is more appropriate to assume that the government has a budget that is already financed by other means and that the government returns the tariff revenue to consumers in one way or another. In addition, by assuming that the government returns the tariff revenue to consumers, we do not have to introduce an arbitrary assumption about the use of the tariff revenue—the social indifference map can be used for this purpose also.

Finally, it should be clear that the discrepancy between the value of production and the value of consumption arises only when both aggregates are evaluated at domestic prices. When the world prices are used, the two aggregates are necessarily equal, as illustrated by the fact that in Figure 8-1 both the production point (P_1) and the consumption point (C_1) lie on broken line ST. The simplest way to verify this is to observe that the consumption point *must* lie on line ST: Irrespective of any taxes or subsidies imposed by the small economy, *the value of exports of the rest of the world must be equal to the value of imports of the rest of the world, with both aggregates evaluated at international prices.*

The Effect on the Volume of Trade

When the government redistributes the tariff revenue to private consumers, the tariff causes the volume of trade of the small country to shrink. This is an important effect of the tariff, and it deserves careful consideration.

Since world prices are assumed constant, we can find out what happens to the volume of trade of the small country by concentrating on either the volume of exports of food or the volume of imports of clothing. We choose the latter.

The volume of imports of clothing is given by the difference between the domestic consumption of clothing and the domestic production of clothing. As we have seen, the tariff affects both the domestic production and the domestic consumption of clothing (and food for that matter). How does the tariff affect the domestic production and the domestic consumption?

As we have seen, the tariff causes the domestic production of clothing (importables) to increase (protective effect). Thus, the production effect tends to reduce the volume of imports—other things being equal, the increase in the domestic production of clothing leaves a smaller gap between domestic consumption and domestic production to be filled with imports. The consumption effect is more complicated and could go either way. Nevertheless, even if the domestic consumption of clothing were to increase, it could never increase sufficiently to outweigh the production effect.

The change in the domestic consumption of clothing can be broken down into a *substitution effect* plus an *income effect*. Thus, the imposition of the tariff makes clothing relatively more expensive, causing consumers to substitute food for clothing, as illustrated in Figure 8-1 by the movement from C_0 to C'' along indifference curve I_3. In addition to the change in relative prices, the tariff causes the real income of the small country to fall, as illustrated by the movement from indifference curve I_3 to indifference curve I_1. This income effect is not as reliable as the substitution effect, however. When clothing is a *normal* commodity, its consumption tends to fall as income falls. In this case, the income effect reinforces the substitution effect, and thus the domestic consumption of clothing clearly falls. Accordingly, when the imported good (clothing) is normal, the tariff causes the volume of imports (and thus the volume of trade) to fall as domestic consumption falls and domestic production rises.

Difficulties arise only when the imported good is *inferior*.[1] In this case, as income falls, its domestic consumption increases. Nevertheless, the volume of trade falls again. This is shown in Figure 8-2. Lines MN and ST coincide with the synonymous lines of Figure 8-1. Their common slope gives the relative price of food in world markets. Initially the economy produces at P_0 and consumes at C_0. (In order to keep the diagram simple, the production-possibilities frontier is not drawn.) The tariff causes the small economy's budget line to shift

---

[1] The reader who is not interested in the rare phenomenon of inferiority may skip the rest of this subsection. As it turns out, the tariff causes the small country's volume of trade to shrink irrespective of whether the imported good is normal or inferior.

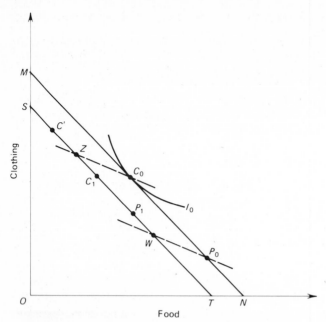

Figure 8-2 *The effect of a tariff on the volume of trade.*
Initially the economy produces at P_0 and consumes at C_0. The tariff causes the economy's budget line to shift from MN to ST, and the domestic price ratio to fall from the slope of parallel lines MN and ST to the slope of broken parallel lines ZC_0 and WP_0. The production point shifts above and to the left of W, as shown by P_1, since the value of domestic production at domestic prices must be higher at P_1 than at P_0. Similarly, the consumption point shifts below and to the right of Z, as shown by C_1—otherwise the social indifference curves would intersect. The volume of trade declines because $P_0C_0 = WZ > P_1C_1$.

from MN to ST and the domestic price ratio to fall to the common slope of parallel lines ZC_0 and WP_0. The initial volume of trade is given by distance P_0C_0, which is equal to WZ by construction. We wish to show that the posttariff production and consumption points will always lie between W and Z, as illustrated by points P_1 and C_1, respectively, so that the posttariff volume of trade P_1C_1 is lower than the free-trade volume of trade $P_0C_0 = WZ$.

Consider first the production point. Recall that the value of output produced evaluated at domestic prices is necessarily higher at the posttariff production point (P_1) than at the free-trade point (P_0). Hence, P_1 must lie above and to the left of W, as shown in Figure 8-2. (The reader may wish to return to Figure 8-1 and verify that P_0 lies inside line DF.)

Turn now to the consumption point. Posttariff equilibrium cannot possibly lie in region SZ. If it did—as illustrated, for instance, by point C'—the indifference curve through C' would definitely intersect indifference curve I_0, because the former must lie totally above broken line ZC_0. We therefore conclude that the posttariff consumption point must lie below and to the right of Z, as shown by C_1.

Accordingly, we conclude that the tariff causes the volume of trade to fall, because $P_1C_1 < WZ = P_0C_0$.

The Prohibitive Tariff

As we have just seen, the tariff causes the volume of trade to shrink. In fact, by following the steps in the preceding argument, the reader can easily prove an additional proposition: As the small economy raises the ad valorem tariff rate, the volume of trade shrinks further. When the ad valorem tariff rate is raised too high, the volume of trade drops to zero; that is, the tariff becomes *prohibitive*. In other words, a prohibitive tariff forces the country to return to autarky.

The prohibitive tariff is illustrated in Figure 8-3. Curve UV is the production-possibilities frontier, while curves I_1 and I_2 are two social indifference curves. The world relative price ratio is given by the slope of line MN. Initially the economy produces at P_0 and consumes at C_0. The country imposes a tariff that reduces the domestic price ratio to the slope of DF. Apparently, all trade ceases completely as the economy produces and consumes at P_1. The tariff is prohibitive.

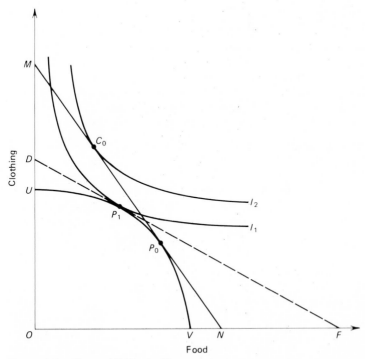

Figure 8-3 *The prohibitive tariff.*
Initially the economy produces at P_0 and consumes at C_0. A tariff that causes the domestic price ratio to fall from the slope of *MN* (world price ratio) to the slope of *DF* is prohibitive, because then the economy produces and consumes at P_1.

Figure 8-3 illustrates the *minimum* ad valorem rate at which the tariff becomes prohibitive. Obviously, raising the tariff above this minimum level changes nothing—the tariff continues to be prohibitive.

The Effect on the Internal Distribution of Income: The Stolper-Samuelson Theorem

We saw in Chapter 2 that one commonly used argument against free trade is the "cheap foreign labor" argument for protection. This argument is based on the empirical observation that real wages are much higher in industrial nations, such as the United States, than in less developed countries, such as India. If American workers, the argument goes, are subjected to the competition of cheap foreign labor, the American real wage rate will be drastically reduced. Thus, tariffs are needed to protect the American standard of living from the cheap foreign labor.

As we pointed out in Chapter 2, the "cheap foreign labor" argument for protection is a pseudo argument that does not stand up to scientific scrutiny. The higher American wage rate stands on the firm foundation of higher American labor productivity—American workers have better skills and cooperate with much larger amounts of capital. Cheap foreign labor is no threat to the American standard of living.

Yet there is a grain of truth in the "cheap foreign labor" argument. As we have seen, a tariff imposed by a small country raises the relative price of the imported commodity (clothing) and shifts resources from the export industry (food) to the import-competing industry (clothing). The tariff forces a drastic reorganization of the small country's structure of production. Not only do resources shift from one industry to the other, but also the optimal methods of production, the optimal factor proportions, and the marginal productivities of both factors in both industries—and thus the internal distribution of income—all change with the tariff. The essence of this complex reorganization is captured by the Stolper-Samuelson theorem.

Theorem 8-1 (Stolper-Samuelson theorem)   An increase (decrease) in the relative price of a commodity raises (lowers) the real wage of the factor used intensively in its production. (In other words, an increase in the relative price of a commodity raises the marginal physical product of the factor used intensively in its production in *every* line of production.)

The proof of the Stolper-Samuelson theorem is implicit in our discussion of the Heckscher-Ohlin model (Chapter 5). Thus, as the price of clothing rises with the tariff, resources shift from the food industry to the clothing industry. Recall that clothing is labor intensive relative to food. Accordingly, the food industry releases more units of land per unit of labor (or, alternatively, fewer units of labor per unit of land) than the clothing industry is willing to absorb. As a result, there emerges an excess demand for labor and/or an excess supply of land, causing the wage rate to rise and the rent to fall. Does it follow then that the *real* wage for labor services rises? Be careful, because in addition to the wage rate, the price of clothing rises also. As it turns out, the wage rate rises faster than the price of clothing.

As labor becomes more expensive relative to land, both industries substitute the cheaper factor, land, for the more expensive factor, labor; that is, both industries become less labor intensive or more land intensive. Consequently, the marginal physical product of labor (that is, the factor used intensively in the commodity whose price increases) *rises* in *both* industries. Similarly, the marginal physical product of land (that is, the factor used intensively in the commodity whose relative price decreases) *falls* in *both* industries.

We therefore conclude that as the tariff causes clothing to become more expensive relative to food, the real wage rate for labor (that is, the factor used intensively in clothing) rises, and the real rent for land (that is, the factor used intensively in food) falls.

The implication of the Stolper-Samuelson theorem is that even though the small country as a whole loses from the imposition of the tariff, the factor used intensively by the import-competing industry becomes better off. In our example, a worker can buy more food and more clothing after the tariff. Hence, it is to the advantage of the factor used intensively by the import-competing industry to demand tariff protection, even though the rest of the country will be worse off.

Redistribution of the Tariff Revenue

The Stolper-Samuelson theorem ignores the redistribution of the tariff revenue. Suppose that the government actually redistributes all tariff revenue to the factor whose income is actually reduced by protection. Is it possible for this factor also to become better off after the tariff? Unfortunately, when the tariff-levying country is small, the answer is "no." The reason is simple. As we have seen, the tariff reduces the value of output produced at world prices. Since the real income of the factor used intensively by the import-competing industry increases while the real income of the economy as a whole decreases, it follows that a small country will never be able to compensate (by means of tariff-revenue redistribution) the factor whose income has been reduced by protection.

8-3 THE EFFECTS OF THE TARIFF ON A LARGE COUNTRY

The preceding analysis rests on the assumption that the tariff-levying country is small, that is, a price taker in world markets. Yet that analysis is essential in understanding the effects of a tariff levied by a large country.

When the tariff-levying country is large, her commercial policy necessarily disturbs world markets and brings about a change in her terms of trade. In general, the tariff tends to improve the large country's terms of trade. In fact, in the absence of retaliation, a large country can always impose an appropriate tariff and improve her welfare, even though the tariff is always detrimental to the welfare of a small country.

This section explores the nature and implications of the terms-of-trade effect of the tariff within the standard two-country, two-commodity model developed in Part 1 of the book.

The Terms-of-Trade Effect

Assume again two countries, America (home country) and Britain (foreign country). Either country's actions are substantial enough to influence international prices. The initial free-trade equilibrium position can be shown in terms of the familiar offer curves, as illustrated in Figure 8-4. Free-trade equilibrium occurs at the intersection of the free-trade offer curves, that is, point E_0. America exports OF_0 units of food to Britain in exchange for OC_0 units of clothing. The slope of terms-of-trade line TOT_0 (that is, OC_0/OF_0) gives the relative price of food in terms of clothing, which is America's free-trade terms of trade. How does a tariff levied by America affect the initial free-trade equilibrium?

When a country levies a tariff, her offer curve shifts, giving rise to a new equilibrium. In particular, when the government redistributes the tariff revenue to the private sector (an assumption that we maintain throughout our discussion), the offer curve shifts toward the origin, as illustrated in Figure 8-4 by

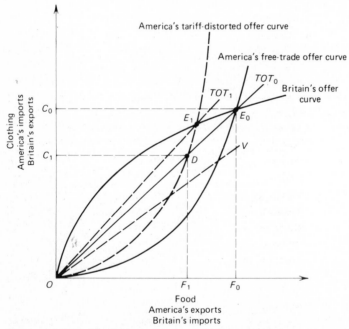

Figure 8-4 *The effect of a tariff on the terms of trade.*
The initial free-trade equilibrium at E_0 is disturbed by an American tariff. America's offer curve shifts toward the origin, as shown by her broken tariff-distorted offer curve. Thus, equilibrium shifts to E_1. America's terms of trade improve, as shown by the fact that line TOT_1 is steeper than line TOT_0.

America's *tariff-distorted offer curve*. This result follows from the analysis of Section 8-2. There we saw that a tariff by a small country causes her desired volume of trade to shrink. For instance, if America were a small country, and TOT_0 were the foreign offer curve, a tariff levied by America would cause her free-trade volume of trade OE_0 to shrink to, say, OD. But this must be true for any given linear foreign offer curve. Accordingly, the tariff-distorted offer curve must lie closer to the origin than the free-trade offer curve, as illustrated in Figure 8-4.

After the tariff, international equilibrium shifts to point E_1, where America's tariff-distorted offer curve intersects Britain's offer curve. Observe carefully that *America's terms of trade improve:* terms-of-trade line TOT_1 is steeper than terms-of-trade line TOT_0. This is a necessary result.

The large country (America) is able to improve her terms of trade by levying a tariff because she exploits her monopoly-monopsony power in world markets. Recall that at the initial free-trade prices (OC_0/OF_0), America's desired volume of trade contracts (from OE_0 to OD). In particular, America's supply of exports of food decreases by F_1F_0, while her demand for imports of clothing decreases by C_1C_0. In other words, in the market for food, America acts like a monopolist who restricts supply in order to raise price; and in the market for clothing, America acts like a monopsonist who restricts demand in order to buy the product at a lower price. As a result of the excess demand for (that is, shortage of) food (F_1F_0) as well as the excess supply (that is, surplus) of clothing (C_1C_0) in the world markets, the relative price of food (America's exportables) tends to rise, as illustrated by the slope of terms-of-trade line TOT_1 at tariff-ridden equilibrium point E_1.

Note that a small country lacks any monopoly-monopsony power in world markets. Therefore, the small country is in the same position as a perfect competitor who cannot affect market prices. This is the fundamental reason a small country cannot affect her terms of trade while a large country can.

The Effect of a Tariff on Domestic Prices

For problems of domestic resource allocation and income distribution, what is important is not whether the terms of trade of the tariff-levying country improve after the imposition of the tariff but rather whether the domestic price ratio falls below or rises above the free-trade equilibrium price ratio. Does the imported commodity become more expensive, after the imposition of the tariff, in the tariff-levying country? In other words, does the tariff actually protect the import-competing industry?

When the tariff-levying country is small (and thus her terms of trade are fixed), the tariff causes the price of the imported commodity to rise in the domestic market proportionally to the tariff. When the tariff-levying country is large, there is a second influence that must be considered before we can decide what happens to the domestic relative price of the imported commodity: the resultant reduction in the relative price of the imported commodity in world markets (that is, the terms-of-trade improvement we studied in the previous subsection). Is it possible for the terms-of-trade improvement that accompanies the tariff to reverse the initial, direct increase in the domestic price of the imported commodity with the result that the imported commodity actually becomes cheaper, not only in world markets but also in the domestic economy? In general, anything is possible.

Normally the tariff protects the domestic import-competing industry. That is, normally the imported commodity becomes more expensive in the tariff-levying country while it becomes cheaper in world markets. This normal case is illustrated in Figure 8-4 by vector OV, whose slope shows America's domestic price ratio after the imposition of the tariff. Free-trade vector TOT_0 lies between vector OV and tariff-ridden vector TOT_1.

Metzler (1949) discovered the paradoxical case in which the tariff makes the imported commodity cheaper all around (that is, both in world markets and domestically). Known as Metzler's paradox (or Metzler case), this curious possibility arises when (1) the foreign demand for imports is inelastic and (2) the tariff-levying country's marginal propensity to import is very low. Under these circumstances, the price of the imported commodity in the world market may fall by more than the amount of the tariff. As a result, the imported commodity may become cheaper in the tariff-levying country also.

Metzler's case is illustrated in Figure 8-5, which is similar to Figure 8-4 except that now Britain's offer curve is very inelastic at the free-trade equilibrium point (E_0), and vector OV, whose slope indicates America's posttariff domestic price ratio, is steeper than free-trade vector TOT_0. As we have seen, had America's terms of trade remained constant at the initial level indicated by terms-of-trade line TOT_0, America's domestic relative price of food would have fallen, as illustrated by the slope of broken line OV'. However, as America's terms of trade improve, the terms-of-trade line rotates counterclockwise from TOT_0 to TOT_1, pulling with it vector OV'. Because the foreign offer curve is highly inelastic and America's marginal propensity to import is low (by assumption), the improvement of America's terms of trade, and thus the counterclockwise rotation of the terms-of-trade line, is rather substantial, pulling eventually vector OV' *above* free-trade vector TOT_0, as shown by vector OV. As a result, the imported commodity (clothing) becomes cheaper in America after the tariff.

The important implication of Metzler's case is, of course, the *negative* protection provided by the tariff to the import-competing industry. Thus, the domestic production of the imported commodity *falls* in the tariff-levying country after the tariff—resources shift out of the import-competing industry and into the export industry. This is indeed a paradoxical phenomenon, because tariffs are usually advocated by politicians who want to protect the import-competing industries. It seems ironic that when a country is very successful in improving her terms of trade through commercial policy, the import-competing industry suffers from the effects of negative protection.

The interested reader may refer to Chacholiades (1978, pp. 473–482) for more details on Metzler's paradox.

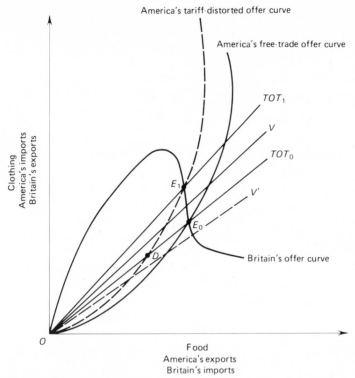

Figure 8-5 *Metzler's paradox.*
Because Britain's offer curve is highly inelastic at free-trade equilibrium point E_0, an American tariff now causes America's importables (that is, clothing) to become cheaper not only in Britain but also in America. Note that both vector OV (whose slope shows America's relative price of food) and TOT_1 (whose slope shows Britain's relative price of food) are steeper than TOT_0 (whose slope shows the relative price of food before the tariff).

8-4 THE OPTIMAL TARIFF

Free trade is not always the best policy from a *national* point of view. For instance, a "large" country may exploit her monopoly-monopsony power in international trade by imposing an *optimal tariff*. This maximizes the tariff-levying country's own national welfare. Apparently, the optimal tariff rate for a "large" country must lie somewhere between zero and the minimum prohibitive rate (that is, the tariff rate that eliminates all trade and gains from trade). On the other hand, the optimal tariff rate for a "small" country is zero—any positive tariff imposed by a small country necessarily reduces her welfare. This section clarifies the problem of the optimal tariff and shows how to determine a large country's optimal tariff rate.

The Small-Country Case Again

We saw in Section 8-2 that free trade is the best policy for a small country which by definition lacks monopoly-monopsony power in international trade. In other words, the optimal tariff for a small country is zero. To understand well the large country's optimal-tariff problem, it is necessary to go a little deeper into the conditions for welfare maximization in a small country.

Free trade leads to the following fundamental equation:

(Social) marginal rate of substitution = (social) marginal rate of transformation = terms of trade

This equation is necessary for maximizing a small country's welfare. We can understand why this is so by considering a situation in which the above equation does not hold. The tariff provides an excellent example.

As we have seen, the tariff creates a wedge (or divergence) between domestic and foreign prices. For instance, suppose that 1 unit of food exchanges for 2 units of clothing in world markets and that a small country, America, finds it profitable to export food and import clothing. Under free-trade conditions, the world prices must rule in America also. Suppose, however, that America imposes an ad valorem tariff of 100 percent on the imports of clothing. Under these circumstances, the price of clothing in America doubles, with the result that in America 1 unit of food exchanges for 1 unit of clothing only. Accordingly, America transfers resources from the production of food to the production of clothing until the marginal rate of transformation (or the opportunity cost of food in terms of clothing) is reduced to 1 (that is, America's domestic price ratio); and America's consumers substitute food for clothing until the marginal rate of substitution of food for clothing is also reduced to 1. As we saw in Section 8-2, this internal reorganization of America's production and consumption causes both America's volume of trade and welfare to fall. Let us see why.

In America, after the tariff, 1 unit of clothing is worth 1 unit of food—the marginal rate of substitution of food for clothing is 1. Yet in the international market 1 unit of clothing exchanges for only one-half of 1 unit of food. Accordingly, America can benefit from additional trade: The value of an additional unit of imported clothing (= 1 unit of food) is higher than the cost of obtaining it from the international market (one-half of 1 unit of food).

We therefore see that the tariff prevents the small country (America) from taking advantage of the opportunity to trade—the tariff *reduces* the volume of *profitable* trade.

The Large-Country Case

When the tariff-levying country is large, the tariff gives rise to two conflicting effects: (1) the volume of trade tends to fall, which tends to reduce welfare; and (2) the terms of trade tend to improve, which tends to increase welfare. Welfare is maximized when an appropriate tariff is chosen to balance these opposing tendencies.

Why is it that free trade does not maximize the welfare of a large country? To see clearly what is involved, we must draw a distinction between the *average* terms of trade and the *marginal* terms of trade. The former (average) is the concept we have been using all along: It shows the number of units of imports that, *on the average*, a country obtains per unit of exports, and it is given graphically by the slope of the terms-of-trade line. The latter (marginal) shows the number of additional units of imports that the country obtains by increasing exports *at the margin* by 1 unit. The marginal terms of trade are given by the slope of the foreign offer curve at the equilibrium point.

Figure 8-6 illustrates the difference between America's average and marginal terms of trade. Free-trade equilibrium occurs at *E*, where America exports *OF* units of food to Britain in exchange for *OC* units of clothing. Thus, *on the average*, America obtains *OC/OF* units of imports of clothing per unit of exports of food, as revealed by the slope of terms-of-trade line *TOT*. Ratio *OC/OF* (that is, the slope of *TOT*) is America's average terms of trade.

America's marginal terms of trade are given, on the other hand, by the slope of the tangent to Britain's offer curve at *E*, that is, the slope of *UV*. In par-

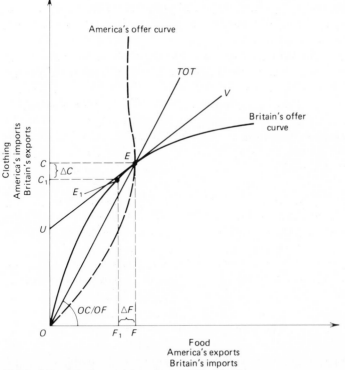

Figure 8-6 *Average and marginal terms of trade.*
Suppose that equilibrium occurs currently at *E*, where America exports *OF* units of food to Britain in exchange for *OC* units of clothing. The ratio *OC/OF*, given by the slope of *TOT*, shows America's average terms of trade. America's marginal terms of trade, on the other hand, are given by the slope of Britain's offer curve at *E* (or by the slope of *UV*, which is merely the tangent to Britain's offer curve at *E*).

ticular, the slope at E shows the number of units of clothing that Britain would refuse to export to America if America reduced her exports of food to Britain by 1 unit. For instance, if America reduced her exports of food from OF to OF_1 (that is, by $\Delta F = OF - OF_1$), Britain would trade at E_1, that is, Britain would reduce her exports of clothing from OC to OC_1 (by $\Delta C = OC - OC_1$). Accordingly, *at the margin*, Britain would reduce her exports of clothing by $\Delta C/\Delta F$ per unit of export reduction by America. Graphically, the ratio $\Delta C/\Delta F$ gives the slope of straight line E_1E (not drawn). The limit of this ratio, as F_1F tends to zero, is given by the slope of the tangent (UV) at E—as E_1 moves closer and closer to E, the slope of E_1E tends to become equal to the slope of UV.

Free trade equalizes the domestic price ratio (and thus the domestic marginal rates of substitution and transformation) to the average terms of trade. However, welfare maximization requires the equalization of the domestic price ratio to the marginal terms of trade—as we have seen for welfare maximization, trade must continue up to the point where the *value* of the last unit of imports (as revealed by the domestic marginal rate of substitution, which is equal to the domestic price ratio) is equal to its *marginal cost* (as revealed by the reciprocal of the marginal terms of trade). For a small country, the average and marginal terms of trade are equal, and therefore free trade maximizes social welfare. For a large country, the marginal terms of trade are, in general, lower than the average, and therefore free trade pushes the volume of trade beyond its optimal point. It is no wonder then that an optimal tariff may be needed to restrict the volume of trade and maximize the large country's welfare.

The principle that welfare is maximized at the point where the value of the last unit of imports is equal to its marginal cost is reminiscent of the principle that monopoly profits are maximized at the point where marginal revenue equals marginal cost.

Graphical Illustration[2]

Consider Figure 8-7. Free-trade equilibrium occurs at E, which is the intersection between America's and Britain's free-trade offer curves. At E, America reaches broken trade indifference curve I_1^a. Note that terms-of-trade line TOT is tangent to America's trade indifference curve I_1^a at E. This means, of course, that America's marginal rate of substitution (and transformation) of food for clothing equals America's average terms of trade. Now assume that Britain continues to remain a free-trade country irrespective of America's commercial policy. (This is an important assumption, the implications of which are explored further in the next subsection.) What is America's optimal tariff policy?

America maximizes her social welfare by trading not at free-trade point E but at the point where Britain's offer curve becomes tangent to America's highest possible trade indifference curve, as shown by point G. Thus, at G

---

[2] This subsection presupposes knowledge of the concept of trade indifference curves. Therefore, the reader who omitted the appendix to chapter 4 may wish to omit this subsection also.

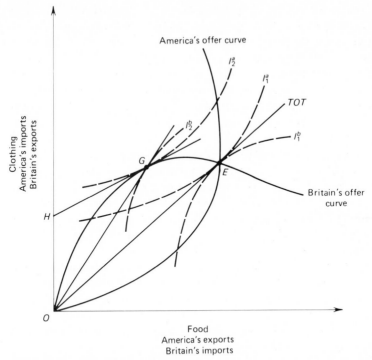

Figure 8-7 *The optimal tariff rate.*
America can maximize her welfare by imposing that (optimal) tariff rate which causes
America's offer curve to pass through point G, where Britain's offer curve is tangent to the
highest possible trade-indifference curve, I_2^a, of America. At G, America's domestic price ratio
is given by the slope of *HG*, which is actually America's marginal terms of trade; and Britain's
price ratio is given by the slope of *OG*, which is America's average terms of trade.

America reaches the trade indifference curve I_2^a, which is higher not only than
I_1^a but also than any other trade indifference curve intersected by Britain's offer
curve. Accordingly, on the assumption that Britain remains a free-trade
country and therefore continues to trade along her free-trade offer curve,
America can impose an optimal tariff and force Britain to trade at G, where
America's welfare is maximized.

Note that at G, America's marginal rate of substitution (given by the slope
of trade indifference curve I_2^a) equals America's marginal terms of trade (given
by the slope of Britain's offer curve).

Of course, America's marginal rate of substitution (and transformation) of
food for clothing, and thus America's marginal terms of trade, must be equal to
America's domestic price ratio. Accordingly, America's relative price of food
(p_a) must be given by the slope of line HG. America's average terms of trade,
which are equal to Britain's relative price of food (p_b), are given by the slope of
vector OG. These two price ratios (that is, p_a and p_b) can be used to determine
precisely America's optimal tariff rate. By rearranging the equation

$p_a = p_b/(1 + t)$, we obtain $t = (p_b - p_a)/p_a$, where p_a is given by the slope of HG, p_b is given by the slope of OG, and t is America's optimal tariff rate.

If Britain's offer curve were a straight line, as shown by free-trade equilibrium terms-of-trade line TOT, America's optimal tariff rate would be zero— America would maximize social welfare at E. This confirms our earlier conclusion regarding a small country (America) that takes international prices as given: the small country's optimal tariff rate is zero.

Retaliation

The preceding discussion is based on the assumption that while America imposes an optimal tariff rate, Britain passively continues to maintain a free-trade policy. Nevertheless, both countries can play the game. In fact, retaliatory measures from Britain can be expected if only because America's optimal tariff rate reduces Britain's welfare. Returning to Figure 8-7, the reader should observe that America's optimal tariff rate forces Britain to shift from trade indifference curve I_1^b to the lower trade indifference curve I_2^b.

Unfortunately, when Britain retaliates, perhaps by imposing a tariff that maximizes her (Britain's) welfare, it is no longer clear that America (that is, the country which initiated the tariff war) can benefit. Many outcomes are possible. Either country may benefit from such a tariff war while the other losses, or both countries may lose. What is *not* possible, though, is for both countries to benefit. This becomes clear in the next section.

8-5 TARIFFS AND WORLD WELFARE

Free-trade advocates always emphasize the deleterious effects of tariffs on world welfare. In particular, a tariff creates a wedge between foreign and domestic prices and interferes with the maximization of the welfare of the world in the following fundamental ways:

1 *It reduces the world output of commodities by merely reversing the process of international division of labor, which is dictated by the law of comparative advantage.*
2 *It forces a suboptimal allocation of commodities among consumers.*

The purpose of this section is to clarify these inefficiencies of tariffs.

Tariffs and World Output

In our discussion of comparative advantage, we saw that when each country specializes in the production of that commodity in which she has a comparative advantage, the world output of every commodity increases (potentially). Tariffs, in general, prevent the world from maximizing these production gains.

Maximization of world output occurs when the marginal rates of transformation (that is, opportunity costs) are equalized between countries. What is the common-sense meaning of this condition? We can discover its meaning and significance by considering a situation in which it is *not* satisfied.

Suppose that America's opportunity cost of food in terms of clothing is 3 and Britain's is 2. If America reduces her production of food by 1 unit while Britain increases her production of food by 1 unit, the total world production of food remains constant. What happens to the world output of clothing? Since America's opportunity cost of food is 3 units of clothing, America's output of clothing increases by 3 units. Similarly, Britain's output of clothing falls by 2 units because Britain's opportunity cost of food in terms of clothing is 2. Accordingly, the world output of clothing increases by $3 - 2 = 1$, which is merely the difference between America's and Britain's opportunity cost of food.

We therefore reach an important conclusion: *When the marginal rates of transformation (that is, opportunity costs) are different between countries, the world can always increase the output of one commodity without reducing the output of any other commodity.* Alternatively, when America's and Britain's opportunity costs are equal, the world cannot achieve further production gains; that is, the world output is already at its maximum.

Free trade equalizes commodity prices between countries. Given that commodity prices are equal to opportunity costs, it follows that free trade leads to equalization of opportunity costs between countries. Accordingly, free trade maximizes world output. In other words, under free-trade conditions it is impossible to increase the world output of one commodity without reducing the output of another commodity.

It must be clear by now why tariffs reduce world output. As we have seen, a tariff creates a wedge (or divergence) between foreign and domestic commodity prices. Because commodity prices are equal to opportunity costs, it follows that a tariff creates a divergence between the opportunity costs (or marginal rates of transformation) of countries. A tariff prevents the world from maximizing world output.

In fact, the higher the ad valorem tariff rate, the higher the divergence between the opportunity costs of countries, and, therefore, the higher the loss in world output due to the tariff.

The loss of world output due to a tariff is illustrated in Figure 8-8. Britain's production block (that is, production-possibilities frontier) HNM is drawn upside down (or rotated by 180°) and superimposed on America's production block OUV so that the production points of the two countries coincide, as illustrated by point P. By assumption, food is relatively cheaper in America (presumably because of an American tariff on imports of clothing), as illustrated by the fact that America's production block is flatter than Britain's at P. America's outputs of food and clothing are given by the coordinates of vector OP. Similarly, Britain's outputs of food and clothing are given by vector PH. Accordingly, the world outputs of food and clothing are given by vector OH (which is the vector sum of OP plus PH). How can we show that world output is not maximized at H? Merely shift Britain's production block upward and to the right until it becomes tangent to America's production block, as shown by $H'N'M'$. It is evident that when both America and Britain produce at E, the total world output of food and clothing is given by point H'. But at H' the world enjoys a larger output of food and clothing compared with tariff-ridden point H.

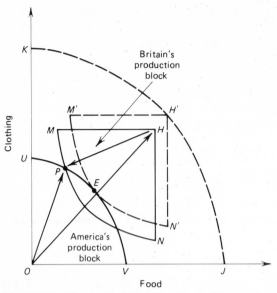

Figure 8-8 *The world-output loss of a tariff.*
Britain's production block *HNM* is drawn upside down and superimposed on America's production block *OUV* so that the production points of the two countries, in the presence of a tariff, coincide, as illustrated by point *P*. The world outputs of food and clothing are given by vector *OH*, which is the sum of production vectors *OP* and *PH* of America and Britain, respectively. Because of the tariff, the world suffers a production loss at *H*. Thus, by shifting Britain's production block upward and to the right until it becomes tangent to America's production block at *E*, as shown by *H'N'M'*, the world production point can shift to *H'*, where more food and more clothing is available than at *H*. In fact, we can slide Britain's production block *H'N'M'* along America's (*OUV*), keeping them tangent at all times, and then let the corner of Britain's block (that is, point *H'*) trace out world production-possibilities frontier *KH'J*. Point *H* necessarily lies inside frontier *KH'J* implying a production loss.

Note that at *E* the two production blocks are tangent to each other; that is, the marginal rates of transformation of America and Britain are equal. As we have seen, this is the condition for world output maximization.

What precisely do we mean when we say that world output is maximized? Further, is world output maximized at *H'* only? Slide Britain's production block *H'N'M'* along America's production block *OUV* in such a way that curve *M'EN'* remains tangent to *UEV* at all times; and let the corner of Britain's block (that is, point *H'*) trace out broken curve *KH'J*, which is simply the world production-possibilities frontier. The latter shows the *maximum* amount of clothing the world as a whole can produce given the world output of food. By world output maximization we merely mean production at any point (not just *H'*) that lies *on* the world production frontier—not inside it. Note that point *H'* does lie on the world production frontier, whereas the tariff-ridden point *H* does not.

Free trade does enable the world to produce *on* the world frontier, because it equalizes opportunity costs between countries (as illustrated by the tangency at *E*). Tariffs, on the other hand, force the world to produce *inside* the world frontier because they give rise to a divergence between the marginal rates of transformation of countries, as shown by points *P* and *H*. This is the first inefficiency of tariffs.

Tariffs and Consumption

In addition to preventing the world from producing on the world production-possibilities frontier, a tariff interferes with the optimal allocation of commodities among consumers. How does this second inefficiency of tariffs come about?

A fixed bundle of commodities (for example, 1,000 bushels of wheat and 2,000 yards of cloth) is optimally allocated between two consumers (or countries) when it is no longer possible to make, with the same bundle of commodities, one consumer (or country) better off without making the other worse off. Optimality is attained when the marginal rates of substitution in consumption are equal between consumers (or countries).

Assume that America's marginal rate of substitution of food for clothing is 2 and Britain's is 3. We can make Britain better off without reducing America's welfare merely by transferring 1 unit of food from America to Britain and 2 units of clothing from Britain to America. America's welfare remains constant, because America exchanges 1 unit of food for 2 units of clothing and America's marginal rate of substiution of food for clothing is 2. On the other hand, Britain becomes better off. While she is willing to give up 3 units of clothing for the extra unit of food—Britain's marginal rate of substitution of food for clothing is 3—Britain actually exports only 2 units of clothing to America. Accordingly, Britain is made better off while America's welfare remains constant.

Alternatively, we could transfer 3 units of clothing from Britain to America (as we also transfer 1 unit of food from America to Britain) and thus make America better off as we keep Britain's welfare the same. Finally, if we transfer something between 2 and 3, say, 2.5, units of clothing from Britain to America, then both countries become better off.

The welfare gains are possible, of course, in the preceding example because of the initial divergence between the marginal rates of substitution of America and Britain. When these marginal rates of substitution are equalized, the allocation of commodities becomes optimal in the sense that it is no longer possible to make one country better off without making the other worse off.

Figure 8-9 illustrates the optimal allocation of commodities among countries (or consumers). It is a box diagram similar to the one we studied in Chapter 3 (see Figure 3-5) in relation to production. Food is measured horizontally and clothing vertically. The sides of the box show the total amounts of food and clothing available to the world economy. Measure America's consumption of food and clothing with respect to origin O_a and Britain's with respect to origin O_b. Draw America's social indifference curves with respect to O_a, as illustrated by curves I_a^1 and I_a^2. Similarly, draw Britain's social indifference curves with respect to O_b, as illustrated by curves I_b^1 and I_b^2. Finally, trace

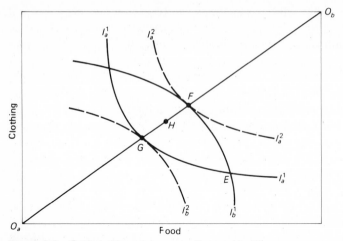

Figure 8-9 *Optimization of consumption and tariffs.*
The sides of the box show the fixed world outputs of food and clothing. Consumption is optimized only along contract curve O_aGHFO_b, which is merely the locus of tangencies between America's (I_a^1, I_a^2) and Britain's (I_b^1, I_b^2) social indifference curves. While free trade makes it possible for countries to consume along the contract curve, a tariff creates a wedge between foreign and domestic prices, and thus marginal rates of substitution, and pulls consumption off the contract curve, as shown by point E. Surely point E is inferior to a point such as H, which implies higher welfare for both countries compared to E.

out the locus of tangencies between the two sets of indifference curves, as shown by *contract curve* $O_a \, GHFO_b$.

It must be evident that consumption is optimized along the contract curve only. That is, when food and clothing are allocated between America and Britain at a point along the contract curve, such as G, it is not possible to reallocate commodities and make, say, America better off without making Britain worse off. Thus, any point above and to the right of America's social indifference curve I_a^1 necessarily lies on a social indifference curve for Britain that is lower than I_b^2.

On the other hand, when food and clothing are allocated at a point, such as E, that lies off the contract curve, it is possible to make one country better off without making the other country worse off. For instance, if we shift the allocation of food and clothing from E to F, we make America better off (I_a^2 is higher than I_a^1), while Britain remains on the same indifference curve, I_b^1. Alternatively, if we shift the allocation from E to G, we make Britain better off (I_b^2 is higher than I_b^1), while America remains on the same indifference curve, I_a^1; and finally if we shift from E to a point on the contract curve between G and F, as illustrated by H, we make both countries better off.

Note that the marginal rates of substitution of America and Britain are equal only along the contract curve. At any other point that lies off the contract curve, these marginal rates of substitution are not equal. For instance, at E America's marginal rate of substitution of food for clothing is lower than Britain's, as illustrated by the fact that I_a^1 is flatter at E than I_b^1.

Free trade makes it possible for countries to consume along the contract curve. As we have seen, each country consumes at the point where her marginal rate of substitution of food for clothing is equal to the relative price of food. Free trade equalizes commodity prices between countries. Therefore, free trade equalizes the marginal rates of substitution between countries and enables countries to consume along the contract curve. In short, under free trade it is not possible to reallocate a fixed bundle of commodities and make one country better off without making the other country worse off.

A tariff, on the other hand, creates a wedge between foreign and domestic prices, and thus marginal rates of substitution. Therefore, the tariff prevents the world from consuming along the contract curve. The tariff forces the world to consume at a suboptimal point off the contract curve, as illustrated by point E. This is the second inefficiency introduced by tariffs and reinforces the loss of world output that we studied in the preceding subsection.

The Tariff as a Production Subsidy plus a Consumption Tax

As we have seen, the tariff interferes with the optimization of both production and consumption. This is the clue to the relationship between the tariff, on the one hand, and production and consumption taxes and subsidies, on the other. Consumption taxes and subsidies interfere only with the optimization of consumption. Production taxes and subsidies interfere only with the optimization of production. Accordingly, tariffs combine elements of both production and consumption taxes and subsidies. In particular, *a tariff is equivalent to a consumption tax plus a production subsidy on importables.* This idea is pursued further in Chapter 9.

8-6   EFFECTIVE PROTECTION

This section deals with the relatively new concept of the *effective rate of protection,* which differs from the "nominal" rate (published in the country's tariff schedule) when a protected import-competing industry utilizes imported inputs (that is, intermediate products imported from the rest of the world) that are themselves subject to duty. The effective rate is usually, but not necessarily, much higher than the nominal rate.

Intermediate Products in International Trade

In the real world, commodities are not usually produced by the direct application of the primary factors labor and land alone. In addition, actual production processes frequently require *intermediate products,* that is, goods produced for the purpose of being used as inputs in the production of other goods. For instance, steel is used in the production of automobiles, coal is used in the production of steel, oil is used in the production of electricity, flour is used in the production of bread, leather is used in the production of shoes, and so on.

Intermediate products also play a significant role in international trade—a very large proportion of world trade is in intermediate products. The introduction of intermediate products gives rise to many interesting problems in the theory of international trade. These problems are, however, beyond the scope of this book, and the interested reader is referred to Chacholiades (1979). This section deals only with the concept of the effective rate of protection.

Nominal versus Effective Tariff Rates

When a protected import-competing industry utilizes imported inputs that are themselves subject to duty, the nominal tariff rate does not convey the true level of protection which is provided to the domestic producers and which, in the final analysis, affects resource allocation. The basic reason for this anomaly is the fact that nominal rates apply to the *total* value of imports, while the true level of protection (which is relevant to domestic producers and resource allocation) applies only to the "value added" by domestic producers. "Value added" is the difference between the total value of goods produced and the value of imported inputs, and represents the amount of money paid to the domestic primary factors of production, labor, and land (or capital). Two examples should clarify the issue.

Example 1 Suppose that the price of shoes on world markets is $40 a pair and that to produce one pair of shoes, America (home country) must import $30 worth of leather from abroad. Accordingly, America's shoe industry creates $10 worth of "value added" [that is, price of shoes ($40) less value of imported leather ($30)]. Assume now that America imposes a 25 percent "nominal" tariff on imported shoes, raising their domestic price to $50 [that is, foreign price ($40) plus tariff per pair ($10)]. What is the effective rate of protection provided to the domestic producers of shoes? The 25 percent nominal tariff rate raises the value added from the original level of $10 to the higher level of $20 (that is, $50 − $30). Thus, *the value added increases by 100 percent, and this is the effective rate of protection that America provides to her shoe-making activity.*

Example 2 Assume now that in addition to the 25 percent nominal tariff rate on imported shoes, America imposes a 10 percent tariff on the imports of leather. What happens to the effective rate of protection of America's shoe-making activity? Again we must determine the percentage change in the value added of America's shoe industry. We already know that the initial value added is $10. The tariff on shoes raises their price to $50 (that is, $40 + 0.25 × $40). However, the tariff on leather raises the cost of leather per pair of shoes from $30 to $33. Accordingly, the value added increases to $17 (that is, $50 − $33). Thus, the value added increases by 70 percent [that is 100 × ($17 − $10)/$10]. This effective rate of 70 percent is certainly lower than the rate of 100 percent that ruled before the imported leather was taxed. Note carefully the inverse effect of the tariff on imported inputs (leather) on the effective rate of protection accorded to final products (shoes).

Mathematical Formulation

With very little effort and a little high school algebra, we can formalize the preceding discussion. By so doing, we shall be able to derive easily some important conclusions concerning the theory of effective protection.

The preceding examples show that the effective rate of protection gives the percentage increase in domestic value added over the free-trade level, an increase made possible by the country's tariff structure. The effective rate of protection (e) depends on three parameters:

1. the nominal tariff rate on the final product (t)
2. the nominal tariff rate on imported inputs (t_m)
3. the share of the imported inputs in the total value of the final product in the absence of tariffs (α)

Suppose that the fixed world price of a final imported commodity (for example, shoes) is p. The domestic production of shoes requires a fixed amount of an imported intermediate product (for example, leather) whose price on world markets is also fixed. In the absence of tariffs, the value of imported leather that goes into the domestic production of one pair of shoes is αp. Accordingly, under free-trade conditions the value added in the shoe industry is

$$v = p - \alpha p = p(1 - \alpha) \qquad (8\text{-}1)$$

Suppose now that the country taxes the imports of both shoes and leather. The domestic price of shoes rises to $(1 + t)p$; and the cost of imported leather per pair of shoes rises to $(1 + t_m)\alpha p$. Accordingly, the value added in the domestic shoe industry changes to

$$v' = (1 + t)p - (1 + t_m)\alpha p \qquad (8\text{-}2)$$

By definition, the effective rate of protection (e) is

$$e = \frac{v' - v}{v} \qquad (8\text{-}3)$$

Substituting equations (8-1) and (8-2) into equation (8-3) and simplifying, we obtain

$$e = \frac{v' - v}{v} = \frac{(1 + t)p - (1 + t_m)\alpha p - p(1 - \alpha)}{p(1 - \alpha)}$$

or

$$e = \frac{(1 + t) - (1 + t_m)\alpha - (1 - \alpha)}{1 - \alpha}$$

or

$$e = \frac{1 + t - \alpha - \alpha t_m - 1 + \alpha}{1 - \alpha}$$

or

$$e = \frac{t - \alpha t_m}{1 - \alpha} \qquad (8\text{-}4)$$

In our first numerical example, we had $t = .25$, $t_m = 0$, and $\alpha = .75$. The effective tariff rate was 100 percent, which is consistent with equation (8-4): $e = \frac{.25 - 0}{1 - .75} = 1$. Similarly, in our second numerical example, we had $t = .25$, $t_m = .1$, and $\alpha = .75$. The effective tariff rate was 70 percent, which is again consistent with equation (8-4): $e = \frac{.25 - .75 \times .1}{1 - .75} = \frac{.175}{.25} = .7$.

We can now use equation (8-4) to establish some important propositions concerning the theory of effective protection, as follows:

1 *When the nominal tariff rates on the final product and the imported inputs are equal (that is, when $t = t_m$), the effective tariff rate (e) becomes equal to the nominal rate.* Thus, when $t = t_m$, equation (8-4) becomes: $e = \frac{t - \alpha t}{1 - \alpha} = \frac{t(1 - \alpha)}{1 - \alpha} = t$.

2 When the nominal tariff rates on the final product and the imported inputs are not equal (that is, $t \neq t_m$), then we distinguish between two cases, as follows:

(a) *The effective tariff rate is higher than the nominal tariff rate on the final product (that is, $e > t$) when the nominal tariff rate on the final product exceeds the rate levied on the imported inputs (that is, when $t > t_m$).*

(b) *The effective tariff rate is lower than the nominal tariff rate on the final product (that is, $e < t$) when the nominal tariff rate on the imported inputs exceeds the nominal rate levied on the final product (that is, when $t_m > t$).*

This proposition is easily proved. Rewrite equation (8-4) as follows:

$$e = \frac{t - \alpha t_m}{1 - \alpha} = \frac{t - \alpha t + \alpha t - \alpha t_m}{1 - \alpha} = t + \frac{\alpha}{1 - \alpha}(t - t_m) \qquad (8\text{-}5)$$

Since $0 < \alpha < 1$, it follows that $\frac{\alpha}{1 - \alpha} > 0$.

Accordingly, when $t > t_m$, the term $\frac{\alpha}{1 - \alpha}(t - t_m)$ is positive, causing the effective rate e to be larger than the nominal rate t. For instance, return for a moment to our second numerical illustration where $t = .25 > .10 = t_m$, and $\alpha = .75$. In this case, the effective rate is necessarily higher than the nominal rate:

$$e = .25 + \frac{.75}{1 - .75} (.25 - .10) = .25 + 3(.15) = .70 > .25 = t$$

On the other hand, when $t < t_m$, the term $\frac{\alpha}{1 - \alpha} (t - t_m)$ is negative, causing the effective rate e to be lower than the nominal rate t. For instance, assume that $t = .25 < .30 = t_m$, and $\alpha = .75$. Now the effective rate is necessarily lower than the nominal rate:

$$e = .25 + \frac{.75}{1 - .75} (.25 - .30) = .25 + 3(-.05) = .10 < .25 = t$$

3   *The effective tariff rate may even become negative!* This occurs when $\alpha t_m > t$, as can be easily seen from equation (8-4). In other words, *negative effective protection occurs when the nominal tariff rate on the final product is lower than the nominal tariff rate on key imported inputs weighted by the share of imported inputs in the total value of the final product.* For instance, assume again that $t = .25$ and $\alpha = .75$, but let $t_m = .50$ so that $\alpha t_m = (.75) (.50) = .375 > .25 = t$. A simple application of equation (8-4) gives: $e = \dfrac{.25 - .75 \times .50}{1 - .75} = \dfrac{-.125}{.25} = -.5$. Thus, even though the nominal tariff rate is 25 percent, in the final analysis the industry is provided with a *negative* effective rate of protection of 50 percent, that is, the industry's "value added" is cut in half. Many instances of negative effective protection have been observed in less developed countries (for example, Pakistan).

4   *The effective tariff rate e increases either when the nominal tariff rate on the final product t increases or when the nominal tariff rate on the imported input t_m decreases.* This proposition must be obvious from equation (8-4). Thus, when either t increases or t_m decreases, the numerator $t - \alpha t_m$ increases, causing the effective rate e to increase. The reader may wish to return to our earlier numerical illustrations and try different values for t and t_m in order to verify this proposition.

Empirical Evidence

The theory of effective protection has received much attention during the last two decades. As was natural, many researchers provided empirical estimates of effective rates for many industries and countries. A highly selective sample of these empirical findings (based on post–Kennedy Round data) is presented in Tables 8-1 and 8-2.

It is evident from Table 8-1 that the effective tariff rates bear little resemblance to the corresponding nominal tariff rates. Some effective rates are as much as ten to thirteen times higher than the corresponding nominal rates,

Table 8-1 Nominal and Effective Tariff Rates after the Kennedy Round

Commodity group	EEC Tariff rate Nominal	EEC Tariff rate Effective	Japan Tariff rate Nominal	Japan Tariff rate Effective	United States Tariff rate Nominal	United States Tariff rate Effective	Free trade share of value added
Foods and feeds							
Meat and meat products	19.5	36.6	17.9	69.1	5.9	10.3	0.250
Preserved sea foods	21.5	52.6	13.6	34.7	6.0	15.6	0.300
Preserved fruits and vegetables	20.5	44.9	18.5	49.3	14.8	36.8	0.270
Milk, cheese, and butter	22.0	59.9	37.3	248.8	10.8	36.9	0.143
Manufactured and processed foods*	14.6	17.7	24.0	59.3	5.0	1.0	0.228
Flour, cereal, and bakery products	16.1	24.9	22.4	46.4	6.9	15.6	0.320
Cocoa products and chocolate	12.8	34.6	22.8	80.7	4.2	16.2	0.210
Soft drinks	14.9	−19.8	35.0	41.0	1.0	−9.5	0.400
Mill products and prepared feeds	11.4	31.6	13.8	32.2	23.4	111.0	0.270
Wood, paper, and rubber products							
Wood products	8.2	9.5	12.4	22.0	10.4	18.3	0.445
Paper products and wood pulp	7.4	20.1	6.6	12.1	2.7	5.5	0.415
Rubber products	8.3	19.0	9.3	20.2	6.1	12.5	0.360
Yarn, fabrics, and clothing							
Yarns and threads	6.2	19.4	9.9	24.2	19.5	37.1	0.280
Fabrics and clothing	14.3	29.1	13.0	22.0	27.3	40.4	0.340
Jute sacks, bags, and woven fabrics	18.2	42.9	27.1	65.0	1.4	3.2	0.330
Vegetable and animal oils							
Plant and vegetable oils†	11.1	138.0	10.1	64.9	9.4	17.7	0.055
Cottonseed oil	11.0	79.0	25.8	200.3	59.6	465.9	0.120
Rapeseed oil	9.0	57.2	15.1	22.3	20.8	60.9	0.150
Soya bean oil	11.0	148.1	25.4	286.3	22.5	252.9	0.070
Animal and marine fats and oils	5.2	−26.8	5.1	−1.9	4.2	10.7	0.200
Leather, tobacco, and soap							
Leather and leather products	7.8	14.6	14.8	22.6	7.0	12.8	0.397
Cigars and cigarettes	87.1	147.3	339.5	405.6	68.0	113.2	0.530
Soaps and detergents	7.5	14.4	16.6	44.4	7.9	19.3	0.230
Median tariff rate‡	12.2	33.1	16.5	45.4	8.6	18.0	

* Includes roasted coffee.
† Consists of both crude and refined palm kernel oil, groundnut oil, and coconut oil.
‡ Median rates for the 123 individual products on product groupings.

Table 8-2 Escalation of Tariff Protection in the EEC, Japan, and the United States

Production process	EEC Nom-inal	EEC Ef-fective	Japan Nom-inal	Japan Ef-fective	United States Nom-inal	United States Ef-fective
Groundnut oil						
Groundnuts, green	0.0	. . .	0.0	. . .	18.2	. . .
Groundnut oil, crude and cake	7.5	92.9	7.6	93.7	18.4	24.6
Groundnut oil, refined	15.0	186.4	10.1	324.8	22.0	64.9
Paper and paper products						
Logs, rough	0.0	. . .	0.0	. . .	0.0	. . .
Wood pulp	1.6	2.5	5.0	10.7	0.0	−0.5
Paper and paper articles	13.1	30.2	5.9	17.6	5.3	12.8
Wood products						
Logs, rough	0.0	. . .	0.0	. . .	0.0	. . .
Sawn wood	1.9	4.9	0.7	2.0	0.0	0.0
Wood manufactures	7.4	10.7	9.8	15.3	7.4	8.4
Dairy products						
Fresh milk and cream	16.0	. . .	0.0	. . .	6.5	. . .
Condensed and evaporated milk	21.3	44.3	31.7	154.8	10.7	30.1
Cheese	23.0	58.8	35.3	175.6	11.5	34.5
Butter	21.0	76.6	45.0	418.5	10.3	46.7
Wool fabrics						
Raw wool	0.0	. . .	0.0	. . .	21.1	. . .
Wool yarn	5.4	16.0	5.0	9.3	30.7	62.2
Wool fabrics	14.0	32.9	14.7	35.1	46.9	90.8
Cotton fabrics						
Raw cotton	0.0	. . .	0.0	. . .	6.1	. . .
Cotton yarn	7.0	22.8	8.1	25.8	8.3	12.0
Cotton fabrics	13.6	29.7	7.2	34.9	15.6	30.7
Leather products						
Bovine hides	0.0	. . .	0.0	. . .	0.0	. . .
Leather	7.0	21.4	6.2	20.2	17.8	57.4
Leather goods excluding shoes	7.1	10.3	10.5	15.8	22.4	32.5
Jute products						
Raw jute	0.0	. . .	0.0	. . .	0.1	. . .
Jute fabrics	21.1	57.8	20.0	54.8	0.0	−0.9
Jute sacks and bags	15.3	9.8	34.3	75.2	2.8	7.3
Palm kernel oil						
Palm nuts, kernels	0.0	. . .	0.0	. . .	0.0	. . .
Palm kernel oil, crude and cake	7.0	87.1	6.4	79.1	4.2	52.3
Palm kernel oil, refined	14.0	195.9	8.0	79.2	3.4	6.1
Chocolate						
Cocoa beans	5.4	. . .	0.0	. . .	0.0	. . .
Cocoa powder and butter	13.6	76.0	15.0	125.0	2.6	22.0
Chocolate products	12.0	−6.8	30.6	36.3	5.7	10.3

Source: A. J. Yeats (1974). "Effective Tariff Protection in the United States, the European Economic Community, and Japan." The Quarterly Review of Economics and Business, vol. 14 (Summer), p. 47.

while other effective rates are actually negative. Granted that the effective rates give a more accurate picture of the true level of protection afforded any given industry,[3] it becomes evident that the nominal rates cannot be trusted as indicators of protection. Thus, before we can pass a judgment as to how high a country's tariff wall is, we must convert the nominal tariff rates into effective rates.

The median effective tariff rates (see the last line of Table 8-1) seem to suggest that effective protection is much higher in Japan and the European Economic Community than in the United States.

Table 8-2 suggests that both the nominal and the effective rates tend to increase with each stage of processing. Less developed countries often complain about this bias in the tariff structure of developed nations. They claim that this bias encourages the flow of raw materials and semifinished products into the advanced countries and thus inhibits industrialization in less developed countries.

8-7 SUMMARY

1 Nations impede the free flow of trade by means of several devices— such as tariffs and quotas—known as commercial policies.

2 The tariff is a tax (or duty) levied on a commodity when it crosses a national boundary. The most common instrument of commercial policy is the tariff on an imported commodity. A less common tariff is the export duty.

3 Tariffs originated as a source of government revenue. Even today many less developed countries impose tariffs to raise revenue. Industrial nations impose tariffs mainly to protect their domestic industries from foreign competition.

4 In general, taxes (whether on imports or exports) can be imposed as (a) ad valorem rates, (b) specific rates, or (c) compound rates.

5 There are some important differences between specific and ad valorem rates. Administratively, specific rates are easier to apply—they do not require knowledge of the commodity value, as the ad valorem rates do. However, the *ad valorem* incidence of a specific tax tends to fall (rise) with inflation (deflation). In addition, when various qualities of a commodity exist, a flat ad valorem rate is more equitable than a specific rate—a flat specific rate is heavier on the cheaper qualities.

6 A convenient assumption (followed throughout this book) is that the government returns the tariff revenue to its private citizens (in the form of either lump-sum transfers or a general income-tax reduction).

7 A tariff imposed by a small country has the following effects: (a) it raises domestically the price of the imported commodity by the full extent of the tariff; (b) it causes resources to shift from the export industry into the import-competing industry; (c) it reduces the value of output produced at world prices (because the value of output produced is maximized at the free-trade

---

[3] Nominal tariff rates, of course, are important insofar as the effects on consumption and demand generally are concerned.

production point); (d) it causes welfare to decline; and (e) it causes the volume of trade to shrink (whether the imported commodity is "normal" or "inferior").

8 At domestic prices, the value of consumption (aggregate expenditure) is higher than the value of production (national income at factor cost) by the amount of the tariff revenue. However, the two aggregates become equal when they are evaluated at world prices.

9 The tariff that reduces the volume of trade to zero is called prohibitive.

10 The Stolper-Samuelson theorem states that an increase (decrease) in the relative price of a commodity raises (lowers) the real wage of the factor used intensively in its production. When tariff protection raises the price of importables, the factor used intensively by the import-competing industry becomes better off; and the second factor becomes worse off, even if the government were to redistribute all tariff revenue to this second factor.

11 When a country levies a tariff, its offer curve shifts toward the origin—its volume of trade falls at all terms of trade. When the tariff-levying country is "large" (that is, it has monopoly-monopsony power in international trade), the tariff causes the imported commodity to become relatively cheaper in the rest of the world (that is, the country's terms of trade improve).

12 There is a paradoxical case (the Metzler case) in which the tariff causes the price of the imported commodity to fall in the world market by more than the tariff, with the result that the imported commodity becomes cheaper in the tariff-levying country also. This paradox arises when (a) the foreign demand for imports is inelastic and (b) the tariff-levying country's marginal propensity to import is very low. The implication of Metzler's case is that the "protection" provided to the import-competing industry is *negative* (or perverse).

13 Free trade equalizes the domestic price ratio (and thus the marginal rates of substitution and transformation) to the average terms of trade. However, welfare maximization requires the equalization of the domestic price ratio to the marginal terms of trade.

14 For a small country, the average and marginal terms of trade are equal; therefore, free trade maximizes its social welfare.

15 For a large country, the marginal terms of trade are, in general, lower than the average; free trade does *not* maximize its social welfare.

16 The optimal tariff restricts the volume of trade appropriately and maximizes the large country's welfare. The optimal tariff for a small country is zero.

17 When foreign countries retaliate, the country that initiates the tariff war (by imposing an optimal tariff first) may become worse off.

18 A tariff creates a wedge between foreign and domestic prices and interferes with the maximization of world welfare in two ways: (a) it forces the world to produce inside the world production frontier (because it creates a divergence between the marginal rates of transformation of countries) and (b) it forces the world to consume at a suboptimal point, off the contract curve (because it creates a divergence between the marginal rates of substitution of countries).

19 A tariff is equivalent to a production subsidy plus a consumption tax on importables.

20 The effective tariff rate (e) is higher than, equal to, or lower than, the nominal tariff rate on the final product (t) according to whether the latter (that is, t) is higher than, equal to, or lower than, the nominal tariff rate on the imported inputs (t_m), respectively. The effective tariff rate becomes negative when the nominal tariff rate on the final product (t) is lower than the nominal tariff rate on imported inputs (t_m), with the latter (that is, t_m) being weighted by the share of imported inputs in the total value of the final product (α); that is, the effective rate is negative when $t < \alpha t_m$.

SUGGESTED READING

Balassa, B. (1965). "Tariff Protection in Industrial Countries: An Evaluation." *Journal of Political Economy,* vol. 73 (December), pp. 573–594.

Black, J. (1959). "Arguments for Tariffs." *Oxford Economic Papers* (N.S.), vol. 11, pp. 191–208.

Chacholiades, M. (1978). *International Trade Theory and Policy.* McGraw-Hill Book Company, New York, chaps. 17–19.

————. (1979). "Intermediate Products in the Theory of International Trade." *Economic Perspectives,* vol. 1, pp. 151–172.

Metzler, L. A. (1949). "Tariffs, the Terms of Trade, and the Distribution of National Income." *Journal of Political Economy,* vol. 57, pp. 1–29. Reprinted in AEA *Readings in International Economics.* Richard D. Irwin, Inc., Homewood, Ill., 1968.

Stolper, W. F. and P. A. Samuelson (1941). "Protection and Real Wages." *Review of Economic Studies,* vol. 9, pp. 50–73. Reprinted in H. S. Ellis and L. A. Metzler (eds.), AEA *Readings in the Theory of International Trade.* Richard D. Irwin, Inc., Homewood, Ill., 1950.

Yeats, A. J. (1974). "Effective Tariff Protection in the United States, the European Economic Community, and Japan." *The Quarterly Review of Economics and Business,* vol. 14 (Summer), pp. 41–50.

Chapter Nine

Domestic Distortions and Noneconomic Objectives

The standard theory of tariffs that we discussed in Chapter 8 shows that, in general, tariffs reduce world efficiency and welfare. Yet, as we pointed out earlier, the flow of international trade has been impeded for hundreds of years by several trade barriers, such as tariffs, quotas, and exchange control. This chapter deals with the most common arguments for trade intervention and attempts to identify the conditions under which a tariff may be preferable to either nothing (that is, laissez faire) or some other policy.

9-1 THE THEORY OF DOMESTIC DISTORTIONS

The desire to accelerate the pace of economic development of the less developed countries and raise their standards of living (through increased capital formation, industrialization, and a larger share of the gains from international trade) gave rise to a renewed interest in the *economic arguments* for protection in the postwar economic writings. The traditional *infant-industry argument* for protection was restated and expanded to include the whole industrial sector, and many new arguments for protection were advanced by several distinguished economists, most notably Lewis (1954), Myrdal (1956), Hagen (1958), and Prebisch (1959). For the most part, these arguments rest on the existence of *external economies* and *factor-price differentials,* which in turn give rise to *domestic distortions* (that is, divergences between market prices and opportunity costs).

The *theory of domestic distortions* is a direct outgrowth of this activity in the area of economic development and deals primarily with (1) the various distortions that prevent the market mechanism from achieving Pareto optimality and (2) the policy recommendations for the neutralization of the domestic distortions and the restoration of Pareto optimality. (As it turns out, trade intervention should not be adopted as a means of correcting domestic distortions.) The main proposition of the theory of domestic distortions is that *policy intervention must take place at the exact point at which the distortion occurs.*

Domestic distortions are usually classified into *endogenous distortions* and *policy-induced distortions*. *Endogenous distortions* are those distortions that are primarily due to market imperfections, such as external economies and monopolistic or oligopolistic market structures. *Policy-induced distortions,* on the other hand, are those distortions that are the result of economic policies, such as tariffs, production subsidies, and consumption taxes. This chapter deals only with endogenous distortions, because the optimal policy to correct a policy-induced distortion is merely the elimination of the policy that caused the distortion in the first place.

The theory of domestic distortions is *not* an argument for protection. Domestic distortions violate Pareto optimality, but trade intervention is not the remedy.

In general, there are four points of intervention through taxes and subsidies: (1) international trade (through export and import taxes and subsidies), (2) domestic production (through production taxes and subsidies), (3) domestic consumption (through consumption taxes and subsidies), and (4) employment of factors (through taxes and subsidies on factor use).

Intervention is optimal when it restores Pareto optimality by completely offsetting the existing distortion without giving rise to a new distortion in the process. This is accomplished when *policy intervention takes place at the exact point at which the underlying market imperfection occurs and is equal to the degree of distortion,* thus offsetting the distortion completely. This is the *general rule for optimal intervention,* and it is applied below to specific market imperfections.

In the rest of this chapter, we deal primarily with "first-best" policies, that is, those policies that restore Pareto optimality and maximize social welfare. Nevertheless, where it appears useful, we also consider whether alternative, suboptimal policies may still improve the level of welfare attainable under laissez-faire. This problem becomes important when for one reason or another, the policy maker is actually denied the use of the policy instrument required for a first-best solution.

9-2 THE OPTIMAL TARIFF AGAIN

The theory of the optimal tariff studied in Chapter 8 rests on the existence of a *foreign distortion,* that is, a distortion in international markets. This foreign distortion occurs when an open economy is "large", that is, when a country has monopoly-monopsony power in international trade. Under these circumstances, free trade equalizes the domestic price ratio to the *average* terms of trade. However, national welfare maximization requires equality between the domestic price ratio and the *marginal* terms of trade. Accordingly, in the presence of monopoly-monopsony power in international trade, free trade violates Pareto optimality. *The optimal tariff can be viewed, then, as the first-best policy to offset the foreign distortion.*

Many small countries lack the ability to influence their terms of trade by means of commercial policy simply because they do not control a large enough share of world markets. For these small countries, free trade is, of course, Pareto optimal. Yet there are countries that do control a large share of the world market for some commodity or commodities, such as Brazil in coffee and Japan in automobiles and TV sets. These large countries possess monopoly-monopsony power in international trade. For them free trade is not Pareto optimal. They can benefit from trade intervention as they are able to shift the (average) terms of trade in their favor.

It is important to emphasize that the existence of monopoly-monopsony power in international trade results in a distortion *from the national standpoint only*. As we saw in Chapter 8, free trade is absolutely necessary for maximization of world welfare. In particular, trade barriers introduce two important inefficiencies into the world economy: (1) They prevent the world from producing on the world production-possibilities frontier, and (2) they prevent the allocation of commodities between countries from taking place on the contract curve. Accordingly, an optimal tariff by, say, America, is a very inefficient instrument for transferring real income from the rest of the world to America—the welfare loss to the rest of the world is much higher than the gain to America.

Clearly, when there are ethical grounds for redistributing income between countries, the first-best policy is not the tariff; rather, it is a direct income transfer that violates none of the first-order conditions for maximization of world welfare.

What lessons can be drawn from the preceding analysis? Perhaps the following:

1   Laissez faire is a first-best policy for a perfectly competitive economy with no monopoly-monopsony power in international trade.

2   Laissez faire is a first-best policy for the world as a whole.

3   In the presence of monopoly-monopsony power in international trade, Pareto optimality (from the national viewpoint) is attained by means of the optimal tariff, which attacks the distortion at the source and at the appropriate rate.

4   It is not true that a tariff always increases national welfare. The result depends on circumstances. For instance, a prohibitive tariff eliminates all trade and all the gains from trade.

Having discussed the foreign distortion (monopoly-monopsony power in trade) at some length, we shall assume for the rest of the analysis of this chapter that world prices are fixed (that is, that our open economy possesses no monopoly-monopsony power in trade). Alternatively, we may assume that our open economy always imposes the optimal tariff.

9-3 DISTORTIONS IN DOMESTIC PRODUCTION AND TRADE INTERVENTION

So far we have been assuming that domestic prices are always equal to marginal opportunity costs in production and social marginal rates of substitution in consumption. On the basis of this assumption, we have been able to show that except for the optimal tariff argument, free trade is a first-best policy. What happens when, as a result of externalities in production or consumption, or because of monopolistic or oligopolistic market structures, domestic prices are not equal to marginal opportunity costs in production and/or social marginal rates of substitution in consumption? It has been argued that in such cases of domestic distortions, free trade is not an optimal policy and that tariffs (and perhaps export and import subsidies) may be beneficial, after all.

A Production Distortion in a Closed Economy

We begin our discussion of domestic distortions by assuming that our home country, America, is initially a closed economy. We further assume that the relative price of food is always lower than the opportunity cost of food. This situation could occur in either of the following instances:

    1 *Monopolistic or oligopolistic market structures.* Clothing is produced under monopolistic or oligopolistic conditions.
    2 *Production externalities.* Either the production of clothing generates external economies or the production of food generates external diseconomies.

    When clothing is produced under monopolistic conditions, the price of clothing is higher than the marginal cost of clothing, since a monopolist sets the marginal cost equal to the marginal revenue—not the price. Assuming that food is produced under perfectly competitive conditions, and thus the price of food is equal to its marginal cost, it follows that:

$$\frac{\text{Price of food}}{\text{Price of clothing}} < \frac{\text{marginal cost of food}}{\text{marginal cost of clothing}}$$

In other words, the relative price of food is lower than the opportunity cost of food. (Recall that the opportunity cost of food is given by the absolute slope of the production-possibilities frontier, which in turn is given by the ratio of marginal costs.)

    Similarly, when both industries are purely competitive but the production of clothing generates *economies* (that is, reductions in costs) that are *external* to the individual firms and, therefore, not included in their cost-revenue calculations, the price of clothing is necessarily higher than its social marginal cost. As a result, the relative price of clothing is higher than its opportunity cost, or, what amounts to the same thing, the relative price of food is lower than its opportunity cost.

Finally, when both industries are purely competitive but the production of food generates *diseconomies* (that is, increases in costs) that are *external* to the individual firms and, therefore, not included in their cost-revenue calculations (as when a corporation pollutes the air or the water but does not pay for the damage), the price of food will be lower than its social marginal cost. As a result, the relative price of food will be lower than its opportunity cost.

Figure 9-1 illustrates the implications of a production distortion in our closed economy, America. Ideally, America should produce and consume at E, where her production-possibilities frontier UV touches the highest possible social indifference curve, I_a^2. Because of the distortion in domestic production, however, America produces and consumes at P_0, where the relative price of food (given by the slope of DD') is lower than the opportunity cost of food (given by the slope of the production-possibilities frontier at P_0). Accordingly, America fails to maximize her social welfare.

How will America react to the opportunity to trade? Will America specialize in the commodity in whose production she has a comparative advantage? Will America benefit from free trade? Is free trade an optimal policy for America? Should America impose a tariff? These are important questions, and they demand our immediate attention. As it turns out, America could specialize in the right or the wrong commodity, the introduction of international trade may reduce America's welfare, and a tariff may either improve or worsen America's welfare. As we shall see, however, a tariff is never a first-best policy.

Specialization in the Wrong Commodity

Suppose now that America is given the opportunity to trade food and clothing at fixed world prices. In particular, assume that the international price ratio lies between America's autarkic price ratio and domestic marginal rate of transformation, as illustrated in Figure 9-1 by broken line WW'.

Obviously, America's *true* comparative advantage lies in the production of clothing, because America's opportunity cost of clothing is lower than the relative price of clothing in world markets—line WW' is flatter than the production-possibilities frontier at P_0. Nevertheless, America's *apparent* comparative advantage lies in food, because the domestic relative price of food is lower than the relative price of food in world markets—line WW' is steeper than line DD'. Accordingly, under laissez faire America will specialize in the production of food, which is the *wrong* commodity. What is particularly bad is that *the introduction of international trade could make America worse off*, as shown in Figure 9-1. Thus, as production moves to P_1, consumption shifts to a point, such as C_1, which necessarily lies on a lower social indifference curve than I_a^1.

In the terminology of Chapter 4, we can say that the introduction of international trade causes America to enjoy a *consumption gain* and suffer a

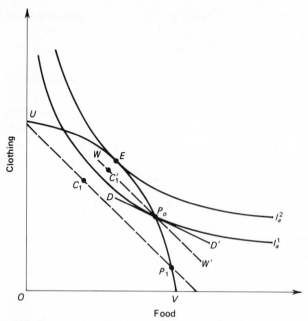

Figure 9-1 *Distortion in domestic production leading to specialization in the wrong commodity.*
Because of a distortion in domestic production, America produces and consumes, before trade, at P_0, where the relative price of food (given by the slope of DD') is lower than the opportunity cost of food (given by the slope of production-possibilities frontier UV at P_0). When she is given the opportunity to trade in world markets at the fixed price ratio given by the slope of WW', America shifts production to P_1 (because WW' is steeper than DD'). Nevertheless, America's true comparative advantage lies in clothing (because the production frontier is steeper at P_0 than WW'). Consumption shifts to C_1, which lies on a lower indifference curve than I_a^1.

production loss. If production were frozen at the autarkic point P_0, the economy's consumption would shift from P_0 to, say, C_1', which must lie on a higher social indifference curve. This is the consumption gain. However, production does not remain at P_0—it moves to P_1. America's income falls and causes the consumption equilibrium to move from C_1' to C_1. This is the production loss. *In general, when the economy specializes in the wrong commodity, the introduction of free trade may make the economy better off or worse off depending on whether the consumption gain is larger or smaller than the production loss.*

We have seen that in the present case free trade causes America to specialize in the wrong commodity (food). Should America then impose a tariff to protect her clothing industry, where her true comparative advantage lies? Certainly a tariff on imports raises their domestic price above the world price, encourages their production, and tends to eliminate the divergence between the terms of trade and the domestic marginal rate of transformation. Unfortunately, trade intervention is not the optimal policy in the present case. In fact, it may be even detrimental to national welfare. We return to the optimal policy a little later in this section.

Overspecialization in the Right Commodity

If the international price ratio does *not* lie between the autarkic market price ratio and the domestic marginal rate of transformation, our economy will specialize in the right commodity, but the degree of specialization will be either higher or lower than the optimum.

Consider Figure 9-2, which is similar to Figure 9-1. In autarky, America produces and consumes at P_0, where the relative price of food (that is, the slope of DD') is lower than the opportunity cost of food (that is, the slope of production-possibilities frontier UV at P_0). Assume that the world relative price of food is higher than America's opportunity cost of food under autarky, as shown by line WW'. Now America's true comparative advantage lies in the production of food, and America actually specializes in its production. However, because of the distortion, America overspecializes in food.

As we know, America's optimal production occurs at point E, where America's opportunity cost of food equals the world relative price of food. However, because of the distortion, America's production must occur

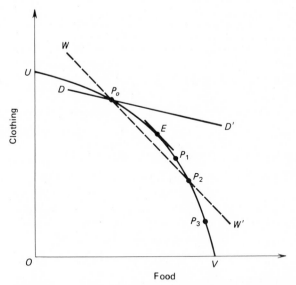

Figure 9-2 *Domestic distortion in production leading to overspecialization in the right commodity.*
Because of a distortion in domestic production, America produces and consumes, before trade, at P_0, where the relative price of food (given by DD') is lower than the opportunity cost of food at P_0 (that is, the slope of UV at P_0). When she is given the opportunity to trade in world markets at the fixed price ratio indicated by WW', America overspecializes in the right commodity (food), as illustrated by points P_1, P_2, and P_3. Because of the distortion, America cannot produce at optimal point E; rather, she produces at a point where the opportunity cost of food is higher than the world price ratio (that is, some point in region EV but beyond E).

southeast of E, as illustrated by points P_1, P_2, and P_3. Why does America over-specialize in food?

After the opening up of trade, America's domestic price ratio becomes equal to the international price ratio. Competition guarantees this result. However, because of the domestic distortion (say, external economies in the production of clothing), America's relative price of food is *always* lower than America's opportunity cost of food. Accordingly, America must produce at a point where the opportunity cost of food is higher than the world relative price of food. In other words, America must produce at a point where the tangent to the production-possibilities frontier is steeper than line WW', as illustrated by points P_1, P_2, and P_3. (Note that in region UE, the tangent to the production-possibilities frontier is necessarily flatter than line WW'.) As a result, America *overspecializes* now in the *right* commodity.

How does free trade compare with autarky in the present case? The introduction of trade again causes America to enjoy a consumption gain. Nevertheless, contrary to the previous case, in which America necessarily suffered a production loss, the production effect on welfare in the present case may be positive—that is, a gain (as illustrated by point P_1), negative—that is, a loss (as illustrated by point P_3), or zero (as illustrated by point P_2). When the country does not suffer a production loss, the introduction of trade necessarily increases national welfare. Otherwise, the overall effect of trade on welfare is indeterminate.

In the present case, the argument for protection appears to be rather strong. By means of an appropriate tariff, America could shift her production to optimal point E. Should we then conclude that America must impose a tariff? Unfortunately, the tariff is again a second-best policy and may even reduce national welfare.

It is true, of course, that America should shift her production to point E. The tariff, however, is not the instrument to do this. What the tariff actually does is to replace the initial distortion (that is, the gap between the world relative price of food and America's opportunity cost of food) by another distortion. As we have seen, a tariff creates a wedge between foreign and domestic prices and thus gives rise to a gap between foreign prices and the domestic marginal rate of substitution in consumption. Accordingly, while the tariff may shift America's production to point E, it also injects an inefficiency into the consumption pattern of America. The final effect of the tariff on welfare is, therefore, indeterminate.

Underspecialization in the Right Commodity

Consider finally Figure 9-3, which is similar to Figures 9-1 and 9-2. Assume that in autarky America produces and consumes at P_0, where the relative price of food (given by the slope of DD') is lower than the opportunity cost of food. The divergence between relative prices and opportunity costs is due to the existence of an external economy in the production of clothing. Assume further that the fixed world relative price of food is lower than America's autarkic

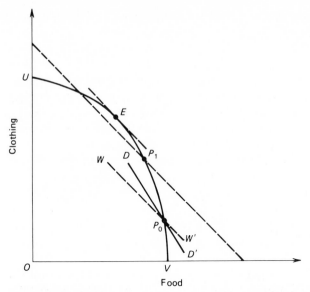

Figure 9-3 *Domestic distortion in production leading to underspecialization in the right commodity.*
In autarky, America produces and consumes at P_0, where the relative price of food (given by the slope of DD') is lower than the opportunity cost of food, because the production of clothing is subject to external economies. When she is given the opportunity to trade in world markets at the fixed price ratio indicated by WW', America shifts her production to P_1—not to E—because of the distortion that always makes food's price lower than food's opportunity cost. Thus, America underspecializes in the production of clothing.

price, as shown by broken line WW'. After the introduction of international trade, America specializes in the production of clothing. Thus, America specializes in the right commodity, that is, the commodity in whose production she has a true comparative advantage. However, because of the distortion, America underspecializes in the production of clothing.

Because of the distortion, America's relative price of food is always lower than America's opportunity cost of food. Therefore, after the introduction of trade, America must produce at a point where the slope of the production-possibilities frontier (that is, opportunity cost of food) is steeper than line WW' (that is, America's relative price of food after trade), as illustrated by point P_1. Note carefully that America cannot produce in region EU, because there the production-possibilities frontier is flatter than line WW'. In particular, America cannot produce at optimal production point E. Accordingly, point P_1 must lie southeast of E, as shown in Figure 9-3. This means that America does not transfer enough resources from the production of food to the production of clothing; that is, America underspecializes now in the right commodity.

Note that in the present case the introduction of trade necessarily makes America better off. The reason must be obvious: The consumption gain is now supplemented by a meager but nevertheless positive production gain.

As with the preceding two cases, trade intervention continues to be a second-best policy because of the consumption inefficiency introduced by tariffs.

Optimal Policy

We now turn briefly to the question of optimal policy. In all three cases studied above, we concluded that because of the distortion in domestic production, laissez faire does not maximize America's welfare. By the same token, the effects of a tariff on America's welfare are uncertain: Even though it may remove the distortion in domestic production, the tariff introduces a distortion in domestic consumption, and thus the effect on welfare may be either positive or negative. What is absolutely certain is that a tariff cannot possibly be an optimal policy because of the inefficiency it injects into the consumption pattern. What, then, is America's optimal policy?

America's optimal policy is to intervene directly at the source of the distortion, namely, *production*. The idea is to remove the distortion in domestic production without creating another distortion anywhere else. Obviously, we must reject tariffs, which, by correcting the distortion in domestic production, create a new distortion in domestic consumption. America must use *production taxes or production subsidies at an appropriate rate to offset the distortion completely*. These production taxes (or subsidies) have the important feature that they offset the distortion in domestic production *without creating a new distortion*.

In particular, America's optimal policy consists of the following alternatives: (1) a production subsidy to clothing or (2) a production tax on food. Either of these policies, or a combination of the two, can restore full Pareto optimality when either the production of clothing generates external economies or the production of food generates external diseconomies.

In the case of external diseconomies, the general rule is either to tax the commodity that generates external diseconomies or to subsidize the production of the other commodity. Similarly, in the case of external economies, the general rule is either to subsidize the commodity whose production generates external economies or to tax the production of the other commodity.

America's optimal policy is illustrated in Figure 9-4, which merely reproduces the basic structure of Figures 9-1 through 9-3. Under laissez faire, America produces at P_1 and consumes somewhere along broken line WW' (whose slope indicates the fixed world price ratio). A production subsidy to the clothing industry, or a production tax on food, administered at the appropriate level shifts America's production point from P_1 to E, where the marginal rate of transformation (that is, the opportunity cost of food) equals the fixed world price ratio—line MEN is parallel to WW'. Because the production subsidy (or tax) does not disturb the prices paid by consumers, which continue to be equal to the fixed world prices, America consumes at C, where the marginal rate of substitution in consumption equals the fixed world price ratio. Because production taxes and subsidies attack the production distortion at the source, they re-

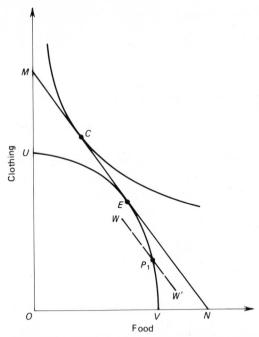

Figure 9-4 *Optimal policy in the presence of a distortion in domestic production.*
This diagram reproduces the basic structure of Figures 9-1 through 9-3. Under laissez faire,
America produces at P_1 and consumes somewhere along *WW'*. A production subsidy to the
clothing industry, or a production tax on food, shifts production to *E* and consumption to *C*,
where America's welfare is at a maximum.

store Pareto optimality. By producing at E and consuming at C, America now
maximizes her welfare.

9-4 OTHER DOMESTIC DISTORTIONS

In addition to distortions in domestic production, an economy can experience
distortions in domestic consumption and factor employment.

Distortions in domestic consumption usually arise from either external
economies or external diseconomies in the consumption of some commodity or
commodities. In such cases, the optimal policy is either a *consumption subsidy*
(consumption tax) to the commodity whose consumption is subject to the external economy (external diseconomy), or a *consumption tax* (consumption subsidy) on the other commodity.

Distortions in the employment of factors arise from factor-price differentials (and particularly wage differentials) and certain types of production externalities that are known as *factor-generated production externalities*. In these
cases, the rule for optimal intervention calls for the use of taxes or subsidies on
the uses of factors.

Concern over wage differentials is not new. Nevertheless, in the postwar economic writings the subject of factor-price differentials received a great impetus as a result of the increased interest in the economics of less developed countries. Two different types of factor-price differentials are usually cited. First, there may be a differential between the reward of a particular factor in different industries. For example, it is usually alleged that industrial wages are higher than agricultural wages by a margin which is greater than what can be accounted for by such factors as higher skill, disutility of urban living, investment in human capital (by training), and moving costs from the rural to the urban sector. Second, factor prices may be equal in all lines of production, but factor rewards may not correspond to marginal productivity. For example, wages may be equal between industry and agriculture, but wages in agriculture may be higher than the marginal productivity of labor there.

Factor-price differentials that may indicate genuine distortions (that is, differentials that cannot be accounted for by higher skills, investment in human capital, moving costs, disutility of urban living, and so on) may be due to any number of reasons. Some of these reasons are: lack of information, discrimination (age, sex, or race), seniority that does not reflect economic superiority, trade union intervention, differential factor taxation or subsidization, factory legislation, and imperfect capital markets.

The discussion of the welfare effects of factor-price differentials dates back to Manoilesco (1931), who observed that the average income in industry exceeds that in agriculture and concluded that agricultural countries can benefit by providing tariff protection to industry in order to shift workers out of agriculture into industry. This argument has been revived by Lewis (1954) and Hagen (1958).

Genuine factor-price differentials give rise to two major distortions. First, they prevent equality between the marginal rate of substitution of labor for land in the food and clothing industries. As a result, they cause a misallocation of resources—the economy does not operate on the contract curve, and the production-possibilities frontier is pulled in toward the origin (except at the intercepts). Second, they give rise to a divergence between the commodity market price ratio and the domestic marginal rate of transformation, as in the case of production distortion.

Can protection improve national welfare in the present case of factor-price differentials? It may and it may not. What is absolutely certain in this case is that protection cannot possibly restore Pareto optimality, since it cannot restore equality between the marginal rate of substitution of labor for land in the two industries. Hence, with protection, the allocation of resources continues to remain inefficient, and the economy continues to produce on the shrunk-in production-possibilities frontier. Moreover, it must be clear from our earlier discussion of distortions in domestic production that protection may even reduce welfare below the free-trade level.

A production subsidy to the commodity overpriced by the distortion, or a production tax on the underpriced commodity, though still not optimal (or first-best), is nevertheless superior to both protection and laissez faire. The reason is simple: *The production tax (or subsidy) maximizes national welfare subject to the shrunk-in production-possibilities frontier.* This policy does not restore Pareto optimality fully, of course. But it does eliminate the divergence between the market price ratio and the domestic marginal rate of transformation. For this reason, the production tax (or subsidy) enables the economy to increase national welfare above the level attained under laissez faire or any scheme of protection.

How can the economy restore Pareto optimality in the presence of distortionary factor-price differentials? The answer must be clear from the general rule for optimal intervention: The economy must attack the distortion at the source, which is the *inefficient use of factors of production*. This can only be accomplished by means of *appropriate taxes or subsidies on the uses of factors*.

For further details, see Chacholiades (1978, Chapter 20).

9-5   THE INFANT-INDUSTRY ARGUMENT

The infant-industry argument is an argument for *temporary* protection to correct a distortion which does not last forever but which disappears gradually with the passage of time. This argument, which has always had great appeal to young and developing nations, is said to have been formulated in 1791 by Alexander Hamilton, George Washington's Secretary of the Treasury; developed further by H. C. Carey and others; and later transplanted to Germany by Friedrich List. However, Viner (1965, pp. 71–72) provides evidence to the effect that this argument is of much earlier origin.

The Formulation of the Infant-Industry Argument by John Stuart Mill

Perhaps the clearest formulation of the infant-industry argument is provided by John Stuart Mill (1904, pp. 403–404). Since Mill's exposition is very concise indeed, it is quoted in full:

> The only case in which, on mere principles of political economy, protecting duties can be defensible, is when they are imposed temporarily (especially in a young and rising nation) in hopes of naturalizing a foreign industry, in itself perfectly suitable to the circumstances of the country. The superiority of one country over another in a branch of production often arises only from having begun it sooner. There may be no inherent advantage on one part, or disadvantage on the other, but only a present superiority of acquired skill and experience. A country which has this skill and experience yet to acquire, may in other respects be better adapted to the production than those which were earlier in the field; and besides, it is a just remark of Mr. Rae, that nothing has a greater tendency to promote improvements in any branch of production, than its trial under a new set of conditions. But it cannot be expected that individuals should, at their own risk, or rather to their certain loss, introduce a new manufacture, and bear the burden of carrying it on, until the producers have

been educated up to the level of those with whom the processes are traditional. A protecting duty, continued for a reasonable time, will sometimes be the least inconvenient mode in which the nation can tax itself for the support of such an experiment. But the protection should be confined to cases in which there is good ground of assurance that the industry which it fosters will after a time be able to dispense with it; nor should the domestic producers ever be allowed to expect that it will be continued to them beyond the time necessary for a fair trial of what they are capable of accomplishing.

Thus, the "Mill test" for infant-industry protection is whether the infant will eventually overcome its historical handicap and grow up to compete effectively and without protection against early starters.

Bastable (1903, p. 140; 1923, pp. 140–143), however, objected that the Mill test, though necessary, is not sufficient, and claimed that, in addition, the infant industry must eventually be able to generate sufficient savings in costs to compensate the economy for the losses (due to higher costs to the consumers) it suffers during the learning period when protection is necessary. Bastable correctly considered the incurring of costs during the learning period as a type of investment whose returns, it is hoped, accrue to the economy in the form of future cost reductions (relative to the costs that would have to be incurred in the absence of the development of the domestic industry). The "Bastable test," then, requires that the present discounted value of the future benefits be at least as high as the initial cost incurred to help the infant grow.

Johnson (1965, p. 27) notes that even when the Bastable test is passed, the infant-industry argument reduces essentially to the assertion that free competition produces a socially inefficient allocation of investment resources. For the validity of the argument, Johnson continues, "it must be demonstrated either that the social rate of return exceeds the private rate of return on the investment, or that the private rate of return necessary to induce the investment exceeds the private and social rates of return available on alternative investment, by a wide enough margin to make a socially profitable investment privately unprofitable." But even if these additional conditions are satisfied, the optimal policy is *not* tariff protection but rather some sort of *subsidy* to the infant industry, since a domestic, not foreign, distortion is involved.

Economies of the Learning Process and Optimal Policy

Central to the infant-industry argument is the notion that practice makes perfect; during the initial stages of development, the "infants" are assumed to learn both from their own experiences and from each other. This learning process, which generally (but not necessarily) involves external economies, is *irreversible*. This important feature of the infant-industry argument distinguishes it from the case of static external economies discussed earlier in this chapter. As we have seen, static externalities (economies or diseconomies) form a *permanent* characteristic of the economy's technology and call for *permanent* government intervention. The infant-industry argument, on the other hand, is based on a dynamic learning process that generates external economies over a certain period of time, and thus calls for only *temporary* government intervention.

When the economies generated during the learning period are *internal* to the firm (for example, economies of scale), Adam Smith's invisible hand can, in general, be counted on to produce a socially efficient allocation of investment resources, and there is no need for government intervention to protect any "infants." There are, of course, exceptions—the capital market may be imperfect, and as a result the cost of financing investment in new industries may be excessively high; or there may be a difference between social and private time preference, assessment of risk, availability of information, foresight, and so on. But even in these exceptional cases, tariff protection is not the answer. In fact, tariff protection is a second-best policy and may even reduce welfare. The first-best policy follows from the general rule for optimal intervention: The government should intervene at the precise point where the distortion occurs. For instance, in the case in which an imperfect capital market makes the cost of financing investment in new industries excessively high, the optimal policy is to subsidize the provision of capital to such industries.

Two major varieties of the externality argument are usually found in the literature. First, it is claimed that because of the absence of the necessary labor skills, the pioneering entrepreneur of a particular industry must train the labor force. However, the argument goes, the return from the improvement of labor skills cannot be appropriated by the entrepreneur but is rather imputed to the labor force, since the workers, after gaining the necessary skills, might be lured away by other entrepreneurs who enter the field later and are willing and able to pay a higher wage. Accordingly, the private rate of return to the pioneering entrepreneur (who cannot be certain of appropriating all the fruits of his or her investment) is necessarily lower than the social rate of return. Obviously, the optimal policy in the present case is not tariff protection but rather subsidy to the training of the labor force.

The second externality argument deals with the acquisition of knowledge of production technique. The acquisition of such knowledge necessarily involves the incurring of costs in the present in the hope of reaping profits in the future. But once created, such knowledge cannot be effectively guarded by the pioneering entrepreneur. Others who enter the field subsequently can certainly make use of it. Once again, the pioneering entrepreneur cannot appropriate all the fruits of his or her investment, and therefore the private rate of return is necessarily lower than the social rate of return. Tariff protection is again a second-best policy and could hurt the country instead of benefiting it. The optimal policy is merely a direct subsidy to the learning process itself.

Writers in the field of economic development have extended the infant-industry argument to the whole industrial sector. They claim that the external economies generated by firms in one industry are not confined to that particular industry alone but instead spread over the whole "infant manufacturing sector." Thus, they think in terms of "infant-economy protection" rather than "infant-industry protection."

Graphical Illustration[1]

The infant-industry argument is illustrated in Figure 9-5. The initial production-possibilities frontier is given by curve UV and the international price ratio (which remains constant throughout by assumption) by the absolute slope of lines L_1P_1, and L_2P_2, and L_3P_3. Before protection is provided to the infant clothing industry, the economy produces at P_1 and consumes at C_1. After protection, however, the production-possibilities frontier shifts outward gradually, as a result of the continuous improvement in skills and production techniques, until it eventually attains the position shown by curve $U'V$. Figure 9-5 illustrates the most favorable case in which the infant industry grows to become a net exporter. Thus, eventually the economy produces at P_3 and consumes at C_4.

The adjustment process is most interesting but cannot be studied in detail without a lot of additional information. Within our limited scope, however, we can offer some insights. Thus, immediately after a protective tariff is imposed on the imports of clothing and before any improvement in skills and production techniques takes place, production equilibrium shifts to, say, P_2, and consumption equilibrium to C_2. Note that the marginal rate of substitution at C_2 equals the short-run domestic marginal rate of transformation at P_2.

Suppose that instead of a protective tariff, the country pursues a policy of an equivalent subsidy to the production of clothing. Production still shifts to P_2; but consumption shifts to C_3, where the marginal rate of substitution equals the terms of trade. Thus, the production subsidy to the infant clothing industry is definitely superior to the tariff (basically because of the consumption inefficiency introduced by the tariff but not the production subsidy), and this superiority continues over time.

Imagine now the initial production-possibilities frontier shifting gradually outward, and let broken line P_1P_3 be the locus of points on the successive frontiers where the domestic marginal rate of transformation equals the fixed terms of trade (that is, line P_1P_3 is the locus of points on the successive frontiers where the slopes are equal to the slope of UV at P_1). In addition, let broken line $C_3C_1KC_4$ indicate the income-consumption curve through C_3, where the marginal rate of substitution of food for clothing equals the given relative price of food in world markets.

The economy will actually follow consumption-equilibrium path $C_3C_1KC_4$ when the policy of a production subsidy to clothing is pursued. When a tariff is actually imposed, the economy will follow a different consumption-equilibrium path, illustrated by broken line C_2KC_4. The precise consumption-equilibrium path under a protective tariff is not unique, however, since it depends on the particular tariff policy pursued over time. Nevertheless, one thing is clear: When point K (that is, the intersection of broken lines P_1P_3 and $C_3C_1KC_4$) is reached, the country becomes self-sufficient in clothing; and beyond point K, the country is a net exporter of clothing. (Assume that the tariff, or production

---

[1] This subsection may be omitted without interrupting the continuity of the book.

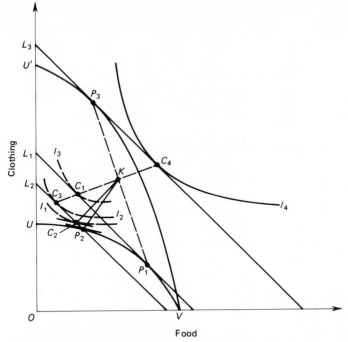

Figure 9-5 *The infant-industry argument.*
The initial production-possibilities frontier is given by curve *UV* and the fixed world price ratio by the slope of L_1P_1. Before protection, the economy produces at P_1 and consumes at C_1. After protection, the production frontier shifts to *U'V*, production to P_3, and consumption to C_4.

    Immediately after the imposition of a tariff on the imports of clothing, production shifts to P_2 and consumption to C_2. An equivalent production subsidy, however, which shifts production to P_2, would shift consumption to C_3. Thus, the production subsidy is superior to the tariff, and this superiority continues over time.

subsidy, is reduced gradually through time until it is totally removed when point *K* is reached). Finally, the production-equilibrium path is illustrated by curve P_2KP_3.

Does the economy become better off by assisting the infant industry to grow? We cannot tell from Figure 9-5 alone. All we know is that *eventually* welfare will rise above the initial level at C_1. We do not know, however, whether the present discounted value of the future gains in welfare is actually higher than the welfare losses suffered during the transitional period until social indifference curve I_3 is reached.

The problem is actually a little more complex. There is not a single consumption path that moves the economy from the initial equilibrium at C_1 to the long-run equilibrium at C_4, but many. In fact, there may be an infinite number of such paths, each one depending on a specific economic policy through time. Our analysis clearly shows that a protective tariff can never be the optimal policy, since there is always a production subsidy that can do better. But even if attention is confined to policies involving a production subsidy only, a real problem remains: How do we choose the "best" production subsidy scheme? The solution to this problem requires knowledge regarding the effect of each alternative production subsidy scheme on labor skills and production techniques over time. This problem, though interesting, is not pursued any further here.

One very interesting feature of the infant-industry argument that must be emphasized is the shift from *static* to *dynamic* comparative advantage.

9-6   IMMISERIZING GROWTH AND DISTORTIONS

In Chapter 7 we considered the paradoxical phenomenon known as *immiserizing growth,* in which a country actually becomes worse off with growth. We pointed out at the time that, in general, immiserizing growth occurs because of the existence of a distortion (either foreign or domestic) that *is not offset by an optimal policy.* In Chapter 7 we considered only the case of a large growing country (with monopoly-monopsony power in international trade) that does not pursue an optimal tariff policy. Here, we consider briefly the case of a "small" country (with no monopoly-monopsony power in international trade) that either provides tariff protection to her import-competing industry before and after growth or suffers from a production externality.

Tariff Protection

Consider Figure 9-6. Before growth, the "small" country, America, which provides tariff protection to her clothing industry, produces at P_0 and consumes at C_0. Thus, America's domestic relative price of food (given by the absolute slope of parallel broken lines 1, 2, 3, and 4) is lower than the fixed world price of food (given by the absolute slope of parallel lines P_0K and P_1N). Note that both America's marginal rate of transformation (that is, the slope of the production-possibilities frontier at P_0) and America's marginal rate of substitution of food for clothing (that is, the slope of social indifference curve I_0 at C_0) are equal to America's domestic relative price of food. Note also that America consumes along line P_0K, where the value of exports of the rest of the world is equal to the value of imports of the rest of the world. Finally, because of the tariff, America is *not* maximizing her social welfare.

Suppose now that because of technical progress, America's production-possibilities frontier shifts outward, as illustrated by broken curve $U'V'$. In particular, assume that *America's technical progress is now predominantly concentrated in the import-competing industry (clothing).* This assumption is in sharp contrast with the assumption we made earlier in Chapter 7 in relation to immiserizing growth experienced by a "large," laissez-faire country, namely, that the technical progress is concentrated predominantly in the export sector.

What happens to America's production, consumption, and welfare after growth? America's production shifts from P_0 to P_1 (where the opportunity cost of food is again equal to America's relative price of food); and America's con-

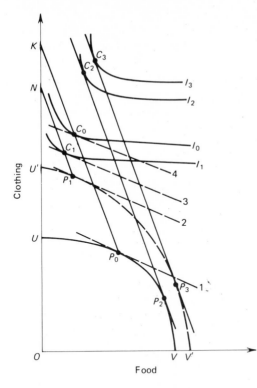

Figure 9-6 *Immiserizing growth in the presence of tariff protection.*
Because of a tariff on the imports of clothing, America produces initially at P_0 (on production frontier UV) and consumes at C_0. Technical progress, predominantly concentrated in the import-competing industry (clothing), causes the production frontier to shift to $U'V'$. Production shifts to P_1, where the value of America's production at the fixed world prices (given by P_0K and P_1N) is lower than before growth (at P_0). Consumption shifts to C_1, which lies on a lower social indifference curve than C_0. If the tariff did not exist, production and consumption would have occurred at P_2 and C_2, respectively, before growth; and growth would have shifted them to P_3 and C_3, respectively.

sumption shifts from C_0 to C_1 (where the marginal rate of substitution of food for clothing equals America's domestic relative price of food and the value of exports equals the value of imports at world prices). Our diagram illustrates the case in which *the value of America's production at world prices is lower after growth (at P_1) than before (at P_0)*: line P_1N lies closer to the origin than line P_0K. As a result, America consumes at a lower indifference curve (I_1) after growth than before (I_0). That is, growth reduces America's welfare.

Distortion in Domestic Production

Immiserizing growth can also be experienced by a "small" country in the presence of a distortion in domestic production (or even a distortion in the domestic employment of factors). This is illustrated in Figure 9-7. Before growth, America again produces at P_0 and consumes at C_0. Because of a production externality (either an external economy in the production of food or an external diseconomy in the production of clothing), America's opportunity cost of food at P_0 (given by the slope of production-possibilities frontier UV at P_0) is less than the fixed world price of food (given by the slope of MN or $M'N'$). However, because foreign prices are equal to domestic prices, America's marginal rate of substitution of food for clothing at C_0 equals the relative price of food—line MN is tangent to social indifference curve I_0 at C_0.

Technical progress, which is predominantly concentrated in the import-

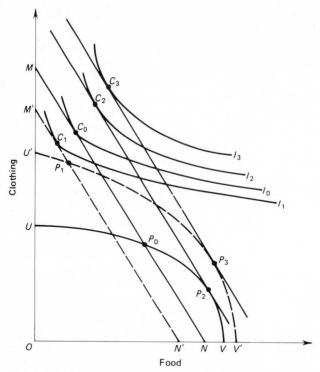

Figure 9-7 *Immiserizing growth due to a distortion in domestic production.*
Because of a production externality, America produces initially at P_0 and consumes at C_0.
Technical progress, which is predominantly concentrated in the import-competing industry
(clothing), causes production frontier UV to shift to $U'V'$. Production shifts from P_0 to P_1 and
consumption from C_0 to C_1. America's welfare falls with growth, because C_1 lies on a lower
social indifference curve than C_0.

Had America pursued an optimal policy (production subsidy) throughout, production
and consumption would have shifted from their respective pregrowth points P_2 and C_2 to P_3
and C_3. Thus, America's welfare would have increased with growth.

competing industry (clothing), shifts America's production-possibilities frontier
outward, as illustrated by broken curve $U'V'$. America's production shifts from
P_0 to P_1 and America's consumption from C_0 to C_1. As in the preceding case,
the value of America's production at P_1 (after growth) is lower than its value at
P_0 (before growth). Consequently, America's welfare falls—C_1 lies on a lower
social indifference curve than C_0.

Conclusion

Immiserizing growth is a phenomenon that occurs only when a distortion,
foreign or domestic, is not offset by means of an optimal policy. If the distortion
is actually corrected by means of an optimal policy, as explained in Sections
9-2 through 9-4, then immiserizing growth cannot occur.

For instance, consider the cases illustrated in Figures 9-6 and 9-7. An optimal policy (either removing an existing tariff, as in Figure 9-6, or imposing an

optimal production tax, as in Figure 9-7) shifts production and consumption, before growth, to P_2 and C_2, respectively (in both diagrams). Similarly, after growth, production and consumption shift to P_3 and C_3, respectively. Note that while C_2 lies on a higher social indifference curve than C_0 (or C_1), C_3 lies on a still higher social indifference curve than C_2.

We therefore conclude that economic growth may become immiserizing only if a distortion (foreign or domestic) exists. When the distortion is corrected by means of an optimal policy, economic growth always improves welfare.

9-7 NONECONOMIC ARGUMENTS FOR PROTECTION

The theory of endogenous distortions has a direct application to various noneconomic arguments for protection. The purpose of this last section is to consider these noneconomic arguments.

Noneconomic Objectives

So far in this book, we have pretended that the only objective of a nation is to maximize her economic welfare. However, economic welfare is not the sole goal of life. Political, cultural, and sociological objectives are also important. Such noneconomic objectives may make it desirable to pursue activities that are not economically efficient. Even Adam Smith himself stated in a famous passage that national defense matters more than national opulence.

The case of oil production illustrates the point well. The United States is presently heavily dependent on foreign oil that is controlled by the Organization of Petroleum Exporting Countries (OPEC). For political reasons, the oil-producing nations may discontinue their supply of oil to the United States in the future. It is common knowledge that in 1973 OPEC imposed an oil embargo; and when the embargo was finally lifted, OPEC quadrupled the dollar price of crude oil (from \$2.59 to \$11.65 a barrel), shaking the economic stability of the world economy. To guard against such a contingency, it may be argued that tariff protection is needed to increase the domestic production of oil (since the capacity to produce oil cannot be increased substantially overnight). This is a powerful argument. However, as we shall see, the optimal policy is a production subsidy—not tariff protection.

The rest of this section deals with the desirability of tariffs and alternative policy measures for the achievement of four specific objectives: (1) a certain level of *production* (perhaps for military reasons); (2) a certain level of *consumption* (usually to restrict the consumption of luxury goods on social grounds); (3) a certain level of *self-sufficiency* (to reduce the dependency on imports for political or military reasons); and (4) a certain level of *employment of a factor of production*, such as labor (to preserve the national character and the traditional way of life). These objectives are called noneconomic because they essentially originate outside the economic model. We need not concern ourselves with either the nature or the rationality of these noneconomic objectives.

The attainment of a noneconomic objective has an economic cost (in the form of a welfare loss), since it generally involves the violation of one or more Pareto optimality conditions. The object of our investigation, then, is to determine that policy which achieves the noneconomic objective at the least welfare loss, that is, the optimal policy.

General Rule for Optimal Intervention

We have seen in this chapter that the optimal policy for correcting a distortion is to intervene at the exact point of the distortion. For instance, to remove a distortion in domestic production, the government must intervene with a production tax or subsidy. This optimal rule is also the key to the present case of noneconomic objectives.

When the government pursues a certain policy for achieving a noneconomic objective, it necessarily introduces into the economy a (policy-induced) distortion. The resultant welfare loss is minimized when the government actually intervenes at the exact point where the noneconomic objective lies. For instance, if the *production* of a commodity must be encouraged for military reasons, the optimal policy is a *production* subsidy—not a tariff. Similarly, if the *consumption* of a commodity must be restricted, the optimal policy is a *consumption* tax, and so on. The following discussion clarifies this important rule.

Achievement of a Production Goal

Suppose that production in an industry considered vital to national defense must be encouraged above the level attained under laissez faire. What is the least-cost method for the achievement of this goal?

Consider Figure 9-8. Initially the country produces at P_0 and consumes at C_0. By assumption, the world price ratio is fixed and given by the absolute slope of parallel lines L_0P_0 and L_1P_1. Note that both the marginal rate of transformation (that is, the absolute slope of production-possibilities frontier UV at P_0) and the marginal rate of substitution (that is, the absolute slope of social indifference curve I_0 at C_0) are equal to the fixed world price ratio. Accordingly, the economy is initially maximizing the social welfare. Suppose now that the government wishes to shift production from P_0 to P_1 because for some reason, such as national defense, the production of clothing must not be permitted to fall below level OJ.

A tariff could achieve the production goal but would lead to an additional, unnecessary, and costly distortion in consumption—it would cause production to shift to P_1 and consumption to C_2 (where the marginal rate of substitution equals the *domestic* marginal rate of transformation).

The optimal policy is to *subsidize the production of clothing* so that the marginal rate of substitution in consumption remains equal to the fixed world price ratio. Accordingly, with an appropriate production subsidy to clothing (or production tax on food), production would shift to P_1 and consumption to C_1, which lies on a higher social indifference curve than C_2.

When the economy has monopoly-monopsony power in international

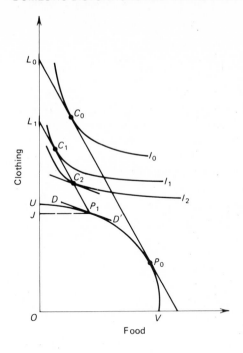

Figure 9-8 *Tariff versus production subsidy to achieve a production goal.*
For a noneconomic reason (for example, national defense), the country wishes to shift production from laissez faire point P_0 to P_1 on production-possibilities frontier *UV*. A tariff is not optimal for this purpose, because it introduces an unnecessary distortion in consumption, as illustrated by point C_2. A production subsidy, on the other hand, maximizes welfare subject to production at P_1, as illustrated by C_1.

trade, the optimal policy involves a combination of a tariff plus a production subsidy (or tax).

Achievement of a Consumption Goal

Alternatively, suppose that the government wishes to restrict the consumption of, say, luxuries, below the level attained under laissez faire conditions. What is the optimal policy to achieve this goal? With fixed world prices, the optimal policy is a consumption tax. The tariff is again inferior.

Consider Figure 9-9, which shows the same laissez faire equilibrium as Figure 9-8. Given the fixed world price ratio (shown by the absolute slope of lines L_0Z and C_1P_1), the economy produces at P_0 and consumes at C_0. Suppose, however, that the government wants to restrict the domestic consumption of clothing to level *OJ*. Draw a horizontal line through *J* and let it intersect line L_0Z at C_2. Given production-possibilities frontier *UV*, the fixed world price ratio, and the additional constraint on the domestic consumption of clothing, it becomes apparent that the economy must maximize social welfare subject to constraint JC_2Z. Such welfare maximization must occur at C_2, since line segment C_2Z intersects all (and is never tangent to any) indifference curves.

How can equilibrium at C_2 be reached? The economy must continue to produce at P_0, and, therefore, tariffs and production taxes and subsidies must be ruled out. An appropriate *consumption tax* that makes the price ratio to the domestic consumers equal to the absolute slope of line L_2C_2 (which is tangent

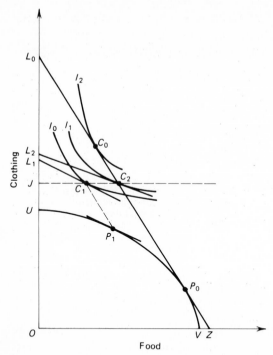

Figure 9-9 *Tariff versus consumption tax to achieve a consumption goal.*
For a noneconomic reason, the country wishes to reduce the consumption of clothing from
the laissez faire level attained at C_0 to OJ. A tariff is not optimal for this purpose, because it attracts resources into the production of clothing and inflicts a needless additional welfare loss
on the economy, as illustrated by points P_1 (production) and C_1 (consumption). The optimal
policy is a consumption tax on clothing that leaves production at P_0 (where the slope of
production-possibilities frontier UV is equal to the fixed world price ratio given by the slope of
L_0P_0) but shifts consumption to C_2.

to indifference curve I_1), and therefore equal to the marginal rate of substitution
of food for clothing at C_2, achieves the desired result.

A tariff to reduce the consumption of clothing is inefficient, since it also attracts resources into the production of clothing and inflicts a needless additional welfare loss on the economy. For instance, as Figure 9-9 illustrates, with
an appropriate tariff, production shifts to P_1 and consumption to C_1 (where the
marginal rate of substitution equals the domestic marginal rate of transformation, and the consumption of clothing is OJ). But C_1 is certainly inferior to C_2.
The latter (C_2), as we have seen, can be reached by imposing an appropriate
consumption tax.

When the economy also has monopoly-monopsony power in international
trade, the optimal policy involves a combination of a tariff plus a consumption
tax.

Other Noneconomic Objectives

There is no need to pursue other noneconomic objectives in detail, since the
principle involved should be clear by now. Accordingly, when the noneconom-

ic objective is to reduce the volume of imports, the optimal policy is an appropriate tariff on imports. Similarly, when the noneconomic objective is to raise the employment of a factor, such as labor, in certain activities, the optimal policy is a direct subsidy to the use of labor in those activities.

9-8 SUMMARY

1   Domestic distortions prevent the market mechanism from achieving Pareto optimality.

2   Endogenous domestic distortions are due to market imperfections. They may occur in production, consumption, or factor employment.

3   Policy-induced distortions are the result of economic policies, such as tariffs and other taxes or subsidies.

4   To restore Pareto optimality, policy intervention (equal to the degree of distortion) must occur at the exact point at which the underlying market imperfection prevails. This is the general rule for optimal intervention.

5   To correct a policy-induced distortion, the optimal policy is obviously to eliminate that policy which causes the distortion in the first place.

6   The theory of the optimal tariff rests on the existence of a foreign distortion (from the national viewpoint). The optimal tariff itself may be viewed as the optimal policy to correct the foreign distortion.

7   A production distortion (that is, a divergence between the marginal rate of transformation and the domestic price ratio) could occur as a result of production externalities or imperfect market structures.

8   An open economy subject to a production externality may specialize in either commodity. If it specializes in the right commodity, it may either overspecialize or underspecialize. When it underspecializes in the right commodity, it becomes better off with free trade; but in all other cases, it *may* become worse off.

9   The optimal policy to correct a *production* distortion is a *production* tax (or subsidy). A tariff is a second-best policy, because it introduces a consumption distortion.

10   A consumption distortion (that is, a divergence between the marginal rate of substitution in consumption and the domestic price ratio) usually arises from the existence of externalities in the consumption of some commodity.

11   The optimal policy to correct a *consumption* distortion is a *consumption* subsidy (or tax).

12   Distortions in the employment of factors arise from factor-price differentials (particularly wage differentials) or factor-generated externalities.

13   Factor-price differentials occur when a factor is rewarded differently in different industries (for example, industrial wages may be higher than agricultural wages) or when factor rewards, though equal between industries, do not correspond to marginal productivity.

14   Distortions in the employment of factors prevent the economy from producing on its production-possibilities frontier; and, in addition, they create a divergence between the commodity-price ratio and the marginal rate of transformation.

15   The optimal policy to correct distortions in the employment of factors is to use appropriate taxes (or subsidies) on the uses of factors. Though superi-

or to protection, a production subsidy is not optimal, because it does not restore production on the production-possibilities frontier.

16 Static externalities form a permanent characteristic of technology and call for permanent intervention. The infant-industry argument, however, rests on a dynamic and irreversible learning process that generally generates external economies only over a specific period of time and thus calls for only *temporary* government intervention.

17 The Mill test for infant-industry protection is whether the "infant" will eventually grow to compete, without protection, against early starters. The Bastable test requires further that the present discounted value of the future benefits be at least as high as the initial cost incurred to help the infant grow.

18 Because an infant industry involves a domestic (not foreign) distortion, the optimal policy is *not* tariff protection but rather some sort of subsidy to the infant industry.

19 In the presence of a distortion (foreign or domestic) that is not corrected by an optimal policy, a growing country ("large" or "small") may experience immiserizing growth.

20 Any policy to achieve a noneconomic objective introduces a distortion and results in a welfare loss. To minimize the welfare loss, intervention must occur at the exact point where the noneconomic objective lies. Thus, to achieve a production (consumption) goal, the optimal policy is a production (consumption) subsidy or tax; to reduce the volume of imports, the optimal policy is a tariff; and to raise the employment of a factor in certain activities, the optimal policy is a direct subsidy to the use of that factor in those activities.

SUGGESTED READING

Bastable, C. F. (1903). *The Theory of International Trade,* 4th ed. Macmillan & Co., Ltd., London.

—— (1923). *The Commerce of Nations,* 9th ed. (rev.). Methuen & Co., Ltd., London.

Bhagwati, J. and V. K. Ramaswami (1963). "Domestic Distortions, Tariffs, and the Theory of Optimum Subsidy." *Journal of Political Economy,* vol. 71, no. 1 (February), pp. 44–50. Reprinted in R. E. Caves and H. G. Johnson (eds.). *Readings in International Economics,* Richard D. Irwin, Inc., Homewood, Ill., 1968.

Black, J. (1959). "Arguments for Tariffs." *Oxford Economic Papers* (N.S.), vol. 11, pp. 191–220.

Cairnes, J. E. (1974). *Some Leading Principles of Political Economy.* Macmillan and Company, Ltd., London.

Corden, W. M. (1957). "Tariffs, Subsidies and the Terms of Trade." *Economica* (N.S.), vol. 24 (August), pp. 235–242.

—— (1974). *Trade Policy and Economic Welfare.* Oxford University Press, London.

Eckaus, R. S. (1955). "The Factor-Proportions Problem in Underdeveloped Areas." *American Economic Review,* vol. 45 (September), pp. 539–565. Reprinted in A. N. Agarwala and S. P. Singh (eds.), *The Economics of Underdevelopment.* Oxford University Press, London, 1958.

Hagen, E. (1958). "An Economic Justification of Protectionism." *Quarterly Journal of Economics,* vol. 72 (November), pp. 496–514.

Johnson, H. G. (1965). "Optimal Trade Intervention in the Presence of Domestic Distortions." In R. E. Baldwin et al. (eds.). *Trade, Growth and the Balance of Payments: Essays in Honor of Gottfried Haberler*. Rand McNally & Company, Chicago.

——— (1967). "The Possibility of Income Losses from Increased Efficiency or Factor Accumulation in the Presence of Tariffs." *Economic Journal*, vol. 77, no. 305 (March), pp. 151–154. Reprinted in H. G. Johnson, *Aspects of the Theory of Tariffs*. Harvard University Press, Cambridge, Mass., 1972.

Lewis, A. (1954). "Economic Development with Unlimited Supplies of Labour." *Manchester School* (May), pp. 139-191. Reprinted in A. N. Agarwala and S. P. Singh (eds.). *The Economics of Underdevelopment*. Oxford University Press, London, 1958.

Magee, S. P. (1976). *International Trade and Distortions in Factor Markets*. Marcel Dekker, Inc., New York.

Manoilesco, M. (1931). *The Theory of Protection and International Trade*. P. S. King and Son, Ltd., London.

Mill, J. S. (1904). *Principles of Political Economy*, vol. II. J. A. Hill and Company, New York. (The first edition of *Principles* appeared in 1848.)

Myint, H. (1963). "Infant Industry Arguments for Assistance to Industries in the Setting of Dynamic Trade Theory." In R. Harrod (ed.). *International Trade Theory in a Developing World*. St. Martin's Press, Inc., New York.

Myrdal, G. (1956). *An International Economy*. Harper and Row, Publishers, New York.

Prebish, R. (1959). "Commercial Policy in Underdeveloped Countries." *American Economic Review*, Proceedings, vol. 49 (May), pp. 251–273.

Viner, J. (1965). *Studies in the Theory of International Trade*. Augustus M. Kelley, Publishers, New York.

Chapter Ten

Other Trade Barriers and U.S. Commercial Policy

The tariff is the most common instrument of protection, but it is not the only one. Nations may restrict their foreign trade in many other ways. Indeed, as the tariff walls continue to come down as a result of multilateral trade negotiations, the significance of the nontariff barriers to international trade grows.

After a brief discussion about export taxes (Section 10-1) and export and import subsidies (Section 10-2), we will survey some of the most important nontariff barriers affecting trade. Section 10-3 deals with the theory of quantitative restrictions (quotas) and brings out their similarities to, and differences from, tariffs. Section 10-4 presents the theory of international cartels, whose relevance must be obvious to everyone if only because of the tremendous success of OPEC in the 1970s. Section 10-5 deals with the various forms of dumping (that is, international price discrimination) and the economic problems that dumping gives rise to. Section 10-6 considers briefly several other nontariff barriers, such as technical and administrative regulations and government procurement policies. The chapter concludes in Section 10-7 with some highlights of the U.S. tariff history (mainly for the period after 1934) plus some discussion about the trade negotiations that have taken place during the postwar era under the aegis of the General Agreement on Tariffs and Trade (GATT).

10-1 EXPORT TAXES

Nations may restrict their foreign trade by interfering with either their flow of imports or their flow of exports. Nations may impose import duties or import quotas in order to restrict the free flow of their imports, and they may impose export duties or export quotas in an effort to restrict the free flow of their exports. This section deals briefly with export duties (that is, taxes on exported commodities).

Export taxes are relatively rare phenomena among industrial nations. Nevertheless, primary product–exporting nations often impose export duties to either raise revenue or improve their terms of trade (by creating scarcity in world markets and increasing the prices of their exported commodities). For instance, Brazil taxes her exports of coffee, Ghana taxes her exports of cocoa, and Thailand and Burma tax their exports of rice.

As we noted earlier, the Constitution of the United States prohibits the imposition of export taxes. For this reason, the U.S. government resorts to other forms of export restriction, such as export quotas, whenever economic conditions call for such trade intervention. For instance, in years of bad harvests consumer groups seek export quotas in order to keep the cost of food as low as possible.

The effects of export taxes on the allocation of resources are symmetrical to the corresponding effects of import taxes. Lerner (1936) showed that in a long-run, static-equilibrium model (ignoring possible transitional difficulties, such as unemployment and balance-of-payments disequilibria) *a general export tax has the same effect as a general import tax of the same ad valorem percentage*.

Lerner's symmetry theorem is valid within the context of long-run equilibrium only. In the short run, as we will see in Chapter 19, an import tax tends to operate in an expansionary, stimulating fashion (and, in general, tends to improve the balance of payments as well). On the other hand, an export tax tends to operate in an anti-inflationary, depressive manner (and, in general, tends to worsen the balance of payments).

We can demonstrate the symmetry between export and import taxes by showing that their effects on domestic relative prices are identical. For this purpose, we pursue a little further the numerical illustration we discussed in Section 8-2.

Suppose that our "small' country exports food and imports clothing at the current world prices: $p_f = \$10$ and $p_c = \$50$, respectively. Under free-trade conditions, the prices that prevail in world markets prevail in our small economy as well. Thus, 1 unit of clothing exchanges for 5 units of food ($\$50/\$10 = 5$).

Assume first that our small economy imposes a 20 percent tax on the imports of clothing. As we saw in Chapter 8, this import tax causes the domestic price of clothing to rise to $1.20 \times \$50 = \$60$. This is the price that must be paid by domestic consumers and received by domestic producers. While in the world markets 1 unit of clothing continues to exchange for 5 units of food (that is, \$50/\$10), in our small country 1 unit of clothing exchanges now for 6 units of food (that is, \$60/\$10). As we have seen, this change in the domestic relative price of clothing has profound effects on the domestic organization of the economy of the small country—on the pattern of production, the pattern of consumption, the distribution of income, and so on.

Alternatively, assume that the small economy imposes a 20 percent tax on the exports of food. How does the export tax affect the domestic price of food? Evidently, the small economy can continue exporting food if the domestic price of food falls sufficiently so that the cost of food to foreign importers, inclusive of the export tax, continues to be \$10. In particular, the domestic price of food (that is, the price paid by domestic consumers and received by domestic producers) must drop to \$10/1.20 = \$8.33. What is the relative price of clothing after the imposition of the export tax? It is \$50/\$8.33 = 6.

We therefore conclude that whether the small country imposes a 20 percent tax on the imports of clothing or a 20 percent tax on the exports of food, the domestic relative price of clothing rises from 5 to 6. Thus, 1 unit of clothing exchanges for 6 units of food after the imposition of the export or import tax, as compared with 5 units of food before the imposition of the tax.

Because the effect on the all-important *relative* price of clothing is the same for the export tax on food as it is for the import tax on clothing, the general microeconomic effects of the export tax must be identical to the corresponding effects of the import tax. It must be clear that this important conclusion remains valid when the tax-levying country is "large." Accordingly, no further discussion is needed on the effects of export taxes.

10-2 EXPORT AND IMPORT SUBSIDIES

Trade subsidies are merely *negative* trade taxes. That is, an import subsidy is a negative import tax, and an export subsidy is a negative export tax. For this reason, a detailed analysis of export and import subsidies is redundant. In general, the microeconomic effects of trade subsidies can be expected to be the opposite of the corresponding effects of trade taxes (that is, import taxes and export taxes).

Import subsidies are a good deal less common than export subsidies. For this reason, the following brief discussion concentrates exclusively on export subsidies. Further discussion of export subsidies, particularly insofar as their effects on national income and the balance of payments are concerned, can be found in Chapter 19.

As we will see in Chapter 19, the primary purpose of an export subsidy is to increase exports by switching foreign spending to domestic products. This is accomplished, of course, by effectively reducing the prices that foreigners have to pay for the subsidized exported commodities. Accordingly, the terms-of-trade effect of export subsidies is, in general, unfavorable.

Export subsidies may be overt or covert. An overt export subsidy involves a direct payment by the government to the exporter of the subsidized commodity in direct proportion to either the volume or the value of the exports. Covert export subsidies, on the other hand, are schemes that provide financial assistance to the exporter indirectly. Such indirect financial assistance is often provided, for instance, through subsidization of credit conditions and of export shipping services in ships of the national flag.

Export subsidies are usually considered the equivalent of "dumping" (that is, selling cheaper abroad than at home, a phenomenon we will discuss in Section 10-5). Frequently, foreign countries retaliate by imposing "countervailing," or "antidumping," duties. When this happens, the country that initiates the export subsidy program actually becomes worse off. This conclusion follows easily from the observation that when foreign countries retaliate by imposing "antidumping" duties, the export subsidy program really amounts to a direct income transfer by the export-subsidizing country to the rest of the world.

An important case in which an export subsidy may be granted occurs when the export industry uses imported inputs that are subject to import duties. In this case, which is frequently observed in less developed countries, the export industry is granted an export subsidy, which in effect is a rebate of the tariff paid by the same industry on imported inputs. This type of export subsidy is indeed very sensible. Otherwise, the export industry would be at a disadvantage in world markets.

Finally, note that the symmetry we observed earlier between export and import taxes also exists between export and import subsidies. Thus, in the long run a general export subsidy has the same effects as a general import subsidy of the same ad valorem percentage.

10-3 QUANTITATIVE RESTRICTIONS

Nations may also restrict their foreign trade by directly limiting the physical volume (or value) of either their imports (*import quota*) or their exports (*export quota*). Our discussion in this section shows that the microeconomic effects of these quantitative restrictions are very similar to the effects of import and export taxes. However, our discussion also shows that there are some important differences between quantitative restrictions and trade taxes. Indeed, it is because of these differences that quantitative restrictions are often preferred to trade taxes.

Like trade taxes, quantitative restrictions are frequently used to protect domestic industries from foreign competition. However, both trade taxes and quantitative restrictions have important macroeconomic effects (which we will study in Chapter 19). Accordingly, quantitative restrictions and trade taxes may sometimes be used to correct a balance-of-payments disequilibrium or even raise the level of domestic employment.

Types of Import Quotas

A quantitative restriction on the imports of a particular commodity may be administered either through an *open quota* (also known as a *global quota*) or through import licenses. A global quota allows a specified amount of imports of a particular commodity per year (or some other time period) but does not specify where the product may come from or who is entitled to import it. As soon as the specified amount is actually imported, further imports into the country are prohibited for the rest of the time period.

The disadvantages of a global quota are obvious. Merchants (domestic importers and foreign exporters) rush to get their shipments into the country before the limit is reached. Those who are lucky enough to receive their goods in time enjoy abnormal profits—after the quota is filled, domestic prices rise because of the increased scarcity. Those who are late suffer losses—storage costs and even reshipment to the country of origin may be involved. Goods originating in distant places are discriminated against because of the longer transport time involved and the higher loss (the result of higher transport costs) in the event they arrive late. Also, large importing firms that are able to order sizable quantities on short notice (because of trade connections and good credit) have a distinct advantage over small importers. Finally, the rush to get commodities into the quota country as soon as possible may result in greater price fluctuation over the year, especially in the case of perishable goods.

To avoid the chaos of a global quota, governments usually issue import licenses, which they either sell to the importers at a competitive price (or simply for a fee) or just give away on a first-come, first-served basis. The licenses may or may not specify the source from which the commodity is to be procured. Unfortunately, *real* resources are used up as people compete for import licenses.

Equivalence between Import Taxes and Import Quotas

For every import quota there is an *equivalent import tax*. We can understand the various microeconomic effects of import quotas by exploiting this equivalence. As it turns out, partial equilibrium analysis is sufficient for this purpose.

Consider Figure 10-1, which illustrates the market for an imported commodity, such as steel. The domestic demand-for-imports schedule is given by DD', while the foreign supply-of-exports schedule is given by SS'. Under free-trade conditions, equilibrium occurs at E, where the domestic demand-for-imports schedule intersects the foreign supply-of-exports schedule. Under free-trade conditions the home economy imports 50,000 units (per month) at $12 per unit.

Suppose now that the authorities impose an import quota equal to 40,000 units (per month). This quota is *effective* because it is lower than the free-trade flow of imports (that is, 50,000). The import quota is represented in Figure 10-1 by vertical line QFH. Immediately after the imposition of the import quota, the price in the home market *rises* to $13 (see point F), while the price in the rest of

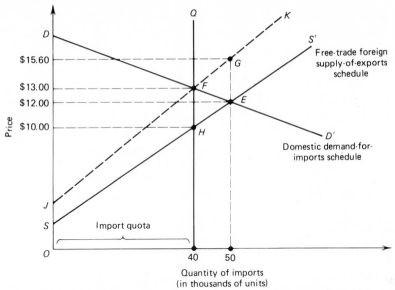

Figure 10-1　*Equivalence between an import quota and an import tax.*
Under free-trade conditions, equilibrium occurs at *E*, where the domestic demand-for-imports schedule intersects the foreign supply-of-exports schedule. Thus, the country imports 50,000 units at $12 per unit. A quota equal to 40,000, represented by vertical line *QFH*, raises the domestic price to $13 (see point *F*) and lowers the foreign price to $10 (see point *H*). A 30 percent import tax achieves the same results as the 40,000 import quota by causing the foreign supply-of-exports schedule to shift upward by 30 percent, as shown by broken line *JK*.

the world *falls* to $10 (see point *H*). Like an import tax, an import quota creates a wedge between the domestic price and the corresponding foreign price.

Evidently, the authorities can achieve the same results by imposing a 30 percent import tax. This causes the foreign supply-of-exports schedule to shift upward by 30 percent, as shown by broken line *JK*. Observe that the vertical distance *EG* (that is, $3.60) is 30 percent of the price at *E* (that is, $12), and the vertical distance *HF* (that is, $3) is 30 percent of the price at *H* (that is, $10). The same relationship holds, of course, for all points along the two schedules. After the imposition of the import tax, the volume of imports falls to 40,000, the domestic price rises to $13, and the foreign price falls to $10—exactly as in the case of the import quota.

We must therefore conclude that the microeconomic effects of an import quota (on domestic and foreign production, consumption, imports, exports, terms of trade, factor prices, and so on) are exactly the same as those of an equivalent import tax.

Differences between Import Quotas and Import Taxes

Even though the preceding discussion leads to the conclusion that the effects of an import quota are exactly the same as those of an equivalent tariff, there are still some important differences between quotas and tariffs.

One considerable difference lies with the *revenue effect*. In the case of the tariff, the government will collect $3 per unit of imports (that is, $3 × 40,000 = $120,000). In the case of the import quota, the outcome is not so certain. To implement the import quota, governments usually issue import licenses, which they either sell to the importers at a competitive price (or simply for a fee) or just give away on a first-come, first-served basis. *If* the license fee per unit of imports is actually determined (by competition or otherwise) to be $3, the import quota will bring into the government treasury the same amount of revenue as the equivalent tariff (that is, $120,000). In this case, the economic effects of the import quota are identical to those of the equivalent tariff, except for the insignificant difference that under an import quota the government revenue is called "license fees" and under an import tax "tariff revenue."

However, depending on how the licensing system actually works, the amount of $120,000 may accrue to the domestic importers, to consumers, to government officials (who may have to be bribed before they will issue the necessary licenses), or to the foreign exporters or even the foreign governments. For instance, if the domestic importers obtain the necessary licenses free of any fees and then organize themselves into a monopoly while the foreign exporters remain unorganized, the domestic importers are likely to get the profit. It is, of course, conceivable that the domestic government, through effective price-control measures, may prevent the importers from raising the price of imports to consumers; in that case all the profit may accrue to the consumers. On the other hand, if the foreign exporters are organized while the domestic importers are not, the profit may accrue to the foreign exporters. Finally, foreign governments may impose an equivalent export tax and collect all the revenue. When the revenue (or profit) actually accrues to the foreigners, the home economy becomes worse off.

Kindleberger (1975, pp. 8–9) emphasizes another important difference between an import quota and a tariff. Even though for every import quota there is always an equivalent tariff, the practical estimation of the equivalent tariff rate is not easy, because the supply and demand curves are not known in advance. Thus, an import quota appears to be a more *certain* measure than a tariff.

Moreover, under specific conditions a tariff may not work at all. For instance, when the goal of the government is to raise the domestic price of imports in order to protect the domestic producers, and in addition the foreign supply-of-exports schedule is perfectly inelastic (or very inelastic), the government must impose an import quota—no tariff can do the job. Return to Figure 10-1, and imagine that the foreign supply-of-exports schedule is given by the vertical dotted line through E. Further, suppose that the government wishes to raise the domestic price from $12 to $13. To accomplish its goal, the government must impose an import quota equal to 40,000 per period of time. Under the postulated circumstances, no tariff can affect the initial equilibrium at E. To be sure, a tariff will cause the vertical foreign supply schedule to shift upwards. Since it is vertical, however, the shift will change nothing, and the foreigners will merely absorb the import tax.

Kindleberger illustrates his point with a historical example. When the increase in the U.S. tariff diverted the 1929–1930 bumper Australian wheat crop to Europe, the French, who wanted higher wheat prices for French peasants, had to impose an import quota—no simple tariff could keep the Australian wheat out because of the inelastic supply of wheat from Australia to Europe once wheat was excluded from America.

A third important difference between an import quota and a tariff is this: An import quota may convert a potential into an actual monopoly, while a tariff cannot. In the presence of a tariff, even a monopolist cannot charge more than the world price plus the tariff. In the presence of a quota, however, most of the foreign competitive pressure is removed and the potential monopolist may become an actual monopolist by raising the price well above the world price plus the equivalent tariff.

Consider Figure 10-2, where the domestic industry of some imported commodity is a potential monopoly. The solid MC curve is the domestic monopolist's marginal cost curve. Similarly, the solid AR curve is the domestic demand schedule. The world price of this imported commodity is OP_w. Assume that the

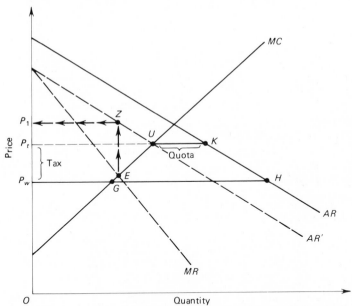

Figure 10-2 *Potential monopoly converted to actual monopoly under import quota.*
The foreign supply of exports is infinitely elastic at price OP_w. With free trade, the domestic consumers purchase a total of P_wH units. The domestic monopolist produces only P_wG (see point G, where the monopolist's marginal cost equals the world price), and the country imports the additional amount GH from abroad. With the imposition of a specific import tax equal to P_wP_t, the equilibrium price rises to OP_t, consumption falls to P_tK, imports fall to UK, and domestic production expands to P_tU. When the import tax is converted into a quota allowing only UK units of imports, the domestic monopolist reduces production to P_1Z (see point E, where the monopolist's marginal cost curve intersects broken marginal revenue curve MR), and raises price to OP_1.

foreign supply-of-exports schedule is infinitely elastic at OP_w. Before the domestic government interferes with either tariffs or quotas, the domestic price coincides with world price OP_w. Thus, the domestic consumers consume a total of P_wH units, with P_wG produced by the domestic potential monopolist and GH units imported from the rest of the world. When the government imposes a specific import tax of P_wP_t, the world price *inclusive of the import tax* becomes equal to OP_t. Consequently, the domestic price rises to OP_t. At this higher price, the domestic consumers reduce their consumption to P_tK units, while the potential monopolist raises production to P_tU units. As a result, imports fall to UK units.

Suppose now that the government converts the tariff into an import quota, allowing only UK units to be imported from the rest of the world. Displace demand schedule AR to the left by the amount of the import quota, as shown by broken curve AR'. This curve is now the relevant demand schedule for the domestic monopolist—at least for prices higher than the world prices. To determine the profit-maximizing output of the monopolist, draw the marginal revenue curve, as shown by broken curve MR. Profit maximization occurs at E, where the monopolist's marginal cost curve intersects the marginal revenue curve. To determine the monopoly price, move upwards to curve AR', as shown by the arrows from E to Z. Thus, the monopolist reduces output to P_1Z units and raises the price to OP_1. We therefore conclude that in this case the conversion of the tariff into a quota transforms the potential monopolist into an actual monopolist.

There are several other, perhaps less important, differences between import quotas and import taxes. First, when a quota is imposed, the equivalent ad valorem tariff rate tends to change with every shift in the foreign supply-of-exports schedule and the domestic demand-for-imports schedule. An ad valorem import tax, on the other hand, always remains constant (unless, of course, it is changed by the government). Similarly, when a tariff is imposed, the quantity of imports tends to change with every shift in the foreign supply-of-exports schedule and the domestic demand-for-imports schedule. Second, when a quota is imposed on an imported raw material (such as steel), it raises the costs of production of other final commodities (in whose production it is used as an input) and reduces their profitability on world markets, pretty much like a tariff on raw materials. But while the import taxes on raw materials are often returned to the producers of final goods in the form of export subsidies, no such subsidies are given in the case of quotas. Third, while the cost of a high tariff is quite visible from the consumer's point of view, the cost of a quota is not so visible, as the equivalent tariff rate is not easily calculated. Thus, while consumers may complain about tariffs, they may ignore quotas. Finally, quotas are much more difficult to administer than tariffs. Thus, the valuable import licenses are arbitrarily allocated among importers who may be willing to go so far as to bribe eager government officials. Quantitative restrictions tend to suspend the market mechanism and often carry the seeds of corruption and fraud.

Export Quotas

A nation may also exploit its monopoly power in foreign trade by controlling directly the volume (or value) of its exports. The government may decree that only a given quantity (export quota) may be exported per unit of time. For this purpose, the government may issue export licenses, which it either sells to the country's exporters or simply gives away on a first-come, first-served basis.

In general, an export quota causes the price of the restricted commodity to rise in the foreign markets and fall in the domestic market. An export quota tends to create a margin between the price at which the exporters in the restricting country are willing to sell the commodity and the price the foreign consumers are willing to pay for it. This margin may accrue to the government of the restricting country in the form of export-license fees. If the government of the restricting country does not charge a fee for the issue of export licenses, the "margin" may accrue to domestic producers, to intermediaries, to foreign consumers, or even to the government officials who issue the licenses.

As we saw earlier, for every import quota there is an equivalent import tax. The reader can easily show that for every export quota there is an equivalent export tax. Because of this equivalence between export quotas and export taxes, and because of the symmetry between export taxes and import taxes, it must be obvious that there exists also a symmetry between export and import quotas.

Voluntary Export Restraints

Voluntary export restraints are closely related to export and import quotas—the importing country (or countries) uses the threat of import taxes or import quotas to persuade foreign countries to "voluntarily" curtail their exports. This paradoxical situation usually combines elements of protectionist lobbying pressures with a desire on the part of the government of the importing country to conceal its protectionist intentions. For instance, since the 1950s the U.S. government has solicited the cooperation of foreign countries, particularly Japan, to voluntarily curb their exports to the United States of textiles, steel, and other commodities. Apparently, the U.S. government, which was under heavy lobbying pressure to protect domestic producers, ruled out the usual protectionist devices of import taxes and import quotas and instead sought voluntary export restraints, because of her role as the champion of free trade.

Voluntary export restraints are very inefficient. When implemented successfully, they have all the economic effects of import quotas except that the "tariff equivalent revenue" usually accrues to the foreigners. The foreign suppliers are likely to collude and charge a monopoly price instead of charging the competitive price that exists in world markets. Because of this, the effect of voluntary export restraints on the importing country's welfare is quite unfavorable.

10-4 INTERNATIONAL CARTELS

So far we have studied cases in which a single country restricts its foreign trade unilaterally in one way or another. Yet nations may also restrict their trade multilaterally. Governments, or even private corporations located in various countries, may form an international cartel, that is, agree to effectively restrict competition among themselves in an effort to exploit their joint monopoly power.

The world economy has a long history of international cartels in many goods and services, such as bauxite, coffee, diamonds, tobacco, and airline and railway services. The majority of cartels tend to disintegrate rapidly. The most notable exeption is the Organization of Petroleum Exporting Countries (OPEC), which since 1973 has maintained the most lucrative monopoly in world history.

This section deals briefly with the economic principles that govern such international monopolies.

Maximization of Monopoly Profits

The formation of an international cartel is in the first instance an attempt to reap greater profits. How can the cartel members maximize their aggregate profits? Merely by acting as a single profit-maximizing monopolist.

Figure 10-3 illustrates the maximization of the cartel's profits. Schedule SS' shows the willingness of the cartel members as a group to supply (or export) to the rest of the world alternative quantities of the cartelized commodity (such as oil) at alternative prices. As the reader may recall from a course in price theory, this supply schedule is nothing but the marginal cost curve of the cartel members as a group (that is, schedule SS' is the horizontal summation of the marginal cost curves of the cartel members).

Demand schedule DD' shows the willingness of the rest of the world to import alternative quantities from the cartel at alternative prices. Thus, demand schedule DD' shows, at each price, the excess of the total domestic consumption over the total domestic production (of the cartelized commodity) of all nonmember countries as a group.

Apparently, under perfect competition, international equilibrium occurs at point E, where demand schedule DD' intersects supply schedule SS'. Accordingly, under perfectly competitive conditions the cartel members as a group export to the rest of the world amount Q_1 at equilibrium price P_1.

Suppose now that the cartel acts like a single monopolist. Draw the marginal revenue curve, as shown by broken curve DJ, and let it intersect the cartel's marginal cost curve at F. To maximize profits, the cartel must curtail its exports to Q_0 and raise its price to P_2. (Monopoly output is determined by the intersection of the marginal cost curve and the marginal revenue curve, that is, point F; and the monopoly price is determined from the demand curve at the monopoly output, that is, point G).

Shaded triangular area FEJ shows the *increase* in the total profits of the

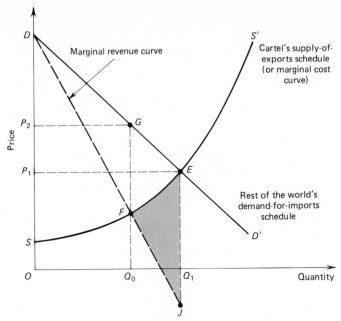

Figure 10-3 *Maximization of the cartel's profits.*
Perfect competition leads to equilibrium at *E*, where the cartel's supply-of-exports schedule intersects the rest of the world's demand-for-imports schedule. To maximize profits, the cartel reduces exports from Q_1 to Q_0 and raises its price from P_1 to P_2. In particular, the cartel determines its monopoly exports at the intersection (*F*) of its marginal cost curve (which coincides with the supply-of-exports schedule) and marginal revenue curve *DJ*. The total profits of the cartel increase by shaded triangular area *FEJ*.

cartel members as a group. Thus, at competitive equilibrium point *E*, the cartel's marginal cost (Q_1E) is much higher than the marginal revenue. (Actually, in Figure 10-3 the marginal revenue is negative at the perfectly competitive exports of Q_1.) In fact, marginal cost is higher than marginal revenue for all units between Q_1 and Q_0. By curtailing its exports, the cartel "saves" each unit's marginal cost but "loses" the marginal revenue. Since between Q_1 and Q_0 each unit's marginal cost is higher than its marginal revenue, it follows that the cartel's profits continue to increase by the difference between marginal cost and marginal revenue until the cartel reduces its output to Q_0. Shaded triangular area *FEJ* merely shows the total increase in profits that results from the reduction in exports from Q_1 to Q_0.

It must be clear from our analysis in Chapter 9 that monopoly pricing by an international cartel interferes with the objective of maximizing world efficiency and potential welfare. Monopoly pricing violates an important Pareto optimality condition, namely, the equality between marginal cost and price. Under monopoly pricing, the price is always higher than marginal cost, and this results in a suboptimal allocation of resources.

Note that the loss to the world is necessarily much bigger than the increase in the cartel's profits, that is, area *FEJ*. Resources would continue to be misallocated even if the cartel were to give back to the rest of the world the additional profits. Put differently, the rest of the world would be better off by making a direct income transfer to the cartel equal to area *FEJ* with the understanding that the cartel would return to the competitive equilibrium at *E*.

A Formula for the Cartel Markup[1]

Before we consider the conditions necessary for a successful international cartel, we derive an important formula that summarizes the economic factors which determine the optimal cartel markup.

A monopoly markup is defined as follows:

$$\text{Markup} = \frac{\text{price minus marginal cost}}{\text{price}} \tag{10-1}$$

For instance, if the monopoly price is \$10 and the marginal cost (of the last unit sold) is only \$2, the markup is 80 percent.

There is a close relationship between the markup and the elasticity of demand. As any price-theory textbook shows, the elasticity of demand is related to the price and the marginal revenue by the formula:

$$\text{Elasticity} = \frac{\text{price}}{\text{price minus marginal revenue}} \tag{10-2}$$

For instance, if the price is \$10 and the marginal revenue (which is always lower than the price) is only \$8, the elasticity is 5 (that is, $\frac{10}{10-8} = \frac{10}{2} = 5$).

Further, at the point where monopoly profits are maximized, marginal revenue equals marginal cost.[2] Combining the equality "marginal cost = marginal revenue" with equations (10-1) and (10-2), we finally obtain

$$\text{Markup} = \frac{1}{\text{elasticity}} \tag{10-3}$$

In other words, the monopoly markup is equal to the reciprocal of the elasticity of demand (in absolute terms). Thus, to achieve a high markup, the elasticity of demand must be low. For instance, when the elasticity of demand is 20, the markup is only 5 percent (that is, $1/20 = .05 = 5$ percent). On the other hand, when the elasticity of demand falls to 2, the markup increases to 50 percent (that is, $1/2 = .5 = 50$ percent).

---

[1] The reader may skip this subsection, as it is slightly more technical than the rest of this chapter.

[2] At the point where monopoly profits are maximized, the elasticity of demand is greater than unity (in absolute terms). This follows from equation (10-2) plus the fact that at the equilibrium point, price > marginal revenue = marginal cost > 0.

For an international cartel (such as OPEC), the relevant elasticity is, of course, the elasticity of demand for imports by the rest of the world (e_m). This elasticity (e_m) depends on the elasticity of the demand for total consumption by the rest of the world (e_c), the elasticity of supply by nonmember countries (e_s), and the cartel's share (k) of the total consumption of the cartelized commodity (such as oil), as summarized by the equation

$$e_m = \frac{e_c + (1 - k)e_s}{k} \tag{10-4}$$

How is equation (10-4) derived? First, note that the demand for imports by the rest of the world (M) equals the difference between total consumption (C) and total production (S) by the rest of the world; that is:

$$M = C - S \tag{10-5}$$

Further, any change in imports (ΔM), following a change in price (ΔP), must also reflect changes in total consumption (ΔC) and production (ΔS) by the rest of the world. More specifically:

$$\Delta M = \Delta C - \Delta S \tag{10-6}$$

Accordingly,

$$\frac{\Delta M}{\Delta P} = \frac{\Delta C}{\Delta P} - \frac{\Delta S}{\Delta P} \tag{10-7}$$

Now recall the following definitions of elasticities:

$$e_m = -\frac{\Delta M}{\Delta P} \cdot \frac{P}{M} \tag{10-8}$$

$$e_c = -\frac{\Delta C}{\Delta P} \cdot \frac{P}{C} \tag{10-9}$$

$$e_s = \frac{\Delta S}{\Delta P} \cdot \frac{P}{S} \tag{10-10}$$

(All demand elasticities—that is, e_m and e_c—are given in absolute terms, that is, as positive numbers.)

Substituting from equations (10-8) to (10-10) into equation (10-7) and simplifying, we obtain

$$M e_m = C e_c + S e_s$$

or

$$e_m = \frac{e_c + (S/C)e_s}{(M/C)} \tag{10-11}$$

Finally, note that the cartel's share (k) in total world consumption is defined by the equation

$$k = \frac{M}{C} \tag{10-12}$$

Substituting equation (10-12) into equation (10-11), keeping in mind that $S = C - M$, we obtain equation (10-4).

Given equations (10-3) and (10-4), we finally conclude that the cartel markup is given by the formula

$$\text{Cartel markup} = \frac{k}{e_c + (1 - k)e_s} \tag{10-13}$$

This last formula is important, because it summarizes for us the factors that determine the optimal cartel markup. Thus, a high markup requires a low demand elasticity for total consumption (e_c), a low supply elasticity by nonmembers (e_s), and a high cartel share (k) in the world market.

Conditions Necessary for a Successful Cartel

Economic theory identifies two conditions that are necessary for the success of an international cartel. They are:

1   The elasticity of demand for imports by the rest of the world must be low in the relevant price range.
2   The cartel members should adhere to the official set of policies (with respect to price and output) voted by the cartel members.

We will examine each of these conditions briefly.

The first condition is obvious from equation (10-3), which shows that the monopoly markup is equal to the reciprocal of the elasticity of demand for imports by the rest of the world at the monopoly price. To be able to achieve a substantial markup, the cartel must face a low elasticity of demand. This condition is actually a combination of the following three conditions:

1   The elasticity of demand for total consumption (*not* imports) by the rest of the world must be low.
2   The elasticity of supply of the cartelized commodity by the rest of the world (that is, nonmembers of the cartel) must also be low.
3   The cartel must control a very large share of the world market for the cartelized commodity.

The significance of these three conditions becomes obvious when we look at equation (10-13): A high cartel markup requires a low elasticity of demand for total world consumption (e_c), a low supply elasticity by nonmember countries (e_s), and a high cartel share (k) of the world market.

It is interesting to note that the above three conditions are satisfied in the case of OPEC and that this actually explains its success. OPEC controls over 50 percent of world crude-oil production, and in addition the rest of the world is unable, at least in the short run, to respond to high prices by increasing substantially its own production of oil. More importantly, however, in the short run there are no good substitutes for oil. The development of alternative energy sources, such as solar energy, is painfully slow. Of course, it is hoped that sooner or later the world will develop alternative energy sources, and perhaps much more efficient automobiles, and thus end its strong dependence on OPEC oil. In the meantime, however, the world is trying to learn how to live with an ever-rising cost of oil.

Turn now to condition 2. An international cartel can maintain a high monopoly price if individual cartel members do not selfishly attempt to capture more profits for themselves by behaving competitively. Each cartel member *does* face such a temptation. The reason is simple: At the monopoly equilibrium, the marginal cost (which presumably is the same for all cartel members) is much lower than the price. Hence, each individual cartel member has the illusion that he can increase his own profits by raising his *own* output—an illusion based on the naive assumption that other cartel members will not attempt to cheat in the same manner. When greedy cartel members behave in this manner, it becomes obvious that the cartel will not be able to effectively restrict output and raise the price. Experience shows that this is a most important reason for the eventual collapse of a cartel.

10-5 DUMPING

Dumping is international *price discrimination*. It takes place when a commodity is sold to foreign buyers at a price that is lower (net of transportation costs, tariffs, and so on) than the price charged domestic customers for the same (or a comparable) commodity.

As the reader may recall from a course in price theory, there is an important condition that is absolutely necessary for successful price discrimination: *The different markets must be separated from one another.* It should not be possible for traders to purchase from the monopolist commodities sold in the cheaper market and then resell them in the dearer market. Similarly, customers in the dearer market should not be able to transfer themselves into the cheaper market in order to benefit from the lower price.

The above condition is usually satisfied in international trade, as the domestic and foreign markets are separated from each other geographically and by tariff walls or other barriers to trade. Accordingly, the cost (transportation costs, tariffs, and so on) of transferring goods from the cheap, foreign market to the dearer, domestic market is usually prohibitive.

This section deals with the various forms of dumping and the economic policy problems that dumping raises.

Types of Dumping

Economists usually distinguish among three different types of dumping: *persistent dumping, predatory dumping,* and *sporadic dumping.*

Persistent dumping arises from the pursuit of maximum profits by a monopolist who realizes that the domestic and foreign markets are disconnected by transportation costs, tariffs, and other trade barriers. Because the elasticity of demand for a commodity is usually higher in the world market than in the domestic market (mainly because of the greater availability of substitutes in the world market relative to the domestic market), the monopolist maximizes profits by charging a higher price to domestic customers (where the demand elasticity is low) than to foreign buyers (where the demand elasticity is high). This proposition will be explained graphically in the next subsection.

Predatory dumping is usually classified as an "unfair method of competition" and the most harmful form of dumping. Predatory dumping occurs when a producer, in an effort to eliminate competitors and gain control of the foreign market, deliberately sells abroad at a reduced price for a short period of time. Assuming that this dumping practice is successful and that all competitors go out of business, the producer later exploits the newly acquired monopoly power by substantially raising the price. Thus, predatory dumping is only *temporary* price discrimination; the main objective of the producer is to maximize long-run profits by increasing his monopoly power, even though this may involve short-run losses.

Sporadic dumping is occasional price discrimination by a producer who happens to have an occasional surplus due to overproduction (presumably because of excess capacity or unanticipated changes in market conditions or just bad production planning). To avoid spoiling the domestic market, the producer sells the occasional surplus to foreign buyers at reduced prices. Thus, sporadic dumping is very similar to "going out of business" sales by domestic department stores.

It is interesting to note that export subsidies may be considered a form of (official) dumping, because they effectively lower the prices charged to foreign buyers. For this reason, GATT prohibits export subsidies with respect to manufactures, except when they happen to be rebates of indirect taxes, such as sales taxes or import taxes on raw materials, as we saw earlier in this chapter.

Further, because of the special status of agriculture, governments frequently practice dumping in order to dispose of accumulated surpluses of agricultural products. Thus, in an effort to support the domestic farmers, a government may institute a *price floor* well above the equilibrium price and purchase from the farmers, at the stipulated price floor, any quantity they cannot sell. Surely the government cannot sell any accumulated surplus to the domestic buyers, who buy all they want at the price floor from the farmers. The only viable option for the government is to sell the surplus to foreign buyers at reduced prices.

The Theory of Persistent Dumping

Figure 10-4 illustrates the theory of persistent dumping, that is, international price discrimination in the pursuit of maximum profits.

Panel (a) gives initially domestic demand schedule AR_d (or average revenue curve). From this demand schedule, we obtain the domestic marginal revenue curve, as shown by broken curve MR_d.

Panel (b) gives initially foreign demand schedule AR_f (or average revenue curve) from which we obtain the foreign marginal revenue curve, as shown by broken curve MR_f. By assumption, foreign demand schedule AR_f is much more elastic than domestic demand schedule AR_d in the relevant price range.

Panel (c) gives initially monopolist's marginal cost curve MC. In the absence of price discrimination, a monopolist maximizes profits by producing that output indicated by the intersection of the marginal cost and marginal revenue curves. Basically, the same principle applies for a discriminating monopolist, except that we must be careful with the meaning of marginal revenue. What is the discriminating monopolist's marginal revenue curve?

Profit is the difference between total revenue and total cost. To maximize profit, the monopolist must maximize total revenue and minimize total cost at

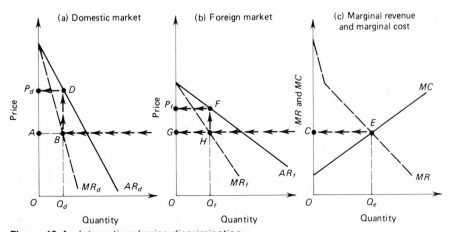

Figure 10-4 *International price discrimination.*
Panel (a) shows domestic average revenue schedule AR_d along with the corresponding marginal revenue curve, MR_d. Panel (b) shows foreign average revenue schedule AR_f along with its marginal revenue curve, MR_f. Panel (c) gives the monopolist's marginal cost curve, MC, plus the "total" marginal revenue curve, MR, which is the horizontal summation of MR_d and MR_f. The monopolist maximizes profits at point E in panel (c), where the marginal cost curve intersects the total marginal revenue curve. Thus, the monopolist produces Q_e units; Q_d units are sold to domestic buyers at price P_d, while Q_f units are sold to foreign buyers at the lower price of P_f.

every level of output and then select that output where the difference between total revenue and total cost is the greatest. To simplify the problem initially, suppose that the monopolist has a fixed amount of output to sell (and, therefore, the costs are fixed). How should the output be allocated between the two markets in order to maximize total revenue?

Apparently, the monopolist must allocate the fixed output between the domestic and foreign markets in such a way that *the marginal revenue of the last unit sold in the domestic market is equal to the marginal revenue of the last unit sold in the foreign market*. Otherwise, the total revenue can always be increased by transferring sales from the market in which the marginal revenue is low to the market in which the marginal revenue is high.

To solve the revenue maximization problem for all "fixed" amounts of output once and for all, add horizontally the domestic and foreign marginal revenue curves, as shown in panel (c) by broken curve MR. Given this total marginal revenue curve in panel (c), the monopolist can quickly discover the optimal allocation of any fixed output between the two markets. For instance, for fixed output Q_e, the monopolist determines from the total marginal revenue curve common marginal revenue Q_eE, which is then carried into panels (a) and (b), as shown by the arrows, to determine the optimal allocation of Q_d (domestic sales) and Q_f (foreign sales). Note that, by construction, the sum of distance AB (that is, Q_d) plus GH (that is, Q_f) equals distance CE (that is, Q_e). Note also that in this specific case the prices the monopolist must charge are P_d (domestic price) and P_f (foreign price), with $P_d > P_f$.

Consider now the general case in which production is also variable. We already know how the monopolist should allocate a fixed quantity. The question now is: How much should the monopolist produce in the first place? The answer is given in panel (c). To maximize profits, the monopolist must produce output Q_e indicated by intersection E of marginal cost curve MC and total marginal revenue curve MR. The sole purpose of panel (c) is to enable the monopolist to determine the optimal output. Once the monopolist knows how much has to be produced he or she can treat that amount as a fixed output and proceed, as above, to determine its optimal allocation between the two markets. As we have seen, the monopolist must sell Q_d units in the domestic market at the price P_d and Q_f units in the foreign market at the price P_f.

Note carefully that since the marginal revenue is the same in both markets at the optimal allocation, the price is necessarily higher in the market with the lower demand elasticity, which is usually the domestic market.

Economic Policy toward Dumping

Dumping, in all its forms, violates fundamental Pareto optimality conditions, and for this reason it is harmful to world welfare. On the one hand, a producer practicing dumping raises prices above the marginal cost (which is the basic evil of monopoly) and, on the other, charges different prices to different consumers.

Of course, sporadic dumping is only a temporary phenomenon, and economists tend to regard its (possible) effects on economic welfare as an insignificant nuisance. In fact, from the point of view of the importing country, sporadic dumping is not all that bad, since it provides benefits to the consumers (who temporarily pay lower prices) without causing any serious damage to the domestic industry.

Predatory dumping, on the other hand, may have serious consequences on the welfare of the importing country by driving domestic producers out of business and penalizing consumers (in the long run) with much higher prices. Indeed, predatory dumping is the most harmful form of dumping.

Persistent dumping lies between the extremes of sporadic dumping and predatory dumping insofar as its effects on the welfare of the world in general and on the welfare of the importing country in particular are concerned.

Unfortunately, in practice it is extremely difficult to distinguish among the three types of dumping. As a result, economic policy is usually directed toward all dumping.

At least in the short run, any kind of dumping benefits the consumers of the importing country. Indeed, excluding the case of predatory dumping, one could argue that dumping raises the potential welfare of the importing country. Yet importing countries typically retaliate against dumping either by imposing antidumping, or countervailing, duties to offset the price differential or by threatening to do so. The main justification for this is the immense pressure put on the governments of the importing countries by their domestic producers, who seek protection against the unfair foreign competition.

In the United States, antidumping legislation dates back to the Anti-Dumping Act of 1921. The 1974 Trade Act provides that the U.S. government may impose countervailing duties or other restrictions under two conditions: (1) The U.S. Treasury Department must first determine that an imported commodity is sold in the United States at a price which is lower than the price prevailing in the exporting country, and (2) the International Trade Commission must testify on the basis of an extensive investigation that American industry "is being or is likely to be *injured* or is prevented from being established" by reason of such imports (italics added).

During the turbulent 1970s, we experienced many cases of dumping. Japan was accused of dumping steel and television sets, and European automobile manufacturers were accused of dumping cars. Most of these dumpers eventually raised their prices in order to avoid countervailing duties. Nevertheless, countervailing duties were applied against several commodities, such as Brazilian handbags and Italian glass.

10-6 OTHER NONTARIFF BARRIERS

Nations may interfere with the free flow of trade in several other ways. These additional nontariff barriers include exchange control (used extensively by less developed countries), technical and administrative protection, and government procurement policies. Since we discuss exchange control in Chapter 19, we shall restrict our comments here to technical and administrative protection and government procurement policies.

Technical, Administrative, and Other Regulations

There are countless government rules and regulations that either intentionally or unintentionally impede the free flow of trade. Such technical and administrative rules include formalities of customs clearance, safety regulations (such as safety specifications for automobiles, tractors, and electrical equipment), health regulations (such as laws that provide for the production of food under hygienic conditions), labeling requirements (such as mark of origin), and technical standards. While many of these regulations serve legitimate objectives, they are frequently offered as an excuse for restricting trade.

Government Procurement Policies

Governments buy huge amounts of goods and services, and their procurement policies have a substantial effect on the free flow of trade. All governments tend to buy domestic products. This tendency was intensified in the 1930s under the slogans "Buy American," "Buy British," and "Buy French."

Under our Buy American Act of 1933, the U.S. government is required to favor domestic suppliers unless their prices are unreasonably high. But what is an "unreasonably high" price? Initially, a domestic price was considered unreasonable if it was higher than a corresponding foreign price by more than 6 percent. Since 1962 the price differential has been raised to 50 percent, at least for defense contracts. However, in December 1979 the United States (and other nations) formally signed the Tokyo Round trade liberalization agreement, which repealed "Buy American" laws.

Besides the desire to protect domestic producers, there are several reasons a government may want to do its shopping at home. In the first place, the government pays no tariffs. In the second place, for political and military reasons a government may just refuse to buy military equipment from a foe. Finally, for reasons of national prestige a government may prefer to use domestically produced commodities, such as automobiles and airplanes. In doing so, however, the government pays a higher price, which is economically inefficient.

10-7 HIGHLIGHTS OF U.S. TARIFF HISTORY AND TRADE LIBERALIZATION

Since the Great Depression of the 1930s, the nations of the world have made tremendous progress toward trade liberalization. This progress is fundamentally due to two factors: (1) the liberal mood of the United States embodied in the Reciprocal Trade Agreements Act of 1934 and later legislation and (2) the development, after World War II, of international organizations, such as the General Agreement on Tariffs and Trade (GATT), which have provided the institutional framework for multilateral negotiations. In this section, we review briefly some of the important developments in the formulation of commercial policy during the past four decades.

The Trade Agreements Act of 1934

During the early 1930s, U.S. exports fell sharply. There were two reasons for this. First, the total volume of world trade declined significantly because of the Great Depression. Second, the Smoot-Hawley Tariff Act of 1930 raised the average duty on imports to an all-time high (53 percent) and provoked foreign retaliation, which in turn caused a further reduction in U.S. exports. Accordingly, the U.S. relative share of world trade declined in the face of a dwindling absolute volume of world trade. Against this background, and in an effort to boost the sagging U.S. exports, the U.S. Congress passed in 1934 the Trade Agreements Act, which basically reflected the change in U.S. attitudes toward free trade. The principles embodied in the Trade Agreements Act have remained the basis of U.S. commercial policy in all subsequent legislation.

To begin with, the Trade Agreements Act of 1934 removed the formulation of U.S. commercial policy from the political atmosphere of the Congress and transferred it to the President. Further, the bill authorized the President to negotiate agreements with foreign nations to lower tariff rates as much as 50 percent of the rates set under the Smoot-Hawley Act.

The trade Agreements Act was founded on two important principles: First, any tariff reductions should be mutual; and second, the bilaterally agreed-upon tariff cuts should be extended to all trading partners—a provision that became known as the *most-favored-nation principle*.

The Trade Agreements Act of 1934 was repeatedly renewed (a total of 11 times), until it was finally replaced by the Trade Expansion Act of 1962 (see below). Under the authority of the Trade Agreements Act and its renewals, the United States achieved significant tariff reductions. By 1940 the United States had signed bilateral trade agreements with 20 foreign nations, and by 1947 the tariff rates that prevailed in 1934 had been cut in half.

Despite the apparent success of the Trade Agreements Act, it soon became evident that the trade liberalization process suffered from a severe drawback: Because of both the *bilateral approach* to tariff reductions and the most-favored-nation principle, there were in general too many third countries that benefited from the bilateral trade agreements between the United States and its partners. These free-rider countries were the beneficiaries of the lower tariff rates negotiated between the United States and its partners—without having to make any reciprocal concessions of their own. To avoid this drawback, the United States and its partners restricted their tariff concessions to commodities that typically dominated bilateral trade, so that only minor suppliers could benefit from the most-favored-nation rule. This severe constraint imposed by the bilateral approach was eventually removed as countries adopted the *multilateral approach* to tariff bargaining.

The General Agreement on Tariffs and Trade (GATT)

After World War II and against the background of the international upheaval of the 1930s, the trading nations of the world proposed (at the 1947–1948 UN Conference on Trade and Employment in Havana) the creation of an International Trade Organization (ITO) to promote international cooperation in trade, to settle disputes over commercial policy, and to move toward freer trade. The U.S. Congress, however, refused to ratify this proposal, and the International Trade Organization never became fact. As a substitute for the stillborn ITO, the trading nations negotiated successfully the formation of another organization, known as the General Agreement on Tariffs and Trade (GATT). This new organization (which is headquartered in Geneva, Switzerland) was created by an executive intergovernmental agreement that did not require congressional approval, as its authority emanated from the Trade Agreements Act of 1934 and later legislation.

Although GATT is not a comprehensive commercial policy code, it rests on three fundamental principles:

1 *The principle of nondiscrimination that is embodied in the unconditional most-favored-nation clause.* This principle is the cornerstone of GATT. Its significance is due to two factors: first, discrimination interferes with the efficient allocation of resources and the maximization of world welfare; and second, discrimination provokes retaliation. However, there are some important exceptions to most-favored-nation treatment: customs unions, free-trade areas, and preferential treatment for trade between a country and its colonies or dominions.

2 *The principle that countries must use tariffs rather than nontariff means (such as quotas) to protect their domestic industry.* There are, however, two important exceptions to this principle: first, countries may use quotas to protect their domestic agriculture; and second, countries may use nontariff measures (such as quotas and export subsidies) to deal with balance-of-payments difficulties.

3 *The principle of consultation in solving disputes among nations over commercial policy.* Indeed, GATT has provided the institutional framework within which the nations of the world have conducted important multilateral negotiations on tariff reductions.

Note also that GATT has special provisions for the less developed countries. Thus, on the one hand, the less developed countries receive preferential treatment by the industrial nations (which actually is a violation of the most-favored-nation principle), and on the other, they obtain all concessions exchanged among industrial nations without any reciprocity.

Under the aegis of GATT, nations have successfully negotiated significant tariff cuts during the postwar era. The first major tariff cut occurred in 1947; the average U.S. tariff dropped by about 20 percent. In each of the following four rounds of negotiations (1947–1962) there were small tariff reductions (4 percent or less).

Economists cite several factors for the meager tariff cuts at these multilateral negotiations. First, in 1947 many tariffs were abnormally high. After these high tariffs were negotiated down to normal levels, import-competing producers began to complain against further cuts, and governments became reluctant to bargain further significant cuts. This lobbying effort actually suited the purposes of governments that wanted to maintain some tariffs for future bargaining. Further, countries whose tariffs were already reduced to low levels could not induce foreigners to negotiate further cuts—they had very little to offer in exchange. Also, the formation of the Common Market in 1957 complicated matters further, as the members of the Common Market were reluctant to reduce their common external tariff on a product-by-product basis. Finally, the U.S. Congress attached restrictive provisions (escape clause and peril point provisions) to renewals of the Trade Agreements Act of 1934, which made it very difficult for the President to negotiate significant tariff reductions.

Escape Clause and Peril Point Provisions

As we have just seen, the trend toward trade liberalization that began in the 1930s was suppressed in the 1950s by the protectionist devices that the U.S. Congress tagged on to renewals of the Trade Agreements Act. These protectionist devices were of two types: general and specific. General protectionist devices were those which offered protection to all domestic inductries "injured" by import competition; they included the *escape clause* and the *peril point provisions,* which we discuss further below. Specific protectionist devices, on the other hand, were those which offered protection to particular industries, such as agriculture.

Incidentally, an important example of a specific protectionist device is the *national security clause,* which blocks action to reduce a duty and even permits withdrawal of concessions when the import-competing industry is essential to national defense. Nevertheless (as we may recall from Chapter 9), tariff protection is not the best policy for the achievement of a production goal, because it involves an unnecessary and costly distortion in consumption. The most efficient policy to achieve a production goal is a direct production subsidy to the affected industry.

Peril point provisions essentially prevented the President from negotiating reductions that could bring the U.S. tariff rates to such low levels as to cause serious damage to the domestic industry.

The escape clause went further than the peril point provisions. Thus, *after* the negotiations were concluded, the escape clause permitted any domestic industry that claimed injury from import competition to petition the U.S. Tariff Commission (now known as the International Trade Commission) for relief. In those cases in which the Tariff Commission determined that serious injury had occurred, it recommended to the President to raise the tariff again. (Actually, until 1962, domestic industries could claim serious injury on the basis of a shrinking market share alone, irrespective of whether their absolute volume of production had also *increased.*)

The escape clause dealt a devastating blow to the trade liberalization process. In essence, the escape clause was promising foreign nations no less than this: that no tariff concessions would be permitted to remain effective unless such concessions were considered to be insignificant.

The 1962 Trade Expansion Act and the Kennedy Round

Partly because of the no-injury doctrine that was embodied in the peril point provisions and the escape clause, and partly because of the formation of the Common Market, which created a new situation and posed a new negotiating challenge, the U.S. Congress passed in 1962 the Trade Expansion Act.

The Trade Expansion Act of 1962, which carved a new direction, had two important features:

1 It gave the President the authority to negotiate *across-the-board* tariff reductions of as much as 50 percent of their 1962 level. This across-the-board approach replaced the product-by-product approach of the Trade Agreements Act that was choking tariff negotiations.

2 It also launched, for the first time, an *adjustment assistance program* to relocate and retrain workers who became unemployed because of tariff concessions and to provide aid (such as low-interest loans, technical assistance, and tax relief) to eligible firms. The 1962 act recognized the superiority of direct adjustment assistance, over import restriction, to those workers and firms injured by increased imports. For this reason, it did not include any peril point provisions.

The principle of adjustment assistance is most significant. As we have seen, free trade improves the potential welfare of the world as well as the welfare of each trading country. However, free trade necessarily hurts some domestic groups, as the Stolper-Samuelson theorem reminds us, even though the welfare of the entire nation improves. In principle, those who gain from free trade can indeed compensate those who lose so that free trade can improve the welfare of everybody. Nevertheless, until 1962 such compensation was discussed as a theoretical possibility only. In actual practice, the losers had to swallow their pride and their losses and move along to other, more profitable ventures while the rest of the society enjoyed the benefits of free trade. No wonder, then, that there have always been groups which opposed free trade and lobbied for trade restriction. The main objective of the adjustment assistance program was to correct this anomaly.

The adjustment assistance program that was launched by the 1962 act did not become a success overnight, particularly because of the narrow eligibility criteria used by the Tariff Commission. Indeed, until 1969, nobody qualified for aid, and frustrated labor unions complained that the displaced workers had been betrayed. Fortunately, in the following years the eligibility criteria were relaxed, and adjustment assistance was provided generously.

Under the aegis of GATT and the authority of the 1962 Trade Expansion Act, the United States and other industrial nations negotiated wide-ranging tariff reductions in the Kennedy Round, which was completed in 1967. In particular, the industrial nations of the world agreed to cut their 1962 tariff rates an average of approximately 35 percent. Although this agreed-upon reduction fell short of the maximum reduction of 50 percent that was authorized by Congress, the Kennedy Round was justifiably considered to be a remarkable achievement.

The Trade Reform Act of 1974 and the Tokyo Round

The 1962 Trade Expansion Act was replaced in 1974 by the Trade Reform Act, which gave the President the authority to negotiate tariff reductions up to a maximum of 60 percent of the post–Kennedy Round rates (and to eliminate completely rates of 5 percent or less). In addition, the act authorized the President to negotiate the reduction of nontariff barriers—a major innovation.

Several other provisions of the 1974 act are also noteworthy. The new legislation liberalized considerably the eligibility criteria for adjustment assistance. Indeed, the 1974 act reaffirmed the superiority of adjustment assistance over trade restriction and did not include any peril point provisions. Further, it changed the antidumping provisions to conform with the rules of GATT. (Essentially, as was pointed out in Section 10-5, this means that countervailing duties can be imposed only after determining that the domestic producers have actually been injured by foreign price discrimination.) The act also authorized the President to extend most-favored-nation treatment to foreign countries that in 1974 did not enjoy such treatment (such as Communist China). Finally, the act offered a "Generalized System of Preferences" to "beneficiary" developing nations with respect to "eligible" products. In particular, it granted duty-free entry to the exports of developing countries with respect to manufactures, semimanufactures, and selected other products. However, the definitions of "beneficiary country" and particularly "eligible product" are quite restrictive. For instance, duty-free treatment cannot be given to textiles and apparel, watches, shoes, certain kinds of electronic products, steel, and glass products, nor to any other article subject to import-relief measures. Indeed, the act requires the withdrawal of preferential treatment from any article that becomes subject to import-relief or national security actions.

Under the authority of the Trade Reform Act of 1974, the United States participated in the Tokyo Round of multilateral trade negotiations. These negotiations, which were concluded in Geneva in April 1979, were conducted within the famework of GATT. (The Tokyo Round received its name from the fact that these negotiations were formally inaugurated in Tokyo in September 1973, even though the actual negotiations took place in Geneva.) The Tokyo Round negotiations were conducted on the basis of broad commodity categories rather than on a product-by-product basis. In December 1979, the United States, the European Common Market nations, Japan, and other countries (Austria, Argentina, Canada, Chile,[3] Finland, Hungary, New Zealand,

---

[3] Chile signed in October 1979.

Norway, Sweden and Switzerland) formally signed the agreement in Geneva. The agreed-upon measures are expected to affect more than $125 billion in annual world trade. The United States has agreed to an average tariff cut of about 31 percent, the European Economic Community to one of 27 percent, Japan to one of 28 percent, and Canada to one of 34 percent. Most of the cuts will be phased in over a period of eight years beginning January 1, 1980.

It may be noted that in the Tokyo Round every country, including the United States, took special care to protect certain "sensitive" industries from sharp tariff reductions. For example, U.S. tariff cuts on textiles, steel and some chemical products will not take place until January 1, 1982—two years later than the rest.

10-8 SUMMARY

1 To restrict the flow of their imports, nations may impose import duties or import quotas; to restrict the flow of their exports, nations may impose export duties or export quotas.

2 Trade subsidies are negative trade taxes, and their microeconomic effects are opposite to the corresponding effects of trade taxes. The terms-of-trade effect of export subsidies is generally unfavorable.

3 In a long-run, static-equilibrium model, a general export tax has the same effects as a general import tax of the same ad valorem percentage (Lerner's symmetry theorem). A similar symmetry exists between export and import subsidies as well as between export and import quotas.

4 A quantitative restriction on the imports of a commodity may be administered either through an open (or global) quota (with many disadvantages) or through the issue of import licenses.

5 For every import quota there is an equivalent import tax. The microeconomic effects of an import quota are the same as those of an equivalent import tax. However, there are important differences between quotas and tariffs: The quota profit need not accrue to the domestic government; an import quota is more certain than a tariff; when the foreign supply-of-exports schedule is perfectly inelastic, a tariff cannot raise the domestic price; and an import quota may convert a potential into an actual monopoly, while a tariff cannot.

6 Under a voluntary export restraint, the importing country solicits the cooperation of foreign countries to voluntarily curb their exports. The effect on the importing country's welfare is unfavorable—the "tariff equivalent revenue" usually accrues to the foreigners.

7 Two conditions are necessary for the success of an international cartel: (a) the elasticity of demand for imports by the rest of the world must be low; and (b) the cartel members should adhere to the official set of policies, that is, they should avoid cheating. Condition (a) is a combination of three conditions: (i) the demand elasticity for total consumption by the rest of the world must be low; (ii) the elasticity of supply by the rest of the world must be low; and (iii) the cartel must control a very large share of the world market.

8 Dumping is international price discrimination (that is, selling a commodity to foreign buyers at a price that is lower than the price charged to domestic customers). Dumping is possible because the foreign and domestic markets are separated from each other geographically and by tariff walls or other barriers to trade—the cost of transferring goods from the cheap, foreign market to the dearer, domestic market is prohibitive.

9 Dumping can be: (a) persistent (arising from the pursuit of maximum profits and from the fact that the foreign demand elasticity is higher than the domestic); (b) predatory (occurring when a producer sells abroad at reduced prices until control is gained of the foreign market, at which point the producer raises the price substantially); or (c) sporadic (occurring when a producer sells an occasional surplus to foreigners at reduced prices in order to avoid spoiling the domestic market).

10 Dumping violates Pareto optimality conditions and is harmful to world welfare. At least in the short run, however, dumping benefits the consumers of the importing countries. Yet importing countries typically retaliate against dumping because of the pressure put on them by domestic producers who seek protection.

11 Other nontariff barriers to trade include exchange control, technical and administrative protection, and government procurement policies.

12 The Trade Agreements Act of 1934 was founded on two principles: (a) tariff reductions should be mutual and (b) bilateral tariff reductions should be extended to all trading partners (most-favored-nation principle).

13 The General Agreement on Tariffs and Trade (GATT) rests on three principles (a) nondiscrimination, (b) consultation, and (c) use of tariffs rather than nontariff measures. [This last principle applies to a country's protecting its industry (except agriculture)—however, the country may use nontariff measures to cope with balance-of-payments difficulties.]

14 In the 1950s the U.S. Congress tagged on to renewals of the Trade Agreements Act two types of protectionist devices: (a) general (such as the escape clause and the peril point provisions) and (b) specific (such as protection to agriculture and the national security clause).

15 The Trade Expansion Act of 1962 (which replaced the Trade Agreements Act of 1934) had two features: (a) it gave the President the authority to negotiate across-the-board tariff reductions of as much as 50 percent of their 1962 level, and (b) it provided for adjustment assistance to workers and firms injured by increased imports (a major innovation). It did not include any peril point provisions. Under the aegis of GATT and the authority of the Trade Expansion Act, the United States negotiated with other industrial nations tariff cuts of 35 percent of the 1962 tariff rates (Kennedy Round).

16 The Trade Reform Act of 1974 (which replaced the Trade Expansion Act) gave the President the authority to negotiate: (a) tariff reductions of as much as 60 percent of the post–Kennedy Round rates and (b) the reduction of nontariff barriers (a major innovation). In addition, the 1974 act liberalized the eligibility criteria for adjustment assistance and did not include any peril point provisions. Under the authority of the Trade Reform Act, the United States participated in the Tokyo Round of multilateral trade negotiations.

SUGGESTED READING

Adams, W., et al. (1979). *Tariffs, Quotas and Trade: The Politics of Protectionism.* Institute for Contemporary Studies, San Francisco.

Baldwin, R. E., and J. D. Richardson (1974). *International Trade and Finance: Readings,* part 2. Little, Brown and Company, Boston.

Bhagwati, J. (1965). "On the Equivalence of Tariffs and Quotas." In R. E. Baldwin et al. (eds.). *Trade, Growth and the Balance of Payments: Essays in Honor of Gottfried Haberler.* Rand McNally & Company, Chicago.

Curzon, G. (1965). *Multilateral Commercial Diplomacy.* Michael Joseph, London.

Golt, S. (1978). *The GATT Negotiations 1973–79: The Closing Stage.* National Planning Association, Washington.

Kindleberger, C. P. (1975). "Quantity and Price, Especially in Financial Markets." *The Quarterly Review of Economics and Business* (Summer), pp. 7–19.

Kindleberger, C. P., and P. H. Lindert (1978). *International Economics,* 6th ed. Richard D. Irwin, Inc., Homewood, Ill., chaps. 8, and 10–12.

Lerner, A. P. (1936). "The Symmetry between Import and Export Taxes." *Economica,* vol. 3, no. 11 (August), pp. 306-313. Reprinted in R. E. Caves and H. G. Johnson (eds.). AEA *Readings in International Economics.* Richard D. Irwin, Inc., Homewood, Ill., 1968.

Meier, G. M. (1973). *Problems of Trade Policy.* Oxford University Press, New York.

Vernon, R. (ed.) (1976). *The Oil Crisis.* W. W. Norton and Company, Inc., New York.

Chapter Eleven

Customs Unions

Basically there are two approaches to international trade liberalization: the international approach and the regional approach. The international approach involves international conferences under the aegis of GATT, such as the Kennedy Round and the Tokyo Round. The purpose of these international conferences is to reduce tariffs and other nontariff barriers to international trade worldwide. The regional approach involves agreements among small numbers of nations whose purpose is to free trade among themselves while maintaining barriers to trade with the rest of the world. Such agreements include *preferential trading clubs, free-trade areas, customs unions, common markets,* and *economic unions.*

Even though the formation of preferential trading arrangements, as these agreements are collectively known, may be influenced more by political factors than by economic factors, such regional trading groups raise a number of interesting economic questions. Does the formation of regional trading groups represent a movement toward freer trade or greater protection? Do preferential trading arrangements enhance the economic efficiency and welfare of the world as a whole? Does the formation of a preferential trading arrangement benefit each participating country? Does the rest of the world lose?

This chapter deals with the partial-equilibrium approach to preferential trading, as the general-equilibrium approach is beyond the scope of the book. After defining the various types of preferential trading arrangements (Section 11-1) and explaining the general nature of preferential trading (Section 11-2), we consider briefly the main propositions of the theory of the second best (Section 11-3), which is directly applicable to the theory of preferential trading, and then inspect the theory of customs unions (Section 11-4). Section 11-5 provides a numerical illustration of the important concepts of trade creation and trade diversion. Section 11-6 generalizes the analysis by bringing together both the production and the consumption effects of customs unions. Section 11-7 examines briefly the so-called dynamic effects of customs unions, such as increased competition, stimulus to technical change, stimulus to investment, and economies of scale. Section 11-8 illustrates some of the practical problems that member countries face in the formation of customs unions, such as the determination of a common external tariff and the special regime for agriculture. Finally, Section 11-9 deals with the special problems that arise in relation to preferential trading among less developed countries.

11-1 PREFERENTIAL TRADING ARRANGEMENTS: SOME DEFINITIONS

Preferential trading arrangements may assume several forms. We can distinguish among five such arrangements: *preferential trading club, free-trade area, customs union, common market,* and *economic union.* In this section we explore the meaning of these forms of regional integration and introduce several terms that have come into fairly standard usage.

Preferential Trading Club

Two or more countries form a preferential trading club when they *reduce* their respective import duties on imports of all goods (except the services of capital) from each other; that is, when they exchange small tariff preferences. The member countries retain their original tariffs against the outside world.

In 1932, Great Britain and her Commonwealth associates, encompassing approximately one-fourth of the earth's land surface and population, established a system of trade known as the *Commonwealth Preference System.* Under it, the Commonwealth countries lowered their tariff rates on their mutual trade (that is, imports from other Commonwealth countries) but retained their higher tariff rates on imports from the rest of the world. The Commonwealth Preference System is a good historical example of a preferential trading club.

Free-Trade Area (or Association)

Two or more countries form a free-trade area, or a free-trade association, when they *abolish* all import duties (and all quantitative restrictions) on their mutual trade in all goods (except the services of capital) but retain their original tariffs against the rest of the world.

An example of a free-trade area is the European Free Trade Area (EFTA), originally consisting of the "Outer Seven": Austria, Denmark, Norway, Portugal, Sweden, Switzerland, and the United Kingdom. On July 1, 1977, when Denmark and the United Kingdom (as well as Ireland) joined the European Economic Community, the membership to the European Free Trade Area shrank to five. Headquartered in Geneva, EFTA is indeed a free-trade area. It has neither a common external tariff nor a common economic policy, and it does not participate in GATT negotiations as a single bargaining unit.

When a group of countries form a free-trade area by eliminating all import duties on their mutual trade but without establishing a common external tariff (on imports from the rest of the world), a *policing problem* arises: imports from the rest of the world may enter a high-duty member country through a low-duty member country, thus avoiding the high import duty. This phenomenon is known as "trade deflection."

For instance, consider three countries: A (home country), B (partner country), and C (representing the rest of the world). While trade between A and B is free, imports from C are subject to import duties. In particular, assume that country A levies a duty of, say, 60 percent on imports of commodity X from C. On the other hand, country B levies a duty of only 10 percent on such imports from C. Under these circumstances, there is a strong incentive to import commodity X into country A (high-duty member) through country B (low-duty member) and pay an import duty of only 10 percent, since trade between A and B is free.

To correct the problem of "trade deflection," member countries must be able to distinguish effectively (perhaps through a detailed examination of the certificates of origin as the commodities cross the national frontiers) between goods originating in the free-trade area and goods originating in the rest of the world. Actually, the problem is not that simple, as illustrated by the case of an outside producer who builds just a "final" assembly plant in the low-duty member country and then exports from that plant to the rest of the free-trade area.

Trade deflection also occurs in the case of preferential trading clubs, which do not have a common external tariff, either. However, because trade among the club members is not completely free—they exchange only *small* tariff preferences—the incentive to beat the system is not as strong as in the case of free-trade areas.

Customs Union

Two or more countries form a customs union when they abolish all import duties on their mutual trade in all goods (except the services of capital) and, in addition, adopt a common external tariff schedule on all imports of goods (except the services of capital) from the rest of the world.

A customs union is also a free-trade area, because trade among the member countries is free. On the other hand, a free-trade area need not be a customs union, because a free-trade area need not have a common external tariff.

Also note that the adoption of a common external tariff by a customs union eliminates the phenomenon of trade deflection together with the policing problem of intraunion trade of commodities originating in the rest of the world.

There are many historical examples of customs unions. For instance, in 1834 a large number of sovereign German states formed a customs union known as the Zollverein. (The Zollverein would prove significant in Bismarck's unification of Germany in 1870.) A more recent example is the European Economic Community (EEC), which was founded by the Treaty of Rome (signed in March 1957). The European Economic Community, also known as the Common Market, originally included six countries: Belgium, France, West Germany, Italy, Luxembourg, and the Netherlands. The membership has increased to 10 as Denmark, Ireland, and the United Kingdom joined the Community in 1977, and Greece in 1979.

Common Market

Two or more countries form a common market when they form a customs union and, in addition, allow free movement of all factors of production among them. Thus, the common-market countries abolish all trade restrictions on their mutual trade and also establish a common external tariff, as a customs union. Accordingly, a common market is also a customs union (and a free-trade area). However, a customs union need not be a common market, because the latter allows free movement of all factors of production (labor and capital) among the common-market countries. The European Economic Community is working toward the implementation of the concept of a common market.

Economic Union

An economic union is the most complete form of economic integration. Two or more countries form an economic union when they form a common market and, in addition, proceed to unify their fiscal, monetary, and socioeconomic policies.

An example of an economic union is the Benelux, which was the economic union formed by Belgium, the Netherlands, and Luxembourg. (The term *Benelux* is made up of the first letters of each country's name.) These three countries formed a customs union in 1948; this was converted into an economic union in 1960 (as a result of the 1958 Benelux Treaty). As we noted earlier, Belgium, the Netherlands, and Luxembourg became part of the European Economic Community, which is also moving gradually into an economic union.

The United States serves an an excellent example of an economic union. Fifty states are joined together in a complete economic union, with a common currency (which implies permanently fixed rates of exchange among the fifty states) and a single central bank (that is, the Federal Reserve System). Trade is free among the states, and both capital and labor move freely in pursuit of maximum returns. Fiscal and monetary policy, as well as international affairs, military expenditures, retirement and health programs, and so on, are pursued by the federal government. Other programs, such as education, police protection, and cultural affairs, are pursued by state and local governments, so that states can maintain their "identity" within the union.

An economic union is the ultimate form of economic integration. Whether the European Economic Community will eventually attain the status of an economic union remains to be seen. The obstacles are great. Unlike the United States, the European Economic Community consists of different sovereign nations with different languages, customs, and heritages. Nationalism runs deep in their peoples' minds, and memories of violent wars still prevent them from discarding their individual national identities and joining hands in the pursuit of a common goal.

Concluding Remarks

The preferential trading arrangements we have discussed in this section represent various degrees of economic integration. These trading arrangements start at the lowest degree of economic integration (that is, preferential trading club) and go through progressively higher stages to the most complete degree of economic integration (that is, economic union).

11-2 THE NATURE OF PREFERENTIAL TRADING

The theory of customs unions, which we discuss below, does not deal solely with the economic effects of customs unions narrowly defined. It deals also with the economic effects of free-trade areas, common markets, preferential trading clubs, and even economic unions. In short, the theory of customs unions deals with the economic effects of discriminatory systems in general.

We begin our discussion of the theory of customs unions by considering the general nature of preferential trading.

Commodity versus Country Discrimination

The standard theory of tariffs surveyed in Chapter 8 rests on the simplifying assumption that import duties are imposed in a nondiscriminatory fashion; that is, a uniform ad valorem tariff rate is levied on *all* imports irrespective of the imported commodity or the country of origin.

In practice, however, discrimination does occur. It takes one of two forms: (1) *commodity discrimination* or (2) *country* (or *geographical*) *discrimination*. Commodity discrimination occurs when different ad valorem import duties are levied on different commodities (for example, 20 percent on oil and 50 percent on cameras). Country discrimination, on the other hand, occurs when different ad valorem import duties are levied on the same commodity imported from different countries (for example, 10 percent on cameras imported from Germany and 60 percent on cameras imported from Japan).

Customs Unions as Country Discrimination

The theory of customs unions is a relatively new branch of the theory of tariffs and deals primarily with the effects of geographical discrimination. In particular, the theory of customs unions deals with the effects of preferential trading.

As we have seen, a group of countries may decide to form a preferential trading arrangement. This means that all member countries agree to lower (or eliminate) their respective tariff rates on imports from each other but not on imports from the rest of the world. Such reciprocal tariff reductions necessarily discriminate against imports from the rest of the world.

How is trade between the union members affected? How is trade between the union members and the rest of the world affected? How is the welfare of the member countries, individually and as a group, as well as the welfare of the rest of the world, affected by this geographical discrimination? All these are important questions, and we will discuss them in the rest of this chapter.

The Two Opposing Tendencies of a Customs Union

The pioneer in the theory of customs unions was Jacob Viner (1950). He put forth the major proposition that a customs union (or any other form of preferential trading) combines elements of freer trade with elements of greater protection, and he argued convincingly that it is not clear that such an arrangement increases (potential) welfare.

In particular, Viner argued that a customs union (or any other form of preferential trading) gives rise to two opposing tendencies. On the one hand, *a customs union tends to increase competition and trade among the union member countries,* and this represents a movement toward freer trade. On the other hand, *a customs union tends to provide relatively more protection against trade and competition from the rest of the world,* and this represents a movement toward greater protection.

It is interesting to note that in the field of customs unions, free traders and protectionists often agree with each other. This paradoxical agreement between the two opposing camps is actually the result of the strange coexistence of elements of freer trade with elements of greater protection, which we noted above. In their calculations, the free traders tend to exaggerate the elements of freer trade, while the protectionists tend to exaggerate the elements of greater protection.

Customs Unions and Pareto Optimality

The theory of customs unions is *not* concerned with the Pareto-optimum conditions, that is, the conditions which lead to maximum welfare. The formation of a customs union necessarily violates the Pareto-optimum conditions because of the existence of tariffs. In fact, the Pareto-optimum conditions are violated even before the formation of the customs union—tariffs exist before the customs union is formed. Accordingly, the theory of customs unions deals with nonoptimal situations, and it is therefore a special case of the *theory of the second best.* (The main propositions of the theory of the second best are reviewed briefly in Section 11-3).

Customs Unions and the Theory of the Second Best

The theory of the second best warns us that no general conditions can be specified under which the formation of a preferential trading arrangement leads always to an increase (or a decrease for that matter) in welfare. This makes the theory of customs unions relatively more difficult than other branches of economic theory. Every case must be analyzed on its own merits—the approach must be taxonomic. Such a taxonomic approach is, of course, very cumbersome, and it cannot be exhaustive. Our object in this chapter is to provide the necessary analytical framework within which any particular situation may be studied.

11-3 THE THEORY OF THE SECOND BEST: A DIGRESSION

The theory of the second best deals with suboptimal situations, that is, situations in which not all Pareto-optimum conditions are satisfied. The beginnings of this theory can be traced back to the pathbreaking book of Viner (1950). The theory was fully developed a few years later by James Meade (1955b). Shortly after Meade's contribution, Richard Lipsey and Kelvin Lancaster (1956) restated and generalized it.

What is the theory of the second best? Its main theorem is simple. Consider an economy that is prevented from fulfilling one Paretian condition. Then the other Paretian conditions, although still attainable, are in general no longer desirable. That is, when one Paretian condition cannot be fulfilled—and thus maximum welfare cannot be reached—maximization of *attainable* welfare requires in general the violation of the other Paretian conditions.

From the above general theorem follows a very important corollary. Consider an economy in a suboptimal situation in which several Paretian conditions are violated (because, say, of the existence of taxes). Suppose now that one or more, but not all, of the previously violated conditions were to be fulfilled (because, say, some of the initial taxes are now removed). Would welfare increase? One might be tempted to answer "yes," since such a change seems to bring the economy closer to Pareto optimality—more Pareto-optimum conditions are satisfied after than before the removal of some taxes. Yet the theory of the second best teaches us that such a conclusion is simply wrong. The precise effect on welfare depends on circumstances. When two suboptimal situations are compared, there are no general rules in judging which is better than the other.

Meade (1955b, p. 7) offers an illuminating analogy. He imagines a person who wishes to climb to the highest point on a range of hills. Not every step upward helps the person reach the summit, however. Walking uphill, the person can reach only the summit of the particular hill he or she happens to be on—not the summit of the highest hill. Similarly, while it may be possible to tell that an infinitesimal change in a tariff actually increases welfare (that is, a small step upward brings the person higher on the particular hill he or she happens to be on), there is no way of predicting that the elimination of tariffs on trade between the customs union members will actually increase welfare (that is, there is no way of predicting "in a dense fog and without elaborate instruments"—Meade's phrase—that when the person switches to another hill that he or she will actually be higher).

As noted in the preceding section, the theory of the second best is directly applicable to the theory of customs unions, since the latter theory, by definition, deals with suboptimal situations.

11-4 AN OUTLINE OF THE THEORY OF CUSTOMS UNONS

Before turning to a detailed analysis of the theory of customs unions, it is useful to consider a broad outline. The purpose of this section is to provide such an outline.

What are the effects of customs unions on the international allocation of resources? Does the formation of a customs union improve or worsen resource allocation and welfare? Before the publication of Viner's classic book, it was generally believed that the formation of a customs union was a step toward free trade and that it therefore tended to increase welfare. Viner showed that this view is not necessarily correct. In particular, Viner showed that the formation of a customs union combines elements of freer trade with elements of greater protection and may either improve or worsen resource allocation and welfare.

Viner's main tools of analysis were the concepts of *trade creation* and *trade diversion*. In particular, Viner demonstrated that the formation of a customs union may lead to either trade creation or trade diversion; but whereas trade creation is good and tends to increase welfare, trade diversion is bad and tends to decrease welfare. The final effect on welfare depends on which of these two opposing influences, trade creation or trade diversion, is stronger.

What do the terms *trade creation* and *trade diversion* mean? Even though the next two sections of this chapter clarify these concepts, it is not difficult to grasp their intuitive meaning. The formation of a customs union, such as the European Economic Community, normally shifts the national locus of production of some commodities. When the shift in the national locus of production of a certain commodity is such as to *create* some *new* trade, we say that the customs union gives rise to trade creation. On the other hand, when the shift in the national locus of production is such as to merely *divert* some *old* trade from one country to another, we say that the customs union gives rise to trade diversion.

For instance, consider the European Economic Community and suppose that before its formation France and Germany were self-sufficient in the production of commodity X. In particular, assume that before the formation of the Community, neither France nor Germany imported commodity X because of their existing high tariffs. However, suppose that after the formation of the Community and following the elimination of tariffs on intra-Community trade, France finds it cheaper to import commodity X from Germany, because presumably Germany is more efficient than France in the production of X. Accordingly, the national locus of production of commodity X shifts from the *higher*-cost French producers to the *lower*-cost German producers, and as a result *new* trade is generated between France and Germany. This is a case of trade creation.

Note carefully that trade creation improves the international allocation of resources by shifting the national locus of production from a high-cost producer to a low-cost producer. Thus, trade creation increases welfare by reducing costs or, alternatively, by increasing world income. It is in this sense that trade creation is conceived to be beneficial to welfare.

Turn now to an illustation of trade diversion. Suppose that before the formation of the European Economic Community, France imported commodity Y from the United States, presumably because the United States was the most efficient (lower-cost) producer of commodity Y in the world. Suppose further that after the formation of the Community and following the elimination of tariffs on intra-Community trade, France finds it cheaper to import commodity Y from Germany, because imports from Germany are duty-free. Thus, thanks to the newly formed geographical tariff discrimination, the national locus of production of commodity Y shifts from the *lower*-cost producer, that is, the United States, to the *higher*-cost producer, that is, Germany. France's imports of Y are diverted from the United States to Germany. This is clearly a case of trade diversion.

Again note carefully that trade diversion worsens the international allocation of resources by shifting the national locus of production from a low-cost producer (for example, the United States) to a high-cost producer (for example, Germany). Thus, trade diversion reduces welfare by increasing costs or, alternatively, by reducing world income. It is in this sense that trade diversion is detrimental to welfare.

In summary, the formation of a customs union causes some products that were formerly produced domestically (say, in France) to be imported from other partner countries (say, Germany)—the tariffs on such imports have been eliminated. Here the shift in production is from a higher-cost domestic producer to a lower-cost producer in a partner country: trade creation. But, in addition, the formation of a customs union causes some products that were formerly imported from the rest of the world (say, the United States) to be imported from a partner country, thanks to the newly formed geographical tariff discrimination. Here the shift in production is from a lower-cost producer in the rest of the world to a higher-cost producer in a partner country: trade diversion. The final effect on welfare is indeterminate. Welfare improves only when trade creation outweighs trade diversion. When trade diversion outweighs trade creation, welfare deteriorates. Indeed, one partner country may lose even though the other partner countries gain.

11-5 AN ILLUSTRATION OF TRADE CREATION AND TRADE DIVERSION

The concepts of trade creation and trade diversion are best illustrated by a numerical example. Consider three countries: A (home country), B (partner country), and C (representing the rest of the world). Suppose that each country produces commodity X at constant average cost, as shown in Table 11-1.

Under free-trade conditions, country C would export commodity X to both A and B ($30 < $40, $30 < $50). Suppose, however, that country A imposes a 100 percent uniform ad valorem tariff on all imports. While the cost of

Table 11-1   Trade Creation
(Average Cost of Production of Commodity X in Countries A,
B, and C; and A's Cost of Importing X from B and C)

Country	Average cost of production, $ (1)	A imposes a uniform 100% import duty, $ (2)	A removes the duty on imports from B but not from C, $ (3)
A	50	50	50
B	40	80	40
C	30	60	60

production of X in A remains at $50, the cost (inclusive of the tariff) of importing X from B and C increases to $80 and $60, respectively, as shown in column (2) of Table 11-1. Since $50 < $80 and $50 < $60, country A will produce commodity X domestically.

Now let countries A and B form a customs union and eliminate all import duties on imports from each other (but not on imports from C). The relevant costs to A are shown in column (3) of Table 11-1. Thus, A's domestic cost of production of importing X from B falls to $40 (since country A eliminates now the tariff on imports from B), and the cost of importing X from C (inclusive of the tariff) remains at $60. Obviously, after the formation of the customs union, country A ceases to produce X and imports it from country B (the other union member). This is an example of trade creation. That is, before the formation of the customs union, country A domestically produces X at $50. After the formation of the customs union, country A stops production of X and imports it from B. Since B's cost of production is lower than A's ($40 < $50), such a shift in the national locus of production represents trade creation and improves the allocation of resources.

Table 11-2 gives an example of trade diversion. The cost of production of commodity Y in the three countries is exactly the same as the cost of X in Table 11-1. The only difference from the preceding illustration is that A's initial import duty is 50 percent. Accordingly, before the formation of the customs

Table 11-2   Trade Diversion
(Average Cost of Production of Commodity Y in Countries A,
B, and C; and A's Cost of Importing Y from B and C)

Country	Average cost of production, $ (1)	A imposes a uniform 50% import duty, $ (2)	A removes the duty on imports from B but not from C, $ (3)
A	50	50	50
B	40	60	40
C	30	45	45

union, country A imports Y from C, since \$45 < \$50 < \$60 [see column (2)]. However, after the formation of the customs union, country A imports Y from B, since \$40 < \$45 < \$50 [see column (3)]. The shift in production is now from the low-cost producer, C (\$30), to the high-cost producer, B (\$40). This shift in production represents trade diversion and is detrimental to resource allocation and welfare.

In this illustration, higher protection is necessarily offered to B's high-cost producers. This is done not in the customary fashion of a reduction in B's imports of Y but rather through price discrimination in country A in B's favor. This type of protection offered to B's producers enables them to extend their sales to country A by replacing, unfortunately, a more efficient producer (C).

11-6 CONSUMPTION EFFECTS

Viner's innovative analysis of customs unions, as presented in Sections 11-4 and 11-5, deals only with the *production effects* of preferential trading. However, the formation of customs unions gives rise to *consumption effects* also. These consumption effects were emphasized by Meade (1955a), Lipsey (1957, 1960, 1970), and Gehrels (1956). In this section, we follow Johnson (1962) and bring together both the production and consumption effects of customs unions.

The Nature of the Consumption Effects

What is the nature of the consumption effects of customs unions? Return to the examples of trade creation and trade diversion given in Tables 11-1 and 11-2. In *both* cases, after country A removes its tariff on imports from B (but not from C), *the price paid by A's consumers falls*. In particular, in the trade-creation example of Table 11-1, the price of X falls from \$50 (A's domestic cost of X) to \$40 (B's average cost of X). Similarly, in the trade-diversion example of Table 11-2, the price of Y falls from \$45 (C's average cost of Y plus import duty) to \$40 (B's average cost of Y). Accordingly, unless A's demand for either X or Y is perfectly inelastic, *A's consumption of both X and Y must increase*. This resultant increase in consumption is actually the consumption effect of customs unions—an element overlooked by Viner.

In our discussion of the theory of customs unions, we must take into consideration this new (consumption) effect, since it tends to expand trade and improve welfare. We do this in the rest of this section.

Trade Creation Again

Figure 11-1 illustrates both the production and consumption effects of customs unions. Downward-sloping line DD' is A's demand schedule (for a certain commodity, say, X). Similarly, upward-sloping line SS' is A's domestic supply schedule (for X). To simplify our analysis, we assume that the supply schedule of B (that is, the partner) is infinitely elastic, as shown by horizontal line PP'. Adding A's tariff to B's supply schedule, we obtain horizontal schedule TT'. Thus, before the formation of the customs union (and assuming that C's average cost of production is higher than OP), country A consumes OQ_3, with

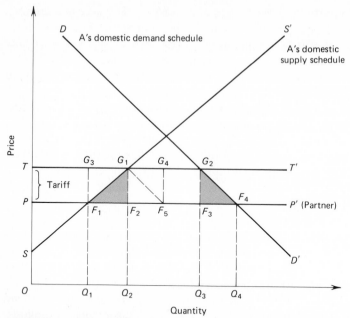

Figure 11-1 *Trade creation.*
Before the formation of the customs union, country A consumes OQ_3, with OQ_2 produced by A and Q_2Q_3 imported from B (partner). After the formation of the customs union between A and B and the elimination of A's tariff PT, A's consumption increases to OQ_4, A's domestic production falls to OQ_1, A's imports increase to Q_1Q_4, and A's tariff revenue $G_1F_2F_3G_2$ disappears. The net gain to A is represented by the areas of the two shaded triangles, $F_1F_2G_1$ and $F_3F_4G_2$. Triangle $F_1F_2G_1$ illustrates the production effect and triangle $F_3F_4G_2$ the consumption effect.

OQ_2 produced by A's domestic producers and Q_2Q_3 imported from B. The area of rectangle $G_1F_2F_3G_2$ gives A's tariff revenue.

What happens after the formation of the customs union and the elimination of A's tariff? A's consumption increases to OQ_4, A's domestic production falls to OQ_1, A's imports increase to Q_1Q_4, and A's tariff revenue disappears.

A's consumers benefit from the elimination of A's tariff. By how much? By area PF_4G_2T. But not all of this is net gain to country A. For one thing, area PF_1G_1T is a producers' surplus enjoyed by A's producers before the elimination of A's tariff, and it is now lost (to A's consumers). For another, the area of rectangle $G_1F_2F_3G_2$ represents the tariff revenue collected by A's government before the formation of the customs union. This tariff revenue is now lost. Accordingly, the net gain to country A is represented by the areas of the two shaded triangles, $F_1F_2G_1$ and $F_3F_4G_2$.

Shaded triangle $F_1F_2G_1$ represents A's saving of real cost on domestic production replaced by imports and illustrates Viner's *production effect* of a customs union leading to trade creation. Amount Q_1Q_2 was formerly produced domestically at a total cost given by area $Q_1Q_2G_1F_1$. This same amount (Q_1Q_2)

is now imported from a lower-cost country at a total cost given by area $Q_1Q_2F_2F_1$. Obviously, there is a net gain of $F_1F_2G_1$.

Similarly, shaded triangle $F_3F_4G_2$ represents a net gain in consumers' surplus. It is this *consumption* effect that Viner ignored. Meade (1955a) classifies this gain as something different from the production gain and in fact states that this gain is due to *trade expansion* (because it represents a *net* increase in A's consumption that is satisfied from imports and is not just a mere replacement in domestic consumption of goods formerly produced in A, as is the production gain.) Johnson (1962) adds the two triangles together to obtain the total gain from trade creation.

The total gain from trade creation, as represented in Figure 11-1 by the sum of the areas of the two shaded triangles, $F_1F_2G_1$ and $F_3F_4G_2$, depends on three parameters: (1) A's initial tariff (that is, distance PT), (2) A's supply elasticity at preunion production point G_1, and (3) A's demand elasticity at preunion consumption point G_2. In general, the higher the initial level of A's tariff and the more elastic A's domestic supply and demand curves, the larger the gain from trade creation.

Draw broken line G_1F_5 parallel to G_2F_4 (Figure 11-1). Then the sum of the two shaded triangles is equal to the area of triangle $F_1F_5G_1$, which is half the area of rectangle $F_1F_5G_4G_3$ (that is, the increase in imports times the tariff). This provides a convenient formula for empirical measurement of the trade-creation gains from the customs union. Actually, empirical estimates of this figure run extremely low—1 or 2 percent of the gross national product of the participating countries, sometimes even less. To understand why, assume that a country whose imports (M) are 30 percent of her gross national product (I) imposes a 40 percent tariff (t) on imports. Assume further that the foreign price of imports is p_m and, as the tariff is eliminated, imports increase by 50 percent. The total gain, given by the earlier formula, becomes: $(tp_m\Delta M)/2 = (0.4 \times 0.5Mp_m)/2 = (0.4 \times 0.5 \times 0.3I)/2 = 0.03I$. Thus, even with such an optimistic example, the total gain amounts to only 3 percent of gross national product.

Trade Diversion Again

Turn now to the case of trade diversion. Before the formation of the customs union, country A imports commodity Y from the relatively more efficient country C (representing the rest of the world). However, after the formation of the union, country A imports Y from its partner, country B, which, though less efficient than C, can sell Y to A's consumers cheaper than C, since A's tariff schedule discriminates aginst C.

Consider Figure 11-2, which illustrates the case of trade diversion. As before, lines DD' and SS' represent A's domestic demand and supply schedules, respectively. Similarly, horizontal lines BB' and CC' represent the infinitely elastic supply schedules (*before* the addition of A's tariff) of countries B and C, respectively. By assumption, C's average cost of production (OC) is lower than B's (OB). Adding A's tariff to C's supply schedule CC', we obtain

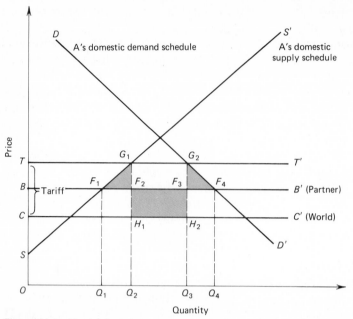

Figure 11-2 *Trade diversion.*
Before the formation of the customs union, country A consumes OQ_3, of which OQ_2 is produced domestically and Q_2Q_3 is imported from C (representing the rest of the world). After the formation of the customs union and the elimination of A's tariff on imports from B, A diverts its purchases from C to B (because $OB < OT$). A's consumption increases to OQ_4, A's production decreases to OQ_1, A's imports increase to Q_1Q_4, and A's tariff revenue $G_1H_1H_2G_2$ vanishes. The two shaded triangles, $F_1F_2G_1$ and $F_3F_4G_2$, represent gain. Shaded rectangle $F_2H_1H_2F_3$ represents the loss from diverting the initial amount of imports Q_2Q_3 from a lower-cost source (C) to a higher-cost source (B).

schedule TT'. (B's supply schedule, including the tariff, is not needed. Why not?) Before the formation of the customs union, country A consumes OQ_3, of which OQ_2 is produced domestically by A's producers and Q_2Q_3 is imported from C. A's tariff revenue is given by area $G_1H_1H_2G_2$.

After the formation of the customs union and the elimination of A's tariff on imports from B, country A finds it cheaper to import Y from B ($OB < OT$). Thus, A's consumption increases to OQ_4, A's domestic production decreases to OQ_1, A's imports increase to Q_1Q_4 (that is, A's imports increase by the decrease in domestic production, Q_1Q_2, plus the increase in domestic consumption, Q_3Q_4), and A's tariff revenue vanishes. The consumers' surplus increases again by area TBF_4G_2. On the other hand, the producers' surplus decreases by area TBF_1G_1.

Divide A's tariff-revenue loss (that is, area $G_1H_1H_2G_2$) into two parts: $G_1F_2F_3G_2 + F_2H_1H_2F_3$. Subtract the loss of producers' surplus (that is, area TBF_1G_1) as well as the first part of the tariff-revenue loss (that is, area $G_1F_2F_3G_2$) from the gain of consumers' surplus (that is, area TBF_4G_2) to obtain the two shaded triangles, $F_1F_2G_1$ and $F_3F_4G_2$. The sum of these two shaded triangles represents a gain that we must compare with the remaining loss of the second part of the tariff revenue (that is, shaded area $F_2H_1H_2F_3$). If the sum of the two shaded triangles (that is, $F_1F_2G_1 + F_3F_4G_2$) is larger than shaded rectangle $F_2H_1H_2F_3$, then trade diversion actually results in a net social gain. On the other hand, if $F_1F_2G_1 + F_3F_4G_2 < F_2H_1H_2F_3$, trade diversion results in a net social loss.

What is the meaning of triangles $F_1F_2G_1$ and $F_3F_4G_2$ and of rectangle $F_2H_1H_2F_3$? Well, rectangle $F_2H_1H_2F_3$ represents the net loss from diverting the *initial* amount of imports (Q_2Q_3) from a lower-cost source (country C) to a higher-cost source (country B). This is primarily the detrimental effect of trade diversion referred to by Viner. But as we have just seen, this is not the only effect. There are two beneficial effects represented by triangles $F_1F_2G_1$ and $F_3F_4G_2$. Triangle $F_1F_2G_1$ represents a *production gain*, while triangle $F_3F_4G_2$ represents a *consumption gain*. In particular, triangle $F_1F_2G_1$ represents the net reduction of social cost that results from shifting the locus of production of the amount Q_1Q_2 from country A, where its total cost is given by area $F_1Q_1Q_2G_1$, to country B, where its total cost is given by area $F_1Q_1Q_2F_2$. Similarly, triangle $F_3F_4G_2$ represents the net increase in consumers' surplus brought about by the increase in A's consumption by Q_3Q_4. (Recall that country B produces amount Q_3Q_4 at a total cost given by area $F_3Q_3Q_4F_4$.)

Trade-Diverting Customs Unions and Welfare Improvement[1]

Implicit in the preceding analysis is the notion that trade diversion need not have a net detrimental effect on welfare, contrary to Viner's original view. Thus, turning again to Figure 11-2, if the sum of the two shaded triangles (that is, $F_1F_2G_1 + F_3F_4G_2$) is larger than the area of shaded rectangle $F_2H_1H_2F_3$, then trade diversion actually results in a net social gain. Indeed, many economists have attempted to show that a trade-diverting customs union may increase welfare. This is not the place to review the literature on this puzzle. We only wish to point out that the dispute over the possibility that, or the conditions under which, a trade-diverting customs union may increase welfare is a sham dispute—a semantic problem.

The problem arises from a definition of trade diversion that includes, on the one hand, diversion of *initial* trade from a lower-cost source (country C) to a higher-cost source (partner country B) and, on the other hand, creation of *new* trade between the home country (A) and the partner country (B), resulting both from the adjustment in A's consumption and from the replacement of A's domestic production by B's production. Analytically, these two elements must be kept apart.

The diversion of *initial* trade from a lower-cost source to a higher-cost source is called *pure trade diversion*. On the other hand, the creation of *new* trade between the home country and the partner country must be considered as *trade creation and must be added to the trade creation proper*. Once this is

---

[1] The reader may omit this subsection.

done, we can always say that trade creation is a "good thing" (that is, welfare increasing) and trade diversion a "bad thing" (that is, welfare reducing) with the net effect of the customs union depending on which of these two effects (properly defined) is stronger.

If the above reconciliation is accepted, we can return to Figure 11-2 and claim that the sum of the areas of the two shaded triangles, $F_1F_2G_1$ and $F_3F_4G_2$, is actually trade creation, and that only rectangle $F_2H_1H_2F_3$ represents trade diversion.

Some Limitations

The preceding analysis concentrated on the effects of a customs union on a single commodity. But the formation of a customs union will, in general, affect many commodities. When many commodities are introduced, various secondary repercussions must be added to the analysis. Thus, various degrees of complementarity and substitutability will exist on the demand side. On the supply side, costs need not be constant.

The preceding analysis also assumes implicitly that the increase in imports (following the formation of a customs union) is matched by a corresponding increase in exports at the given terms of trade so that trade remains balanced. This need not be the case, however. In general, the terms of trade will have to change also to reestablish the balance between exports and imports.

These limitations of the partial-equilibrium approach to the theory of customs unions point to the need for a general-equilibrium analysis. However, a general-equilibrium analysis is beyond the scope of this book. The interested reader may consult M. Chacholiades (1978), Chapter 23.

11-7 DYNAMIC EFFECTS OF CUSTOMS UNIONS

Besides the static effects of trade creation and trade diversion, whose magnitude, as we have seen, is no more than a negligible percentage of the national income of the participating countries, customs unions have some interesting *dynamic effects,* such as increased competition, stimulus to technical change, stimulus to investment, and economies of scale. These so-called dynamic effects do not lend themselves easily to systematic analysis. As a result, widespread disagreement and controversy surrounds them. We will discuss these effects briefly. For more information, the reader is referred to Balassa (1961), Corden (1972), and Scitovsky (1958).

Increased Competition

Competition in this context does not mean many firms selling a homogeneous product. Rather, it refers to the ability and willingness of producers to encroach upon each other's markets. Scitovsky (1958, pp. 19–48) argued that increased competition was very significant in the European Economic Community.

As tariffs are removed and the market expands, the number of potential competitors increases. Monopolistic and oligopolistic market structures become exposed to outside pressures. Inefficient firms must either become efficient or close down. Competition becomes less personal and more effective and leads to research and development of new products.

Technical Change

To repeat, the enlargement of the market leads to increased competition, and this in turn stimulates research and development. This creates a climate that is conducive to increased technical change and faster economic growth.

Investment

The increase in competition and technical change leads to additional investment, which is necessary in order to take advantage of the newly created opportunities. To be sure, certain import-competing industries are hard hit by the extra competition from more efficient producers located in other union countries. In these industries, a certain amount of disinvestment must be expected. This disinvestment must be subtracted from the positive investment activity in other flourishing industries in order to determine the net effect on investment. The latter is very hard to estimate.

Some union countries may also experience an increase in investment from the rest of the world. Thus, existing foreign firms in the union may expand or regroup in order to take advantage of the newly created opportunities. In addition, foreign firms, which in the past used to serve the union countries by exports, may now decide to build plants in the union countries—after all, as we saw earlier in the discussion of trade diversion, these foreign producers are discriminated against after the formation of the customs union. This actually may have been the reason for the massive American investment in Europe after 1955, although there are those who believe that this phenomenon was due to a sudden awareness on the part of American corporations of the existence of a growing, vigorous market from which they did not wish to be excluded.

Economies of Scale

We briefly discussed the phenomenon of economies of scale in Chapter 4. Here it is sufficient to note that the creation of a large market leads to a greater degree of specialization, which results in a reduction in costs for several reasons: fuller utilization of plant capacity, learning by doing, and development of a pool of skilled labor and management.

It has been argued that a great advantage of the U.S. economy is its huge internal market, which facilitates the exploitation of economies of scale. Nevertheless, critics observe that, on the one hand, many small companies are efficient, while at the same time some large ones are sluggish; and, on the other, countries with relatively small internal markets, like Sweden and Switzerland, have highly efficient industries and are very affluent.

Economies of scale are particularly important to the less developed countries. (See Section 11-9.)

11-8 OTHER PROBLEMS OF CUSTOMS UNIONS

The actual formation of a customs union usually faces enormous difficulties. This section illustrates these difficulties by discussing briefly the determination of the common external tariff and the special regime for agriculture.

The Common External Tariff[2]

The determination of a common external tariff by a customs union is not always an easy matter. Aside from the real problem of arriving at a common tariff nomenclature, the union members must also reach agreement on the height of the common tariff as well as the distribution of the tariff proceeds among the member countries.

In the case of the European Economic Community, the Treaty of Rome set the common external tariff equal to the arithmetical average of the import duties of the member nations—a procedure that was consistent with the rules of GATT. Initially, this simple average of members' duties resulted in lower tariffs for France and Italy but higher tariffs for Germany and the Benelux countries.

The simple arithmetical average of the import duties of the member nations is not the only way to determine the common external tariff. Perhaps a better approach would be to take a weighted average. But what weights should be used? If the existing import duties are weighted by the *actual* volume of trade, the resultant average would be rather biased—the higher the import duty, the lower the volume of imports and hence its weight. In the extreme case of a prohibitive tariff, its weight would be zero, which is ludicrous. Conceivably, the *free-trade* volume of trade may generate a much better system of weights. Yet the free-trade weights are not available—at least not before the union members complete an enormous amount of econometric work to estimate elasticities.

Turn now to the question of distributing of the tariff proceeds among the member countries. How should this be done? Perhaps the simplest solution would be to allow each member country to keep all tariff proceeds it collects as goods (shipped from the rest of the world to the customs union) cross its borders. Yet this is not necessarily an equitable system. A union member's imports from the rest of the world may have to enter through another member's customs first, such as Germany's imports, which arrive through either the Netherlands or Italy. A more equitable system would be to distribute the tariff proceeds on the basis of the country that actually consumes the imported goods from the rest of the world. Unfortunately, tracing imported goods to the country of consumption requires a prohibitive bureaucratic machinery.

Because the solution to the above problems is vital to the welfare of each member country, negotiations tend to last for a long time. Each individual

---

[2] This subsection is influenced by Kindleberger and Lindert (1978), Chapter 9.

country's objective in these negotiations is to maximize its own share of the net welfare gains.

Common Agricultural Policy

Without question, one of the most difficult problems in the formation of the European Economic Community has been the establishiment of a common agricultural policy. Because the national agricultural programs of the original Community members were markedly different from each other, agreement on a common agricultural policy was not easy to achieve.

Eventually, the European Economic Community adopted a unique system known as the *variable levy* (*prélèvement*). The basic idea of the system is simple. First, the Community determines in advance the desired internal price (for each agricultural product) that it wishes to maintain. This support price, known as the *target price* (*prix indicatif*), determines the level of internal consumption and production and, therefore, the volume of imports of each commodity. Second, the Community imposes a sliding tariff (or variable levy) equal to the difference between the (lowest) price on the world market and the target price. Any change in the world price, or the target price, gives rise to a corresponding change in the variable levy. Apparently, the variable levy shifts the entire burden of adjustment to variations in the Community's consumption and production on third-country suppliers. In addition, the variable levy discourages foreign countries from subsidizing their exports and foreign producers from absorbing part of the import duty in order to maintain (or increase) their sales.

Agreement on the system of the variable levy was relatively easy. Agreement on the desired levels of the support prices, however, proved much more difficult. Indeed, a direct conflict arose between France and West Germany. In particular, West Germany, which is relatively inefficient in the production of wheat, demanded a high support price for wheat, especially because German farmers were politically powerful. On the other hand, France, with a more efficient agricultural sector, demanded a lower support price for wheat. Eventually, the Community reached agreement on a support price between the two extremes.

The common agricultural policy was also a major obstacle in Britain's entry into the European Economic Community. Britain supported its agricultural sector with direct subsidies to the British farmers. Essentially, the British system, known as a "deficiency payment" system, allowed supply and demand conditions to determine their food prices. For this reason, the food prices the British consumers paid, as well as the British agricultural incomes, were generally low. The British then made up the "deficiency" in agricultural incomes by means of direct cash payments to their farmers. Britains's entry into the European Economic Community and the acceptance of the Community's price support system in lieu of their own deficiency payment system generated a sharp rise in the cost of living in Britain. Ironically, the large increase in the price of foodstuffs essentially subsidized French, West German, and Italian farmers.

Incidentally, note that the deficiency payment system is superior to the price support system for various reasons. First, the deficiency payment system does not generate any unwanted surplus production. Second, the deficiency payment system keeps the prices low for consumers. Finally, the deficiency payment system makes public the total cost of this form of aid. Thus, the system is continuously under budgetary control and public scrutiny.

11-9 PREFERENTIAL TRADING AMONG LESS DEVELOPED ECONOMIES

Among the less developed countries there exists an understandable desire to accelerate the pace of their economic development and to raise their standards of living. To achieve this goal, the less developed countries often pursue a policy known as import-substituting industrialization. As we saw in Chapter 7, though, this policy often means heavy losses to the countries involved, as excessive import-substituting industrialization goes against the law of comparative advantage and generates economic inefficiency.

An important economic factor that may account for the failure of import-substituting industrialization in many less developed countries is the small size of national markets. Less developed countries suffer from low per capita incomes. In addition, the populations of many of these countries are very small. For these reasons, each individual less developed country is not able to support efficient industries. A modern industry must serve a large market in order to achieve economies of scale and become efficient and viable in the long run.

To overcome the obstacle of their small national markets, the less developed countries often resort to regional integration. For instance, suppose that each of five countries, such as Costa Rica, El Salvador, Guatemala, Honduras, and Nicaragua, are too small to support five modern industries, say X_1, X_2, X_3, X_4, and X_5. These five countries could form a customs union and agree to assign only one industry to each country. For example, they could assign industry X_1 to Costa Rica, industry X_2 to El Salvador, industry X_3 to Guatemala, industry X_4 to Honduras and industry X_5 to Nicaragua. In this way, each individual country could develop an efficient industry to serve all five countries—a much larger market than any of the five national markets.

Actually, the above five countries did establish in 1960 the Central American Common Market (CACM); and customs unions and free-trade areas among less developed countries have been established in various parts of the world. For instance, the Latin American Free Trade Association (LAFTA) was established in 1960; the Caribbean Free Trade Association (CARIFTA) was formed in 1968 and transformed in 1973 into a common market (CARICOM); the East African Community was established in 1967; the Customs and Economic Union of Central Africa was organized in 1966; and the Economic Community of West Africa was formed in 1974.

Note carefully that the trend toward regional integration among less developed economies is the result of their realizing that they cannot succeed in their efforts to industrialize unless they achieve economies of scale, which requires large markets. Thus, their interest does not lie in trade creation. Indeed, these countries seem to be more interested in trade diversion! In other words, because of their interest in enlarging the size of their markets, the less developed countries are actually interested in diverting at least part of their purchases from the industrial nations to their partner countries. After all, the labor that goes into the trade-diverting activities is seldom withdrawn from other useful activities. More often than not, such labor is drawn from the ranks of the unemployed or underemployed, and its opportunity cost is very low, near zero.

Unfortunately, regional integration has not been very successful. Various reasons are responsible for this fact. First, there are political difficulties. Governments, especially those of newly founded nations, are not eager to sacrifice their freedom, sovereignty, and autonomy. Second, there is the problem of transportation. Despite their geographical proximity, the less developed economies lack adequate transportation facilities necessary for making the enlarged market meaningful. The lack of adequate transportation facilities, plus the fact that their overall market remains actually small even after integration, limits the scope of economies of scale as well as the scope of competition. Third, as Kindleberger and Lindert (1978, p. 184) point out, there is always the apprehension among the relatively poorer countries that the relatively more advanced countries of the group may eventually dominate the entire customs union. That is, the relatively poorer countries feel that once they open their doors to their partners, they will never be able to build their own industry. To cope with this problem, several customs unions, such as the Central American Common Market, tried, with very limited success, the approach of industrial planning. This involves the assignment of certain industries to certain countries. But while each country may be happy with its own monopoly, some countries may not resist the temptation to encroach upon the other countries' monopolies. This is actually what happened with the Central American Common Market, where industrial planning broke down even before the outbreak of the dismal "soccer war" between Honduras and El Salvador in 1969.

In conclusion, it may be fair to say that if the less developed countries are determined to industrialize irrespective of the social cost, industrialization through regional integration should be preferred where feasible. The reason is simple: Regional integration can support larger and more efficient production units.

11-10 SUMMARY

1 The theory of customs unions deals with the economic effects of preferential trading arrangements, such as preferential trading clubs, free-trade areas, customs unions, common markets, and economic unions.

2 While the members of preferential trading clubs exchange small tariff preferences, the members of a free-trade area abolish all import duties on their mutual trade.

3   A customs union is a free-trade area with a common external tariff schedule. The union members must agree on both the height of the common tariff and the distribution of the tariff proceeds.

4   Unlike customs unions, preferential trading clubs and free-trade areas do not have a common external tariff. For this reason, a policing problem arises: Imports from the rest of the world may enter a high-duty member country through a low-duty member country (trade deflection).

5   A common market is a customs union whose members allow, in addition, free movement of all factors of production among them.

6   An economic union is a common market whose members unify their fiscal, monetary, and socioeconomic policies.

7   A preferential trading arrangement gives rise to two opposing tendencies: (a) it increases competition and trade among the member countries (movement toward freer trade), and (b) it increases protection against trade and competition from the rest of the world (movement toward greater protection).

8   The theory of customs unions is a special case of the theory of the second best, whose main proposition states that when one Paretian condition is violated, all other Paretian conditions, although still attainable, are no longer desirable. The theory of the second best warns us that no general conditions can be specified under which the formation of a preferential trading arrangement always leads to an increase in welfare.

9   Viner demonstrated that the formation of a customs union generates two static effects: trade creation and trade diversion. He dealt only with the production effects (which arise from the shift in the national locus of production). Meade added the consumption effects (which arise from the cheapening of goods in member countries).

10   When properly defined, trade creation (diversion) is always beneficial (detrimental) to welfare. Thus, welfare increases (decreases) when trade creation is larger (smaller) than trade diversion.

11   Customs unions also generate dynamic effects, such as increased competition, stimulus to technical change, stimulus to investment, and economies of scale.

12   One of the most difficult problems in the formation of the European Economic Community has been the establishment of a common agricultural policy. The Community eventually adopted a unique system known as the variable levy.

13   To overcome the obstacle of their small national markets and achieve economies of scale, the less developed countries often resort to regional integration. These countries are interested less in trade creation than in trade diversion (that is, diversion of at least part of their purchases from the industrial nations to their partners). Such regional integration schemes have not been very successful.

SUGGESTED READING

Balassa, B. (1961). *The Theory of Economic Integration*. Richard D. Irwin, Inc., Homewood, Ill.

———— (1974). "Trade Creation and Trade Diversion in the European Common Market: An Appraisal of the Evidence." *Manchester School of Economic and Social Studies*, vol. 42 (June), pp. 93–135.

Cooper, C. A., and B. F. Massell (1965). "A New Look at Customs Union Theory." *Economic Journal*, vol. 75 (December), pp. 742–747.

Corden, W. M. (1972). "Economies of Scale and Customs Union Theory." *Journal of Political Economy*, vol. 80 (March), pp. 465–475.

Gehrels, F. (1956). "Customs Union from a Single-Country Viewpoint." *Review of Economic Studies*, vol.24, pp. 61–64.

Johnson, H. G. (1958). "The Gains from Freer Trade with Europe: An Estimate." *Manchester School of Economic and Social Studies*, vol. 26 (September), pp. 247–255.

——— (1962). *Money, Trade and Ecomomic Growth.* Harvard University Press, Cambridge, Mass., chap. 3.

Kindleberger, C. P., and P. H. Lindert (1978). *International Economics*, 6th ed., Richard D. Irwin, Inc., Homewood, Ill., chap. 9.

Lipsey, R. G. (1957). "The Theory of Customs Unions: Trade Diversion and Welfare." *Economica*, vol. 24 (February), pp. 40–46.

——— (1960) "The Theory of Customs Unions: A General Survey." *Economic Journal*, vol. 70, no. 279 (September), pp. 496–513. Reprinted in R. E. Caves and H. G. Johnson (eds.). AEA *Readings in International Economics*. Richard D. Irwin, Inc., Homewood, Ill., 1968.

——— (1970). *The Theory of Customs Unions: A General Equilibrium Analysis.* Weidenfeld and Nicolson, London.

——— and K. Lancaster (1956). "The General Theory of the Second Best." *Review of Economic Studies*, vol. 24, pp. 11–32.

Meade, J. E. (1955a). *The Theory of Customs Unions*, North-Holland Publishing Company, Amsterdam.

——— (1955b). *The Theory of International Economic Policy*, vol. 2: *Trade and Welfare.* Oxford University Press, London.

Scitovsky, T. (1958). *Economic Theory and Western European Integration.* Stanford University Press, Stanford, Calif.

Viner, J. (1950). *The Customs Union Issue.* Carnegie Endowment for International Peace, New York, especially chap. 4.

Part Three

The International Adjustment Process

Chapter Twelve

The Foreign Exchange Market

The first two parts of this book dealt with the *real* economic forces that in the long run determine the structure of production, consumption, and trade in the international economy. Throughout, money was seen in its classical role as a veil of real economic phenomena and as such was ignored.

The time has come to put money under special scrutiny. Our main interest now shifts to *international finance*. In particular, we are concerned with the foreign exchange market and the balance of payments. The short-run adjustment processes (which we took for granted in Parts 1 and 2) now assume great significance. Also of central importance are the difficulty of attaining international equilibrium and the economic policies that may be necessary for the achievement of international equilibrium when the automatic processes either are too slow or are not working properly.

International finance is full of strange terms: arbitrage, speculation, hedging, forward contracts, the adjustable peg, the crawling peg, the Snake in the Tunnel, Special Drawing Rights (SDR's), and many, many more. This jargon, combined with tales about international financial markets, creates an atmosphere of mystery, which is mainly responsible for the apprehension of the student who approaches the subject for the first time. It is hoped that this book will eradicate such apprehension. The rest of this book will show how the main principles and tools of economic analysis (with which the student is already familiar) can be applied to the area of international finance.

We begin the story of international finance by giving in this chapter a brief account of the foreign exchange market. In particular, this chapter deals with the nature, organization, and functions (international clearing, hedging, and speculation) of the foreign exchange market; the forward market and its relationship to the spot market; and, finally, the Eurodollar market.

12-1 THE BASIS OF THE FOREIGN EXCHANGE MARKET

We start our discussion of the foreign exchange market by considering the fundamental cause for its existence and the basic function it performs.

The Multitude of National Currencies

What is the foreign exchange market? Why is it needed?

The *foreign exchange market* is nothing more than the market where national currencies are bought and sold against one another. There is a need for a foreign exchange market because there are as many national currencies as there are sovereign nations. In fact, the main distinguishing feature of international finance is the existence of many national currencies and monetary policies. If a single currency were used throughout the world there would be no need for a foreign exchange market, and trade among nations would resemble trade among the various states of the United States.

The multitude of national currencies provides an extra dimension to every international economic transaction (that is, every economic transaction between a resident of one country and a resident of another); every international transaction requires the conversion of one currency into another (that is, a *foreign exchange transaction*). The primary function of the foreign exchange market is to perform the conversion of (or the transfer of purchasing power from) one currency into another.

Exports, Imports, and Foreign Exchange

In general, *the flow of goods and services between countries requires the conversion of the currency of the importing country into the currency of the exporting country.* For instance, consider the case of an American corporation that sells (exports) computers to a British importer. The American corporation must be paid in dollars, while the British importer has pounds sterling only. Somehow the pounds sterling of the British importer must be converted into dollars. It is immaterial, of course, as to whether the American exporting corporation or the British importer goes to the trouble of actually converting pounds sterling into dollars. [If the American corporation accepts payment in pounds sterling, it is that corporation's responsibility to go into the foreign exchange market and sell pounds for dollars. On the other hand, if the American corporation insists on being paid directly in dollars, the responsibility of selling pounds for dollars (or buying dollars with pounds) is assigned to the

British importer.] The important point is that *the flow of goods and services from America to Britain generates a supply of pounds (the importer's currency) and a demand for dollars (the exporter's currency).*

Consider another example. Suppose that an American importer buys British automobiles from a British exporter. If the American importer is allowed to pay in dollars, the British exporter must sell the dollars for pounds in the foreign exchange market. On the other hand, if the British exporter insists on being paid in pounds, it is the American importer who must enter the foreign exchange market and exchange dollars for pounds.

Finally, consider America's exports and imports of goods and services at the same time. America's exports require the conversion of foreign currencies (foreign exchange) into dollars. That is, *America's exports give rise to a supply of foreign exchange and a demand for dollars.* On the other hand, America's imports require the conversion of dollars into foreign exchange. That is, *America's imports give rise to a demand for foreign exchange and a supply of dollars.*

Other International Transactions and Foreign Exchange

The flow of goods and services among sovereign nations generates a large part of the supply and demand for currencies in the foreign exchange market. Nevertheless, the flow of goods and services among countries is not the only type of activity that gives rise to foreign exchange transactions. People may demand foreign currencies because, for instance, they want to buy assets from foreigners. Tourists traveling abroad also come into contact with the foreign exchange market, usually upon their arrival at the foreign airport, where they rush to the exchange counter to convert their own currency into the foreign currency. Also, many people in Italy and Greece who receive remittances from their relatives who emigrated to the United States, Canada, or Australia enter the foreign exchange market to exchange the foreign currencies for their domestic currency (lira or drachma, as the case may be).

The Need for a Market Mechanism

It would be very difficult for an American importer in need of pounds sterling to seek out an American exporter with the necessary amount of pounds for sale. Surely exporters and importers in all countries are willing to pay a small commission for the convenience of making currency exchanges on a smoothly working, impersonal market. An important function of the foreign exchange market is to bring together all buyers and sellers of each national currency and carry out all currency exchanges quickly and efficiently.

A Hypothetical Clearing House

The foreign exchange market solves the conversion problem by performing an important *clearing function.* We can understand this clearing function by imagining that a clearing house is set up with small working balances of all currencies. To keep the discussion simple, however, assume that there are only two currencies: dollars and pounds. The clearing house announces that it is willing to exchange either currency for the other at a certain rate (say, $2 per £1) and hopes, of course, that the inflow of each currency will approximately match the outflow. The initial cash balances of the clearing house actually become a revolving fund.

The clearing function is shown schematically in Figure 12-1. The initial working balances of the clearing house are represented by the level of the water in the middle tank. Actually, this tank consists of two chambers. The level of

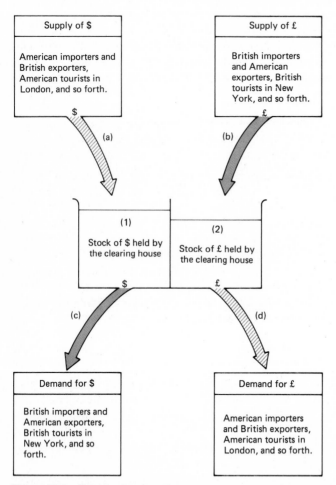

Figure 12-1 *The clearing function.*
The level of the water in middle chambers 1 and 2 represents the initial stock of dollars and pounds, respectively, held by the clearing house. Striped arrows *a* and *d* show, respectively, the inflow (supply) of dollars into and the outflow of (demand for) pounds from the clearing house. Similarly, dark arrows *b* and *c* show, respectively, the inflow (supply) of pounds into and the outflow of (demand for) dollars from the clearing house. Note the strict correspondence that must exist between arrows *a* and *d*, and between arrows *b* and *c*.

the water in chamber 1 shows the initial stock of dollars held by the clearing house, and the level of the water in chamber 2 shows the initial stock of pounds.

Striped arrow *a* at the upper-left-hand corner shows the flow of dollars into chamber 1 that results from the activity of American importers and British exporters, American tourists in London, etc. As we saw earlier, this group of people needs to convert dollars into pounds; that is, they supply dollars and demand pounds. The group's demand for pounds is shown by striped arrow *d* at the lower-right-hand corner, which represents an outflow of pounds from the clearing house. Note carefully that arrows *a* and *d* (that is, the inflow of dollars and the outflow of pounds, respectively) are similarly striped in order to emphasize the strict correspondence that exists between them—the same group of transactors turn them on and off simultaneously.

Dark arrows *b* and *c* at the upper-right-hand and the lower-left-hand corners, respectively, represent the conversion of pounds into dollars that is required by British importers and American exporters, British tourists in New York, etc. In particular, arrow *b* shows the inflow (supply) of pounds into chamber 2 of the middle tank, and arrow *c* shows the outflow of (demand for) dollars from chamber 1. Again, both of these arrows bear the same appearance in order to emphasize the strict relationship that exists between them.

When the inflow of a currency into the clearing house does not completely match its outflow, the difference is reflected in the level of the stock of that currency held by the clearing house. When the inflow is larger than the outflow, the stock held by the clearing house tends to rise; when the inflow is smaller than the outflow, the stock tends to fall.

Temporary versus Fundamental Disequilibrium

Besides facilitating currency exchanges, the initial stock of dollars and pounds of the clearing house can be used to bridge *temporary* gaps between the inflow and the outflow of either currency. *Permanent* or *persistent* gaps, however, which may arise from time to time, cannot be dealt with in this manner. When a persistent gap arises, economists say that a *fundamental disequilibrium* exists. At the risk of oversimplifying, we may say that the rest of the book discusses the various causes and cures of this phenomenon. Essentially, a fundamental disequilibrium can be corrected by means of some adjustment that brings about a better synchronization between the inflows and the outflows of the clearing house.

12-2 ORGANIZATION OF THE MARKET

So far we have used the term *clearing house* to characterize a function rather than a particular institution. In reality, the clearing function is performed by banks, partly because most foreign exchange transations of any size take the form of an exchange of bank deposits and partly because, in case the importer needs credit to finance his or her imports, it is convenient to combine the foreign exchange transaction with the credit transaction.

To understand the actual orgainization of the foreign exchange market, examine Figure 12-2. The various transactors in the foreign exchange market are presented as four layers of a pyramid. At the bottom (layer 1) we find those businesses and individuals (for example, exporters, importers, and tourists) whose activities generate either a supply of or demand for foreign exchange. As a rule, these ultimate users and suppliers of foreign exchange do not deal directly with one another but use the services of the commercial banks, which are represented by layer 2.

For instance, the American corporation that sells computers to a British importer will first receive a promissory note from the importer for the amount of the purchase. Then the American corporation will sell ("discount") the note to an American bank.

Similarly, the American importer of British cars may purchase from an American commercial bank the necessary amount of sterling.

To meet the needs of their customers, commercial banks usually maintain deposits with foreign banks. Thus, the American commercial bank will accept the American importer's dollars (or reduce his or her checking account balance) and at the same time instruct its correspondent bank in London to make a transfer from the American bank's account to the account of the British exporter.

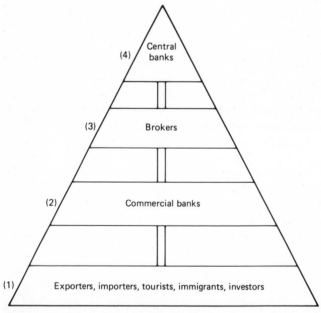

Figure 12-2 *Organization of the foreign exchange market.*
The four layers of the pyramid portray the four types of transactors and their relationship to one another. In layer 1, we find the ultimate users and suppliers of foreign exchange; these transactors use the services of commercial banks (layer 2). To iron out their net balances, commercial banks use the services of brokers (layer 3). The latter are also the link between commercial banks and central banks (layer 4).

In the course of their foreign exchange dealings, commercial banks purchase foreign exchange from some of their customers while they sell it to others. Accordingly, each commercial bank acts to some extent as a clearing house, partially offsetting sales with purchases. However, this clearing process cannot be expected to be perfect, because for some banks the total purchases of foreign exchange exceed their sales, while for other banks the total purchases fall short of their sales. To iron out their net balances, commercial banks use the services of foreign exchange brokers. The latter are represented by layer 3 in the pyramid of Figure 12-2. In effect, these brokers offer to commercial banks the same type of services as those offered by commercial banks to the ultimate users and suppliers of foreign exchange. The brokers keep in constant touch with commercial banks. Competition among brokers is rather keen.

The brokers are also the link between central banks and commercial banks. In Figure 12-2, central banks are represented by the top layer. The foreign exchange activities of central banks mainly involve intervention to influence market conditions or exchange-rate fluctuations. In addition, they may also reflect government transactions (as central banks serve as the principal banker of their governments) and transactions with various international organizations and other central banks. The activities of central banks are considered later in this chapter as well as in the rest of the book.

The student should resist the feeling that the four layers of Figure 12-2 stand for the chronological order of the various transactions. The truth of the matter is that all types of transactions ususally take place simultaneously.

In this book we are not interested in the various means of payment in international transactions (for example, bills of exchange, checks, telegraphic transfers, and cash). The distinction between them is legal—not economic. It is sufficient for our purposes to note that because of the keen competition which exists among these different means of payment, we can speak of the supply and demand for foreign money without paying much attention to the particular document used.

12-3 THE INTERNATIONAL CHARACTER OF THE FOREIGN EXCHANGE MARKET

What is a market? Does a market have to be housed in a single building? Does a market have to be limited to a particular locality? Certainly, national currencies are traded at many spots on the globe: for example, New York, Chicago, London, Zurich, Hong Kong, Singapore, and Tokyo. Is each one of these geographic places a separate market? If not, why not? These are important questions, and the purpose of this section is to consider all of them briefly.

The Foreign Exchange Market as an International Market

By the term *market,* economists mean any organization in which the buyers and sellers of a commodity are kept in constant touch with each other. There is no need for a market to be housed in a single building.

The foreign exchange dealers of commercial banks keep in constant touch with brokers and with each other by cable, teletype, and telephone, and they are constantly alert to the latest quotations in the various geographic spots of the market. As a result, the foreign exchange market embraces all financial centers of the world. It is not limited to a particular locality; it is, rather, an *international* market where national currencies are traded.

Arbitrage

The economic force that keeps the various financial centers around the world united as a single market is known as *arbitrage*. By definition, arbitrage is the simultaneous purchase and sale of foreign currencies for the sake of profit. Profitable arbitrage opportunities arise either because the price of one currency in terms of another (that is, the rate of foreign exchange) differs from one financial center to another or because the various rates of exchange are inconsistent, as explained below.

Two-Point Arbitrage

Suppose that the pound sterling exchanges for $2 in New York and for $2.10 in London. An arbitrageur (usually a foreign exchange dealer of a commercial bank) can make a profit by buying pounds in New York at $2 and simultaneously selling them in London at $2.10. This kind of arbitrage tends to draw the two prices together by forcing up the dollar price of the pound sterling in New York and depressing it in London. Even small discrepancies between the exchange rates quoted in various financial centers give rise to voluminous arbitrage—which practically wipes out the discrepancies within minutes.

The above example illustrates what is usually referred to as *two*-point arbitrage simply because it involves *two* currencies only.

Three-Point (or Triangular) Arbitrage

Profitable arbitrage due to the inconsistency of the uniformly quoted rates is a bit more difficult, since it involves at least three currencies. We shall explain it by means of an example.

Consider three currencies: the dollar, the pound, and the yen. All three currencies are traded in New York, London, and Tokyo. Suppose that the following prices (or rates of exchange) prevail currently in all three financial centers:

£1 sells for either $2 or 390 yen
$1 sells for 200 yen

Because, by assumption, the same prices prevail in all financial centers, it is no longer possible for an arbitrageur to make a profit by buying a currency where it is cheap and selling it where it is expensive. Nevertheless, the quoted prices (or rates) are inconsistent, and an arbitrageur can make a profit as follows:

1. Sell £1 for $2.

2. Then sell each $1 for 200 yen to collect a total of 400 yen.
3. Finally, buy back the initial £1 for 390 yen, and pocket 10 yen.

This type of arbitrage is known as *three*-point (or triangular) arbitrage, because it involves *three* currencies.

Indirect (or Cross) Rates of Exchange

The rates (or prices) used in the preceding example are usually called *direct*. To gain further insight into the problem of consistency of exchange rates, we pursue the above example of three-point arbitrage a little further.

First, we must introduce the concept of an *indirect* (or *cross*) *rate* of exchange. What is an indirect rate? Suppose you want to convert £1 into yen. The direct rate gives the number of yen (390) that a bank can give you in exchange for £1. However, you may obtain yen for your pound by first exchanging it for dollars (2) and then exchanging the dollars for yen (400). The number of yen you obtain in this indirect fashion is the indirect rate. In our illustration, the direct rate (390 yen) is lower than the indirect rate (400 yen). Hence, you can make a profit by selling your pound indirectly for 400 yen and buying in back directly for 390 yen.

Many-Currency Arbitrage

In the real world, other, more complicated forms of arbitrage—involving four, five or more currencies—can take place. Nevertheless, the relatively simple three-currency arbitrage illustrated above is sufficient to establish consistent rates of foreign exchange. Accordingly, when it works well, the three-currency (or three-point) arbitrage eliminates the profitability of these more complicated forms of arbitrage, which only rarely take place.

12-4 EXCHANGE RISK

We mentioned earlier in this chapter that the main distinguishing feature of international finance is the existence of many national currencies. In a deeper sense, however, it is not really the multitude of national currencies per se that constitutes the distinguishing feature of international finance but rather the possibility of exchange rate fluctuations. Exchange rates are prices for currencies expressed in terms of other currencies. It is a basic fact of international finance that these prices can change depending on supply and demand conditions, even though such changes may be restricted by the institutional constraints of the international monetary system that happens to prevail at the time (as is explained later on in this book). The purpose of this section is to consider the implications of this additional dimension of international finance.

Statement of the Problem and Some Definitions

The fact that exchange rates can change creates serious problems for exporters and importers. Ordinarily, export and import transactions involve periods of waiting, and the future rate of exchange is not completely certain. As a result, the slightest unfavorable change in the exchange rate may involve exporters and importers in losses completely unrelated to their normal business. This possibility of loss suffered from an unfavorable change in the exchange rate is usually referred to as *exchange risk.*

In general, foreign assets may appreciate or depreciate in value as the price of the foreign currency increases or decreases, respectively. As a result, some people (known as *hedgers*) who dislike exchange risk insist on maintaining an exact balance between their assets and liabilities in foreign currencies. Others (known as *speculators*) who think they know what the future rate of exchange will be and are willing to gamble, hold their assets in that currency which they expect to appreciate in value.

Note that even though we often speak of *hedgers* and *speculators,* it is more accurate to refer to the *activities* of *hedging* and *speculation.* It is the activities, not the persons, that are important from an economic viewpoint, because the same person may actually act as a hedger in some cases while acting as a speculator in others.

The foreign exchange market provides useful services to both hedgers and speculators, as illustrated in the following examples.

Hedging

Consider first the case of an Amercian exporter of computers who has just received £100,000 in the form of a checking deposit with a London bank. Suppose that the American exporter wants to maintain his funds in liquid form for 3 months but does not wish to run an exchange risk. For instance, if in 3 months the pound sterling were to fall to $1.80 from its current price of $2, the dollar equivalent of the American exporter's deposit would fall from $200,000 to $180,000—a loss of $20,000 in just 3 months. To avoid the exchange risk, the American exporter must sell his £100,000 today in the foreign exchange market and invest his dollars ($200,000) in the United States.

As a second illustration, assume that the American exporter expects to receive £100,000 in 3 months. Since the pounds are not available today, how can the exporter hedge against the possible depreciation of the pound? The answer is implicit in what we said earlier: The exporter must generate a liability in pounds of exactly the same amount as the expected sales proceeds. To accomplish this, the exporter borrows £100,000 in London for 3 months; then he sells it in the foreign exchange market for $200,000, which he invests in the United States. Now he has his funds in dollars, as in the first illustration, but in addition he has an asset of £100,000 (the expected payment by the British importer) plus a liability of £100,000 (the loan in London). Since both the asset and liability in sterling mature in 3 months, it follows that *irrespective of what the price of the pound is in 3 months, the exporter can use the sales proceeds to pay off the loan.* (In this example we ignored the interest charges for the sake of simplicity.)

Note that even though in the above illustration he is able to eliminate the exchange risk, the American exporter is required to have credit facilities in

London. This is, of course, a severe drawback, which usually forces the American exporter to work with the forward market, as is explained in the following section.

As a third and final illustration, consider the case of an American importer of British automobiles who must pay the British exporter £100,000 in 3 months. To hedge against this sterling liability, the importer can buy sterling today in the foreign exchange market, deposit it with a British bank, and use it (along with the interest accrued) in 3 months to pay off the debt. Of course, this type of hedging requires the importer to have either idle cash or credit facilities. For this reason, the American importer usually prefers to work with the forward market, as is explained in the next section.

Speculation

Speculation is the deliberate assumption of exchange risk in the expectation of a profit. The speculator has definite expectations about future rates of exchange and is interested in making a profit by buying foreign exchange when it is cheap and selling it when it is expensive. If the speculator is right in her expectations, she makes a profit; but if she is wrong, she suffers a loss. The possibility of a loss often restrains speculators in their activities.

Note carefully that speculation is the opposite of hedging. While hedging means some action that tends to eliminate exchange risk, speculation means the deliberate assumption of exchange risk.

Speculation also ought to be distinguished from arbitrage. Arbitrage also involves the principle of buying a currency where it is cheap and selling it where it is expensive. Nevertheless, arbitrage is riskless, because for all practical purposes the purchase and sale take place at the same moment and all prices are known to the arbitrageur. The activities of the speculator, on the other hand, are necessarily subject to exchange risk. Indeed, the element of exchange risk is *the* characteristic feature of speculation.

Speculators are usually portrayed as greedy and antisocial individuals whose subversive activities generate total chaos in international financial markets from time to time. In fact, these mysterious gnomes of Zurich are supposed to perform their subversive activities during major financial crises. With respect to such tales, the reader must keep in mind two things. First, in the broad form in which we are using the term, speculation can be practiced by many types of individuals and businesses: exporters and importers of goods and services, bankers, tourists, and so on. Anybody whose total assets in a foreign currency do not match his or her liabilities in that same currency is a speculator. Second, whether speculation is responsible for the crises that arise from time to time in the international financial markets is an empirical question. While it may be responsible for some crises, speculation need not, and in fact does not, always create chaos. It is at least theoretically possible for speculation to perform the highly useful function of ironing out exchange-rate fluctuations through time. As Milton Friedman points out, speculators will continue in the business only so long as it is profitable. This will be the case if, as a rule, they can buy cheap and sell dear. But to buy cheap and sell dear is to iron out exchange-rate fluctuations through time. (See also Section 21-5.)

A speculator with pessimistic expectations about the future price of a currency is called a *bear;* one with optimistic expectations, a *bull.* For example, a bull of sterling (that is, one who expects the pound sterling to become more expensive in the future) buys sterling now when it is cheap and plans to sell it later on when it becomes expensive. In technical jargon, the bull of sterling takes a *long position* (that is, his sterling assets are larger than his sterling liabilities).

Similarly, a bear of sterling (that is, one who expects the price of sterling to fall in the future) takes a *short position* (that is, her sterling assets are smaller than her sterling liabilities). For instance, an American speculator who expects the pound sterling to depreciate in the near future can borrow pounds sterling in London and sell them for dollars in the foreign exchange market. In this fashion she creates a sterling liability without a matching sterling asset. If she is right in her expectations, she buys sterling in the future at a lower price and pays off her debt, pocketing in the meantime a handsome profit in dollars.

Trader Speculation

As noted earlier, exporters and importers who either expect to receive or make payment in a foreign currency in the future are running an exchange risk. These traders can speculate merely by not covering their exchange risk. The decision by a trader not to cover his or her exchange risk is certainly similar to the decision of a pure speculator to deliberately open a long or a short position in a foreign currency in order to make a profit.

Nevertheless, not covering the exchange risk is not the only form of trader speculation (that is, speculation by an importer or exporter). Another important form of trader speculation is what is usually referred to as *leads and lags.* This term refers to the adjustment that importers and exporters make in the timing of payments, the placement of orders, and the making of deliveries for the purpose of avoiding losses or making profits from an anticipated change in the rate of foreign exchange.

Suppose, for instance, that a substantial depreciation of the pound sterling is expected. A British exporter of goods invoiced in dollars will be anxious to delay (*lag*) receiving payment in the hope of selling his dollar revenue at an exchange rate that is more favorable than the present one. He can do so merely by extending credit to foreign importers, perhaps at very attractive terms. He may accomplish the same result merely by delaying his deliveries.

If the British exports are invoiced in pounds sterling instead of dollars, the outcome is the same except that the American importer assumes the initiative now. Thus, when a depreciation of the pound sterling is expected, the American importer will delay (lag) her payment and placement of order in the hope of buying pounds sterling cheaper in the future.

British importers of goods invoiced in dollars will be anxious to accelerate (*lead*) their payments and placement of orders merely to avoid being caught with dollar obligations in the event of a depreciation of the pound sterling. Again, if the goods are invoiced in pounds sterling, it is the American exporters who will take the initiative to accelerate their receipts. In addition, the American exporters may offer better terms to the British importers and induce the latter to accelerate their orders as well.

12-5 FORWARD EXCHANGE

Foreign exchange transactions are usually divided into two major classes: *spot* transactions (requiring immediate delivery) and *forward* transactions (which are merely agreements for future exchanges of currencies). Because of this basic distinction, we often distinguish between the *spot market* and the *forward market,* as well as between the *spot rate* (that is, the price of a foreign currency in the spot market) and the *forward rate* (that is, the price of a foreign currency in the forward market).

The purpose of this section is to clarify the difference between spot transactions and forward transactions, to introduce the reader to the mechanics and conventions of forward exchange, and to explain the economic significance of the forward market. The following section examines briefly the relationshp that exists between spot rates and forward rates.

Spot Transactions

All the foreign exchange transactions we have considered so far in this chapter are spot transactions. Their distinguishing feature is that they require *immediate delivery,* or *exchange of currencies on the spot.* (This is not exactly accurate. In practice, the settlement of spot transactions usually requires a couple of days. Nevertheless, for our purposes we ignore this minor complication and proceed on the assumption that spot transactions are indeed settled on the spot.)

The rate of exchange used in the settlement of spot transactions is called the spot rate; the market for spot transactions, the spot market.

Forward Transactions

Consider again the case of the American importer of British automobiles who must pay £100,000 to the British exporter in 3 months, say, on April 10. Suppose that today, January 10, the spot rate of sterling is $2, but the American importer is uncertain what the rate will be in 3 months. For this reason, he wants to hedge against this sterling liability (or cover his exchange risk, as it is usually expressed).

We have seen how the American importer can cover his exchange risk by using the facilities of the spot market (spot covering). Thus, he can buy sterling today in the spot market, deposit it with a British bank, and use it (along with the interest accrued) in 3 months to pay off his debt. Nevertheless, as we pointed out earlier, this type of spot covering has a severe drawback: It requires the American importer to have either large amounts of idle cash or credit facilities. The forward market, on the other hand, requires neither cash nor credit facilities. In addition, covering the exchange risk through the forward market (forward covering) is much simpler and is usually preferred. How can the American importer cover his exchange risk in the forward market?

All the American importer has to do is to sign a contract (known as a *forward contract*) with his bank, according to which the bank agrees to deliver to him £100,000 on April 10. The price per pound (that is, the forward rate) that the American importer agrees to pay his bank may or may not be equal to the current spot rate ($2). The American importer may agree to pay, say, $1.90 or $2.05 per pound to be delivered on April 10 depending on what the current forward rate is. The important thing to note, though, is the fact that by signing the forward contract and agreeing to the forward rate, the American importer removes the uncertainty surrounding his liability. If, for instance, the current forward rate is $2.05, the American importer knows at the very moment he signs the forward contract that on April 10 he will be required to pay $205,000 exactly, irrespective of what the actual spot rate, or forward rate, is on April 10.

Note carefully that today (January 10) the American importer only signs a contract. Neither pounds nor dollars change hands. (In practice, the American importer may be required by his bank to put up 10 percent of the value of the contract as security.) The exchange of currencies will take place 3 months later, on April 10. In other words, the forward market deals in present commitments to buy and sell currencies at some specified future time.

As a second illustration, consider the case of the American exporter who expects to receive £100,000 in 3 months, say, on April 10. As we have seen in the preceding section, the American exporter can cover her exchange risk in the spot market (spot covering): She can borrow £100,000 in London for 3 months and sell it in the spot market for, say, $200,000; and on April 10 she can use her sales proceeds of £100,000 to pay off her debt. (Recall that, for simplicity, we ignore any interest charges.) This is spot covering, and, as we have seen, it has the drawback that the American exporter must have credit facilities in London. Again, forward covering is much simpler.

The American exporter can easily cover her risk in the forward market by selling £100,000 forward. In other words, she must sign a contract with her bank today, according to which the bank agrees to buy £100,000 from her on April 10. Again, the forward rate need not be, and in general is not, equal to either the current spot rate or the spot rate that will actually prevail in the spot market on April 10. It is conceivable that the American exporter may have to sell her expected sales proceeds of £100,000 at a price that is lower than the current spot rate. Nevertheless, by signing the forward contract today, the American exporter protects herself against the risk of an unfavorable change of the rate of exchange.

On the basis of the preceding illustrations, we can conclude that a forward transaction is merely an agreement (called the forward exchange contract, or forward contract) between two parties (either a bank and a customer or two banks) that calls for delivery at some prescribed time in the *future* of a specified amount of foreign currency by one of the parties against payment in domestic currency by the other party at a price (called the forward exchange rate, or forward rate) agreed upon *now* when the contract is signed. The market for forward transactions is known as the *forward market*.

The Basis of the Forward Market

It is important to remember that the main function of the forward market, its raison d'être, is to enable businesspeople to cover their exchange risks. As the above illustrations show, the forward covering of exchange risks essentially enables exporters and importers alike to eliminate the uncertainty of the foreign exchange element from international transactions.

Note also that the exchange risk is not eliminated if the exporters and importers of one country insist on dealing in terms of their own domestic currency. In this case, the exchange risk is simply shifted to the foreigners. Since this procedure might discourage the foreigners, it is almost certain that some advantageous transactions would be ruled out. Thanks to forward exchange, however, this great loss to the international economy can be averted.

Types of Forward Contract

Ordinarily, forward contracts are quoted for 1-, 3-, or 6- month delivery, as illustrated in Figure 12-3, for the pound sterling, the Canadian dollar, the French franc, the Japanese yen, the Swiss franc, and the German mark. All the other rates quoted in Figure 12-3 are spot rates.

The maturity of each individual forward contract is usually tailored to the needs of the parties involved, as each forward contract calls for delivery at a prescribed date, which need not coincide with any one of the above even maturities. As a result, a separate forward rate is usually negotiated for each forward contract depending on its maturity.

In addition to the forward contract, which calls for delivery at a specified future date, another, more flexible type of contract is available, namely, the *forward-option contract,* which ordinarily calls for delivery at the beginning of the month (that is, from the 1st to the 10th), the middle of the month (that is, from the 11th to the 20th), or the end of the month (that is, from the 21st to the 31st). Option contracts are necessarily more expensive, because the banks work on the assumption that the customer will ask for, or make, the delivery on the day that is the least favorable from the bank's point of view.

Forward Premium and Forward Discount

The forward rate for a currency, say, the pound sterling, is said to be at a premium with respect to the spot rate when £1 buys more units of another currency, say, the dollar, in the forward market than in the spot market. Conversely, the forward rate for pounds is said to be at a discount with respect to the spot rate when £1 buys fewer dollars in the forward market than in the spot market. For instance, when the spot rate is $2 and the 3-month forward rate is $2.025, we say that the pound sterling is at a forward premium because

Foreign Exchange

Friday, April 4, 1980

The New York foreign exchange selling rates below apply to trading among banks in amounts of $1 million and more, as quoted at 3 p.m. Eastern time by Bankers Trust Co. Retail transactions provide fewer units of foreign currency per dollar.

Country	U.S. $ equiv. Fri.	U.S. $ equiv. Thurs.	Currency per U.S. $ Fri.	Currency per U.S. $ Thurs.
Argentina (Peso)				
Financial	.00058	.00058	1745.00	1745.00
Australia (Dollar)	1.0750	1.0715	.9302	.9332
Austria (Schilling)	.0712	.0714	14.05	14.01
Belgium (Franc)				
Commercial rate	.0316957	.031827	31.55	31.42
Financial rate	.031007	.031007	32.25	32.25
Brazil (Cruzeiro)	.0215	.0215	46.60	46.60
Britain (Pound)	2.1375	2.1410	.4678	.4670
30-Day Futures	2.1420	2.1452	.4669	.4661
90-Day Futures	2.1454	2.1487	.4661	.4653
180-Day Futures	2.1503	2.1535	.4651	.4643
Canada (Dollar)	.8390	.8383	1.1919	1.1928
30-Day Futures	.8402	.8397	1.1902	1.1909
90-Day Futures	.8448	.8443	1.1837	1.1844
180-Day Futures	.8503	.8498	1.1761	1.1767
China-Taiwan (Dollar)	.0279	.0279	35.85	35.85
Colombia (Peso)	.0253	.0253	39.50	39.50
Denmark (Krone)	.1639	.1644	6.1025	6.0825
Ecuador (Sucre)	.0375	.0375	26.75	26.75
Finland (Markka)	.2549	.2553	3.9230	3.9180
France (Franc)	.2208	.22143	4.5300	4.5190
30-Day Futures	.2220	.2226	4.5035	4.4930
90-Day Futures	.2228	.2246	4.4875	4.4525
180-Day Futures	.2261	.2266	4.4230	4.4125
Greece (Drachma)	.0247	.0247	40.50	40.50
Hong Kong (Dollar)	.1968	.1966	5.0825	5.0870
India (Rupee)	.1240	.1240	8.064	8.064
Indonesia (Rupiah)	.00162	.00162	618.00	618.00
Iraq (Dinar)	3.40	3.40	.2941	.2941
Ireland (Pound)	1.9200	1.9200	.57291	.5729
Israel (Pound)	.024	.024	41.65	41.65
Italy (Lira)	.001101	.001103	908.20	906.20
Japan (Yen)	.003865	.003890	258.70	257.05
30-Day Futures	.003887	.003912	251.30	255.65
90-Day Futures	.003911	.003936	255.70	254.05
180-Day Futures	.003949	.003975	253.25	251.60
Lebanon (Pound)	.2928	.2928	3.4160	3.4160
Malaysia (Ringgit)	.4335	.4331	2.3076	2.3090
Mexico (Peso)	.04386	.04386	22.80	22.80
Netherlands (Guilder)	.4667	.4680	2.1425	2.1370
New Zealand (Dollar)	.9370	.9325	1.0672	1.0723
Norway (Krone)	.1918	.1928	5.2130	5.1865
Pakistan (Rupee)	.1015	.1015	9.852	9.852
Peru (Sol)	.004	.004	250.00	250.00
Philippines (Peso)	.1360	.1360	7.353	7.353
Portugal (Escudo)	.0194	.0194	51.50	51.50
Saudi Arabia (Riyal)	.3003	.3003	3.3300	3.3300
Singapore (Dollar)	.4357	.4354	2.2950	2.2970
South Africa (Rand)	1.2370	1.2355	.8084	.8093
South Korea (Won)	.00174	.00174	576.25	576.25
Spain (Peseta)	.013624	.0137	73.40	73.00
Sweden (Krona)	.2208	.2149	4.5280	4.5150
Switzerland (Franc)	.5359	.5374	1.8660	1.8610
30-Day Futures	.5420	.5435	1.8450	1.8400
90-Day Futures	.5526	.5542	1.8095	1.8045
180-Day Futures	.5663	.5679	1.7660	1.7610
Thailand (Baht)	.05	.05	20.00	20.00
Uruguay (New Peso)				
Financial	.1170	.1170	8.55	8.55
Venezuela (Bolivar)	.2329	.2329	4.2930	4.2930
West Germany (Mark)	.5081	.5097	1.9680	1.9620
30-Day Futures	.5127	.5143	1.9505	1.9445
90-Day Futures	.5201	.5217	1.9227	1.9167
180-Day Futures	.5298	.5315	1.8875	1.8815

Figure 12-3 Foreign Exchange Quotation from *The Wall Street Journal*, April 4, 1980.

$2.025 > $2. On the other hand, when the spot rate is $2 and the forward rate is only $1.975, we say that the pound sterling is at a forward discount, since $1.975 < $2.

The forward premium or forward discount is usually expressed as a percentage deviation from the spot rate on a per annum basis (like the rate of interest). For instance, when the spot rate is $2 and the 3-month forward rate is $2.025, the pound sterling is at a 5 percent forward premium:

$$\frac{\$2.025 - \$2}{\$2} \times \frac{12 \text{ (months)}}{3 \text{ (months)}} \times 100 = +5 \text{ (premium)}$$

Similarly, when the spot rate is $2 and the 3-month forward rate is only $1.975, the pound sterling is at a 5 percent forward discount:

$$\frac{\$1.975 - \$2}{\$2} \times \frac{12 \text{ (months)}}{3 \text{ (months)}} \times 100 = -5 \text{ (discount)}$$

Finally, note carefully that when the pound is at a forward premium, the dollar is necessarily at a forward discount. Similarly, when the pound is at a forward discount, the dollar is at a forward premium.

Forward Speculation

We saw earlier how a speculator can speculate in the spot market. For instance, an American speculator who expects the pound sterling to appreciate in terms of the dollar may buy sterling now in the spot market in the hope of selling it later at a higher price. This is spot speculation; it has the drawback that the speculator must have with either idle cash or access to credit facilities. Accordingly, the speculator may prefer to speculate in the forward market precisely because forward speculation requires neither command over cash nor access to credit facilities.

The speculator who expects the pound sterling to appreciate in the near future simply buys sterling forward. For instance, if today, January 10, the current *forward rate* for 3-months sterling is $2.05 and the speculator expects the *spot rate* to rise to $2.40 on April 10, he can buy £100,000 forward. (The bank may require the speculator to put down 10 percent of the contract as collateral.) On April 10 the speculator must pay $205,000 to the bank in exchange for £100,000. If he is right in his expectations and the spot rate on April 10 is indeed $2.40, the speculator can turn around and sell to the same bank his £100,000 for $240,000. Thus, he can make a profit of $35,000 (that is, $240,000 − $205,000). In fact, on April 10, the speculator can walk into the bank without any cash and merely collect his profit of $35,000, since the bank can combine the two transactions and just pay the difference.

Of course, if on April 10 the spot rate is less than $2.05, the speculator will suffer a loss. For instance, if it is $1.90, the speculator will lose $15,000.

Similarly, the speculator who expects the pound sterling to depreciate in the near future can sell pounds sterling forward. For instnace, suppose that on January 10 the current forward rate is $2.05 and a speculator expects the spot rate to be $1.80 on April 10. She sells, say, £100,000, forward at the current forward rate of $2.05. If she is right in her expectations and the spot rate actually falls down to $1.80, on April 10 she can buy £100,000 in the spot market at a total cost of $180,000. Then she can deliver £100,000 to the bank with which she signed the forward contract on January 10 and collect a total of $205,000. Actually, the speculator can do all her business with the same bank. Thus, on April 10 she may walk into the bank and simply collect her profit of $25,000 (that is, $205,000 − $180,000).

Banks and Exchange Risk

How do banks cover the risks they assume as they sign forward contracts? They do it in three steps.

First, forward purchases and sales of a particular currency by a particular bank ordinarily match to a considerable extent. Hence, a large portion of the risk involved is automatically offset.

Second, banks deal among themselves (with the help of brokers) to iron out their net individual positions. Hence, another large portion of risk is cancelled by means of trading between banks.

Third, banks use spot covering for any residual amount of forward sales or forward purchases that remains after the first two steps. Suppose, for instance, that a bank finds itself with a residual amount of forward sterling liabilities. The bank can cover its residual exchange risk merely by buying sterling spot and investing it in London. Accordingly, when the forward contracts become due, the bank can use the London funds to honor its forward commitments.

In the same way, banks can cover their working balances of foreign exchange. Essentially, the procedure boils down to a swap of demand deposits between, say, the New York banks and the London banks, with a forward contract to reverse the exchange of deposits in, say, 3 months. These transactions are repeated, of course, every 3 months, or whatever the maturity of the forward contract is.

There is an important application of the above principle in the so-called swaps, through which the monetary authorities of two countries acquire claims on each other. For instance, suppose that the pound sterling is under heavy pressure and the Bank of England needs foreign exchange (dollars) to support it. For this purpose, the Bank of England may enter into an agreement with the Federal Reserve to exchange ("swap") demand deposits. This swapping of demand deposits places additional foreign exchange reserves in the hands of both monetary authorities. Such swaps may be irreversible. However, as a rule they are accompanied by a forward contract that reverses the initial transaction at a future date (usually within a maximum of 12 months).

Forward Arbitrage

Profitable arbitrage opportunities arise in the forward market as well. However, our earlier discussion of (spot) arbitrage is sufficient, since no new considerations are introduced by forward arbitrage. It is left up to the interested reader to provide the necessary details.

12-6 COVERED INTEREST ARBITRAGE

Even though we speak of the spot market and the forward market, we must resist the feeling that these markets are unrelated. The fact of the matter is that the spot and forward markets are very closedly linked and that the spot and forward rates of exchange are simultaneously determined.

The link between the spot and forward rates of exchange is provided by a form of arbitrage known as *covered interest arbitrage*. The theory of covered interest arbitrage was first expounded clearly by John M. Keynes (1923, pp. 115–139). It rests on the simple proposition that funds available for short-term investments, say, 3 months, are placed in that center (at home or abroad) which yields the highest return. This is actually part of the normal process of maximizing earnings from investment.

The purpose of this section is to acquaint the reader with the rudiments of the theory of covered interest arbitrage. For a more extended discussion, the reader is referred to M. Chacholiades (1978).

Short-Term Investments and Exchange Risk

In a closed economy with a single national currency the problem of interest arbitrage is trivial: Funds move from the region where the interest rate is low to the region where the interest rate is high until the same interest rate prevails everywhere.

In the world economy, the problem of interest arbitrage becomes more complicated because of the existence of exchange risk. In the presence of exchange risk, the comparison between interest rates is no longer a sufficient guide for the allocation of funds between financial centers.

Suppose that the interest rate is 10 percent per annum in New York and 12 percent in London. An American investor who invests her funds in London will not necessarily earn 12 percent per annum, however. She will do so only if the price of the pound sterling in terms of dollars (that is, the rate of exchange) remains constant. If the pound actually depreciates, she will make less. In general, *the American investor's rate of return on the funds that she invests in London is roughly equal to the rate of interest that prevails in London less any depreciation of the pound (or plus any appreciation of the pound)*. We can illustrate this basic result by means of a simple example.

Suppose that the current spot rate is $2 and the American investor wants to invest $10,000 in London. To do so, she must first sell her dollars for pounds in the spot market (that is, she must buy pounds). Thus, she obtains £5,000, which she invests in London for 3 months at 12 percent per annum. Accordingly, by the end of the 3 months her investment has increased to £5,150. Indeed, her investment in pounds grows at 12 percent per annum, which is the rate of interest in London.

Nevertheless, the American investor is not actually interested in pounds; rather, she is interested in dollars. To obtain dollars, however, in 3 months, she must sell her £5,150 in the foreign exchange market. If the exchange rate continues to be $2, our investor will obtain $10,300, which means that she will indeed make a return of 12 percent per annum on her initial investment of $10,000.

Suppose, however, that the pound depreciates in 3 months to $1.975, which actually represents a depreciation of the pound at the rate of 5 percent per annum. In this case, at the end of the 3-month period, the American investor will receive only $5,150 × 1.975 = $10,171.25. Accordingly, the American investor now makes $171.25 on her initial investment, which corresponds to an annual rate of return of $171.25 $\times \frac{12}{3} \times \frac{1}{10,000} \times 100 = 6.85$ percent. Thus, in the final analysis, the American investor makes (approximately) 7 percent per annum, which is actually the difference between the annual interest rate in London (12 percent) and the depreciation of the pound (5 percent).

It is apparent from the preceding illustration why the rate of return of the American investor is the difference between the rate of interest that exists in London and the depreciation of the pound. On the one hand, the American investor earns interest at the rate of 12 percent per annum on the funds she invests in London. On the other hand, she buys the pounds at $2 and sells them later at $1.975 only; that is, she loses 5 percent per annum in the foreign exchange market. Accordingly, her net return is roughly equal to the difference between the rate of interest that prevails in London and the percentage depreciation of the pound. Of course, if sterling appreciates instead, the return to the American investor (on her initial dollar funds) becomes higher than the London interest rate by the percentage of sterling appreciation.

The Keynesian Theory of Covered Interest Arbitrage

As we have just seen, investing funds in a foreign financial center involves an exchange risk. To be rid of the exchange risk, the American investor (usually a bank) has to make use of the facilities of the forward market. In particular, the investor must cover his or her position by selling forward the sterling he or she expects to receive in the future (hence the term "covered" interest arbitrage). Under these circumstances, the percentage sterling depreciation or appreciation used in the previous example is now reflected by the forward discount or forward premium, respectively. Accordingly, if the forward rate is equal to the spot rate, it is certainly profitable to transfer funds to London (that is, the center with the highest interest rate). Further, if the pound sterling is at a forward premium, it is even more profitable to do so, because, in addition to the gain due to the favorable interest-rate differential, the investor makes an additional gain by buying sterling in the spot market, where it is cheap, and selling it in the forward market, where it is expensive. However, if the pound is at a forward discount, the gain from the favorable interest-rate differential must be weighed against the loss suffered from buying sterling in the spot market, where it is expensive, and selling it in the forward market, where it is cheap. Whether the investor's return is higher than the New York interest rate depends on which of these two elements (that is, the gain from the interest-rate differential or loss on the purchase and sale of sterling) is stronger. Accordingly, if the interest-rate differential is higher than the forward discount, it is profitable to transfer funds to London. If the interest-rate differential is smaller than the forward discount, it is not. On the contrary, in the latter case, *it is profitable to transfer funds from London to New York.*

If it is profitable for an American investor to transfer funds to London, it is necessarily profitable for an English investor to do so as well. The only difference between the two is that the American investor starts with dollars and ends with dollars, while the English investor starts with pounds and ends with pounds. Thus, the English investor has to borrow dollars in the New York money market, use the dollars to buy sterling in the spot market, and invest the sterling in London. In addition, the English investor has to sell forward a sufficient amount of sterling to be able to repay the loan (principal plus interest) when it becomes due. Of course, his or her profit is in sterling; it is the difference between the amount of sterling received from the loan made to the London money market (principal plus interest) and the amount of sterling sold forward to repay the loan (principal plus interest) received from the New York money market. The significance of this observation is that it is unnecessary for us to distinguish between arbitrageurs according to their nationality.

Under normal circumstances, covered interest arbitrage proceeds until the forward difference (premium or discount, as the case may be) equals the interest-rate differential. This means that the interest-rate differential is exactly balanced by the loss (or gain, as the case may be) of buying sterling in, say, the spot market and selling it in the forward market. Under these circumstances, it is no longer profitable to transfer funds from one financial center to another, and we say that the forward rate is at *interest parity,* or simply that interest parity prevails.

The fact that the movement of fully covered funds from one financial center to another depends not only on the interest-rate differential but also on the forward difference is of great significance to economic policy. Mainly because of the important role the interest rate plays in maintaining full employment and a healthy rate of economic growth, it is important to know that the movement of arbitrage funds can be influenced through the forward market. For this reason, the forward rate becomes an important instrument of economic policy—it frees the interest rate to attend to other domestic goals.

12-7 THE EURODOLLAR MARKET

We conclude this chapter with a brief discussion of the Eurodollar. In particular, we will examine the nature of Eurodollars and the Eurodollar market, the main causes for the development of the Eurodollar market, how Eurodollars are created, and the issue of whether the Eurodollar market creates dollars.

What Are Eurodollars?

Exactly what are Eurodollars? They are deposit liabilities, denominated in U.S. dollars, of banks located outside the United States. In other words, Eurodollars have two basic characteristics: (1) they are *short-term obligations* to pay U.S. dollars and (2) they are obligations of *banks located outside the United States.*

The banks themselves need not be just foreign. They are often European branches of major U.S. commercial banks. Further, their depositors may be of any nationality. In fact, the depositors range from European central banks and European and non-European firms and individuals to U.S. banks, corporations, and residents.

(We may note in passing that there also exists a counterpart long-term market for Eurobonds, that is, bonds offered in Europe but denominated in U.S. dollars).

Note that the term *Eurodollars* has recently come to be a little misleading. In the 1970s the European banks expanded their operations to accept deposits and make loans in currencies other than the dollar. Further, the practice of accepting deposits in dollars and other foreign currencies has spread to other parts of the world, such as Hong Kong and Singapore. For this reason, one often hears the terms *Asia-currency* and *Asia-currency market* as well as *Eurocurrency* and *Eurocurrency market*. For simplicity, we shall refer to the Eurodollar market only.

Causes of the Eurodollar Market

What were the main causes for the development of the Eurodollar market? Eurodollars originated in the 1950s with the Russians, who wanted to hang on to their dollar balances but did not want to keep them in the United States out of fear that the U.S. government might one day freeze them. In effect, the Russians wanted dollar claims that were not subject to any control by the U.S. government. They solved their problem merely by depositing their dollar earnings in special accounts with European banks. These Russian deposits marked the birth of the Eurodollar market. Through the 1960s and 1970s the Eurodollar market grew very rapidly.

In a deeper sense, the fundamental cause for the development of the Eurodollar market was the special position of the dollar as a *key,* or *vehicle, currency.* In other words, the whole international monetary system revolved around the dollar; the dollar was the main currency that was (and still is) used to carry out international transactions. In addition, governments around the world used the dollar as the main intervention currency for the purpose of maintaining the external value of their currency within the so-called *support points or intervention points* (usually set at 1 percent on either side of the officially agreed upon parity, that is, the dollar price of each foreign currency). Because of this special role of the dollar, dollar balances were held by both non-U.S. private individuals and corporations (to finance their foreign transactions) and foreign central banks (as part of their international reserves).

The special role of the dollar as a vehicle currency indeed explains why foreign individuals, corporations, and governments would want to hold dollar balances. Nevertheless, this important role by itself does not really explain why these funds were deposited with European rather than American banks. What additional reason was there for the rapid development of the Eurodollar market?

The most important additional reason was Regulation Q, which was a Federal Reserve regulation fixing a ceiling for the interest rate that the member banks could pay on time deposits. As interest rates in Europe grew higher than the ceiling placed by the Federal Reserve, Eurodollar deposits became more profitable than U.S. deposits, and so the Eurodollar market grew rapidly.

The Eurodollar market continued to grow with the increase of world trade. After the oil-price increase of 1973, the Eurodollar market experienced phenomenal growth as the oil-exporting countries began to deposit large amounts of dollars in European banks. (In 1974 alone the dollar holdings of the OPEC countries increased by $60 billion.) The total Eurodollar deposits (including Eurocurrencies other than the dollar) grew from about $1 billion in 1960 to $25 billion in 1968, to $90 billion in 1972, and to about $400 billion by the end of 1977.

Creation of Eurodollars

How are Eurodollars created? Do European banks have the capacity to create dollars? These are important questions.

Eurodollars are created when someone who owns dollars deposits them with a European bank. A few examples can illustrate the point. First consider the case of an Arab sheik who transfers $1 million from his checking account with the Morgan Guaranty Trust Company of New York to a bank in London, say, Barclays Bank, which has an account with Morgan Guaranty. The New York bank transfers $1 million from the account of the sheik to the account of Barclays Bank, leaving the total U.S. money supply (which includes deposits of foreign banks and other foreigners) unchanged. On the other hand, Barclays Bank experiences an increase in both its dollar assets (its demand deposits with Morgan Guaranty increase by $1 million) and dollar liabilities (its deposit liabilities to the sheik increase by $1 million). Accordingly, $1 million Eurodollars are created, as reflected by the increase in the deposit liabilities of Barclays Bank.

As a second illustration, consider the case of a European bank that in some way acquires dollar deposits on a New York bank. The European bank may acquire dollar deposits either from a European exporter or from anyone else who happens to own dollars, such as the sheik of the first illustration. The important point now is that the European bank can create Eurodollars by simply lending the acquired dollars to someone else at interest. (In principle, this process of Eurodollar creation is identical to the ordinary process of money creation by commerical banks.) For instance, to pursue the first illustration a little further, Barclays Bank could loan $900,000 to a British corporation, keeping as reserve only 10 percent of its newly acquired demand deposits on Morgan Guaranty.

The last illustration shows clearly that the Eurodollar market can potentially create dollars in exactly the same way that commercial banks create money, that is, by making loans which are redeposited in the same banking system. In fact, there are those who believe that the money multiplier in the Eurodollar market is very high because of the absence of any minimum reserve requirements beyond those imposed by prudence. The leading proponent of this view is Milton Friedman. However, Friedman's views have not gone unchallenged. Other economists have pointed out that the multiplier process to which Friedman refers is fundamentally correct in principle only. In particular, severe leakages weaken substantially the capacity of the Eurodollar market to create dollars, and thus dampen the multiplier process.

It has been pointed out, for instance, that the dollars loaned by the Eurobanks are not always deposited back into the system. They are often sold to European central banks for local European currencies. As it turned out, since 1971 European central banks have tended to hold their dollar assets in the form of deposits with U.S. banks or U.S. treasury bills; and, therefore, the multiplier process has been cut short.

The view now is that the Eurodollar market can indeed create money but that the money multiplier is rather low. The Eurodollar banks behave more like the savings and loan associations rather than the commercial banks of the United States.

Some Concluding Remarks

We conclude this section with some additional observations on the Eurodollar market.

In the first place, note that a Eurobank is not subject to foreign exchange risk: its dollar assets are equal to its dollar liabilities. This does not mean that Eurobanks cannot speculate. Rather, it means that by merely operating in the Eurodollar market the Eurobanks do not necessarily assume an open position, long or short.

Second, the Eurodollar market is a highly organized capital market that facilitates the financing of international trade and investment. Competition in the Eurocurrency markets is quite keen, with banks carrying on arbitrage operations between the dollar and other markets. Interest parity is usually maintained.

Finally, the Eurodollar market has not been subject to any overall official regulation even though some spotty requirements have marred, from time to time, the rather free character of the market.

12-8 SUMMARY

1   The foreign exchange market embraces all financial centers of the world; and it enables all buyers and sellers of each national currency to carry out all currency exchanges quickly and efficiently.

2   Arbitrage (that is, the simultaneous purchase and sale of foreign currencies for the sake of profit) is the force that keeps the various financial centers around the world united as a single market. Arbitrage is riskless.

3 Profitable arbitrage opportunities arise because the rates of exchange either differ between financial centers or are inconsistent.

4 Three-point arbitrage (involving three currencies) is sufficient to establish consistent rates of exchange.

5 Speculation is the deliberate assumption of exchange risk in the expectation of profit. A speculator takes a long position (short position) in that currency which he or she expects to appreciate (depreciate) in value.

6 Hedging is the opposite of speculation. Hedgers avoid the exchange risk by maintaining an exact balance between their assets and liabilities in foreign currencies.

7 Exporters and importers can speculate by not covering their exchange risks.

8 The term *leads and lags* refers to the adjustment that importers and exporters make in the timing of payments, the placement of orders, and the making of deliveries, for the purpose of avoiding losses or realizing profits from an anticipated change in the rate of exchange.

9 Spot transactions require immediate delivery. Forward transactions, on the other hand, are agreements (forward contracts) for future exchanges of currencies.

10 The main function of the forward market (that is, the market for forward transactions) is to enable businesspeople to cover their exchange risks.

11 Spot speculation has the drawback that the speculator must have either idle cash or access to credit facilities. Forward speculation requires neither, and for this reason it is preferred.

12 To cover the exchange risks that arise from their forward contracts, banks (with the aid of brokers) deal among themselves to iron out their individual positions. For any remaining balances, banks use spot covering.

13 Swaps are a means by which two central banks acquire claims on each other—they swap equivalent amounts of their own currencies. Swaps may be irreversible, but as a rule, they are accompanied by a forward contract that reverses the initial transaction at a future date.

14 Covered interest arbitrage provides the link between the spot rate of exchange and the forward rate of exchange. Under normal circumstances, covered interest arbitrage (that is, the movement of funds between financial centers with the exchange risk covered) proceeds until the forward difference equals the interest-rate differential. Then the forward rate is said to be at interest parity.

15 The forward rate is an important instrument of economic policy.

16 Eurodollars are deposit liabilities, denominated in U.S. dollars, of banks located outside the United States. In the 1970's the practice of accepting deposits in foreign currencies spread to many parts of the world and applied to currencies besides the dollar.

17 Eurodollars originated in the 1950s with the Russians, who deposited their dollar earnings in special accounts with European banks because they wanted dollar claims not subject to any control by the U.S. government.

18 In a deeper sense, the fundamental cause for the development of the Eurodollar market was the special role of the dollar as a key currency; the fact that interest rates were higher in Europe than in the United States because of Regulation Q was also important.

19   The Eurodollar market can potentially create dollars in the same way commercial banks create money. Because of severe leakages, however, the money multiplier is rather low.

20   A Eurobank is not subject to exchange risk—its dollar assets are equal to its dollar liabilities.

21   The Eurodollar market is a highly organized capital market but is not subject to any overall official regulation.

SUGGESTED READING

Chacholiades, M. (1978). *International Monetary Theory and Policy.* McGraw-Hill Book Company, New York, chap. 1.

Coninx, R. G. F. (1978). *Foreign Exchange Today.* Woodhead-Faulkner, Ltd., London.

Friedman, M. (1969). "The Euro-Dollar Market: Some First Principles," *Morgan Guaranty Survey (October),* pp. 4–14. Reprinted in R.E. Baldwin and J.D. Richardson (eds.). *International Trade and Finance.* Little, Brown and Company, Boston, 1974.

Keynes, J. M. (1923). *A Tract on Monetary Reform.* Macmillan & Co., Ltd., London, pp. 113–139.

Kubarych, R. M. (1978). *Foreign Exchange Markets in the United States.* Federal Reserve Bank of New York.

Chapter Thirteen

The Balance of Payments

This chapter deals mainly with the accounting balance of payments; that is, the basic accounting record of a country's economic transactions with the rest of the world. After clarifying the basic balance-of-payments accounting principles and conventions, the chapter proceeds to illustrate these principles as well as the usual reporting difficulties with examples from the actual construction of the U.S. balance of payments. The discussion then moves to the concept of balance-of-payments equilibrium and later to various accounting balances (that is, merchandise balance, balance on goods and services, current account balance, basic balance, liquidity balance, and official settlements balance). The chapter concludes with a brief discussion of the international investment position (also known as balance of international indebtedness). Examples taken from the recent experience with the U.S. balance of payments illustrate all the new concepts.

13-1 DEFINITIONS AND CONVENTIONS

The *accounting balance of payments* of a country is a systematic record of all *economic transactions* between the residents of the reporting country and the residents of the rest of the world over a specified *period of time*. This definition raises several questions. Who is a resident? What is an economic transaction? What is the relevant period of time?

Residency

Like all other forms of social accounting, the (accounting) balance of payments records the transactions of a *group* of persons and institutions, namely, those who are identified with the reporting country. For this identification, residency is used as the main criterion.

Obvious examples of resident individuals and institutions are citizens of the country living there permanently, central and local governments, and business enterprises and nonprofit organizations located in the country. Less obvious examples are tourists, diplomatic and military personnel stationed abroad, citizens studying or undergoing medical treatment abroad, and foreign branches and subsidiaries of domestic companies. These classifications are arbitrary, of course.

International institutions (that is, political, administrative, or financial organizations in which members are governments or official institutions) are not considered residents of the country of their location. They are treated instead as international areas outside national boundaries. Therefore, their transactions with residents of the country of their location are considered international and are recorded as such in its balance of payments. As examples one could cite the International Monetary Fund, the International Bank for Reconstruction and Development, and the United Nations.

Economic Transactions

Economic transactions are exchanges of value. For instance, people enter into an economic transaction when they buy groceries: they exchange their money for the groceries. In general, economic transactions comprise transfers of ownership of goods, rendering of services, and transfers of money and other assets (including all financial claims, whether equity or creditor, and immovable property). International economic transactions are economic transactions between residents of different countries.

Normally, economic transactions involve the exchange of goods, services, or money or other assets against one another. Nevertheless, some transactions involve the transfer of goods, services, or money or other assets from residents of one country to residents of another *as a gift,* without expectation of payment.

Further, an economic transaction need not involve money, as in the case of barter, in which goods are exchanged for goods. Thus, the balance of payments does not record only those transactions that are cleared through the foreign exchange market. Conversely, there are international transactions (such as gross capital flows) that are cleared through the foreign exchange market and yet are not recorded in the balance of payments, as is explained on the next page.

Accounting versus Economic Time Period

The accounting balance of payments is drawn over a specified time period known as the *accounting time period*. This time period actually determines the total population of transactions recorded in the balance of payments. For this reason, it is very crucial. The statistical measurement of the balance-of-payments deficit or surplus is inherently related to the length of the accounting time period. In effect, the accounting deficit or surplus can be increased or decreased arbitrarily by changing the length of the accounting time period.

Economists usually distinguish between the accounting time period and the *economic time period*. The latter is that period over which the balance of payments must be in equilibrium on economic grounds; it need not coincide with the accounting time period.

What is the appropriate length of the economic time period? Is it a day, a week, a month, a year, a decade? The answer to this question is of paramount importance, because on it depends not only the correct diagnosis of the balance-of-payments problem but also the formulation of economic policy. Usually economists point out that the economic time period should be long enough to even out the effects of self-correcting, short-term disturbances of a daily, weekly, monthly, or seasonal nature. As a result, the year is considered to be the minimum acceptable economic time period.

It is important to realize that there is no unique way to specify the economic time period. Such specification necessarily involves a subjective judgment, and thus differences of opinion (especially in the formulation of economic policy) arise from time to time between equally competent and honest people.

13-2 THE PRINCIPLES OF BALANCE-OF-PAYMENTS ACCOUNTING

In principle, the balance of payments is constructed on the basis of double-entry bookkeeping similar to that used by business firms. Thus, an international economic transaction gives rise to two entries in the balance of payments: a debit entry and a credit entry of equal amounts. This section explains first the general principles of balance-of-payments accounting and then shows how these principles are used in the actual construction of the U.S. balance of payments.

Debit and Credit Entries: Definitions

In ordinary business accounting, the following convention is adopted: *A debit entry is used to show an increase in assets or a decrease in liabilities, while a credit entry is used to show an increase in liabilities or a decrease in assets.* The same elementary principles can be applied to the recording of transactions in the balance of payments. In principle, a debit entry is made in the U.S. balance of payments when an international transaction gives rise to a debit entry in the books of a U.S. resident. Similarly, a credit entry is made in the U.S. balance of payments when an international transaction gives rise to a credit entry in the books of a U.S. resident.

For example, when a U.S. resident exports goods to a foreigner on credit, a debit entry is made to show the increase in the foreign assets held by U.S. residents, and a credit entry (merchandise exports) is made to show the decrease in the stock of goods held by U.S. residents. Conversely, when a U.S. resident imports goods from a foreigner on credit, a debit entry (merchandise imports) is made to show the increase in the stock of goods held by U.S. residents, and a credit entry is made to show the increase in the stock of U.S. liabilities to foreigners.

Transactions such as gifts and donations (that is, transactions not involving a *quid pro quo*) give rise to only one entry, a debit or a credit, as the case may be. However, these transactions are treated as exceptions, and by accounting convention a second entry is made (as shown below) to keep the books in balance.

For instance, suppose that a U.S. resident of Greek origin makes a gift of money to her relatives in Greece by transferring to them a U.S. demand deposit held with a foreign bank. A credit entry must be made in the U.S. balance of payments showing the decrease in liquid claims on foreigners. Since the U.S. resident receives nothing in return, however, no debit entry can be made. Yet to fulfill the principle of double-entry bookkeeping, which states that for every credit entry there must be a corresponding debit entry and vica versa, a debit entry ("Unilateral transfers to foreigners: Immigrants' remittances") is made in the U.S. balance of payments by convention.

There is an alternative and often useful way of looking at the debit and credit entries of the balance of payments. We can imagine that each *debit entry* in the U.S. balance of payments gives rise to a dollar *outpayment* (*negative* item); and that each *credit entry* gives rise to a dollar *inpayment* (*positive* item). In a general sense, the dollar outpayments represent the *actual purchases* of foreign exchange by the U.S. residents (and monetary authorities) in order to finance their imports of goods and services, lending to foreigners, repayments of loans that the U.S. residents received from foreigners in the past, and so on. Similarly, the dollar inpayments represent the *actual sales* of foreign exchange that the U.S. residents received during the accounting time period for their exports of goods and services, borrowing from foreigners, loan repayments by foreigners, sale of assets to foreigners, and so on.

The U.S. Balance of Payments

Table 13-1 is a highly condensed version of the U.S. balance of payments for 1977. This simplified version has been adapted from the more detailed statement of U.S. international transactions for 1977 reported by the U.S. Department of Commerce in its *Survey of Current Business* (June 1978), which is reproduced in its entirety as Table 13-2. To facilitate the comparison of the tables, the numbers in parentheses at the end of each entry in Table 13-1 give the corresponding entries (lines) in Table 13-2.

Table 13-1   Summary of U.S. Balance of Payments, 1977
(Billions of U.S. Dollars)

Debit entries or outpayments (−)		Credit entries or inpayments (+)	
Current account			
1. Imports of goods (18)	152	6. Exports of goods (2)	121
2. Imports of services (19–31)	42	7. Exports of services (3–15)	63
3. Net unilateral transfers to foreigners (32,34–36)	5		
(Capital outflow)		**Capital account**	
		(Capital inflow)	
4. Net increase in U.S. assets abroad other than official reserves (43, 47)	34	8. Net increase in foreign assets in the United States other than official reserves (64)	14
Official reserve account			
5. Net increase in U.S. official reserve assets (38)	0	9. Net increase in foreign official assets in the United States (57 less 55)	35
Total debits	233	Total credits	233
Balances			
10. Balance on merchandise trade (76)	−31		
11. Balance on goods and services (77)	−11		
12. Balance on current account (79)	−15		
13. Official settlements balance (80, 81)	+35		

Source: Adapted from U.S. Department of Commerce, *Survey of Current Business,* June 1978, Table 1, pp. 16–17.

On the debit (−) side of Table 13-1, we find five entries. The first entry ("Imports of goods") is by far the largest item. In 1977 the United States imported goods worth $152 billion. A debit entry is made in the U.S. balance of payments for merchandise imports because the acquisition of goods by U.S. residents involves an increase in U.S. assets.

The second entry on the debit side of Table 13-1 ("Imports of services") is also large. This entry shows that in 1977 U.S. residents received (from foreigners) services worth $42 billion. As is shown in Table 13-2 (see lines 19–31), these services included *travel abroad* by U.S. tourists, *passenger fares* and other *transportation* services, *fees and royalties, interest and dividends* to foreign holders of domestic bonds, stocks, and other assets (essentially for the use of foreign capital that was made available to U.S. residents), and so on. In each case, a debit (−) entry is made for the value of services rendered to U.S. residents by foreigners.

The third debit entry ("Net unilateral transfers to foreigners") shows the value of the "gifts" that U.S. residents made to foreigners during 1977. This is the fictitious entry referred to earlier. This entry is made in the balance of payments merely to fulfill the principle of double-entry bookkeeping. These "gifts" (or unilateral transfers) of $5 billion consist of U.S. military grants of goods and services, U.S. government grants (excluding military grants) and

Table 13-2   U.S. International Transactions, 1977
(Billions of U.S. Dollars)

Line	(Credits +; debits −)[a]	1977
1	**Exports of goods and services**[b]	**183,214**
2	Merchandise, adjusted, excluding military[c]	120,585
3	Transfers under U.S. military agency sales contracts	7,079
4	Travel	6,164
5	Passenger fares	1,366
6	Other transportation	6,983
7	Fees and royalties from affiliated foreigners	3,767
8	Fees and royalties from unaffiliated foreigners	958
9	Other private services	3,728
10	U.S. government miscellaneous services	485
	Receipts of income on U.S. assets abroad:	
11	Direct investment	19,851
12	Interest, dividends, and earnings of unincorporated affiliates	12,540
13	Reinvested earnings of incorporated affiliates	7,312
14	Other private receipts	10,881
15	U.S. government receipts	1,368
16	**Transfers of goods and services under U.S. military grant programs, net**	**194**
17	**Imports of goods and services**	**−193,727**
18	Merchandise, adjusted, excluding military[c]	−151,644
19	Direct defense expenditures	−5,745
20	Travel	−7,451
21	Passenger fares	−2,843
22	Other transportation	−7,263
23	Fees and royalties to affiliated foreigners	−253
24	Fees and royalties to unaffiliated foreigners	−194
25	Private payments for other services	−2,383
26	U.S. government payments for miscellaneous services	−1,359
	Payments of income on foreign assets in the United States:	
27	Direct investment	−2,829
28	Interest, dividends, and earnings of unincorporated affiliates	−1,257
29	Reinvested earnings of incorporated affiliates	−1,572
30	Other private payments	−6,224
31	U.S. government payments	−5,540
32	**U.S. military grants of goods and services, net**	**−194**
33	**Unilateral transfers (excluding military grants of goods and services), net**	**−4,708**
34	U.S. government grants (excluding military grants of goods and services)	−2,776
35	U.S. government pensions and other transfers	−973
36	Private remittances and other transfers	−959
37	**U.S. assets abroad, net (increase/capital outflow (−))**	**−34,650**
38	U.S. official reserve assets, net[d]	−231
39	Gold	−118
40	Special drawing rights	−121
41	Reserve position in the International Monetary Fund	−294
42	Foreign currencies	302

Line	(Credits + ; debits −)[a]	1977
43	U.S. government assets, other than official reserve assets, net	−3,679
44	U.S. loans and other long-term assets	−6,445
45	Repayments on U.S. loans[e]	2,720
46	U.S. foreign currency holdings and U.S. short-term assets, net	47
47	U.S. private assets, net	−30,740
48	Direct investment	−12,215
49	Equity and intercompany accounts	−4,094
50	Reinvested earnings of incorporated affiliates	−7,312
51	Foreign securities	−5,398
	U.S. claims on unaffiliated foreigners reported by U.S. nonbanking concerns:	
52	Long-term	25
53	Short-term	−1,725
	U.S. claims reported by U.S. banks, not included elsewhere:	
54	Long-term	−751
55	Short-term	−10,676
56	**Foreign assets in the United States, net (increase/capital inflow (+))**	**50,869**
57	Foreign official assets in the United States, net	37,124
58	U.S. government securities	32,602
59	U.S. Treasury securities[f]	30,294
60	Other[g]	2,308
61	Other U.S. government liabilities[h]	1,644
62	U.S. liabilities reported by U.S. banks, not included elsewhere	773
63	Other foreign official assets[i]	2,105
64	Other foreign assets in the United States, net	13,746
65	Direct investment	3,338
66	Equity and intercompany accounts	1,766
67	Reinvested earnings of incorporated affiliates	1,572
68	U.S. Treasury securities	563
69	U.S. securities other than U.S. Treasury securities	2,869
	U.S. liabilities to unaffiliated foreigners reported by U.S. nonbanking concerns	
70	Long-term	−620
71	Short-term	877
	U.S. liabilities reported by U.S. banks, not included elsewhere:	
72	Long-term	373
73	Short-term	6,346
74	**Allocations of special drawing rights**	
75	**Statistical discrepancy (sum of above items with sign reversed)**	**−998**
	Memoranda:	
76	Balance on merchandise trade (lines 2 and 18)	−31,059
77	Balance on goods and services (lines 1 and 17)[j]	−10,514
78	Balance on goods, services, and remittances (lines 77, 35, and 36	−12,445
79	Balance on current account (lines 77 and 33)[j]	−15,221

Table 13-2 (continued)

Line	(Credits + ; debits −)[a]	1977
	Transactions in U.S. official reserve assets and in foreign offical assets in the United States:	
80	Increase (−) in U.S. official reserve assets, net (line 38)	−231
81	Increase (+) in foreign official assets in the United States (line 57 less line 61)	35,480

Source: U.S. Department of Commerce, *Survey of Current Business,* June 1978, pp. 16–17.

[a]Credits, +: exports of goods and services; unilateral transfers to United States; capital inflows (increase in foreign assets (U.S. liabilities) or decrease in U.S. assets); decrease in U.S. official reserve assets.

Debits, −: imports of goods and services; unilateral transfers to foreigners; capital outflows (decrease in foreign assets (U.S. liabilities) or increase in U.S. assets); increase in U.S. official reserve assets.

[b]Excludes transfers of goods and services under U.S. military grant programs (see line 16).

[c]Excludes exports of goods under U.S. military agency sales contracts identified in Census export documents, excludes imports of goods under direct defense expenditures identified in Census import documents, and reflects various other adjustments (for valuation, coverage, and timing) of Census statistics to a balance of payments basis; see table 3.

[d]For all areas, amounts outstanding March 31, 1978, were as follows in millions of dollars: line 38, 19, 192; line 39, 11,718; line 40, 2,693; line 41, 4,701; line 42, 80.

[e]Includes sales of foreign obligations to foreigners.

[f]Consists of bills, certificates, marketable bonds and notes, and nonmarketable convertible and nonconvertible bonds and notes.

[g]Consists of U.S. Treasury and Export-Import Bank obligations, not included elsewhere, and of debt securities of U.S. government corporations and agencies.

[h]Includes, primarily, U.S. government liabilities associated with military sales contracts and other transactions arranged with or through foreign official agencies; see table 4.

[i]Consists of investment in U.S. corporate stocks and in debt securities of private corporations and State and local governments.

[j]Conceptually, the sum of lines 79 and 74 (total, all areas) is equal to "net foreign investment" in the national income and product accounts (NIPA's) of the United States. However, the foreign transactions account in the NIPA excludes reinvested earnings of incorporated foreign affiliates of U.S. direct investors and of incorporated U.S. affiliates of foreign direct investors; beginning with 1973-IV, shipments and financing of extraordinary military orders placed by Israel are also excluded. Line 77 (total, all areas) differs from "net exports of goods and services" in the NIPA due to the omission in the NIPA of net reinvested earnings, shipments of extraordinary military orders placed by Israel, and U.S. government interest payments to foreigners. The latter payments are classified in a separate category in the foreign transactions account in the NIPA's. A reconciliation table of the international accounts and the NIPA's foreign transactions accounts will appear in table 4.3 in the presentation of the NIPA's in the July 1978 *Survey of Current Business.*

pensions, and private remittances (see lines 32 and 34–36 of Table 13-2). Note, for instance, that in the case of a U.S. military grant, another entry is made on the credit side of Table 13-1, namely, exports of goods. Similarly, a credit entry is made for all other types of unilateral transfers to foreigners.

The first three debit entries (and the corresponding credit entries—that is, entries 5 and 6) constitute the *current account,* as shown in Table 13-1.

The fourth debit entry of Table 13-1 ("Net increase in U.S. assets abroad other than official reserves") shows the net increase in the stock of foreign assets held by U.S. residents. Insofar as the balance-of-payments accounting is concerned, a debit entry is made in the U.S. balance of payments whether U.S. residents acquire goods, services, financial assets, or immovable property from foreigners. In particular, the fourth debit entry includes: (1) U.S. government loans to foreign countries less repayment of loans by foreigners; (2) private direct investment abroad by U.S. corporations (such as the establishment of foreign branches and subsidiaries); (3) purchases of foreign securities by U.S. residents; (4) acquisition of demand and time deposits in foreign banks by U.S.

residents; (5) open book credit extended to foreigners by U.S. corporations; and so on. See lines 43–55 of Table 13.2.

The fourth debit entry together with the corresponding credit entry (entry 8) constitute the capital account, as shown in Table 13-1. Note carefully that the capital account records the capital flows into and out of the United States. But it does not record the *gross* flows—it only records the *net* changes in foreign claims and liabilities. This practice is due to the fact that bonds, stocks, and other assets may be sold and bought several times during a year, and the *turnover* is of less interest than the net change. Also, it is difficult to collect data on the gross amounts traded. As a result, here is a notable example of international transactions that go through the foreign exchange market but fail to be recorded in the balance of payments.

Note also that valuation changes, such as changes in the market values of securities, are *not* recorded in the balance of payments because they are not international transactions.

The capital account is usually broken down into short-term and long-term accounts, depending on the nature of the credit instruments involved. Short-term capital is embodied in credit instruments with original maturity of one year or less, such as deposits, commercial and financial paper and acceptances, loans and commercial book credits, and items in the process of collection. Long-term capital consists of ownership instruments (such as equity holdings of shares and real estate) plus credit instruments with original maturity greater than one year.

Long-term capital is further divided into direct investment and portfolio investment. Direct investment is defined as investment in enterprises located in one country but effectively controlled by residents of another country. Direct investment as a rule takes the form of investment in branches and subsidiaries by parent companies located in another country. Thus, the U.S. direct investments abroad are the U.S.-owned portions of foreign business enterprises in which U.S. residents are deemed to have an important voice in management. Similarly, foreign direct investments in the U.S. are those that involve an important foreign managerial interest. Any other long-term investment is classified as portfolio investment. Accordingly, portfolio investment includes long-term securities, commercial credits and bank loans, mortgages, equities in trusts and estates, and miscellaneous other long-term claims.

The final debit entry ("Net increase in U.S. official reserve assets") of Table 13-1 shows an insignificant increase in U.S. official reserve assets, such as gold, foreign currencies, Special Drawing Rights (SDRs)[1], and reserve position in the International Monetary Fund (IMF).

The fifth debit entry together with the corresponding credit entry (entry 9) constitute the *official reserve account*. Even though it deals with changes in claims and liabilities as the capital account, the official reserve account is

---

[1]Special Drawing Rights (SDRs), also known as *paper gold,* are assets created by the International Monetary Fund (IMF) and distributed to its member countries. The monetary authorities of member countries accept SDRs from one another in settling debts.

recorded separately because of its significance to the international monetary reserve position of the United States.

All debit (−) entries give rise to dollar outpayments (or actual purchases of foreign exchange). How are these dollar outpayments financed? This is shown by the credit entries that represent dollar inpayments (or actual sales of foreign exchange). Thus, the $233 billion outpayments were financed by means of (1) exports of goods (entry 6), $121 billion; (2) exports of services (entry 7), $63 billion; (3) net increase in the stock of U.S. assets held by foreigners (entry 8), $14 billion; and (4) net increase in U.S. assets held by foreign central banks (entry 9), $35 billion.

There is no need for a detailed interpretation of the credit entries of Table 13-1. They correspond to debit entries in the balances of payments of foreign countries, and we have already discussed the nature of debit entries.

13-3 REPORTING DIFFICULTIES

Putting together a balance of payments raises questions of *residency* (that is, how to *identify* international transactions), *coverage* (that is, how to accurately collect data on *all* international transactions), *valuation* (that is, how to *value* international transactions, especially those that do not go through the marketplace), and finally, *timing* (that is, *when* to make the necessary entry in the balance of payments). This section examines these problems. The student who is in a hurry may skip this section and proceed directly to the following section, which deals with the concept of balance-of-payments equilibrium

Errors and Omissions

The fact that the balance of payments is theoretically constructed on the basis of double-entry bookkeeping implies that the sum of total debits must necessarily be equal to the sum of total credits. This is usually expressed by saying that *the balance of payments always balances.* In practice, however, the collection of statistical data for the construction of the balance of payments is inherently imperfect, for reasons given below. Therefore, it is not improbable—in fact it is the rule—to get in practice a sum of debits that is unequal to the sum of credits. In this case, an additional entry is made in the balance of payments to restore the equality between the two sides—to fulfill the accounting principle that total credits equal total debits. In the United States this entry used to be called "errors and omissions." Recently, the U.S. Department of Commerce changed it to "statistical discrepancy" in order to identify it clearly as a residual. This entry is shown in line 75 of Table 13-2.

Residency

Theoretically, the balance of payments is defined as a systematic record of all transactions between the residents of the reporting country and foreigners. In practice, there are several exceptions and borderline cases.

For instance, until recently the U.S. Department of Commerce did not include in the U.S. balance of payments the undistributed profits of foreign subsidiaries of U.S. corporations. This practice understated, of course, both investment earnings and capital flows and was abandoned by the U.S. Department of Commerce in June of 1978.

On the other hand, sales of gold by the U.S. monetary authorities to U.S. residents are included in the U.S. balance of payments (despite the fact that no international transaction is involved), because such purchases and sales affect the stock of international monetary reserves of the United States.

Coverage

In principle, the balance of payments is supposed to record *all* international economic transactions. In practice, however, many international economic transactions are hard to capture through any systematic procedures of data collection. As a result, they go unreported.

Consider, for instance, merchandise trade. This item is usually based on customs returns. There are many reasons why these returns do not, as a rule, cover all transactions of merchandise trade. In the first place, when the formal border procedures are inadequate to cope with the volume of traffic (as is the case of U.S. exports over the Canadian border), several important transactions are by necessity omitted from the statistics. Further, certain items regarded as merchandise (such as goods sent by parcel post; ships and aircraft; and fish and other marine products caught in the open sea and sold directly in foreign ports) are often omitted from the customs reports.

Usually, for most service items there are no comprehensive reports of individual transactions as there are for merchandise exports and imports. Therefore, the data on services are usually arrived at by *estimation* rather than *enumeration*. This is the main reason for the imperfect coverage of services.

Estimates for tourist expenditures, for example, are based in part on the number of travelers and on a sample of voluntary returns showing destination, length of stay, and expenditures. For a wide variety of other service items (such as commissions and royalties) there are little or no data.

Finally, note that the collection of data on movements of private long-term portfolio capital and short-term capital presents serious problems of coverage. It is usually extremely difficult to obtain reports of all such movements from all individuals and firms engaging in international transactions. As a rule, no estimates of unreported transactions can be made because the universe of transactors and transactions is not known. The size of omissions is not known, even roughly. It is for this reason that it is usually thought that the entry "errors and omissions" is due to unrecorded capital movements.

However, even though its coverage is imperfect, the balance of payments is accurate enough and remains a highly useful instrument.

Valuation

Essentially, the balance-of-payments statisticians attempt to measure the value of the resources transferred from one country to another. To the extent that regular market transactions are involved, resource value is best represented by the actual amount paid (or agreed on), with appropriate treatment of transportation and other related expenses. In practice, however, the actual amounts paid are not always easily available.

For instance, a U.S. importer must file an "import-entry" form with the Customs Bureau on the arrival of the goods from abroad. On the basis of this document, the Customs Bureau determines whether the goods are dutiable and, if so, the amount due. In addition, this document forms the basis for the balance-of-payments entry. It is obvious that if the value figure is not involved in the calculation of duty, there is little incentive for accuracy on the part of the importer—especially if the correct figure is not conveniently available.

Even greater valuation difficulties arise when there is no market transaction, as in the case of shipments between affiliated companies or branches, immigrants' household effects, gifts, barter transactions, and so on. Such transactions enter the trade figures at nominal or arbitrary values.

Timing

At what point should merchandise trade be recorded in the balance of payments? When the importer's liability is incurred (when he or she places the order or signs the contract)? When the importer actually pays for the goods? Or when the goods actually move from the exporter to the importer—and in this case should the entry be made when the goods leave the exporter or when they reach the importer? Each of these points has its merits, of course. For instance, the time that payment is made is important to the foreign exchange market and the reserves of the countries involved.

In practice, the entries in the merchandise trade account are based on customs returns, which generally record merchandise as it crosses the customs frontier of the reporting country. Most countries assume that, in general, their customs returns provide a reasonably accurate record of changes in ownership. Further, they assume that services should be recorded when they are actually rendered; unilateral transfers, when the gift is legally made; and capital flows, when the ownership of assets is transferred from residents of one country to residents of another.

13-4 BALANCE-OF-PAYMENTS EQUILIBRIUM

As we saw earlier in this chapter, the balance of payments is constructed on the basis of double-entry bookkeeping. As a result, the balance of payments always balances in an accounting sense (that is, total debits equal total credits). (For the moment ignore any statistical deficiencies giving rise to "errors and omissions.") Does this accounting balance mean that the balance of payments is also in equilibrium? In other words, does the identity "total debits = total credits" mean that the reporting country never experiences any balance-of-payments difficulties? Unfortunately, this is not the case, as any casual observer of international affairs would know.

Autonomous versus Accommodating Transactions

In principle, the transactions recorded in the accounting balance can be divided into two major categories: *autonomous* and *accommodating*. Autonomous transactions are those that are undertaken for their own sake, usually in response to business considerations and incentives but sometimes in response to political considerations as well. Their main distinguishing feature is that they take place independently of the balance-of-payments position of the reporting country. All other transactions are called accommodating. Accommodating transactions do not take place for their own sake. Rather, they take place because other (autonomous) transactions are such as to leave a *gap to be filled*.

Examples of autonomous transactions include virtually all exports of goods and services undertaken for profit, unilateral transfers, and most long-term capital movements as well as many short-term capital movements motivated by a desire either to earn a higher return or to find a safe refuge. On the other hand, examples of accommodating transactions include the sale of gold or foreign currencies by the central bank in order to fill the gap between the receipts and payments of foreign exchange by the private residents of the country in question and a gift or loan received by the authorities of a country from foreign governments for the express purpose of filling a gap in the autonomous receipts and payments.

Imagine that a horizontal line is drawn through a balance-of-payments statement. Above this imaginary line, place all autonomous transactions (or entries); below the line, place all accommodating transactions (or entries). When the balance on autonomous transactions is zero (that is, when autonomous payments equal autonomous receipts), the balance of payments is in equilibrium. When the sum of autonomous receipts is greater than the sum of autonomous payments, there is a *surplus;* and when the sum of autonomous receipts falls short of the sum of autonomous payments, there is a *deficit.* In each case, the accounting measure of disequilibrium (surplus or deficit) is given by the difference between the sum of autonomous receipts and the sum of autonomous payments.

Because the balance of payments is an identity, we always have

Sum of autonomous transactions +
sum of accommodating transactions = 0

or

Sum of autonomous transactions = −sum of accommodating transactions.

Accordingly, the accounting measure of balance-of-payments disequilibrium can also be determined as the *negative* of the difference between accommodating receipts and payments.

Difficulties with Autonomous and Accommodating Transactions

All this appears easy and straightforward. But actually the analytical distinction between autonomous and accommodating transactions, although sound in principle, faces insurmountable difficulties in practical applications.

First, there is the possibility of international inconsistency. A transaction may be regarded autonomous for one country but accommodating for another. This is the case, for instance, when in the face of balance-of-payments difficulties the monetary authorities of a country borrow in the private financial market of another country.

Second, the distinction between autonomous and accommodating transactions is an ex ante concept depending ultimately on *motives,* which cannot be observed in an ex post statisitical statement like the balance of payments. The problem would not be as difficult if it were possible to infer the motive either from the type of the transaction or the type of the transactor. But this is not the case. As a result, in any practical application a subjective judgment must be made regarding the ultimate motive behind each transaction. The subjective element necessarily gives rise to differences of opinion among equally competent and honest people.

A very subtle difficulty arises in relation to monetary policy. For instance, suppose that the U.S. monetary authorities are successful in attracting substantial amounts of short-term capital from foreign financial centers by simply raising their interest rate. What is the nature of this short-term capital inflow: autonomous or accommodating? Certainly from the point of view of private arbitrageurs these transactions are motivated by profit considerations and ought to be classified as autonomous. But their profitability is actually influenced by the action of the U.S. monetary authorities, who presumably are concerned about the state of the U.S. balance of payments. Thus, from the viewpoint of the U.S. monetary authorities these transactions are accommodating—they are prompted by monetary policy to fill a gap left by other transactions.

We must therefore conclude that the ex post grouping of transactions into autonomous and accommodating is not unambiguous. The horizontal line through the balance-of-payments entries may be drawn in a number of arbitrary ways, none of which can be considered the correct one. Accordingly, we must reach the negative conclusion that there is no unique accounting measure of balance-of-payments disequilibirium. To be sure, several measures can be developed, each one serving a particualr purpose. (Several measures are discussed in the next section.) But the feeling must be resisted that a single number can be relied upon to show the precise degree of balance-of-payments disequilibrium.

13-5 ACCOUNTING BALANCES

In this section, we describe several accounting balances in relation to the U.S. balance of payments. These balances and the ensuing discussion highlight some of the difficulties involved in any effort to determine the balance-of-payments deficit or surplus. Each balance provides the analyst with some useful information. Nevertheless, none of these (or any other) balances can adequately describe the international position of the United States during any given period. For this reason, the most controversial balances have now been abondoned by the U.S. Department of Commerce.

The Merchandise Balance

The *merchandise balance* is the difference between exports and imports of goods. For instance, Table 13-1 shows that in 1977 the United States exported $121 billion and imported $152 billion worth of goods. Accordingly, in 1977 the United States suffered a merchandise-balance *deficit* of $31 billion ($121 − $152). This deficit is shown in Table 13-1 (line 10). It is also shown in Table 13-2 (line 76) as well as in Table 13-3 [last entry in column (4)].

The merchandise balance is available on a monthly basis, as the customs officials can rapidly collect and report merchandise trade data. The "trade balance" that we hear in the news every month is actually the merchandise balance. It has very limited value as a guide to policy.

The merchandise balance of the United States for the years 1960–1977 is given in column (4) of Table 13-3. Until 1970 the United States enjoyed a merchandise-balance surplus. Beginning with 1971, however, the U.S. merchandise balance turned negative (deficit), with the exception of the years 1973 and 1975. In 1977 the United States suffered a huge merchandise-balance deficit of $31 billion.

Balance on Goods and Services

The *balance on goods and services* is the difference between exports and imports of goods and services. Thus, the horizontal line through Table 13-1 is now drawn right after entries 2 and 7. Above the line we have exports and imports of goods and services (that is, entries 1, 2, 6, and 7). The U.S. balance on goods and services for the year 1977 was negative (deficit) to the amount of $11 billion ($121 + $63 − $152 − $42). (The difference of $1 billion arises because of rounding.) This is shown in line 11 of Table 13-1. It is also shown in line 77 of Table 13-2, and in column (5) of Table 13-3.

Table 13-3 gives in columns (2), (3), and (5) U.S. exports of goods and services, U.S. imports of goods and services, and balance on goods and services, respectively, for the years 1960–1977. Aside from the small deficit ($2 billion) in 1972, the United States enjoyed a healthy positive balance on goods and services until 1976. In 1977, however, the United States suffered a deficit of $11 billion, which incidentally was dramatically smaller than the U.S. merchandise-balance deficit of $31 billion of the same year. The most important contributor to this difference between the two balances was the income from U.S. investments abroad (see Table 13-2, lines 11–14).

The balance on goods and services provides an important link between the balance of payments and national income. (This is explained at some length in Chapter 16.) For the moment, it is sufficient to note that the balance on goods

Table 13-3 U.S. International Transactions in Selected Years
(Billions of U.S. Dollars)

Year (1)	Exports of goods and services (2)	Imports of goods and services (3)	Balance of merchandise trade (4)	Balance on goods and services (5)	Balance on current account (6)	Increase (−) in U.S. official reserve assets (7)	Increase (+) in foreign official assets in the United Sates (8)
1960	29	−24	5	5	3	2	1
1961	30	−24	6	6	4	1	1
1962	32	−26	5	6	3	2	1
1963	34	−27	5	7	4	0	2
1964	39	−29	7	10	7	0	1
1965	41	−33	5	8	5	1	0
1966	45	−39	4	6	3	1	−1
1967	47	−42	4	6	3	0	3
1968	52	−49	1	4	1	−1	−1
1969	58	−54	3	3	0	−1	−2
1970	66	−60	3	6	2	2	7
1971	69	−66	−2	2	−1	2	27
1972	77	−79	−6	−2	−6	0	10
1973	110	−99	1	11	7	0	5
1974	146	−137	−5	9	2	−1	10
1975	156	−133	9	23	18	−1	5
1976	171	−162	−9	9	4	−3	13
1977	183	−194	−31	−11	−15	0	35

Source: U.S. Department of Commerce, *Survey of Current Business,* June 1978, pp. 16–17.

and services (or net exports, for short) is a major component of the aggregate demand for (expenditure on) the reporting country's aggregate output.

Even though it is more useful and inclusive than the merchandise balance, the balance on goods and services is not inclusive enough. Therefore, like the merchandise balance, the balance on goods and services has only limited usefulness—the analyst must carefully combine it with additional information before it can be put to use to shed light on policy questions.

The Current Account Balance

One of the most important balances is the *current account balance,* which puts above the line all entries related to exports and imports of goods and services and unilateral transfers. In other words, the current account balance is the sum of the balance on goods and services plus the balance on unilateral transfers (gifts).

Table 13-1 (line 12) shows that in 1977 the United States had a current account *deficit* of $15 billion (that is, the sum of debit entries 1–3 was larger than the sum of credit entries 6–7 by $15 billion).

Table 13-3 shows in column (6) the U.S. current account balance for the years 1960–1977. With the exception of the years 1971, 1972, and 1977, the United States had a positive current account balance (that is, a surplus) throughout this period.

What is the economic meaning of the current account balance? In searching for an answer, we get an important clue by looking at the entries below the line. It is an accounting fact that the current account balance is the mirror image of the capital account balance (including official reserves). This must be so because the sum of all debit entries equals the sum of all credit entries; and thus the balance on all entries *above* any horizontal line drawn through the balance-of-payments entries must be equal to the balance on all entries *below* the line, except for sign. Accordingly, a current account *deficit* of $15 billion coincides with a capital account *surplus* (including reserves) of $15 billion. As it turns out, we can discover the meaning of the current account deficit by looking at its mirror image, the capital account surplus. What does a capital account surplus (or deficit) mean?

The capital account *surplus* (that is, net credit balance) of $15 billion which the United States experienced in 1977 simply means that the (net) liabilities of the United States to the rest of the world increased by $15 billion. In other words, in 1977 the United States received $15 billion credit from the rest of the world. Why was this credit necessary? To finance the current account deficit of $15 billion, that is, the *net* U.S. outpayment for goods, services, and gifts. Accordingly, a *current account deficit is tantamount to an increase in the international indebtedness of the reporting country.* This is very much like the family that either goes into debt or uses some of its accumulated wealth to finance the excess of its spending over its income.

Conversely, a *current account surplus represents an increase in the net foreign wealth of the reporting country.* The current account surplus is the mirror image of a capital account (including reserves) deficit, that is, net debit balance, which evidently means that the reporting country's *net* foreign assets increase (or its net foreign liabilities decrease). This is very similar to the family that uses part of its income to increase its assets (or reduce its debts).

In summary, the current account balance shows the change in the reporting country's net foreign wealth. A current account surplus tends to increase the country's net foreign wealth, and it is usually called *net foreign investment*. A current account deficit, on the other hand, represents a reduction in the reporting country's net foreign wealth, and it is referred to as *net foreign disinvestment*.

The Basic Balance

The *basic balance* places above the line exports and imports of goods and services, unilateral transfers, and long-term capital movements. The basic balance is given by the sum of the current account balance plus the balance on long-term capital movements.

The basic balance grew out of the preoccupation of economists with the *transfer problem*. Briefly, the question is whether a country making a unilateral transfer (or a long-term loan) to another would develop an export surplus such as to enable her to make the transfer in *real* terms.

It is often thought that the transactions which the basic balance places above the line (that is, exports of goods and services, unilateral transfers, and long-term capital movements) depict the workings of some basic, long-run forces and that the basic balance measures these underlying trends, abstracting from such "volatile" transactions as short-term capital movements and errors and omissions. This thesis is not very convincing, however. Experience shows that the flows of goods and services (above the line) have experienced sharp short-run fluctuations, whereas short-term financial obligations (below the line) have exhibited important long-run trends.

The statistical separation of short-term from long-term capital is imperfect and of limited analytical significance. Large flows of short-term capital lurk within direct investments and transactions in long-term securities, while credits that are nominally short-term may be repeatedly renewed. Moreover, movements of certain types of short-term capital are often closely related to merchandise trade and to other "basic" transactions which they finance so that it cannot be said that the two generally respond to different sets of forces.

The Liquidity Balance

About 1955, concerned over the gradually mounting volume of U.S. liabilities to foreigners, the Department of Commerce adopted a new accounting balance, the *liquidity balance*. The main objective of the new measure was to show changes in the liquidity position of the United States.

The liquidity balance places above the line exports of goods and services, unilateral transfers, long-term capital movements, errors and omissions, and changes in U.S. claims against foreigners. It places below the line changes in

U.S. liquid liabilities to all foreigners (both private and official) and changes in U.S. monetary reserves.

The liquidity balance deficit or surplus is usually defined in terms of the flows placed below the line. Accordingly, a *liquidity balance deficit shows the net decrease in U.S. official reserves plus the net increase in U.S. liquid liabilities to foreigners* (private and official). Similarly, a *liquidity balance surplus shows the net increase in U.S. official reserves plus the net decrease in U.S. liquid liabilities to foreigners* (private and official).

Note the sharp asymmetry in the treatment of foreign and domestic short-term capital flows. While changes in short-term liquid liabilities to foreigners are placed below the line, changes in U.S. short-term claims against foreigners are placed above the line. This asymmetry was defended on the ground that the balance of payments should reflect the ability of U.S. monetary authorities to defend the exchange value of the dollar. From this point of view, all U.S. liquid liabilities to foreigners pose a potential danger for U.S. official reserves, and for this reason changes in them are placed below the line. On the other hand, the argument goes, it is not certain that U.S. monetary authorities will be able to liquidate U.S. private liquid claims on foreigners and use them to offset U.S. liquid liabilities. For this reason, changes in U.S. liquid claims on foreigners are placed above the line.

The liquidity balance has been severely criticized. In the first place, the basic rationale for it is concerned with the relationship between two stocks: U.S. official reserves and U.S. liquid liabilities. The balance of payments, on the other hand, records only changes (flows) in these stocks. Further, the claim that the liquidity balance is a barometer of the ability of U.S. monetary authorities to defend the exchange value of the dollar is ill founded. Thus, on the one hand, many of the U.S. liquid liabilities to foreigners are really locked in, representing minimum working balances, compensating balances that must be held against U.S. loans to foreigners, balances required to maintain future lines of credit, and so on. On the other hand, in the event of a crisis in the confidence of the dollar, the dollar balances held by U.S. residents might pose a much bigger threat than dollar balances held by foreigners. If foreign residents can convert their dollar balances into foreign currencies, U.S. resident can do so, too.

The Official Settlements Balance

General concern about the large and continuing deficit (on the liquidity definition) in the U.S. balance of payments since 1958, and persistent and justifiable criticism of the liquidity definition itself, prompted the U.S. government in 1963 to appoint a committee chaired by Edward M. Bernstein to review balance-of-payments statistics. The committee correctly stressed that "no single number can adequately describe the international position of the United States during any given period..." (Review Committee 1965, p. 101). Nevertheless, despite this strong opposition to a single number, surplus or deficit, the committee contributed a new accounting measure known as the *official settlements balance*.

The official settlements balance is a variant of the liquidity balance. Whereas the liquidity balance places below the line changes in U.S. liabilties to *all* foreigners, the review committee proposed to split U.S. liabilities to foreigners into *official* (that is, due to foreign central banks) and *private* (that is, due to foreign private individuals, banks, and corporations), with the former placed below and the latter above the line. Thus, to transform the liquidity balance into the official settlements balance, we must transfer from below to above the line the change in U.S. liquid liabilities to foreign *private* residents.

In particular, the *official settlements balance deficit shows the net decrease in U.S. official reserves plus the net increase in U.S. liquid liabilities to official foreigners.* Similarly, the *official settlements balance surplus shows the net increase in U.S. official reserves plus the net decrease in U.S. liquid liabilities to official foreigners (central banks).*

The basic rationale for the offical settlements balance is the same as that for the liquidity balance: to serve as a barometer of the ability of U.S. monetary authorities to defend the exchange value of the dollar. Being a variant of the liquidity balance, the official settlements balance suffers from the same drawbacks as the liquidity balance.

Recent Developments in U.S. Official Reporting

Partly because of the above criticisms of the basic, liquidity, and official settlements balances, and partly because of recent major changes in the world economy and the international monetary system (most notably the widespread substitution of "dirty" floating for the regime of par values), the U.S. Department of Commerce has abandoned the official reporting of overall balances (that is, basic balance, liquidity balance, and official settlements balance). Instead, the Department now presents the balance of payments in a rather neutral way: It retains only the merchandise balance, the balance on goods and services, and the current account balance, largely because of their relationship to other macroeconomic accounting systems.

Accounting Balances under Flexible Exchange Rates

Since 1973 most major currencies have been allowed to "float," but not entirely freely. Governments do intervene frequently to maintain orderly markets and often to support the external value of their currencies. This system has come to be known as *dirty*, or *managed, floating.* How should an accounting balance be interpreted under this new regime?

Under a *freely fluctuating exchange-rate system* there is absolutely no government intervention in the foreign exchange market, and the rate of exchange is left free to equate autonomous supply with autonomous demand for foreign exchange. It is axiomatic that under a freely fluctuating exchange-rate system accommodating transactions are totally absent and the balance of payments can register neither a surplus nor a deficit. Any disturbances, real or monetary, that may give rise to balance-of-payments disequilibria under a *fixed-* exchange-rate system are now reflected in exchange-rate fluctuations.

The regime of "dirty," or managed, floating is a mixture of the fixed and freely fluctuating exchange-rate systems. Here the authorities do intervene to iron out wide fluctuations in the exchange rate. Such intervention, though, is discretionary—not mandatory. Any deficits or surpluses must be interpreted now with extreme care because they reflect a mixture of such discretionary intervention *plus* positive investment behavior. Accordingly, a change in the reserve position of a country can no longer be interpreted as the passive consequence of all other "autonomous" international economic transactions.

13-6 THE INTERNATIONAL INVESTMENT POSITION

The *international investment position* (also known as the *balance of international indebtedness*) is a statement of the stock of total foreign assets and liabilities of the reporting country at a particular time. Its usefulness derives mainly from the fact that it provides a basis for projecting future flows of investment income. Unfortunately, there are enormous difficulties for its practical evaluation. Since total foreign assets need not be equal to total foreign liabilities, it is not even possible to say how accurate such a statement is.

The international investment position is, in principle, related to the balance of payments. Essentially, the capital account of the balance of payments records *changes* in the reporting country's stocks of foreign assets and liabilities. (Recall the earlier comments on the current account balance.) Therefore, under ideal conditions the international investment position could be derived as a summation of *all* past debits and credits in the capital account of the balance of payments. In practice, however, ideal conditions are never realized so that the international investment position summarizes, in addition to the combined cumulative effects of international capital flows, the effects of a number of other factors over the years, such as changes in foreign exchange rates and changes in prices of domestic and foreign securitites. (Recall that valuation changes in claims and liabilities are not included in the balance of payments because they are not international transactions.)

Figure 13-1 shows the international investment position of the United States for the years 1973—1977. Note that traditionally the United States has been a net creditor to the rest of the world, even though recently the U.S. short-term liabilities have become a multiple of the U.S. official reserves and one often hears in the news about the "dollar overhang" and the "dollar glut."

13-7 SUMMARY

1   The balance of payments is a systematic record of all economic transactions between the residents of the reporting country and the residents of the rest of the world over a specified period of time (known as the accounting period).

2   The economic time period is that period during which the balance of payments must be in equilibrium on economic grounds.

3   In principle, the balance of payments is constructed on the basis of

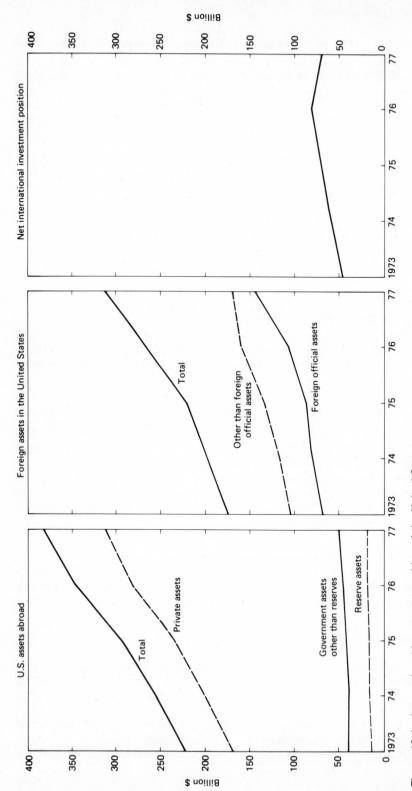

Figure 13-1 *International investment position of the United States.*

double-entry bookkeeping. For this reason, it always balances, that is, total debits equal total credits. (Any statistical deficiencies are reported separately as "errors and omissions" or "statistical discrepancy.")

4   Debit (credit) entries give rise to dollar outpayments (inpayments) and represent actual purchases (sales) of foreign exchange by domestic residents, including the monetary authorities.

5   The balance of payments is divided into three accounts: the current account (consisting of the entries for exports and imports of goods and services plus unilateral transfers), the capital account (consisting of the entries that indicate the net changes in foreign claims and liabilities), and the official reserve account (consisting of those entries that indicate changes in the official reserve assets).

6   The capital account is divided into short-term and long-term accounts. The long-term account is further divided into direct investment and portfolio investment.

7   The construction of a balance of payments raises questions of residency, coverage, valuation, and timing.

8   In principle, the transactions recorded in the balance of payments can be divided into autonomous (undertaken for their own sake) and accommodating (undertaken to fill a gap left by the autonomous transactions).

9   When autonomous payments equal autonomous receipts, the balance of payments is in equilibrium. Otherwise, there exists either a deficit (autonomous payments > autonomous receipts) or a surplus (autonomous receipts > autonomous payments).

10   The ex ante distinction between autonomous and accommodating transactions cannot be observed in an ex post accounting balance of payments. Accordingly, several accounting measures of disequilibrium can be developed, each one serving a particular purpose.

11   The merchandise balance (available on a monthly basis) is the difference between exports and imports of goods. Its usefulness is limited.

12   The balance on goods and services is the difference between exports and imports of goods and services. It provides an important link between the balance of payments and national income.

13   The important current account balance shows the change in the reporting country's net foreign wealth.

14   The basic balance is given by the sum of the current account balance plus the balance on long-term capital movements.

15   The liquidity balance places below the line changes in U.S. liquid liabilities to all foreigners (private and official) plus changes in U.S. monetary reserves.

16   The official settlements balance is a variant of the liquidity balance. It places below the line changes in U.S. monetary reserves plus changes in U.S. liquid liabilities to official foreigners only.

17   The rationale for both the liquidity balance and the offical settlements balance is the same: to serve as a barometer of the ability of U.S. monetary authorities to defend the exchange value of the dollar. Both balances suffer from the same severe drawbacks, and along with the basic balance they have been abandoned by the Department of Commerce.

18   The international investment position (or balance of international indebtedness) is a statement of the stock of total foreign assets and liabilities of the reporting country at a particular time. It provides a basis for projecting future flows of investment income but faces enormous difficulties of statistical estimation.

SUGGESTED READING

Chacholiades, M. (1978). *International Monetary Theory and Policy*. McGraw-Hill Book Company, chap. 2.

Cooper, R. N. (1966). "The Balance of Payments in Review," *Journal of Political Economy* (August), pp. 379–395.

Fieleke, N. S. (1971). "Accounting for the Balance of Payments," *New England Economic Review*, (May–June), Federal Reserve Bank of Boston, pp. 3–15.

International Monetary Fund, (1949). Balance of Payments Yearbook, 1938-1946-1947. The International Monetary Fund, Washington.

―――― (1977), *Balance of Payments Manual*, 4th ed. The International Monetary Fund, Washington.

Kemp, D. S. (1975). "Balance-of-Payments Concepts—What Do They Really Mean?" *Review* (July). Federal Reserve Bank of St. Louis, pp. 14–23.

Kindleberger, C. P. (1965). *Balance-of-Payments Deficits and the International Market for Liquidity*. Princeton Essays in International Finance, no. 46. International Finance Section, Princeton University, Princeton, N.J.

―――― (1969). "Measuring Equilibrium in the Balance of Payments," *Journal of Political Economy*, 77 (November–December), pp. 873–891.

Review Committee for Balance of Payments Statistics 1965. *The Balance of Payments Statistics of the United States: A Review and Appraisal*. Washington.

Chapter Fourteen

The Balance-of-Payments Problem: A Basic Model

The preceding two chapters dealt with the basic concepts of foreign exchange and the balance of payments. These concepts are indispensable when dealing with the great issues of international finance. Throughout Chapters 12 and 13 there were repeated references to exchange rates and balance-of-payments equilibrium. Nevertheless, there was no systematic discussion of the economic forces that keep the foreign exchange market and the balance of payments in equilibrium. The time has come to begin such a discussion.

It is indeed ironic that the complex issues of international finance can be tackled successfully by means of an uncomplicated model. Nevertheless, it is true. Our main objective in this chapter is to carefully describe this model and then use it to illustrate various aspects of the balance-of-payments problem. In this sense this chapter serves as a general introduction to the rest of the book.

The simplified model introduced in this chapter draws on concepts that were developed in the first part of the book, especially in Chapters 2 through 4. The student who has mastered that analysis should have no trouble with the present discussion.

This chapter begins with a clear, concise statement of the basic assumptions of our simplified model. It then proceeds to describe briefly international equilibrium in the sense of Part 1 of this book, that is, as a long-run phenomenon. It continues with various situations of international disequilibrium and describes the difficulties of returning to international equilibrium. A final section deals with the famous *transfer problem* and brings out its relationship to the balance-of-payments problem.

The model in this chapter serves as a general framework for the analysis of the rest of the book. As a result, the main concern is with the general nature of the problem and the issues involved rather than with any specific solution to the model. Any specific results brought out by the present discussion are only incidental, and the student should not let them overshadow his or her understanding of the main issues.

14-1 THE BASIC ASSUMPTIONS

Most of the important issues of international finance can be studied successfully within the context of a two-country model. Accordingly, we shall assume that there are two countries, America (home country) and Britain (foreign country, or the rest of the world), with national currencies, the dollar and the pound sterling, respectively. We shall further assume that each of these two countries specializes completely in the production of a single commodity (or class of commodities). In particular, we shall assume that America specializes completely in the production of (that is, produces only) *A-exportables* and Britain in the production of *B-exportables*.

This model is simpler than the models of Part 1 of the book (where normally each country produced both commodities), because our main concern here is with the balance-of-payments problem, not comparative advantage.

We shall also assume that each country produces its output by means of a single factor of production, labor. Further, each country's supply of homogeneous labor is fixed, and constant returns to scale prevail everywhere. In particular, we shall assume that the units of measurement are such that each country's labor coefficient of production is unity. In other words, America uses 1 unit of labor to produce 1 unit of A-exportables, and Britain uses 1 unit of labor to produce 1 unit of B-exportables. Needless to say, this is a harmless, simplifying assumption.

The interest rate in each country is given; perfect competition prevails everywhere; and transportation costs as well as barriers to trade (for example, tariffs) are zero. Tastes in each country are represented by a nonintersecting social indifference map with regular convexity. Commodity exports are the only source of supply of foreign exchange, and commodity imports are the only purpose of demand for foreign exchange.

For the moment there is no need to make any specific assumption regarding the flexibility of the money-wage rate or the relationship between aggregate spending and national income in each country. We shall return to these issues later.

The present model has several limitations. For instance, it excludes the possibililty of diversification in production, the existence of nontraded goods, capital markets, and the multiplicity of factors of production, to mention only a few. There are, however, reasons for using this model. First, such simplifications permit us to cut through much detail and go directly to the real issues—any complications can be introduced at a later stage. (Indeed, most of the assumptions enumerated presently are modified in later chapters.) Second, none of the important conclusions of the model is destroyed when any or all simplifying assumptions are dropped. From the point of view of balance-of-payments theory, nothing is gained by unnecessarily introducing more complications into our basic model.

14-2 INTERNATIONAL EQUILIBRIUM

Before commenting on the adjustment process, it is natural to consider briefly the general equilibrium of our basic model. For this purpose, we tentatively assume that in each country *aggregate expenditure on commodities equals aggregate income*. This is the same assumption that we made in Part 1 in the context of the pure theory of trade. We drop this restrictive assumption later in this chapter.

Equilibrium in the Factor and Commodity Markets

General equilibrium requires that supply equals demand in all markets—the labor markets, the commodity markets, and the foreign exchange market. This is illustrated by the box diagram of Figure 14-1. Distance O_aO shows America's output of A-exportables when America's supply of labor is fully employed. Similarly, distance O_bO shows Britain's output of B-exportables when Britain's supply of labor is fully employed. Draw America's social indifference map with respect to origin O_a, as illustrated by indifference curve I_aI_a'. Similarly, draw Britain's social indifference map with respect to origin O_b, as illustrated by indifference curve I_bI_b'. The coordinates of any point in the box with respect to O_a and O_b give the amounts of A-exportables and B-exportables allocated to A and B, respectively. Given the assumption of free trade and the absence of transportation costs, the commodity prices, and therefore the marginal rates of substitution, must be the same in the two countries. Accordingly, general equilibrium must occur somewhere along contract curve O_aEO_b, which is nothing but the locus of tangencies between the two sets of indifference curves, as illustrated by point E. Which point along the contract curve represents general equilibrium?

By assumption, aggregate income equals aggregate expenditure in both countries. This means that both America's and Britain's budget lines must pass through point O at all prices. Imagine that a budget line through O rotates continuously from the position OO_a to OO_b, and determine the two *price-consumption curves*, PCC_a and PCC_b. Curve PCC_a is the locus of tangencies between the rotating budget line and America's indifference curves, while PCC_b is the locus of tangencies between the rotating budget line and Britain's indifference curves. As is well known, these two price-consumption curves necessarily

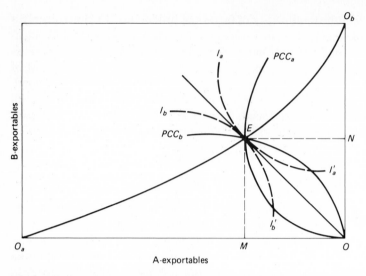

Figure 14-1 *International equilibrium.*
Distance O_aO shows America's full-employment output of A-exportables. Similarly, distance O_bO shows Britain's full-employment output of B-exportables. General equilibrium occurs at the intersection of America's and Britain's price-consumption curves (PCC_a and PCC_b). America exports MO units of A-exportables to Britain in exchange for ON units of B-exportables. America's terms of trade are given by the slope of line OE.

intersect along the contract curve, as illustrated in Figure 14-1 by point E. In fact, the intersection of the two price-consumption curves (that is, point E) is the general equilibrium point.

The coordinates of general equilibrium point E with respect to origin O_a (that is, distances O_aM and ME) show America's *absorption* of A-exportables and B-exportables, respectively. Similarly, the coordinates of E with respect to origin O_b (NE and O_bN) show Britain's absorption of A-exportables and B-exportables, respectively. Accordingly, out of her total production of O_aO units of A-exportables, America uses O_aM units for domestic consumption and investment (that is, domestic absorption) and exports the rest (MO) to Britain. Similarly, out of her total production of O_bO units of B-exportables, Britain uses O_bN units for domestic absorption and exports the rest (ON) to America. Essentially, America exchanges MO units of A-exportables for ON units of Britain's B-exportables.

On the basis of the preceding interpretation, it is evident that the coordinates of general equilibrium point E with respect to O (OM, ON) show America's exports of A-exportables and Britain's exports of B-exportables, respectively. In fact, price-consumption curves PCC_a and PCC_b viewed from origin O become our familiar offer curves, as the reader should verify. It is true that the "offer curves" of Figure 14-1 are drawn in the second quadrant, while the offer curves of Part 1 of this book were always drawn in the first quadrant. This is an insignificant difference, however.

Note also that line OE is actually the equilibrium terms-of-trade line (drawn in the second quadrant, not the first). Accordingly, the slope of line OE gives America's equilibrium terms of trade (that is, the relative price of A-exportables).

Equilibrium in the Foreign Exchange Market

Even though we have no information concerning absolute prices or the rate of exchange, it is important to note that general equilibrium point E establishes equilibrium not only in the factor and commodity markets but also in the foreign exchange market.

For instance, let p_a and p_b indicate the dollar prices of A-exportables and B-exportables, respectively, that prevail in equilibrium in America. Similarly, let p_a^* and p_b^* indicate the prices (in pounds sterling) of A-exportables and B-exportables, respectively, that prevail in equilibrium in Britain. (From now on we shall use asterisks to indicate Britain's prices, or prices expressed in pounds.) Finally, assume that £1 sells for $\$R$ (the rate of exchange is R). In the absence of transportation costs, tariffs, and other barriers to trade, perfect competition (or rather *commodity arbitrage*) establishes the equalities $p_a = Rp_a^*, p_b = Rp_b^*$.

In general, we can write America's terms of trade (p) as follows:

$$p = \frac{p_a}{p_b} = \frac{R \cdot p_a^*}{R \cdot p_b^*} = \frac{p_a^*}{p_b^*} = \frac{p_a}{R \cdot p_b^*} \tag{14-1}$$

Note that in forming the terms of trade (a ratio of money prices), we must express both money prices in terms of the *same* currency.

Further, we have seen that America's equilibrium terms of trade are given by the slope of vector OE (Figure 14-1). That is,

$$p = \frac{ON}{MO} = \frac{\text{America's volume of imports}}{\text{America's volume of exports}} \tag{14-2}$$

Combining equations (14-1) and (14-2), we obtain:

$$\frac{p_a}{R \cdot p_b^*} = \frac{ON}{MO}$$

or

$$p_a \cdot MO = R \cdot p_b^* \cdot ON \tag{14-3}$$

or

$$\frac{p_a}{R} \cdot MO = p_b^* \cdot ON \tag{14-4}$$

Equation (14-3) merely says that the value of American exports equals the value of American imports (British exports) when both aggregates are evaluated in dollars. Similarly, equation (14-4) says that the value of American exports equals the value of American imports when both aggregates are evaluated in pounds. By assumption, the quantity of foreign exchange (pounds) supplied coincides with the value (in pounds) of American exports; and the quantity of foreign exchange (pounds) demanded coincides with the value (in pounds) of American imports. Accordingly, general equilibrium point E (Figure 14-1) implies equilibrium in the foreign exchange market as well.

14-3 THE ADJUSTMENT PROCESS:
(1) INCOME = ABSORPTION

Can the long-run equilibrium of Figure 14-1 be attained automatically? That is, does a disequilibrium state automatically generate forces that tend to restore equilibrium? If such automaticity exists, what is the precise adjustment process? On the other hand, if such automaticity does not exist, what policy measures must be pursued to restore equilibrium? These are important questions. The rest of the book is devoted to them. The rest of the present chapter gives only tentative answers and prepares the ground for subsequent discussion.

Types of Disequilibria

We are concerned primarily with the problems of equilibrium and adjustment in the foreign exchange market. The foreign exchange market is not an ordinary market, because it provides the link among the economies of the world. Long-run equilibrium in the foreign exchange market is indeed akin to general equilibrium; *long-run* equilibrium in the foreign exchange market requires that all other markets also be in equilibrium. The adjustment process of the foreign exchange market is inherently much more complicated than the adjustment process of any other market.

Disequilibrium in the foreign exchange market may coincide with (or reflect) a disequilibrium in some other market or markets. But this is not necessary. As shown in Section 14-4, disequilibrium in the foreign exchange market may exist even when all other markets are in equilibrium. The present section deals with disequilibrium states in which, in addition to the foreign exchange market, some other market is out of equilibrium. Section 14-4 deals with the important case in which only the foreign exchange market is out of equilibrium.

Disequilibrium in the Commodity Markets

To maintain continuity with the analysis of Part 1 of the book, we describe in this section that type of balance-of-payments disequilibrium which reflects disequilibrium in the commodity markets. Throughout this discussion a crucial assumption is maintained: *national income equals desired spending* (or *absorption*) in each country. We will remove this assumption in Section 14-4.

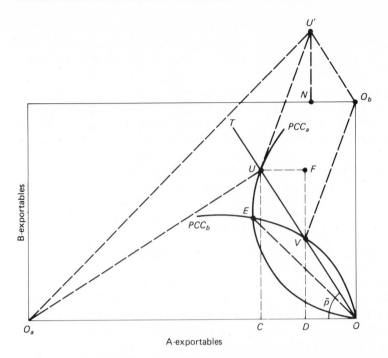

Figure 14-2 *Disequilibrium in the commodity markets and the foreign exchange market.*
At the current terms of trade indicated by *OT*, America wants to buy (absorb) bundle *U* and
Britain bundle *V*. Assuming that all buyer plans are realized, both countries end up at *F*, where
America runs a balance-of-trade deficit of *UF* (in A-exportables) or *VF* (in B-exportables).
America's inventories of A-exportables increase by *UF* (or *NO_b*), and Britain's inventories of
B-exportables decrease by *VF* (or *NU'*), per unit of time.

Consider Figure 14-2, which is similar to Figure 14-1. The contract curve
and the social indifference curves have been omitted for simplicity. Long-run
equilibrium occurs at *E*. However, the current price ratio ($\bar{p}$), given by the
slope of vector *OT*, is by assumption higher than the long-run equilibrium price
ratio. This is clearly a disequilibrium situation.

There are, of course, many types of disturbances (for example, changes in
tastes, technology, and factor supplies) that can cause a system to be out of
long-run equilibrium. For our present purposes, the cause of disequilibrium is
irrelevant.

What is the nature of the disequilibrium state portrayed in Figure 14-2?
That is, what markets are out of equilibrium? Clearly, the labor markets are in
equilibrium. Nevertheless, at the current price ratio ($\bar{p}$), America wants to buy
bundle *U* and Britain bundle *V*. The aggregate quantities of A-exportables and
B-exportables demanded by both countries are given by vector $O_a U'$, which is
the vector sum of vectors $O_a U$ and $V O_b$. This vector addition is carried out by
completing parallelogram UVO_bU'. Thus, the coordinates of point *U'* with respect to O_a show the total quantities of A-exportables and B-exportables

demanded by both America and Britain. On the other hand, the total supplies of A-exportables and B-exportables are given by the coordinates of point O_b with respect to O_a (that is, the sides of the box). Accordingly, there exists an excess demand for B-exportables (given by vertical distance NU') and an excess supply of A-exportables (given by horizontal distance NO_b).

For the moment assume that *all buyer plans are realized.* That is, America's buyers (consumers, producers, and government) are allowed to buy bundle U and Britain's buyers bundle V. *America's producers use the excess supply of A-exportables (NO_b) to increase their inventories; and Britain's producers meet the excess demand for B-exportables (NU') out of inventories.* Thus, the disequilibrium in the commodity markets reflects *unplanned inventory changes.*

Disequilibrium in the Foreign Exchange Market

What is the situation in the foreign exchange market? Observe that America actually exports to Britain only DO units of A-exportables, while Britain exports to America CU (or DF) units of B-exportables. Given that the current price ratio ($\bar{p}$) is given by the slope of vector OT—that is, $\bar{p} = DV/DO$—it follows that the value of American exports falls short of the value of American imports—in short, America is running an import surplus or a balance-of-payments deficit. This is verified as follows:

$$\bar{p} = \frac{DV}{DO}$$

or

$$\bar{p} \cdot DO = DV$$

or

$$\left(\frac{p_a}{Rp_b^*}\right)DO = DV$$

or

$$\left(\frac{p_a}{R}\right)DO \equiv \text{supply of pounds sterling} = p_b^* \cdot DV < p_b^* \cdot DF \equiv$$
$$\text{demand for pounds sterling}$$

Desired Absorption versus Actual Absorption

Actually Figure 14-2 teaches us more. While America's *desired* absorption is indicated by point U, her *actual* absorption is given by point F.

Thus, America produces O_aO units of A-exportables and exports DO units to Britain. This means that America actually keeps O_aD units of A-exportables for domestic use even though her consumers and producers desire only O_aC units. As we have seen, the difference, CD, represents unplanned inventory accumulation in America. On the other hand, America desires and actually imports $CU = DF$ units of B-exportables.

Accordingly, even though America desires bundle U, she actually buys bundle F, with the difference, CD, reflecting unplanned inventory accumulation of A-exportables.

Similarly, while Britain's *desired* absorption is indicated by point V (which lies on Britain's offer curve), her *actual* absorption is given by point F (that is, the same as America's *actual* absorption point). The difference between Britain's actual and desired absorption points reflects the fact that America imports more B-exportables than Britain's exporters expected to export. Britain's exporters expected to export only DV units of B-exportables, but the American importers actually imported $CU = DF$ units. The British importers had to dig into their inventories in order to meet the unexpected, larger demand by the American importers. The difference, VF, between points V (Britain's desired absorption) and F (Britain's actual absorption) reflects the unintended reduction in Britain's inventories.

Note carefully that America's balance of payments *deficit* is given by the difference between America's desired absorption and America's actual absorption. We saw earlier that:

Demand for pounds sterling $= p_b^* \cdot DF$

Supply of pounds sterling $= p_b^* \cdot DV$

Accordingly,

America's deficit $= p_b^* \cdot DF - p_b^* \cdot DV = p_b^* \cdot VF = p_a^* \cdot UF$

(Recall that $p_a^*/p_b^* = VF/UF$.)

Similarly, Britain's *surplus* is equal to the excess of Britain's desired absorption over Britain's actual absorption, that is $p_b^* \cdot VF$.

Actually, the above results are special cases of a more general identity:

Balance of trade = national income − actual absorption   (14-5)

(The term *balance of trade* is used here in the same sense as the term *balance on goods and services* was used in Chapter 13.) This is easily seen when it is realized that in the present type of disequilibrium, national income equals desired absorption by assumption. The identity (14-5) may be obvious to some students from Figure 14-2. It is, however, studied further in Chapter 16.

Summary of Disequilibrium Signs

In summary, the disequilibrium portrayed in Figure 14-2 implies disequilibrium in both commodity markets, and also disequilibrium in the foreign exchange market. In particular, there exist:

1 An excess supply of A-exportables ($CD = UF = NO_b$), which is reflected in an increase in American inventories per unit of time

2 An excess demand for B-exportables ($VF = NU'$), which is reflected in a decrease in British inventories per unit of time

3 An excess demand for pounds sterling ($p_b^* \cdot VF = p_a^* \cdot UF$), which is reflected in a decrease (increase) in America's (Britain's) foreign exchange reserves. In effect, in this disequilibrium state, America converts her foreign exchange reserves into unwanted inventories of A-exportables. On the other hand, Britain reluctantly converts her commodity inventories (of B-exportables) into foreign exchange reserves.

How can this disequilibrium be corrected?

Tendencies toward General Equilibrium

The disequilibrium of Figure 14-2 could be corrected if America's terms of trade (that is, the relative price of A-exportables) were allowed to fall, as illustrated by broken vector OE. Are there any economic forces that may automatically bring about this result?

First, recall that America's terms of trade are given by $p = p_a/Rp_b^*$ [see equation (14-1)]. Accordingly, a reduction in p may be accomplished by any one of the following three ways (or any combination):

1 A reduction in the dollar price of A-exportables (p_a)
2 An increase in the pound sterling price of B-exportables (p_b^*)
3 An increase in the rate of exchange (R)

Are there any economic signs that may lead us to believe that these changes will actually take place?

Based on the disequilibrium states in the markets for A-exportables, B-exportables, and foreign exchange (pounds sterling), a classical economist would hasten to point out that in the current disequilibrium state there are indeed strong economic forces at work that will restore international equilibrium. In particular, the classical economist would argue, because of the observed excess supply of A-exportables, there exists a tendency for their price (p_a) to fall. Similarly, because of the observed excess demand for B-exportables (and the depletion of Britain's inventories), there exists a tendency for their price (p_b^*) to rise. Finally, because of the existence of an excess demand for pounds sterling, there is a tendency for the rate of exchange (R) to rise. Accordingly, in the classical world of perfect price flexibility one would expect the price system to adjust quickly and restore equilibrium promptly. In fact, we accepted this much ourselves in Parts 1 and 2 of this book! Unfortunately, the world economy of today does not justify such optimism. Let us consider each one of these prices separately.

Adjustment in the Commodity and Labor Markets

We consider first the tendencies for change in the commodity markets. Discussion of exchange-rate changes is postponed until the next subsection.

As we have just seen, the disequilibrium state illustrated in Figure 14-2 involves a positive excess *supply* of A-exportables plus a positive excess *demand* for B-exportables. Ordinarily, the price of A-exportables would tend to fall, and the price of B-exportables would tend to rise. Or would they?

Consider the price of A-exportables. In equilibrium, it must be equal to the cost of labor that is needed to produce 1 unit of A-exportables. In turn, this labor cost depends on the amount of labor needed for the production of 1 unit of A-exportables (that is, *the labor coefficient of production*) as well as the money-wage rate in America. Now the labor coefficient is a technological constant whose value cannot vary at will. In fact, it may be recalled that for simplicity we have assumed that the labor coefficients in both America and Britain are unity. Under these circumstances, the average labor cost of production of A-exportables (in dollars) coincides with America's money-wage rate. [Similarly, the average labor cost of production of B-exportables (in pounds) coincides with Britain's money-wage rate.] Consequently, *a reduction in the price of A-exportables requires a prior reduction in the American money-wage rate.* Is a reduction in the American money-wage rate possible?

Unfortunately, reductions in money-wage rates are always resisted by powerful labor unions. Indeed, it is a common observation that the money-wage rate is notoriously inflexible in the downward direction. If this is the case, how will equilibrium in the market for A-exportables be restored?

If the money-wage rate cannot be reduced, then America's producers will simply have to cut their production of A-exportables—they cannot be expected to accumulate inventories indefinitely. Thus, America's producers will start laying off workers. America's rate of unemployment will start rising as production and national income fall.

The student probably knows already that when a country's national income falls, the demand for commodities in general (that is, aggregate expenditure) also falls. Therefore, the reduction in America's national income will cause a *reduction in America's demand for both A-exportables and B-exportables.* If allowed to proceed far enough, *such a process can restore equilibrium in both the commodity markets and the foreign exchange market.* However, this process cannot restore general equilibrium because of the massive unemployment that emerges in America.

The preceding process is illustrated in Figure 14-3, which is similar to Figure 14-2. Vector OT and points U and V of Figure 14-2 are transferred to Figure 14-3. Curve O_aU is America's income-consumption curve for the initial disequilibrium terms of trade (given by vector OT). Now allow America's production to fall by $O_aO'_a$, and shift (1) America's origin from O_a to O'_a and (2)

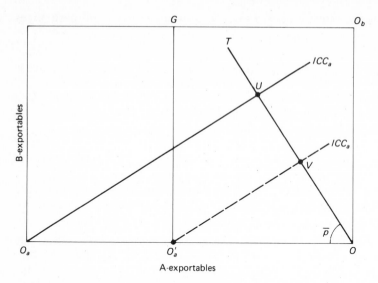

Figure 14-3 *Balance-of-payments equilibrium established by means of changes in produc-tion and income.*
As America's production of A-exportables falls to O'_aO, the box diagram shrinks to O'_aOO_bG, and America's income-consumption curve passes through Britain's absorption point V, as shown by broken curve O'_aV. Balance-of-payments equilibrium now prevails at V, but America suffers from massive unemployment.

America's income-consumption curve O_aU to O'_aV, as shown in Figure 14-3. Note carefully that at the current terms of trade (given by vector OT), point V is not only Britain's desired absorption point, it is America's desired absorption point as well. In other words, point V becomes an equilibium point similar to point E of Figures 14-1 and 14-2. At V both the commodity markets and the foreign exchange market are in equilibrium. Of course, massive unemployment prevails in America now, and unfortunately there exists no automatic mecha-nism to eliminate it.

Once equilibrium is established in the commodity markets and the foreign exchange market, there will be no further tendency for either the price of B-ex-portables or the rate of exchange to change.

Exchange-Rate Adjustment

Return to Figure 14-2 and recall that there exists initially an excess demand for pounds. Will the rate of exchange rise sufficiently and restore general equilibrium?

The question of an exchange-rate adjustment depends largely on the insti-tutional arrangement of the foreign exchange market. Broadly speaking, there are two basic systems: (1) the *fixed-exchange-rate system* and (2) the *flexible-exchange-rate system*. These two systems are actually polar cases. Between them there are many compromises. For instance, there is the *wide band*, where the rate of exchange is flexible within wide limits but is prevented from moving outside those limits. There is also the *crawling peg,* according to which the rate of exchange changes continuously but by very small amounts; that is, it "crawls".

Under a fixed-exchange-rate system the rate of exchange is kept fixed. This system has taken several forms. Before World War I, it took the form of an international *gold standard,* according to which all countries tied their monies to gold and allowed the unrestricted import and export of gold.

The essence of the gold standard was that the rates of exchange were fixed. For instance, suppose that the American monetary authorities agreed to buy and sell unlimited amounts of gold at $200 per ounce. Assume also that the British authorities agreed to buy and sell gold at £100 per ounce. Then the rate of exchange would be $2 per pound (*mint parity*). Any excess demand for pounds at this rate would merely cause gold to be exported from America to Britain. Thus, economic units in need of pounds would simply turn their dollars in for gold at the Federal Reserve and then sell the gold to the Bank of England for pounds. Similarly, an excess supply of pounds (that is, an excess demand for dollars) would cause gold to be exported from Britain to America. Under the gold standard, exchange-rate adjustments (prompted by changes in the official price of gold) were unthinkable.

After World War II, and in particular between 1944 and 1971, the free world sought the advantages of the fixed-exchange-rate system in the so-called Bretton Woods system, also known as the system of the *adjustable peg.* This system was similar to the gold standard with respect to the determination and maintenance of the spot-exchange rates in the short run. Thus, the dollar was pegged to gold at the fixed parity of $35 per ounce of gold, and dollars held by official monetary institutions were convertible freely into gold, as the United States was prepared to buy and sell unlimited amounts of gold at the official rate. Every other country was required to (1) declare the *par value* (or *parity*) of its currency in terms of gold or the U.S. dollar and (2) stand ready to defend the declared parity in the foreign exchange market by buying or selling dollars, at least in the short run. Accordingly, the currencies of member countries were kept stable in terms of dollars and thus in terms of each other. Exchange rates were thereby *fixed,* but only in the short run.

In the long run, a country whose balance of payments was in *fundamental disequilibrium* was allowed to change the dollar parity of its currency. For instance, a country experiencing a balance-of-payments *deficit* (surplus) was allowed to *devalue* (*revalue*) its currency. Exchange-rate adjustment did not work well in practice, however, and deficit countries had many reasons, rational and irrational, to avoid the drastic measure of devaluation.

Note that both *depreciation* and *devaluation* of a currency mean that the currency becomes cheaper relative to other currencies. Similarly, *appreciation* and *revaluation* (or *upvaluation*) mean that the currency becomes more expensive relative to other currencies. Nevertheless, the terms *devaluation* and *revaluation* usually refer to *deliberate government policy actions,* while the terms *depreciation* and *appreciation* refer to *exchange-rate changes in response to market forces.*

Under a flexible-exchange-rate system, the rate of exchange is determined daily by the forces of supply and demand. When government intervention is completely absent and the rate of exchange is determined by the market forces, we speak of *clean floating*. On the other hand, when monetary authorities intervene either to move the rate or to prevent it from moving freely in response to supply and demand, we speak of *dirty floating*.

Return now to the disequilibrium state of Figure 14.2. We may conclude that if the foreign exchange market is organized on the basis of a fixed-exchange-rate system, the rate of exchange will not change even though there may exist an excess demand for pounds. What if a flexible-exchange-rate system is actually adopted, or if the monetary authorities of the deficit country (America) devalue their currency? Will the system return then to long-run equilibrium point E smoothly?

It certainly seems plausible that an increase in the rate of exchange (depreciation of the dollar) could restore general equilibrium in Figure 14-2. However, aside from the issue of destabilizing speculation, there are reasons to believe that general equilibrium cannot be restored by a mere exchange-rate adjustment.

In the first place, an exchange-rate adjustment may affect aggregate spending. If this is so, the system will not move to point E, simply because aggregate spending will not remain equal to the full-employment income in either country.

More important, a devaluation (or depreciation) of the dollar is equivalent to a reduction in America's real income because of the deterioration of America's terms of trade. Such real-income reductions are usually resisted by workers. Thus, American workers will probably attempt to negotiate higher money wages in order to recover their losses caused by the devaluation. If the American workers are successful in raising their money wages, the cost of production, and thus the price, of A-exportables will increase and offset completely the adverse effect of the devaluation of the dollar on the American terms of trade. [Equation (14-1) shows that as p_a and R increase by the same percentage, America's terms of trade (p) remain constant.] Without a deterioration in the American terms of trade, there can be no movement toward the long-run equilibrium point E of Figure 14-2.

We may therefore conclude that adjustment through exchange-rate variations is not that simple. Later in the book, we shall pursue the influence of the exchange rate and its variations on the behavior of the world economy.

14-4   THE ADJUSTMENT PROCESS: (2) INCOME $\neq$ ABSORPTION

So far we have assumed that in each country national income equals desired absorption (or spending). The time has come to drop this assumption. This opens the way for a new type of balance-of-payments disequilibium—a disequilibrium in the foreign exchange market that does not coincide with a disequilibirum in any other market.

Policies for Internal Balance

Return to the initial disequilibium of Figure 14-2. *Desired* absorption equals full-imployment income in each country. But in America *actual* absorption is higher than desired absorption, which leads to an undesired accumulation of inventories. In Britain *actual* absorption is lower than desired absorption, which leads to an undesired decumulation of inventories. These undesired (or unintended) changes in inventories in the two countries tend to reduce production and employment in America and possibly produce inflation in Britain. (In the preceding section we saw how a cut in America's production and employment can bring about equilibrium in the foreign exchange market.) How will the American and British authorities react to this situation?

According to current macroeconomic thinking, the American authorities, fearing unemployment, will increase aggregate spending by means of expansionary fiscal and monetary policies. Thus, the American authorities may encourage domestic investment by reducing the rate of interest. Or they may encourage domestic consumption by reducing income taxes, thus placing more purchasing power in the hands of the consumers. Or finally, they may step up government purchases of goods and services.

The British authorities, fearing inflation, may reduce aggregate spending by means of deflationary fiscal and monetary policies. Thus, they may raise the interest rate and/or income taxes; and they may also reduce government spending on goods and services.

Under certain conditions, which are specified below, such policies for *internal balance* (that is, full employment without inflation) pursued by America and Britain simultaneously can restore equilibrium in the commodity markets and eliminate unintended inventory changes. Nevertheless, they give rise to a "fundamental disequilibrium" in the foreign exchange market (and, of course, the balance of payments).

Fundamental Disequilibrium

Consider Figure 14-4. Vector OT and points U and V correspond to the synonymous vector and points of Figures 14-2 and 14-3. Thus, at the current terms of trade and levels of spending, America desires bundle U and Britain bundle V. Draw America's income-consumption curve through point U and Britain's through point V, as shown by broken curves O_aUE and O_bEV. [Recall that an income-consumption curve is the locus of points where the marginal rate of substitution (or absolute slope of indifference curves) remains equal to a given price ratio—in our case, the initial terms of trade.] These income-consumption curves intersect at E.

If America increases her spending to O_aC (that is, by OC) and Britain reduces her spending to O_bD (that is, by OD), then point E will indicate both countries' desired absorption, and both commodity markets will clear. Accordingly, at point E there will exist equilibrium in the commodity markets and the labor markets.

Is there also equilibrium in the foreign exchange market at E? Unfortu-

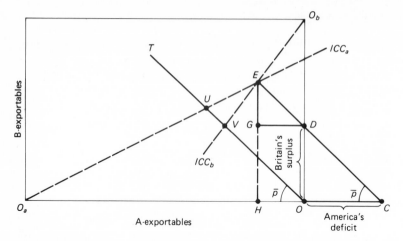

Figure 14-4   *Disequilibrium in the foreign exchange market alone.*
At the current terms of trade ($\bar{p}$), America wants to consume at U and Britain at V. America,
fearing unemployment, increases spending by OC; and Britain, fearing inflation, cuts spending by OD. Equilibrium occurs at E, where America runs a balance-of-payments deficit of OC
(in A-exportables).

nately, this is not the case. At E, America exports GD (or HO) units of A-exportables to Britain in exchange for HE or $(OD + GE)$ units of B-exportables.
Clearly, the value of GD units of A-exportables equals the value of only GE
units of B-exportables. Hence, America suffers from an import surplus of OD
units of B-exportables (which is equivalent to OC units of A-exportables).

It is interesting to note again that America's deficit is equal to the excess of
America's absorption over America's income. Similarly, Britain's surplus is
equal to the excess of Britain's income over Britain's absorption. This is shown
clearly in Figure 14-4, which the reader must study carefully, bearing in mind
that here actual absorption equals desired absorption.

Since both the commodity and labor markets are in equilibrium at point E
(Figure 14-4), there is no reason to expect any change in either the commodity
prices or the money-wage rates. Further, at point E there are no unintended inventory changes. Accordingly, neither the American nor the British producers
have any incentive to change their production plans. Every consumer and
every producer is in equilibrium. Yet the foreign exchange market is out of
equilibrium: The American monetary authorities lose reserves to the British
authorities in every period. Since reserves are limited, this situation cannot
continue for long. Can a devaluation (or depreciation) of the dollar restore general equilibrium? No, even though it is the commonsense medicine that is often
applied to cure a fundamental balance-of-payments disequilibrium.

Expenditure Adjusting versus Expenditure Switching

How can America and Britain correct the disequilibrium of Figure 14-4? First,
both America and Britain must reverse the earlier expenditure changes and
return to the disequilibrium state of Figure 14-2. That is, both countries must

pursue an *expenditure-adjusting policy* (that is, a policy that affects aggregate expenditure) to shift the budget line of Figure 14-4 from *CE* to *OT*. In addition, America and Britain must pursue an *expenditure-switching policy* (that is, a policy that "switches" expenditure from B-exportables to A-exportables), such as a devaluation of the dollar, to restore full general equilibrium at *E*.

The above prescription may sound easy, but it is not. The main reason for this is the fact that normally expenditure-adjusting policies also have an element of expenditure switching. Similarly, expenditure-switching policies have an element of expenditure adjusting. The art of economic policy is to determine the correct mix of expenditure-adjusting and expenditure-switching policies, as is shown in Part 4 of the book.

A Final Note

In the preceding discussion, we took it for granted that an intersection between the two income-consumption curves (Figure 14-4) always exists above and to the right of vector *OT*, as illustrated by point *E*. But this is the case only when America's income-consumption curve is flatter than Britain's, as shown in Figure 14-4. When America's income-consumption curve happens to be steeper than Britain's, no intersection exists above and to the right of *OT*, although one may exist below and to the left of *OT*. In general, the two income-consumption curves may intersect any number of times, or not at all.

14-5 THE TRANSFER PROBLEM

So far in this chapter, we have focused on exports and imports of goods and services only. Of course, these are typically the largest entries in the balance of payments. Nevertheless, our analysis has ignored completely other major categories of transactions. We now wish to extend the scope of our investigation to encompass *unilateral transfers* and *long-term capital movements*. These have attracted a great deal of attention since the beginning of economic science.

What do the entries of unilateral transfers and long-term capital movements have in common to deserve our considering them simultaneously? Simply this: Even though a unilateral transfer is a *gift* (a movement of assets from one country to another without expectation of payment) while a capital movement creates future obligations (for example, interest or dividends plus the expectation that in the future the borrower will return to the lender the initial funds received), *in the current period they both give rise to the need to transfer purchasing power from one country to another* (from the donor to the beneficiary or from the lender to the borrower).

In fact, we can break down a capital movement into two transfers: a transfer of the original capital from the lender to the borrower and a reverse transfer (or sequence of transfers) of the principal and interest (or dividends) from the borrower to the lender.

The difficulties that arise when a country needs to transfer purchasing power to another country form the main elements of the *transfer problem*. Accordingly, both the current problem of the *dollar overhang* (that is, the massive amounts of dollar claims that the rest of the world has accumulated against the United States in the postwar period) and the difficulties surrounding the "pe-trodollars" (that is, the huge excess of foreign exchange earnings of a small number of Middle Eastern and other oil-producing nations) come under the umbrella of the transfer problem, which is actually the subject of the present discussion.

In general, transfers of purchasing power, or *transfer payments,* from one country to another may occur for the following various reasons:

    1 *Borrowing* by economic units in a poor country from economic units in richer countries
    2 *Reparations* made to the victors by defeated countries (for example, by France after the Franco-Prussian War of 1870–1871 and by Germany after World War I)
    3 *Grants* supplied by developed nations to industrially backward countries
    4 Settlement of old debts
    5 Immigrants' transfer payments

The reason we now turn to the transfer problem is the fact that the transfer problem is merely an inversion of the balance-of-payments problem. This important relationship is explained below.

Financial Transfer versus Real Transfer

An important distinction that we must always keep in mind is between the *financial* transfer and the *real* transfer. The financial transfer refers to the movement of financial assets from the transferor to the transferee, and the conversion of the currency of the transferor into the currency of the transferee through the foreign exchange market. The real transfer, on the other hand, refers to the induced movement of goods between countries.

As we shall see, the financial transfer and the real transfer are interrelated. In general, the real transfer may precede, accompany, or follow the financial transfer.

A crucial question that has attracted much attention is whether a financial transfer of, say, $1 million from America to Britain will result in the subsequent movement of $1 million worth of goods from America to Britain. When this is actually the case (that is, when $1 million worth of goods are actually shipped from America to Britain), we say that the transfer is *effected.* On the other hand, when the financial transfer induces a *smaller* flow of goods (say, $800,000), we say that the transfer is *undereffected.* And when the financial transfer induces a *larger* flow of goods (say $1,300,000), we say that the transfer is *overeffected.*

When the transfer is actually effected, there is no transfer problem; that is, an effected transfer results in no balance-of-payments difficulties—the financial flows match the commodity-trade flows precisely. On the other hand, when a transfer is either undereffected or overeffected, there is a transfer problem; that is, a transfer that is not exactly effected creates a state of balance-of-payments disequilibrium, which must be corrected somehow.

The degree to which a transfer is actually effected depends on the manner in which the financial assets are raised in the transferor country and also how they are used in the transferee country. For instance, if the funds come out of past savings in the transferor country and go into savings in the transferee country, there will be no effect on the commodity flows. The same will be true if the transferor country actually prints new money that finds its way into the transferee's stockpile of foreign currency. On the other hand, if the funds are actually raised by taxation in the transferor country and spent on goods and services in the transferee country, there will be definite repercussions on the flows of goods and services between the two countries, and the transfer may be effected, undereffected, or overeffected, depending on circumstances.

Note carefully that the real transfer is actually effected when the transferor country develops an export surplus, and the transferee country an import surplus, equal to the transfer. Thus, the real transfer may take the form of either *increased exports* or *reduced imports* by the transferor country, or both. This is the only way in which real capital may be transferred between countries.

Also note that the goods transferred need not be capital goods, even though the transfer may be the result of a long-term loan by a rich country to a poor country for the purpose of assisting the poor country to build a factory, a dam, or some other project. Even in such cases consumption goods and services may indeed be transferred by the transferor country to the transferee. These consumption goods and services enable the transferee country to free resources and channel them into the production of capital goods (for example, a dam or a factory). We therefore conclude that the nature of the goods transferred is immaterial. In general, these goods reflect the comparative advantages and disadvantages of the countries involved.

Finally, it is important to emphasize that the transfer problem is *not* concerned with the long-run effects of the movement of real capital between countries, such as the effect on the production-possibilities frontier, comparative advantage, marginal productivity of factors, and income distribution. Rather, the transfer problem is a standard exercise in the balance-of-payments adjustment mechanism and is mainly concerned with the difficulties and manner in which real capital is transferred between countries as a result of borrowing, reparations, aid, and so on. This actually explains why unilateral payments, such as reparations, which do not necessarily result in capital formation in the recipient country, are lumped together with payments, such as corporate borrowing and direct investment, which do give rise to capital formation.

The Transfer Problem as the Inversion of the Balance-of-Payments Problem

The transfer problem may be viewed as the inversion of the balance-of-payments problem. Thus, any actual balance-of-payments disequilibrium involves a real transfer from the surplus country to the deficit country. The cor-

rection of the balance-of-payments disequilibrium, brought about either automatically or by means of planned government policies, can be viewed as the
problem of generating either a real transfer of equal amount in the opposite direction (that is, from the deficit to the surplus country) or a money transfer from
the surplus to the deficit country. The latter case is illustrated below with the
recycling of petrodollars.

Consider again the balance-of-payments disequilibrium illustrated in Figure 14-4. America is running a deficit of OC (measured in A-exportables). In
particular, America's expenditure on goods and services is given by O_aC, while
America's income is given by O_aO (both aggregates measured in A-exportables). The difference between America's income and expenditure, that is,
$OC = O_aC - O_aO$, is made good by means of an import surplus. Accordingly,
we can say that Britain is actually transferring to America OC units of A-exportables per unit of time. This is a real transfer. Nevertheless, we have a
balance-of-payments problem, because the real transfer from Britain to
America is not accompanied by a financial transfer.

The balance-of-payments problem can be solved in one of two ways: (1) by
reversing the real transfer or (2) by inducing a financial transfer from the
surplus country (Britain) to the deficit country (America). As we saw earlier,
the reversal of the real transfer (that is, the elimination of America's import
surplus) requires a combination of expenditure-adjusting policies (in both countries) and expenditure-switching policies. On the other hand, the inducement of
a financial transfer involves a loan (or grant) from Britain to America. The
reversal of the real transfer implies a return to the long-run equilibrium portrayed in Figure 14-1. The loan from Britain to America maintains the state of
Figure 14-4 by making it possible for America to finance its deficit (without
running out of reserves).

Consider now the transfer problem proper. Starting from the long-run
equilibrium of Figure 14-1, let Britain make a financial transfer to America.
The transfer will be totally effected only when a new state of equilibrium is
reached in which America develops an import surplus equal to the transfer, as
illustrated in Figure 14-4. Accordingly, effecting a transfer means that we shift
from the equilibrium of Figure 14-1 to that of Figure 14-4. This is exactly the
opposite, of course, of what we must do in the absence of any transfer to correct the balance-of-payments disequilibrium portrayed in Figure 14-4.

The Secondary Burden of the Transfer

In general, effecting a transfer requires (1) an adjustment in each country's
aggregate expenditure and (2) a change in relative prices. The required change
in relative prices (terms of trade) attracted too much attention in the past, especially in relation to the German reparations.

It may be recalled that after World War I Germany was made at Versailles
to pay war reparations to the Allies. Lord John M. Keynes upheld the so-called
orthodox position, namely, the view that the transfer problem causes the terms
of trade of the transferor to deteriorate, and claimed that Germany would have

to experience a severe terms-of-trade deterioration in order to generate the necessary export surplus and effect the transfer. He even expressed fears that Germany would not be able to make the transfer at all because of the low elasticity of demand for her exports. Bertil Ohlin opposed Keynes by advocating that a transfer need not necessarily worsen the terms of trade of the transferor country.

The issue of whether the terms of trade of the transferor country deteriorate with the transfer is clearly an empirical one. No amount of a priori reasoning can tell us what will actually happen in any particular situation. Each case must be studied on its own by means of patient econometric work.

When the transfer actually causes her terms of trade to deteriorate, the transferor country apparently suffers a *secondary burden*. Nevertheless, the whole question of secondary burdens (and benefits for that matter) seems semantic or artificial. Certainly, what is important is the total effect of the transfer on the economic welfare of the transferor country and the transferee. One would then expect governments engaged in negotiating reparations payments to take into consideration the effects of the transfer on the terms of trade, although this argument need not apply to transfers effected by private economic units, which behave as price takers.

The Recycling of Petrodollars

The 1973 oil-price increase caused the transfer of huge amounts of purchasing power (petrodollars) from the oil-importing nations to the oil-exporting countries. In 1974 alone, the members of OPEC developed a surplus of almost $60 billion. Ipso facto, the surplus funds of the oil-exporting countries were equal to the current account deficits of the rest of the world.

Apart from the frightening question of whether the oil-exporting countries would continue to exchange their deposits of oil for liquid claims and securities, there was the basic question of the *recycling* of petrodollars: the distribution of oil-surplus monies back to the deficit countries in order to close the circle. Many financial analysts were very nervous and jittery, and indeed they saw in their crystal balls the specter of the early 1930s, when huge monetary transfers played havoc with the international financial mechanism and threw the international economy into a tailspin. Fortunately, nothing of the sort happened.

The oil-exporting countries had a strong preference for liquidity and placed their surpluses in highly liquid, low-risk investments. On the other hand, the oil-importing countries sought to finance their deficits by liquidating longer-term and riskier assets. Accordingly, the short-term investments of the OPEC members were completely unrelated to the balance-of-payments needs of the oil-importing countries. The financial markets that looked attractive to OPEC were not necessarily located in those deficit countries that actually needed the funds to finance their deficits. Consequently, a heavy recycling burden fell upon the international financial community.

As it turned out, the Eurodollar market did most of the recycling. After all, the Eurodollar market was the principal outlet for OPEC surplus funds. Even though many Eurodollar banks experienced considerable strain during this process of international financial intermediation, the overall performance of the market was remarkable.

It may be noted that some recycling assistance came from official arrangements, such as the 1974 oil facility that was set up by the International Monetary Fund in an effort to assist less developed countries hit hard by the oil-price increase.

14-6 CONCLUSION

The discussion of this chapter leads to an important conclusion: Adjustment may proceed either through *prices* (such as exchange-rate adjustments, and money-wage changes) or through *incomes* (that is, aggregate spending, production, and employment). The next two chapters deal with both of these aspects of the international adjustment mechanism. In particular, Chapter 15 discusses exclusively the price-adjustment mechanism, while Chapter 16 concentrates mainly on the income-adjustment mechanism.

14-7 SUMMARY

1   Most issues of international finance can be clarified by a simple model of two countries, say, America and Britain. America produces only A-exportables with labor (which is in fixed supply) and under constant returns to scale. Britain produces only B-exportables. Each country's tastes are given by a social indifference map.

2   General equilibrium requires that supply equals demand in all markets: the labor markets, the commodity markets, and the foreign exchange market. A necessary condition for general equilibrium is that aggregate income equals aggregate expenditure in each country. When this condition is satisfied, general equilibrium can be portrayed graphically by means of a box diagram, as in a two-consumer exchange economy.

3   Assuming that national income equals desired spending (or absorption) in each country, a balance-of-payments disequilibrium must reflect disequilibrium in the commodity markets and (when all buyer plans are realized) unplanned inventory changes, with the deficit country converting her foreign exchange reserves into unwanted inventories of goods, and the surplus country converting her commodity inventories into foreign exchange reserves. This disequilibrium can be corrected by allowing the deficit country's terms of trade to worsen sufficiently, but without disturbing the equality between national income and desired absorption.

4   A reduction in America's terms of trade can be accomplished in one of three ways: (a) a reduction in the money price of A-exportables, (b) an increase in the money price of B-exportables, or (c) a depreciation of America's currency.

5   A reduction in the money prices of the deficit country's exportables requires a reduction in that country's money-wage rate. Since the latter is

inflexible in the downward direction, production and income in the deficit country will fall instead—producers cannot be expected to accumulate inventories indefinitely. Such income reduction can restore equilibrium in both commodity markets as well as the foreign exchange market, but at the expense of massive unemployment in the deficit country.

6 Whether the currency of the deficit country depreciates or not depends on the existing exchange-rate system. Between the polar cases of the fixed- and flexible-exchange-rate systems there are many compromises, such as the wide band and the crawling peg.

7 Even if we ignore the issue of destabilizing speculation, a depreciation of the deficit country's currency need not restore equilibrium. Thus, a currency depreciation may affect aggregate spending and thus destroy the equality between national income and desired spending. More important, a currency depreciation may induce the deficit country's workers to demand higher money wages in order to maintain their standard of living. Such wage increases, however, neutralize the effect of currency depreciation on the terms of trade. But equilibrium cannot be restored without a change in the terms of trade.

8 When the (deficit) country with unplanned inventory accumulation increases its spending (by means of expansionary fiscal and monetary policies), while at the same time the (surplus) country with unplanned inventory decumulation decreases its spending, equilibrium in the commodity markets could be restored; but a "fundamental disequilibrium" would arise in the foreign exchange market. Actual absorption would be equal to desired absorption in each country, but absorption would be different from national income. A deterioration in the deficit country's terms of trade (brought about by devaluation or otherwise) would no longer restore general equilibrium, because income does not equal absorption.

9 To correct a "fundamental disequilibrium," the two countries must combine expenditure-adjusting policies (to bring their expenditures into equality with their respective full-employment incomes) with expenditure-switching policies (to shift the terms of trade to their equilibrium value).

10 The transfer problem is a standard exercise in the balance-of-payments adjustment mechanism. It is concerned with the difficulties and manner in which real capital is transferred between countries as a result of borrowing, reparations, aid, and so on.

11 The transfer is effected, overeffected, or undereffected when the flow of goods (real transfer) from the transferor to the transferee is equal to, larger than, or smaller than, the financial transfer that induces it. The nature of the goods transferred is immaterial. There is a transfer problem (that is, balance-of-payments difficulties) when the transfer is not exactly effected.

12 The degree to which a transfer is actually effected depends on the manner in which the financial assets are raised in the transferor country and used in the transferee.

13 In general, effecting a transfer requires (a) an adjustment in each country's aggregate spending and (b) a change in the terms of trade.

14 The orthodox position (Keynes) holds that the transfer causes the terms of trade of the transferor to deteriorate (secondary burden). The modern position (Ohlin) holds that the transfer need not make worse the transferor's terms of trade.

15 The transfer problem is the inverse of the balance-of-payments problem.

16 The "recycling" problem (that is, the distribution of the oil-surplus monies of the OPEC members back to the oil-importing nations) arose from the fact that the countries in which OPEC members invested their funds did not coincide with the oil-importing countries that actually needed the funds to finance their deficits. The Eurodollar market did most of the recycling.

SUGGESTED READING

Alexander, S. S. (1952). "Effects of a Devaluation on a Trade Balance." *IMF Staff Papers*, vol. 2 (April), pp. 263–278. Reprinted in R. E. Caves and H. G. Johnson (eds.). AEA *Readings in International Economics*. Richard D. Irwin, Inc., Homewood, Ill., 1968.

Chacholiades, M. (1978). *International Monetary Theory and Policy*. McGraw-Hill Book Company, New York, Chaps. 9 and 12.

Johnson, H. G. (1961). *International Trade and Economic Growth: Studies in Pure Theory*. Harvard University Press, Cambridge, Mass., chap. 6. Reprinted in R. E. Caves and H. G. Johnson (eds.). AEA *Readings in International Economics*. Richard D. Irwin, Inc., Homewood, Ill., 1968.

Keynes, J. M. (1929). "The German Transfer Problem." *Economic Journal*, vol. 39 (March), pp. 1–7. Reprinted in H. S. Ellis and L. A. Metzler (eds.). AEA *Readings in the Theory of International Trade*. Richard D. Irwin, Inc., Homewood, Ill., 1950.

Ohlin, B. (1929). "The Reparation Problem: A Discussion. I. Transfer Difficulties, Real and Imagined." *Economic Journal*, vol. 39 (June), pp. 172–178. Reprinted in H. S. Ellis and L. A. Metzler (eds.). AEA *Readings in the Theory of International Trade*. Richard D. Irwin, Inc., Homewood, Ill., 1950.

Pearce, I. F. (1970). *International Trade*. W. W. Norton and Company, Inc., New York, chaps. 1–6.

Chapter Fifteen

The Price-Adjustment Mechanism

The analysis of the previous chapter leads to two fundamental conclusions:

    1 *Balance-of-payments* adjustment may proceed through either prices or incomes (or both).
    2 *Price adjustment* may take the form of either exchange-rate changes or price-level changes (that is, general inflation and deflation).

This chapter deals exclusively with the price-adjustment mechanism, while the income-adjustment mechanism is considered in the next chapter. In particular, the first five sections of this chapter lay the foundations of the price-adjustment mechanism and provide a detailed discussion of the effects of exchange-rate changes on the balance of payments and the terms of trade. The discussion is deliberately cast in very general terms, simply because it is immaterial whether an exchange-rate change is the result of government policy (such as devaluation or revaluation under the adjustable peg) or reflects market supply and demand conditions. The economic effects of, say, a 10 percent devaluation under the adjustable peg are identical to the economic effects of a 10 percent depreciation under the flexible-exchange-rate system.

Exchange-rate adjustments have very profound effects on the international economy. A change in the rate of foreign exchange throws all commodity markets out of equilibrium. As the commodity markets adjust slowly to a new equilibrium, each country experiences dramatic changes in domestic production, consumption, exports, imports, supply of foreign exchange, demand for foreign exchange, and terms of trade. Indeed, the effects of an exchange-rate adjustment are so extensive that they sooner or later filter down to each and every citizen. The multifarious effects of an exchange-rate adjustment are discussed in Section 15-4.

The main concern of this chapter is whether a devaluation (or depreciation) of the currency of a deficit country will actually reduce the balance-of-payments deficit. As it turns out, devaluation (or depreciation) may either improve or make worse the deficit country's balance of payments—it all depends on circumstances. Crucial to the outcome of devaluation are the import-demand elasticities. The implications of this important conclusion are far reaching, as is explained in Sections 15-4, 15-5 and 15-9.

Section 15-6 considers briefly the special problems that are created by the presence of nontraded goods, that is, goods which are not traded internationally between countries but rather are purely domestic goods because of prohibitive transportation costs. This is a digression from the main theme, and the student may omit it.

Sections 15-7 and 15-8 show briefly how to extend the analysis of exchange-rate changes to price-level changes under fixed exchange rates. In particular, Section 15-7 deals with David Hume's price-specie-flow mechanism, and Section 15-8 deals with the purchasing-power-parity theory.

The final section (15-9) discusses the econometric difficulties in estimating import-demand elasticities and provides some recent estimates of these elasticities for 15 industrial countries.

With the minor exception of Section 15-6, the analysis of this chapter rests heavily on the so-called partial-equilibrium model, the main architects of which were Bickerdike (1920), Robinson (1937), and Machlup (1939, 1940), even though others have generously contributed to its development. For this reason, the first two sections of this chapter review the basic assumptions of this model and derive the supply-of-exports and demand-for-imports schedules that form the raw material of the partial-equilibrium model.

15-1 THE PARTIAL-EQUILIBRIUM MODEL

Before we can study the effects of exchange-rate adjustments, we must choose a model for commodity trade. Because of our primary interest in the price-adjustment mechanism, we choose the partial-equilibrium model. What are the assumptions of this model?

As before, assume that there are two countries, America (home country) and Britain (foreign country, or rest of the world) with national currencies the dollar and the pound sterling, respectively. Aggregate America's exports into a single homogeneous commodity and call them for convenience A-exportables. Similarly, aggregate Britain's exports into another homogeneous commodity and call them B-exportables. Observe that A-exportables and B-exportables are *different* commodities. In contrast to the model of Chapter 14, assume that each country produces *both* A-exportables and B-exportables. This last assumption provides greater generality, of course.

Also, in order to concentrate on commodity trade only, assume as before that the net balance of capital movements plus unilateral transfers is always zero.

We now come to the heart of the partial-equilibrium model. In complete contrast to the model of Chapter 14, assume that each country has supply and demand schedules showing the quantities of A-exportables and B-exportables supplied by domestic producers and demanded by domestic consumers, respectively, at alternative prices expressed in *domestic* currency. It is this assumption that is mainly responsible for the name *partial-equilibrium* model.

Panel (*a*) of Figure 15-1 illustrates America's domestic supply and demand schedules for B-exportables. In particular, supply schedule *SS'* shows the quantities of B-exportables supplied by American producers at alternative *dollar* prices. For instance, when the price of B-exportables is $60, American producers as a group are willing to supply 14,000 units. On the other hand, when the price rises to $120, American producers are willing to supply the larger quantity of 18,000 units.

Note that America's supply schedule slopes upwards because normally American producers can produce larger quantities of B-exportables only at higher costs.

Similarly, America's domestic demand schedule, *DD'*, shows the quantities of B-exportables that American consumers are willing to purchase at alternative *dollar* prices. This demand curve slopes downward, because American consumers are willing to purchase larger quantities of B-exportables only at lower prices. For instance, when the price is $120, American consumers are willing to buy 18,000 units of B-exportables. On the other hand, when the price falls to $60, American consumers are willing to purchase the larger quantity of 20,000 units.

Similar domestic supply and demand schedules exist in America for A-exportables. Also, such domestic schedules for A-exportables and B-exportables exist in Britain. The only difference is that Britain's schedules give prices in *pounds,* not dollars.

An important assumption of the partial-equilibrium model is that the various domestic supply and demand schedules are largely independent of each other. For instance, we must insist that the demand schedules for A-exportables remain unaltered as the price of B-exportables changes, even though in reality one commodity may be substituted for another as *relative* prices change. This is, of course, a drawback of the partial-equilibrium model that we can justify by assuming that such substitution, if any, is rather negligible.

This is the basic skeleton of the partial-equilibrium model. Before we can put it to work, it is necessary to go through the preliminary exercise of deriving the demand-for-imports and supply-of-exports schedules, as shown in the next section.

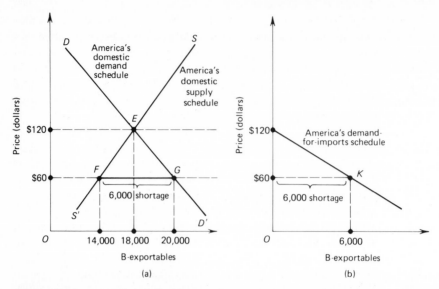

Figure 15-1 *Derivation of America's demand-for-imports schedule.*
Panel (*a*) shows America's domestic supply schedule (*SS'*) and demand schedule (*DD'*) for A-exportables. Panel (*b*) gives America's demand-for-imports schedule. For each price below $120 (say, $60), determine in panel (*a*) America's domestic supply (14,000) and demand (20,000) of B-exportables. America's excess demand for B-exportables (that is 20,000 − 14,000 = 6,000) is America's demand for imports at the selected price ($60), as shown in panel (*b*).

15-2 SCHEDULES FOR IMPORTS AND EXPORTS

A commodity market is in equilibrium when the price is such that one country's desired volume of imports matches the other country's desired volume of exports. For this reason, we cannot show international equilibrium in the commodity markets unless we have each country's *demand-for-imports schedule* and *supply-of-exports schedule*. We can obtain these from the domestic supply and demand schedules, as explained below.

The demand-for-imports schedule is part of what is ordinarily called in price theory the *excess-demand curve*. Similarly, the supply-of-exports schedule is part of what is ordinarily known as the *excess-supply curve*. The only new element is that America's consumers and producers are interested in prices expressed in dollars, while Britain's consumers and producers are interested in prices expressed in pounds. Fortunately, this is not an insurmountable difficulty.

The Demand-for-Imports Schedule

Consider again Figure 15-1, which shows how to derive America's demand-for-imports schedule. Panel (*a*) shows America's domestic supply and demand schedules for B-exportables. Panel (*b*) gives America's demand-for-imports schedule.

Consider panel (*a*) first. When the price of B-exportables is $120, American consumers are willing to buy 18,000 units, which is exactly the number of units American producers are willing to sell at that price. When the price drops below $120, America develops a shortage (excess demand) of, or a *demand for imports* for, B-exportables. For instance, when the price drops to $60, American consumers are willing to purchase 20,000 of B-exportables, but American producers are willing to sell 14,000 units only; thus, America develops a shortage (demand for imports) of 6,000 units. Panel (*b*) gives this information directly; it shows that America's demand for imports is zero when the price is $120 but increases to 6,000 units when the price falls to $60.

In general, America's demand-for-imports schedule in panel (*b*) gives directly the horizontal differences between the domestic demand and supply schedules of panel (*a*) for all prices below $120.

It is extremely important to note that because it is derived from the domestic demand *and* supply schedules, the demand-for-imports schedule depends on all those parameters that lie behind the domestic supply and demand schedules. Accordingly, like America's domestic demand for B-exportables, the demand-for-imports schedule depends on tastes, incomes, and other prices. But unlike America's domestic demand for B-exportables, the demand-for-imports schedule depends also on technology and factor prices—the parameters that lie behind America's domestic supply schedule.

In the same way, we can derive Britain's demand-for-imports schedule (for A-exportables). There is no compelling reason to repeat this exercise. We must only remember that Britain's demand-for-imports schedule gives the quantities of A-exportables that Britain is willing to import at alternative prices *expressed in pounds.*

The Supply-of-Exports Schedule

Turn now to Figure 15-2, which shows how to derive America's supply-of-exports schedule. Panel (*a*) shows again America's domestic supply (*SS'*) and demand (*DD'*) schedules for A-exportables. Panel (*b*) gives America's supply-of-exports schedule.

Consider panel (*a*) first. When the price of A-exportables is $42, American consumers are willing to buy 1,300 units, which is exactly the amount American producers are willing to sell at that price. Therefore, when the price is $42, America's supply of exports is zero, as shown in panel (*b*). As the price rises above $42, however, America develops a *surplus* of A-exportables. For instance, when the price rises to $72, America's consumers reduce their consumption of A-exportables to 800 units, while America's producers increase their production to 3,000 units. Accordingly, when the price rises to $72, America develops a surplus of 2,200 units of A-exportables. Put differently, at $72 America is willing to export 2,200 units of A-exportables, as shown again in panel (*b*).

Panel (*b*) gives directly all the information concerning America's surpluses of A-exportables at prices higher than $42. In general, America's supply-of-ex-

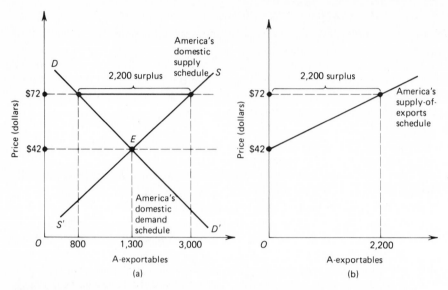

Figure 15-2 *Derivation of America's supply-of-exports schedule.*
Panel (*a*) shows America's domestic supply schedule (*SS'*) and demand schedule (*DD'*) for A-exportables. Panel (*b*) gives America's supply-of-exports schedule. For each price above $42 (say, $72), determine in panel (*a*) America's domestic supply (3,000) and demand (800) of A-exportables. America's excess supply of A-exportables (that is, 3,000 − 800 = 2,200) is America's supply of exports at the selected price ($72), as shown in panel (*b*).

ports schedule in panel (*b*) gives directly the horizontal differences between the domestic supply and demand schedules of panel (*a*) for all prices above $42.

Note again that America's supply-of-exports schedule does not depend only on those parameters that lie behind the domestic supply schedule in panel (*a*)—that is, technology and factor prices. It depends also on all those parameters that lie behind America's domestic demand schedule—that is, tastes, incomes, and prices of other commodities.

We could follow the above procedure to derive Britain's supply-of-exports schedule, but there is no need to do so. We must always remember, however, that Britain's supply-of-exports schedule gives the quantities of B-exportables that Britain is willing to export at alternative prices *expressed in pounds*.

15-3 EQUILIBRIUM IN THE COMMODITY MARKETS

Given America's and Britain's demand-for-imports and supply-of-exports schedules, we can proceed to determine equilibrium in the commodity markets. We must do this before we can find out whether the balance of payments is in equilibrium. When we know the equilibrium volumes of exports and imports as well as the equilibrium prices of A-exportables and B-exportables, we can determine each country's export revenue and expenditure on imports (in either dollars or pounds). The difference between a country's export revenue and expenditure on imports is, of course, the country's balance-of-trade deficit or surplus, as the case may be.

The Need to Express All Prices in Terms of the Same Currency

As we pointed out earlier, a commodity market is in equilibrium when the price of the commodity is such that one country's desired volume of imports matches the other country's volume of exports.

If America and Britain were two regions of a single country using a common currency, we could easily determine equilibrium in a commodity market: We could superimpose one country's (region's) demand-for-imports schedule on the other country's (region's) supply-of-exports schedule and then determine the point of intersection between the two schedules.

However, America and Britain are different nations with different national currencies. As a result, our search for commodity-market equilibria is now slightly complicated by the fact that America's schedules express all prices in dollars, and Britain's schedules express all prices in pounds sterling.

Obviously, before we can determine the commodity-market equilibria, we must express all prices in terms of the same currency. We can choose either currency for this purpose, although here we choose to express all prices in terms of pounds mainly because of our interest in the supply and demand for foreign exchange (pounds).

Conversion of American (Dollar) Prices into Pounds

Britain's demand-for-imports and supply-of-exports schedules give prices in pounds to begin with. Accordingly, in Figure 15-3 we have drawn Britain's schedules as they were originally derived. The rate of foreign exchange simply has no influence on Britain's schedules, which remain unaltered throughout our discussion.

However, the original demand-for-imports and supply-of-exports schedules of America (see Figures 15-1 and 15-2) give all prices in dollars. Therefore, we must transform America's schedules in order to make them give prices in pounds. For this transformation, we must know the rate of foreign exchange.

Suppose that the rate of exchange is $2, that is, £1 sells for $2. How can we convert the dollar prices given by the original demand-for-imports and supply-of-exports schedules of America (Figures 15-1 and 15-2) into pounds? Simply by dividing each dollar price by 2, since $2 is equivalent to £1. This is actually shown by America's schedules in Figure 15-3.

On the assumption that £1 sells for $2, America's demand-for-imports and supply-of-exports schedules given in Figure 15-3 give exactly the same information as the corresponding schedules of Figures 15-1 and 15-2. For instance, America's demand-for-imports schedule in Figure 15-1, panel (*b*), shows that America is willing to import 6,000 units of B-exportables *at $60 per unit*. In Figure 15-3, panel (*a*), America's demand-for-imports schedule shows that America is willing to import 6,000 units of B-exportables *at £30 per unit*. Since £1 sells for $2, by assumption, the price of $60 is equivalent to the price of £30 and vice versa.

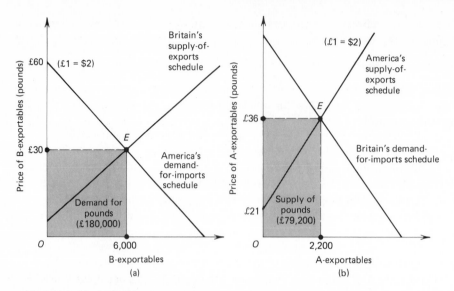

Figure 15-3 *Equilibrium in the commodity markets.*
After transforming America's schedules of Figures 15-1(*b*) and 15-2(*b*) to give prices in pounds, we superimpose them on Britain's schedules to determine equilibrium in the commodity markets. Panel (*a*) shows that equilibrium in the market for B-exportables occurs at *E*, where the price of B-exportables is £30, and that the quantity imported by America is 6,000 units. America's expenditure on imports—that is, £30 × 6,000 = £180,000—is the demand for pounds, as shown by the shaded rectangle.
   Panel (*b*) shows that equilibrium in the market for A-exportables occurs at *E*, where the price of A-exportables is £36 and the quantity exported by America is 2,200 units. America's export revenue—that is, £36 × 2,200 = £79,200—is the supply of pounds, as shown by the shaded rectangle.

   The same relationship holds, of course, between all prices along America's demand-for-imports schedule in Figure 15-1, panel (*b*), and the corresponding prices along America's schedule in Figure 15-3, panel (*a*). For any volume of imports, the dollar price (Figure 15-1) is *twice* as high as the price in pounds (Figure 15-3), because $2 is equivalent to £1.
   Similarly, America's supply-of-exports schedule in Figure 15-2, panel (*b*), shows that America is willing to export 2,200 units of A-exportables at $72 per unit. On the other hand, America's supply-of-exports schedule of Figure 15-3, panel (*b*), shows that America is willing to export 2,200 units of A-exportables at £36 per unit. Again, since £1 sells for $2, by assumption, the price of $72 is equivalent to the price of £36 and vice versa.
   The same relationship holds, of course, between all prices along America's supply-of-exports schedule in Figure 15-2, panel (*b*), and the corresponding prices along America's schedule in Figure 15-3, panel (*b*). For any volume of exports, the dollar price (Figure 15-2) is *twice* as high as the price in pounds (Figure 15-3), because $2 is worth £1.
   Note carefully that America's demand-for-imports and supply-of-exports schedules in Figure 15-3 are good only when £1 sells for $2. If the rate of

exchange were different, these schedules would also be different, as shown in Section 15-4. To remind the reader of this important truth, the equation £1 = $2 is printed next to America's schedules.

Commodity-Market Equilibrium with Prices in Pounds

We are finally ready to determine equilibrium in the markets for A-exportables and B-exportables. This is shown in Figure 15-3. Panel (a) illustrates the market for B-exportables and panel (b) the market for A-exportables.

Consider panel (a) first. Equilibrium occurs at point E, that is, the intersection of Britain's supply-of-exports schedule and America's demand-for-imports schedule. Thus, at the equilibrium price of £30, Britain exports 6,000 units of B-exportables to America. This means that America spends £180,000 on imports. Alternatively, we can say that at the current rate of exchange (£1 = $2), there is a demand for £180,000 (foreign exchange), as shown by the shaded rectangle in panel (a).

Turn now to panel (b), which shows the market for A-exportables. Equilibrium occurs at E, that is, the intersection of America's supply-of-exports schedule and Britain's demand-for-imports schedule. Accordingly, at the equilibrium price of £36, America exports 2,200 units of A-exportables to Britain. America's export revenue is £79,200, which is actually the amount of pounds supplied in the foreign exchange market at the current rate of exchange ($2 = £1).

Knowing the equilibrium prices in pounds and the rate of foreign exchange, we can easily infer the equilibrium prices in dollars as well as America's export revenue and expenditure on imports in dollars. Thus, the equilibrium prices of A-exportables and B-exportables are, respectively, $2 × 36 = $72 and $2 × 30 = $60. Similarly, America's export revenue is $2 × 79,200 = $158,400, while America's expenditure on imports is $2 × 180,000 = $360,000.

We should also emphasize that given the equilibrium prices, we can go back to each country's domestic supply and demand schedules to determine each country's domestic production and consumption of A-exportables and B-exportables. We leave this as an exercise for the reader.

In the current illustration, America suffers from an import surplus of £100,800 (that is, £180,000 − £79,200). Will a devaluation (or depreciation) of the dollar reduce (or eliminate) America's import surplus? This is a critical question, and we consider it in the next section.

15-4 THE EFFECTS OF DEVALUATION

At the commodity-market equilibrium state illustrated in Figure 15-3, America is running a balance-of-trade deficit. Under a flexible-exchange-rate system, the dollar will depreciate automatically; that is, the price of the pound in terms of dollars will tend to rise. Even under the adjustable peg, America may decide to devalue the dollar, or Britain may decide to revalue the pound. In any case, the rate of exchange (dollars per pound) will increase. What are the effects of this exchange-rate adjustment?

As we pointed out earlier, the effects of devaluation are rather extensive. The purpose of this section is to enable the reader to obtain a general understanding of them.

Effects on Commodity-Market Equilibria

Return to Figure 15-3, and suppose that the rate of exchange increases from $2 to $3. What happens to the initial commodity-market equilibria?

It must be obvious that when the dollar depreciates, the equilibria (E) shown in the two panels of Figure 15-3 can no longer persist. This must be clear from our earlier discussion. America's demand-for-imports and supply-of-exports schedules in Figure 15-3 are drawn on the assumption that £1 = $2. *When the dollar depreciates, America's schedules become obsolete and must be redrawn.* As a result, the commodity-market equilibria will shift to new points along the unmodified schedules of Britain.

For instance, consider the market for B-exportables. Before the depreciation of the dollar, equilibrium occurs at E, where Britain exports to America 6,000 units of B-exportables at £30 per unit. Of course, we know from Figure 15-1, panel (*b*), that America is willing to import 6,000 units of B-exportables at $60 per unit; since $2 = £1, it follows that America is indeed willing to pay £30 (that is, $^{60}/_2$) per unit. When the dollar depreciates, Britain will no longer export 6,000 units of B-exportables to America. For this volume (6,000 units), Britain demands £30 per unit and America offers $60 per unit. Since now $3 = £1, it follows that America is willing to pay only £20 (that is, $^{60}/_3$) per unit, which is, of course, less than the £30 per unit that Britain wants. Alternatively, Britain can receive £30 per unit only if America pays $90 (that is, 3 × 30 instead of 2 × 30) per unit. But America is not willing to import 6,000 of B-exportables at $90 per unit. At that high price, America is willing to import much *less* (see Figure 15-1).

Similarly, America's volume of exports of A-exportables cannot remain at 2,200 units—it will tend to increase. The reason is simple. For the volume of 2,200 units of A-exportables, America is willing to accept $72 per unit, while Britain is willing to offer £36. When £1 = $2, Britain's offer of £36 is equivalent to America's demand for $72. However, when the exchange rate rises to £1 = $3, the price of £36 that Britain is willing to pay becomes much higher than $72, that is, the price America is willing to accept. In fact, after the dollar depreciates, America is willing to export 2,200 units of A-exportables at only £24 (that is, $^{72}/_3$) per unit; at this low price (in pounds), Britain is willing to import much *more* (see Figure 15-2).

We therefore conclude that the depreciation of the dollar disturbs the initial commodity-market equilibria. In particular, America's *volume of imports tends to fall as the British goods become more expensive in dollars.* On the other hand, America's *volume of exports tends to rise as the American goods become cheaper in pounds.*

How can we determine the new commodity-market equilibria after the dollar depreciates? We must first redraw America's demand-for-imports and supply-of-exports schedules on the assumption that the rate of exchange is £1 = $3. This is shown in Figure 15-4, which gives all the schedules shown in Figure 15-3 plus America's new schedules (see broken lines) for the new rate of exchange (£1 = $3). Once America's schedules are redrawn, the commodity-market equilibria are determined as before, as illustrated by points G in both markets (panels).

Note carefully that as the dollar depreciates, America's new (broken) schedules necessarily lie below the corresponding initial schedules. The reason must be clear: The dollar prices along America's schedules (see Figures 15-1 and 15-2) are now divided by $3—not $2—to obtain the corresponding prices in pounds.

Summary of the Effects of Devaluation

Having determined the postdevaluation commodity-market equilibria, we can use Figure 15-4 to identify clearly the various effects of devaluation. In general, we can expect the following eight effects.

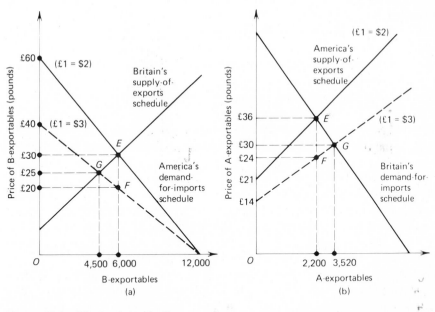

Figure 15-4 *Effects of devaluation.*
As the rate of exchange increases from $2 to $3 per pound (that is, as the dollar depreciates), America's schedules shift downward, as illustrated by the broken schedules in both panels. Equilibrium shifts from E to G in both panels. The demand for pounds (that is, America's expenditure on imports of B-exportables decreases from £30 × 6,000 = £180,000 to £25 × 4,500 = £112,500. The supply of pounds (that is, America's export revenue) increases from £36 × 2,200 = £79,200 to £30 × 3,520 = £105,600, because the elasticity of Britain's demand for imports is greater than unity.

1 The Effect on Commodity Flows In general, the volume of imports of America (that is, the country which devalues her currency) decreases, while her volume of exports increases. In Figure 15-4, America's volume of imports decreases from 6,000 to 4,500 units of B-exportables, while her volume of exports increases from 2,200 to 3,520 units of A-exportables.

2 The Effect on Foreign Prices In general, devaluation depresses foreign prices. In Figure 15-4 the prices of A-exportables and B-exportables, expressed in pounds (foreign currency), fall. In particular, the price of B-exportables falls from £30 to £25, and the price of A-exportables falls from £36 to £30.

3 The Effect on Domestic Prices In general, devaluation has an inflationary effect on domestic prices. Even though Figure 15-4 does not directly show the dollar prices of A-exportables and B-exportables, we can easily infer that both these dollar prices increase with the devaluation of the dollar.

How can we infer that the dollar price of B-exportables rises with devaluation (even though the price of B-exportables in pounds actually falls)? By observing that America's volume of imports falls. At a lower volume of imports, America must be paying a higher dollar price (see America's downward-sloping demand-for-imports schedule in Figure 15-1).

How can we infer that the dollar price of A-exportables also rises with devaluation (even though the price of A-exportables in pounds actually falls)? By observing that America's volume of exports increases. At a higher volume of exports, America must be receiving a higher dollar price (see America's upward-sloping supply-of-exports schedule in Figure 15-2).

4 The Effect on the Quantity of Foreign Exchange Demanded What is the quantity of pounds (foreign exchange) demanded? It is America's expenditure on imports (expressed in pounds). Now both America's volume of imports and the price of B-exportables (in pounds) fall. Therefore, America's expenditure on imports, and thus the quantity of pounds demanded, must also fall. In particular, in Figure 15-4, panel (*a*), America's expenditure on imports falls from £180,000 (that is, 30 × 6,000) to £112,500 (that is, 25 × 4,500).

5 The Effect on the Quantity of Foreign Exchange Supplied Unfortunately, this effect is indeterminate. Essentially because of this, the analysis of the foreign exchange market as well as the effect of devaluation on the balance of trade become complicated.

The quantity of pounds (foreign exchange) supplied coincides with America's export revenue (in pounds): price of A-exportables in pounds times America's volume of exports. As the dollar depreciates, the price of A-exportables (in pounds) falls, while America's volume of exports increases. Hence, America's export revenue (and thus the supply of pounds) may increase, decrease, or remain constant.

In Figure 15-4 America's export revenue actually increases from £79,200 (that is, $36 \times 2,200$) to £105,600 (that is, $30 \times 3,520$). However, this favorable outcome is the result of an implicit assumption: that the elasticity of Britain's demand for imports is greater than unity.

As the dollar depreciates, equilibrium shifts from E to G along Britain's demand-for-imports schedule. As we already know (See Section 4-3), such a movement along a demand curve causes the total revenue to increase only when the elasticity of demand is greater than unity. If Britain's demand-for-imports schedule were actually inelastic, such a movement would have caused America's export revenue to fall.

6 The Effect on America's Terms of Trade Does a devaluation (or depreciation) of the dollar improve or make worse America's terms of trade? Anything is possible.

As we saw earlier, the devaluation of the dollar causes the prices of *both* A-exportables *and* B-exportables to rise in America (where they are expressed in dollars) and fall in Britain (where they are expressed in pounds). Therefore, it is not possible to predict the effect of devaluation on America's terms of trade, that is, the ratio of the price of A-exportables to the price of B-exportables.

Figure 15-4 illustrates the limiting case in which America's terms of trade remain constant, as the reader should verify.

The appendix to this chapter shows rigorously that the effect of devaluation on America's terms of trade depends on the various import-demand elasticities and export-supply elasticities. In particular, the appendix shows that America's terms of trade improve, deteriorate, or remain constant according to whether the product of the supply elasticities of exports is respectively smaller than, larger than, or equal to the product of the demand elasticities for imports.

7 The Effect on the Balance of Trade This is the most important effect of devaluation. A country devalues her currency because her balance of trade (or, in general, balance of payments) is in deficit. Does devaluation improve the balance of trade? Not always. The effect of devaluation on the balance of trade is indeterminate.

We can easily understand why the balance-of-trade effect of devaluation is indeterminate. As we saw earlier, an increase in the rate of exchange (that is, devaluation of the dollar) causes the demand for foreign exchange (that is, America's expenditure on imports expressed in pounds) to fall. This reduction in the demand for foreign exchange works, of course, in the direction of reducing America's deficit. However, before we can say whether America's balance of trade improves, we must also know what happens to the supply of foreign exchange. If the supply of foreign exchange increases, we must unequivocally conclude that the deficit falls. But the supply of foreign exchange may also fall (when Britain's demand for imports is inelastic). Evidently, when the supply of foreign exchange falls, it is not at all obvious that America's deficit decreases with devaluation. In particular, if the reduction in the supply of foreign exchange is larger than the reduction in the demand for foreign exchange, America's deficit actually becomes larger.

Economists have shown that the balance-of-trade effect of devaluation depends in a rather complex fashion on the import-demand and export-supply elasticities. Nevertheless, there is an important and less complicated condition, known as the *Marshall-Lerner condition,* whose satisfaction guarantees that devaluation actually improves the balance of trade (that is, reduces the deficit).

Marshall-Lerner Condition: When the sum of the two demand elasticities for imports (that is, America's and Britain's), in absolute terms, is greater than unity, devaluation reduces the balance-of-trade deficit.

For a proof of the Marshall-Lerner condition, see the appendix to this chapter.

We have already met an example in which the Marshall-Lerner condition is satisfied and devaluation reduces the deficit. This is the example of Figure 15-4, where Britain's demand elasticity for imports is greater than unity (and thus the Marshall-Lerner condition is satisfied irrespective of what America's demand elasticity for imports is). The devaluation of the dollar reduces America's deficit from £100,800 (that is, $36 \times 2,200 - 30 \times 6,000$) to £6,900 (that is, $30 \times 3,520 - 25 \times 4,500$).

As an example in which the Marshall-Lerner condition is *not* satisfied and devaluation *increases* the deficit, return to Figure 15-4, and assume that each country's elasticity of demand for imports is zero; that is, each country's demand-for-imports schedule is vertical. When the dollar depreciates, America's schedules [that is, America's import-demand schedule in panel (*a*) and America's supply-of-exports schedule in panel (*b*)] shift downward.

In the market for A-exportables, equilibrium will shift from *E* to *F*, since Britain's demand-for-imports schedule is now assumed to be given by the vertical line through *E*. Thus, America's export revenue will fall from £79,200 to £52,800.

On the other hand, equilibrium in the market for B-exportables, panel (*a*), will continue to remain at *E*, since a vertical shift of a vertical line will leave the vertical line in the same position. Accordingly, the demand for pounds will remain at its initial value of £180,000, and America's deficit will *increase* by the amount by which America' export revenue falls. In particular, America's balance-of-trade deficit will *increase* from £100,800 (that is, $79,200 - 180,000$) to £127,200 (that is, $52,800 - 180,000$).

Unfortunately, even when the Marshall-Lerner condition is indeed satisfied, the beneficial effect of devaluation on the balance of trade may be frustrated by labor-union demands for higher money wages. Recall our earlier conclusion that devaluation has an inflationary impact on domestic prices. When labor unions are successful in maintaining their *real* wages at the predevaluation level (by forcing the same percentage increase in their money-wage rates as the percentage increase in the rate of foreign exchange), the beneficial effects of devaluation are completely wiped out. When America experiences cost-push inflation at the same percentage rate as the devaluation of the dollar, America's broken schedules in Figure 15-4 will shift back to their initial position shown by the solid schedules.

8 The Effect on Domestic Consumption and Production Devaluation has some predictable effects on domestic production and consumption of both countries. As we saw, the devaluation of the dollar causes the prices of A-exportables and B-exportables to rise in America (where they are expressed in dollars) and fall in Britain (where they are expressed in pounds). In general, therefore, we must expect the consumption of both A-exportables and B-exportables to fall in America (where they become more expensive) and rise in Britain (where they become cheaper). On the other hand, we must expect the production of both A-exportables and B-exportables to rise in America and fall in Britain.

15-5 SUPPLY AND DEMAND FOR FOREIGN EXCHANGE

We have already learned how to determine the quantities of foreign exchange demanded and supplied at any given rate of exchange and how these quantities are likely to change as the rate of exchange changes. This section completes the analysis by introducing explicitly the supply and demand schedules for foreign exchange. These schedules show the various quantities of foreign exchange demanded and supplied at alternative rates of exchange.

Supply and Demand Schedules for Foreign Exchange

Figure 15-5 gives the supply and demand schedules for pounds sterling. In principle, these schedules are derived from the demand-for-imports and supply-of-exports schedules of America and Britain. For each rate of exchange, we determine the quantities of foreign exchange (pounds) supplied and demanded, as we did earlier in Figures 15-3 and 15-4. This information enables us to determine a point on the supply schedule for foreign exchange and another point on the demand schedule for foreign exchange. By repeating this exercise many times, we can determine as many points as we wish on the supply and demand schedules for foreign exchange. When we have enough points, we can trace the continuous curves shown in Figure 15-5.

Normally, the demand curve for foreign exchange slopes downward. This is implicit in our earlier conclusion that a devaluation of the dollar (that is, an *increase* in the rate of exchange) *decreases* the quantity of foreign exchange (pounds) demanded.

The supply curve for foreign exchange is normally *backward bending*. This is again consistent with our earlier conclusion that a devaluation of the dollar may cause the quantity of pounds supplied to either *increase* (when Britain's demand for imports is *elastic*) or *decrease* (when Britain's demand for imports is *inelastic*).

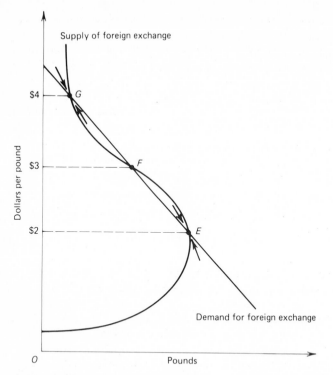

Figure 15-5 *Supply and demand schedules for foreign exchange.*
For each rate of exchange, the downward sloping demand schedule for foreign exchange
gives the quantity of pounds demanded by America's importers and British exporters. The
supply schedule for foreign exchange gives, for each rate of exchange, the quantity of
pounds supplied by American exporters and British importers. Normally, the supply curve is
backward bending, giving rise to multiple equilibria, such as *E, F,* and *G*. Points *E* and *G* are
stable, while point *F* is unstable.

In particular, for "low values" of the rate of exchange, America's supply-
of-exports schedule intersects Britain's demand-for-imports schedule very
high, closer to the vertical axis, where Britain's demand for imports is elastic.
Thus, for "low values" of the rate of exchange, the supply schedule for pounds
slopes upward.

On the other hand, for "high values" of the rate of exchange, America's
supply-of-exports schedule intersects Britain's demand-for-imports schedule
very low, closer to the horizontal axis, where Britain's demand for imports is
inelastic. Thus, for "high values" of the rate of exchange, the supply schedule
for pounds bends backward. [Return again to Figure 15-4, panel (*b*), and verify
these conclusions.] This explains why the supply schedule for foreign
exchange is normally backward bending, as shown in Figure 15-5.

Equilibrium in the Foreign Exchange Market

Equilibrium in the foreign exchange market occurs when the rate of exchange is
such that the quantity of foreign exchange demanded equals the quantity

supplied. Graphically, equilibrium occurs at the point of intersection of the supply and demand schedules for foreign exchange.

Because the supply schedule for foreign exchange is normally backward bending, equilibrium in the foreign exchange market need not be unique. This is shown in Figure 15-5, which illustrates the case of three equilibria: *E, F,* and *G.* Accordingly, in Figure 15-5 the foreign exchange market can be in equilibrium when the rate of exchange assumes any one of the following three values: $2, $3, or $4.

The multiplicity of equilibrium in the foreign exchange market creates several difficulties. In the first place, some of the equilibria are necessarily *unstable,* as explained below.

Second, from the point of view of social desirability, each country may rank these equilibria differently. For instance, America may prefer point *G* to *E* (or *F*), while Britain may prefer point *E* to *G* (or *F*). This situation may lead to conflicting policies between countries, with deleterious effects.

Finally, private speculative activity may be such as to cause the system to switch from one (stable) equilibrium to the other, giving rise to unnecessary and wasteful reallocation of resources within each country. (Recall the discussion of Section 15-4, which showed, among other things, how an exchange-rate adjustment affects each country's domestic production of A-exportables and B-exportables.)

Stability in the Foreign Exchange Market

When a market is in equilibrium, each potential buyer can find a seller and each seller can find a buyer. Every market participant does what he or she desires to do, and no buyer or seller has any incentive to change his or her behavior. If not disturbed, equilibrium can last forever. But is there any guarantee that a market will be in equilibrium if it is not already? What happens when a market (or a system of markets) is out of equilibrium? Will the market return to equilibrium?

The behavior of a market (or a system of markets) out of equilibrium is the subject matter of *stability analysis.* Are there economic forces at work that will automatically bring the market (or the system of markets) back to equilibrium? If there are such forces and the market (or system) does tend to return to equilibrium, then that equilibrium is called *stable;* otherwise, the equilibrium is called *unstable.* Clearly, the concept of stability is an important one because equilibrium cannot be taken seriously unless it is stable.

How can we tell whether an equilibrium point is stable or unstable? To answer this question, we need to know how the buyers and sellers react when the current price is not an equilibrium one.

It is commonly believed that if the quantity supplied is larger than the quantity demanded, the price will tend to fall, presumably because the suppliers who are unable to sell all they want at the current price will lower their bids. On the other hand, if the quantity supplied is smaller than the quantity demanded, the price will tend to rise, presumably because the buyers who are unable to buy all they want at the current price will raise their bids. For instance, in Figure 15-5, the rate of exchange will tend to fall when it is either higher than $4 or between $2 and $3. When it is between $3 and $4, or lower than $2, the rate of exchange will tend to rise.

Points such as E and G (Figure 15-5) are *stable*. When the rate of exchange happens to be in the neighborhood of $2 (say, $2.10 or $1.80), the tendency is to move *toward* the equilibrium value of $2, as illustrated by the arrows above and below point E. Similarly, when the rate of exchange is in the vicinity of $4, either above or below, the tendency is to move *toward* the equilibrium value of $4, as illustrated by the arrows above and below point G.

The middle equilibrium point, F, is *unstable*. When the rate of exchange is in the vicinity of $3, the tendency is to move *away* from the equilibrium value of $3, as illustrated by the arrows above and below point F. For instance, if the current rate of exchange is $3.10, it will tend to move toward $4; and if it is $2.80, it will tend to move toward $2.

Of course, if the exchange rate were to move promptly to a stable equilibrium and remain there, the existence of multiple and unstable equilibria would not cause much concern. Unfortunately, both speculation and balance-of-payments disturbances (such as bumper crops or crop failures in an agricultural country or business cycles in an industrial nation) may cause wide fluctuations in the rate of exchange.

Consider speculation first. Return to Figure 15-5, and suppose that the rate of exchange *increases* from $2 to, say, $2.10. If the speculators interpret this small increase to mean that the rate of exchange will increase further, they will start buying pounds (in the hope of selling them later at a higher price). These speculative purchases will certainly cause the rate of exchange to rise further, and if it increases beyond the unstable point, F (that is, $3), it will certainly continue to climb all the way to $4. When the rate stabilizes at $4, the speculators will sell their pounds (and make a handsome profit). In so doing, however, the speculators will cause the rate of exchange to fall, perhaps all the way to $2. Accordingly, this self-fulfilling, profitable speculation will cause wide fluctuations in the rate of exchange; and as we have seen, these fluctuations will result in unnecessary and wasteful shifts of resources into and out of the export and import-competing sectors in each country.

Figure 15-6 illustrates another form of instability: *wide fluctuations in the exchange rate caused by exogenous balance-of-payments disturbances*. Equilibrium occurs initially at G, where the solid schedules intersect. Note that this equilibrium is unique and stable (see arrows). Suppose that as a result of a recession in America (causing America's demand for imports to fall), the demand schedule for pounds shifts to the left, as shown by the broken line through E. Equilibrium moves to E, which is also unique and stable. Note, however, the wide swing in the rate of exchange, which falls from $4 to $2. What is responsible for this tremendous depreciation of the pound? The *backward bending* supply schedule for pounds. If the supply schedule were upward sloping and very elastic, as shown by broken line HG, the pound would have depreciated only slightly.

These are some of the most important reasons why flexible exchange rates cannot be counted on to work efficiently in practice.

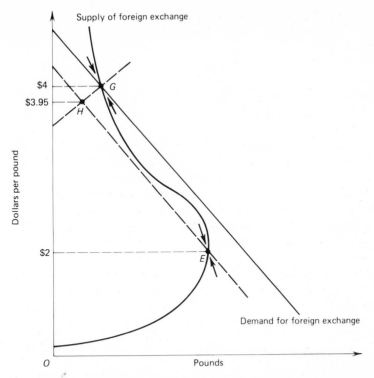

Figure 15-6 *Exchange-rate fluctuations caused by shifts in exports and imports.*
Because the supply-of-foreign-exchange schedule is backward bending at the initial (unique
and stable) equilibrium point *G*, a shift of the demand schedule to the left, as shown by
broken curve *HE*, causes a tremendous depreciation of the pound as the foreign exchange
market adjusts to the new equilibrium point, *E*. If the supply schedule were upward sloping,
as shown by broken line *HG*, the pound would have depreciated only slightly.

15-6 NONTRADED GOODS: A DIGRESSION[1]

As we saw in Section 15-4, a devaluation of the dollar causes the prices of A-
exportables *and* B-exportables to rise in America and fall in Britain. Accordingly, the production of both A-exportables and B-exportables expands in
America and falls in Britain. The partial-equilibrium model does not explain
where the American producers of A-exportables and B-exportables find the additional resources that are necessary for the expansion of their production.
Similarly, our model fails to explain what actually happens to the resources that
Britain's producers of A-exportables and B-exportables release as they reduce
their production.

If we allow unemployment in each country as a possibility, we could argue
that America's producers bring into the production process resources (such as
labor) that were previously unemployed, while the resources the British producers release remain idle (or unemployed). We shall explore this possibility

[1] This section may be skipped.

further in the next chapter. For the moment, we would like to concentrate on a different explanation—an explanation that is consistent with full employment in both countries.

An implicit assumption of the partial-equilibrium model is that each country possesses another industry (in addition to the industries of A-exportables and B-exportables). This third industry (or sector) produces other goods and services, such as haircuts and houses, which are not traded internationally because of prohibitive transportation costs. These goods and services are usually called *domestic* or *nontraded goods.*

Given the existence of nontraded goods, it appears that we could argue that a devaluation of the dollar causes American resources to shift out of the nontraded-goods sector and into the export and import-competing sectors (or the traded-goods sector), that is, into the industries of A-exportables and B-exportables. In Britain, of course, where the production of A-exportables and B-exportables falls, we could argue that the released resources flow into the nontraded-goods sector.

There is a difficulty, however, with this argument that needs further clarification. As we argued above, America must transfer resources from the nontraded-goods sector to the traded-goods sector, and Britain must do the opposite—that is, transfer resources from the traded-goods sector to the nontraded-goods sector. Now our analysis in Part 1 of this book shows clearly that such transfers of resources can take place only if the prices of the traded goods (that is, A-exportables and B-exportables) rise in America, and fall in Britain, relative to the prices of nontraded goods. Is it reasonable to expect such relative-price changes after the devaluation of the dollar?

Immediately after the devaluation of the dollar, the money prices of the traded goods (that is, A-exportables and B-exportables) rise in America and fall in Britain. Accordingly, there seems to be a tendency for the traded goods to become more expensive relative to the nontraded goods in America, and cheaper in Britain. These are, of course, the relative-price changes that are necessary in both countries for the transfer of resources between sectors, as explained in the preceeding paragraph. But are such relative-price changes viable in the long run? Will America's and Britain's markets for nontraded goods continue to remain in equilibrium at these altered relative prices?

Consider America's market for nontraded goods first. America transfers resources from the nontraded-goods sector to the traded-goods sector. Hence, *America's output of nontraded goods necessarily falls.* What happens to America's demand for nontraded goods? As the nontraded goods become relatively cheaper, rational Americans want to substitute nontraded goods for traded goods. (Recall that the devaluation of the dollar also causes America's consumption of A-exportables and B-exportables to fall.) Accordingly, *the quantity of nontraded goods demanded in America must rise.* If America's market for nontraded goods was in equilibrium to begin with, it cannot remain so as nontraded goods become relatively cheaper *because their supply falls while their demand increases.* Consequently, the initial reduction in the relative price of nontraded goods generates an excess demand for nontraded goods that tends to push their relative price back to its initial level. (By definition, equilibrium in the market for nontraded goods requires that the domestic demand be equal to the domestic supply—there can be no exports or imports of nontraded goods.) But without a permanent reduction in the relative price of nontraded goods, no permanent transfer of resources can take place from the nontraded-goods sector to the traded-goods sector.

We observe exactly the opposite tendencies in Britain. Initially, the devaluation of the dollar causes the traded goods to become cheaper relative to the nontraded goods. Such a relative-price change is, of course, necessary for the needed transfer of resources from the traded-goods sector to the nontraded-goods sector. Unfortunately, this relative-price change is not viable in the long run, as it generates forces for its elimination. Thus, the initial increase in the relative price of nontraded goods causes their supply to increase and their demand to fall; and the resultant excess supply of nontraded goods tends to force their relative price down to its initial level.

Our analysis seems to have reached an impasse. After the devaluation of the dollar, the relative price of nontraded goods must change in both America and Britain in order to facilitate the transfer of resources between sectors (in each country separately). Yet such relative-price changes do not seem to be viable in the long run. Without permanent relative-price changes, no permanent transfers of resources can take place. How can we resolve this apparently difficult issue?

The solution is implicit in our discussion in Chapter 14. Recall that devaluation alone cannot restore balance-of-payments equilibrium and maintain full employment at the same time. The deficit country (which spends more on goods and services than her national income) must, in addition, reduce her aggregate spending. Similarly, the surplus country (whose national income is higher than her aggregate spending) must, in addition, increase her spending. This is necessary because balance of payments equilibrium requires that each country's aggregate spending equals that country's national income.

Thus, simultaneously with the devaluation of the dollar, America must *reduce* her aggregate spending on *all* goods and services (including nontraded goods). This expenditure reduction eliminates, in turn, the excess demand for nontraded goods, which we observed earlier, and removes the tendency for the reversal of the initial reduction in the relative price of America's nontraded goods.

Similarly, Britain must *increase* her spending on *all* goods and services (including nontraded goods). This increase in Britain's spending eliminates, in turn, the excess supply of nontraded goods, which we observed earlier, and removes the tendency for the reversal of the initial increase in the relative price of Britain's nontraded goods.

We therefore conclude that when devaluation is combined with the appropriate expenditure changes in the countries involved, the necessary relative-price changes can indeed take place and facilitate the required transfer of resources between sectors (in each country separately) as envisaged by the partial-equilibrium model.

15-7 THE PRICE-SPECIE-FLOW MECHANISM

So far we have discussed the price-adjustment mechanism in relation to exchange-rate changes. How does price adjustment work under a fixed-exchange-rate system, such as the gold standard?

Two centuries ago, the Scottish philosopher David Hume argued that there was an automatic self-correcting "price-specie-flow mechanism" at work that guaranteed balance-of-payments equilibrium. Hume's explanation was that gold flows tended to produce price-level changes (according to the quantity theory of money), which in turn tended to restore equilibrium in the balance of payments and eventually check the flow of gold.

For instance, suppose that America and Britain are on the gold standard and that at the existing rate of exchange of $2 (per pound) America runs a balance-of-payments deficit. Because the rate of exchange cannot rise (to, say, $3), America's import surplus will lead to a gold flow from America to Britain, as shown in Figure 15-7 (see distance *CD*). According to the rules of the game, America's money supply will contract, while Britain's money supply will expand. The precise changes of the money supplies will depend, of course, on the

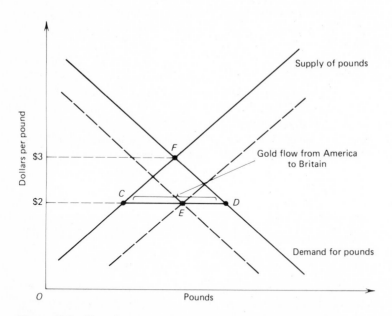

Figure 15-7 *The price-specie-flow mechanism.*
At the fixed rate of $2 per pound, America is running a deficit given by distance *CD*. America finances her deficit by exporting gold to Britain. Britain's money supply expands, causing Britain's cost structure and prices to rise. Similarly, America's money supply contracts, causing America's cost structure and prices to fall. As a result, America's exports increase, causing the supply-of-pounds schedule to shift to the right, as shown by the broken supply curve; and America's imports decrease, causing the demand-for-pounds schedule to shift to the left, as shown by the broken demand curve. Equilibrium is finally reestablished at *E* (that is, at the fixed rate of $2).

structures of the banking systems of the two countries. For our purposes, however, it is sufficient to know that America's money supply will contract and Britain's expand.

Given the classical world of complete wage and price flexibility (and full employment), the reduction in the American money supply will cause, according to the quantity theory of money, America's cost structure and prices to fall. Similarly, the expansion in the British money supply will cause Britain's cost structure and prices to rise. In terms of our partial-equilibrium model, this means that America's demand-for-imports and supply-of-exports schedules will shift downward and that Britain's schedules will shift upward. With *high elasticities*, these shifts will

1   increase America's exports (as America becomes a cheaper place to buy) and cause the supply-of-pounds schedule to shift to the right, as shown by the broken supply curve in Figure 15-7
2   reduce America's imports and cause the demand-for-pounds schedule to shift to the left, as shown by the broken demand curve in Figure 15-7

In this way, the flow of gold will cease and equilibrium in the foreign exchange market will occur at the existing rate of exchange (see point *E*).

It is often erroneously stated that there is a presumption in the price-specie-flow mechanism that the gold-losing country will experience a worsening in her terms of trade. This conclusion is wrong. Inflation and deflation, as implied by the classical economists, are equivalent to exchange-rate changes. As we have seen, the terms-of-trade effect of an exchange-rate adjustment is indeterminate. The same must be true for the price-specie-flow mechanism as well. The explanation for this phenomenon is simple. While it is true that America's gold exports to Britain cause prices to fall in America and rise in Britain, it is the prices of *both* A-exportables *and* B-exportables that fall in America and rise in Britain. Thus, it is unwarranted to jump to the conclusion that A-exportables become cheaper relative to B-exportables.

Modern economists emphasize that national income changes play a major stabilizing role in the adjustment process under an international gold standard. This fact was widely recognized after Keynes published his *General Theory* in 1936. There is no particular urgency to discuss the importance of national income changes at this point. The next chapter studies the income-adjustment mechanism in detail.

15-8   THE PURCHASING-POWER-PARITY THEORY: ANOTHER DIGRESSION[2]

The purchasing-power-parity (PPP) theory is an attempt to explain, and perhaps more importantly measure statistically, the equilibrium rate of exchange and its variations by means of the price levels and their variations in

[2]The reader may skip this section.

different countries. This theory, which is usually associated with the Swedish economist Gustav Cassel, is based on the simple idea that a certain amount of money should purchase the same representative bundle of commodities in different countries—hence Cassel's term *purchasing-power parity*. The PPP theory has been severely criticized through the years.

There are two versions of the purchasing-power-parity theory: the *absolute* version and the *relative* (or *comparative*) version. While the absolute version is useless, the relative version does have some validity, as explained below. This section deals with both versions.

The Absolute Version of the PPP Theory

Consider again the two countries, America and Britain. The absolute version of the PPP theory declares that the equilibrium rate of exchange (that is, dollars per pound) is equal to the ratio of America's price level to Britain's price level (or, in symbols, P_a/P_b). How valid is this proposition? Can we really abandon our supply-and-demand analysis of the foreign exchange market and use instead the ratio of price levels to determine the equilibrium rate of exchange? Unfortunately, this is not the case.

In our discussion of the partial-equilibrium model, we pointed out that for *any* rate of exchange (whether it is the equilibrium rate or not), the dollar price of each traded good equals its price in pounds times the rate of exchange. For instance, if the price of A-exportables is $10 in America and the rate of exchange is $2 (per pound), the price of A-exportables in Britain must be £5 (that is, $10 = 2 \times 5$). In the absence of transportation costs and trade impediments (such as tariffs and quotas), this strict relationship holds for each traded good. Accordingly, it follows that when all goods are traded internationally, the same strict relationship must hold trivially between any *equally weighted* price index numbers for America and Britain.

For instance, suppose that the current rate of exchange is $2 (per pound) and that the prices of A-exportables and B-exportables, respectively, are $10 and $40 in America and £5 and £20 in Britain. For simplicity, suppose that the weights of A-exportables and B-exportables are equal in the construction of America's and Britain's price index numbers. Accordingly, America's price index number (P_a) is $25 (that is, $0.5 \times \$10 + 0.5 \times \$40$), and Britain's price index number (P_b) is £12.5 (that is, $0.5 \times £5 + 0.5 \times £20$). Obviously, $2 = $25/£12.5; that is, rate of exchange $(R) = P_a/P_b$.

The relationship $R = P_a/P_b$ must hold trivially for *any* rate of exchange—not just the equilibrium rate. Accordingly, we cannot use it to determine *the* equilibrium rate. This is a devastating blow to the absolute version of the PPP theory.

In the real world there are, of course, transportation costs and trade impediments. In fact, as we pointed out in Section 15-6, there is a whole class of *nontraded* (purely domestic) goods in each country that is not traded internationally particularly because of prohibitive transportation costs. Now there is no simple relationship between the prices of these nontraded goods in the various countries. Accordingly, in this general case, the equation $R = P_a/P_b$ cannot hold even when the current rate of exchange (R) happens to be the equilibrium rate.

We need not go into any further detail. The absolute version of the PPP theory is useless, and we reject it.

The Relative Version of the PPP Theory

The relative version of the PPP theory, which incidentally received more attention than the absolute version, is a comparative-statics proposition. In particular, the relative version is concerned with *the effects of inflation on an initial equilibrium rate of exchange.* Essentially, Cassel invoked the quantity theory of money and proposed that money is neutral.

We can again use our partial-equilibrium model to illustrate the relative version of the PPP theory. Suppose that at the current rate of exchange of, say, $2 (per pound), the value of American exports of A-exportables equals the value of American imports of B-exportables, as shown in Figure 15-8 by the initial equilibrium points, E, in the two panels. Now let America increase her money supply by, say, 50 percent, and wait until the international economy reaches a new equilibrium. What will be the relationship between the new equilibrium rate of exchange and the initial rate of $2? Cassel's theory predicts that the new equilibrium rate must be higher than the old by the percentage rate of inflation in America, say, 50 percent. That is, the new equilibrium rate of exchange must be $3 (that is, $2 + 0.50 \times $2). Let us see why.

As we learned in our discussion of the price-specie-flow mechanism (see Section 15-7), the expansion in the American money supply causes America's cost structure and prices to rise. Accordingly, America's demand-for-imports and supply-of-exports schedules shift upward, as illustrated in Figure 15-8 by the broken schedules.

Note that because of inflation, America's prices (in both pounds and dollars) increase by 50 percent at all volumes of exports and imports. For instance, at the initial volume of imports of 5,000 units of B-exportables, America is now willing to pay £30, which is 50 percent higher than the initial price of £20. Similarly, for the initial volume of exports of 20,000 units of A-exportables, America now demands £7.5, which is also 50 percent higher than the initial price of £5.

If the rate of exchange remains constant at $2 (per pound), equilibrium in the markets for A-exportables and B-exportables will shift to point G in both panels, and America's balance of trade will register a deficit (assuming that each country's elasticity of demand for imports is higher than unity). Is it possible to change the rate of exchange and shift America's broken schedules back to their initial position? If this is actually done, equilibrium in the markets for A-exportables and B-exportables will return to points E, where America's balance of trade is zero. As it turns out, America's broken schedules will shift back to their initial position when the rate of exchange also rises by 50 percent, that is, from $2 to $3, as the student should be able to verify.

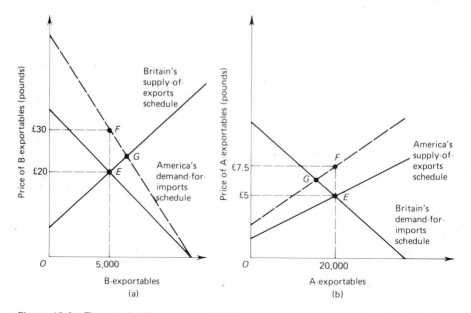

Figure 15-8 *The purchasing-power-parity theory.*
At the current rate of exchange ($2 = £1), the value of American exports ($5 × 20,000) equals the value of American imports (£20 × 5,000). As America undergoes 50 percent inflation, her demand-for-imports and supply-of-exports schedules shift upward, as shown by the broken schedules. By itself, the American inflation would cause the commodity-market equilibria to shift from E to G in both panels and generate a deficit in America's balance of payments. However, when the rate of exchange increases by 50 percent also, that is, from $2 to $3, the American schedules return to their original position and equilibrium returns in both panels to E, where America's balance of payments is in equilibrium again.

Note carefully that the existence of nontraded commodities does *not* affect the preceding conclusion at all.

A problem similar to the above actually occurred after World War I. The war had disrupted trade between allies and had halted it completely between enemies. When the war was finally over and trade started to flow again, there was a need to establish new rates of exchange. Many countries thought they could return to the prewar rates. Unfortunately, the prewar rates were inappropriate, particularly because the various countries had experienced quite different degrees of inflation. Cassel suggested that the prewar rates of exchange must be so adjusted as to take into account these divergent degrees of inflation. In particular, he suggested the following formula for the case of two countries, say, America and Britain:

$$R' = \frac{P_a'/P_a^o}{P_b'/P_b^o}R^o \qquad (15\text{-}1)$$

where R^o = rate of exchange before the war

R' = recommended rate of exchange after the war

P_a^o, P_a' = America's price level before and after the war, respectively

P_b^o, P_b' = Britain's price level before and after the war, respectively

It must be clear by now that the relative version of the PPP theory is no longer a truism. It makes the valid point that monetary conditions exert an important influence on the rate of exchange. Yet this theory suffers from a severe drawback: Aside from difficulties of statistical verification, it rests on the crucial assumption that technology, tastes, factor supplies, levels of employment, trade impediments, and capital movements do not change during the transition period. Such changes no doubt take place incessantly in the international economy and do exert a profound influence on the rate of exchange. This is especially true when the transition involves a major war.

15-9 EMPIRICAL EVIDENCE

The discussion in this chapter makes it abundantly clear that the price-adjustment mechanism can function smoothly only if the elasticities of demand for imports are high. Devaluation, for instance, cannot be successful unless the Marshall-Lerner condition is satisfied, that is, unless the sum of the devaluing country's elasticity of demand for imports plus the foreign elasticity of demand for the devaluing country's exports is greater than unity in absolute terms.

This final section deals briefly with the empirical estimates of these import-demand elasticities. Since this is not a book on econometrics, the following discussion considers only the most rudimentary problems of empirical estimation. The interested reader may find additional discussion of these problems in Orcutt (1950) and Leamer and Stern (1970, Chapter 2).

Empirical Estimates

Table 15-1 summarizes the empirical estimates of elasticities published in a study by Houthakker and Magee (1969). These findings seem to be in general agreement with the results of other empirical studies.

A quick glance at Table 15-1 reveals the following facts:

1   The elasticity of demand for imports, shown in column (2), is less than −1 (that is, greater than unity in absolute terms) for three countries only (Belgium-Luxembourg, Canada, and Denmark). For five countries (Australia, France, the Netherlands, South Africa, and the United Kingdom), the elasticity of demand for imports has the wrong sign (positive). For the rest of the countries, the elasticity coefficient is negative but less than unity in absolute terms.

2   The foreign elasticity of demand for a country's exports, shown in column (3), is less than −1 for three countries only (France, South Africa, and the United States). (These three countries are incidentally *different* from the three countries whose elasticities of demand for imports are less than −1.) For four countries (Belgium-Luxembourg, Germany, Norway, and Sweden), the foreign elasticity of demand for their exports has the wrong sign (positive). For the rest of the countries, the elasticity coefficient is negative but less than unity in absolute terms.

3   Column (4) gives for each country the sum of the elasticities of imports and exports listed in columns (2) and (3). The Marshall-Lerner condition is satisfied for seven countries only (Canada, Denmark, France, Japan, South Africa, Switzerland, and the United States). While this finding is comforting,

Table 15-1 Elasticities for Total Imports and Exports of 15 Industrial Countries
(Annual Data, 1951–1966)

Country (1)	Elasticity of imports (2)	Elasticity of exports (3)	Sum of elasticities [col. (2) + col. (3)] (4)
Australia	0.83*	−0.17*	0.66
Belgium-Luxembourg	−1.02	0.42*	−0.60
Canada	−1.46	−0.59	−2.05
Denmark	−1.66	−0.56*	−2.22
France	0.17*	−2.27	−2.10
Germany	−0.24*	1.70*	1.46
Italy	−0.13*	−0.03*	−0.16
Japan	−0.72	−0.80*	−1.52
The Netherlands	0.23*	−0.82*	−0.59
Norway	−0.78	0.20*	−0.58
South Africa	1.04*	−2.41	−1.37
Sweden	−0.79*	0.67*	−0.12
Switzerland	−0.84*	−0.58	−1.42
United Kingdom	0.22*	−0.44*	−0.22
United States	−0.54*	−1.51	−2.05

*These coefficients are not statistically significant from zero at the 5 percent level of confidence.
   Source: H. S. Houthakker and S. P. Magee (1969). "Income and Price Elasticities in World Trade." *Review of Economics and Statistics,* vol. 51 (May), p. 113.

we must also note that there are important countries, such as Australia, Germany, Italy, the Netherlands, Norway, Sweden, and the United Kingdom, that do *not* satisfy the Marshall-Lerner condition.

Elasticity Pessimism and Optimism

In the 1930s and 1940s economists feared that elasticities were very low and that the Marshall-Lerner condition was not generally satisfied. This "elasticity pessimism" gave way to "elasticity optimism" in the 1960s and 1970s. Although such elasticity optimism cannot be fully supported by the empirical studies, such as that of Houthakker and Magee (1969), Orcutt (1950) gave several reasons why the empirical estimates actually *underestimated* the true elasticities. In effect, in his path-breaking paper, Orcutt provided sufficient hope that the true elasticities are high enough to satisfy the Marshall-Lerner condition. Orcutt's reasons are as follows.

   1 The Identification Problem The observed time-series price and quantity data that econometricians use to estimate the various elasticities of demand for imports refer to intersections of supply and demand schedules, such as those illustrated in Figures 15-3, 15-4, and 15-8. An important precondition for time-series estimation is that these underlying supply and demand schedules for exports and imports shift over time. Otherwise, the same prices and quantities would prevail always, thus generating only one point on each schedule, which obviously is not sufficient for a successful estimation of the entire schedules.

When the demand schedule is relatively stable over time and only the supply schedule shifts, the observed price and quantity data will represent points along the demand schedule. In this case the econometrician will be able to estimate the true demand schedule correctly.

On the other hand, when the supply schedule remains relatively stable over time and the demand schedule shifts, the observed price and quantity data will actually represent points along the supply schedule—not the demand schedule. Therefore, in this particular case the econometrician's estimate of the "demand schedule" will in effect identify the supply schedule—not the true demand schedule.

Finally, when both the supply and demand schedules shift over time, the observed price and quantity data will not represent points along any particular supply or demand schedule. Accordingly, a brave econometrician who attempts to estimate a "demand schedule" from such observations will actually obtain a spurious (or hybrid) schedule. Evidently, this estimated schedule corresponds to neither the supply schedule nor the demand schedule but something in between. Because of this, the slope of the estimated spurious schedule may be either negative or positive. Even when it is negative, it is less (in absolute terms) than the slope of the true demand schedule. The result, of course, is a low estimate of the true elasticity.

2 The Aggregation Problem The empirical estimates of import-demand elasticities are made on the basis of highly aggregative data. Unless the demand elasticity is the same for all commodities that enter into the aggregates, the empirical estimates will be biased in the downward direction. What is the reason for this bias?

Commodities with relatively low elasticities typically experience larger price fluctuations than commodities with relatively high elasticities. Accordingly, the aggregate data exaggerate the importance of the low-elasticity commodities with the result that the estimated elasticities understate the true elasticities.

3 Errors of Measurement It is a well-known econometric fact that when there are errors of measurement (due to misclassification, falsification, or faulty methods of index number construction) in the *explanatory* variables, the estimates are biased. For further discussion of this technical point, see Orcutt (1950).

4 Short-Run versus Long-Run Elasticities Orcutt argued that the estimated elasticities are basically short-run elasticities. Accordingly, they are necessarily lower than the true long-run elasticities.

Recall that a country's demand for imports depends on the demand schedule of domestic consumers as well as the supply schedule of domestic producers of importables. On the demand side, consumers typically react slowly to price changes because it takes time for habits to adjust. Therefore, the short-run demand schedules are more inelastic than the corresponding long-run demand schedules. On the supply side, the reader is probably more familiar with the fundamental distinction between short-run supply curves versus long-run supply curves, with short-run supply elasticities being much smaller than their long-run counterparts. Accordingly, the true long-run elasticities of imports (and exports) must be substantially larger than the estimates of the corresponding short-run elasticities.

5 Small versus Large Price Changes Orcutt also argued that the elasticity of the demand for imports is probably larger for large price changes than for small price changes. He went on to say that the estimates were actually made during a period in which price changes were rather small. As a result, the estimated elasticities were biased in the downward direction.

15-10 SUMMARY

1 The partial-equilibrium model assumes that each country has supply and demand schedules giving the quantities of goods supplied by domestic producers and demanded by domestic consumers, respectively, at alternative prices expressed in domestic currency. These schedules are assumed to be independent of each other.

2 A country's demand-for-imports schedule gives the quantities (domestic shortages) that the country is willing to import at alternative prices expressed in domestic currency. This schedule depends on both the parameters that lie behind the domestic demand schedule (that is, tastes, incomes, and other commodity prices) and those that lie behind the domestic supply schedule (that is, technology and factor prices).

3 A country's supply-of-exports schedule gives the quantities (domestic surpluses) that the country is willing to export at alternative prices expressed in domestic currency. This schedule also depends on the parameters that lie behind the domestic supply schedule and those that lie behind the domestic demand schedule.

4 A commodity market is in equilibrium when the price of the commodity is such that one country's desired volume of imports matches the other country's desired volume of exports.

5 Before determining the commodity-market equilibria, it is necessary to express all prices in the same currency. For this purpose, it is necessary to know the rate of foreign exchange.

6 A country's export revenue (expenditure on imports) is given by the product of the country's equilibrium volume of exports (imports) and their equilibrium price in either domestic currency or foreign exchange. The difference between a country's export revenue and expenditure on imports gives that country's balance-of-trade deficit or surplus.

7 In general, a change in the rate of exchange disturbs an initial commodity-market equilibrium by causing one country's demand-for-imports and supply-of-exports schedules to shift.

8 In general, a devaluation has many effects: the devaluing country's volume of imports (exports) decreases (increases); the prices of traded goods fall (rise) in the rest of the world (in the devaluing country), causing their production to fall (expand) and their consumption to increase (decrease); the

demand for foreign exchange (that is, the devaluing country's expenditure on imports expressed in foreign currency) falls; the supply of foreign exchange (that is, the devaluing country's export revenue expressed in foreign exchange) may increase, decrease, or remain constant according to whether the foreign demand for imports is elastic, inelastic, or unit-elastic, respectively; the devaluing country's terms of trade may improve, deteriorate, or remain constant according to whether the product of the export-supply elasticities is respectively smaller than, larger than, or equal to the product of the import-demand elasticities; and the balance of trade may either improve or deteriorate.

    9 Devaluation improves the balance of trade when the sum of the two import-demand elasticities (in absolute terms) is greater than unity. This is the Marshall-Lerner condition.

    10 By plotting the quantities of foreign exchange supplied (demanded) against alternative rates of exchange, we obtain the supply (demand) schedule for foreign exchange. Usually, the demand schedule is downward sloping, while the supply schedule is backward bending.

    11 Equilibrium in the foreign exchange market occurs at the intersection of the supply and demand schedules for foreign exchange. When the supply schedule is backward bending, there may be multiple equilibria.

    12 When the supply schedule for foreign exchange is backward bending, speculation and other disturbances (for example, bumper crops, crop failures, and business cycles) may cause wide fluctuations in the rate of exchange, giving rise to unnecessary and wasteful reallocation of resources within each country.

    13 The partial-equilibrium model becomes consistent with full employment when each country possesses an additional industry producing nontraded goods. However, devaluation must then be combined with appropriate expenditure adjustments in both countries: the deficit (surplus) country must reduce (increase) its aggregate spending.

    14 Hume's automatic, self-correcting "price-specie-flow mechanism" rests on the idea that gold flows between countries tend to produce price-level changes, which in turn tend to restore equilibrium in the balance of payments. The mechanism assumes wage and price flexibility and high elasticities. The gold-losing country need not experience a terms-of-trade deterioration.

    15 The absolute version of the purchasing-power-parity theory asserts that the equilibrium rate of exchange is equal to the ratio of the price levels of the countries involved, that is, $R = P_a/P_b$. This theory is useless. In the absence of transportation costs and other trade impediments, the equation $R = P_a/P_b$ holds trivially for any rate of exchange—not just the equilibrium rate. In the presence of transportation costs, the equation $R = P_a/P_b$ cannot hold even when R is the equilibrium rate.

    16 The relative version of the PPP theory has some validity. This version is concerned with the effects of inflation on an initial equilibrium rate of exchange and rests on the neutrality of money and the quantity theory. Its drawback is that it also rests on the assumption that technology, tastes, etc., do not change during the transition period.

    17 The empirical estimates of the import-demand elasticities underestimate the true elasticities for various reasons, such as the identification problem, the aggregation problem, errors of measurement, and the fact that short-run elasticities are normally lower than the true long-run elasticities.

APPENDIX: Devaluation

This appendix deals with the effects of devaluation on the balance of trade and the terms of trade in the context of the partial-equilibrium model.

The Effect of Devaluation on the Balance of Trade

Write America's balance of trade in pounds $(T^£)$ as follows:

$$T^£ = S^£(R) - D^£(R) = \text{(America's export revenue)}$$
$$- \text{(America's expenditure on imports)} = \bar{p}_a^* M_b (\bar{p}_a^*) - \bar{p}_b^* X_b (\bar{p}_b^*) \qquad \text{(A15-1)}$$

where $S^£(R)$ = supply of pounds as a function of the rate of exchange (R)
$\quad D^£(R)$ = demand for pounds as a function of R
$\quad \bar{p}_a^*, \bar{p}_b^*$ = *equilibrium* prices in pounds of A-exportables and B-exportables, respectively
$\quad M_b(\bar{p}_a^*)$ = Britain's imports of A-exportables at the equilibrium price $\bar{p}_a^*$
$\quad X_b(\bar{p}_b^*)$ = Britain's exports of B-exportables at the equilibrium price $\bar{p}_b^*$

A bar $(-)$ on any price indicates that it is an equilibrium price. An asterisk $(*)$ on any price indicates that it is expressed in pounds. A price without an asterisk means that it is in dollars.

Throughout our discussion remember that the following equations hold:

$$p_a = R p_a^* \qquad \text{(A15-2)}$$

$$p_b = R p_b^* \qquad \text{(A15-3)}$$

Also note carefully that equilibrium prices $\bar{p}_a^*$ and $\bar{p}_b^*$ depend on the rate of exchange, as explained in Sections 15-3 and 15-4.

We are now ready to study the effect of a devaluation of the dollar (that is, an increase in R) on America's balance of trade. Differentiate equation (A15-1) with respect to R to obtain

$$\frac{dT^£}{dR} = \frac{dS^£}{dR} - \frac{dD^£}{dR} = (1 + e_{mb}) M_b \frac{d\bar{p}_a^*}{dR} - (1 + e_{xb}) X_b \frac{d\bar{p}_b^*}{dR} \qquad \text{(A15-4)}$$

where $e_{mb} = \dfrac{dM_b}{d\bar{p}_a^*} \dfrac{\bar{p}_a^*}{M_b}$ = Britain's elasticity of demand for imports

$\qquad e_{xb} = \dfrac{dX_b}{d\bar{p}_b^*} \dfrac{\bar{p}_b^*}{X_b}$ = Britain's elasticity of supply of exports

To make any progress, we must evaluate derivatives $d\bar{p}_a^*/dR$ and $d\bar{p}_b^*/dR$. For this purpose, we must turn to the commodity markets.

Equilibrium in the market for A-exportables prevails when the price of A-exportables is such that the following equation is satisfied:

$$X_a(R\bar{p}_a^*) = M_b(\bar{p}_a^*) \qquad \text{(A15-5)}$$

where X_a = America's exports as a function of $p_a = R\bar{p}_a^*$. Similarly, equilibrium in the market for B-exportables requires that the following equation be satisfied:

$$X_b(\bar{p}_b^*) = M_a(R\bar{p}_b^*) \tag{A15-6}$$

where M_a = America's imports as a function of $p_b = Rp_b^*$. For each value of R, equation (A15-5) gives the equilibrium price of A-exportables, that is, $\bar{p}_a^*$, and equation (A15-6) gives the equilibrium price of B-exportables, that is, $\bar{p}_b^*$.

Differentiate equation (A15-5) totally with respect to R to obtain

$$\frac{dX_a}{d\bar{p}_a}\left(\bar{p}_a^* + R\,\frac{d\bar{p}_a^*}{dR}\right) = \frac{dM_b}{d\bar{p}_a^*}\,\frac{d\bar{p}_a^*}{dR}$$

or

$$\frac{d\bar{p}_a^*}{dR} = \frac{\bar{p}_a^*}{R}\,\frac{e_{xa}}{e_{mb} - e_{xa}} \tag{A15-7}$$

where $e_{xa} = \dfrac{dX_a}{d\bar{p}_a}\,\dfrac{\bar{p}_a}{X_a}$ = America's elasticity of exports, and $X_a = M_b$.

Similarly, differentiate equation (A15-6) totally with respect to R to obtain

$$\frac{dX_b}{d\bar{p}_b^*}\,\frac{d\bar{p}_b^*}{dR} = \frac{dM_a}{d\bar{p}_b}\left(\bar{p}_b^* + R\,\frac{d\bar{p}_b^*}{dR}\right)$$

or

$$\frac{d\bar{p}_b^*}{dR} = -\frac{\bar{p}_b^*}{R}\,\frac{e_{ma}}{e_{ma} - e_{xb}} \tag{A15-8}$$

where $e_{ma} = \dfrac{dM_a}{d\bar{p}_b}\,\dfrac{\bar{p}_b}{M_a}$ = America's elasticity of demand for imports, and $M_a = X_b$.

Finally, substitute equations (A15-7) and (A15-8) into equation (A15-4) to obtain

$$\frac{dT^{\mathcal{L}}}{dR} = \frac{\bar{p}_a^* M_b}{R}\left[\frac{e_{xa}(1 + e_{mb})}{e_{mb} - e_{xa}} + \frac{\bar{p}_b^* X_b}{\bar{p}_a^* M_b}\,\frac{e_{ma}(1 + e_{xb})}{e_{ma} - e_{xb}}\right] \tag{A15-9}$$

A devaluation of the dollar improves America's balance of trade when the bracketed expression on the right-hand side of equation (A15-9) is positive. This is indeed the most general condition for a successful devaluation.

When America's balance of trade is initially zero (that is, $\bar{p}_b^* X_b = \bar{p}_a^* M_b$) and the supply elasticities of exports are infinite (that is, $e_{xa} = e_{xb} = \infty$), the bracketed expression on the right-hand side of equation (A15-9) reduces to $[-(1 + e_{mb}) - e_{ma}]$, as the reader should verify. Accordingly, for a successful devaluation in this case it is necessary that $(-1 - e_{ma} - e_{mb}) > 0$, or

$$+ e_{ma} + e_{mb} < -1 \tag{A15-10}$$

Inequality (A15-10) is the *Marshall-Lerner condition*.

When the Marshall-Lerner condition is satisfied—that is, when inequality (A15-10) holds—the right-hand side of equation (A15-9) is positive, assuming only that initially America's balance of trade is either zero or negative (deficit), that is, $\bar{p}_b^* X_b \geq \bar{p}_a^* M_b$. This we can show rather easily.

First, observe that when $\bar{p}_b^* X_b > \bar{p}_a^* M_b$ the following inequality is a sufficient condition for $dT^\pounds/dR > 0$:

$$\frac{e_{xa}(1 + e_{mb})}{e_{mb} - e_{xa}} + \frac{e_{ma}(1 + e_{xb})}{e_{ma} - e_{xb}} > 0$$

Given that $e_{mb} - e_{xa} < 0$ and $e_{ma} - e_{xb} < 0$, the last inequality simplifies to

$$-e_{xa}e_{xb}(1 + e_{ma} + e_{mb}) + e_{ma}e_{mb}(1 + e_{xa} + e_{xb}) > 0 \tag{A15-11}$$

Since $e_{ma}e_{mb}(1 + e_{xa} + e_{xb}) \geq 0$, it follows that inequality (A15-11) is satisfied whenever the Marshall-Lerner condition is satisfied.

The Effect of Devaluation on the Terms of Trade

Turn now to the effect of the devaluation of the dollar on America's terms of trade ($\bar{p}$).

Write America's terms of trade as follows:

$$\bar{p} = \frac{\bar{p}_a^*}{\bar{p}_b^*} \tag{A15-12}$$

Differentiate $\bar{p}$ with respect to R to obtain:

$$\frac{d\bar{p}}{dR} = \left(\frac{1}{\bar{p}_b^*}\right) \left[\frac{d\bar{p}_a^*}{dR} - \frac{\bar{p}_a^*}{\bar{p}_b^*} \frac{d\bar{p}_b^*}{dR} \right] \tag{A15-13}$$

Finally, substitute from equations (A15-7) and (A15-8) to obtain:

$$\frac{d\bar{p}}{dR} = \left(\frac{\bar{p}_a^*}{R\bar{p}_b^*}\right) \left(\frac{e_{xa}}{e_{mb} - e_{xa}} + \frac{e_{ma}}{e_{ma} - e_{xb}} \right)$$
$$= \left(\frac{\bar{p}_a^*}{R\bar{p}_b^*}\right) \left[\frac{e_{ma}e_{mb} - e_{xa}e_{xb}}{(e_{mb} - e_{xa})(e_{ma} - e_{xb})} \right] \tag{A15-14}$$

From equation (A15-14) it follows that:

1 America's terms of trade *improve* with the devaluation of the dollar, that is, $(d\bar{p}/dR) > 0$, when $e_{ma}e_{mb} > e_{xa}e_{xb}$; that is, when the product of the demand elasticities for imports is higher than the product of the supply elasticities of exports.

2 America's terms of trade *deteriorate*, that is, $d\bar{p}/dR < 0$, when $e_{ma}e_{mb} < e_{xa}e_{xb}$.

3 Finally, America's terms of trade remain unaltered, that is, $d\bar{p}/dR = 0$, when $e_{ma}e_{mb} = e_{xa}e_{xb}$.

SUGGESTED READING

Bickerdike, C. F. (1920). "The Instability of Foreign Exchange." *Economic Journal,* vol. 30 (March), pp. 118–122.

Chacholiades, M. (1978). *International Monetary Theory and Policy.* McGraw-Hill Book Company, New York, chaps. 3–8.

Houthakker, H. S., and S. P. Magee (1969). "Income and Price Elasticities in World Trade." *Review of Economics and Statistics,* vol. 51 (May), pp. 111–125.

Leamer, E. E., and R. M. Stern (1970). *Quantitative International Economics.* Allyn and Bacon, Inc., Boston, chap. 2.

Machlup, F. (1939 and 1940). "The Theory of Foreign Exchanges." *Economica,* vol. 6 (new series), November 1939, and February 1940. Reprinted in H. S. Ellis and L. A. Metzler (eds.). AEA *Readings in the Theory of International Trade.* Richard D. Irwin, Inc., Homewood, Ill., 1950.

Orcutt, G. H. (1950). "Measurement of Price Elasticities in International Trade." *The Review of Economics and Statistics,* vol. 32, no. 2 (May). Reprinted in R. E. Caves and H. G. Johnson (eds.). AEA *Readings in International Economics.* Richard D. Irwin, Inc., Homewood, Ill., 1968.

Robinson, J, (1939). "The Foreign Exchanges." In J. Robinson. *Essays in the Theory of Employment.* Macmillan & Co., Ltd., London. Reprinted in H. S. Ellis and L. A. Metzler (eds.). AEA *Readings in the Theory of International Trade.* Richard D. Irwin, Inc., Homewood, Ill., 1950.

Chapter Sixteen

The Income-Adjustment Mechanism

Our discussion in Chapter 14 showed that international adjustment may proceed either through *prices* or through *incomes* (that is, through aggregate spending, production, and employment). While Chapter 15 examined the *price-adjustment mechanism,* this chapter deals mainly with the *income-adjustment mechanism.*

Most of the analysis of this chapter rests on the simplifying assumption that all prices (for example, commodity prices, money-wage rates, the rate of exchange, and the rate of interest) remain constant. This assumption is convenient because now we wish to study the important relationship that exists between a country's national income and the foreign-trade sector.

The income-adjustment mechanism is a direct outgrowth of Keynes's *General Theory,* even though Keynes himself had little to do with it. This powerful mechanism yields two important propositions:

   1 *International trade is a significant vehicle for the transmission of business cycles between countries.* This proposition comes under the *national-income multiplier theory.*
   2 *Balance-of-payments disturbances that affect the circular flow of income give rise to national-income changes that tend to bring about partial (not*

complete) adjustment in the balance of payments. This proposition comes under the *balance-of-trade multiplier theory.*

The present chapter deals with both propositions.

Section 16-1 reviews the basic Keynesian model of income determination in a closed economy. Section 16-2 expands the analysis to the determination of national income in a small open economy. The term *small open economy* refers to an open economy whose foreign trade (that is, exports and imports of goods and services) is a negligible fraction of total world output, so that changes in its imports do not have any appreciable effect on total world expenditure. Section 16-3 deals with the foreign-trade multiplier of a small open economy. Finally, Section 16-4 generalizes the discussion to a two-country model and considers the implications of foreign repercussions. The appendix to this chapter deals with the derivation of the foreign-trade multiplier formulas in the presence of foreign repercussion.

16-1 INCOME DETERMINATION IN A CLOSED ECONOMY

Even though it is assumed that students are familiar with the basic Keynesian model of income determination in a closed economy, a brief review of such a model would be helpful before we expand it to the world economy. The purpose of this section is to provide such a review. For simplicity, we ignore the government sector.

The Circular Flow of Income

In any closed economy, it is important to distinguish among three economic flows, as follows:

1 *Aggregate demand D.* This flow refers to the aggregate expenditure that all economic units (for example, consumers and producers) are willing to incur for consumption C or investment I. That is, $D = C + I$.

2 *Aggregate output Q.* This flow refers to the aggregate production of investment goods plus consumption goods. Accordingly, aggregate output (or *gross national product*) stands for the annual flow of goods supplied by the business sector of the economy.

3 *National income Y.* This flow refers to the aggregate income earned by the factors employed in the production of aggregate output. In particular, national income is the sum of all factor earnings; that is, $Y =$ wages + interest + rents + profits.

The relationship among aggregate demand D, aggregate output Q, and national income Y may be clarified further by means of the *circular flow of income* in the economy, as illustrated in Figure 16-1. It does not matter where we start, as long as we follow the direction of the arrows. For instance, start with aggregate output Q, which generates national income Y. National income Y, in

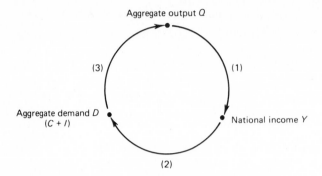

Figure 16-1 *The circular flow of income.*
It does not matter where we start on this circular-flow-of-income diagram as long as we follow the direction of the arrows. For instance, aggregate output Q generates national income Y, national income generates aggregate demand D, aggregate demand generates aggregate output, and so on, ad infinitum.

turn, generates aggregate demand D, and demand gives rise to output, and so on, ad infinitum.

Let us consider the circular flow of income a little more closely. As factors of production are used in the production of output Q, they earn incomes (that is, wages, interest, rents, and profits) for their services. Therefore, the production of output Q generates the national income Y, as shown by arrow (1).

It is an accounting fact that the aggregate income earned by all factors of production during any given year (or some other time period) must be identically equal to the value of output produced. In symbols, $Y = Q$. The identity $Y = Q$ follows from the fact that while the first three categories of factor earnings (that is, wages, interest, and rents) are *contractual,* the last category (profits) is a *residual.* In particular, profits are given by the difference between the value of output produced (sales revenue) and the contractual payments to factors (cost of production); that is:

$$\text{Profits} = Q - (\text{wages} + \text{interest} + \text{rents}) \qquad (16\text{-}1)$$

But this latter identity can be rearranged as follows:

$$Q = \text{wages} + \text{interest} + \text{rents} + \text{profits} = Y \qquad (16\text{-}2)$$

Because of this fundamental identity, we can drop the distinction between aggregate output and national income, and we can also use the symbol Y to represent both national income and aggregate output.

Turn now to arrow (2), which shows that national income Y determines aggregate demand $D = C + I$. What can we say about the two components of aggregate demand (C and I)?

As a first approximation, we may assume that the *desired* (or planned) flow of investment expenditure I is exogenous. That is, desired investment I is independent of the level of national income Y; that is, $I = \bar{I}$, where the bar (−) indicates that investment is exogenous (or constant).

The desired level of consumption, on the other hand, depends on the level of national income, that is, $C = C(Y)$. This is the crucial *consumption function* that plays a very significant role in the Keynesian macroeconomic system.

As national income Y increases, desired consumption increases also. The extra amount by which desired consumption increases when national income goes up by one unit (for example, $1) is known as the *marginal propensity to consume* (MPC). As a rule, the marginal propensity to consume is positive and less than unity. Thus, even though desired consumption increases when national income increases, the increase in consumption ΔC is not as big as the increase in income ΔY; that is, $\Delta C < \Delta Y$. In fact, MPC $= (\Delta C/\Delta Y) < 1$.

The part of national income that is not spent on consumption is called *saving* S. Put another way, $S = Y - C(Y) = S(Y)$.

As we have seen, consumption increases when income increases; but the increase in consumption ΔC is always smaller than the increase in income. The extra income that is not spent on consumption, that is, $\Delta Y - \Delta C$, represents additional saving ΔS. In other words, we always have $\Delta Y - \Delta C = \Delta S$ or $\Delta Y = \Delta C + \Delta S$. Further, the fraction of each extra dollar of income that goes into saving, that is, $\Delta S/\Delta Y$, is known as the *marginal propensity to save* (MPS). Because of the identity $\Delta Y = \Delta C + \Delta S$, it is evident that *the sum of the marginal propensity to consume (MPC) plus the marginal propensity to save (MPS) equals 1.* Or:

$$\text{MPC} + \text{MPS} = 1 \tag{16-3}$$

So far we have seen how the production of aggregate output Q gives rise to national income Y, as shown in Figure 16-1 by arrow (1), and also how national income Y gives rise to aggregate demand $D = C(Y) + \bar{I}$, as shown by arrow (2). To complete the circle, we must finally consider the link between aggregate demand D and aggregate output Q.

The producers do not produce the aggregate output Q for its own sake. Rather, they produce output because they expect to sell it. That is, producers in general produce output only to the extent that there exists a demand for it. When aggregate demand increases, the producers sooner or later increase their production in order to meet the increased demand. On the other hand, when aggregate demand decreases, the producers sooner or later decrease their production. It is therefore apparent that in the final analysis the desired volume of aggregate demand determines aggregate output, as shown in Figure 16-1 by arrow (3).

Determination of National Income

We now proceed with the determination of national-income equilibrium in the simple Keynesian model of a closed economy.

As the student may recall from introductory economics, national-income equilibrium occurs when *desired* aggregate demand D, that is, $C(Y) + \bar{I}$, equals aggregate output (or supply) Q, that is, Y (recall that $Q = Y$). In other words, national-income equilibrium prevails when the three flows of Figure 16-1 are perfectly synchronized; that is, when

$$Y = C(Y) + \bar{I} \tag{16-4}$$

We can rearrange equation (16-4) as follows:

$$S(Y) = Y - C(Y) = \bar{I} \tag{16-5}$$

The left-hand side of equation (16-5) gives the desired level of *saving* $S(Y)$, that is, that part of national income not spent on consumption. Accordingly, equation (16-5) tells us that national-income equilibrium prevails when the desired flow of saving equals the desired flow of investment. If we think of saving as a *leakage* from the income stream (that is, as a portion of national income which is not spent and which is therefore lost to the income stream) and of investment as an exogenous *injection* into the income stream, we can then say that *national-income equilibrium occurs when the injections match the leakages.*

Figure 16-2 illustrates the determination of national-income equilibrium in a closed economy. The top panel gives the solution in terms of equation (16-4). We first add vertically desired level of investment $\bar{I}$ to desired consumption $C(Y)$ to obtain aggregate expenditure (or absorption) schedule $C(Y) + \bar{I}$. National-income equilibrium occurs at E, where aggregate expenditure schedule $C(Y) + \bar{I}$ intersects the 45° line. (The 45° line is the locus of points whose distances from the two axes are equal.) The lower panel gives the solution in terms of equation (16-5). Equilibrium occurs at F, where saving schedule $S(Y)$ intersects investment schedule $\bar{I}$. In both panels, the equilibrium level of income is 900.

Note the strict relationship between the saving schedule of panel (*b*) and the consumption schedule of panel (*a*). When national income is zero, the economy still wishes to consume 100, as shown in panel (*a*), merely by using up (that is, dissaving) 100 of accumulated past savings, as shown in panel (*b*). When income rises to 300, the economy wishes to spend all of it on consumption, as shown by point H in panel (*a*). This means that when income is 300 the economy's desired saving is zero, as shown by point K in panel (*b*). For levels of income higher than the critical level of 300, desired saving is positive (that is, the economy saves); for income levels lower than 300, desired saving is negative (that is, the economy dissaves). In general, the vertical distances between consumption schedule $C(Y)$ and the 45° line in panel (*a*) are always equal to the corresponding vertical distances between the saving schedule and the horizontal axis in panel (*b*). The saving schedule may be viewed as the twin of the consumption schedule.

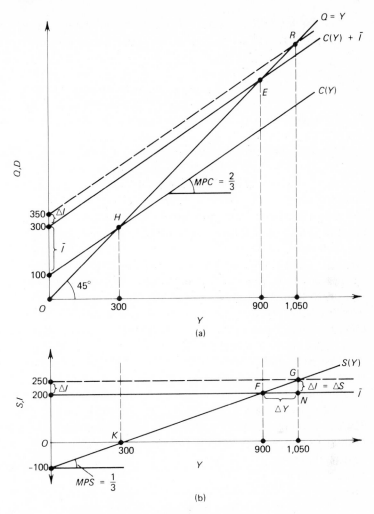

Figure 16-2 *National-income equilibrium in a closed economy.*
In panel (a) we add vertically the desired level of investment to consumption function $C(Y)$ to obtain aggregate expenditure schedule $C(Y) + \bar{I}$. National-income equilibrium occurs at E, where the $C(Y) + \bar{I}$ schedule intersects the 45° line. In panel (b), equilibrium occurs at F, where saving schedule $S(Y)$ intersects horizontal investment schedule $\bar{I}$. In both panels the equilibrium level of income is 900.

Why is it that equilibrium prevails when national income is at 900 (Figure 16-2)? Because at that point both consumers and producers are content with what they are doing, and they will continue doing the same thing. In particular, consumers spend on consumption what they actually wish to spend on consumption (that is, 700). Similarly, business firms invest exactly what they want to invest (that is, 200). Finally, producers sell exactly what they produce (that is, 900). Neither consumers nor firms have any incentive to change their behavior.[1]

Stability of Equilibrium

What if national income is actually different from the level indicated by the intersection of the saving schedule and the investment schedule [or, alternatively by the intersection of aggregate expenditure schedule $C(Y) + \bar{I}$ and the 45° line]? Will there by any economic forces to push national income toward its equilibrium level? In other words, is the national-income equilibrium stable?

Return to Figure 16-2. At levels of national income below 900, aggregate demand $C(Y) + \bar{I}$ exceeds aggregate supply Y, as shown in panel (a); and alternatively, desired investment $\bar{I}$ exceeds desired saving $S(Y)$, as shown in panel (b). Accordingly, business firms will experience a continuous reduction in their inventories because sales exceed production. As a result of this *unplanned* (or involuntary) inventory decumulation, business firms will eventually revise upward their production plans, and national income will rise.

At levels of national income above 900, aggregate demand falls short of aggregate supply, or, alternatively, desired saving exceeds desired investment. Business firms will be unable to sell all they want. Thus, they will experience a continuous involuntary inventory accumulation that will eventually force them to revise downward their production plans. National income will fall.

We therefore conclude that the equilibrium depicted in Figure 16-2 is indeed stable.

It is interesting to note that the stability of equilibrium is guaranteed by the fact that the marginal propensity to consume is less than 1. This makes aggregate demand schedule $C(Y) + \bar{I}$ flatter than the 45° line and thus ensures that the equilibrium is stable. [Since investment is exogenous, the slope of the aggregate demand schedule is the same as the slope of the consumption schedule, that is, the marginal propensity to consume (MPC).]

The Multiplier

Suppose now that the annual level of (desired) investment rises from 200 to 250. What happens to the equilibrium level of national income? Apparently income will rise. But this is not the whole story. Income will not just rise by the increase in investment (that is, $50 = 250 - 200$). Income will actually rise by much more than the increase in investment. How can that be?

Return again to Figure 16-2. In the top panel, the increase in investment causes the aggregate demand schedule to shift upward, as shown by the broken line. Equilibrium shifts to point R, where the new aggregate demand schedule intersects the 45° line. In the lower panel, the increase in investment causes the investment schedule to shift upward, as shown by the broken horizontal line. Equilibrium now shifts to point G, where the saving schedule intersects the

---

[1] Of course, if the equilibrium income (900) is less than the full-employment income, there will be general discontent with the existing unemployment.

new investment schedule. In either case, national income increases by 150 (that is, $1050 - 900$), which is 3 times as large as the increase in investment. The number 3, which shows what multiple of the increase in investment ΔI is the increase in income ΔY, is called the *multiplier*. Put another way:

$$\Delta Y = \text{multiplier} \times \Delta I \tag{16-6a}$$

or

$$\text{multiplier} = \frac{\Delta Y}{\Delta I} \tag{16-6b}$$

What determines the multiplier? Why is the multiplier greater than unity? To answer these questions, consider again the lower panel of Figure 16-2. As investment increases by 50, the investment schedule shifts upward by 50, and equilibrium shifts from F to G. Note carefully that equilibrium is reestablished only when national income rises sufficiently to generate additional saving ΔS (leakage) to match precisely the autonomous increase in investment (injection). Put differently, $\Delta S = \Delta I = 50$. By how much should income increase so that $\Delta S = \Delta I$? Because $\Delta S = \text{MPS} \times \Delta Y$, we must have

$$\Delta I = \Delta S = \text{MPS} \times \Delta Y$$

or

$$\Delta Y = \left(\frac{1}{\text{MPS}}\right) \Delta I$$

Therefore

$$\text{Multiplier} = \frac{\Delta Y}{\Delta I} = \left(\frac{1}{\text{MPS}}\right) \tag{16-7}$$

That is, *the multiplier is equal to the reciprocal of the marginal propensity to save*. Since $0 < \text{MPS} < 1$, it follows that the multiplier is higher than 1. In the example of Figure 16-2, the marginal propensity to save is $1/3$; therefore, the multiplier is 3.

The common-sense meaning of the multiplier is not difficult to capture. As businesses build more factories and buy more equipment, they generate extra income. This extra income goes to those factors (such as workers) who actually produce the additional factories and equipment. In turn, these income recipients, who find their incomes increased, spend part of their new revenues on consumption. How large their increase in consumption is depends, of course, on their marginal propensity to consume. The crucial consideration, however, remains the fact that extra consumption means extra production and, therefore, extra income, which leads again to further consumption, and so on, ad infinitum. Thus, we see that national income does not just rise by the increase in investment; it rises by much more. When does this process end? When national income rises by the increase in investment times the multiplier.

16-2 INCOME DETERMINATION IN AN OPEN ECONOMY

We are now ready to consider the determination of national income in an open economy. For the most part we shall concentrate on an open economy that is "small" in the sense that changes in its imports do not have any appreciable effect on total world expenditure. This means that for the moment we shall ignore all foreign repercussions from induced changes in the circular flow of income of the rest of the world. We shall consider the "large" country case, where foreign repercussion is important, in Section 16-4.

This section deals primarily with the determination of national-income equilibrium in a small open economy. The next section considers the foreign-trade multiplier theory as well as the balance-of-trade multiplier theory for domestic and foreign disturbances.

Aggregate Absorption versus Aggregate Demand

In a closed economy, aggregate demand for the economy's output coincides with aggregate expenditure (or absorption) by the economy's residents. This is not so in an open economy. Accordingly, we must first clarify the distinction between aggregate absorption and aggregate demand. In view of the significance of the difference between these two aggregate flows, from now on we shall use two separate symbols: D for aggregate demand (as before) and Z for aggregate absorption.

First, consider aggregate absorption (or spending), which is simpler. As with the closed economy, aggregate absorption Z is the sum of consumption and investment expenditures; that is, $Z = C + I$. (When the government sector is included, Z must include government expenditure G as well; that is, $Z = C + I + G$.) As before, we shall assume that desired investment is exogenous, while desired consumption depends on national income.

What is aggregate demand D for the open economy's aggregate output? When the economy is open, the aggregate demand is the sum of two major components: a domestic demand component plus a foreign demand component. The foreign demand component is merely the open economy's *exports* X to the rest of the world. The domestic demand component, on the other hand, is that portion of aggregate absorption Z that is spent on domestic products.

The domestic demand component does not coincide with the economy's aggregate expenditure Z because part of that expenditure goes to purchase foreign products (imports). To arrive at the domestic demand component, we must subtract from Z the open economy's expenditure on imports; that is, domestic demand component $= Z - M$.

We therefore conclude that aggregate demand D for the open economy's output is equal to $Z - M + X$; that is,

$$D = Z + (X - M) = C + I + (X - M) \qquad (16\text{-}8)$$

Equation (16-8) reveals that the *aggregate demand for the open economy's output equals the economy's aggregate absorption ($C + I$, or Z) plus the economy's balance of trade ($X - M$)*.

Note carefully that imports M act as "leakages," just like saving. On the other hand, exports act as exogenous "injections" into the expenditure stream, just like investment.

We have already seen that desired consumption depends on national income, while desired investment is exogenous. Because our present interest is with a "small" open economy, we can also take exports of goods and services as exogenous, like investment. Exports depend on foreign economic conditions that our open economy is too small to influence.[2] Imports, on the other hand, depend positively on domestic national income. Before we show how to determine the equilibrium level of national income in an open economy, we must take a closer look at this important relationship between imports M and national income Y. This relationship is known as the *import function*.

The Import Function

In general, an open economy imports goods and services from the rest of the world for two different reasons.

1 An open economy may import foreign goods for direct domestic consumption or investment. For instance, a country may import final consumption goods (such as food and clothing) as well as capital goods (such as machinery).

2 An open economy may also import raw materials (such as oil, steel, and lumber) for use as inputs into the domestic production of goods and services.

Each of these reasons provides some economic justification for the observed positive dependence of imports M on national income Y.

Figure 16-3 illustrates a hypothetical import schedule. The desired level of imports M depends on the current level of national income Y. The import schedule slopes upward because, in general, imports tend to increase as national income increases. For instance, when national income is 700, the desired level of imports is 75; when national income increases to 800, the desired level of imports increases to 85. Thus, as income increases by 100, imports increase by 10.

Of special significance is the ratio of the change in imports ΔM to the

---

[2] Note that within the context of the Keynesian model under consideration, all outputs are demand-determined.

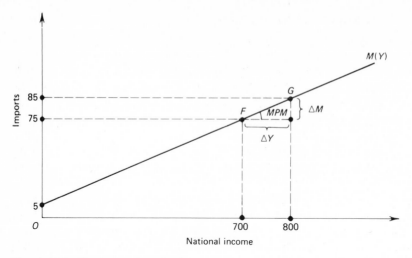

Figure 16-3 *The import function.*
When national income is 700, the desired level of imports is 75; and when national income increases to 800, the desired level of imports increases to 85. Thus, as income increases by 100, imports increase by 10. The ratio 10/100 is the *marginal propensity to import* (MPM); it is given graphically by the slope of the import function.

change in national income ΔY, that is, $\Delta M/\Delta Y$. This ratio is known as the *marginal propensity to import* (MPM) and gives the extra amount of imports caused by a one-unit increase in national income. For instance, in Figure 16-3 imports increase by 10 when national income increases by 100. This means that the marginal propensity to import is 0.10; that is, for each dollar increase in national income ($\Delta Y = \$1$), the economy increases her spending on imports by 10 cents. The marginal propensity to import (MPM) is given graphically by the slope of the import function, as illustrated in Figure 16-3.

The ratio of imports M to national income Y, that is, M/Y, is known as the *average propensity to import*. For instance, in Figure 16-3 the average propensity to import is 75/700 at F, and 85/800 at G.

The ratio of the marginal propensity to import to the average propensity to import is the *income elasticity of demand for imports*.

Table 16-1 summarizes the empirical estimates of the three parameters of the import functions of various countries. Column (1) gives the estimates of the income elasticity of demand for imports of various countries [published in a study by Houthakker and Magee (1969)]. Column (2) gives the average propensity to consume of various countries. [The estimates of column (2) are based on the data on imports and gross domestic product reported in the IMF *International Financial Statistics*, September 1967, for the year 1960.] Finally, column (3) gives the marginal propensity to import on the basis of the formula MPM = (income elasticity) × (average propensity). All marginal and average propensities to import reported in Table 16-1 are positive and less than unity.

National-Income Equilibrium

We are now ready to determine the equilibrium of national income in an open economy.

As with a closed economy, national income equilibrium in an open economy occurs when desired aggregate demand D, that is $C(Y) + \bar{I} + \bar{X} - M(Y)$, equals aggregate output (or supply) Q, that is, Y (recall that $Q = Y$). In other words, national-income equilibrium in a small open economy prevails when

$$Y = C(Y) + \bar{I} + \bar{X} - M(Y) \tag{16-9}$$

In what follows, we find it more convenient to use equation (16-9) in either of the following forms:

$$S(Y) + M(Y) = \bar{I} + \bar{X} \tag{16-10}$$

$$S(Y) - \bar{I} = \bar{X} - M(Y) \tag{16-11}$$

where saving function $S(Y)$ is given by the difference $Y - C(Y)$, as before. We obtain equation (16-10) from equation (16-9) merely by transferring consumption function $C(Y)$ and import function $M(Y)$ to the left-hand side, and then substituting saving function $S(Y)$ for the difference $Y - C(Y)$. Finally, we obtain equation (16-11) from equation (16-10) merely by transferring desired investment $\bar{I}$ to the left-hand side and import function $M(Y)$ to the right-hand

Table 16-1 Estimates of the Marginal and Average Propensities to Import

Country	Income elasticity of imports (1)	Average propensity to import (2)	Marginal propensity to import (3) = (1) × (2)
Australia	0.90	0.15	0.14
Canada	1.20	0.15	0.18
Denmark	1.31	0.30	0.40
France	1.66	0.10	0.17
Germany	1.80	0.14	0.26
Italy	2.19	0.14	0.31
Japan	1.23	0.11	0.13
The Netherlands	1.89	0.41	0.77
Norway	1.40	0.32	0.45
South Africa	1.13	0.21	0.23
Sweden	1.42	0.24	0.33
Switzerland	1.81	0.26	0.48
United Kingdom	1.66	0.18	0.30
United States	1.51	0.03	0.05

Sources: (1) H. S. Houthakker and S. P. Magee. "Income and Price Elasticities in World Trade." *Review of Economics and Statistics,* vol. 51, no. 2, May 1969, table 1, p. 113. (2) Estimated for 1960 from IMF, *International Financial Statistics,* vol. 20, no. 12, December 1967.

side. Mathematically, equations (16-9) to (16-11) are all equivalent. They all determine the same equilibrium level of national income.

Equation (16-10) relates the endogenous leakages, $S(Y)$ and $M(Y)$, out of the income stream to the exogenous injections, $\bar{I}$ and $\bar{X}$, into the income stream. Thus, national-income equilibrium occurs when the injections match the leakages.

Equation (16-11), on the other hand, relates the excess of saving over domestic investment (that is, the *net* domestic leakage) to the balance-of-trade surplus (that is, the *net* foreign injection). Of course, domestic investment may exceed domestic saving in any national-income equilibrium situation. In that case, imports must also exceed exports; and the excess of domestic investment over saving (that is, the *net* domestic injection) must match the balance-of-trade deficit (that is, the *net* foreign leakage).

The virtue of equation (16-11) is that it gives directly the balance-of-trade surplus or deficit.

Figure 16-4 illustrates the determination of national-income equilibrium in a small open economy. The top panel gives the solution in terms of equation (16-10). The lower panel gives the solution in terms of equation (16-11). In both panels, the equilibrium level of income is Y_0.

In the top panel, we first add vertically exogenous exports $\bar{X}$ to exogenous investment $\bar{I}$ to obtain horizontal schedule $\bar{I} + \bar{X}$. We also add vertically import function $M(Y)$ to saving function $S(Y)$ to obtain upward-sloping schedule $S(Y) + M(Y)$. National-income equilibrium occurs at intersection E of the $\bar{I} + \bar{X}$ schedule and the $S(Y) + M(Y)$ schedule. At that equilibrium point, economy's saving S_0 and imports M_0 are given, respectively, by vertical distances Y_0G and GE. The economy's balance of trade is in deficit, as shown by vertical distance GF, which is equal to both $M_0 - \bar{X}$ and $\bar{I} - S_0$.

Note carefully that the slope of the $S(Y) + M(Y)$ schedule is equal to the sum of the marginal propensity to save (MPS) plus the marginal propensity to import (MPM), that is, the sum of the individual slopes of the saving function and the import function. This observation becomes important in the next section, which deals with the foreign-trade multiplier.

In the lower panel, we arrive at the national-income equilibrium as follows. First, we subtract vertically import function $M(Y)$ from exogenous exports $\bar{X}$ to obtain downward-sloping schedule $\bar{X} - M(Y)$. We further subtract vertically exogenous investment $\bar{I}$ from saving function $S(Y)$, that is, we shift the saving function downward by the amount of exogenous investment, to obtain upward-sloping schedule $S(Y) - \bar{I}$. National-income equilibrium occurs at intersection H of the $\bar{X} - M(Y)$ schedule and the $S(Y) - \bar{I}$ schedule. Again national income is Y_0; and vertical distance HY_0 shows the balance-of-trade deficit that coincides with the deficit shown in the top panel.

Compare Figure 16-4 to Figure 16-2, and argue, as before, that national-income equilibrium is "stable." That is, for levels of national income *below* Y_0, show that business firms will experience *involuntary inventory decumulation* and that they will revise upward their production plans, causing national in-

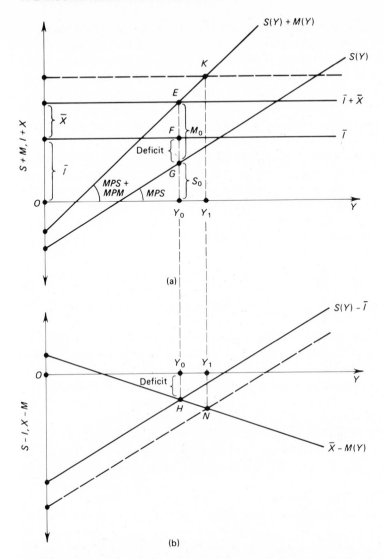

Figure 16-4 *National-income equilibrium in a small open economy.*
In panel (*a*) we add vertically exogenous exports $\bar{X}$ to exogenous investment $\bar{I}$ to obtain horizontal schedule $\bar{I} + \bar{X}$. We also add vertically import function $M(Y)$ to saving function $S(Y)$ to obtain schedule $S(Y) + M(Y)$, whose slope gives the sum of the marginal propensity to save (MPS) plus the marginal propensity to import (MPM). Equilibrium occurs at the intersection of the $\bar{I} + \bar{X}$ schedule and the $S(Y) + M(Y)$ schedule. In panel (*b*) we subtract vertically import function $M(Y)$ from exogenous exports $\bar{X}$ to obtain downward-sloping schedule $\bar{X} - M(Y)$. We also subtract vertically exogenous investment $\bar{I}$ from saving function $S(Y)$ to obtain upward-sloping schedule $S(Y) - \bar{I}$. Equilibrium occurs at H, which is the intersection of schedules $\bar{X} - M(Y)$ and $S(Y) - \bar{I}$. In both panels, the equilibrium level of income is Y_0. The balance-of-trade deficit is given in panel (*a*) by distance GF and in panel (*b*) by distance HY_0, with $GF = HY_0$. An increase in investment by ΔI causes the $\bar{I} + \bar{X}$ schedule in panel (*a*) to shift upward and the $S(Y) - \bar{I}$ schedule in panel (*b*) to shift downward, as illustrated by the broken lines. National income increases to Y_1 in both panels, and the balance-of-trade deficit increases to NY_1, as shown in panel (*b*)

come to *rise*. On the other hand, for levels of national income *above* Y_0, show that business firms will experience *involuntary inventory accumulation* and that they will revise downward their production plans, causing national income to *fall*. Only when national income is equal to Y_0 will the business firms be content with their production plans.

Further, note carefully that the equilibrium level of income Y_0 need not coincide with the full employment level of income. National-income equilibrium may indeed coincide with widespread unemployment.

Finally, note that there is no need for the balance of trade to be in equilibrium when national income is at its equilibrium level. The national-income equilibrium condition, as illustrated by equation (16-11), is *not* the same thing as the balance-of-trade equilibrium condition (that is, $X - M = 0$). Therefore, national-income equilibrium may indeed coexist with balance-of-trade disequilibrium. This is actually the case in Figure 16-4.

16-3　THE FOREIGN-TRADE MULTIPLIER

How do exogenous disturbances, such as autonomous changes in domestic investment, exports, and imports, affect the open economy's national income and balance of trade? This section deals exclusively with this crucial question. Our discussion proceeds as follows. First, we derive a general formula for the foreign-trade multiplier. Second, we provide a general discussion of the effects of autonomous disturbances on the balance of trade. Finally, we illustrate the principles involved by means of several specific examples.

Derivation of the Foreign-Trade Multiplier

Drawing on the discussion of the closed economy in Section 16-1, it must be clear that any autonomous disturbance that causes aggregate demand $D = C(Y) + \bar{I} + \bar{X} - M(Y)$ to change by, say, ΔD, must also cause national income to change. In particular, the change in national income ΔY must be a *multiple* of the change in aggregate demand ΔD. The ratio $\Delta Y/\Delta D$ is the *open-economy multiplier*.

Also known as the *foreign-trade multiplier*, the open-economy multiplier is greater than 1 but smaller than the multiplier of a corresponding closed economy. We have seen that the multiplier of a closed economy is given by the reciprocal of the marginal propensity to save. We wish to derive a similar formula for the foreign-trade multiplier.

Before proceeding with the derivation of the foreign-trade multiplier, however, it is important to note that an autonomous increase in aggregate demand may reflect an autonomous change in any of the components of aggregate demand. In other words, the autonomous increase in aggregate demand ΔD may reflect:

1　An autonomous *increase* in desired investment, that is, $\Delta D = \Delta I$.
2　An autonomous *increase* in exports, that is, $\Delta D = \Delta X$.

3 An autonomous *increase* in desired consumption, that is, $\Delta D = \Delta C$. This implies an upward shift of the consumption schedule. Thus, at *any* level of national income, desired consumption increases by ΔC.

4 An autonomous *decrease* in imports, that is, $\Delta D = -\Delta M$. This implies a downward shift of the import schedule. That is, at *any* level of income, imports fall by ΔM. Note carefully that this reduction in imports by ΔM tends to increase aggregate demand D to the extent that the open economy shifts expenditure ΔM toward the consumption of domestic goods and away from imports, with aggregate saving $S(Y)$ and consumption $C(Y)$ remaining constant. If the reduction in imports actually reflects a genuine reduction in consumption (that is, $\Delta C = \Delta M$), neither aggregate demand D nor national income will change.

We shall return to these specific cases toward the end of this section. For our present purposes, the origin of the increase in aggregate demand ΔD is immaterial. How does the change ΔD affect income?

We have seen that national-income equilibrium occurs when the leakages, $S(Y) + M(Y)$, out of the income stream match exactly the exogenous injections, $\bar{I} + \bar{X}$, into the income stream. When an exogenous disturbance causes the aggregate demand to increase by ΔD at *every* level of income, there emerges, at the *initial* level of income, an excess of autonomous injections over leakages equal to the autonomous increase in aggregate demand. Equilibrium is therefore restored when an increase in income ΔY *induces* the leakages, $S(Y) + M(Y)$, to increase by ΔD, so that total endogenous leakages equal total exogenous injections once again. For any change in income ΔY, the leakages change by $(MPS + MPM)\Delta Y$. (Recall that MPS stands for the marginal propensity to save, and MPM for the marginal propensity to import.) Accordingly, national-income equilibrium is restored when

$$\Delta D = (MPS + MPM)\Delta Y \tag{16-12}$$

A simple rearrangement of equation (16-12) gives:

$$\text{Foreign-trade multiplier} = \frac{\Delta Y}{\Delta D} = \frac{1}{MPS + MPM} \tag{16-13}$$

The foreign-trade multiplier is smaller than the closed-economy multiplier. This result is mathematically trivial because

$$\frac{1}{MPS} > \frac{1}{MPS + MPM}$$

What is the common-sense explanation for this result? The obvious reason is that the open economy has an extra leakage for imports. But there is a deeper reason. From the point of view of the world economy as a whole, imports are *not* a leakage—only saving is a leakage. The world is indeed a closed economy!

Accordingly, as autonomous spending increases in our economy, a new equilibrium is established only when a corresponding amount of saving is generated in the world economy. But whereas in a closed economy the additional saving is generated only at home, in an open economy the additional saving is generated both at home and abroad. Consequently, following an increase in autonomous spending, the increase in the closed economy's national income must be larger than the income increase of a corresponding open economy, because the closed economy must generate more saving than the open economy.

The Balance-of-Trade Effect

An exogenous disturbance may affect the balance of trade in two ways:

1 The disturbance may originate in the foreign sector and thus affect the balance of trade directly (or autonomously). This *autonomous effect* occurs when either exports or imports change autonomously (at each level of income), as explained below.

2 In addition, whether it originates in the foreign sector or not, a disturbance *induces* a further change in the balance of trade through its effect on national income. This *induced effect* occurs when a disturbance causes the aggregate demand to change by, say, ΔD, at every level of national income. As we have seen, change in aggregate demand ΔD causes national income to change (by a multiple of ΔD); and change in income ΔY induces a change in imports ($MPM \times \Delta Y$).

We therefore conclude that the overall effect of a disturbance on the balance of trade is the sum of two separate effects: (1) the autonomous effect (if any) and (2) the induced effect. As we shall see, the induced effect of a disturbance that originates in the foreign sector tends to work against the autonomous effect, with the result that the overall balance-of-trade effect of the disturbance is much smaller than its initial direct (or autonomous) effect. In other words, *the national-income adjustment mechanism is a powerful stabilizing mechanism of the balance of payments.*

Specific Illustrations

To gain further insight into the above propositions, we now turn to concrete examples. In particular, we wish to consider briefly the effects on national income and the balance of trade of the following disturbances:

1 An increase in desired investment
2 An increase in exports
3 An increase in imports
4 An improvement in the balance of trade brought about by devaluation

Throughout our discussion, we assume that the marginal propensity to save is 0.10 and that the marginal propensity to import is 0.15. Therefore, the foreign-trade multiplier is $1/(0.10 + 0.15) = 4$. In all examples, we assume that the open economy's national income is in equilibrium before the disturbance.

1   An Increase in Desired Investment   Suppose that domestic investment $\bar{I}$ increases by 100. Determine the effect on national income and the balance of trade.

Since the foreign-trade multiplier is 4, the increase in national income must be $4 \times 100 = 400$.

In terms of Figure 16-4, the increase in investment ΔI causes the $\bar{I} + \bar{X}$ schedule (top panel) to shift upward by ΔI, as illustrated by the broken schedule. Alternatively, in the lower panel, the increase in investment ΔI causes the $S(Y) - \bar{I}$ schedule to shift downward, as shown again by the broken schedule. Equilibrium shifts from E to K in the top panel and from H to N in the lower panel. The increase in national income ΔY is the same in both panels, as it should be.

The increase in investment causes the balance of trade to deteriorate. Note that in the present case there is only the induced effect. (The autonomous effect is missing because the change in investment does not affect the balance of trade directly.) In particular, the increase in investment causes imports to increase by:

$$\text{MPM} \times \Delta Y = 0.15 \times 400 = 60$$

This is illustrated in Figure 16-4, panel (b), by the fact that distance NY_1 is larger than distance HY_0.

2   An Increase in Exports   Suppose that exports increase by 100. Determine the effect on national income and the balance of trade.

The effect on national income is again equal to $4 \times 100 = 400$. In terms of Figure 16-4, panel (a), the increase in exports causes the $\bar{I} + \bar{X}$ schedule to shift upward, as shown by the broken line. In panel (b), we must shift the $\bar{X} - M(Y)$ schedule upward (not shown).

The balance-of-trade effect consists now of the autonomous effect (that is, the increase in exports by 100) plus the induced effect (that is, the increase in imports induced by the increase in income). Thus,

$$\begin{aligned}
\text{Balance-of-trade effect} &= \Delta X - \Delta M \\
&= \Delta X - \text{MPM} \times \Delta Y \\
&= 100 - 0.15 \times 400 = 100 - 60 = 40
\end{aligned}$$

Accordingly, the overall improvement in the balance of trade (that is, 40) is much smaller than the initial autonomous effect (that is, 100). This is an important result, and it verifies our earlier conclusion that the income-adjustment mechanism acts as a powerful stabilizing mechanism.

In general, the balance-of-trade effect of a change in exports ΔX is given by $\Delta X - \Delta M = \Delta X - \text{MPM} \times \Delta Y = \Delta X - [\text{MPM}/(\text{MPS} + \text{MPM})]\Delta X = [\text{MPS}/(\text{MPS} + \text{MPM})]\Delta X$, where $\Delta Y = [1/(\text{MPS} + \text{MPM})]\Delta X$. Because $\text{MPS}/(\text{MPS} + \text{MPM}) < 1$, the overall effect on the balance of trade is always less than the initial increase in exports.

The preceding result is illustrated in Figure 16-5, which is similar to Figure 16-4, panel (*b*). National-income equilibrium occurs initially at E, where the $S(Y) - \bar{I}$ schedule intersects the $\bar{X} - M(Y)$ schedule. Initially, the balance of trade is zero—point E lies on the horizontal axis. Exports increase autonomously by EH, causing the $\bar{X} - M(Y)$ schedule to shift upward, as shown by the broken schedule. Equilibrium shifts to F. Note carefully that the final balance-of-trade improvement, shown by distance GF, is necessarily smaller than the initial, autonomous improvement, shown by distance EH.

3 An Increase in Imports Suppose that the open economy reduces an existing tariff and thus causes domestic consumers to divert 100 of their consumption expenditures from domestic to foreign products. Determine the effect on national income and the balance of trade.

The shift from domestic to foreign products causes the aggregate demand for domestic output to *fall* by the increase in imports (100). Thus, national income *falls* by $4 \times 100 = 400$. [That is, $\Delta Y = 4 \times \Delta D = 4 \times (-\Delta M) = -4 \times 100 = -400$.]

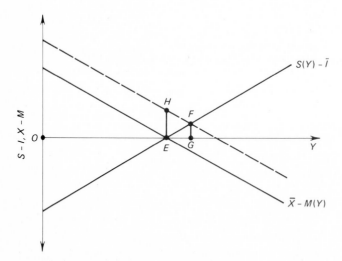

Figure 16-5 *Comparison between the initial and final balance-of-trade effects of disturbances that originate in the foreign sector.*
Equilibrium occurs initially at E, where the balance of trade is zero; that is, $\bar{X} - M(Y) = 0$. Exports increase by EH and cause the $\bar{X} - M(Y)$ schedule to shift upward, as shown by the broken schedule. Equilibrium shifts to F. The final balance-of-trade improvement (GF) is smaller than the initial improvement (EH).

The overall balance-of-trade deterioration is again less than the initial autonomous increase in imports. This is due to the reduction in national income, which induces a reduction in imports. This induced reduction in imports is equal to MPM $\times \Delta Y = 0.15(-400) = -60$. Accordingly, the overall balance-of-trade deterioration is only $100 - 60 = 40$.

The reader may illustrate in Figure 16-4, panel (b) the above conclusion by shifting downward the $\bar{X} - M(Y)$ schedule.

4 Devaluation Finally, suppose that the open economy devalues its currency and that the devaluation improves *initially* the balance of trade by 100. What additional effects, if any, will the open economy experience?

Since the balance of trade is a component of aggregate demand (recall that $D = Z + T$), it follows that the initial balance-of-trade improvement (at the initial level of national income) constitutes an increase in aggregate demand. Accordingly, national income will increase by $4 \times 100 = 400$. Further, the increase in income will induce an increase in imports equal to MPM $\times \Delta Y = 0.15 \times 400 = 60$. Therefore, the *final* balance-of-trade improvement will be $100 - 60 = 40$, which again is less than the initial improvement.

Figure 16-5 illustrates again the above results. As before, equilibrium occurs initially at E. Devaluation shifts the schedule $\bar{X} - M(Y)$ upward, as shown by the broken schedule. Equilibrium shifts to F. Thus, national income increases by EG. The national-income increase induces an additional flow of imports. As a result, final balance-of-trade improvement GF is smaller than initial improvement EH.

16-4 FOREIGN REPERCUSSION

In our discussion so far, we have assumed that imports are a leakage, while exports are given exogenously on the argument that exports depend on events that occur in the rest of the world. This assumption works well for a "small" country, whose exports and imports of goods and services are actually negligible fractions of total world output. For a "large" country, however, whose international trade (that is, whose value of exports and imports of goods and services) is a respectable percentage of world income, our analysis needs drastic modification.

A country's imports are the exports of the rest of the world. Similarly, a country's exports are the imports of the rest of the world. Accordingly, an open economy is economically interdependent with the rest of the world; we cannot ignore this interdependence, especially when the open economy is large. Economic events, such as investment booms or recessions, in a large country influence the economies of other nations; similarly, such events occurring in the rest of the world exert influence on an open economy. As the saying goes, when America sneezes, Europe and Japan catch cold (and nowadays vice versa). This was illustrated vividly by the Great Depression of the 1930s. The sharp reduction in U.S. national income, caused by a severe decline in U.S. investment, induced a large decline in U.S. imports, that is, foreign exports, and threw the world economy into a tailspin.

The purpose of this section is to consider this additional dimension of the income-adjustment mechanism. As should be expected, foreign repercussions give rise to rather complicated multiplier formulas, which are best derived separately (see the Appendix to this chapter). Our main concern in this section is to clarify the strong economic interdependence that exists among nations and also to show that this expanded income-adjustment mechanism continues to serve as a strong balance-of-payments stabilizer.

A Two-Country Model

Consider again a world of two countries, America (home country) and Britain (foreign country, or rest of the world). According to the analysis of Section 16-2, we can write an income equilibrium condition for each country as follows:

$$\bar{I}_a + X_a = S_a(Y_a) + M_a(Y_a) \tag{16-14}$$

$$\bar{I}_b + X_b = S_b(Y_b) + M_b(Y_b) \tag{16-15}$$

where the subscripts a and b refer to America and Britain, respectively.

If each country's exports were exogenous (that is, constant), we would be able to treat each country as a "small" economy and solve each equation by itself, essentially as we did in Section 16-2. However, this procedure would ignore completely the strong interdependence between countries and would fail to take into consideration the foreign-income repercussions.

How does the interdependence between America and Britain manifest itself in terms of equations (16-14) and (16-15)? These equations cannot be solved independently of each other. Recall that each country's exports are the same thing as the other country's imports; that is, $X_a = M_b(Y_b)$ and $X_b = M_a(Y_a)$. Substituting the identities $X_a = M_b(Y_b)$ and $X_b = M_a(Y_a)$ into equations (16-14) and (16-15), we obtain

$$\bar{I}_a + M_b(Y_b) = S_a(Y_a) + M_a(Y_a) \tag{16-14$'$}$$

$$\bar{I}_b + M_a(Y_a) = S_b(Y_b) + M_b(Y_b) \tag{16-15$'$}$$

It is now clear that we must solve equations (16-14)$'$ and (16-15)$'$ simultaneously in order to determine the equilibrium incomes of America (Y_a) and Britain (Y_b).

Note carefully that when America's and Britain's incomes are in equilibrium, the following equalities hold:

$$\begin{aligned}
\text{America's balance of trade } (T_a) &= M_b(Y_b) - M_a(Y_a) \\
&= S_a(Y_a) - \bar{I}_a = \bar{I}_b - S_b(Y_b)
\end{aligned} \tag{16-16}$$

$$\bar{I}_a + \bar{I}_b = S_a(Y_a) + S_b(Y_b) \qquad\qquad (16\text{-}17)$$

Equation (16-16) follows easily from equations (16-14)' and (16-15)' after a simple rearrangement of terms. This equation is important because it reveals to us that at any national-income equilibrium, we can measure America's balance of trade surplus (or deficit) in three different ways:

1 As the difference between Britain's desired imports and America's desired imports, that is, $M_b(Y_b) - M_a(Y_a)$
2 As the difference between America's desired saving and investment, that is, $S_a(Y_a) - \bar{I}_a$
3 As the difference between Britain's desired investment and saving, that is, $\bar{I}_b - S_b(Y_b)$

Equation (16-17) also follows from equations (16-14)' and (16-15)'. Add equation (16-14)' to equation (16-15)' and then cancel the term $M_a(Y_a) + M_b(Y_b)$ found on both sides of the equation. The significance of equation (16-17) must be apparent—that *in a world economy aggregate desired saving by all countries must equal aggregate desired investment by all countries.* This is nothing else but a straightforward generalization of the simple Keynesian condition "desired saving equals desired investment" in a closed economy. The world economy is indeed a closed economy; and in a closed economy only saving is a leakage, so that in equilibrium the total endogenous leakages $(S_a + S_b)$ must equal the total exogenous injections $(\bar{I}_a + \bar{I}_b)$.

Transmission of Business Cycles between Countries

Economic observers usually point out that the business cycles of the major industrial nations move in unison. The correlation is not perfect, of course; but the tendency toward synchronized cycles is strong. Our theory can help explain this uniformity.

Suppose that America experiences a boom in domestic investment. The reasons for the boom need not concern us. They may range from technical progress and optimistic entrepreneurial expectations to an expansionary monetary policy. If America were a *small* economy, her national income would increase by the change in investment (ΔI_a) times America's foreign-trade multiplier $[1/(MPS_a + MPM_a)]$; and her balance of trade would deteriorate by the increase in her imports $\{MPM_a \times \Delta Y_a = [MPM_a/(MPS_a + MPM_a)]\Delta I_a\}$. What happens now when America is *large?*

The increased American imports (British exports) raise British incomes and create British jobs. In fact, even if nothing else happens in America, Britain's national income will increase by the change in Britain's exports times the British foreign-trade multiplier. The chain of events will not stop here, however. As Britain's national income and, therefore, imports (American exports) rise, America's income and imports will begin to rise again, thus setting off a new cycle. This process will continue until the combined increase in saving in both America and Britain becomes equal to the initial increase in American investment; that is, until $\text{MPS}_a \times \Delta Y_a + \text{MPS}_b \times \Delta Y_b = \Delta I_a$.

It is apparent that the investment boom in America brings prosperity throughout the world. British incomes rise in harmony with American incomes. Foreign trade channels part of the American prosperity to the rest of the world. As we pointed out at the beginning of this chapter, international trade is a significant vehicle for the transmission of business cycles between countries. This is an important economic phenomenon.

Observe carefully that the increase in America's national income must be larger when foreign repercussions are taken into account than when they are absent. The reason is that British income increases, causing British imports (American exports) to increase, which in turn causes American income to increase further, beyond the level indicated by the foreign-trade multiplier without foreign repercussion.

Nevertheless, it remains true that the foreign-trade multiplier even *with* foreign repercussion falls short of the closed-economy multiplier. The reason, as we explained earlier, is that in a closed economy the additional saving is generated only at home, whereas in an open economy the additional saving is generated both at home and abroad.

Finally, consider the effect of America's investment boom on America's balance of trade. As we saw earlier, in the absence of foreign repercussion America's balance of trade deteriorates. What happens now when foreign repercussion is present? Does America's balance of trade deteriorate in the present case as well? If it does, how does the present deterioration with foreign repercussion compare with the deterioration without foreign repercussion?

We first show that America's balance of trade deteriorates. For this purpose, it is convenient to infer the change in America's balance of trade from the change in Britain's income. Equation (16-16) shows that America's balance of trade T_a is given by the difference $\bar{I}_b - S_b(Y_b)$. Therefore, the change in T_a must be given by the change in the difference $\bar{I}_b - S_b(Y_b)$; that is, $\Delta T_a = \Delta \bar{I}_b - \Delta S_b = \Delta \bar{I}_b - \text{MPS}_b \times \Delta Y_b$. Further, $\Delta \bar{I}_b = 0$ because Britain's desired investment remains constant by assumption. Accordingly, $\Delta T_a = -\text{MPS}_b \times \Delta Y_b < 0$ (since $\Delta Y_b > 0$).

Next we show that the deterioration in America's balance of trade *with* foreign repercussion is *smaller* than the corresponding deterioration *without* foreign repercussion. To accomplish this, we now choose a different expression from equation (16-16) to represent America's balance of trade: $T_a = S_a(Y_a) - \bar{I}_a$. Therefore, *whether foreign repercussion is present or not*, $\Delta T_a = \Delta S_a - \Delta I_a = \text{MPS}_a \times \Delta Y_a - \Delta I_a$. We have seen that ΔY_a is bigger when foreign repercussion is present than when it is absent. Accordingly, the increase in domestic saving $\Delta S_a = \text{MPS}_a \times \Delta Y_a$ is larger when foreign repercussion is present. Since ΔI_a is the same in both cases, we must conclude that *America's balance-of-trade deterioration is indeed smaller when foreign repercussion is taken into account*. Once more, we see that the income-adjustment mechanism acts as a stabilizing mechanism of the balance of payments.

Switching Policies

During the 1930s, the years of the Great Depression, countries sought to at least partially solve their problem of domestic unemployment by means of diverting expenditure from foreign products and channeling it toward their own domestic products. For this purpose, countries used a whole arsenal of policy weapons. Such measures are now known as *switching policies* because they *switch* expenditure away from the products of one country and channel it toward the products of another country. These switching policies can range from devaluation, tariffs, and nontariff barriers to international trade to mere political propaganda, which may take the form of such slogans as "Buy American," "Buy French," "Buy British," and so on.

The distinguishing feature of expenditure-switching policies is that they primarily affect the aggregate demand for the products of the country pursuing such policies *through changes in her balance of trade.* As we will see below, such policies tend to expand domestic income and employment at the expense of foreign incomes and employment. In effect, the country adopting an expenditure-switching policy is exporting unemployment to the rest of the world. For this reason, expenditure-switching policies are usually referred to as *beggar-thy-neighbor* policies. When all countries suffer from the same ills, beggar-thy-neighbor policies usually provoke retaliation. Thus, as soon as one country succeeds in increasing her balance of trade, other countries retaliate with the result that the volume of international trade relative to world activity continually shrinks. Political, strategic, and sentimental considerations add fuel to the fire, and the flames of economic nationalism blaze ever higher and higher.

Our analysis has proceeded far enough for us to be able to understand the consequences of expenditure-switching policies. As a final exercise, we consider the effects of a switching policy, such as the imposition of a tariff, on the national incomes of America and Britain as well as on the balance of trade.

An Illustration of a Switching Policy

Return now to our two-country model, and suppose that because of the imposition of higher tariffs, America switches part of her spending away from imports from Britain and toward her own domestic products. How does this autonomous reduction in American imports affect the national incomes of America and Britain as well as America's balance of trade?

We wish to show that:

1 The national incomes of America and Britain will move in *opposite* directions. In particular, America's income Y_a will increase and Britain's income Y_b will decrease.

2 America's balance of trade will improve. However, the final improvement will be much smaller than the initial reduction in American imports.

Let us begin with the income changes. Because the reduction in American imports has no effect on the desired level of investment either in America ($\bar{I}_a$)

or in Britain ($\bar{I}_b$), it follows that at the new equilibrium total world (desired) saving must be the same as before the change in imports. This follows from equation (16-17), which shows that aggregate desired saving by all countries must, in equilibrium, be equal to aggregate desired investment by all countries. Since $S_a(Y_a) + S_b(Y_b)$ must remain constant, the national incomes of America and Britain *must* change in *opposite* directions, if at all. For if both Y_a and Y_b increase (decrease), the sum $S_a(Y_a) + S_b(Y_b)$ will also increase (decrease).

We next show that Y_a will increase and Y_b will decrease. Suppose for the moment that we arbitrarily keep Y_b fixed at its original level. This means that we also keep Britain's imports (American exports) at their original level while we allow America's national income to reach a new equilibrium. Then America's national income and balance of trade will change in exactly the same way as if America were a "small" country. Thus, drawing on our analysis in Section 16-3, America's income will *increase* [by $\Delta Y_a = (1/\mathrm{MPS}_a + \mathrm{MPM}_a) \times \Delta M$, where ΔM = reduction in American imports in absolute terms]. More important, America's balance of trade will *improve* (by $\Delta S_a = \mathrm{MPS}_a \times \Delta Y_a$), which means that *Britain's balance of trade will deteriorate.*

Return now to Britain's national income. Recall that we kept it fixed at its original level. Can Britain's income remain actually at that level? No, there will be a tendency for Britain's national income to fall. Thus, the deterioration in the British balance of trade implies that the aggregate demand for the British products will be lower than Britain's aggregate supply. (Recall that aggregate demand equals aggregate absorption plus balance of trade.) We therefore conclude that *Britain's national income will eventually fall.* Since America's national income must move in the opposite direction, we also conclude that *America's income will eventually increase.*

We could reach the same conclusion by initially keeping Y_a constant and allowing Y_b to reach a new (lower) equilibrium after the reduction in America's imports. Britain's balance of trade would again deteriorate with the result that the aggregate demand for America's products would be higher than America's aggregate supply. America's income would tend to rise; hence, Britain's income would tend to fall.

Turn now to the effect on America's balance of trade, which must eventually improve. In particular, the final improvement in America's balance of trade is given by the increased saving in America, that is, $\Delta S_a = \mathrm{MPS}_a \times \Delta Y_a$. Further, the improvement in America's balance of trade must be *smaller* than the initial autonomous reduction in America's imports. This is due to the income changes. Thus, America's income increases, inducing additional imports into America. In addition, Britain's income falls, inducing a reduction in Britain's imports (= America's exports).

16-5 SUMMARY

1 In any closed economy, there exist three economic flows: aggregate demand ($C + I$), aggregate output (Q), and national income (Y). Because of the residual character of profits, aggregate output is identical to national income (earned). In turn, national income generates aggregate demand, and demand gives rise to output.

2 In a closed economy, national-income equilibrium occurs when desired aggregate demand $C(Y) + \bar{I}$ equals aggregate output; that is, $Y = C(Y) + \bar{I}$, or $Y - C(Y) \equiv S(Y) = \bar{I}$ (that is, leakages equal injections). Because the marginal propensity to consume is less than 1, equilibrium is stable.

3 The closed-economy multiplier is equal to the reciprocal of the marginal propensity to save (MPS). Since MPS $<$ 1, the multiplier is higher than 1.

4 The aggregate demand for the open economy's output equals the economy's aggregate absorption $(Z = C + I)$ plus its balance of trade $(T = X - M)$.

5 The marginal propensity to import (that is, the ratio of the change in imports to the change in national income) is given graphically by the slope of the import schedule.

6 The ratio of imports to national income (that is, M/Y) is the average propensity to import; and the ratio of the marginal to the average propensity to import is the income elasticity of demand for imports.

7 In a "small" open economy, national-income equilibrium prevails when aggregate output equals desired aggregate demand; that is, when $Y = C(Y) + \bar{I} + \bar{X} - M(Y)$. The last equation can take either of the following forms: (a) $S(Y) + M(Y) = \bar{I} + \bar{X}$ (that is, leakages equal injections) or (b) $\bar{X} - M(Y) = S(Y) - \bar{I}$ (that is, balance of trade equals excess saving).

8 National-income equilibrium may coexist with balance-of-trade disequilibrium $(X - M \neq 0)$ or unemployment or both.

9 The foreign-trade multiplier without foreign repercussion ("small" open economy) is given by 1/(MPS + MPM).

10 The overall effect of a disturbance on the balance of trade is the sum of two effects: (a) the induced effect (which works through national income and the resultant change in imports) plus (b) the autonomous effect (which exists only when the disturbance originates in the foreign sector and results in a change in exports or imports at the *initial* level of national income).

11 The induced effect of a disturbance that originates in the foreign sector tends to work against the autonomous effect with the result that the overall balance-of-trade effect is much smaller than the initial autonomous effect. (This is true both in the presence and absence of foreign repercussion.) Thus, the national-income adjustment mechanism is a powerful stabilizing mechanism of the balance of payments.

12 For a "large" country, it is necessary to take into account foreign income repercussion, which gives rise to rather complicated multiplier formulas. Yet the expanded income-adjustment mechanism continues to serve as a strong balance-of-payments stabilizer.

13 Foreign repercussion can be studied with a model of two countries (America and Britain). For each country, there is a national-income equilibrium equation (as with a "small" open economy). In addition, each country's imports are the other country's exports. The two equations must be solved simultaneously for the equilibrium levels of incomes.

14 In the world economy, desired aggregate saving by all countries equals desired aggregate investment by all countries.

15 The business cycles of the industrial nations move in unison. An investment boom in one country brings prosperity throughout the world.

16 A boom in a country causes its balance of trade to deteriorate. But such deterioration is smaller when foreign repercussion is present than when it is absent.

17 The closed-economy multiplier is larger than the corresponding foreign-trade multiplier with or without foreign repercussion (because in a closed economy the additional saving is generated only at home, while in an open economy the additional saving is generated both at home and abroad).

18 The foreign-trade multiplier is larger when foreign repercussion is present than when it is absent.

19 The increase in the national income of a country is larger when the initial autonomous change occurs in the demand for that country's products than for foreign products. Accordingly, a diversion of spending from foreign products to domestic products increases domestic income and employment and reduces foreign incomes and employment.

20 Expenditure-switching policies (also known as beggar-thy-neighbor policies) switch (that is, divert) expenditure from the products of one country and channel it toward the products of another country. When all countries suffer from the same ills, beggar-thy neighbor policies provoke retaliation.

APPENDIX: Foreign-Trade Multipliers

This appendix deals with the derivation of the foreign-trade multiplier formulas in the presence of foreign repercussion. The model used for this purpose is the two-country model of Section 16-4.

Recall that both national incomes (Y_a and Y_b) are in equilibrium when the following equations are satisfied:

$$\bar{I}_a + M_b(Y_b) = S_a(Y_a) + M_a(Y_a) \tag{16-14$'$}$$

$$\bar{I}_b + M_a(Y_a) = S_b(Y_b) + M_b(Y_b) \tag{16-15$'$}$$

Consider now an autonomous increase in the aggregate demand for America's products, such as an increase in America's desired investment (ΔI_a). A new equilibrium is attained when the following equations are satisfied:

$$\Delta I_a + \text{MPM}_b \times \Delta Y_b = \text{MPS}_a \times \Delta Y_a + \text{MPM}_a \times \Delta Y_a \tag{A16-1}$$

$$0 + \text{MPM}_a \times \Delta Y_a = \text{MPS}_b \times \Delta Y_b + \text{MPM}_b \times \Delta Y_b \tag{A16-2}$$

Dividing both equations by ΔI_a and then solving them for $\Delta Y_a/\Delta I_a$ and $\Delta Y_b/\Delta I_a$, we obtain:

$$k_{aa} \equiv \frac{\Delta Y_a}{\Delta I_a} = \frac{\text{MPS}_b + \text{MPM}_b}{\text{MPS}_a(\text{MPS}_b + \text{MPM}_b) + \text{MPM}_a\text{MPS}_b} \tag{A16-3}$$

$$k_{ba} \equiv \frac{\Delta Y_b}{\Delta I_a} = \frac{\text{MPM}_a}{\text{MPS}_a(\text{MPS}_b + \text{MPM}_b) + \text{MPM}_a\text{MPS}_b} \tag{A16-4}$$

It is convenient to adopt the symbol k_{ij} for the multiplier relating the total change in the national income of the ith country to the autonomous change in the demand for the products of the jth country, as shown by equations (A16-3) and (A16-4).

There is no need to derive separately the foreign-trade multipliers for an autonomous change in the aggregate demand for Britain's products, such as an increase in $\bar{I}_b$ by ΔI_b. We can obtain these multipliers directly from equations (A16-3) and (A16-4) merely by reversing the roles of the two countries, that is, by switching the subscripts a and b. Thus,

$$k_{bb} \equiv \frac{\Delta Y_b}{\Delta I_b} = \frac{\text{MPS}_a + \text{MPM}_a}{\text{MPS}_b(\text{MPS}_a + \text{MPM}_a) + \text{MPM}_b\text{MPS}_a} \tag{A16-5}$$

$$k_{ab} \equiv \frac{\Delta Y_a}{\Delta I_b} = \frac{\text{MPM}_b}{\text{MPS}_b(\text{MPS}_a + \text{MPM}_a) + \text{MPM}_b\text{MPS}_a} \tag{A16-6}$$

The reader can easily prove the following propositions:

1 The closed-economy multiplier is larger than the corresponding foreign-trade multipler with or without foreign repercussion. In other words, $1/\text{MPS}_i > k_{ii}$ and $1/\text{MPS}_i > 1/(\text{MPS}_i + \text{MPM}_i)$.

2 The foreign-trade multiplier with foreign repercussion (k_{ii}) is larger than the foreign-trade multiplier without foreign repercussion. In other words, $k_{ii} > 1/(\text{MPS}_i + \text{MPM}_i)$.

3 The foreign-trade multiplier k_{ii} is larger than the foreign-trade multiplier k_{ij}. That is, the increase in the national income of a country, say, America, is larger when the initial autonomous change occurs in the demand for American products than for British products.

4 A diversion of either country's spending from British products to American products reduces income and employment in Britain and increases income and employment in America. (This is actually a corollary to proposition 3.) This is a composite case: An autonomous *increase* in the aggregate demand for America's products is combined with a simultaneous *decrease* in the aggregate demand for Britain's products. Hence, America's foreign-trade multiplier is now given by the *difference* $k_{aa} - k_{ab} > 0$; and Britain's, by $k_{ba} - k_{bb} < 0$.

SUGGESTED READING

Black, J. (1957). "A Geometrical Analysis of the Foreign Trade Multiplier." *Economic Journal* (June), pp. 240–243.

Chacholiades, M. (1978). *International Monetary Theory and Policy*. McGraw-Hill Book Company, New York, chap. 10.

Houthakker, H. S., and S. P. Magee. (1969). "Income and Price Elasticities in World Trade." *The Review of Economics and Statistics*, vol. 51, no. 2, pp. 111–125.

Kindleberger, C. P. (1973). *International Economics*, 5th ed. Richard D. Irwin, Inc., Homewood, Ill., chap. 20 and app. H.

Machlup, F. (1943). *International Trade and the National Income Multiplier*. The Blakiston Company, Philadelphia.

Meade, J. E. (1951). *The Theory of International Economic Policy*, vol. 1, *The Balance of Payments*. Oxford University Press, New York, parts 2 and 3.

Robinson, R. (1952). "A Graphical Analysis of the Foreign Trade Multiplier." *Economic Journal* (September), pp. 546–564.

Chapter Seventeen

Money and the Balance of Payments

For pedagogical reasons, we have ignored up until this point the intimate relationship that exists between the balance of payments and the money supply. However, to understand fully the balance-of-payments problem, it is necessary to introduce *money* explicitly into our discussion.

To be sure, the significance of money surfaced earlier during our discussion of the price-specie-flow mechanism and the purchasing-power-parity theory (see Chapter 15). But that discussion was not very systematic. The primary purpose of this chapter is to provide a systematic discussion of the relationships that exist between the money supply and the balance of payments and to clarify the short-run and long-run consequences of money and monetary policy. This is a crucial step. In fact, this chapter sets the stage for the discussion of the main policy issues of international finance in the last part of the book. Throughout the present chapter, it is assumed that the rate of foreign exchange is fixed.

There is a mutual interaction between the money supply and the balance of payments. In the first place, payments imbalances (deficits or surpluses) represent net flows of money between nations and tend to affect each nation's money supply, as we saw earlier in our discussion of the price-specie-flow mechanism. Here the direction of causation runs from the balance of payments to the money supply.

On the other hand, changes in the supply of money affect the balance of payments, as we also saw in our discussion of the price-specie-flow mechanism and the purchasing-power-parity theory. Here the direction of causation is reversed; that is, now the direction of causation runs from the money supply to the balance of payments.

The mutual interaction between the money supply and the balance of payments makes the adjustment mechanism more difficult but also more interesting.

Section 17-1 provides a general discussion of how the balance of payments affects the money supply and then explains how the monetary authorities can actively sterilize any payments imbalances, that is, prevent them from influencing the money supply. The rest of the chapter focuses primarily on the influence that the money supply exerts on the balance of payments. After a brief introductory sketch of how changes in the money supply affect the balance of payments (Section 17-2), we develop separately the *IS-LM* apparatus (Sections 17-3–17-5) and the external balance schedule (Section 17-6). Our discussion culminates in Section 17-7, where we bring together the *IS-LM* apparatus and the external-balance schedule. In Section 17-8, we review briefly the monetary approach to the balance of payments.

17-1 PAYMENTS IMBALANCES AND THE SUPPLY OF MONEY

Payments imbalances (that is, deficits and surpluses) have definite and direct effects on the supply of money. For instance, a balance-of-payments deficit tends to reduce the money supply of the deficit country, and a balance-of-payments surplus tends to increase the money supply of the surplus country. The precise changes in the money supply depend on the specific structure of the banking system of the country involved, as explained below. (The study of banking systems is a rather complicated subject and cannot be undertaken here. It is assumed that the reader is already familiar with the functioning of modern banking systems, which is explained in most introductory textbooks on economics.[1] Our discussion surveys only those principles that are of paramount importance to international finance.)

The 100-Percent-Money Principle

The simplest banking system, although not necessarily the best, is that system in which the money supply (M_s) is always equal to the stock of international reserves. Such a system is said to be based on the *100-percent-money principle*, which actually means that the money supply is backed by reserves (say, gold) 100 percent.

The 100-percent-money principle is illustrated by the *gold-specie standard*, where the actual currency in circulation consists of gold coins of a certain fixed gold content. The coins are freely minted at standard rates. They are also

---

[1] For instance, see P. A. Samuelson (1980). *Economics*, 11th ed., McGraw-Hill Book Company, New York, chaps. 15–17.

freely meltable and exportable. Under the gold-specie standard, payments imbalances (deficits or surpluses) give rise to gold movements (gold exports or imports, as the case may be). In turn, *gold movements imply changes in the*
money supply on a one-to-one basis.

Note carefully that the above conclusion continues to hold even when gold
certificates with 100 percent gold backing actually form the circulating medium
of exchange.

The U.S. Money Supply

Modern banking systems are much more complicated than the gold-specie
standard. To appreciate the problem, we now consider briefly the banking system of the United States.

Today in the United States there are three major types of money: *coins,*
paper money, and *checking deposits* (or *demand deposits* in commercial
banks). Coins are only a negligible percentage of the total money supply. Paper
money consists mostly of Federal Reserve notes issued by the 12 Federal
Reserve banks and accounts for roughly 25 percent of the total U.S. money
supply. Demand deposits in the 14,700 U.S. commercial banks account for the
rest of the U.S. money supply. Accordingly, demand deposits are by far the
largest component of the U.S. money supply. (Here ignore "near moneys,"
such as time deposits and savings deposits.)

The 12 Federal Reserve banks nominally are private corporations. Their
stock is owned by the commercial banks they serve. Their policy, however, is
controlled by the Board of Governors of the Federal Reserve System who are
appointed by the President of the United States. All national commercial banks
are members of the Federal Reserve System. Nevertheless, there are many
smaller commercial banks that are not members. These nonmember banks account for about 25 percent of total demand deposits. The following discussion
ignores nonmember banks.

Commercial banks operate on the *fractional-reserve principle:* Member
banks are required to maintain reserves in the form of deposits at the Federal
Reserve bank in their district. A bank's reserve deposits must be equal to a certain percentage of that bank's demand liabilities.

When it is unable to meet its reserve requirements, a member bank can
borrow from the Federal Reserve bank in its district. The rate of interest the
Federal Reserve banks charge member banks is usually called the *discount*
rate.

The total volume of demand deposits the commercial banks can create
depends on (1) the volume of bank reserves and (2) the required-reserve ratio.
In particular,

$$\text{Demand deposits} = \frac{\text{reserves}}{\text{required-reserve ratio}} \tag{17-1}$$

Note that the reciprocal of the required-reserve ratio is usually referred to as the *money multiplier*. Thus, equation (17-1) can also be written as:

Demand deposits = money multiplier × reserves   (17-2)

The Federal Reserve System can control the total volume of demand deposits by controlling its determinants, that is, the reserve ratio and the volume of bank reserves. For instance, the Federal Reserve System can increase the money supply by reducing the required-reserve ratio. The reduction in reserve requirements leaves commercial banks with *excess* reserves and induces them to make additional loans. As banks make additional loans, the total volume of demand deposits increases.

Alternatively, the Federal Reserve System can increase the money supply by increasing the volume of reserves of member banks. In particular, the Federal Reserve System may either reduce the discount rate or purchase government securities from the public. The reduction in the discount rate tends to increase the member banks' *borrowed* reserves because it makes it more profitable for commercial banks to borrow from the Federal Reserve System. On the other hand, the purchase of government bonds increases the member banks' *un*borrowed reserves. Eventually the seller of the securities obtains a demand deposit in a commercial bank, while the commercial bank experiences an increase in its reserve deposit account with the Federal Reserve bank. Accordingly, both the reduction in the discount rate and the purchase of government securities tend to increase the total volume of reserves of member banks, causing a multiple expansion in the money supply.

To decrease the money supply, the Federal Reserve System must either *increase* reserve requirements, *raise* the discount rate, or *sell* government securities to the public.

Federal Reserve purchases and sales of U.S. securities are usually called *open-market operations*.

In summary, the major policy instruments at the disposal of the Federal Reserve System are:

1   The required-reserve ratio
2   The discount rate
3   Open-market operations

Varying the required-reserve ratio is a drastic measure, however. For this reason, the Federal Reserve Board relies primarily on the discount rate and open-market operations, changing reserve requirements only infrequently.

Payments Imbalances and Demand Deposits

How do balance-of-payments deficits and surpluses affect the supply of money when a modern banking system, such as that of the United States, is in operation? We shall answer this question within the context of a rather simplified modern banking system.

Assume that the total supply of money consists of demand deposits only. The exclusion of coins and paper money merely simplifies matters without affecting seriously any fundamental conclusions. Assume further that all international reserves, such as gold and foreign currencies, are in the hands of the monetary authorities, that is, the central bank and treasury, even though in practice commercial banks may also hold international reserve assets.

Broadly speaking, the assets of commercial banks consist of (1) reserve deposit accounts with the central bank and (2) domestic assets, such as stocks, bonds, and loans to corporations. By accounting necessity, the total assets of commercial banks (that is, reserves plus domestic assets) are equal to the total liabilities of commercial banks (that is, demand deposits in commercial banks, which we have already identified with the total supply of money). Accordingly, we always have the identity:

Money supply = bank reserves + domestic assets   (17-3)

Note carefully that while equation (17-3) is always true (by definition), equations (17-1) and (17-2) give the *maximum* volume of demand deposits the commercial banks can legally create. Accordingly, equations (17-1) and (17-2) are true only when the commercial banks are fully loaned up. When the commercial banks have excess reserves, the actual volume of demand deposits falls short of the maximum volume indicated by equations (17-1) and (17-2).

Consider now the effects of payments imbalances on the money supply. Because equation (17-3) is always true, it follows that the change in the money supply must be equal to the change in bank reserves plus the change in domestic assets held by the commercial banks. A payments imbalance changes bank reserves directly. In fact, we now define a payments imbalance to be equal to the change in international reserves, which in turn must be equal to the change in bank reserves. In other words,

Payments imbalance = change in bank reserves   (17-4)

Now the change in bank reserves brings about a direct change in demand deposits, as shown by equation (17-3).

However, this is not all. The change in bank reserves also represents a change in the monetary base. *If* the commercial banks are always fully loaned up, the change in bank reserves must eventually lead to a *multiple* change in the money supply. Thus, the change in bank reserves induces the commercial banks to adjust their holdings of domestic assets (loans and securities) as well, as we explained earlier.

We can clarify the preceding discussion by means of a concrete example. Suppose that the required-reserve ratio is 0.2 (that is, the money multiplier is 5) and the country suffers from a balance-of-payments deficit of $100. In particular, assume that the exporters receive $1,900 (in foreign exchange), which they sell to the central bank through their commercial banks. On the other hand, the importers pay $2,000 (in foreign exchange) for their imports. The importers buy the foreign exchange they need from the central bank through their commercial banks.

The above transactions result in the following direct changes:

1 *Change in demand deposits in commercial banks.* . . . . −$100
   (The exporters' demand deposits *increase* by $1,900
   while the importers' demand deposits *decrease* by $2,000.)
2 *Change in international reserves* . . . . −$100
   (The central bank purchases $1,900 and sells $2,000.)
3 *Change in bank reserves* . . . . −$100
   (The commercial banks' reserve deposit account in
   the central bank increases by $1,900 and decreases by $2,000.)

The above are only the direct effects of the deficit. Assuming that all commercial banks were fully loaned up to begin with, a multiple contraction process of the money supply would follow as the commercial banks reduced their holdings of domestic assets in order to satisfy the legal reserve requirements. Eventually, the money supply would *fall* by $500 (reduction in bank reserves $100 + reduction in bank domestic assets $400). In other words, the reduction in the money supply would be equal to the reduction in bank reserves ($100) times the money multiplier (5).

Of course, it is conceivable that initially the commercial banks may have excess reserves. In that case, the multiple contraction process of the money supply will not take place. The commercial banks will merely experience a reduction in their excess reserves and the money supply (demand deposits) will only fall by $100 (direct effect).

Sterilization Operations

The preceding discussion shows how payments imbalances affect the money supply *when the monetary authorities react passively, that is, do nothing.* However, the money supply is under the control of the monetary authorities; and the monetary authorities may actively seek to sterilize the payments imbalance, that is, prevent the payments imbalance from having any net effect on the money supply.

Historically, such sterilization operations were not uncommon even during the gold-standard era (1870–1914). Nevertheless, they became widespread in the 1920s, and especially after World War II when full employment became a primary objective of economic policy. Thus, monetary policy, the main instrument of the balance-of-payments adjustment process under the gold-standard rules of the game, was diverted from its initial function of keeping the balance of payments in equilibrium (external balance) toward the achievement of full employment (internal balance).

How do the monetary authorities carry out their sterilization operations? To sterilize a balance-of-payments deficit, they must purchase government bonds in the open market, reduce the discount rate, or lower reserve requirements. To sterilize a balance-of-payments surplus, they must do the opposite; that is, they must either sell government securities, raise the discount rate, or raise reserve requirements.

Apparently, there are limits to the ability of the monetary authorities to sterilize payments imbalances. For instance, the monetary authorities cannot continue sterilizing a chronic (or fundamental) deficit indefinitely, because they will sooner or later run out of international reserve assets. Similarly, the monetary authorities cannot continue sterilizing a chronic surplus indefinitely—sooner or later their stock of international reserve assets will become equal to the domestic money supply, and further surpluses will raise the money supply on a one-to-one basis, as in the case of the gold-specie standard.

We therefore conclude that in the long run chronic payments imbalances are likely to affect the money supply. In the short run, however, the monetary authorities have plenty of leeway, and they actually do offset payments imbalances by means of their sterilization operations.

17-2 EFFECTS OF THE MONEY SUPPLY ON THE BALANCE OF PAYMENTS (INTRODUCTION)

As we stated earlier, there is a mutual interaction between the balance of payments and the money supply. The balance of payments influences the money supply and, at the same time, is influenced by it. So far in this chapter we have studied the influence the balance of payments exerts on the money supply. In the rest of this chapter, we focus our attention on the influence the money supply exerts on the balance of payments. To facilitate our discussion, we present in this section, by a way of introduction, a brief sketch of how changes in the money supply affect the balance of payments.

Economists generally agree that an increase in the money supply tends to worsen the balance of payments and that a decrease tends to improve it. They differ only on the mechanism through which the money supply exerts its influence. On the one hand, the *monetarists* believe that the money supply exerts its influence on the balance of payments *directly*. On the other hand, the *Keynesians* argue that the money supply affects the balance of payments *indirectly*, through its influence on the rate of interest.

The View of the Monetarists

David Hume was the first successful monetarist. His price-specie-flow mechanism (see Chapter 15) was the first successful refutation of the mercantilist thesis that a country could continually generate large balance-of-payments surpluses by means of import restrictions and export subsidies. Hume argued that balance-of-payments surpluses as well as deficits are only ephemeral phenomena—they last only until domestic prices adjust according to the quantity theory of money and restore external equilibrium.

The automatic self-correcting price-specie-flow mechanism of Hume is based on a direct link between the money supply and the balance of payments.

As we explained in Chapter 15, changes in the money supply affect directly the supply and demand schedules for commodities and thus the balance of payments. In particular, an increase in the money supply tends to raise domestic prices and worsen the balance of payments, and a decrease tends to lower domestic prices and improve the balance of payments.

Monetarists have had only limited success in their efforts to provide a solid theoretical foundation for the quantity theory. As a result, the alleged direct link between the money supply and the balance of payments rests on rather shaky grounds. Despite this state of affairs, however, contemporary monetarists have given a new twist to the older ideas and constructed the so-called new monetary approach to the balance of payments. Section 17-8 briefly reviews this new approach.

The View of the Keynesians

The Keynesians agree with the monetarists that an increase in the money supply tends to worsen the balance of payments and that a decrease tends to improve it. However, the Keynesians argue that the money supply affects the balance of payments indirectly, through its influence on the rate of interest.

The bare elements of the Keynesian view are easy to grasp. For instance, an increase in the money supply makes credit loans more plentiful to investors and lowers the rate of interest. Investors undertake additional investment projects which, as a result of the reduction in the interest rate, have become more profitable. Finally, the increase in domestic investment increases national income and imports (see Chapter 16), and thus worsens the balance of trade.

To the extent that capital is mobile between countries, the interest-rate reduction also induces a capital outflow (or reduces an existing capital inflow). Essentially, some holders of domestic financial assets seek to exchange them for foreign financial assets, which, as a result of the reduction in the domestic interest rate, have become relatively more attractive. The shift, if any, from domestic to foreign financial assets (capital outflow) puts an additional strain on the balance of payments.

We therefore conclude that an increase in the money supply reduces the rate of interest and worsens the balance of payments for two reasons:

1 *It worsens the balance of trade.* The reduction in the interest rate induces an increase in domestic investment, which in turn increases the domestic national income and imports.

2 *It worsens the capital account.* The reduction in the interest rate induces a capital outflow as some lenders switch their lending from the domestic economy to the rest of the world.

Conversely, a reduction in the money supply improves the balance of payments. Thus, as the supply of money falls and credit loans become scarce, the interest rate rises. The increase in the interest rate has two favorable effects on the balance of payments:

   1 *It improves the balance of trade* by reducing domestic investment, national income (through the foreign-trade multiplier), and thus imports.

   2 *It improves the capital account* by inducing a *capital inflow.* Lenders who find the higher domestic interest rate more attractive switch their lending from the rest of the world to the domestic economy.

The overall balance-of-payments improvement is, of course, the sum of the balance-of-trade improvement plus the capital-account improvement.

   The next five sections probe more deeply into the Keynesian mechanism.

17-3   EQUILIBRIUM IN THE MONEY MARKET: THE *LM* CURVE

As we have seen, the money supply affects the balance of payments through its influence on the rate of interest. To understand this Keynesian mechanism more fully, we must develop the *IS-LM* model of intermediate macroeconomics, properly modified to suit the needs of an open economy. This section develops the *LM* curve, while Section 17-4 develops the *IS* curve. Section 17-5 brings these two curves together and deals with the problem of general macroeconomic equilibrium. Section 17-6 introduces the balance of payments and develops the external balance schedule. Finally, Section 17-7 brings together the *IS-LM* apparatus and the external-balance schedule and shows how the money supply affects the balance of payments.

The Supply of Money

We are now concerned with the conditions under which the money market is in equilibrium. For this purpose, we must first consider both the supply of money and the demand for money. We begin with the supply of money, which is easier.

   As we saw earlier (see Section 17-1), payments imbalances do affect the money supply, particularly when the monetary authorities react passively to deficits and surpluses (that is, do nothing). Nevertheless, the monetary authorities can, and often do, sterilize the effects of payments imbalances in the manner described in Section 17-1. In what follows, we find it convenient to assume that the monetary authorities do indeed sterilize the effects of payments imbalances. In other words, we initially assume that the monetary authorities keep the supply of money fixed, by "immunizing" it against balance-of-payments deficits and surpluses. We will relax this assumption in Section 17-7.

The Demand for Money

Broadly speaking, people can keep their accumulated wealth in three forms: (1) money; (2) interest-earning assets, which, for convenience, we call "securities" (such as bonds, stocks, and savings accounts); and (3) physical assets (such as houses, factories, machinery, and inventories—and human capital). The decision to invest in physical assets (and human capital) evidently comes under the domain of the theory of investment (see Section 17-4). What really concerns us here is the choice between money and interest-earning assets (or securities).

Like money, securities are highly liquid assets. Nevertheless, securities seem to be superior to money because they yield interest. We can say that holding money is expensive: When people hold their wealth (or part of it) in the form of money, they lose the interest they could earn by holding securities instead. In effect, the rate of interest measures the opportunity cost of holding money instead of securities.

If securities are indeed superior to money, why is it that people hold money? Compared with money, securities have two significant drawbacks: (1) they are not a medium of exchange, and (2) they are more risky than money (that is, their prices fluctuate through time). Even in the absence of any risk of default, the prices of securities fluctuate in response to interest-rate changes, as shown below. We are forced to conclude, then, that economic units determine their demand for money by balancing the benefits it yields against the cost of holding it, that is, the rate of interest.

Keynes suggested three motives for holding money: (1) the transactions motive, (2) the precautionary motive, and (3) the speculative motive. The transactions motive refers to the use of money as a medium of exchange and actually represents money in *active* circulation. The precautionary and speculative motives, on the other hand, represent money held as *inactive* balances. Keynes's main contribution in this area was his rational explanation of why people keep inactive balances, particularly speculative balances. We examine each of these motives for holding money separately.

The Transactions Motive

The transactions motive for holding money arises from the fact that economic units do not usually enjoy perfect synchronization between their streams of revenue (income) and their streams of expenditure. Thus, economic units do not normally pay all their bills on payday. Indeed, they need money for executing transactions every day between paydays. In other words, each economic unit needs money to bridge the gap between its income stream and its expenditure stream.

Broadly speaking, the aggregate demand for money for transactions purposes depends on the cost of holding money (that is, the rate of interest) and the institutional arrangements (such as society's habits of payment, degree of vertical integration, and the like), which in the final analysis determine the degree of synchronization between the various streams of receipts and payments in the society. Given the institutions, the *aggregate demand for transactions balances is roughly proportional to national income.*

The accepted opinion is that the effect of the rate of interest on the demand for transactions balances is negligible, particularly when the rate of interest is within a normal range. This is due to the fact that shifting wealth from transactions balances to interest-earning assets, and from interest-earning assets to transactions balances, involves costs, such as the inconvenience of making extra trips to the savings bank (for individuals), bookkeeping expenses, brokerage fees, and the like (for corporations). The interest rate must be sufficiently high before economic units find it profitable to economize on their transactions balances by making several short-term investments within each payment period. Nevertheless, *at very high interest rates,* we should expect an inverse relationship between the demand for transactions balances and the rate of interest.

The Precautionary Motive

The precautionary motive for holding money emanates from the uncertainty that exists in the real world. It is usually a wise precaution to guard against unforeseen events by holding extra cash instead of planning to spend the last dollar just before payday. Precautionary balances enable people to meet unanticipated increases in expenditure prompted by such adverse developments as illness, a car breakdown while on a trip, and the like. In addition, the precautionary balances enable people to take advantage of unanticipated bargains and other opportunities.

The total amount of money held for precautionary purposes is primarily a function of national income. The influence of the cost of holding money (that is, the rate of interest) is rather limited. For this reason, we can combine the precautionary balances with the transactions balances and consider their sum to be roughly proportional to national income.

The Speculative Motive

Uncertainty is also responsible for the speculative motive for holding money. Even though money does not earn interest, it may still constitute a particularly attractive investment outlet at times of uncertainty. At such times, money provides protection against capital losses that could be brought about by adverse market conditions. Accordingly, economic units hold speculative balances because they are uncertain about the future prices of securities and also about the exact time they will have to sell the securities, that is, when they will need liquidity.

The prices of securities depend profoundly on the rate of interest. To appreciate this dependence, consider one particular type of security—the British Consol—which pays a fixed coupon return to the bearer but never matures. For instance, a 10 percent British Consol of £1,000 denomination is in effect a promise to pay the bearer £100 each year forever! Thus, the person who buys this British Consol for £1,000 earns 10 percent per year on his or her investment. However, if the market rate of interest is less than 10 percent, the price of the British Consol must adjust (increase) so that the coupon rate equals the rate of interest. For example, if the interest rate falls from 10 percent to 5 percent, the price of the British Consol must rise from £1,000 to £2,000 so that the person who buys it continues to earn the market rate of interest. Of course, if the rate of interest rises, the price of the British Consol must fall. In general, the price of the British Consol is equal to the ratio of fixed coupon (£100) to rate of interest. Accordingly, there exists an inverse relationship between the price of the British Consol and the rate of interest. When the interest rate is high, the price of the British Consol is low; and when the interest rate is low, the price of the British Consol is high. This inverse relationship is typical between the prices of securities and the rate of interest.

Observe carefully that when the interest rate rises, the prices of securities fall. Thus, those investors who must turn their securities into cash necessarily suffer a capital loss. *The demand for speculative balances arises actually from the fear of capital loss.*

The volume of money that economic units hold for speculative purposes depends on their assessment of market conditions. When the interest rate appears to be low, that is, when economic units *expect* the interest rate to rise (and thus the prices of securities to fall) in the future, they shift from securities to money because of the fear of capital losses. After all, these capital losses could easily outweigh the interest that securities yield. On the other hand, when the interest rate appears to be high, that is, when economic units expect the rate of interest to fall (and thus the prices of securities to rise) in the future, they shift from money to securities because, in addition to the interest they earn by holding securities, they also expect capital gains.

We therefore conclude that the speculative demand for money is negatively (or inversely) related to the rate of interest.

Derivation of the *LM* Curve

We now proceed to determine the conditions under which the money market is in equilibrium. For this purpose, we must bring together the two components of the money market: the demand for money and the supply of money.

Evidently, equilibrium in the money market prevails when the demand for money equals the supply of money. The supply of money is exogenous; we assume that it is under the control of the monetary authorities. The demand for money, on the other hand, depends positively on the level of national income (transactions demand) and negatively on the rate of interest (speculative demand). Accordingly, equilibrium in the money market prevails when the level of national income and the interest rate are such that the demand for money equals the given supply of money.

Actually, there is an infinite number of combinations of income levels and interest rates that make the demand for money equal to the supply of money. The locus of all these combinations of income levels and interest rates that are consistent with equilibrium in the money market is known as the *LM* curve.

Figure 17-1 shows how to derive the *LM* curve. Consider downward-sloping curve V_1U_1 in panel 1, which shows the speculative demand for money (L_s). When the rate of interest is 15 percent or higher, the speculative demand for money is zero. As the rate of interest drops below 15 percent, the speculative demand for money becomes positive; it increases when the rate of interest decreases. Finally, the speculative demand for money becomes infinitely elas-

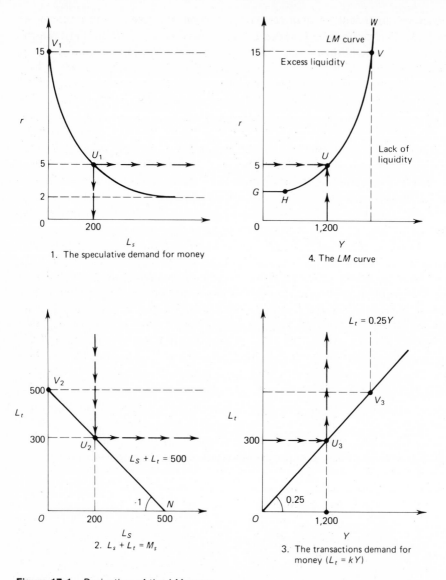

Figure 17-1 *Derivation of the LM curve.*
For any arbitrary point on the speculative demand for money, say, U_1, we complete rectangle $U_1U_2U_3U$, whose corner (U) in panel 4 gives a point on the *LM* curve. In this manner, we can determine as many points as we please on the *LM* curve.

tic (that is, the curve becomes horizontal) when the rate of interest drops to 2 percent. This illustrates the case of the *liquidity trap*: Because securities are "inferior" to money, people prefer to keep all their nonphysical wealth in the form of money when the rate of interest drops to a certain minimum (2 percent in our illustration).

Straight line U_3V_3 through the origin in panel 3 shows the demand for money for transactions (plus precautionary) purposes (L_t). This is in line with our earlier argument that the transactions demand for money is proportional to national income.

Straight line V_2U_2N in panel 2 shows the infinite number of ways in which the given money supply ($M_s = 500$) can be split into speculative balances (L_s) and transactions balances (L_t), according to the equilibrium condition $L_s + L_t = M_s$.

Finally, from the information given in panels 1 to 3, we derive the *LM* curve (see panel 4). For any arbitrary point on the speculative demand for money, say, U_1, we complete rectangle $U_1U_2U_3U$, whose corner (U) in panel 4 gives a point on the *LM* curve. In this manner, we can determine as many points as we please on the *LM* curve. When we have enough points, we can trace out the *LM* curve, as shown in panel 4.

The justification for this geometrical procedure is rather simple. At U_1 the rate of interest is 5 percent and the speculative demand for money is 200. Moving horizontally to the right, we register the 5 percent interest rate, that is, the height of corresponding point U on the *LM* curve (panel 4). To obtain the income coordinate of point U, we return to point U_1 and move vertically downward to point U_2, whose height gives the amount of money that is left for transactions purposes (that is, $500 - 200 = 300$). Then, we move horizontally to the right, from U_2 to U_3, to determine the level of income (1,200) at which the transactions demand for money is just 300. Finally, we carry the level of income upward to panel 4 to obtain the precise location of point U on the *LM* curve.

Properties of the *LM* Curve

The *LM* curve (Figure 17-1, panel 4) has several important properties, which we now summarize:

I   The *LM* curve consists of three different ranges:

  A   The *classical range*, corresponding to *vertical* portion *VW*. In this range, the rate of interest is so high that the speculative demand for money is zero. The prices of securities are very low and, in general, asset holders expect them to rise. So they keep all their liquid wealth in the form of "securities." All the available supply of money is used for transactions purposes only.

  B   The *normal range*, corresponding to *strictly upward sloping* portion *HV*. Here, as the rate of interest increases, the speculative demand decreases and releases additional amounts of money for transactions purposes. Hence, in complete contrast with the classical range, an increase in the rate of interest is consistent with a higher level of income.

  C   The *liquidity-trap range*, corresponding to horizontal portion *GH*. This range of the *LM* curve corresponds, of course, to the horizontal part of the speculative demand for money.

II The *LM* curve divides the whole quadrant into two regions:

A The region of *excess liquidity*, located above and to the left of the *LM* curve. For combinations of levels of national income and rates of interest in this region, the demand for money falls short of the supply of money. Asset holders attempt to convert their excess money holdings into securities, raising the prices of securities and lowering the rate of interest until a point is reached on the *LM* curve.

B The region of *lack of liquidity*, located below and to the right of the *LM* curve. For combinations of levels of national income and rates of interest in this region, the demand for money exceeds the supply of money. To increase their liquidity, asset holders sell securities, lowering their prices and raising the interest rate until a point is reached on the *LM* curve.

17-4 EQUILIBRIUM IN THE GOODS MARKET: THE *IS* CURVE

We now turn to the goods market. As we saw in Chapter 16, the goods market is in equilibrium when the aggregate demand $(C + I + X - M)$ equals the economy's current level of output or national income (Y). This fundamental equilibrium condition reduces to:

$$I + X = S + M \tag{17-5}$$

That is, national-income equilibrium occurs when the exogenous injections (investment I and exports X) just match the endogenous leakages (saving S and imports M).

In Chapter 16, we assumed that both desired exports X and investment I are exogenous, while desired saving S and imports M depend positively on the level of national income. Now we wish to expand this framework by recognizing the influence of the rate of interest on aggregate spending, particularly desired investment I.

By introducing the rate of interest as a determinant of the desired level of investment (and perhaps saving), we shall be able to establish an important link between the money market and the goods market. It is essentially through this link that the money supply exerts its influence on national income and the balance of trade.

The Marginal Efficiency of Investment

The entrepreneur's decision to invest, that is, to enlarge his or her plant, increase inventories, or buy additional and perhaps more efficient equipment, depends on a comparison between expected costs and revenues. This comparison is slightly complicated by the fact that costs and revenues are not contemporaneous. For instance, an entrepreneur may invest $10,000 in a machine today and receive a stream of *net* revenues of, say, $1,500 over the next 10 years. The fact that the cost of the machine ($10,000) is less than the sum of the future revenues ($15,000) is *not* an indication that the project is profitable. Indeed, if the rate of interest is (approximately) above 8.5 percent per annum (for example, 10 percent), the project will be unprofitable, as the reader should be able to verify.

How does the entrepreneur make the comparison between expected costs and revenues? In one of two ways:

1 The entrepreneur may calculate the *present discounted value* of the stream of net revenues that he or she expects to obtain from the project and compare it with the current cost of the project. The project is undertaken only when the present discounted value of the expected stream of revenues is higher than (or, in the limiting case, equal to) the initial cost of the project.

2 Alternatively, the entrepreneur may calculate the *marginal efficiency* of the investment project (also known as the internal rate of return) and compare it with the market rate of interest. (The marginal efficiency of an investment project is that rate of return, or rate of interest, which makes the present discounted value of the expected stream of net revenues equal to the initial cost of the project.)

An example may clarify the two methods. Suppose that an entrepreneur expects a project whose initial cost is $100 today to generate $110 in 1 year. Suppose, further, that the market rate of interest is 8 percent per year. The present discounted value of the project is $110/1.08 = $101.85, which is higher than the initial cost of the project ($100). On the other hand, the marginal efficiency of the project is 10 percent ($110/1.10 = $100), which is higher than the market rate of interest (8 percent). Accordingly, irrespective of the method followed, the investment project is profitable, and the entrepreneur should undertake it.

Note that the market rate of interest continues to be relevant even when a firm does not borrow the necessary funds but uses retained earnings (internal financing). In this case, the market rate of interest measures the opportunity cost of internal financing, that is, what the firm could earn by investing its funds in interest-earning assets instead.

The Investment-Demand Schedule

At any particular time, each firm is likely to consider a large number of alternative projects. Each firm ranks its projects on the basis of their marginal efficiency. Given any two projects, a firm always ranks as more desirable the project with the higher marginal efficiency. This ranking gives rise to an investment-demand schedule for each firm. When we add horizontally the investment-demand schedules of all firms, we obtain the economy's downward-sloping investment-demand schedule, as shown in Figure 17-2. (Here disregard the possible interdependence that may exist between investment projects either within each firm or among firms.)

For any rate of interest, we can read off the investment-demand schedule the desired level of investment. For instance, when the rate of interest is 10

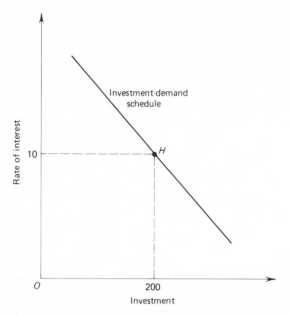

Figure 17-2 *The investment-demand function.*
For any rate of interest, such as 10 percent, we can read off the investment-demand schedule
the desired level of investment (200). The investment-demand schedule slopes downward to
reflect the fact that as the rate of interest falls, the desired level of investment increases.

percent, the economy's desired volume of investment is 200 (billion dollars).
When the rate of interest falls, the desired level of investment tends to increase
as additional projects become profitable.

Derivation of the *IS* Curve

Given that investment is a function of the rate of interest, we cannot determine
the equilibrium level of national income unless we know the rate of interest. As
the rate of interest falls, the desired level of investment increases, causing national income to increase (through the multiplier). The *IS* curve summarizes
this important relationship between the rate of interest and the equilibrium
level of income. In particular, the *IS* curve is the locus of all combinations of interest rate r and national income Y that keep the commodity market in equilibrium, that is, those combinations of r and Y which satisfy equation (17-5).

With a procedure similar to that used to derive the *LM* curve, we show in
Figure 17-3 how to derive the *IS* curve. In panel 1 we add horizontally the investment-demand schedule to the fixed amount of exports ($\bar{X} = 150$) to obtain
the $I + X$ schedule, which shows the desired level of investment plus exports at
alternative interest rates. In panel 2, we draw a 45° line to represent equilibrium
condition $S + M = I + X$. And in panel 3 we simply draw the familiar $S + M$
schedule (see Chapter 16). From the information given in panels 1–3, we finally derive the *IS* curve, which is shown in panel 4. Thus, for any arbitrary point

on the $I + X$ schedule, such as U_1, we complete rectangle $U_1U_2U_3U$, whose corner (U) in panel 4 lies on the *IS* curve.

The justification for the above geometric procedure is simple. At U_1 the rate of interest is 10 percent and the desired volume of exogenous injections ($I + X$) is 350. Moving horizontally to the right, we register the 10 percent interest rate, that is, the height of corresponding point U on the *IS* curve (panel 4). To obtain the income coordinate of point U, we return to U_1 and move vertically downward to U_2, whose height gives the desired volume of endogenous

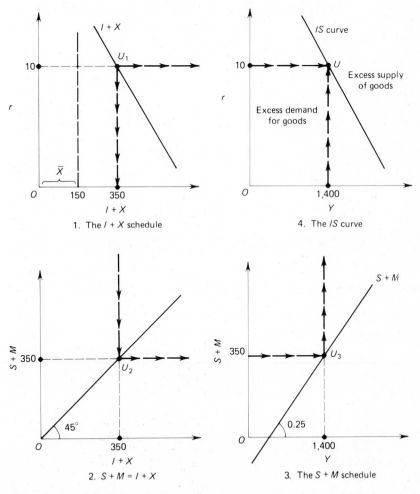

Figure 17-3 *Derivation of the IS curve.*
In panel 1, we add horizontally the investment demand schedule to the fixed amount of exports ($\bar{X} = 150$) to obtain the $I + X$ schedule. In panel 2, we draw a 45° line to represent equilibrium condition $S + M = I + X$. And in panel 3, we draw the $S + M$ schedule. For any arbitrary point on the $I + X$ schedule, such as U_1, we complete rectangle $U_1U_2U_3U$, whose corner (U) in panel 4 lies on the *IS* curve.

leakages $(S + M)$, that is, 350. (In equilibrium, the endogenous leakages must always be equal to the exogenous injections.) From U_2 we move horizontally to U_3 to determine the equilibrium level of income, that is, 1,400. (We assume that the sum of the marginal propensity to save plus the marginal propensity to import is 0.25, and thus the foreign-trade multiplier is 4.) We finally carry the equilibrium level of income upward to panel 4 to determine the precise location of point U on the IS curve. By repeating this exercise many times, we can finally obtain the entire IS curve.

Properties of the *IS* Curve

To the extent that desired investment increases when the rate of interest falls, the IS curve must be sloping downward, as illustrated in Figure 17-3. When desired investment, and in general aggregate spending, is not responsive to the rate of interest, both the $I + X$ schedule (panel 1) and the IS curve (panel 4) become vertical. This case is usually referred to as the extreme *fiscalist case.*

Further, the IS curve divides the whole quadrant into two regions:

1   The region of *excess (commodity) supply*, located above and to the right of the IS curve. For combinations of levels of income and rates of interest in this region, aggregate supply exceeds aggregate demand and inventories tend to pile up. Producers lower production, reducing the level of income until a point is reached on the IS curve.

2   The region of *excess(commodity) demand*, located to the left and below the IS curve. For combinations of levels of income and rates of interest in this region, aggregate demand exceeds aggregate supply and inventories tend to fall. Producers increase production, raising the level of income until a point is reached on the IS curve.

17-5   GENERAL MACROECONOMIC EQUILIBRIUM

To determine general macroeconomic equilibrium, we bring together the LM curve (which represents equilibrium in the money market) and the IS curve (which represents equilibrium in the goods market), as shown in Figure 17-4. The equilibrium rate of interest (r_e) and the equilibrium level of national income (Y_e) are determined simultaneously by the intersection (E) of the IS and LM curves.

Note carefully that the IS and LM curves divide the whole quadrant into four regions, as illustrated in Figure 17-4. In all these regions, we find signs of disequilibrium and tendencies for change. For instance, for any point in region 1 that is located to the right of both the IS curve and the LM curve, there exist: (1) excess supply of goods, causing national income to fall, and (2) lack of liquidity, causing the interest rate to rise. These tendencies for change are illustrated by the pair of arrows drawn in region 1.

The reader should study all four regions and verify both the signs of disequilibrium and the tendencies for change that are registered in each. In the

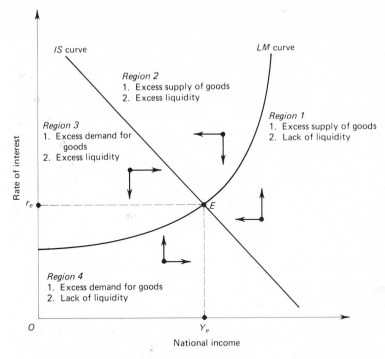

Figure 17-4 *General macroeconomic equilibrium.*
The equilibrium rate of interest r_e and the equilibrium level of national income Y_e are simultaneously determined by intersection E of the IS and LM curves. At any other point, there are signs of disequilibrium and tendencies for change, as shown by the arrows in each of the four regions into which the IS and LM curves divide the whole quandrant.

rest of this book, we assume that the economy moves quickly to the intersection of the IS and LM curves, which is the only equilibrium point.

Having determined the equilibrium level of national income and rate of interest, we can refer back to the individual schedules (or functions) to determine also the equilibrium levels of investment, saving, consumption, imports, and exports, as well as the equilibrium decomposition of the supply of money into transactions balances and speculative balances. We leave this as an exercise for the reader.

Lastly, note that at equilibrium point E (that is, the intersection of the IS and LM curves), there is absolutely no requirement for the economy to be at full employment or for the balance of payments to be in equilibrium.

17-6 BALANCE-OF-PAYMENTS EQUILIBRIUM: THE EXTERNAL BALANCE SCHEDULE

We finally bring into focus the last piece of the puzzle: the balance of payments. Under what conditions is the balance of payments in equilibrium?

External Balance: Definition

We already know (see Chapter 13) that the balance of payments consists of three major accounts: the current account, the capital account, and the official reserve account. For our present purposes, we assume that balance-of-payments equilibrium (or external balance) prevails when the official reserve account balance is zero.

Because it is constructed on the basis of double-entry bookkeeping, the balance of payments always balances. That is, the sum of the three accounts of the balance of payments is always zero. Accordingly, we can express the condition for balance-of-payments equilibrium as follows:

Current account balance + capital account balance = 0   (17-6)

In what follows, we concentrate on the current account balance and the capital account balance.

The current account balance is the sum of two separate balances: (1) the balance on goods and services (that is, exports less imports) and (2) the balance on unilateral transfers. To simplify our exposition, we assume that the balance on unilateral transfers is zero. Thus, in the following discussion the current account balance coincides with the balance on goods and services, and we refer to it as the balance of trade.

Given the above simplification, it becomes apparent that external balance prevails when an *export surplus* (that is, a *positive* current account balance) matches a *net capital outflow* (that is, a *negative* capital account balance); or when an *import surplus* (that is, a *negative* current account balance) matches a *net capital inflow* (that is, a *positive* capital account balance). Under these circumstances, equation (17-6) holds, and the balance on autonomous transactions is zero. Further, the foreign exchange market is in equilibrium and the monetary authorities neither lose nor gain international reserves.

The Determinants of External Balance

Turn now to the determinants of the current account balance and the capital account balance. Recall the *assumption that the rate of foreign exchange is fixed*.

As we saw in Chapter 16, the balance of trade $(X - M)$ depends on the level of national income (Y). As national income rises, imports tend to increase, causing the balance of trade to deteriorate. We have nothing more to add to that discussion.

The capital account balance, however, depends primarily on the rate of interest. As the domestic rate of interest rises, people tend to substitute domestic "securities" (which tend to become cheaper) for foreign securities (whose prices remain unchanged), and thus the capital account improves. On the other hand, as the domestic rate of interest falls, people tend to substitute foreign securities for domestic securities, and thus the capital account deteriorates.

Economists distinguish among three types of capital mobility:

1 *Perfect capital mobility.* In this case, the domestic securities are perfectly substitutable for foreign securities, and their prices (and thus the rate of interest) are determined in world markets. The rate of interest that prevails in the world markets must also prevail in our small open economy.[2]

2 *Perfect capital immobility.* In this case, our open economy's capital market is totally disconnected from the world capital markets. The capital account balance is always zero, irrespective of the domestic rate of interest.

3 *Imperfect capital mobility.* In this case, which we consider as typical, the domestic securities are only imperfectly substitutable for foreign securities. The capital account balance is now a function of the interest-rate differential. As the domestic interest rate rises (assuming that the foreign interest rate remains constant), the capital account improves.

It is also possible that the capital account balance may in addition depend on national income. Thus, an increase in national income may lead to an increase in profitable-investment opportunities and attract foreign direct investment. In an effort to keep our exposition as simple as possible, we shall ignore this possibility.

The External Balance Schedule

Given that the balance of trade is primarily a function of national income, while the net capital flow (that is, capital account balance) is primarily a function of the rate of interest, it is evident that external equilibrium prevails when the level of national income and the interest rate are such that the net capital flow matches the balance of trade. Indeed, there is in general an infinite number of income levels and interest rates that are consistent with external balance, that is, satisfy equation (17-6). The locus of all these combinations of income levels and interest rates that are consistent with balance-of-payments equilibrium is known as the *external balance schedule.* We now wish to derive this important schedule. For this purpose, we use a procedure similar to that used to derive the *IS* and *LM* curves.

Consider Figure 17-5. Panel 1 illustrates the capital account schedule. When the rate of interest is 12 percent, the net capital flow is zero. As the rate of interest drops to 8 percent, the economy develops a *net* capital *outflow* of −100. The economy enjoys net capital *inflows* only when the rate of interest increases above the rate of 12 percent. (Recall that capital *outflows* are *negative* and that capital *inflows* are *positive.*) The 45° line in panel 2 represents the balance-of-payments equilibrium condition, that is, equation (17-6). Note carefully that the 45° line matches positive export surpluses with negative net capital outflows, and negative import surpluses with positive net capital inflows. Panel 3 exhibits the familiar $X − M$ schedule (see Chapter 16).

---

[2]Under fixed exchange rates, perfect capital mobility is inconsistent with sterilization of payments imbalances. Instead, the domestic money supply becomes an endogenous variable and renders the *LM* curve horizontal at the world interest rate.

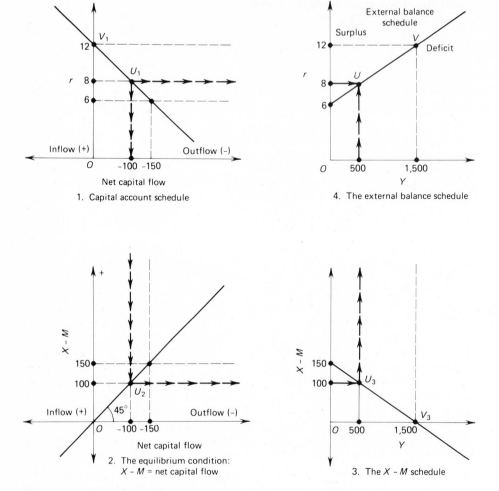

Figure 17-5 *Derivation of the external balance schedule.*
Panel 1 illustrates the capital account schedule. For instance, when the rate of interest is 12 percent, the net capital flow is zero (see point V_1). When the rate of interest drops to 8 percent, the economy develops a net capital outflow of -100 (see point U_1). The 45° line in panel 2 represents the equilibrium condition: $X - M =$ net capital flow. Panel 3 gives the $X - M$ schedule. For any arbitrary point on the capital account schedule, such as U_1, we complete rectangle $U_1U_2U_3U$, whose corner (U) in panel 4 lies on the external balance schedule.

Based on the information given in panels 1 to 3, we finally derive the external balance schedule in panel 4 by completing the various rectangles, as we did earlier with the *IS* and *LM* curves. For instance, for any arbitrary point on the capital account schedule, such as U_1, we complete rectangle $U_1U_2U_3U$, whose corner (U) in panel 4 lies on the external balance schedule. The justification for this geometric procedure is similar to that given earlier in relation to the derivation of the *IS* and *LM* curves. For this reason, we leave the details to the reader.

Properties of the External Balance Schedule

To the extent that the capital account schedule is downward-sloping, as illustrated in Figure 17-5, panel 1, the external balance schedule must be upward-sloping, as shown in panel 4. Thus, as the domestic interest rate rises, the net capital outflow falls (or the net capital inflow rises), and a surplus appears in the balance of payments. To restore external balance, national income must rise to induce an increase in imports equal to the reduction in the net capital outflow. This is the case of imperfect capital mobility.

When capital is perfectly immobile between countries, the capital account schedule becomes vertical, coinciding with the vertical axis. In this case, the external balance schedule becomes vertical also at that level of income at which the balance of trade is zero, that is, at the point of intersection (V_3) between the $X - M$ schedule and the horizontal axis (panel 3).

Finally, when capital is perfectly mobile, the capital account schedule becomes horizontal at the interest rate that prevails in world markets, causing the external balance schedule to also become horizontal at that same rate of interest.

Further, the external balance schedule divides the whole quadrant into two regions:

1 The *region of external deficit*, which lies to the right of the external balance schedule, as shown in Figure 17-5. For any point in this region, the level of national income is too high and/or the rate of interest is too low for external balance. The balance of payments is in deficit and the economy loses international reserves.

2 The *region of external surplus*, which lies to the left of the external balance schedule, as shown in Figure 17-5. For any point in this region, the level of national income is too low and/or the rate of interest is too high for external balance. The balance of payments is in surplus and the monetary authorities gain international reserves.

17-7 THE *IS-LM* APPARATUS AND THE EXTERNAL BALANCE SCHEDULE

In Figure 17-6 we finally bring together the *IS-LM* apparatus and the external balance schedule. The intersection of the *IS* and *LM* curves (that is, point E) determines, as we saw in Section 17-5, the equilibrium level of national income (300) and the rate of interest (8 percent). Point E does not represent balance-of-payments equilibrium, however, because it does not lie on the external balance schedule. The balance of payments must be in deficit because point E lies to the right of the external balance schedule; that is, point E lies in the region of external deficit.

The Size of the Payments Imbalance

On the basis of our assumptions so far, the external balance schedule and equilibrium point E are independent of each other. This means that the external bal-

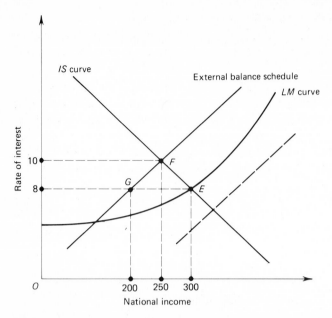

Figure 17-6 *The IS-LM apparatus with the external balance schedule.*
The intersection (*E*) of the *IS* and *LM* curves determines the equilibrium level of income (300)
and the rate of interest (8 percent). Since point *E* lies to the right of the external balance
schedule, the balance of payments is in deficit.

ance schedule could lie either to the left or to the right of point *E* (see broken
schedule). It is even conceivable that the external balance schedule passes
through point *E*, and in that case the balance of payments is in equilibrium simultaneously with the money and goods markets.

Suppose that the external balance schedule does not pass through the intersection of the *IS* and *LM* curves. How can we determine the payments imbalance? Merely by calculating the change in imports that is necessary to restore external balance, assuming that the rate of interest, and thus the capital
account balance, remains constant.

For instance in Figure 17-6 the intersection (*E*) of the *IS* and the *LM*
curves lies to the right of the external balance schedule. Hence, the balance of
payments is in deficit. By freezing the rate of interest at 8 percent and allowing
national income to drop from 300 to 200 (that is, $\Delta Y = -100$), we can restore
external balance (see point *G*). Suppose now that the marginal propensity to import is 0.15. By how much do imports fall as income falls by 100? Imports fall
by 15 (that is, 0.15×100). Hence, the balance-of-payments deficit at *E* must
be 15 also.

The Influence of the Money Supply on the Balance of Payments

In Figure 17-6 we see clearly the influence of the money supply (which determines the location of the *LM* curve) on the balance of payments. Thus, the

money supply is one of the determinants of the rate of interest and the equilibrium level of national income (that is, point E). The location of point E relative to the external balance schedule determines, in turn, the size of the payments imbalance.

An increase in the money supply shifts the LM curve to the right, causing the rate of interest to fall and the level of national income to rise (as equilibrium point E travels southeast along the given IS curve). Accordingly, an increase in the money supply worsens the balance of payments because it worsens both the capital account (through the reduction in the interest rate) and the balance of trade (through the increase in national income).

On the other hand, a reduction in the money supply shifts the LM curve to the left, causing the rate of interest to rise and the level of income to fall (as equilibrium point E travels northwest on the given IS curve). Thus, a reduction in the money supply improves the balance of payments since it improves both the balance of trade and the capital account.

The Effect of Payments Imbalances on the Money Supply Again

In Section 17-1 we studied the influence of payments imbalances on the supply of money. In our discussion since then, however, we have largely ignored this important influence; we have been assuming that the monetary authorities sterilize the effects of payments imbalances, keeping the money supply constant.

Nevertheless, under the gold-standard rules of the game, the deficit country must allow its money supply to fall, and the surplus country must allow its money supply to rise. Indeed, the new monetary approach to the balance of payments (summarized in the next section) is built on the premise that the monetary flows associated with payments imbalances are not sterilized—or cannot be, within the relevant time period—but instead influence the money supply. How does the removal of sterilization operations affect our results?

Return to Figure 17-6, and consider again the intersection (E) of the IS and LM curves. When the balance of payments is allowed to exert its influence on the money supply (as, for instance, in the case of the gold-specie standard), the equilibrium at E cannot last. Rather, it becomes a *temporary* equilibrium. Thus, as the monetary authorities lose international reserves, the money supply falls and the LM curve shifts continuously to the left—at the same interest rate but a smaller supply of money, the money market can remain in equilibrium at a smaller national income. This process eventually comes to an end when the LM curve shifts sufficiently to the left and passes through the point of intersection (F) between the IS curve and the external balance schedule.

Under the present circumstances of no sterilization operations, the long-run equilibrium of the system is determined by the intersection (F) of the unchanging IS curve and the external balance schedule—not the intersection of the IS and LM curves. The money supply ceases to be exogenous. Rather, it becomes an important endogenous variable whose value stabilizes only when the system reaches long-run equilibrium at point F.

Assuming that the full-employment level of income is higher than 300, the passive policy of the monetary authorities penalizes the economy with increased unemployment. Thus, by suspending their sterilization operations, the monetary authorities allow the system to move from E to F. In effect, the monetary authorities sacrifice the goal of full employment at the altar of external balance. This actually explains why monetary authorities refuse to remain passive but rather actively pursue sterilization operations in an effort to "immunize" the money supply against payments imbalances.

17-8 THE MONETARY APPROACH TO THE BALANCE OF PAYMENTS: A DIGRESSION

The monetary approach to the balance of payments is an outgrowth of domestic "monetarism" (that is, the view that the supply of money is the key determinant of aggregate demand) and the intellectual grandchild of Hume's price-specie-flow mechanism (although there are important differences between the two theories, as noted below).

Stemming mainly from the work of Mundell and Johnson, the monetary approach views the balance of payments as a totally monetary phenomenon. Furthermore, the monetary approach maintains that payments imbalances (deficits and surpluses) reflect stock disequilibria between the supply of money and the demand for money, the latter being a stable function of the level of national income. Indeed, the monetary approach views the balance of payments as a safety valve that opens automatically to either release an excess supply of money in the form of a balance-of-payments deficit or allow into the country an additional amount of money in the form of a balance-of-payments surplus in order to satisfy an existing excess demand for money. (Recall our discussion in Section 17-1 concerning the effect of payments imbalances on the supply of money.)

A fundamental premise of the monetary approach is that the monetary authorities cannot, and actually do not, sterilize the monetary flows associated with surpluses and deficits but instead allow them to influence the domestic money supply. As we saw in Section 17-1, there are indeed limits to the ability of the monetary authorities to sterilize payments imbalances, and in the long run chronic payments imbalances are likely to affect the money supply. However, in the short run, the monetary authorities have plenty of leeway and they do offset payments imbalances by means of sterilization operations.

Given the premises of the monetary approach, it must be clear that payments imbalances must be *transitory* phenomena that tend to correct themselves—payments imbalances can last until the supply of money becomes equal to the demand for money. In other words, a payments imbalance (reflecting a disequilibrium between the supply of and demand for money) brings about an adjustment in the supply of money that tends to eliminate the initial disequilibrium in the money market and thus correct the balance-of-payments disequilibrium.

The monetary approach concentrates mostly on the official reserve account of the balance of payments, lumping together all other entries into a single autonomous, above-the-line category. In other words, the monetary approach makes no effort to explain the behavior of individual entries above the line or the behavior of partial balances, such as the balance on goods and services, the current account balance, and so on. Rather, it views the balance of payments "from the bottom up."

The monetary approach is reminiscent of Hume's price-specie-flow mechanism, particularly because both theories deal with a self-correcting mechanism based on the monetary flows associated with deficits and surpluses. However, the two theories differ in at least one important respect: Hume's mechanism works through commodity prices, while the monetary approach works through the supply and demand for money. Thus, the price-specie-flow mechanism starts at the top of the balance of payments, whereas the monetary approach begins at the bottom. As a result, the import-demand elasticities, which are so important for the smooth functioning of the price-specie-flow mechanism, are irrelevant to the monetary approach.

The policy implications of the monetary approach are far-reaching. Viewing payments imbalances as temporary, self-correcting phenomena, the monetary approach leads practically to the conclusion that policy measures to correct balance-of-payments disequilibria are generally unnecessary. If the authorities are patient enough and remain passive, a balance-of-payments disequilibrium will automatically correct itself sooner or later. The trouble, of course, is that such correction may occur much later; and, in the meantime, the economy may suffer from unnecessary adjustment costs.

Even though the final word may not be in yet, the author remains skeptical about the monetary approach, which he considers a dangerous oversimplification of a rather complex economic phenomenon. Whatever its long-run implications, the monetary approach cannot provide a good explanation for actual, short-run deficits and surpluses and thus cannot serve as a guide to balance-of-payments policy. A country that suffers from a severe balance-of-payments deficit may find little relief in the thought that in the long run its deficit will be solved automatically. Perhaps policy makers suffer from myopia. One cannot help but recall Keynes's words: "In the long run we shall all be dead!"

17-9 SUMMARY

1 There is a mutual interaction between the money supply and the balance of payments.

2 A balance-of-payments deficit (surplus) tends to reduce (increase) the money supply. This is obvious in the case of the gold-specie standard, where payments imbalances generate gold movements, which, in turn, imply changes in the money supply on a one-to-one basis.

3 In a modern banking system, such as that of the United States, there are three major types of money: coins, paper money, and demand deposits (the largest component).

4 The major policy instruments at the disposal of the monetary authori-

ties are: the required-reserve ratio, the discount rate, and open market operations.

5   The *maximum* volume of demand deposits (which the commercial banks can create) is given by the product of the volume of bank reserves and the money multiplier (that is, the reciprocal of the reserve ratio). In addition, the *actual* volume of demand deposits is identical to the sum of bank reserves plus domestic assets (held by banks).

6   A payments imbalance leads to a direct change in bank reserves, which, in turn, induces the commercial banks to adjust their holdings of domestic assets. Assuming the banks are always fully loaned up, the change in the money supply (demand deposits) is equal to the change in bank reserves times the money multiplier.

7   The monetary authorities can, and often do, sterilize payments imbalances, even though there are limits to such operations. To sterilize a deficit (surplus), the monetary authorities must either purchase (sell) government bonds in the open market, reduce (raise) the discount rate, or lower (raise) reserve requirements.

8   Economists generally agree that an increase (decrease) in the money supply tends to worsen (improve) the balance of payments. But the monetarists believe that the money supply influences the balance of payments directly, while the Keynesians argue that the money supply affects the balance of payments indirectly, through its influence on the interest rate.

9   Securities seem to be superior to money because they yield interest. Yet compared with money, securities have two significant drawbacks: They are *not* a medium of exchange, and they are more risky. Economic units determine their demand for money by balancing the benefits it yields against the cost of holding it (that is, the interest rate).

10   The demand for money depends positively on the level of national income (transactions plus precautionary balances) and negatively on the interest rate (speculative demand).

11   Equilibrium in the money market prevails when the level of national income and the interest rate are such that the demand for money equals the supply of money.

12   The *LM* curve is the locus of all combinations of income levels and interest rates that are consistent with equilibrium in the money market. It divides the whole quadrant into two regions: the region of excess liquidity (located above and to the left of the *LM* curve) and the region of lack of liquidity (located below and to the right of the *LM* curve).

13   An investment project is profitable when either its current cost is lower than the present discounted value of its future stream of net revenues or the market interest rate is lower than its marginal efficiency.

14   For any interest rate, the downward-sloping investment-demand schedule gives the desired volume of investment (that is, the sum of all investment projects whose marginal efficiency is at least as high as the interest rate). As the interest rate falls, the desired volume of investment increases because additional projects become profitable.

15   The *IS* curve is the locus of all combinations of income levels and interest rates that satisfy the equation $I(r) + \bar{X} = S(Y) + M(Y)$, which is the commodity-market-equilibrium condition. The *IS* curve is either downward-sloping or vertical according to whether aggregate spending (particularly investment) is responsive to the interest rate or not, respectively. Further, the IS curve divides the whole quadrant into two regions: the region of excess commodity supply (located above and to the right of the IS curve) and the region of excess commodity demand (located below and to the left of the IS curve).

16   Assuming that the rate of exchange is fixed, the balance of trade $(X - M)$ depends on the level of national income only. As national income rises, imports increase, causing the balance of trade to deteriorate.

17   The capital account balance depends primarily on the rate of interest. Normally, as the domestic interest rate rises, the capital account improves (assuming the foreign interest rate is constant). This is the case of imperfect capital mobility that lies between the polar cases of perfect capital mobility and perfect capital immobility.

18   The external balance schedule is the locus of all combinations of income levels and interest rates that are consistent with balance-of-payments equilibrium (external balance); that is, those combinations which satisfy the equation: balance of trade + capital account balance = 0 (assuming that the balance on unilateral transfers is zero). The external balance schedule is vertical, upward-sloping, or horizontal, according to whether capital is perfectly immobile, imperfectly mobile, or perfectly mobile, respectively. Further, the external balance schedule divides the whole quadrant into two regions: the region of external deficit (located to its right) and the region of external surplus (located to its left).

19   Assuming that the supply of money is exogenous, the equilibrium interest rate and national income are determined simultaneously by the intersection of the IS and LM curves; and the balance of payments registers a deficit or surplus according to whether the intersection of the IS and LM curves lies in the region of external deficit or surplus, respectively.

20   In the absence of sterilization operations, the intersection of the IS and LM curves corresponds to a temporary equilibrium, because the money supply ceases to be exogenous. Instead, the long-run equilibrium of the system occurs at the intersection of the unchanging IS curve and the external balance schedule—the supply of money stabilizes at that point only.

21   The monetary approach to the balance of payments maintains that payments imbalances are temporary phenomena that reflect stock disequilibria between the supply of money and the demand for money, the latter being a stable function of national income. A fundamental premise of the monetary approach is that the monetary authorities do not sterilize payments imbalances. Finally, the monetary approach views the balance of payments "from the bottom up," and this differentiates it from the price-specie-flow mechanism.

SUGGESTED READING

Chacholiades, M. (1978). *International Monetary Theory and Policy*. McGraw-Hill Book Company, New York, chaps. 17 and 19.

Frenkel, J., and H. G. Johnson, eds. (1975). *The Monetary Approach to the Balance of Payments*. George Allen & Unwin, Ltd., London.

Hansen, A. (1953). *A Guide to Keynes*. McGraw-Hill Book Company, New York, chaps. 5–7.

Hicks, J. R. (1937). "Mr. Keynes and the 'Classics'; A Suggested Interpretation." *Econometrica*, vol. 5, pp. 147–159.

Johnson, H. G. (1961). *International Trade and Economic Growth: Studies in Pure Theory*. Harvard University Press, Cambridge, Mass., chap. 6. Reprinted in R. E. Caves and H. G. Johnson (eds.), AEA *Readings in International Economics*. Richard D. Irwin, Inc., Homewood, Ill., 1968.

——— (1972). "The New Monetary Approach to Balance-of-Payments Theory." *Journal of Financial and Quantitative Analysis* (March), pp. 1555–1572. Reprinted in M. Connolly and A. Swoboda (eds.). *International Trade and Money*. University of Toronto Press, Toronto, 1973.

——— (1976). "Elasticity, Absorption, Keynesian Multiplier, Keynesian Policy, and Monetary Approaches to Devaluation Theory: A Simple Geometric Exposition." *American Economic Review*, vol. 66, no. 3 (June), pp. 448–452.

Kreinin, M. E., and L. H. Officer (1978). *The Monetary Approach to the Balance of Payments: A Survey*. Princeton Studies in International Finance, no. 43, International Finance Section, Princeton University, Princeton, N.J.

Mundell, R. (1968). *International Economics*. The Macmillan Company, New York, chaps. 11 and 15.

Samuelson, P. A. (1980). *Economics*, 11th ed., McGraw-Hill Book Company, New York, chaps. 15–18.

Part Four

Adjustment Policies

Chapter Eighteen

International Economic Policy

So far our discussion of international equilibrium and adjustment has focused on automatic processes only. The rest of the book deals with the formulation of economic policy.

Even though the question of economic policy may seem more interesting and perhaps more relevant, the decision to discuss automatic processes first was deliberate. We cannot hope to be successful in our search for optimal policies unless we have a thorough knowledge of how the international economy actually works and how autonomous or policy-induced changes affect the international economy. But having studied these problems in Part 3 of the book, we now turn in Part 4 to the interesting issue of economic policy.

This chapter deals primarily with some general principles that can serve as a guide in the formulation of economic policy. Section 18-1 deals with the theory of economic policy in rather broad terms. This section discusses the differences between the traditional approach of Part 3 and the policy approach of this last part, and explains the famous rule of Tinbergen.

The following two sections deal with the question of the proper definitions of internal and external balance. In particular, Section 18-2 deals with the important distinction between temporary and fundamental balance-of-payments equilibria, while Section 18-3 deals with the proper meaning of the term *internal balance* in the light of the recent discussions of the Phillips curve.

Finally, the last two sections illustrate the problem of how to apply two mutually independent and effective instruments (such as government spending and exchange-rate adjustments) in order to achieve internal and external balance. Section 18-4 shows how to apply the general principles of economic policy when prices and inflation are largely ignored. Section 18-5 generalizes the discussion to a "Phillips curve world."

18-1 THE THEORY OF ECONOMIC POLICY

This section deals with some general principles that every student of economic policy should know. These principles lay the foundations for our discussion in this last part of the book. These general principles are illustrated in Sections 18-4 and 18-5.

The Abandonment of Automaticity

Before Keynes published his *General Theory of Employment, Interest and Money* in 1936, economists generally believed that automatic economic forces tended to bring about both full employment (internal balance) and balance-of-payments equilibrium (external balance). This is no longer the case, because Keynes shattered the classical belief in automaticity.

Keynes directly attacked the classical notion of automatic full employment. Like an elevator that could stand perfectly still at any floor, the economy, Keynes argued convincingly, could reach equilibrium at any level of national income, not just the full-employment level.

In his *General Theory,* Keynes was not concerned with the balance of payments. As a result, the notion of automatic balance-of-payments equilibrium persisted a bit longer. However, economists gradually came to the realization that external balance, like internal balance, is not normally attained automatically. Rather, external balance should be considered as an objective (or target) of deliberate economic policy. Indeed, this is now the predominant view among economists, even though there are still some lingering doubts in the minds of the proponents of the monetary approach to the balance of payments (see Section 17-8).

We therefore conclude that the general view today is that both internal and external balance are policy objectives (or targets) which must be pursued by means of deliberate economic policy measures.

Targets and Instruments

The traditional approach to international equilibrium and adjustment that we discussed in Part 3 dealt primarily with the effects of changes in any exogenous parameter on such critical variables as national income, employment, terms of trade, and the balance of payments. For instance, in our discussion of the foreign-trade multiplier (Chapter 16), we asked how an autonomous shift in desired investment may affect the level of national income as well as the balance of trade. Similarly, in Chapter 15 we asked how a change in the rate of exchange may affect the balance of trade and the terms of trade as well as the domestic production and consumption of various commodities (such as export-ables, import-competing goods, and nontraded goods). In Chapters 20 and 21, we shall ask how fiscal and monetary policies affect national income and the balance of payments under fixed- or flexible-exchange-rate systems.

The policy-oriented approach, on the other hand, is not concerned directly with the effects of exogenous changes, even though the traditional approach lays the foundations of the policy model. The policy approach takes a diamet-rically opposite view. To begin with, it makes a sharp distinction between *policy targets* (objects of policy)—such as full employment and balance-of-payments equilibrium—and *policy instruments* (vehicles of policy)—such as the money supply, government spending, taxes, tariffs, and rate of foreign exchange. Then, instead of asking how a change in a policy instrument, such as the money supply, will affect the level of, say, national income and the balance of payments, the policy approach takes the targets as given and solves for the required values of the instruments. The fundamental question now is this: What should be the money supply, government spending, rate of foreign exchange, and so on (that is, the instruments) so that external and internal balance (that is, the targets) may prevail simultaneously? The main architects of this policy-oriented approach were Meade (1951) and Tinbergen (1952).

Note carefully the relationship between the traditional approach and the Meade-Tinbergen policy model. To be able to determine the critical values of the instruments (that is, those values which can achieve the various policy ob-jectives), we must first know how a change in the value of an instrument affects the various targets, such as the level of national income and the balance of payments. This explains why we had to study the traditional approach before we considered the policy approach.

Tinbergen's Rule

In searching for the appropriate values of the instruments, we derive invaluable guidance from what is known in the literature as Tinbergen's rule.

Tinbergen's rule: To achieve a given target, we must apply an effective in-strument; and to achieve *n* independent targets, we must apply at least *n* in-dependent and effective instruments.

Tinbergen's rule is a powerful principle. It declares forthrightly that we cannot simultaneously achieve *n* targets unless we simultaneously apply at least as many instruments. For instance, we cannot simultaneously achieve full employment and balance-of-payments equilibrium (two targets) unless we apply at least two independent and effective instruments. Indeed, in the last few decades economists have spent a great deal of time discussing the problem of how expenditure-adjusting policies can be combined with expenditure-switching policies to achieve simultaneously external and internal balance.

In particular, Meade showed that when expenditure-adjusting policies alone are used, *conflicts* arise between internal and external balance. These conflicts arise because there are fewer instruments than targets. When an additional instrument, such as the rate of foreign exchange, is combined with expenditure-adjusting policies, all conflicts are removed and internal and external balance are attainable simultaneously (see Section 18-4).

The targets must be *independent*. For instance, suppose there exists a one-to-one correspondence between two target variables, such as the level of employment and national income. It makes no sense to consider full employment and maximum output as independent (or different) targets. Similarly, in a two-country world (America and Britain), it makes no sense to consider America's external balance as a different target from Britain's external balance—when one balance of payments is in equilibrium, the other is in equilibrium also, ignoring any possible inconsistencies in the two countries' definitions of external balance.

In addition, the instruments must be *effective* and mutually *independent*. An instrument is effective when it affects a target variable (or variables) to an appropriate degree. For instance, a reduction in the interest rate during a deep depression when investment is not interest-elastic (fiscalist case) is an ineffective means of increasing national income and employment. The instruments must also be mutually independent in the sense that their *relative* effectiveness on different target variables is different. For instance, as we shall see in Section 18-4, we cannot achieve internal and external balance simultaneously if we use taxes and government spending as instruments. The reason is simple: Our instruments (taxes and government spending) are not mutually independent—increases in government spending raise income and worsen the balance of trade at the same rate as reductions in taxes. More specifically, if an increase in government spending (say, $50) raises national income by $100 and worsens the balance of trade by $20, an appropriate reduction in taxes that raises national income by $100 will also worsen the balance of trade by $20. The relative influence of taxes and government spending on the two targets (national income and balance of payments) is the same. Therefore, taxes and government spending are not independent instruments; in particular, they are two specific cases of expenditure-adjusting policies.

Note carefully that in the present context "independence" refers to the *effects* of the instruments—not to whether it is feasible to use the instruments independently of each other. Thus, taxes and government spending are not independent instruments neither because tax revenues determine how much the government can spend on goods and services nor because government spending determines how much revenue must be raised in taxes; rather, they are not independent because their relative influence on the two targets (national income and balance of payments) is the same.

On the other hand, we can simultaneously achieve balance-of-payments equilibrium and full employment by combining exchange-rate adjustments with changes in government spending, because the relative effectiveness of these two instruments on the two targets is different. Thus, exchange-rate adjustments are one form of expenditure-switching policy whose relative effectiveness on national income and balance of payments differs from that of an expenditure-adjusting policy. This example is pursued further in Section 18-4.

Before we apply the preceding principles to concrete cases, we must pause to discuss the meaning of our two targets: external and internal balance. We do this in the next two sections.

18-2 TEMPORARY VERSUS FUNDAMENTAL DISEQUILIBRIA

In this section, we discuss briefly the all-important distinction between temporary and fundamental balance-of-payments disequilibria. We show that temporary disequilibria must be financed, while fundamental disequilibria require true adjustment. Indeed, the rest of the book deals mainly with the problem of how to handle fundamental disequilibria.

Some Broad Definitions

As we saw earlier, an external disequilibrium reflects in the first instance a gap between "autonomous" purchases and sales of foreign exchange. This gap is closed by "accommodating" sales or purchases (as the case may be) of foreign exchange by the monetary authorities. But not every gap between autonomous international receipts and payments need present serious problems. In this connection, the distinction between *temporary* and *fundamental* (or persistent) balance-of-payments disequilibria is important.

In principle, temporary balance-of-payments disequilibria (deficits or surpluses) tend to last for a short period of time. Temporary disequilibria are prompted by exogenous disturbances that are of either a purely *transitory* nature (for example, a strike or crop failure) or a *reversible* nature (for example, seasonal or cyclical).

Fundamental disequilibria, on the other hand, are chronic in nature; that is, they tend to persist. The causes of fundamental disequilibria are deep-seated imbalances in the international economy.

Financing Temporary Disequilibria

The main implication of the distinction between temporary and fundamental disequilibria is this: *Temporary disequilibria can and should be financed, while fundamental disequilibria call for true adjustment.*

The argument for financing temporary disequilibria is similar to the argument presented in Section 17-3 for justifying the transactions demand for money. Neither individual economic units nor nations enjoy perfect synchronization between their streams of revenue and their streams of expenditure. To bridge temporary gaps between their streams of revenue and expenditure, economic units need money. When their revenue exceeds their expenditure, economic units let their stock of money absorb their surplus; and when their expenditure exceeds their revenue, economic units use their stock of money to finance their deficit.

Nations use their stocks of international reserves in the same way individual economic units use their stocks of money. Thus, a nation whose autonomous international payments temporarily exceed its autonomous international receipts can finance its deficit by running down its international reserves. Similarly, a nation may finance a temporary surplus merely by increasing its stock of international reserves.

We can strengthen the argument for financing temporary disequilibria by considering the welfare implications of this policy. Suppose America is an agricultural country, exporting grain, such as corn, which is harvested at only one season of the year. America's exports of corn (which are made during the harvest season only) must pay for America's imports of other commodities throughout the year. Without any financing of temporary disequilibria by America's monetary authorities, the rate of exchange would fluctuate from, say, $2 (during the harvest season), to $4 (during the nonharvest season). Financing, on the other hand, stabilizes the rate at, say, $3, and improves America's welfare.

How does financing external disequilibria improve America's welfare? Merely by effecting a better allocation of resources through time. In the absence of financing, foreign exchange is less valuable during the harvest season than during the nonharvest season. Consequently, commodities (domestic and foreign) are more plentiful and cheaper during the harvest season than during the nonharvest season. Apparently, consumer welfare would increase if America were to transfer some consumption from the harvest season (where it is plentiful and its marginal utility is low) to the nonharvest season (where it is less plentiful and its marginal utility is high). Financing accomplishes just this.

During the harvest season, America's monetary authorities buy foreign exchange and raise its price from $2 to $3. As our discussion of the partial-equilibrium model shows, the domestic prices of all commodities, domestic and foreign, rise also. As a result, America's consumers tend to consume less.

On the other hand, during the nonharvest season, America's monetary authorities sell foreign exchange and prevent its price from rising all the way to $4. Accordingly, the prices of all other commodities (domestic and foreign) remain low, and consumers consume more (compared to the case of no financing).

We therefore conclude that financing temporary external disequilibria is indeed a sound policy that tends to raise economic welfare by effecting a better allocation of resources through time.

Temporary Disequilibria and Speculation

It is interesting to note that under the ideal conditions of the preceding example, private speculation may indeed accomplish the same result as official financing.

As long as the balance on autonomous transactions follows a predictable pattern, like the one postulated above for America, private speculators will soon realize that they can make a profit by buying foreign exchange during the harvest season and selling it during the nonharvest season.

Such stabilizing speculation will tend to reduce the amplitude of exchange-rate fluctuations and improve economic welfare in the same way as official financing. In fact, stabilizing speculation reduces substantially, and in the limiting case eliminates completely, the need for official financing of temporary disequilibria.

Difficulties of the Distinction between Temporary and Fundamental Disequilibria

The rule that temporary disequilibria ought to be financed, while fundamental disequilibria call for true adjustment, is simple enough in principle. Its practical application, however, faces insurmountable difficulties. This was indeed evident in the Articles of Agreement of the International Monetary Fund (IMF) signed by the major non-Communist nations of the world at Bretton Woods, New Hampshire, in 1944.

Even though the IMF permitted countries to use exchange-rate adjustment in the case of fundamental disequilibrium, the concept of fundamental disequilibrium was never defined in the Fund Agreement. This was no accident—even though some economists feel that the main reason was the desire to minimize destabilizing speculation.

The truth of the matter is that whether an existing balance-of-payments disequilibrium is fundamental or temporary depends on future events. Economists can, of course, make a prediction as to the future course of the balance of payments, but they can never be absolutely sure that their prediction will indeed be right. In fact, different people are likely to make different predictions and thus reach different policy recommendations. But even in cases of general unanimity among forecasters, the world economy is under no obligation to follow the common forecast; it may very well prove all forecasters wrong. There are events (such as the 1973–1974 Arab oil embargo) that defy all crystal balls.

Some Risks of Temporary Financing

Because of the inherent difficulty of identifying the true nature of an existing payments imbalance, policymakers are bound to make costly mistakes in the application of economic policy. For instance, financing a "temporary" deficit that turns out to be fundamental may involve the authorities (and the economy) in huge losses. Essentially, the monetary authorities sell large amounts of their international reserves at the existing, low price only to have to buy them back later (after they realize that the deficit is fundamental and thus devalue their domestic currency) at a much higher price. The postwar era is full of such policy errors.

Similarly, financing a "temporary" surplus that turns out to be fundamental may involve the authorities in huge losses. In this case, the monetary authorities buy large amounts of foreign exchange at the current, high price only to have to sell them back at a lower price—after they revalue their domestic currency.

A Final Note

For the rest of our discussion we assume that all external disequilibria are fundamental, unless stated otherwise.

18-3   THE MEANING OF INTERNAL BALANCE: A DIGRESSION[1]

Full employment and price stability are two separate and often conflicting objectives of macroeconomic policy. The *Phillips curve* (that is, the tradeoff relationship between unemployment and inflation) is one of the most controversial concepts in economics today. Also controversial are the policy proposals that deal with the twin evils of inflation and unemployment. Under these circumstances, what meaning should we attach to the term *internal balance*? Should we take it to mean full employment or price stability? This is the major concern in this section.

We begin our discussion with the statistical findings of Phillips (1958). We then expand the *IS-LM* model of Chapter 17 to incorporate prices explicitly and talk about demand-pull and cost-push inflation. Next, we study briefly the dynamics of the labor market as well as the Friedman-Phelps thesis on the acceleration of inflation and the natural rate of unemployment. Finally, we explain the approach we plan to follow in the rest of the book.

The Phillips Curve

In a seminal paper, the late Professor A. W. Phillips of the London School of Economics reached the controversial conclusion that there exists a conflict between the goal of full employment and the goal of price stability. Using British observations for the period 1861–1957, Phillips determined a tradeoff relationship between unemployment and the percentage change in money wages. Because changes in wages usually exceed price-level changes by the rate of growth in labor productivity, it soon became apparent to economists that a similar tradeoff relationship exists between unemployment and inflation. Such a tradeoff relationship between unemployment and price-wage changes is known as the *Phillips curve*.

Figure 18-1 illustrates the Phillips curve. Along the horizontal axis we measure the rate of unemployment. Along the vertical scales we measure the annual rate of inflation (left scale) and the annual rate of change in money wages (right scale). It is assumed that the annual rate of growth in labor productivity (which accounts for the difference between the two vertical scales) is 3 percent per year.

---

[1] The reader may skip this section.

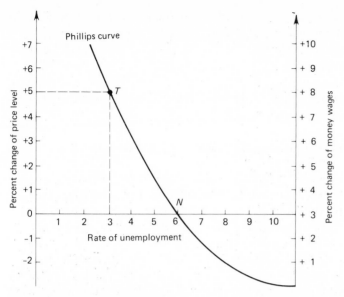

Figure 18-1 *The Phillips curve.*
Along the horizontal axis we measure the rate of unemployment. Along the vertical scales we measure the annual rate of inflation (left scale) and the annual rate of change in money wages (right scale). The Phillips curve implies a conflict between full employment and price stability. For instance, we can "buy" price stability with 6 percent unemployment (see point *N*), or we can reduce unemployment to 3 percent by allowing inflation to rise to 5 percent (see point *T*).

If they were free in their choices, policymakers would certainly prefer full employment with price stability. The Phillips curve, however, implies that high levels of employment coincide with high rates of inflation and that low rates of inflation coincide with high rates of unemployment. Accordingly, the Phillips curve presents policymakers with a powerful dilemma: They must choose between high rates of inflation and high rates of unemployment.

During the 1960s the Phillips curve was viewed as an important relationship. The reason is simple: At that time, the Phillips curve seemed to fit the data well. (Phillips presented his statistical results without any supporting theoretical "explanation.") Nevertheless, during the 1970s high rates of inflation coexisted with high rates of unemployment—a phenomenon that came to be known as *stagflation.* Now stagflation is inconsistent with a stable Phillips curve. As a consequence, economists no longer believe that the original Phillips curve represents a stable relationship. But whether the tradeoff no longer exists is still a highly controversial issue.

Aggregate Demand and Aggregate Supply

It is a fundamental principle of economics that prices are determined jointly by supply and demand. The general price level is determined by aggregate demand and aggregate supply. Accordingly, before we proceed any further with the tradeoff relationship between unemployment and inflation, we must discuss the concepts of aggregate demand and aggregate supply.

In the present context, the term *aggregate demand* refers to a schedule that shows the volumes of real output which the economy (for example, consumers, producers, and government) is willing to purchase at alternative price levels. Similarly, *aggregate supply* is a schedule that shows the volumes of real output which the producers are willing to supply at alternative price levels. As with partial-equilibrium analysis, the equilibrium levels of real output and prices are determined by the intersection of the aggregate demand schedule and the aggregate supply schedule.

In our discussion of the *IS-LM* model in Chapter 17, we assumed that prices were given. In other words, we assumed that the aggregate supply schedule was infinitely elastic at the existing prices (at least up to the point of full employment). The *IS-LM* apparatus merely determined that volume of real output the economy demanded at the given price level.

A more realistic aggregate supply schedule must take into account the fact that prices begin to rise long before the economy reaches full employment. This is illustrated by the aggregate supply schedule of Figure 18-2. In the presence of a substantial amount of unemployment, the economy can increase output without raising prices (see horizontal region *DH*). With relatively little unemployment, the economy can increase output but at the cost of higher

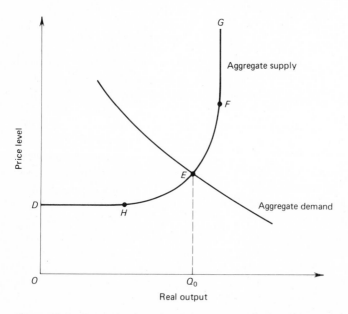

Figure 18-2 *Determination of real output and price level by aggregate supply and aggregate demand.*
Macroeconomic equilibrium occurs at the intersection of the upward-sloping aggregate supply schedule and the downward-sloping aggregate demand schedule, as illustrated by point *E*. Thus, the equilibrium level of real income is Q_0, and the equilibrium price level is Q_0E.

prices (see upward-sloping region *HF*). Finally, when operating at full employment, the economy has no ability to increase output; and increases in aggregate demand result mainly in higher prices (see vertical region *FG*).

The aggregate demand schedule slopes downward, as shown in Figure 18-2. The reason is simple. Return to the *IS-LM* model of Chapter 17, which gives (at the intersection of the *IS* and *LM* curves) the volume of aggregate demand *at the given prices*. What happens to aggregate demand as prices rise? An increase in the general level of prices with the nominal quantity of money remaining constant is equivalent to a reduction in the real supply of money (that is, the stock of money divided by the price level). This causes the *LM* curve to shift to the left (since the *LM* curve is drawn on the assumption that the real quantity of money is given). (Alternatively, we can justify the leftward shift of the *LM* curve merely by noting that higher prices increase the transactions demand for money.) As the *LM* curve shifts to the left, the rate of interest rises and the volume of aggregate demand falls.

There is an additional channel through which an increase in the price level may reduce aggregate demand: the *wealth effect*. As prices rise, the value of cash balances and accumulated government bonds tends to shrink. Private economic units may therefore attempt to restore their accumulated wealth to its original level by reducing their expenditure on goods and services. We ignore the wealth effect mainly because of its transitory nature (it lasts only until the wealth is restored to its initial value) and the fact that its effect on aggregate spending depends on price expectations.

Macroeconomic equilibrium occurs at the intersection of the aggregate supply schedule and the aggregate demand schedule. This is shown by point E in Figure 18-2. Thus, the equilibrium level of income is OQ_0, and the equilibrium-price level is Q_0E.

Demand-Pull versus Cost-Push Inflation

As we have just seen, the price level (as well as real output) is determined by aggregate supply and aggregate demand. Accordingly, an increase in the price level (inflation) may reflect either a rightward shift in the aggregate demand schedule (*demand-pull inflation*) or a leftward (or upward) shift in the aggregate supply schedule (*cost-push inflation*).

Demand-pull inflation may be due to either autonomous increases in aggregate spending (for example, an investment boom) or deliberate expansionary monetary and fiscal policies. Cost-push inflation, on the other hand, may be due to either higher money wages prompted by labor union pressure in a highly unionized economy (or even a reduction in the supply of labor due to an increased desire for leisure) or increases in prices of internationally traded goods (such as crude oil in the 1970s).

Both demand-pull and cost-push inflation tend to raise prices. However, while demand-pull inflation raises real output as well, cost-push inflation causes production and real output to fall. This is illustrated in Figure 18-3. Equilibrium occurs initially at E_0 (as in Figure 18-2), where the price level is P_0 and real out-

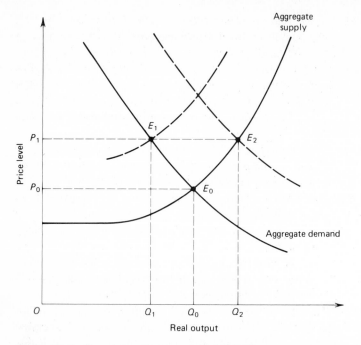

Figure 18-3 *Demand-pull and cost-push inflation.*
Equilibrium occurs initially at E_0. As the demand schedule shifts to the right (demand-pull inflation), equilibrium shifts to E_2; the price level increases to P_1, and output increases to Q_2. Alternatively, as the supply schedule shifts to the left (cost-push inflation), equilibrium moves to E_1; the price level increases again to P_1, but output falls to Q_1.

put is Q_0. When the demand schedule shifts to the right (demand-pull inflation), as indicated by the broken demand schedule, equilibrium moves to E_2; the price level increases to P_1, and output *increases* to Q_2. Alternatively, when the supply curve shifts to the left (cost-push inflation), as shown by the broken supply schedule, equilibrium moves to E_1; the price level increases again to P_1, but output *falls* to Q_1.

Demand-pull inflation seems consistent with the Phillips curve hypothesis: Demand-pull inflation leads to higher prices and higher output and employment, which is the same thing as higher prices and lower employment.

However, demand-pull inflation is not the same thing as the Phillips curve. The reason is simple: The Phillips curve postulates a relationship between the *rate* of inflation and unemployment (or real output), whereas demand-pull inflation, which causes the economy to move along the aggregate supply curve, points to a relationship between the *price level* and real output (as depicted by the aggregate supply schedule).

For instance, in the example of Figure 18-3, as the aggregate demand schedule shifts to the right, equilibrium shifts from E_0 to E_2. The price level increases from P_0 to P_1, as output expands from Q_0 to Q_2 (and the rate of unemployment falls). The rate of inflation is, of course, the percentage rise in the price level, that is, $(P_1 - P_0)/P_0$. Once the economy reaches E_2, however, the rate of inflation drops to zero, even though the price level remains at the higher level, P_1. For prices to continue rising at the initial *rate* of inflation, *it is necessary for the aggregate demand to shift continuously to the right*. But then, of course, the level of output may also continue to expand (and unemployment may continue to fall) as the economy moves along the aggregate supply schedule (unless the aggregate supply schedule is vertical, which presumably occurs at full employment).

Cost-push inflation, on the other hand, is totally inconsistent with the Phillips curve. Indeed, cost-push inflation seems consistent with stagflation. However, it is not the same thing as stagflation. Stagflation means high *inflation* (that is, rate of change in prices) and high unemployment, while cost-push inflation means high *prices* and high unemployment.

Finally, note that in practice demand-pull inflation becomes so intertwined with cost-push inflation that it is extremely difficult to tell them apart. For instance, suppose the authorities pursue an expansionary monetary policy in order to reduce unemployment. This policy causes a rightward shift in the aggregate demand schedule (demand-pull inflation). The rise in the cost of living may prompt labor unions to demand higher money wages. Assuming that the labor unions are successful in their demands, the aggregate supply schedule also shifts upward and to the left, raising prices even further, but also raising unemployment. If the authorities react by expanding the money supply further in the hope of achieving the elusive lower unemployment rate, the economy may eventually run into a wage-price spiral.

We must conclude that although it does shed some light on the problem of inflation and the Phillips curve, our model of demand-pull and cost-push inflation is inadequate. The reason is simple: The model of demand-pull and cost-push inflation is static, while the phenomenon of inflation is dynamic. We must not expect a static model to explain fully a truly dynamic phenomenon.

The Phillips Curve and the Labor Market

One possible explanation of the tradeoff relationship between unemployment and inflation runs in terms of the dynamics of the labor market.

On the one hand, there are always unemployed workers searching for jobs. These workers are unemployed either because they happen to be entering the market for the first time and are still searching for the most profitable employment (for example, people leaving school or the military) or because they are between jobs. Workers between jobs become unemployed either voluntarily (when they quit their jobs to search for better ones) or involuntarily (when they are fired or laid off temporarily because of sluggish demand).

On the other hand, there are always some vacancies, even during periods of recession. These vacancies arise as workers retire, die, or voluntarily quit. As a result, employers are always in the process of searching for qualified workers to fill their vacancies.

It is usually estimated that in a "normal" year about one-fourth of the labor force begins the process of search for new jobs, a process that lasts for approximately 10 weeks. This means that in a "normal" year, the rate of unemployment is about 5 percent:

$$\text{Rate of unemployment} = \frac{\text{number of workweeks lost to unemployment}}{\text{potential number of workweeks}}$$

$$= \frac{1/4 \text{ of labor force} \times 10 \text{ weeks}}{\text{labor force} \times 52 \text{ weeks}} = \frac{(1/4) \times 10}{52} = 0.048$$

In general, the rate of unemployment is given by the formula:

$$\text{Rate of employment} = (\text{search flow}) \times (\text{search duration})$$

where search flow = percentage of labor force that begins the process of search during a year

search duration = fraction of the year spent on search on the average

The number of workers searching for new jobs need not be equal to the number of vacancies. (In fact, "full employment" is often defined as the state in which the number of unemployed workers equals the number of vacancies, with the resultant unemployment called *frictional*.) During periods of recession, the number of unemployed workers tends to be higher than the number of available vacancies. On the other hand, during periods of prosperity, the number of vacancies exceeds the number of unemployed workers.

During periods of prosperity, when aggregate demand is very strong, producers increase production and need more workers. Vacancies rise, and it becomes more difficult for producers to find qualified workers. Producers tend to offer higher wages as the process of search becomes progressively more expensive. Thus, wages tend to rise as the unemployment rate drops.

On the other hand, during periods of recession, when aggregate demand is sluggish, employers have no reason to offer higher wages. In addition, the labor unions themselves become more preoccupied with job security than with higher wages.

We therefore conclude that the dynamics of the labor market can provide a reasonable explanation of the tradeoff relationship between unemployment and inflation. Unfortunately, however, this theory cannot explain the phenomenon of stagflation, which many industrial nations experienced in the 1970s.

The Accelerationists

Headed by Friedman and Phelps, the *accelerationists* are a group of economists who claim that the Phillips curve is a short-run phenomenon that is fundamentally based on the illusion of *unanticipated* inflation. In the long run, this thesis goes, the Phillips curve is *vertical* at some unemployment rate called the *natural rate of unemployment*. Thus, in the long run there can be no tradeoff between unemployment and inflation, because from experience people will learn to anticipate inflation and incorporate it into their decisions. You just cannot fool all the people all the time.

Consider Figure 18-4, which illustrates the Friedman-Phelps argument. The Friedman-Phelps long-run Phillips curve is the vertical line at the natural rate of unemployment of, say, 6 percent. Assume that the economy has remained at point T (where inflation is zero and unemployment is 6 percent) for a long time. As a result, economic units have come to expect stable prices.

Suppose now that policy makers attempt to lower unemployment to 4 percent by increasing the money supply. As aggregate demand increases, producers offer higher money wages in order to hire more workers. (Recall that the labor market is initially in equilibrium at point T.) Since the workers anticipate stable prices (that is, zero inflation), they take the higher money wages to mean higher real wages. Accordingly, in the short run unemployment falls to 4 percent. At the same time, however, inflation rises to 3 percent, as the producers pass the higher costs to the consumers. The economy moves temporarily along the short-run Phillips curve, PC_0, from T to R.

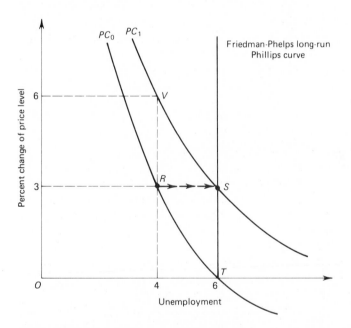

Figure 18-4 *The acceleration of inflation.*
From an initial position of stable prices at T, the authorities increase the money supply in order to reduce unemployment from 6 to 4 percent. In the short run, unemployment does indeed fall to 4 percent and inflation rises to 3 percent; that is, the economy moves along the short-run Phillips curve, PC_0, from T to R. When the workers perceive the higher rate of inflation, they demand higher money wages to compensate for the increase in their cost of living. The Phillips curve shifts upward and to the right, as shown by PC_1 (which is drawn on the assumption that the rate of inflation is 3 percent). Thus, the system returns to point S. To keep unemployment at 4 percent, the authorities must constantly stimulate the economy and accelerate the rate of inflation.

Can the economy remain at point R permanently? No. In the first place, the short-run Phillips curve, PC_0, is drawn on the assumption that the rate of inflation will continue to remain zero. But now inflation runs at 3 percent. Sooner or later, the workers will come to anticipate the higher rate of inflation. They will soon realize that they were actually fooled by the higher money wages since their real wages actually remained the same. To continue offering their services and maintain the unemployment rate at 4 percent, workers will insist that their money wages increase faster by the amount of inflation. This means that the Phillips curve shifts upward and to the right, as shown by curve PC_1 (which is drawn on the assumption that the rate of inflation is 3 percent).

If the authorities do not provide additional stimulus to aggregate demand and producers do not raise the money wages by 3 percent on the average, the economy will slide back to point S along the long-run Phillips curve. To maintain unemployment at 4 percent permanently, the authorities must constantly stimulate the economy by means of fiscal and monetary policy, causing prices and wages to rise at an ever-increasing rate.

The analysis is symmetrical for periods of falling prices: Workers anticipate the falling prices and modify their wage demands accordingly.

The Friedman-Phelps analysis leads to the conclusion that the economy can operate at a *constant* rate of inflation (that is, a rate which neither accelerates or decelerates) only if the unemployment rate coincides with the natural rate—that is, only if the economy operates along the long-run vertical Phillips curve. Accordingly, even though there is a temporary tradeoff between unemployment and inflation, there is no such thing as a permanent tradeoff.

It is now safe to say that economists no longer believe that the initial Phillips curve represents a stable relationship. Economists no longer dispute the fact that the Phillips curve shifts through time. Neither do economists dispute the hypothesis that inflationary expectations are important. But not all economists believe that the long-run Phillips curve is vertical. Of course, the dispute concerning the shape of the long-run Phillips curve is at bottom an empirical issue. For this reason, the dispute cannot be resolved by means of theoretical reasoning. Patient econometric work is of paramount importance for this purpose. Unfortunately, not all the data are available yet.

Conclusion

Economists do not have all the answers to the inflation-unemployment dilemma. There is still a basic disagreement as to whether a tradeoff relationship actually exists between inflation and unemployment. For this reason, a great deal of controversy still surrounds the policy proposals that deal with these twin evils. Because of its significance, this issue will continue to be debated in the professional journals until a consensus is reached. In the meantime, however, we do face a difficulty: How should we proceed?

Because a textbook is not a place to settle a controversial issue, we shall largely ignore it in our future discussion. [The interested reader may benefit from Meade (1978).] For the most part, we shall develop our analysis within the context of the extreme Keynesian assumption of fixed prices (that is, infinitely elastic aggregate supply schedule). We do this for convenience only. Our conclusions, with only slight modification, hold even under the more general assumption of an upward-sloping aggregate supply schedule (see Figures 18-2 and 18-3).

Indeed, the above approach is clearly consistent with the Friedman-Phelps thesis, namely, the proposition that the Phillips curve is vertical at the natural rate of unemployment. We may assume that the economy has experienced stable prices for an extended period of time so that there is no general expectation of future inflation (or deflation). The authorities may then interpret the natural rate of unemployment to mean "full employment." In this case, the economy can reach "full employment" without inflation.

We can follow the same approach even in cases in which we postulate a stable Phillips curve that slopes downward. Again, the authorities may define full employment to coincide with the rate of unemployment at which the Phillips curve crosses the horizontal axis; and in the absence of inflationary expectations, they may pursue policies to achieve that rate.

Occasionally, we may refer to the possibility that the goal of the authorities is to reach some point on a "stable" Phillips curve (that is, the least undesirable combination of inflation and unemployment). In such cases, we shall indicate how to modify our analysis in order to incorporate the phenomenon of inflation.

18-4 POLICY MIX FOR INTERNAL AND EXTERNAL BALANCE

We now turn to the interesting problem of how to apply two mutually independent and effective instruments (government spending and exchange-rate adjustments) to simultaneously achieve external and internal balance.

Some Simplifying Assumptions

To keep our present discussion within manageable proportions, it is convenient to adopt several simplifying assumptions. These are summarized at the start.

We intend to develop our present analysis within the context of the fixed-price model of Chapter 16, in which each nation specializes completely in the production of its exportables. Actually, we shall concentrate on the problems faced by a single open economy, ignoring foreign repercussion.

We shall assume that the monetary authorities keep the domestic interest rate constant by maintaining the supply of money and credit infinitely elastic at the existing rate of interest. This policy is often referred to as the "Keynesian neutral monetary policy." We shall return in Chapter 20 to the "orthodox neutral monetary policy," according to which the monetary authorities hold constant the nominal supply of money.

Also for our present discussion, we shall ignore the capital account of the balance of payments. (The capital account is introduced in Chapter 20.) Accordingly, external balance will correspond to balance-of-*trade* equilibrium.

To be sure, a country may actually aim at either a surplus or deficit in its balance of trade. In that case, external balance should refer to the desired balance-of-trade surplus (or deficit). However, there is no qualitative difference in policy making between the case of aiming at a balance-of-trade surplus and the case of aiming at a zero balance. This becomes clear from our discussion below (see Figure 18-6).

Further, we shall assume that the economy starts from a position in which there exists no expectation of future inflation or deflation and that the economy is able to reach full employment with price stability. We shall return briefly to the Phillips curve modification in Section 18-5.

The Policy Instruments and Their Effects

In our model, we have *two* targets: internal balance and external balance. According to Tinbergen's rule, to achieve these two targets simultaneously we need *two* instruments. For our present discussion, we choose two standard instruments: government spending (G) and the rate of exchange (R). As we already know, government spending represents an expenditure-adjusting policy, while the rate of exchange represents an expenditure-switching policy.

Our discussion in Chapter 16 shows clearly that *each of our two instruments affects both of our targets.* In other words, a change in government spending affects the level of national income *and* the balance of trade. Similarly, a change in the rate of exchange affects the level of national income *and* the balance of trade.

Drawing on the analysis of Chapter 16, we can summarize the effects of changes in government spending and the rate of exchange on internal and external balance as follows:

1 An increase in government spending raises (through the multiplier) national income and employment and worsens the balance of trade (because of the induced increase in imports). The effects for a decrease in government spending are symmetrical.

2 A *devaluation* (that is, an increase in the rate of exchange) improves the balance of trade and raises the level of national income and employment. The effects of a reduction in the rate of exchange (*revaluation*) are symmetrical.

Figure 18-5, which is similar to Figure 16.4, panel (b), and Figure 16-5, reviews briefly the effects of changes in government spending and the rate of exchange. Equilibrium occurs initially at the intersection (E_0) of the S-I and X-M schedules. National income is Y_0, and the balance of trade is in deficit, as indicated by vertical distance $E_0 Y_0$.

An increase in government spending (that is, autonomous expenditure) causes the S-I schedule to shift downward, as shown by the broken line through E_1. Equilibrium shifts to E_1. National income increases to Y_1, and the balance-of-trade deficit worsens to $E_1 Y_1$.

Alternatively, a devaluation causes the X-M schedule to shift upward, as shown by the broken line through E_2. Equilibrium shifts to E_2. National income increases again to Y_1, but the balance-of-trade deficit shrinks to $E_2 Y_1$.

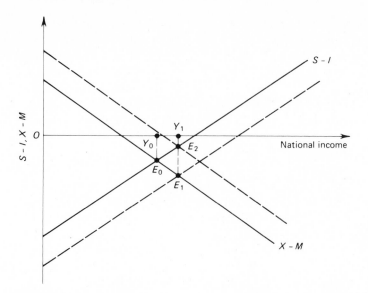

Figure 18-5 *The effects of changes in government spending and the rate of exchange.*
Starting from an initial equilibrium at E_0, an increase in government spending shifts the *S-I* schedule downward (see broken line through E_1) causing national income to increase to Y_1 and the balance-of-trade deficit to worsen to E_1Y_1. Alternatively, a devaluation shifts the *X-M* schedule upward (see broken line through E_2), causing national income to increase to Y_1 and the deficit to fall to E_2Y_1.

It is evident from Figure 18-5 that while the two instruments (government spending and the rate of exchange) have similar effects on the level of national income, they have diametrically opposite effects on the balance of trade. As we shall see below, it is this basic difference that makes it possible for us to combine these two instruments to achieve simultaneously internal and external balance.

Attaining Internal and External Balance

Consider Figure 18-6, which is similar to Figure 18-5. Equilibrium occurs initially at E, that is, the point of intersection between the *S-I* and the *X-M* schedules. We are now interested in the policy mix (that is, the right combination of government spending and the rate of exchange) that can restore internal and external balance. But before we can identify such a policy mix, we must identify on our diagram internal and external balance.

External balance prevails when the balance of trade is zero. This occurs only along the "heavy" horizontal axis. (If a nonzero balance happened to be the target, external balance would occur along a horizontal line whose height would be determined by the size of the desired deficit or surplus.) Accordingly, external balance will prevail if we somehow choose a combination of government spending and rate of exchange such that the corresponding *S-I* and *X-M* schedules intersect along the horizontal axis. Since there is an infinite number

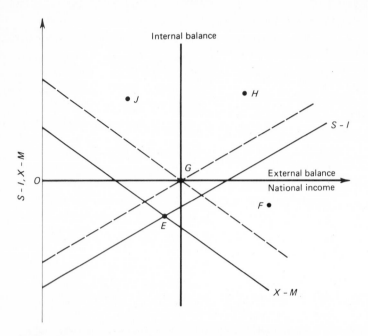

Figure 18-6 *Policies for internal and external balance.*
External balance prevails along the "heavy" horizontal axis. Assuming that *OG* is the full-employment income, internal balance prevails along the "heavy" vertical line through *G*. Internal and external balance prevail simultaneously at point *G* only. To achieve general balance, the authorities must choose that policy mix that causes the *S-I* and *X-M* schedules to pass through point *G*, as illustrated by the broken schedules.

of points along the horizontal axis, it must be evident that *there must also be an infinite number of combinations of levels of government spending and rates of exchange that can bring about external balance.*

Assume now that full employment prevails when national income is *OG*. This means that internal balance will prevail if we somehow choose a combination of government spending and exchange rate such that the corresponding *S-I* and *X-M* schedules intersect along the "heavy" vertical line through *G*. Again, since there is an infinite number of points along this vertical line through *G*, *there must also be an infinite number of combinations of levels of government spending and rates of exchange that are consistent with internal balance.*

Can internal and external balance coexist? How can they be achieved simultaneously? Along the horizontal axis, the economy enjoys external balance; and along the vertical line through *G*, the economy enjoys internal balance. Apparently, internal and external balance cannot occur simultaneously unless the final equilibrium point (that is, the intersection of the *S-I* and *X-M* schedules) lies on both the horizontal axis and the vertical line through *G*. This occurs only at the singular point *G*.

Figure 18-6 illustrates vividly Tinbergen's rule: In general, the economy cannot attain internal and external balance simultaneously by using only one of the two instruments. For instance, changes in government spending shift the *S-I* schedule only and cause the final equilibrium point to travel along the solid *X-M* schedule. Similarly, exchange-rate adjustments shift the *X-M* schedule only and cause the final equilibrium point to travel along the solid *S-I* schedule. To achieve internal and external balance simultaneously, the economy must use both instruments. In particular, the economy must choose that policy mix which causes the *S-I* and *X-M* schedules to pass through point *G*, as illustrated in Figure 18-6 by the broken schedules.

For instance, starting from an initial equilibrium position at *E*, the correct policy is to lower government spending (to shift the *S-I* schedule upward) and raise the rate of exchange, that is, devalue the domestic currency (to shift the *X-M* schedule upward). What policy mixes can restore external and internal balance when the economy starts from an initial equilibrium position at points *F*, *H*, or *J*?

The State of the Economy and Policy Assignment

We often hear of the following *common-sense rule for economic policy:* In the presence of unemployment, increase government spending (or reduce taxes); and in the presence of inflationary pressure, reduce government spending (or raise taxes). Similarly, in the presence of a balance-of-payments deficit, raise the rate of exchange (that is, devalue the domestic currency); and in the presence of a balance-of-payments surplus, lower the rate of exchange (that is, revalue the domestic currency). What does our theory have to say about this common-sense rule? Simply this: It does not always work!

Consider Figure 18-7. Panel (*a*) shows that the vertical line through *G* (internal balance) and the horizontal axis (external balance) divide the whole diagram into four *zones* of economic unhappiness, as follows:

Zone I: When the *S-I* and *X-M* schedules intersect in this zone, as illustrated by point *J*, the economy suffers from *unemployment*, while the balance of trade is in *surplus*.

Zone II: When the *S-I* and *X-M* schedules intersect in this zone, as illustrated by point *H*, the economy suffers from *potential inflationary* pressure, while the balance of trade is in *surplus*.

Zone III: When the *S-I* and *X-M* schedules intersect in this zone, as illustrated by point *F*, the economy suffers from potential *inflationary pressure*, while the balance of trade is in *deficit*.

Zone IV: When the *S-I* and *X-M* schedules intersect in this zone, as illustrated by point *E*, the economy suffers from *unemployment*, while the balance of trade is in *deficit*.

Note carefully that the statistical evidence on employment and balance of payments identifies the zone in which the economy happens to be. The common-sense rule for economic policy is based on the presumption that such knowledge is sufficient for the formulation of the correct economic policy. Unfortunately, this is not the case.

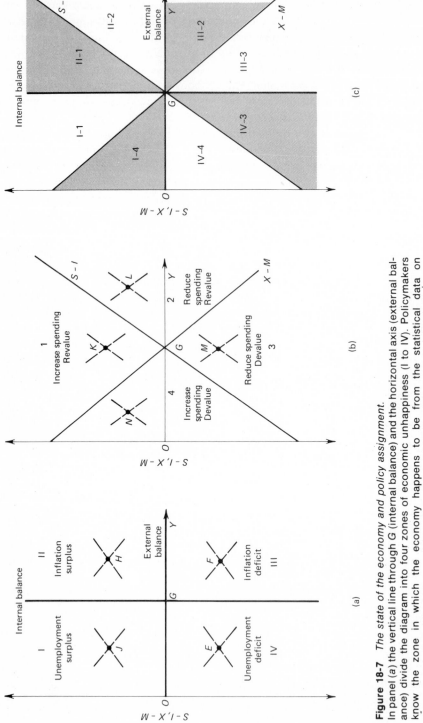

Figure 18-7 *The state of the economy and policy assignment.*
In panel (*a*) the vertical line through *G* (internal balance) and the horizontal axis (external balance) divide the diagram into four zones of economic unhappiness (I to IV). Policymakers know the zone in which the economy happens to be from the statistical data on unemployment and the balance of payments. In panel (*b*) the *S*-*I* and *X*-*M* schedules, drawn through *G* for the optimal policy mix, divide the diagram into four policy regions (1 to 4). To formulate the correct policy mix, the policy makers must know the exact policy region the economy is in, but unfortunately they do not. The shaded areas in panel (*c*) indicate conflicts between the common-sense rule and the correct policy mix.

Turn now to panel (*b*). In this panel, we have drawn the *S-I* and *X-M* schedules through the general balance point, *G. These schedules can prevail only when the authorities actually pursue the "optimal" policy mix.* Of course, the optimal policy mix is not known to the authorities and, therefore, the precise position and shape of these auxiliary *S-I* and *X-M* schedules cannot be known in advance. Nevertheless, this information is of paramount importance to the authorities in their search for the optimal policy mix!

In particular, the "auxiliary" *S-I* and *X-M* schedules divide the entire diagram in panel (*b*) into four *policy regions*, as follows:

Policy region 1: When the *actual S-I* and *X-M* schedules intersect in this region, as illustrated by point *K*, the correct policy is to *increase government spending* (in order to shift downward the *S-I* schedule) and *revalue* the domestic currency (in order to shift downward the *X-M* schedule).

Policy region 2: When the *actual S-I* and *X-M* schedules intersect in this region, as illustrated by point *L*, the correct policy is to *reduce government spending* (in order to shift upward the *S-I* schedule) and *revalue* the domestic currency (in order to shift downward the *X-M* schedule).

Policy region 3: When the *actual S-I* and *X-M* schedules intersect in this region, as illustrated by point *M*, the correct policy is to *reduce government spending* (in order to shift upward the *S-I* schedule) and *devalue* the domestic currency (in order to shift upward the *X-M* schedule).

Policy region 4: When the *actual S-I* and *X-M* schedules intersect in this region, as illustrated by point *N*, the correct policy is to *increase government spending* (in order to shift downward the *S-I* schedule) and *devalue* the domestic currency (in order to shift upward the *X-M* schedule).

Evidently, to formulate the correct policy mix, the policy makers must know the policy region in which the economy happens to be. Unfortunately, such information is not readily available; and the policy makers often rely on the insufficient information contained in the statistical data on unemployment and the balance of payments, which can only determine the zone [see panel (*a*)] the economy is in.

To appreciate the difficulty involved, turn to panel (*c*), which brings together the information given in panels (*a*) and (*b*). The four zones of economic unhappiness overlap with the four policy regions to produce eight areas. Note carefully that the common-sense rule is the wrong medicine in the four shaded areas.

In shaded area I-4 (that is, zone I and policy region 4), the correct policy is to increase spending and *devalue* the domestic currency. But because of the balance-of-trade surplus, the "common-sense" rule calls for a *revaluation* of the domestic currency.

Similarly, in shaded area II-1 (that is, zone II and policy region 1), the correct policy is to *increase government spending* and revalue the domestic currency. However, the "common-sense" rule calls for a *reduction in government spending* because of the existing inflationary pressure.

In shaded area III-2 (that is, zone III and policy region 2), the correct policy is to reduce government spending and *revalue* the domestic currency. However, the "common-sense" rule calls for a *devaluation* of the domestic currency because of the existing balance-of-trade deficit.

Finally, in shaded area IV-3 (that is, zone IV and policy region 3) the correct policy is to *reduce government spending* and devalue the domestic currency. However, the "common-sense" rule calls for an *increase in government spending* because of the existing unemployment. Apparently, in the present case, devaluation in itself provides more than enough stimulation for attainment of internal balance, and fiscal restraint is necessary to counteract it.

It is now apparent that common sense and intuition may lead the system astray. Because the zones of economic unhappiness do not coincide with the policy regions, mistakes are unavoidable. The various conflicts between the common-sense rule and the correct policy mix are the main source of problems and errors of economic policy. When one instrument is substantially out of line, the natural indications for the other may be quite misleading.

A Practical Rule for Policy Making

Return again to Figure 18-7, panel (*c*), and observe carefully that the common-sense directive for at least one of the two instruments is always in the right direction. In other words, *there is always at least one instrument that brings the economy closer to both internal and external balance.* The correct policy, then, is to use that instrument which helps both targets. On this showing, the recommended policy for each of the four zones of economic unhappiness is as follows:

Zone I: In the presence of *unemployment* and a balance-of-trade *surplus*, the authorities should *always increase government spending* (or reduce taxes). The direction of exchange-rate adjustment is ambiguous.

Zone II: In the presence of *inflationary pressures* and a balance-of-trade *surplus*, the authorities should *always revalue their currency*. The direction of change for government spending or taxes is ambiguous.

Zone III: In the presence of *inflationary pressures* and a balance-of-trade *deficit*, the authorities should *always reduce government spending* (or raise taxes). The direction of change for the rate of exchange is ambiguous.

Zone IV: In the presence of *unemployment* and a balance-of-trade *deficit*, the authorities should *always devalue their currency*. The direction of change for government spending is ambiguous.

We can summarize the above results as follows:

State of economy	Fiscal policy	Exchange-rate policy
Unemployment and surplus	Expansionary	?
Inflation and surplus	?	Revaluation
Inflation and deficit	Contractionary	?
Unemployment and deficit	?	Devaluation

In conclusion, note that the above "practical rule" will not usually attain the target. However, it will always bring the economy closer to the target (internal and external balance). In the meantime, the authorities can wait to see in which direction the target will be missed before using the second instrument.

18-5 THE PHILLIPS CURVE IN THE OPEN ECONOMY[2]

So far we have largely ignored the possible tradeoff relationship between unemployment and inflation. But suppose our open economy operates along a stable downward-sloping Phillips curve. How can the authorities use fiscal policy and exchange-rate adjustment to achieve internal and external balance?

One ideal approach would be to recognize explicitly three targets—external balance, full employment, and price stability—and then seek three policy instruments (recall Tinbergen's rule) to achieve the three targets. This is the approach recommended by Meade (1978). In particular, Meade refers to the following three instruments:

1 Fiscal and monetary policy to control aggregate demand (that is, "to prevent excessive inflations or deflations of total money incomes")

2 Modified wage-fixing institutions to control money-wage rates

3 Exchange-rate policy, including exchange control, plus commercial policy to maintain external balance

Meade's proposal, or some other similar proposal, can potentially achieve all three targets simultaneously but *only if the three targets are mutually independent. To the extent that the open economy operates along a stable Phillips curve, inflation and unemployment cannot be considered independent targets.*

The policy makers can, of course, choose one or another point on the Phillips curve on the basis of a social indifference map. Once the policy makers make this choice, however, the selected combination of inflation and unemployment becomes a single target, which we may call "internal balance." The object of economic policy then becomes again the achievement of "internal" and "external" balance. Under these circumstances, the analysis of Section 18-4 can still be applied with only one minor modification:

Starting from a position of general balance (that is, after attaining internal and external balance along the lines of Section 18-4), *the authorities must allow their currency to continuously depreciate at the same rate at which domestic inflation exceeds world inflation. Should the rate of world inflation be higher than the rate of domestic inflation, the authorities must allow their currency to appreciate at the same rate at which world inflation exceeds domestic inflation. If the rate of domestic inflation is equal to the rate of inflation in the rest of the world, no modification is necessary to the analysis of Section 18-4.*

[2]The reader may skip this section.

The preceding conclusion must be clear from our discussion of the purchasing-power-parity theory in Section 15-8.

18-6 SUMMARY

1   Full employment (internal balance) and balance-of-payments equilibrium (external balance) are policy objectives (or targets) that must be pursued by means of deliberate economic policy measures.

2   The policy approach takes the targets as given and solves for the required values of the instruments, such as the money supply, government spending, and taxes.

3   To achieve one target, we need an effective instrument. To achieve *n* independent targets, we need at least *n* independent and effective instruments (Tinbergen's rule).

4   In principle, external disequilibria are classified into temporary (lasting for a short time) and fundamental (lasting for a long time). In practice, predicting the nature of an existing disequilibrium is inherently difficult.

5   Fundamental disequilibria require true adjustment. Temporary disequilibria should be financed, however, in order to achieve a better allocation of resources through time and to raise welfare. Such financing can be done by either the monetary authorities or private speculators.

6   The highly controversial tradeoff relationship between unemployment and inflation is known as the *Phillips curve*. Controversy also surrounds the policy proposals that deal with inflation and unemployment.

7   The static model of demand-pull and cost-push inflation sheds very little light on the dynamic problem of inflation and the Phillips curve.

8   The dynamics of the labor market can provide a reasonable explanation of the tradeoff relationship between unemployment and inflation but cannot explain the phenomenon of stagflation.

9   The *accelerationists* claim that the Phillips curve is a short-run phenomenon based on the illusion of *unanticipated* inflation. In the long run, they assert, the Phillips curve is vertical at the natural rate of unemployment, as people learn to anticipate inflation and incorporate it into their decisions. To maintain unemployment below the natural rate, the authorities must constantly stimulate the economy and accelerate the rate of inflation.

10   In the context of international economic policy, *internal balance* may mean either the rate of unemployment (natural or not) at zero inflation or some combination of unemployment and inflation on a "stable" Phillips curve.

11   In a fixed-price model, full employment with price stability (internal balance) and balance-of-trade equilibrium (external balance) can be achieved simultaneously by a combination of expenditure-adjusting and expenditure-switching policies.

12   The common-sense rule for policy-making—namely, that the authorities should increase (decrease) government spending in the presence of unemployment (inflation) and devalue (revalue) in the presence of an external deficit (surplus)—does not always work.

13   There is always one instrument that brings the economy closer to both internal and external balance. A practical rule is to use first that instrument

which helps both targets, and then wait to see the direction the economy will take before using the second instrument.

14 In a Phillips curve world, the authorities can pursue a combination of inflation and unemployment (internal balance) along with external balance. Once the economy reaches general balance (through the application of expenditure-adjusting and expenditure-switching policies), the authorities must allow the rate of exchange to continuously change by the difference between the domestic and world rates of inflation.

SUGGESTED READING

Chacholiades, M. (1978). *International Monetary Theory and Policy*. McGraw-Hill Book Company, New York, chap. 13.

Friedman, M. (1968). "The Role of Monetary Policy." *American Economic Review* (March), pp. 1–17.

———— (1977). "Inflation and Unemployment." *Journal of Political Economy* (June), pp. 451–472. Nobel lecture.

Johnson, H. G. (1958). *International Trade and Economic Growth: Studies in Pure Theory*. George Allen & Unwin, Ltd., London, chap. 6. Reprinted in R. E. Caves and H. G. Johnson (eds.), AEA *Readings in International Economics*. Richard D. Irwin, Inc., Homewood, Ill., 1968.

Meade, J. E. (1951). *The Theory of International Economic Policy, vol. I, The Balance of payments*. Oxford University Press, London, parts 3 and 4.

———— (1978). "The Meaning of 'Internal Balance.'" *Economic Journal* (September), pp. 423–435. Nobel lecture.

Phillips, A. W. (1958). "The Relation between Unemployment and the Rate of Change of Money Wage Rates in the United Kingdom, 1861–1957." *Economica*, N.S. (November), pp. 283–299.

Swan, T. W. (1955). *Longer-Run Problems of the Balance of Payments*. Paper presented to Section G of the Congress of the Australian and New Zealand Association for the Advancement of Science, Melbourne. Reprinted in R. E. Caves and H. G. Johnson (eds.), AEA *Readings in International Economics*. Richard D. Irwin, Inc., Homewood, Ill., 1968.

Tinbergen, J. (1952). *On the Theory of Economic Policy*. North-Holland Publishing Company, Amsterdam.

Chapter Nineteen

Direct Controls[1]

In the preceding chapter, we saw how expenditure-adjusting policies may be combined with expenditure-switching policies to restore and preserve internal and external balance. We illustrated these two types of policies by means of changes in government spending (expenditure-adjusting) and exchange-rate adjustments (expenditure-switching).

Exchange-rate adjustments are *general* switching policies that influence the balance of payments indirectly, that is, through their effects on national income and the price mechanism. Their primary aim is to divert (or switch) expenditure, *both domestically and in the rest of the world,* from foreign goods to domestic goods.

This chapter deals with *direct controls,* that is, *selective* expenditure-switching policies, whose aim is to control particular elements in the balance of payments. Usually direct controls are imposed on *imports* in an attempt to switch *domestic* expenditure away from foreign goods to home goods. Less common is the use of controls to stimulate *exports* by switching *foreign* spending to domestic products. (Controls may also be imposed on capital flows in an effort to either curb excessive capital outflows or induce capital inflows.)

---

[1] The reader who is in a hurry may skip this chapter and proceed to Chapter 20.

Direct controls can be combined with expenditure-adjusting policies to achieve internal and external balance. This must be clear from the analysis of Section 18-4. The principles involved are the same.

After a brief classification of direct controls in Section 19-1, we discuss the general nature of fiscal controls (Section 19-2) and their general microeconomic and macroeconomic effects (Section 19-3). In the following three sections, we discuss in greater detail the macroeconomic effects of import taxes (Section 19-4) and export subsidies (Section 19-5) and then summarize the important symmetry that exists between import taxes plus export subsidies, on the one hand, and devaluation, on the other (Section 19-6). In the next two sections, we discuss briefly the general nature and effects of the other two major categories of direct controls, commercial controls (Section 19-7) and monetary controls (Section 19-8). We conclude the chapter by considering the merits and demerits of direct controls relative to devaluation.

19-1 CLASSIFICATION OF DIRECT CONTROLS

Following Meade (1951), we classify direct controls as follows:

   1 *Fiscal controls:* Taxes and subsidies on particular items in the balance of payments, mainly merchandise imports and exports
   2 *Commercial controls:* Mainly quantitative restrictions (quotas)
   3 *Monetary controls:* Exchange control, multiple exchange rates, and advance-deposit requirements

In this chapter, we discuss briefly the general nature of these three categories of direct controls, their macroeconomic effects on national income and the balance of payments, and their desirability.

19-2 FISCAL CONTROLS

Fiscal controls include all taxes and subsidies that affect particular items in the balance of payments—usually the exports and imports of merchandise. The reason is simple: Merchandise exports and imports lend themselves more readily to the fiscal devices of taxes and subsidies. Invisible balance-of-payments items, such as tourist expenditure, are more difficult to cover by fiscal controls. Indeed, in the case of capital movements, they tend to break down completely unless they are reinforced by an effective system of exchange control.

The Four Fiscal Controls

Taxes or subsidies may be imposed on exports or imports. Accordingly, we can distinguish among four possible fiscal controls: import tax, export tax, import subsidy, and export subsidy. The most prominent fiscal devices are the import tax and the export subsidy.

The object of the import tax is to switch domestic expenditure from imports and channel it toward domestic output. Similarly, the object of an export subsidy is to stimulate exports by switching foreign spending to domestic output.

The rest of our discussion is restricted to these two important devices, the import tax and the export subsidy.

Ad Valorem, Specific, and Compound Taxes and Subsidies

We may recall from our discussion in Chapter 8 that taxes and subsidies may be fixed legally in any of the following three ways:

1 *The ad valorem basis*, that is, as a percentage on the value of the commodity imported or exported, inclusive or exclusive of transport cost
2 *The specific basis*, that is, as an absolute amount of domestic currency per unit imported or exported
3 *The compound basis*, that is, as a combination of an ad valorem tax (subsidy) *and* a specific tax (subsidy)

Throughout our discussion, we shall make the simplifying assumption that all taxes and subsidies are fixed on the ad valorem basis. This is a harmless assumption because at any given time, there indeed exists a one-to-one correspondence between an ad valorem tax (subsidy) and a specific tax (subsidy). For instance, the import duty on an imported camera whose price is $500 may be specified as either $50 (specific tax) or 10 percent of the price of the camera (ad valorem tax).

The Flexibility of Direct Controls

An important feature of direct controls, as opposed to general switching policies (such as exchange-rate adjustment), is their flexibility in operating differently on exports and imports of particular commodities or on exports to, and imports from, particular countries.

For instance, export subsidies and import taxes are not normally levied indiscriminately on all imports or on all exports. As we saw in Chapter 11, different ad valorem import duties may be levied on different commodities (for example, 20 percent on oil but 50 percent on cameras). Also, different ad valorem import duties may be levied on the same commodity imported from different countries (for example, 10 percent on cameras imported from Germany but 60 percent on cameras imported from Japan).

This flexibility of direct controls enhances their effectiveness as an instrument of balance-of-payments adjustment. Nevertheless, in an effort to simplify our discussion as much as possible, we shall largely ignore this important aspect of direct controls.

19-3 THE GENERAL EFFECTS OF TRADE TAXES AND SUBSIDIES

As we saw in Chapters 8–10, trade taxes and subsidies have several effects. These effects are divided into two major classes: microeconomic (which we studied in Part 2 of the book) and macroeconomic (which we study below).

Microeconomic Effects

We may recall from Chapter 8 that trade taxes and subsidies influence the allocation of resources between countries, the pattern of consumption within each country, the distribution of income between countries through their effect on the terms of trade, the functional distribution of income within each country, etc. Traditionally, these microeconomic effects of trade taxes and subsidies belong to the pure theory of international trade, and we make no attempt here to analyze them further.

As we noted in Part 2, free-trade advocates always emphasize the deleterious effects of tariffs on world welfare. In particular, trade taxes and subsidies interfere with the maximization of world welfare by reversing the process of international division of labor (dictated by the law of comparative advantage) and by forcing a suboptimal allocation of commodities among consumers. The only major qualification to this proposition is the optimal tariff. A large country with monopoly-monopsony power in world trade can improve her welfare (at the expense of the rest of the world) by imposing an optimal tariff, assuming that other countries do not erect retaliatory tariff barriers of their own (see Section 8-4).

If we agree that tariffs are harmful, why are they so widespread? Surely not many tariffs can be justified by the optimum-tariff argument. As it turns out, tariffs often reflect noneconomic arguments for protection (such as national defense). Sometimes tariffs represent "second-best" policies to protect infant industries or to correct other domestic distortions (see Chapter 9). Finally, tariffs may also reflect the relative political power of disparate interests. But we can find additional reasons for the existence of tariffs when we turn to the macroeconomic effects of trade taxes and subsidies.

Macroeconomic Effects

Our present discussion deals mainly with the macroeconomic effects of trade taxes and subsidies, namely, their effects on national income and the balance of payments, and to a lesser extent, the terms of trade.

The strong theoretical justification for free trade is based fundamentally on the assumption of full employment. In the presence of severe unemployment, the argument for free trade seems suspect. During the Great Depression of the 1930s, the main concern was not with the possibility that some resources were not optimally allocated. No, the problem was that a large portion of the economic resources were not allocated at all! Under these circumstances, the first order of business was to increase the level of employment. Improving the allocation of resources was less of a problem. Because aggregate-demand management was not well developed at that time, countries sought to solve their problem of severe unemployment by means of expenditure-switching policies, such as tariffs and devaluations. Such policies prompted, of course, an avalanche of foreign retaliation that led to the competitive devaluations of the early 1930s.

We therefore conclude that countries often use trade taxes and subsidies to bolster the level of domestic employment, especially when fiscal and monetary policies happen to be constrained by other policy objectives. Nevertheless, this is a beggar-thy-neighbor policy that often provokes retaliation.

The next few sections of this chapter discuss the direct and indirect effects of import taxes and export subsidies on national income, the balance of payments, and the terms of trade.

19-4 THE MACROECONOMIC EFFECTS OF IMPORT TAXES

How does the increase in an import tax, or the imposition of a new one, affect the domestic national income and the balance of payments? We answer this question by considering first the *direct* (or impact) effect of import taxes on the balance of payments (and the terms of trade). The basic framework for this type of analysis is the partial-equilibrium model of Chapter 15. Next, we consider the effects of import taxes on national income as well as their induced effects on the balance of payments. The basic model for these latter effects is that of Chapter 16.

Some Simplifying Assumptions

Our entire discussion in the rest of this chapter is based on three simplifying assumptions. They are:

1 The country imposing direct controls is assumed to suffer from a balance-of-payments *deficit*. This is justified by the fact that a balance-of-payments surplus is a less pressing problem. (The reader should be able to apply the present discussion to the case of a surplus country.)
2 The rate of exchange is fixed.
3 Foreign countries do not retaliate.

The third assumption is less justified, since switching policies are, in general, beggar-thy-neighbor policies and as such are likely to provoke retaliation from foreign countries. However, the consideration of retaliation and counter-retaliation would carry us too far afield. For our purposes, it is convenient to consider retaliation and counterretaliation as separate acts of policy and apply the present analysis to determine their effects.

The Direct Effects of Import Taxes

Consider again the partial-equilibrium model of Chapter 15. The home country (America) produces both A-exportables and B-exportables but exports A-exportables to, and imports B-exportables from, Britain (foreign country).

Figure 19-1 illustrates the market for B-exportables. The solid curves show what happens before America imposes an import tax. Equilibrium occurs at the point of intersection (E_0) of America's demand-for-imports schedule, CA, and Britain's supply-of-exports schedule, BS. Thus, America imports OQ_0 units of B-exportables at a price (in pounds) of OP_0. The area of rectangle $OQ_0E_0P_0$ gives America's expenditure on imports. This same area coincides with the demand for pounds at the current rate of exchange.

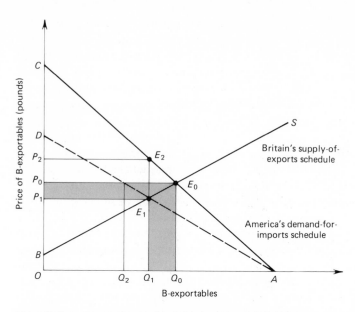

Figure 19-1 *The direct effects of an ad valorem import tax.*
When America imposes an ad valorem import tax, the demand-for-imports schedule rotates counterclockwise through its horizontal-axis intercept, A, as illustrated by broken curve DA. Equilibrium moves to E_1, and America's balance-of-payments improves by the amount indicated by the shaded area.

Suppose now that America suffers from a balance-of-payments deficit (that is, America's export revenue falls short of America's expenditure on imports). Suppose further that to correct the deficit, America imposes an ad valorem import tax. What are the direct effects of the import tax on America's balance of trade and terms of trade? *In general, the tariff reduces the volume of imports and, provided the foreign supply elasticity of exports is not infinite, the price paid to the foreign producers. Hence, both the balance of payments and the terms of trade of the country imposing the tariff tend to improve.*

Consider Figure 19-1 again. When America imposes the import tax, her demand-for-imports schedule rotates counterclockwise through its horizontal-axis intercept (A), as shown by broken curve DA. This new demand-for-imports schedule gives the quantities of B-exportables that America is willing to purchase at alternative prices (in pounds) *net of the tariff*, that is, prices that accrue to Britain's producers. Obviously, equilibrium moves to E_1. America's volume of imports falls to OQ_1, and the price paid to British producers falls to OP_1. America's expenditure on imports falls to $OQ_1E_1P_1$. Hence, America's balance of payments improves by the amount shown by the shaded area.

Note that the actual tax per unit imported is given by distance E_1E_2 (Q_1E_2 is the price paid by America's consumers, while Q_1E_1 is the price received by Britain's producers). The total tariff revenue accrued to America's authorities (revenue effect) is given by the area of rectangle $E_1E_2P_2P_1$.

To the extent that the price paid to Britain's producers falls, America's terms of trade improve. The reduction in the price paid to Britain's producers, and therefore the improvement in America's terms of trade, depends on two elasticities: America's elasticity of demand for imports and Britain's elasticity of supply of exports. In general, the *higher* America's elasticity of demand for imports and/or the *lower* Britain's elasticity of supply of exports, the larger is the terms-of-trade improvement. In the limiting case where Britain's supply elasticity of exports is zero, or America's import-demand elasticity is infinite, the terms-of-trade improvement is maximized—the total burden of the tariff is borne by the foreign producers. At the other extreme, where Britain's supply elasticity of exports is infinite, or America's import-demand elasticity is zero, the terms-of-trade improvement is zero—the total burden of the tariff is borne by the domestic consumers.

The price paid by America's consumers and received by America's producers of B-exportables tends to increase after the tariff (except in the limiting case where Britain's supply elasticity of exports is zero). This encourages America's producers of B-exportables to expand their production (protection effect) and America's consumers to reduce their consumption (consumption effect). The expansion in domestic production plus the reduction in domestic consumption account for the reduction in America's volume of imports.

Import Tax versus Devaluation

Figure 19-1 is similar to Figure 15-4, panel (*a*). The latter shows the effects of a depreciation of the dollar (America's currency) relative to the pound (Britain's currency). Insofar as (1) the volume of America's imports, (2) the net price paid to Britain's producers of B-exportables, and (3) America's expenditure on imports are concerned, an ad valorem tariff of, say, *x* percent, is equivalent to an *x* percent depreciation of the dollar relative to the pound. In this respect, it makes no difference whether America's importers pay a tariff or simply a higher price for Britain's currency.

We therefore conclude that *insofar as the market for B-exportables is concerned, a uniform ad valorem tariff levied on all imports is equivalent to a depreciation of the domestic currency (by the same percentage).*

The Effect of Import Taxes on National Income and the Induced Effect on the Balance of Payments

During the preceding discussion, we implicitly assumed that national income remained constant. On the basis of that assumption, we were able to isolate the direct (or impact) effect of the import tax on the balance of payments.

However, because of its direct effect on the balance of trade (at the initial level of national income), the imposition of the import tax raises the demand for domestic products (by switching domestic expenditure from foreign products toward domestic products). Accordingly, national income tends to rise, inducing additional imports into the country. All this must be clear from our discussion in Chapter 16 (see especially the discussion in Section 16-3).

The overall effect of an import tax on the balance of payments (that is, the sum of the direct effect plus the induced effect) as well as the effect of the import tax on national income depend crucially on how the government uses the tariff revenue. In general, the government may return the additional revenue to the consumers in the form of an income-tax reduction, or it may use it to increase its budget surplus (or reduce its budget deficit) or to finance government purchases of goods and services. Nevertheless, for our present discussion we do not need to consider all these possibilities. The reason is simple: The government's decision to either spend the tariff revenue on goods and services or return it to the consumers in the form of an income-tax reduction *constitutes a separate expenditure-adjusting policy*. We return shortly (see the next subsection) to the use of expenditure-adjusting policies along with direct controls for the attainment of internal and external balance. In the meantime, we assume that the government actually saves the tariff revenue.

Now consider Figure 19-2, which is broadly similar to Figures 16-5 and 18-5. National-income equilibrium occurs initially at the intersection of the X-M and S-I schedules, that is, point E_0. Thus, national income is Y_0, while the balance of trade is in deficit by the amount E_0Y_0. Suppose now that the government imposes an import tax that causes domestic consumers to divert part of their spending from foreign products toward domestic products. In particular,

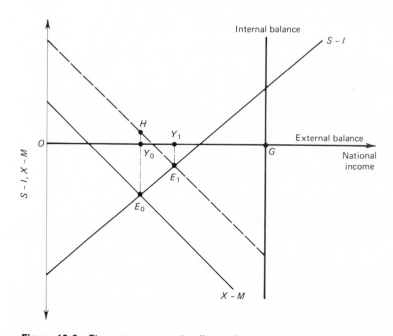

Figure 19-2 *The macroeconomic effects of an import tax.*
The imposition of an import tax disturbs the initial macroeconomic equilibrium at E_0 by causing the X-M schedule to shift upward by amount E_0H (initial impact), as shown by the broken schedule. Equilibrium shifts to E_1, as national income increases to Y_1 and the balance-of-trade deficit decreases to E_1Y_1. To achieve internal and external balance, policymakers must raise import taxes and adjust government spending so that the resultant S-I and X-M schedules pass through general balance point G.

assume that at the initial level of national income, Y_0, the import tax improves the balance of trade by amount E_0H. This means that the import tax causes the X-M schedule to shift upward by balance-of-trade improvement E_0H, as shown by the broken schedule. Equilibrium moves to E_1. Thus, national income increases from Y_0 to Y_1, and the balance-of-trade deficit decreases from E_0Y_0 to E_1Y_1.

Recall from our discussion in Chapter 16 that the overall balance-of-trade improvement $(E_0Y_0 - E_1Y_1)$ is less than the direct improvement (E_0H) at the initial level of national income. This is because of the increase in national income, which induces additional imports. However, note carefully that to the extent that the domestic marginal propensity to save is positive (that is, the S-I schedule is upward sloping), the overall balance-of-trade change is always an improvement. Thus, as the national-income-equilibrium point travels in the northeast direction along an upward-sloping S-I schedule, as illustrated in Figure 19-2 by the movement from E_0 to E_1, the balance-of-trade deficit necessarily decreases (or the surplus increases).

Attaining Internal and External Balance

Following the discussion in Section 18-4, it must be evident that policymakers can combine expenditure-adjusting policies with direct controls—in particular, import taxes—to attain internal and external balance.

For instance, return to Figure 19-2, and suppose that both internal and external balance occur at G, as before. To attain internal and external balance simultaneously, the authorities must (1) raise import taxes and (2) increase government spending, so that the resultant X-M and S-I schedules (not shown) pass through the general balance point, G.

Indeed, the entire analysis of Section 18-4 holds word for word for the present case as well. The only difference is that "import tax" replaces "exchange-rate adjustment."

19-5 THE MACROECONOMIC EFFECTS OF EXPORT SUBSIDIES

We now turn to the macroeconomic effects of export subsidies. How do export subsidies affect the level of national income and the balance of payments? As with import taxes, export subsidies have initially (that is, at the initial level of national income) a direct effect on the balance of trade (and the terms of trade). In turn, the direct effect on the balance of trade causes national income to change. Finally, the national-income change induces a further change in the balance of trade mainly through imports. The purpose of this section is to study these effects of export subsidies.

The Direct Effects of Export Subsidies

As with import taxes, the basic framework for this type of analysis is the partial-equilibrium model of Chapter 15. Recall our simplifying assumptions, particularly that the rate of exchange is fixed and that foreign countries do not retaliate.

Figure 19-3 illustrates the market for A-exportables (that is, America's export commodities). The solid curves show what happens before America (home country) subsidizes exports. Equilibrium occurs at the point of intersection (E_0) of America's supply-of-exports schedule, AS, and Britain's demand-for-imports schedule, BD. Thus, America exports OQ_0 units of A-exportables to Britain at a price (in pounds) of OP_0. The area of rectangle $OQ_0E_0P_0$ shows America's export revenue. This same area coincides with the supply of pounds at the existing rate of exchange.

Suppose now that in an effort to improve her balance of payments, America subsidizes her exports. What are the direct effects of the export subsidy on America's balance of trade and terms of trade? In general, *an export subsidy tends to increase the volume of exports and reduce the price paid by foreigners.* Accordingly, *the terms-of-trade effect of the export subsidy is in general unfavorable.*

What is the balance-of-trade effect? It is indeterminate, for the export revenue can either increase, decrease, or remain constant. In particular, the balance-of-trade effect depends on the foreign elasticity of demand for imports. If the foreign demand for imports is elastic, the export revenue increases with the export subsidy, and the balance of payments improves. But if the foreign

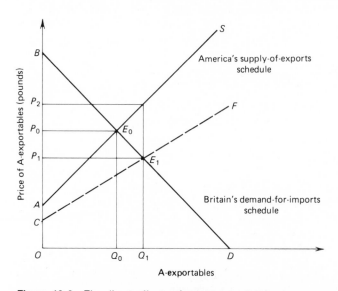

Figure 19-3 *The direct effects of an export subsidy.*
A subsidy to exports causes the supply-of-exports schedule to rotate clockwise, as if the dollar depreciated relative to the pound. This is shown by broken schedule *CF*. Equilibrium moves from E_0 to E_1. The volume of exports increases from OQ_0 to OQ_1. The price received by America's producers (inclusive of the subsidy) increases to OP_2, but the price paid by British consumers fall to OP_1. Whether America's balance of payments improves or not depends on whether the area of rectangle $OQ_1E_1P_1$ is larger or smaller than the area of rectangle $OQ_0E_0P_0$. That depends on Britain's elasticity of demand for imports.

demand for imports is inelastic, the export revenue decreases, and the balance of payments deteriorates.

Note carefully that if the foreign demand is actually inelastic, an export *tax*, not a subsidy, improves the balance of payments. A good case in point is provided by the oil exporting nations, which in the 1970s essentially imposed an exorbitant tax on their exports of oil. Incidentally, other countries have also taxed their exports. For instance, Brazil has taxed its coffee exports, Burma and Thailand have taxed their rice exports, and Ghana has taxed its cocoa exports.

Consider again Figure 19-3. The export subsidy causes America's supply-of-exports schedule to rotate clockwise, as shown by broken schedule CF. This new supply-of-exports schedule gives the quantities of A-exportables that America is willing to export at alternative prices (in pounds) *exclusive of the subsidy,* that is, prices paid by Britain's consumers. Equilibrium moves to E_1. America's volume of exports increases to OQ_1, but the price paid by foreign consumers falls to OP_1. Whether America's balance of payments improves or deteriorates depends on whether the area of rectangle $OQ_1E_1P_1$ is larger or smaller than the area of rectangle $OQ_0E_0P_0$. As we have seen, that depends on Britain's elasticity of demand for imports.

The price received by America's producers (inclusive of the subsidy) increases to OP_2. The higher price, of course, encourages America's producers to increase their production of, and at the same time causes America's consumers to decrease their consumption of, A-exportables. The increase in domestic production plus the decrease in domestic consumption account for the increase in America's volume of exports.

Export Subsidy versus Devaluation

Figure 19-3 is very similar to Figure 15-4, panel (*b*). The latter shows the effects on the market for A-exportables of a devaluation of the dollar relative to the pound. Obviously, insofar as (1) the volume of America's exports, (2) the price paid for A-exportables by Britain's consumers, and (3) America's export revenue are concerned, an *x* percent ad valorem export subsidy is equivalent to an *x* percent depreciation of the dollar relative to the pound. Surely it makes no difference to America's producers of A-exportables whether the higher price (in dollars) they receive for their exports to Britain's citizens is due to an export subsidy or a depreciation of the dollar.

**The Effect of Export Subsidies on National Income
and the Induced Effect on the Balance of Payments**

We can analyze the effect of export subsidies on national income in the same way we analyzed the national-income effect of an import tax. Thus, the direct effect of the export subsidy on the balance of trade (which we discussed above), is equivalent to a change in aggregate demand for domestic output. In turn, the direct change in aggregate demand causes national income to change in the same direction through the foreign-trade multiplier.

As we have seen, the direct effect may be either positive or negative, that is, the export subsidy may cause the balance of trade to either improve (when the foreign demand for imports is elastic) or deteriorate (when the foreign demand for imports is inelastic). Since an export subsidy is not usually granted unless there are reasons to believe that it will cause the balance of trade to improve, we may assume for the rest of this section that the foreign demand for imports is indeed elastic. In other words, we assume that the direct effect of the export subsidy on the balance of trade is positive (that is, favorable).

As with import taxes, the national-income effect of an export subsidy depends, in addition, on the manner in which the subsidy is actually financed. In general, the government may impose an additional income tax to raise the necessary funds, use already-existing general revenues and thus reduce its budget surplus (or increase its budget deficit), or reduce its purchases of goods and services. Again, we do not have to consider all possibilities. We can simply assume that the government actually finances the export subsidy out of already-existing funds. This simplifying assumption is indeed necessary for our policy-oriented approach. Any decision to either raise additional income taxes or reduce government spending on goods and services constitutes a separate act of policy. In particular, it amounts to an expenditure-adjusting policy.

On the assumption that the export subsidy improves the balance of trade at the initial level of income and the government finances the subsidy out of already-existing revenues, it becomes apparent that Figure 19-2 also illustrates both the national-income effect and the overall balance-of-trade effect of the export subsidy. Accordingly, no further discussion is necessary.

19-6   SYMMETRY BETWEEN IMPORT TAXES PLUS EXPORT SUBSIDIES AND DEVALUATION

Given the discussion in the preceding two sections, it becomes apparent that the following proposition is true:

> *Insofar as commodity trade is concerned an x percent depreciation (or devaluation) of a country's currency is equivalent to an x percent ad valorem tax on all imports plus an x percent ad valorem subsidy to all exports.*

19-7   COMMERCIAL CONTROLS

The most important commercial controls are quantitative restrictions on the physical volume or value of imports (import quota) or exports (export quota). The following discussion is therefore restricted to them.

The Import Quota

The most common commercial device is the import quota. We may recall from Chapter 10 that when the government, for one reason or another, desires to control directly the volume (or value) of imports, it may decree that only a given quantity (import quota) may be imported per unit of time.

Even though there are important differences between import taxes and import quotas, it is a theorem that for every import quota there is an equivalent import tax (see Chapter 10). Therefore, it is reasonable to expect that, in general, the macroeconomic effects of an import quota are the same as the macroeconomic effects of the equivalent import tax.[2] Thus, without repeating the analysis of Section 19-4, we may summarize the macroeconomic effects of import quotas as follows:

1   An import quota reduces the volume of imports (at the initial level of national income) and raises their domestic price. (The foreign price falls.)

2   To the extent that the *tariff-equivalent revenue* accrues to domestic economic units (consumers, producers, or government), the import quota always has a *direct* favorable effect on the balance of trade.

3   The direct balance-of-trade effect of the import quota stimulates the domestic economy and causes national income and employment to rise through the foreign-trade multiplier.

4   The increase in national income induces an additional flow of imports. This induced-import effect works against the direct effect of the import quota. However, to the extent that the domestic marginal propensity to save is positive, the overall balance-of-trade effect is always favorable.

5   Policymakers may combine import quotas with expenditure-adjusting policies to simultaneously achieve internal and external balance.

The Tariff Quota

Imports may also be restricted by means of a tariff quota. Under this scheme a certain amount of the commodity is imported free of any duty (or is imported on the payment of a low import duty), while a heavier import duty is imposed on additional quantitites. Thus, the ordinary tariff is the special case of the tariff quota in which the "quota" part is zero. Similarly, the ordinary import quota is the special case of the tariff quota where the import duty of any additional quantities beyond the "quota" part is prohibitively high.

The tariff quota does not raise any additional issues beyond those we studied above in relation to import taxes and simple quotas. For this reason, we shall not discuss the tariff quota any further.

The Export Quota

It is also possible that a country may desire to control directly the volume (or value) of exports. It may therefore decree that only a limited quantity or value of a particular commodity may be exported per unit of time. For this purpose, the government may issue export licenses and either sell them to the country's exporters at a competitive price (or a license fee) or just give away on a first-come, first-served basis.

To the extent that the government sells the export licenses at a competitive

---

[2] The text assumes implicitly that the government uses the "tariff-equivalent revenue" of the import quota in exactly the same way it uses the tariff revenue of the import tax. This assumption is important.

price, the economic effects of an export quota are identical to the effects of an equivalent export tax and *opposite* to the effects of an export subsidy. An export quota tends to raise the price of the restricted commodity in the foreign countries, while it lowers it in the restricting country. The restricting country's export revenue tends to rise only if the foreign demand for imports is inelastic. If the foreign demand for imports happens to be elastic, however, the restricting country's export revenue tends to fall and the balance of trade tends to deteriorate. It is no wonder, then, that export quotas are usually imposed in the face of highly inelastic foreign demand for imports.

19-8 MONETARY CONTROLS

Monetary controls include exchange control, multiple exchange rates, and advance-deposit requirements. This section discusses these monetary devices briefly.

Exchange Control

A deficit country may attempt to solve its balance-of-payments problem by means of exchange control, that is, by arbitrarily *rationing* the limited supply of foreign exchange among all potential buyers at the prevailing rate of exchange. For this purpose, the deficit country may establish an *exchange control authority*. Then the deficit country may proceed to require by law all citizens who receive payment from abroad to sell their foreign currency to the exchange control authority and all citizens who make payments abroad to buy the foreign currency they need from the exchange control authority, at the official rate.

Needless to say, the exchange control authority needs to adopt an inventory policy with respect to foreign exchange and to smooth out any seasonal variations in export revenue and/or expenditure on imports. The object is to keep the *flows* of sales and purchases in line *in the long run*.

An effective system of exchange control requires an elaborate bureaucratic machinery to oversee all foreign exchange dealings. Both exporters and importers have an interest in evading the law—a fact that often leads to black markets, where the domestic currency is traded against foreign exchange at depreciated rates.

An elaborate *postal control* is needed to prevent foreign exchange transactions by mail. Tourists and other travelers should not be allowed to carry currency out of, or into, the country, except in limited amounts. Similarly, all barter transactions should be banned. For this reason, an extensive bureaucratic inquiry at the ports is needed to determine the way all imports and exports are financed.

Further, the exchange control authority must make sure that licensed importers actually use their foreign exchange allotment for the legal purpose for which it is approved. Importers should not be allowed to overstate the price of imported goods and use the surplus of foreign exchange for illegal purposes. Also, exporters should not be permitted to declare an artificially low price for the exported commodities.

Finally, transfers between nonresident accounts (that is, accounts with the domestic banking system held by foreigners, which are freely convertible) and resident accounts (that is, accounts with the domestic banking system held by domestic residents, which are not convertible) must also be controlled. Domestic importers should not be allowed to pay for their imports by means of a transfer to nonresident accounts, unless such a transfer is consistent with the objectives of the exchange control. Similarly, exporters who are paid by means of a transfer from nonresident to resident accounts, and therefore have no foreign exchange to surrender to the exchange control authority, must provide proof that they were actually paid by means of such a transfer.

The administration of an effective system of exchange control is not an easy matter. It is difficult, perhaps impossible, to plug all loopholes. For instance, how can the exchange control authority prevent all leads and lags in international payments?

Multiple Exchange Rates

The preceding discussion assumes that all foreign exchange transactions with the exchange control authority are carried out at a single official rate of exchange. But there is no logical necessity for a uniform rate. The exchange control authority may establish different rates for different transactions. For instance, it may establish relatively high rates for imported luxury goods and relatively low rates for necessities. Similar arrangements may be established for different classes of exports. For our purposes, it is sufficient to note that a system of multiple exchange rates is necessarily equivalent to a system of trade taxes and subsidies.

Advance-Deposit Requirements

Imports may also be discouraged by requiring importers to deposit funds in a commercial bank in an amount equal to some specified percentage of the value of the imported goods for some specified period prior to the receipt of the goods. Such advance-deposit requirements, as they are known, impose an additional cost to the importer, who must tie up his or her funds or borrow the necessary amount. Hence, they are similar to import taxes. One important reason for the adoption of this device is the comparative ease with which it can be administered, especially when international agreements hamper manipulation of other direct controls.

19-9 DESIRABILITY OF CONTROLS

How desirable is the use of direct controls compared with a general switching policy such as devaluation? This question raises two important issues. The first issue involves the effectiveness of controls relative to devaluation: Are controls more effective or less effective relative to devaluation? The second issue concerns the welfare effects of controls relative to devaluation: Do controls interfere more with the maximization of national welfare relative to devaluation? This last section addresses briefly both issues.

Effectiveness of Controls Relative to Devaluation

As we have seen, devaluation is equivalent to an import tax plus an export subsidy. Further, the import tax always reduces the need (or demand) for foreign exchange. The export subsidy, on the other hand, may either increase or decrease the supply of foreign exchange, depending on whether the foreign demand for imports is elastic or inelastic, respectively.

Given the above conclusions, it is evident that an import restriction by itself tends to be more effective than devaluation when the foreign demand for imports is inelastic. On the other hand, when the foreign demand for imports is elastic, devaluation is more effective than mere import restriction.

Nevertheless, an export subsidy by itself can never be more effective than devaluation, since it fails to take into account the favorable effect of devaluation on imports.

In general, controls are more effective than devaluation mainly because of their flexibility. Export and import commodities may be broken down into different classes according to their supply and demand elasticities. Then each class of commodities may be taxed or subsidized at different rates such as to maximize the balance-of-payments improvement.

The Welfare Argument for Controls

Turn now to the second issue, which concerns the effect of controls on welfare relative to devaluation. Consider a deficit country that has the option to use either direct controls or devaluation to correct its balance of payments deficit. Which policy instrument should the country use? Evidently the answer depends on which of the two solutions leaves the country at a higher level of social welfare.

Indeed, Alexander (1951) argued that the choice between controls and devaluation depends on the relation between the existing and the optimal degree of trade restriction. If the current degree of controls falls short of the optimal degree (that is, if the country possesses unexploited monopoly and monopsony power), then controls should be preferred until the optimal degree is reached. If, on the other hand, the current degree of controls lies beyond the optimal degree, devaluation should be preferred. In fact, in the latter case trade restrictions should be relaxed until the optimal degree is reached; then further devaluation of the domestic currency should be used to eliminate the resultant unfavorable effects on the balance of payments. This is the familiar optimal-tariff argument.

Alexander's thesis is interesting, but it has several drawbacks. First, there is the practical difficulty that the optimal degree of trade restriction is neither easily nor uniquely determined. Second, we cannot use trade restriction on a *continuous* basis even if we somehow know what the optimal degree is. For once the optimal degree of trade restriction is reached, the country must turn, according to Alexander, to exchange-rate adjustments. Thus, even though Alexander's argument may be accepted in principle, the *continuous* use of trade restriction must be ruled out, unless it were true that every balance-of-payments deficit necessarily created the required divergence between the existing and optimal degree of trade restriction, which is, of course, absurd.

We therefore conclude that trade restriction to achieve Pareto optimality from the national (not the international) viewpoint is a different issue from the use of trade restriction to correct a balance-of-payments deficit. Whether a country should pursue an optimal-tariff policy or not should be decided irrespective of the state of the balance of payments. Nevertheless, in everyday life political propaganda may be important, and a balance-of-payments deficit may be presented as a justification in intensifying trade restriction perhaps to the degree the authorities perceive as optimal. Under these circumstances, other countries may feel sympathetic toward the deficit country and may not retaliate.

19-10 SUMMARY

1 General switching policies (such as exchange-rate adjustments) switch expenditure, both domestically and in the rest of the world, from foreign goods to domestic goods.

2 Direct controls are selective expenditure-switching policies whose aim is to control particular elements in the balance of payments. They are divided into fiscal controls (such as import taxes and export subsidies), commercial controls (mainly quotas), and monetary controls (such as exchange control, multiple exchange rates, and advance-deposit requirements).

3 An important feature of direct controls is their flexibility in operating differently on exports and imports of particular commodities or on exports to, and imports from, particular countries. This flexibility of direct controls enhances their effectiveness as an instrument of balance-of-payments adjustment.

4 The object of an import tax is to curtail imports by switching domestic expenditure from foreign to domestic products. The object of an export subsidy is to stimulate exports by switching foreign spending to domestic output.

5 An import tax has two effects on the balance of payments: a direct effect (that is, the reduction of imports at the initial level of national income) and an induced effect (that is, the increase in imports induced by the increase in national income). To the extent that the marginal propensity to save is positive, the unfavorable induced effect cannot outweigh the favorable direct effect; so the overall effect is always favorable.

6 An export subsidy has two effects on the balance of payments: a direct effect (that is, the change in export revenue at the initial level of national income) plus an induced effect (that is, the change in imports induced by the change in national income). The direct effect is favorable (unfavorable) when the foreign demand for imports is elastic (inelastic). When the direct effect is fa-

vorable, the overall effect is also favorable (assuming that the marginal propensity to save is positive).

7 Insofar as commodity trade is concerned, an x percent depreciation (or devaluation) of a country's currency is equivalent to an x percent ad valorem tax on all imports plus an x percent ad valorem subsidy to all exports.

8 In general, the macroeconomic effects of an import quota are the same as the macroeconomic effects of an equivalent import tax.

9 A tariff quota allows a certain quantity (quota) of the relevant commodity to be imported free of duty but imposes an import duty on any imports beyond the quota.

10 A country may control directly its volume (or value) of exports by imposing an export quota. The balance-of-payments effect of an export quota is favorable only when the foreign demand for imports is inelastic.

11 Exchange control means arbitrary rationing (through an exchange control authority) of a limited supply of foreign exchange among all potential buyers. The exchange control authority may maintain a single official exchange rate, or it may establish different rates for different transactions. A system of multiple exchange rates is equivalent to a system of trade taxes and subsidies.

12 Policymakers can combine expenditure-adjusting policies with direct controls to attain internal and external balance.

13 An import restriction by itself is more (less) effective than devaluation when the foreign demand for imports is inelastic (elastic). However, an export subsidy by itself can never be more effective than devaluation, because it fails to take into account the favorable effect of devaluation on imports.

14 Trade restriction to achieve Pareto optimality (optimal-tariff argument) is a different issue from the use of trade restriction to correct a balance-of-payments deficit, even though the latter may be used as an excuse to intensify trade restriction (perhaps to the degree the authorities may perceive as optimal).

SUGGESTED READING

Alexander, S. S. (1951). "Devaluation versus Import Restriction as an Instrument for Improving Foreign Trade Balance." *IMF Staff Papers,* vol. 1 (April), pp. 379–396.

Bernstein, E. M. (1950). "Some Economic Aspects of Multiple Exchange Rates." *IMF Staff Papers,* vol. 1, (September), pp. 224–237.

Bhagwati, J. (1965). "On the Equivalence of Tariffs and Quotas." In R. E. Baldwin et al. (eds.). *Trade, Growth and the Balance of Payments: Essays in Honor of Gottfried Haberler.* Rand McNally & Company, Chicago.

——— (1978). *Anatomy and Consequences of Exchange Control Regimes.* Ballinger Publishing Company, Cambridge, Mass.

Chacholiades, M. (1978). *International Monetary Theory and Policy.* McGraw-Hill Book Company, New York, chap. 14.

Hemming, M. F. W., and W. M. Corden (1958). "Import Restriction as an Instrument of Balance-of-Payments Policy." *Economic Journal,* vol. 48 (September), pp. 483–510.

Johnson, H. G. (1958a). *International Trade and Economic Growth: Studies in Pure*

Theory. George Allen & Unwin, Ltd., London, chap. 6. Reprinted in R. E. Caves and H. G. Johnson (eds.), AEA *Readings in International Economics.* Richard D. Irwin, Inc., Homewood, Ill., 1968.

————— (1958b). "The Balance of Payments." *Pakistan Economic Journal,* vol. 8, 2 (June), pp. 16–28. Reprinted in H. G. Johnson. *Money, Trade and Economic Growth.* George Allen & Unwin, Ltd., London, 1962, chap. 1.

Kindleberger, C. P. (1968). *International Economics,* 4th ed. Richard D. Irwin, Inc., Homewood, Ill., chaps. 7 and 8.

————— (1975). "Quantity and Price, Especially in Financial Markets." *The Quarterly Review of Economics and Business* (Summer), pp. 7–19.

Meade, J. E. (1951). *The Theory of International Economic Policy,* vol. 1, *The Balance of Payments.* Oxford University Press, New York, part 5.

Chapter Twenty

Fiscal and Monetary Policy for Internal and External Balance

Tinbergen's rule (see Chapter 18) warns us that to achieve two mutually independent targets, such as internal and external balance, we need two mutually independent and effective instruments, such as an *expenditure-adjusting policy* and an *expenditure-switching policy.*

In our discussion thus far, we have illustrated expenditure-adjusting policies by means of *fiscal policy* (that is, changes in government spending, changes in income taxes, and the like) and *monetary policy* (that is, changes in the supply of money). And we have illustrated expenditure-switching policies by means of *exchange-rate adjustments* (for example, devaluation or revaluation) and *direct controls* (for example, import and export taxes and subsidies, import and export quotas, exchange control, multiple exchange rates, and advance-deposit requirements).

Throughout our discussion, we have seen that the use of expenditure-switching policies is often avoided by policymakers for various reasons, some rational and some irrational. For instance, devaluation is usually identified with loss of national prestige and with failure; exchange control and multiple exchange rates are abhorred because they call for an elaborate bureaucratic machinery to oversee all foreign exchange dealings; import taxes and quotas are dreaded because of the fear of the foreign retaliation they may provoke; and so on.

If expenditure-switching policies (that is, exchange-rate adjustments and direct controls) are actually excluded, how could internal and external balance be attained simultaneously? If the world insists on a fixed-exchange-rate system with free international trade (which, as we have seen, promotes world welfare), do nations have to make the unpleasant choice between the Scylla of unemployment (and inflation) and the Charybdis of balance-of-payments disequilibrium? The possibility of such a conflict was perceived by Meade in the early 1950s. Indeed, this view remained prevalent until the early 1960s when Mundell (1968, pp. 152–176 and 217–271) showed in a series of journal articles that internal and external balance may be attained through an appropriate use of fiscal and monetary policies.

Mundell's solution is possible *only in the presence of capital mobility.* Thus, as we shall see, when capital flows are responsive to interest-rate changes, the impacts of fiscal and monetary policies on national income and the balance of *payments* (including the capital account) are different, mainly because of their opposite effects on the rate of interest. For instance, an expansionary fiscal policy raises the domestic interest rate and attracts capital inflows. On the other hand, an expansionary monetary policy reduces the domestic interest rate and promotes capital outflows. Because of this fundamental difference in their effects on the capital account, policymakers can find a combination of fiscal and monetary policy that is consistent with both internal and external balance simultaneously.

The object of this chapter is to elucidate the Mundellian approach. The first section prepares the ground for this discussion by summarizing briefly the *IS-LM* model of Chapter 17 and by considering the effects of monetary and fiscal policy on national income and the balance of payments. Section 20-2 shows that with the important proviso that capital flows are responsive to interest-rate differentials, policymakers can indeed use fiscal and monetary policy to simultaneously attain internal and external balance. Section 20-3 warns us about the difficulties policymakers actually face in the practice of economic policy, particularly because they lack perfect knowledge of their economic environment. Section 20-4 deals with the assignment problem, which involves the pairing of a particular policy instrument with a particular policy target. As the discussion in that section shows, assigning fiscal policy to internal balance and monetary policy to external balance does not always lead to the smooth attainment of internal and external balance. Sometimes the assignment rule leads to explosive instability. Finally, Section 20-5 summarizes some important criticisms of the Mundellian approach.

20-1 THE *IS-LM* MODEL AGAIN

The main framework of analysis for the Mundellian thesis (on the appropriate use of fiscal and monetary policy to attain internal and external balance simultaneously) is the *IS-LM* model, which we studied in Chapter 17. Before we go any further, it is important that we review briefly the general properties of the *IS-LM* model. That is the purpose of this section. (For more details, the reader is referred to Sections 17-3 to 17-7.)

Equilibrium in the Goods Market

Consider an open economy that produces a homogeneous product (for example, GNP) with labor only and under constant returns to scale. Assume also that the money-wage rate is fixed, so that the aggregate supply schedule is infinitely elastic (that is, horizontal) at the current price. In essence, these assumptions enable us to set prices aside.

Equilibrium in the goods market prevails when the aggregate demand (that is, $C + I + X - M$) equals the economy's current level of output or national income (Y). As we already know, this fundamental equilibrium condition reduces to $I + X = S + M$, or $X - M = S - I$. That is, national-income equilibrium occurs when the exogenous injections (investment I and exports X) just match the endogenous leakages (saving S and imports M).

While exports X are autonomous, investment I depends negatively on the domestic interest rate. On the other hand, saving S and imports M depend on the level of national income Y. As a result, there are an infinite number of combinations of interest rate r and national income Y that preserve the equilibrium condition $I + X = S + M$. The *IS* curve is the locus of all such combinations.

In general, the *IS* curve slopes downward because, as the interest rate falls, the desired level of investment increases, causing national income to increase also (through the multiplier).

Equilibrium in the Money Market

We now turn to the money market. *Throughout this chapter, we assume that the monetary authorities sterilize the effects of payments imbalances.* In other words, we assume that the monetary authorities keep the money supply fixed. The demand for money, on the other hand, depends positively on the level of national income (transactions demand) and negatively on the interest rate (speculative demand).

Equilibrium in the money market prevails when the level of national income and the interest rate are such that the demand for money equals the given supply of money. Evidently there are an infinite number of combinations of income levels and interest rates that make the demand for money equal to the supply of money. The *LM* curve is the locus of all such combinations.

In general, the *LM* curve slopes upward. Thus, as the interest rate increases, the speculative demand decreases and makes more money available for transactions purposes. The economy can absorb the higher transactions balances only if national income rises. Accordingly, an increase in the interest rate requires an increase in the level of national income in order to preserve equilibrium in the money market.

General Macroeconomic Equilibrium and the External Balance Schedule

Consider now Figure 20-1, which brings together the *LM* curve (which represents equilibrium in the money market) and the *IS* curve (which represents equilibrium in the goods market). General macroeconomic equilibrium occurs at intersection *E* of the *IS* and *LM* curves. Accordingly, the current equilibrium interest rate is r_e, and the equilibrium level of national income is Y_e.

Figure 20-1 also illustrates the external balance schedule. This schedule is drawn on the assumption that the rate of exchange is fixed. Its primary purpose is to show us whether, at current equilibrium point *E*, the balance of payments is in deficit or surplus.

External equilibrium prevails when the sum of the current account balance plus the capital account balance is zero. Recall that the balance of trade (and in general the current account balance) is primarily a function of the level of national income, while the capital account balance (that is, net capital flow) is primarily a function of the interest rate (assuming that the foreign interest rate is given). Accordingly, external equilibrium prevails when the level of national income and the interest rate are such that the net capital flow matches the balance of trade. Indeed, there are an infinite number of combinations of income

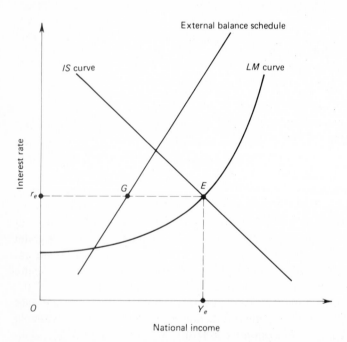

Figure 20-1 *The IS-LM model with the external balance schedule.*
The intersection of the *IS* and *LM* curves determines the equilibrium level of national income (Y_e) and the interest rate (r_e). Since point *E* lies to the right of the external balance schedule, the balance of payments is in deficit. The deficit is actually proportional to horizontal distance *GE*, with the marginal propensity to import being the factor of porportionality.

levels and interest rates that are consistent with external balance. The locus of all these combinations is actually the external balance schedule.

To the extent that capital flows are responsive to interest-rate changes, the external balance schedule is upward sloping, as shown in Figure 20-1. Thus, as the domestic interest rate rises, the capital account balance improves (increases algebraically), and a surplus appears in the balance of payments. To restore external balance at the higher interest rate, national income must rise in order to induce additional imports. Accordingly, an increase in the interest rate must be accompanied by an increase in national income; that is, the external balance schedule must be upward sloping.

Recall also that the external balance schedule divides the whole quadrant into two regions: (1) the region of external deficit (which lies to the right and below of the external balance schedule), and (2) the region of external surplus (which lies to the left and above the external balance schedule). For instance, in Figure 20-1 the economy suffers from a balance-of-payments deficit because equilibrium point E lies to the right of the external balance schedule; that is, level of national income Y_e is too high at current interest rate r_e, or interest rate r_e is too low at current level of national income Y_e. Also, the deficit is equal to horizontal distance GE times the marginal propensity to import.

The Effects of Monetary Policy

How do fiscal and monetary policies (that is, autonomous changes in government spending or income taxes and the supply of money) affect national income and the interest rate as well as the balance of payments? We must answer this question before we consider the use of fiscal and monetary policies for the attainment of internal and external balance.

Consider the effects of monetary policy first. An increase in the money supply causes the LM curve to shift to the right, as shown by the broken curve in Figure 20-2. Equilibrium shifts from E_0 to E_1. The increase in the money supply causes the equilibrium level of national income to increase from Y_0 to Y_1 and the interest rate to fall from r_0 to r_1.

What is the effect on the balance of payments? The *increase* in the money supply *worsens* the balance of payments for two reasons: (1) It worsens the balance of trade through the additional imports that are induced by the increase in national income, and (2) it worsens the capital account through the reduction in the interest rate. In terms of Figure 20-2, the deterioration of the balance of payments is illustrated by the fact that horizontal distance HE_1 (which shows the needed reduction in national income for the restoration of external balance *after* the increase in the supply of money) is necessarily larger than horizontal distance GE_0 (which shows the needed reduction in income for the restoration of external balance *before* the increase in the money supply).

Reversing the above argument, we can easily conclude that a decrease in the money supply causes national income to fall, the interest rate to rise, and the balance of payments to improve (since imports tend to fall and net capital inflow tends to rise).

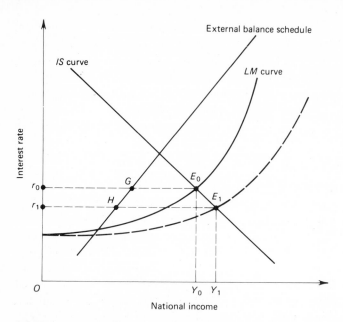

Figure 20-2 *The effects of monetary policy.*
An increase in the money supply causes the *LM* curve to shift to the right, as shown by the broken curve. Equilibrium shifts from E_0 to E_1. Thus, national income increases from Y_0 to Y_1, and the rate of interest falls from r_0 to r_1. The balance of payments deteriorates because of higher imports and lower net capital flows. The balance-of-payments deterioration is illustrated by the fact that distance HE_1 is larger than distance GE_0.

The Effects of Fiscal Policy

Turn now to fiscal policy. An increase in government spending causes the *IS* curve to shift to the right. In general, with a downward-sloping *IS* curve and an upward-sloping *LM* curve, the increase in government spending causes both the level of national income and the rate of interest to rise. This is shown in Figure 20-3. Equilibrium occurs initially at E_0. As the *IS* curve shifts to the right (see broken curve), equilibrium shifts to E_1. Accordingly, the increase in government spending causes the equilibrium level of national income to increase from Y_0 to Y_1. It also causes the interest rate to rise from r_0 to r_1.

What is the effect on the balance of payments? It is indeterminate. Actually, it is two separate, conflicting effects. On the one hand, an expansionary fiscal policy increases the level of national income, which *worsens* the balance of trade (because of increased imports). On the other hand, it raises the interest rate, which *improves* the capital account. The final outcome depends on which of these effects is stronger. This indeterminacy is illustrated in Figure 20-3 by the fact that horizontal distance HE_1 can be either smaller or larger than distance GE_0, depending on the relative slopes of the *LM* curve and the external balance schedule.

Reversing the above argument, we can easily conclude that, in general, a

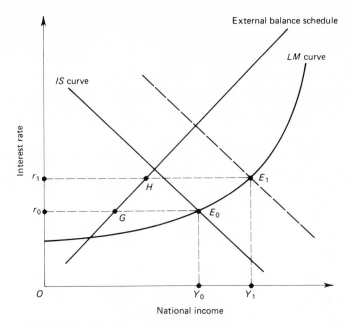

Figure 20-3 *The effects of fiscal policy.*
An increase in government spending causes the *IS* curve to shift to the right, as shown by the broken curve. Equilibrium shifts from E_0 to E_1. Thus, national income increases from Y_0 to Y_1, while the interest rate increases from r_0 to r_1. The balance-of-payments effect is indeterminate, as horizontal distance HE_1 can be either smaller or larger than GE_0, depending on the relative slopes of the *LM* curve and the external balance schedule.

decrease in government spending (that is, a contractionary fiscal policy) causes both the national income and the interest rate to fall. Its effect on the balance of payments is again indeterminate.

20-2   THE COMPATIBILITY OF INTERNAL AND EXTERNAL BALANCE

As we have just seen, *fiscal and monetary policies have diametrically opposite effects on the interest rate* even though they have similar effects on national income. This is the key to the use of fiscal and monetary policies for the attainment of internal and external balance. The only important proviso is that *capital flows are responsive to interest-rate differentials.* The purpose of this section is to elucidate this.

The Internal and External Balance Schedules

Consider Figure 20-4, which illustrates our two targets: internal and external balance. As before, external balance occurs along the upward-sloping external balance schedule. Internal balance, on the other hand, occurs along the vertical line drawn at the full-employment level of national income Y_f. Evidently, inter-

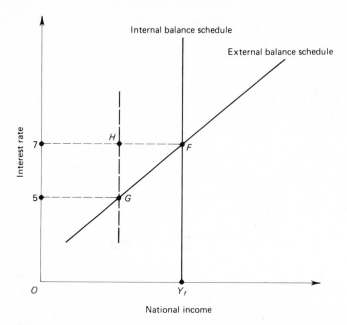

Figure 20-4 *The two targets: internal and external balance.*
External balance occurs along the upward-sloping external balance schedule. Internal balance occurs along the vertical line drawn at full employment income Y_f. Internal and external balance prevail simultaneously at point *F* only. Policymakers must choose that fiscal-monetary mix that causes the *IS* and *LM* curves to pass through general balance point *F*.

nal and external balance occur simultaneously at point *F*, which is the only point that lies on both schedules.

To attain internal and external balance simultaneously, the authorities must take two steps, as follows:

1   They must fix the money supply at an appropriate level so that the *LM* curve passes through general balance point *F*.
2   They must fix government spending at an appropriate level so that the *IS* curve also passes through general balance point *F*.

This solution is discussed below in detail.

The Importance of Capital Mobility

Even at this stage we can understand the implications of the proviso that capital flows are responsive to interest-rate differentials.

Consider point *G* on the external balance schedule. At *G* the balance of payments is in equilibrium. If we shift the economy from *G* to *H* by raising the interest rate from, say, 5 to 7 percent, the balance of payments will register a surplus, *but only when the higher interest rate attracts additional capital inflows.* In that case, we can restore external balance at the higher interest rate by allowing national income to increase. Thus, starting at *H*, we can restore external balance by moving to point F, which lies on the solid upward-sloping external balance schedule.

Suppose now that capital flows are *not* responsive to interest-rate differentials (perfect capital immobility). Begin again at G, where, by assumption, the balance of payments is in equilibrium. Move the economy from G to H by allowing the interest rate to rise from 5 to 7 percent. What is the state of the balance of payments at point H? Since we are now assuming that the change in the rate of interest has no effect on the capital account, and since the balance of trade is a function of national income only (which is the same at H as at G), it follows that the balance of payments must continue to be in equilibrium at H. This means that when capital flows are not responsive to interest-rate differentials, the external balance schedule becomes a *vertical* line (as shown by broken line GH), just like the internal balance schedule.

When the external balance schedule is vertical, as in the case of perfect capital immobility, the economy cannot possibly attain internal and external balance simultaneously by means of fiscal and monetary policies alone. The reason is simple: The internal and external balance schedules (in Figure 20-4) do not cross, as they are parallel vertical lines. At any particular time, the economy can be on either the internal or the external balance schedule *but not on both*. Under these circumstances, a conflict arises between internal and external balance.

How can the economy simultaneously attain internal and external balance in the presence of a conflict? As we saw in Chapters 18 and 19, the economy can simultaneously attain internal and external balance by an appropriate combination of expenditure-adjusting policies (for example, fiscal and monetary policies) and expenditure-switching policies (for example, exchange-rate adjustment and direct controls). In general, expenditure-switching policies cause the external balance schedule to shift. Accordingly, an appropriate expenditure-switching policy can make the vertical external balance schedule coincide with the vertical internal balance schedule and thus remove the potential conflict between internal and external balance. Then, *any* combination of fiscal and monetary policies that brings about internal balance also generates external balance.

20-3 DIFFICULTIES IN THE PRACTICE OF POLICY

Our discussion in the preceding section shows that in the presence of capital mobility, internal and external balance can be attained simultaneously by an appropriate use of fiscal and monetary policy. While this proposition is valid in principle, its practical application is not an easy matter. The purpose of this section is to discuss the various difficulties that arise in the practical application of economic policy.

The Four Zones of Economic Unhappiness

Consider Figure 20-5 (on the next page), which is similar to Figure 20-4. The internal and external balance schedules divide the whole quadrant into four disequilibrium zones, or zones of economic unhappiness. These zones are as follows:

Zone I: Unemployment and balance-of-payments surplus. This zone lies to the left of both the internal balance schedule and the external balance schedule.

Zone II: Potential inflationary pressure and balance-of-payments surplus. This zone lies to the left of the external balance schedule but to the right of the internal balance schedule.

Zone III: Potential inflationary pressure and balance-of-payments deficit. This zone lies to the right of both the internal balance schedule and the external balance schedule.

Zone IV: Unemployment and balance-of-payments deficit. This zone lies to the left of the internal balance schedule and to the right of the external balance schedule.

At any given time, the economy operates in one of the above four zones of economic unhappiness. In particular, the economy operates at the point of intersection of the *IS* and *LM* curves (see Section 20-1). Of course, the authorities cannot be sure of the exact location of the *IS* and *LM* curves or of the external balance schedule. Nevertheless, the authorities can easily infer the zone

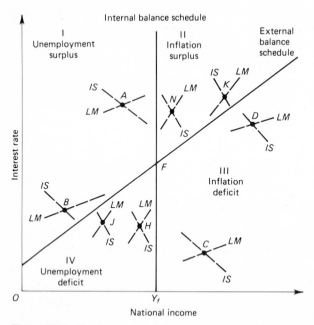

Figure 20-5 *The four zones of economic unhappiness.*
The internal and external balance schedules divide the diagram into four disequilibrium zones. Knowledge of the zone in which the economy happens to be is not sufficient information for the formulation of economic policy.

in which the economy happens to be from the actual data on unemployment-inflation and the balance of payments. Is this knowledge sufficient for the correct formulation of economic policy?

As we explained in Section 20-2, the authorities can attain internal and external balance by adjusting the money supply and government spending in such a way that the resultant *LM* and *IS* curves pass through general balance point *F* (that is, the intersection of the external and internal balance schedules). Knowing just the zone in which the economy happens to be is hardly sufficient for performing this juggling act of simultaneously attaining internal and external balance.

In zones I and III, the authorities are completely in the dark. For instance, points *A* and *B* lie in zone I. If the economy is at point *A*, the authorities must reduce government spending (to shift the *IS* curve downward and to the left) and increase the money supply (to shift the *LM* curve to the right). However, if the economy is at point *B*, which also lies in zone I, the authorities must do the *opposite;* that is, they must increase government spending (to shift the *IS* curve to the right) and reduce the money supply (to shift the *LM* curve to the left). Similarly, points *C* and *D* in zone III imply diametrically opposite policies, as the reader should be able to verify.

The situation is a little better in zones II and IV. In these two zones the direction of change in government spending is known. For instance, in zone II (see points *K* and *N*) the authorities must always reduce government spending (to shift the *IS* curve to the left). Similarly, in zone IV (see points *J* and *H*) the authorities must increase government spending (to shift the *IS* curve to the right).

Unfortunately, the direction of change in the money supply continues to be uncertain in both zone II and zone IV. For instance, points *K* and *N* lie in zone II, but the authorities must increase the money supply at *N* and reduce it at *K*. Similarly, points *H* and *J* lie in zone IV, but the authorities must increase the money supply at *J* and reduce it at *H*.

It is interesting to note that the indeterminacy of monetary policy in zones II and IV is completely removed when the *LM* curve is *flatter* than the external balance schedule. On the other hand, the indeterminacy of monetary policy in zones I and III is removed when the LM curve is *steeper* than the external balance schedule. Unfortunately, the policymakers do not know whether the *LM* curve is flatter or steeper than the external balance schedule.

We therefore conclude that without additional information on the precise location (and slope) of the *IS* and *LM* curves and the external balance schedule, mere knowledge of the zone in which the economy happens to be is not sufficient for the formulation of economic policy.

The Four Policy Regions

To appreciate the difficulties policymakers face, turn to Figure 20-6. Panel (*a*) shows the *IS* and *LM* curves that result from the application of the correct mix of fiscal and monetary policy. These curves, which intersect at general balance point F (see Figure 20-5), divide the diagram into four policy regions. Policymakers must know the precise policy region in which the economy happens to be before they can formulate the correct policy mix. On the assumption that this information is indeed available, the correct policy mix for each policy region is easily determined as follows:

Policy region 1: When the economy is in this region, as illustrated by point A, the authorities must increase both the money supply and government spending. This policy mix will eventually shift the current IS and LM curves (see broken curves through A) to their general-equilibrium position through general balance point F.

Policy region 2: When the economy is in this region, as illustrated by point B, the proper policy mix is to reduce government spending and expand the money supply.

Policy region 3: When the economy is in this region, as illustrated by point C, the proper policy mix is to reduce both the money supply and government spending.

Policy region 4: When the economy is in this region, as illustrated by point

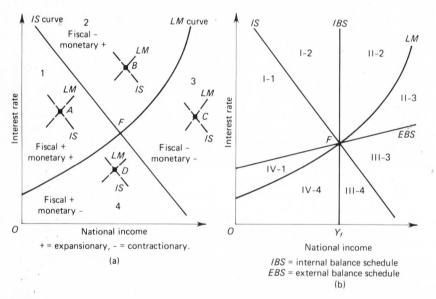

Figure 20-6 *The four policy regions and their relation to the four zones of economic unhappiness.*
Panel (a) shows the IS and LM curves that arise from the application of the correct fiscal-monetary mix. As in Figure 20-5, point F coincides with internal and external balance. These IS and LM curves divide the diagram into four policy regions. To formulate the correct fiscal-monetary mix, policymakers need to know the policy region in which the economy happens to be. Unfortunately, they do not—they only know the zone (see Figure 20-5). Panel (b) brings together the policy regions and the zones. Evidently, the policy regions do not coincide with the zones. In fact, each zone lies in two policy regions. This fact accounts for the uncertainty policymakers face in the formulation of economic policy.

D, the proper policy mix is to increase government spending and reduce the money supply.

Combining Zones with Policy Regions

Unfortunately, the zones of economic unhappiness (see Figure 20-5) do not coincide with the policy regions [see Figure 20-6, panel (a)]—they merely overlap. Now the statistical data on inflation-unemployment and the balance of payments indicate the zone (Figure 20-5) in which the economy happens to be, not the policy region [Figure 20-6, panel (a)]. To understand the implications of this fact, turn to Figure 20-6, panel (b), which is actually a combination of Figure 20-5 and Figure 20-6, panel (a).

The internal and external balance schedules together with the IS and LM curves of panel (a)—that is, the IS and LM curves that are drawn through general balance point F on the assumption that the authorities pursue the correct mix of fiscal and monetary policy—divide the whole diagram into eight areas: area I-1 (that is, zone I and policy region 1), area I-2 (that is, zone I and policy region 2), and so on.

Note carefully that each policy region overlaps two different zones of economic unhappiness and that each zone of economic unhappiness overlaps two different policy regions. For instance, zone I overlaps policy regions 1 and 2, and zone II overlaps policy regions 2 and 3. Similarly, policy region 1 overlaps zones I and IV and policy region 3 overlaps zones II and III.

We therefore conclude that because we cannot associate each zone with just one policy region, there is always uncertainty as to which policy mix is the correct one.

Figure 20-6, panel (b), is drawn on the assumption that the external balance schedule is flatter than the LM curve. This is not necessary. The external balance schedule may be steeper than the LM curve at general balance point F. The reader is encouraged to draw his or her own diagram and verify that in this case zone II lies completely within policy region 2 and zone IV completely within policy region 4. Accordingly, when the external balance schedule is steeper than the LM curve, the correct policy for the twin evils of potential inflationary pressure and balance of payments surplus (zone II) is to increase the supply of money and reduce government spending. Similarly, in the presence of unemployment and a balance of payments deficit, the correct policy is to reduce the money supply and increase government spending.

20-4   THE ASSIGNMENT PROBLEM

Our discussion so far points to a rather gloomy conclusion: Even though the simultaneous attainment of internal and external balance by means of fiscal and monetary policy is in principle feasible, policymakers lack the necessary information for the formulation of the correct policy mix. Are there any policy rules to assist policymakers in their quest for internal and external balance in a world of imperfect information? Indeed there are. This section deals with the famous *assignment problem,* whose proper solution leads to internal and external balance.

Nature of the Assignment Problem

If full information [say, Figure 20-6, panel (*b*)] were available to policymakers, a centralized decision-making process under a unified policy authority for the simultaneous attainment of internal and external balance would be possible.

But information is scarce. What policymakers actually have are only data on national income, unemployment, inflation, the rate of interest, and the state of the balance of payments. Under these circumstances, the fiscal authorities may strongly disagree with the monetary authorities as to the proper policy mix. Differences in political persuasions and ethical beliefs intertwined with imperfect knowledge of the economic system could make the discussion more lively and the disagreement stronger and thus lead to a policy stalemate. Is there an alternative? Yes: policy assignment.

The assignment problem is a product of decentralized decision making and involves the *pairing of a particular policy instrument with a particular policy target.* For instance, the monetary authorities (which control the money supply) may be instructed to attain external balance only, ignoring any side effects of their actions on the level of employment. Similarly, the fiscal authorities may be instructed to use fiscal policy (changes in government spending and taxes) to attain internal balance, ignoring any possible side effects of their actions on the balance of payments. (This policy assignment was proposed by Mundell. Because of its significance, we study it in greater detail below.)

When each arm of policymaking is assigned to a single policy target, the economy does not move to the general balance point in a single stroke. Instead, an adjustment process takes place. The monetary authorities may adjust the money supply to achieve external balance. In so doing, however, they may frustrate the plans of the fiscal authorities, who must adjust their policy in accordance with the new experience. But this action of the fiscal authorities may throw monetary policy off target. Thus, the monetary authorities must again make a change, and so on in an infinite regression. The assignment problem is successfully solved only when this adjustment process leads eventually to the attainment of both targets simultaneously. In technical jargon, the assignment must be "stable."

Mundell's Assignment

Mundell (1968, pp. 152–176 and 233–239) developed a principle (which he called the "principle of effective market classification") according to which *the policy assignment is stable when each policy instrument is assigned to that target on which it has relatively the most influence.* The mathematical underpinnings of this principle are beyond the scope of this book. For our present purposes, we only need to know that *monetary policy should be assigned to external balance and fiscal policy to internal balance* (because monetary policy has a comparative advantage in working on external balance and fiscal policy has a comparative advantage in working on internal balance).

Mundell's assignment rule implies the following prescriptions for specific imbalances:

Zone*	State of the economy	Monetary policy	Fiscal policy
I	Unemployment and surplus	Expansionary	Expansionary
II	Inflation and surplus	Expansionary	Contractionary
III	Inflation and deficit	Contractionary	Contractionary
IV	Unemployment and deficit	Contractionary	Expansionary

*See Figure 20-5.

Advanced treatises on this subject show that when the policy authorities carry out the indicated policy changes smoothly and without lags, Mundell's assignment rule leads to the attainment of internal and external balance. In the presence of lags, however, and discrete policy changes, Mundell's assignment rule may become unstable. These problems are now illustrated.

Two Specific Illustrations

We proceed now with two specific illustrations of Mundell's assignment rule. In the first illustration, the assignment rule is stable and leads to internal and external balance. In the second illustration, the assignment rule is unstable and leads the economy farther and farther from the general balance point. In both illustrations, we assume that both the fiscal and monetary authorities react discontinuously.

Consider Figure 20-7, which initially exhibits the internal and external balance schedules. Suppose that the economy is currently at point A, where broken curves IS_1 and LM_1 intersect. Thus, the economy suffers from unemployment and a balance of payments surplus, since point A lies in zone I. To correct the surplus, the monetary authorities expand the money supply until curve LM_1 shifts sufficiently to the right, as shown by broken curve LM_2. Thus, the economy moves from A to B, as indicated by the heavy arrows. At B the balance of payments is in equilibrium, but the economy still suffers from unemployment. To restore internal balance, the fiscal authorities increase government spending until curve IS_1 shifts sufficiently to the right, as shown by broken curve IS_2. Thus, the economy again moves from B to C, as indicated by the heavy arrows. At C there is full employment, but the balance of payments is in deficit. To correct the deficit, the monetary authorities reduce the money supply sufficiently until curve LM_2 shifts to the left, as shown by broken curve LM_3. Accordingly, the economy moves from C to D, as indicated by the heavy arrows; and so on.

Now return to the initial position at A, and follow the heavy arrows that describe the actual course of the economy. Even though the assignment rule does not take the economy to general balance point F in one step, it is apparent that the economy moves closer and closer to point *F* with every application of the assignment rule. We therefore conclude that Figure 20-7 illustrates the case of a stable assignment.

The example of Figure 20-7 rests on the implicit assumption that the *LM* curve is flatter than the external balance schedule. When this assumption is dropped, an explosive cycle *may* arise. In general, when the *LM* curve is steeper than the external balance schedule, the policy assignment can be either stable or unstable depending on the relative slopes of the *LM* curve, the *IS* curve, and the external balance schedule.

Figure 20-8 illustrates a case in which the assignment rule yields explosive instability. The economy begins at point 1, which lies in zone II. A contractionary fiscal policy (prompted by the existing inflationary pressure) shifts curve *IS₁* down to *IS₂*, and the economy moves to point 2, as shown by the heavy arrows. At point 2, the balance of payments is in deficit, and this prompts a contractionary monetary policy, which shifts curve *LM₁* to the left, as shown by broken curve *LM₂*. As a result, the economy moves to point 3, where unemployment develops. The subsequent expansionary fiscal policy carries the economy to point 4; and so on. In this example, the economy follows an explosive cycle, as indicated by the heavy arrows starting at point 1 and continuing up to point 11 and beyond.

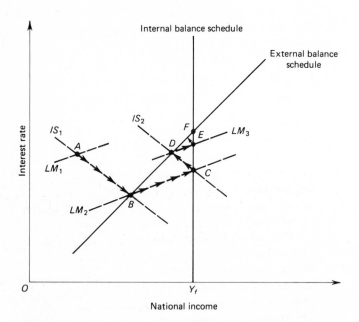

Figure 20-7 *An example of a stable assignment.*
Starting at point *A*, expansionary monetary policy takes the economy to point *B*. Then expansionary fiscal policy (dictated by the existing unemployment at *B*) moves the economy to *C*, where a deficit develops. The deficit prompts a reduction in the money supply, shifting the economy to *D;* and so on. The actual course of the economy is shown by the heavy arrows. Evidently the economy approaches general balance point *F* at a rapid rate.

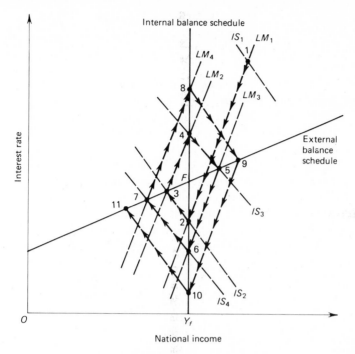

Figure 20-8 *An example of an unstable assignment.*
The interpretation of this diagram is the same as that of Figure 20-7. However, the economy now follows an explosive cycle, as indicated by the heavy arrows starting at point 1 and continuing up to point 11 and beyond.

Conclusion

The assignment rule is a powerful weapon. Yet it does have its drawbacks. As we have seen, in the case of discontinuous adjustment, the assignment rule may not carry the economy to the general balance point. Indeed, there is the real possibility that the assignment rule may lead to explosive instability. Because of this, it is imperative that policymakers seek additional information. On the one hand, opening channels of communication between the various policy authorities may lead to a more balanced approach to the attainment of internal and external balance. On the other hand, econometric research may help policymakers by revealing the position and slope of each of the relevant schedules. The only trouble is that after the policy authorities acquire enough information, they will have no need for any assignment rule—they will be able to go directly to the general balance point in a single stroke, as we explained earlier.

20-5   CRITICISM OF THE FISCAL-MONETARY POLICY MIX

The use of fiscal and monetary policy to attain internal and external balance has been criticized on several points, as follows.

First, fiscal and monetary policies may be subject to constraints, particularly political constraints. For instance, governments may not be willing to either reduce government spending to a low level or raise interest rates to high levels.

Second, even in the absence of political constraints, capital flows may fail to be sufficiently sensitive to interest-rate differentials. In addition, destabilizing speculation may complicate the problem tremendously.

Finally, some economists argue that Mundell's approach is not a true adjustment mechanism. They merely view the fiscal-monetary mix as a method of financing the payments imbalances. In particular, they view the short-term capital flows that are prompted by monetary policy as *accommodating*—not autonomous. These capital flows simply fill a gap left by other transactions. More important, however, the short-term capital flows may be ephemeral. In principle, the short-term capital flows reflect an adjustment in the allocation of *stocks* of assets. When the adjustment proceeds far enough so that the stocks are optimally allocated, the short-term capital flows must cease. (Nevertheless, in a growing world economy, the short-term capital flows may continue forever because the stocks tend to increase over time.) In addition, interest payments on the mounting stock of liabilities to foreigners may eventually sabotage Mundell's solution by reversing the short-term capital flow (that is, by converting an inflow into an outflow), thus aggravating further the payments imbalance.

20-6 SUMMARY

1   An increase in the money supply lowers the interest rate (which worsens the capital account) and increases national income and imports (which worsens the balance of trade). Thus, it worsens the balance of payments. A decrease in the money supply has symmetrical effects.

2   An increase in government spending (or a reduction in taxes) raises both the interest rate and national income. Hence, it improves the capital account and worsens the balance of trade. Its overall balance-of-payments effect is indeterminate. A decrease in government spending (or an increase in taxes) has symmetrical effects.

3   Fiscal and monetary policies have diametrically opposite effects on the interest rate (even though they have similar effects on national income). This difference is the key to their potential use for the attainment of internal and external balance. The only important proviso is that capital flows must be responsive to interest-rate differentials.

4   In terms of the *IS-LM* diagram, internal balance occurs along a vertical line (internal balance schedule) drawn at the full-employment level of national income. To the extent that capital flows are responsive to interest-rate differentials, external balance occurs along an upward-sloping external balance schedule. Internal and external balance occur simultaneously at the point of intersection of the internal and external balance schedules (general balance point).

5   To achieve internal and external balance simultaneously, policy-

makers must set the money supply and government spending at such levels as to make the *LM* and *IS* curves pass through the general balance point.

6   When capital flows are not responsive to interest-rate differentials, the external balance schedule becomes vertical, parallel to the internal balance schedule. In this case, fiscal and monetary policies alone cannot achieve internal and external balance simultaneously (since a general balance point does not exist). Expenditure-switching policies, however, can shift the vertical external balance schedule and make it coincide with the internal balance schedule. Then any combination of fiscal and monetary policies that brings about internal balance generates external balance also.

7   The internal and external balance schedules divide the diagram into four zones of economic unhappiness. At any time, the economy operates in one of these zones (at the intersection of the *IS* and *LM* curves). Indeed, the statistical data on inflation-unemployment and the balance of payments indicate the relevant zone.

8   The *IS* and *LM* curves that result from the application of the correct mix of fiscal and monetary policy divide the diagram into four policy regions. Knowledge of the policy region in which the economy happens to be is necessary for the formulation of the appropriate policy mix.

9   Because each zone of economic unhappiness overlaps two different policy regions, there is always uncertainty as to which policy mix is the correct one—policymakers know only the zone in which the economy happens to be, not the policy region.

10   The assignment problem is a product of decentralized decision making and involves the pairing of a policy instrument with a policy target. Under this scheme, the economy does not move to the general balance point in a single stroke. Instead, an adjustment process takes place. The assignment problem is successfully solved only when this adjustment process is stable.

11   Mundell proposed to assign monetary policy to external balance and fiscal policy to internal balance because monetary policy has a comparative advantage in working on external balance and fiscal policy has a comparative advantage in working on internal balance.

12   With smoothly continuous adjustment, Mundell's assignment is stable. In the presence of lags and discrete policy changes, however, Mundell's assignment may become unstable (when the *LM* curve is steeper than the external balance schedule).

13   Because the assignment rule may lead to explosive instability, policymakers must open channels of communication between the various policy authorities (in the hope of achieving a more balanced approach). In addition, they must use econometric research to determine the position and slope of each of the relevant schedules. However, with full information, there is no need for assignment—the authorities can go directly to the general balance point.

14   The use of fiscal and monetary policy to attain internal and external balance has been criticized on several points: It ignores political constraints; aside from destabilizing speculation, capital flows may not be sufficiently sensitive to interest-rate differentials, or they may dry up quickly (since short-term capital flows reflect an adjustment in the allocation of stocks of assets), or interest payments may sabotage the solution; and, finally, the fiscal-monetary mix is not a true adjustment—it is merely a method of financing payments imbalances.

SUGGESTED READING

Chacholiades, M. (1978). *International Monetary Theory and Policy*. McGraw-Hill Book Company, New York, chaps. 17 and 18.

Mundell, R. A. (1968). *International Economics*. The Macmillan Company, New York.

Stern, R. M. (1973). *The Balance of Payments*. Aldine Publishing Company, Chicago, chap. 10.

Whitman, M. V. N. (1970). *Policies for Internal and External Balance*. Special Papers in International Economics, no. 9, International Finance Section, Princeton University, Princeton, N.J.

Chapter Twenty-One

Flexible Exchange Rates

This chapter deals with the economics of the flexible-exchange-rate system. Under this system the rate of foreign exchange is determined daily in the foreign exchange market by the forces of supply and demand. The daily movements of the exchange rate are not restricted in any way by government policy, although monetary authorities may intervene in the foreign exchange market to iron out wide fluctuations. The freedom of the exchange rate to move daily in response to market forces does not necessarily imply that it will actually move significantly or erratically from day to day. It will do so only if the underlying economic forces are themselves erratic, causing erratic shifts in the supply and demand curves for foreign exchange. By clearing the foreign exchange market, the flexibility of the exchange rate maintains external balance. The authorities may then use other macroeconomic policies to achieve internal balance.

Section 21-1 deals with the theory of employment under flexible exchange rates. Section 21-2 carries the discussion a little further by considering the functioning of the flexible-exchange-rate system within the context of the *IS-LM* model of Chapter 17. After a short digression in Section 21-3 on the difficulties of stabilization policy, Section 21-4 explores the problem of whether the fixed-exchange-rate system or the flexible-exchange-rate system is better at shielding the open economy against the vagaries of economic disturbances. Finally, Section 21-5 summarizes briefly some additional arguments in the continuing debate over fixed and flexible exchange rates.

21-1 THE THEORY OF EMPLOYMENT WITH FLEXIBLE EXCHANGE RATES

In Chapter 16 we studied the income-adjustment mechanism under a regime of fixed rates of exchange and reached the important conclusion that international trade is a significant vehicle for the transmission of business cycles between countries (national-income multiplier theory). Thus, under a regime of fixed rates of exchange a boom (depression) in one country brings about an expansion (contraction) in the rest of the world.

We must now broaden the scope of our investigation by considering the theory of employment under a regime of flexible exchange rates. Under this regime, the rate of foreign exchange adjusts instantaneously and maintains equilibrium in the foreign exchange market continuously. Would such a flexible-exchange-rate system act as a buffer and "insulate" each economy from disturbances that occur in the rest of the world? Would a country now be able to maintain an independent fiscal and monetary policy to stabilize domestic income and employment, ignoring repercussions from foreign disturbances? These are important questions, and we analyze them in this section. (See also Section 21-4.)

National-Income Equilibrium under Flexible Exchange Rates

Return to the income-determination model of Section 16-2. Recall that under a fixed-exchange-rate system, national-income equilibrium in a small open economy prevails when desired aggregate demand $C(Y) + \bar{I} + \bar{X} - M(Y)$ equals aggregate output or national income Y. That is, national-income equilibrium occurs when the level of national income is such that the following equation is satisfied:

$$Y = C(Y) + \bar{I} + \bar{X} - M(Y) \tag{21-1}$$

Assume now that the net balance on international capital flows and unilateral transfers is zero. This simplifying assumption, which we shall drop in the next section, enables us to concentrate on commodity trade only. Thus, equilibrium in the foreign exchange market prevails when the balance of trade is zero; that is, $X - M(Y) = 0$. Now, under a flexible-exchange-rate system, the foreign exchange market is constantly in equilibrium. This means that (with the simplifying assumption that the net balance on capital flows and unilateral transfers is zero) the balance of trade is always zero; that is, $X - M(Y) = 0$. Accordingly, equation (21-1) reduces to:

$$Y = C(Y) + \bar{I} \tag{21-2}$$

Equation (21-2) is exactly the same as the national-income equilibrium condition for a closed economy.

We therefore conclude that the flexibility of the rate of exchange cuts off the *direct* link between national income and the balance of payments and tends to insulate the open economy from disturbances that occur in the rest of the world. In other words, insofar as the equilibrium level of national income (and the multiplier) is concerned, an open economy that adopts the flexible-exchange-rate system appears to behave like a closed economy in which national-income equilibrium prevails when the desired flow of saving—$S(Y) = Y - C(Y)$—equal the desired flow of investment.

The above conclusion need not be universally true, however, because there may also be *indirect* links, such as the terms-of-trade effect (see below), between the balance of payments and national income.

The Open-Economy Multiplier under Flexible Exchange Rates

What is the size of the open-economy multiplier under flexible exchange rates? Ignoring any possible indirect effects between the balance of payments and national income, an open economy with flexible exchange rates behaves like a closed economy. In particular, the open-economy multiplier with flexible exchange rates is equal to the closed-economy multiplier (that is, equal to the reciprocal of the marginal propensity to save) for all those autonomous changes that affect the open economy's desired level of spending at each level of income, such as autonomous changes in the desired flow of either investment I or consumption $C(Y)$ expenditure (as well as government spending). For other autonomous changes, such as changes in exports or imports (see specific illustrations below), the open-economy multiplier with flexible exchange rates is zero.

We can understand the truth of the above proposition and also gain further insights into the mechanism of national-income determination under flexible exchange rates by considering a few specific examples. We should reconsider briefly the effects on national income of the following disturbances, which we studied in Section 16-3:

1 An autonomous increase in exports
2 An autonomous increase in imports
3 An autonomous increase in desired investment

Throughout our discussion, we assume that the marginal propensity to save is 0.10 and the marginal propensity to import 0.15. This is the same assumption we made earlier in relation to the examples of Section 16-3. However, those examples were based on the assumption that the rate of exchange remains fixed always. The present examples, on the other hand, are based on the assumption that the rate of exchange is flexible; that is, the rate of exchange adjusts instantaneously and maintains equilibrium in the foreign exchange market constantly. The reader may want to review his or her understanding of the examples of Section 16-3 before proceeding to the rest of this section, because the discussion presupposes familiarity with that analysis.

1 An Increase in Exports   Suppose that exports increase by 100. What is the effect on national income?

As we saw in Section 16-3, under fixed exchange rates the national-income multiplier is 4 [that is, $1/(0.10 + 0.15) = 4$] and thus national income tends to rise by $4 \times 100 = 400$. Under flexible exchange rates, however, the change in exports cannot have any permanent effect on national income; that is, the multiplier with respect to changes in exports must be zero.

Consider Figure 21-1, which is similar to Figure 16-5. Equilibrium occurs initially at E, where the $S(Y) - \bar{I}$ schedule intersects the $\bar{X} - M(Y)$ schedule along the horizontal axis. (Under flexible exchange rates, national-income equilibrium occurs along the horizontal axis always. Why?) Accordingly, at point E, desired saving $S(Y)$ equals desired investment $\bar{I}$, and exports $\bar{X}$ equal desired imports $M(Y)$. That is, at the initial national-income equilibrium at E, the foreign exchange market is also in equilibrium, and the rate of exchange has no tendency to change from its current level.

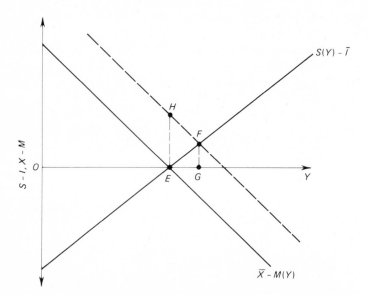

Figure 21-1   *The national-income effect of an increase in exports.*
National-income equilibrium occurs initially at E, where the $S(Y) - \bar{I}$ schedule intersects the $\bar{X} - M(Y)$ schedule along the horizontal axis. Under fixed rates of exchange, an autonomous increase in exports (say, EH) causes the $\bar{X} - M(Y)$ schedule to shift upward, as shown by the broken schedule, shifting equilibrium from E to F and increasing national income by EG. Under flexible exchange rates, equilibrium remains at E, because the initial balance-of-trade surplus, EH, causes the rate of exchange to fall until the broken $\bar{X} - M(Y)$ schedule returns to its initial position through E.

Under fixed rates of exchange, the increase in exports causes the $\bar{X} - M(Y)$ schedule to shift upward, as shown by the broken schedule. Thus, equilibrium shifts from E to F, and national income increases by EG. (In our numerical illustration, EH = increase in exports = 100, and EG = increase in income = 400.)

Under flexible exchange rates, the system cannot settle down at point F. For at F there is a balance of trade surplus, GF, that is, an excess supply of foreign exchange. In fact, under flexible exchange rates, the economy never moves from initial equilibrium point E. In particular, immediately after the increase in exports, the rate of exchange starts falling because of trade surplus EH. As we saw in Chapter 16, a revaluation of domestic currency (that is, a reduction in the price of foreign exchange in terms of domestic currency) causes the $\bar{X} - M(Y)$ schedule to shift downward. The fall in the rate of exchange continues until the broken $\bar{X} - M(Y)$ schedule returns to its initial position through E. Consequently, national-income equilibrium remains at point E.

We therefore conclude that, *under flexible exchange rates, autonomous changes in exports do not have any permanent effects on national income.* In other words, the open-economy multiplier with respect to autonomous changes in exports is zero under flexible exchange rates.

Note that the preceding conclusion holds irrespective of whether or not the Marshall-Lerner condition is satisfied at the initial equilibrium. The reason is simple: If the Marshall-Lerner condition is not satisfied and the initial equilibrium of the foreign exchange market is indeed unstable, the rate of exchange will continue falling until the system arrives at a new stable equilibrium where the Marshall-Lerner condition is satisfied. [For further discussion on this point, see Chacholiades (1978), pp. 244–251.] For this reason, we shall simplify our discussion from now on by assuming that the initial equilibrium is unique and stable.

2 An Increase in Imports   Suppose that the open economy reduces an existing tariff and thus causes its domestic consumers to divert 100 of their consumption expenditures from domestic to foreign products. What is the effect on national income?

As we saw in Section 16-3, under fixed exchange rates the shift from domestic to foreign products causes the aggregate demand for domestic output to fall by the increase in imports (100). Thus, national income *falls* by $4 \times 100 = 400$. [Recall that the open-economy multiplier with fixed rates of exchange is $1/(0.10 + 0.15) = 4$.] Flexible exchange rates, on the other hand, insulate the domestic economy and prevent the shift from domestic to foreign products from having any permanent effect on national income.

Consider Figure 21-2, which illustrates the same initial equilibrium as Figure 21-1 (see point E along the horizontal axis). Under fixed exchange rates, the increase in imports (caused by diversion of spending from domestic to

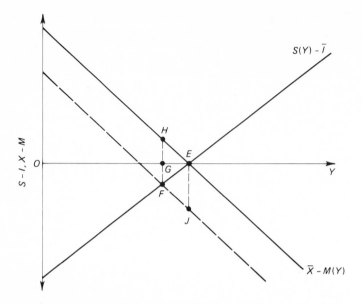

Figure 21-2 *The national income effect of an increase in imports.*
An increase in imports (diversion of domestic spending from domestic to foreign products) disturbs the initial equilibrium at E by shifting the $\bar{X} - M(Y)$ schedule downward, as shown by the broken schedule. Under fixed exchange rates, equilibrium moves from E to F, and national income falls by GE. Under flexible exchange rates, equilibrium remains at E because the initial balance-of-trade deficit, EJ, causes the rate of exchange to increase (depreciation of domestic currency) until the broken $\bar{X} - M(Y)$ schedule returns to its initial position through E.

foreign products) causes the $\bar{X} - M(Y)$ schedule to shift downward, as shown by the broken schedule. Thus, equilibrium shifts from E to F, and national income *falls* by GE. (In our numerical illustration, $FH = increase$ in imports $= 100$, and $GE = reduction$ in national income $= 400$.)

Again, under flexible exchange rates, the system cannot reach equilibrium at F. The reason is simple: At F there is a balance-of-trade deficit, FG (that is, an excess demand for foreign exchange). As with the first illustration (increase in exports), the economy never moves from E under flexible exchange rates. In particular, immediately after the increase in imports, the rate of exchange starts rising because of balance-of-trade deficit EJ. This upward trend in the rate of exchange continues until the broken $\bar{X} - M(Y)$ schedule returns to its initial position through E. Consequently, national-income equilibrium remains at point E.

We therefore conclude that *under a flexible-exchange-rate system, autonomous shifts in domestic expenditure from domestic to foreign products, and vice versa, have no permanent effects on national income.* In this case as well as the previous one concerning autonomous changes in exports, the rate of exchange acts as a perfect automatic stabilizer of the domestic economy.

3 An Increase in Desired Investment Suppose that domestic investment $\bar{I}$ increases by 100. What is the effect on national income?

As we saw in Section 16-3, under fixed exchange rates the increase in domestic investment (100) causes the aggregate demand for domestic output to increase by the same amount. Thus, national income *increases* by $4 \times 100 = 400$. [Recall that the open-economy multiplier with fixed rates of exchange is $1/(0.10 + 0.15) = 4$.] What happens when the rate of exchange adjusts instantaneously and maintains equilibrium in the foreign exchange market continuously?

Consider Figure 21-3, which illustrates the same initial equilibrium as Figures 21-1 and 21-2 (see point E along the horizontal axis). Under fixed exchange rates, the increase in investment causes the $S(Y) - \bar{I}$ schedule to shift downward, as shown by the broken schedule running through points F and J. Thus, equilibrium shifts from E to F, and national income *increases* by EG. (In our numerical illustration, $FH =$ increase in investment $= 100$, and $EG =$ increase in income $= 400$.)

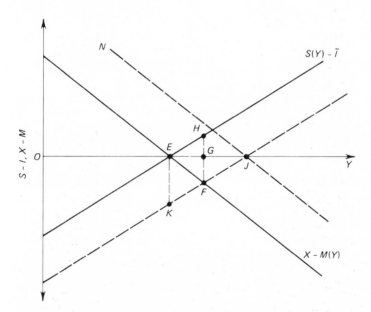

Figure 21-3 *The national income effect of an increase in desired investment.*
The initial equilibrium at E is disturbed by an increase in investment FH, which causes the $S(Y) - \bar{I}$ schedule to shift downward, as shown by broken schedule FJ. Under fixed exchange rates, equilibrium shifts from E to F, and national income increases by EG. Under flexible exchange rates, the economy cannot remain at F, where balance-of-trade deficit FG would prevail. The deficit at F causes the rate of exchange to increase until the $\bar{X} - M(Y)$ schedule shifts upward to intersect the new $S(Y) - \bar{I}$ schedule along the horizontal axis, as shown by broken schedule NJ. Thus, national income increases from OE to OJ. The national-income multiplier is now equal to the reciprocal of the marginal propensity to save (closed-economy multiplier).

Under flexible exchange rates, however, the open economy cannot remain at point F. The reason is simple: At F there is a balance-of-trade deficit, FG (that is, an excess demand for foreign exchange), pulling the rate of exchange up (that is, causing the domestic currency to depreciate). The upward trend in the rate of exchange continues until the $\bar{X} - M(Y)$ schedule shifts upward and to the right and intersects the new $S(Y) - \bar{I}$ schedule along the horizontal axis, as shown by broken schedule NJ. Consequently, national-income equilibrium moves from E to J.

The increase in national income (EJ) under flexible exchange rates is necessarily larger than the corresponding increase (EG) under fixed exchange rates. What is the precise magnitude of the national-income multiplier under flexible exchange rates? Note that in Figure 21-3, the slope of the $S(Y) - \bar{I}$ schedule (which is equal to the marginal propensity to save MPS) is given by the ratio EK/EJ. Since EK = increase in investment ΔI, and EJ = increase in income ΔY, we have

$$\text{MPS} = \Delta I / \Delta Y$$

or

$$\Delta Y = (1/\text{MPS})\Delta I \tag{21-1}$$

Accordingly, *the national-income multiplier under flexible exchange rates is equal to the reciprocal of the marginal propensity to save, as in the case of a closed economy.*

In our numerical illustration, the marginal propensity to save is 0.10. Therefore, the national-income multiplier under flexible exchange rates is $1/0.10 = 10$. Thus, when desired investment increases by 100, the equilibrium level of national income increases by $10 \times 100 = 1,000$.

The Terms-of-Trade Effect

Advanced treatises on the subject point out that the balance of trade may influence national income not only directly but also indirectly through the terms of trade. For instance, consider the previous example of an increase in imports that initially creates a balance-of-trade deficit and causes the domestic currency to depreciate. As we already know, the depreciation of the domestic currency affects the terms of trade. In particular, suppose that the terms of trade of the small open economy deteriorate, which in turn causes the economy's real income to fall—at any level of domestic output, the open economy can consume fewer commodities, both domestic and foreign, after the terms-of-trade deterioration than before. There is a presumption that as real income falls, the open economy may adapt by saving a smaller proportion out of any given money income. Under these circumstances, the $S(Y) - \bar{I}$ schedule of Figure 21-2 would shift downward and to the right, causing national income to eventually increase above the the initial level of OE.

The above terms-of-trade effect was first noted by Laursen and Metzler

(1950). We ignore this effect in this book simply because, though theoretically possible, there does not exist any strong empirical evidence to support it. [For further discussion of the terms-of-trade effect, also known as the Laursen-Metzler effect, see Chacholiades (1978), pp. 235–239.]

21-2 THE *IS-LM* MODEL WITH FLEXIBLE EXCHANGE RATES

We now proceed to consider briefly the functioning of the flexible-exchange-rate system within the context of the *IS-LM* model of Chapter 17. In particular, we wish to find out how fiscal and monetary policies affect the level of national income under flexible exchange rates. Are fiscal and monetary policies relatively more effective under flexible than under fixed exchange rates?

The *IS-LM* Model Again

We can easily expand the *IS-LM* model of Chapter 17 to incorporate flexible exchange rates. Actually, the only modification we must make concerns the state of equilibrium. The flexibility of the rate of exchange guarantees equilibrium in the foreign exchange market. Accordingly, the open economy must always operate on the external balance schedule. This means that general equilibrium cannot prevail unless the external balance schedule passes through the intersection of the *IS* and *LM* curves. Otherwise, in the presence of an external disequilibrium (whether a deficit or surplus), the rate of exchange will continue to change until external balance is restored, as explained below.

Recall that the external balance schedule is the locus of all combinations of income levels and interest rates that are consistent with equilibrium in the balance of *payments* (not balance of *trade,* unless capital movements are absent). Accordingly, *along the external balance schedule the open economy may experience either a balance-of-trade deficit or a balance-of-trade surplus,* depending on whether the net capital flow (which depends on the interest rate only) is positive or negative. Thus, unlike the model of the previous section, the balance of trade does exert a direct influence on national income, and it appears that exogenous changes in exports or imports may affect the equilibrium level of income. That this is *not* so is explained in Section 21-4.

The Effects of Monetary Policy

Consider Figure 21-4. An expansionary monetary policy disturbs the initial equilibrium at point 1 (see solid schedules) by shifting the *LM* curve to the right, as shown by broken curve *LM'*. Under fixed exchange rates, the economy would move to point 2, where national income is higher, the interest rate is lower, and the balance of payments develops a deficit (because point 2 lies to the right of the initial external balance schedule—see solid schedule *EB*). What happens under flexible exchange rates?

Under flexible exchange rates, the incipient deficit at point 2 causes the domestic currency to depreciate. How does this currency depreciation affect

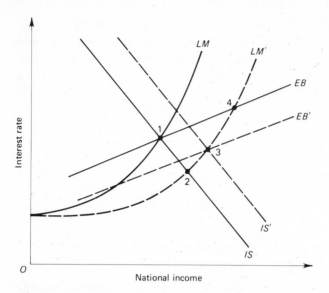

Figure 21-4 *The effects of monetary policy.*
Equilibrium occurs initially at point 1. An expansionary monetary policy shifts the *LM* curve to
the right, as shown by broken curve *LM'*. Under fixed exchange rates, the economy moves to
point 2, where there is a balance-of-payments deficit. Under flexible exchange rates, the deficit at point 2 causes the domestic currency to depreciate, which, in turn, causes the *IS* curve
and the external balance schedule to shift to the right, as shown by broken lines *IS'* and *EB'*.
Equilibrium is finally restored at point 3 (between points 2 and 4), where national income is
higher than at point 2.

the various schedules in Figure 21-4? We must answer this question before we
can determine the final equilibrium under flexible exchange rates.

Although the curve *LM'* may shift slightly to the left (because of the
increase in domestic prices that results from the depreciation of domestic currency), we shall simplify our analysis by assuming that the currency depreciation leaves curve *LM'* unchanged.

On the other hand, both the *IS* curve and external balance schedule *EB*
shift to the right, as shown by broken curve *IS'* and broken schedule *EB'*.
Thus, as the domestic currency depreciates, the balance of trade improves, assuming only that the Marshall-Lerner condition is satisfied. This means that external balance schedule *EB* shifts to the right: At any given interest rate (and
thus given net capital flow), external balance is attained at a higher income level
since at the initial, lower income level there exists an external surplus. The
balance-of-trade improvement caused by the depreciation of the domestic currency also means that the *IS* curve shifts to the right: At every interest rate, the
aggregate demand for the open economy's output tends to increase because of
the balance-of-trade improvement.

Return now to the determination of the final equilibrium (following an
increase in the money supply) under flexible exchange rates. As we have seen,
the incipient deficit at point 2 (Figure 21-4) causes the domestic currency to

depreciate. The currency depreciation, in turn, causes both the *IS* curve and external balance schedule *EB* to shift to the right. The open economy reaches a new equilibrium when its currency depreciates sufficiently so that the new *IS* curve and the new external balance schedule intersect along broken curve *LM'* somewhere between points 2 and 4, as illustrated by point 3. At point 3, the economy reaches a lasting equilibrium. Thus, the foreign exchange market is in equilibrium, and the rate of exchange is stabilized at its new higher level.

It is apparent from Figure 21-4 that monetary policy is more powerful *(insofar as its effects on national income and employment are concerned) under a flexible- than under a fixed-exchange-rate system.* Thus, national income is higher at point 3 (equilibrium point with flexible exchange rates) than at point 2 (equilibrium point with fixed exchange rates).

The Effects of Fiscal Policy

Turn now to fiscal policy. How does an increase in government spending (or a reduction in taxation) affect the level of national income and employment under a flexible-exchange-rate system? Is fiscal policy more or less powerful under flexible exchange rates than under fixed exchange rates?

The case of fiscal policy is a little more complicated than the case of monetary policy. As we saw in Chapter 20, the effect of fiscal policy on the balance of payments is indeterminate under fixed exchange rates, depending on whether the external balance schedule is steeper or flatter than the *LM* curve. Accordingly, under flexible exchange rates, fiscal policy may cause the rate of exchange to either increase or decrease. We illustrate both cases in this section.

Figure 21-5 shows how fiscal policy works when the external balance is steeper than the *LM* curve. An increase in government spending disturbs the initial equilibrium at point 1 (see solid schedules) by shifting the *IS* curve to the right, as shown by broken curve IS'. Under fixed exchange rates, the economy would move to point 2, where national income and the interest rate are higher (relative to the initial equilibrium at point 1), and the balance of payments develops a deficit (because point 2 lies to the right of the initial external balance schedule—see solid schedule *EB*).

With flexible exchange rates, however, the incipient deficit at point 2 causes the domestic currency to depreciate. As we saw earlier in this chapter, the currency depreciation causes both the external balance schedule and curve *IS'* to shift to the right until a new equilibrium is reestablished, as shown by the broken schedules through point 3. By comparing point 2 (equilibrium point under fixed exchange rates) with point 3 (equilibrium point under flexible exchange rates), we reach the following conclusion: *When the external balance schedule is steeper than the LM curve, fiscal policy has a larger effect on national income and employment under a flexible- than under a fixed-exchange-rate system.*

Consider now Figure 21-6, which illustrates how fiscal policy works when the external balance schedule is flatter than the *LM* curve. Again an expansionary fiscal policy disturbs the initial equilibrium at point 1 by shifting the *IS*

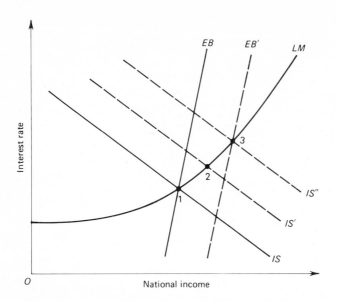

Figure 21-5 *The effects of fiscal policy when the external balance schedule is steeper than the LM curve.*
Equilibrium occurs initially at point 1. An expansionary fiscal policy shifts the *IS* curve to the right, as shown by broken curve *IS'*. Under fixed exchange rates, the economy moves to point 2, where there is a balance-of-payments deficit. Under flexible exchange rates, the deficit at point 2 causes the domestic currency to depreciate; and this depreciation, in turn, causes curve *IS'* and external balance schedule *EB* to shift to the right, as shown by broken lines *IS"* and *EB'*. Equilibrium is finally restored at point 3, where national income is higher than at point 2.

curve to the right, as shown by broken curve *IS'*. Under fixed exchange rates the economy moves to point 2. With flexible exchange rates, however, the incipient balance-of-payments *surplus* at point 2 causes the domestic currency to appreciate in the foreign exchange market. In turn, the appreciation of the domestic currency causes both external balance schedule *EB* and broken curve *IS'* to shift to the left—the effects of currency appreciation are symmetrical to the effects of currency depreciation. The economy eventually reaches equilibrium at some point on the *LM* curve between points 1 and 2, as shown by point 3, where broken curve *IS"* and broken schedule *EB'* intersect.

By comparing point 2 (equilibrium point under fixed exchange rates) with point 3 (equilibrium point under flexible exchange rates), we reach the following conclusion: *When the external balance schedule is flatter than the LM curve, fiscal policy has a smaller effect on national income and employment under a flexible- than under a fixed-exchange-rate system.*

We can summarize the preceding discussion as follows: Whether fiscal policy is more powerful (insofar as its effects on national income and employment are concerned) under a flexible- than under a fixed-exchange-rate system depends on circumstances. In particular, if an expansionary fiscal policy causes a depreciation of the domestic currency, then fiscal policy is more effective

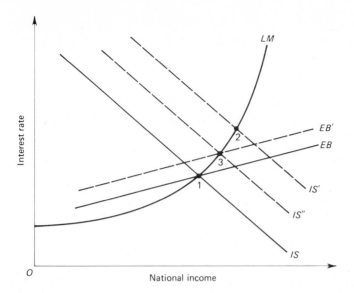

Figure 21-6 *The effects of fiscal policy when the external balance schedule is flatter than the LM curve.*
Equilibrium occurs initially at point 1. An expansionary fiscal policy shifts the *IS* curve to the right, as shown by broken curve *IS'*. Under fixed exchange rates, the economy moves to point 2, where there is a balance-of-payments surplus. Under flexible exchange rates, the surplus at point 2 causes the domestic currency to appreciate; and this appreciation, in turn, causes curve *IS'* and external balance schedule *EB* to shift to the left, as shown by broken lines *IS"* and *EB'*. Equilibrium is finally restored at point 3, where national income is lower than at point 2 (but higher than at point 1).

under a flexible-exchange-rate system. On the other hand, if an expansionary fiscal policy causes an appreciation of the domestic currency, then fiscal policy is more effective under a fixed-exchange-rate system.

Attaining Internal and External Balance

Under flexible exchange rates, external balance prevails constantly as a result of the interplay of free market forces. In other words, the flexibility of the rate of exchange is sufficient to maintain external balance. To attain internal balance as well, the open economy may use either fiscal or monetary policy or any combination of the two. Thus, in the presence of unemployment, the authorities must pursue an expansionary fiscal-monetary policy. On the other hand, in the presence of inflationary pressures, the authorities must pursue a contractionary fiscal-monetary policy. Economists usually count the abundance of policy instruments as a positive advantage of flexible exchange rates.

21-3 STABILIZATION POLICY: A DIGRESSION

Even a casual observer of economic affairs knows that stabilization policy is a rather complicated and often frustrating art. As we explain briefly in this section, fiscal and monetary policies are complicated by lags and uncertainties, and as a rule they do not smoothly stabilize the economy at "full employment." As it turns out, some economic institutions facilitate more than others the task of macroeconomic policy. In fact, the choice of economic institutions is crucial to the success or failure of stabilization policy.

After reviewing in this section the difficulties of stabilization policy, we shall return in Section 21-4 to the question of whether the fixed- or flexible-exchange-rate system makes stabilization policy easier.

Economic Disturbances

Because of incessant disturbances, no economy remains permanently stable at full employment. Rather, a real-world economy tends to fluctuate continuously around its steady-state equilibrium. The main purpose of stabilization policy is to reduce these fluctuations.

Economic disturbances (or autonomous shocks) take place continuously in an economic system. These disturbances usually cause shifts in the various components of aggregate demand. Thus, the consumption function may shift as a result of a change in tastes between consumption and saving. Similarly, the investment function may shift as a result of a change in the optimism (animal spirits) of investors. Government spending and taxes may also change either because of wars or because the government wishes to pursue some socially desirable project(s), such as building a national railroad or highway system, or even sending a person to the moon.

Ironically, policymakers themselves may also introduce further disturbances either because of mistakes (the art of policymaking is extremely difficult) or because of political reasons, as exemplified by the so-called *political business cycle*—an incumbent President may attempt to improve economic conditions right before the election even though such action may destabilize the economy after the election.

The Difficulties of Stabilization Policy

What are the requirements for a successful stabilization strategy? First, the authorities must be able to recognize quickly the occurrence of a disturbance and, more important, predict its effects with sufficient accuracy. Second, they must be able to quickly put into effect economic policy measures that completely neutralize the effects of the disturbance, now and in the future.

Unfortunately, neither requirement is met in the real world. This is due partly to the fact that our knowledge of how the economy actually works is rather limited and partly to the existence of lags in the recognition of a disturbance, in formulating and implementing the correct policy, and in the effects of that policy itself on the economy.

For instance, following an autonomous reduction in aggregate demand, policymakers must first collect data and attempt to make a prediction concerning the ultimate effects of the disturbance on the economy. For this purpose, policymakers must decide whether the disturbance is temporary or permanent. A temporary disturbance, such as a strike, does not usually require any action. Assuming that the disturbance is permanent, however, policymakers must use a sufficiently accurate model of the economy to predict how disruptive the disturbance will be. Then they must decide on the appropriate strategy to minimize the impact of the disturbance. Suppose they decide on fiscal policy action. As the reader may well know, fiscal policy requires new legislation, which must be approved by both houses of Congress. This is often a rather lengthy process. After Congress approves the necessary legislation, it may take some additional time before the policy change goes into effect. For instance, suppose the government decides to build a new highway. It must first survey possible routes, acquire land, listen to public protests, solicit bids, and so on. Ironically, by the time spending starts flowing, a deflationary policy may be needed instead.

Monetary policy action may go into effect much more quickly, of course, than fiscal policy. Nevertheless, the effect on aggregate demand (and specifically investment spending) of an increase in the money supply may take several months, perhaps a year.

The existence of large and variable lags as well as our imperfect knowledge of the workings of the economy and our inability to predict disturbances, such as the 1973–1974 oil embargo, make the task of stabilization policy rather formidable. To appreciate this, simply imagine that you own a car whose brakes and gas pedal take effect only after a significant, but variable, lag. Suppose that you are driving this car along a street full of traffic lights. Suppose further that pedestrians can cross this street any time they want to. Can you really drive this car for long at a reasonable speed without either getting a ticket or running into somebody?

Automatic Stabilizers

Given the difficulties of discretionary macroeconomic policy, it is a great relief to know that modern economies possess *built-in,* or *automatic, stabilizers.* These automatic stabilizers tend to reduce the size of the multiplier and add stability to the economy. Their most important advantage is their automaticity. Immediately after the occurrence of a disturbance, the automatic stabilizers go into action—they are not constrained by any decision lags.

The most important automatic stabilizer is the income tax. For instance, following an inflationary increase in investment, the income tax increases immediately the leakages out of the income stream and provides some cushioning to the upswing. Clearly, a *progressive* income tax is a much stronger automatic stabilizer than a single income-tax rate applying to all income and taxpayers. Another important automatic stabilizer is unemployment compensation.

Because of the difficulties of discretionary stabilization policy, it is understandable that macroeconomists may want to improve the automatic stabilizers. This concern actually extends all the way to international economics.

Thus, international economists are concerned with the problem of choosing the "best" exchange-rate system among various alternatives. Surely in this choice the question of stabilization is of paramount importance.

21-4 EXCHANGE-RATE REGIMES AND STABILIZATION

An open economy may be subject to any number of economic disturbances, such as autonomous shifts in exports, imports, domestic investment, and consumption. Which exchange-rate system better shields the open economy against the vagaries of such exogenous shocks? That is the central concern of this section. As we show below, sometimes the fixed-exchange-rate system and sometimes the flexible-exchange-rate system may act as an automatic stabilizer, depending on the nature of the economic disturbances that afflict the open economy.

A General Proposition

Before proceeding to specific cases, we wish to summarize the essence of the ensuing discussion in the following general proposition. In general, *the flexible-exchange-rate system provides more stability to the open economy in relation to disturbances that originate in the foreign sector*, such as autonomous changes in exports and imports. On the other hand, *the fixed-exchange-rate system provides more stability to the open economy in the presence of disturbances that originate in the domestic flow of spending*, such as autonomous changes in domestic investment, consumption, and government spending. This general proposition is a useful first approximation, even though there may be some exceptions to it.

Disturbances in the Foreign Sector

Consider first the case of disturbances that originate in the foreign sector, such as autonomous shifts in exports and imports. Clearly, the preceding proposition (namely, that the flexible-exchange-rate system provides more stability in relation to disturbances that originate in the foreign sector) is consistent with our discussion in Sections 21-1 and 21-2.

For instance, the analysis of Section 21-1 shows clearly that in the absence of any capital movements, the flexible-exchange-rate system insulates perfectly the domestic economy from autonomous shifts in exports or imports, while the fixed-exchange-rate system allows such autonomous shocks in the foreign sector to exert their full influence on the domestic economy through the open-economy multiplier. Indeed, as we can easily demonstrate, this conclusion remains valid in more general models, such as the *IS-LM* model with interest-sensitive capital movements.

Consider Figure 21-7. Initially, the open economy is in equilibrium at point *E*, where, by assumption, it also enjoys full employment and balance-of-payments equilibrium. Suppose now that the initial equilibrium is disturbed by

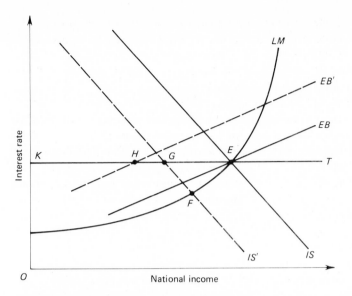

Figure 21-7 *Disturbances in the foreign sector.*
A reduction in exports disturbs the initial equilibrium at *E* by causing the *IS* curve and external balance schedule *EB* to shift to the left, as shown by broken curve *IS'* and schedule *EB'*.
Under a fixed-exchange-rate system, equilibrium shifts to *F*. Under a flexible-exchange-rate
system, however, the economy eventually returns to the initial equilibrium at point *E*.

an autonomous reduction in exports. (Exactly the same analysis holds for an
autonomous increase in imports.) How does this autonomous reduction in exports affect the various schedules?

At the initial rate of exchange, the *IS* curve shifts to the left, as shown by
broken curve *IS'*—at any interest rate, the commodity market can be in equilibrium at a lower income level. This is not all. External balance schedule *EB*
also shifts to the left, as shown by broken schedule *EB'*. Note carefully that the
leftward shift of the external-balance schedule is necessarily larger than the
leftward shift of the *IS* curve. Thus, *at the initial rate of interest (OK) and the
initial rate of exchange,* national income falls by *GE* (which actually represents
the leftward shift of the *IS* curve), but the balance of payments develops a deficit, as the net capital flow remains the same while the balance of trade deteriorates (see example 2 in Section 16-3, even though that example deals with an
*in*crease in exports).

Under a fixed-exchange-rate system, equilibrium will shift to point *F*,
where income is lower than at *E* but higher than at *G*. Under a flexible-
exchange-rate system, the economy will eventually return to point *E*. Thus, immediately after the reduction in exports and the incipient deficit, the domestic
currency will start to depreciate, and it will continue to do so until the external
deficit disappears. Evidently, the economy will reach a new equilibrium only
when the domestic currency has depreciated sufficiently to offset completely
the initial reduction in exports.

To understand the preceding conclusion well in terms of Figure 21-7, assume that the *LM* curve is horizontal, as shown by line *KT*. Under fixed exchange rates, the reduction in exports will shift the economy to *G*. Under flexible exchange rates, the deficit at *G* will cause the rate of exchange to rise until balance-of-payments equilibrium is restored. Now balance-of-payments equilibrium will be restored when the balance of *trade* attains its original value at *E*—since the rate of interest is kept constant, the net capital flow must remain the same. But the balance of trade will indeed attain its original value only when the rate of exchange increases sufficiently to generate a balance-of-trade improvement equal to the initial reduction in exports. Under these circumstances, both curve *IS'* and schedule *EB'* will return to their initial position through *E*. Obviously, this conclusion remains valid even in the general case in which the *LM* curve is upward-sloping, as shown in Figure 21-7.

We must therefore conclude that countries suffering from export instability (such as countries which export only a small number of products that happen to be susceptible to the vagaries of the business cycle in importing countries) can stabilize their domestic economies by adopting the flexible-exchange-rate system. This argument is usually made for countries that export metals, such as Chile (copper) and Malaysia (tin).

Disturbances in the Domestic Flow of Spending

Turn now to internal shocks, such as autonomous shifts in investment spending, government spending, liquidity preference, and supply of money. We are already familiar with the implications of these autonomous shifts from our discussion in Section 21-2. There we saw that monetary policy has a larger impact on national income and employment under a flexible-exchange-rate system than under a fixed-exchange-rate system. Accordingly, internal monetary shocks, such as autonomous shifts in the liquidity preference and changes in the money supply, are likely to be more disruptive (or destabilizing) under the flexible- than under the fixed-exchange-rate system. Therefore, countries that suffer from these internal monetary shocks can facilitate their stabilization policy by adopting the fixed-exchange-rate system.

The effects of internal shocks in domestic spending (such as government spending, investment spending, and consumption spending) are similar to the effects of fiscal policy. As we saw in Section 21-2, whether fiscal policy is more powerful under the flexible- than under the fixed-exchange-rate system depends on the degree of capital mobility. With low capital mobility, fiscal policy is more powerful under the flexible-exchange-rate system (see Figure 21-5). On the other hand, with high capital mobility, fiscal policy is more powerful under the fixed-exchange-rate system (see Figure 21-6). Accordingly, internal shocks in domestic spending are likely to be more disruptive under the flexible-exchange-rate system only when the degree of capital mobility is relatively low. When the degree of capital mobility is relatively high, internal shocks in domestic spending tend to be more disruptive under the fixed-exchange-rate system.

We therefore conclude that countries that suffer from internal shocks in domestic spending and at the same time experience a low degree of capital mobility can facilitate their stabilization policy by adopting the fixed-exchange-rate system. On the other hand, countries that suffer from internal shocks in domestic spending and at the same time experience a high degree of capital mobility can facilitate their stabilization policy by adopting the flexible-exchange-rate system.

Disturbances in International Capital Movements

Finally, we wish to mention the case of autonomous shifts of funds from one financial center to another prompted by political upheavals, rumors, and so on. Assuming that the monetary authorities can sterilize the effects of such movements of funds on the domestic money supply, it must be clear that the fixed-exchange-rate system insulates the domestic economy perfectly in this case. Therefore, countries that experience sudden inflows or outflows of funds should, when feasible, adopt the fixed-exchange-rate system and sterilize any payments imbalances, as explained in Chapter 17. [For further details, see Chacholiades (1978), Chapter 19.]

21-5   FURTHER ARGUMENTS FOR AND AGAINST FLEXIBLE EXCHANGE RATES

We conclude this chapter by summarizing briefly some additional arguments in the continuing debate over fixed and flexible exchange rates. Our discussion begins with the case for flexible exchange rates. We then consider the important issues of uncertainty, destabilizing speculation, and price "discipline."

The Case for Flexible Exchange Rates

As we have seen, under flexible exchange rates external balance is brought about by the free interplay of market forces. The rate of exchange moves freely to equate supply and demand, eliminating continuously external deficits and surpluses. This simplicity of maintaining external balance is an important advantage of the flexible-exchange-rate system. We illustrate the implications of this advantage by considering two alternative situations—a model with flexible domestic prices and a model with fixed domestic prices.

Consider first a classical world in which prices (including factor prices, such as the wage rate) are flexible in both directions. In this classical world, the flexibility of prices alone can maintain internal and external balance. The rate of exchange can remain fixed permanently. Economic disturbances, internal or external, affect prices only. In this case (which we may call the "ideal gold standard"), the argument for flexible exchange rates rests on the notion that changing one price (that is, the rate of exchange) is much simpler (and perhaps more economical) than changing millions of commodity and factor prices in the economy. This argument is similar to the adoption of daylight saving time during the summer months. Instead of rescheduling every single event to occur one hour earlier, it is simpler to move the clock one hour ahead, leaving all schedules unchanged.

Turn now to a Keynesian world of rigid prices. As we saw earlier, a fixed rate of exchange gives rise to external deficits and surpluses because there is no automatic mechanism to achieve external balance. Since their ability to finance external imbalances is rather limited, the authorities must ultimately use deliberate economic policy measures (such as monetary and fiscal policy, direct controls, and exchange-rate adjustment) to restore external balance. Besides any economic inefficiencies that direct controls may entail, the use of discretionary policy to maintain external balance creates additional difficulties for stabilization policy. Essentially, the maintenance of a fixed rate of exchange gives rise to an extra policy target: external balance. As we saw earlier, to simultaneously achieve internal and external balance, the authorities must use two effective and mutually independent instruments. This increases the inherent difficulties of stabilization policy.

The adoption of flexible exchange rates, on the other hand, automatically ensures the preservation of external balance and thereby reduces the tasks of monetary, fiscal, and other policy instruments. The authorities can now direct these instruments toward the preservation of internal balance alone.

The removal of the balance-of-payments motive for restrictions on international trade and payments is an important advantage of flexible exchange rates. Thus, the world can move toward free trade. Each country can be free to specialize in those commodities in whose production she has a comparative advantage. Such international division of labor is fundamental to the maximization of world welfare.

Finally, the adoption of flexible exchange rates provides autonomy to individual countries with respect to their use of public policy. For instance, under fixed exchange rates countries cannot choose points along their respective Phillips curves, implying different rates of inflation. As we saw in Section 18-5, the currency of the country with the higher rate of inflation must be allowed to depreciate at the same rate at which domestic inflation exceeds world inflation. Otherwise, the country cannot preserve both internal and external balance simultaneously. The adoption of flexible exchange rates eliminates the need to coordinate public policy (and particularly monetary policy) among countries. Under flexible exchange rates, countries have more freedom to pursue public policy independently of balance-of-payments considerations.

Uncertainty

The first argument against flexible exchange rates relates to uncertainty. In particular, the critics argue that flexible exchange rates would be highly unstable—exchange rates would fluctuate wildly from day to day. Such instability would lead to increased uncertainty, which, in turn, would seriously reduce the flows of international trade and investment.

The critics usually cite two factors that may account for the alleged instability in the foreign exchange market: elasticity pessimism and destabilizing speculation. (Discussion of destabilizing speculation is postponed until the next subsection.) Elasticity pessimism refers to fears that the price elasticities of import demand for internationally traded goods are very low and that the Marshall-Lerner condition is not generally satisfied. Indeed, when the elasticities are low, balance-of-payments disturbances can still cause wide fluctuations in the exchange rate even though the Marshall-Lerner condition may be satisfied (see Section 15-5).

Elasticity pessimism was prevalent in the 1930s and 1940s but gave way to elasticity optimism in the 1960s and 1970s. Nevertheless, whether the price elasticities of import demand for internationally traded goods are high or low is an empirical question. Unfortunately, as we saw in Section 15-9, empirical studies do not fully support such elasticity optimism, even though there are reasons to believe that the empirical estimates underestimate the true elasticities.

The proponents of flexible exchange rates have three main counterarguments: (1) The fixed-exchange-rate system is not free of risk and uncertainty; (2) flexible exchange rates are not necessarily unstable; and (3) any resultant risk and uncertainty under flexible exchange rates need not have the detrimental effects claimed by the critics. We consider these arguments below.

To the extent the countries cannot, as a practical matter, attain internal and external balance by means of an appropriate use of fiscal and monetary policies (without exchange-rate adjustments), permanently fixed rates impose heavy adjustment costs. Thus, deficit countries must either deflate their economies and generate widespread unemployment or impose restrictions on trade and capital movements. Similarly, surplus countries must eventually accept unwanted inflation.

The adjustable-peg system, on the other hand, reduces substantially the risk of unemployment and inflation (as well as restrictions on trade and capital movements) by allowing countries in fundamental disequilibrium to use exchange-rate adjustment. However, occasional devaluations and revaluations also involve traders and investors in unexpected losses (and gains).

We therefore conclude that the risks and adjustment costs are not necessarily any smaller under a fixed-exchange-rate system than under a flexible-exchange-rate system.

On the positive side, the proponents of flexible exchange rates argue that the freedom of the exchange rates to move daily in response to market forces does not necessarily imply that they will actually move significantly and erratically from day to day. They will do so only if the underlying economic forces are themselves erratic, causing erratic shifts in the supply and demand schedules for foreign exchange. But in that case no international monetary system can function smoothly. The fact of the matter is that the exchange rates will move gradually and predictably, providing gradual adjustment and averting crises. Stabilizing speculation will keep the exchange-rate fluctuations within narrow limits.

Further, risk-averse traders and investors can actually cover their exchange risks in the forward-exchange markets at a moderate cost, as explained in Chapter 12. This is, of course, true for short-term transactions. Admittedly, for long-term transactions, the forward markets are very thin (if they exist at all), and the cost of coverage is very high. Nevertheless, the exchange risk for long-term transactions is highly exaggerated—the world economy tends to provide a substantial amount of automatic hedging. Thus, a country whose currency depreciates steadily over time is likely to be experiencing a steady inflation (relative to the rest of the world). This must be evident from our discussion of the purchasing-power-parity theory (see Section 15-8). For foreign direct investments, this means that any losses due to the depreciation of the foreign currency are likely to be balanced by the increase in foreign earnings due to the higher foreign price level. The same is true of foreign portfolio investments, since the foreign rate of interest is likely to rise to compensate investors for the inflation.

Destabilizing Speculation

Does speculation tend to depress or amplify exchange-rate fluctuations through time? This is an extremely important question. On it depends the success or failure of the flexible-exchange-rate system. As one would expect, the proponents of flexible exchange rates argue that speculation is *stabilizing;* that is, speculation depresses exchange-rate fluctuations. On the other hand, the critics claim that speculation is *destabilizing;* that is, speculation amplifies exchange-rate fluctuations.

Figure 21-8, panel (*a*), illustrates the case of stabilizing speculation. The solid sinewave curve shows the movement of the exchange rate in the absence of speculation. Presumably this cyclical behavior of the exchange rate reflects the influence of cyclical factors on the foreign sector. For simplicity, the trend line is a horizontal straight line. The broken sinewave curve shows how the exchange rate would fluctuate in the presence of stabilizing speculation. The important assumption is that once the rate rises above the trend line, speculators expect the rate to fall and therefore sell foreign exchange (here the pound). Thus, they prevent the rate from rising too much. Similarly, once the rate falls below the trend line, speculators expect the rate to rise and therefore buy foreign exchange. Accordingly, they prevent the rate from falling too much. This sort of stabilizing speculation depresses exchange-rate fluctuations around the trend line, as shown by the broken curve.

Consider now panel (*b*), which illustrates the case of destabilizing speculation. The solid sinewave curve and the trend line are exactly the same as those of panel (*a*). But here, once the rate begins to rise above the trend line, speculators expect it to rise even further. As a result, speculators now *buy* foreign exchange in the hope of selling it in the future at a higher rate. These speculative purchases intensify the rise in the rate of exchange. Conversely, when the rate falls below the trend line, speculators expect it to fall even further. As a result, speculators now *sell* foreign exchange, and they precipitate

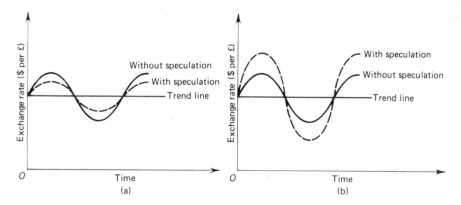

Figure 21-8 *Stabilizing and destabilizing speculation.*
Panel (a) illustrates the case of stabilizing speculation. Once the rate rises above (falls below) the trend line, speculators expect it to fall (rise) and therefore sell (buy) foreign exchange. This stabilizing speculation depresses exchange-rate fluctuations, as shown by the broken curve. Panel (b) illustrates the case of destabilizing speculation. Here, once the rate rises above (falls below) the trend line, speculators expect it to rise (fall) even further and therefore buy (sell) foreign exchange. This destabilizing speculation amplifies exchange-rate fluctuations, as shown by the broken curve.

the fall in the rate. This sort of destabilizing speculation amplifies exchange-rate fluctuations around the trend line, as shown by the broken curve.

How does speculation actually behave under flexible exchange rates? Friedman (1953, p. 175) had a powerful theoretical argument that speculation must be stabilizing. He claimed that "People who argue that speculation is generally destabilizing seldom realize that this is largely equivalent to saying that speculators lose money, since speculation can be destabilizing in general only if speculators on the average sell when the currency is low in price and buy when it is high." Thus, according to Friedman, speculators will continue in the business only so long as it is profitable. This will be the case if they buy cheap and sell dear. But to buy cheap and sell dear is to stabilize.

Friedman's analysis has provoked an interesting controversy as to whether profitable speculation is necessarily stabilizing. Several economists have offered counterexamples in which they attempt to show that destabilizing speculation may be profitable. Other critics have argued that the question of whether destabilizing speculation is profitable or unprofitable is irrelevant. For instance, in the Great Crash of the New York Stock Exchange in October 1929, destabilizing speculators suffered severe losses; but these losses did not prevent them from behaving the way they actually did, precipitating a catastrophe.

The question of whether speculation is stabilizing or destabilizing cannot be settled by recourse to theoretical arguments. Although there may be a presumption that speculation is stabilizing, the question is at bottom an empirical one. Only actual experience with truly flexible exchange rates can resolve the issue.

Price Discipline

Another argument against flexible exchange rates concerns fears that the flexibility of the exchange rate would generate excessive inflation. In particular, the critics of flexible exchange rates claim that fixed exchange rates impose a price "discipline" on the domestic authorities because of the balance-of-payments constraint. Thus, inflationary policies under fixed exchange rates cause external deficits and losses of international monetary reserves. The loss of reserves plus the loss of national prestige in the event of devaluation prevent governments from pursuing inflationary policies. Under flexible exchange rates, on the other hand, governments would no longer be subject to the discipline, as the flexibility of the exchange rate would automatically maintain external balance.

The proponents of flexible exchange rates argue that fixed exchange rates do not really guarantee price stability. To avoid balance-of-payments problems when the exchange rate is fixed, a country must maintain at home that rate of inflation which prevails in the rest of the world (see the discussion of the purchasing-power-parity theory in Section 15-8). Further, the rate of world inflation, which need not be zero, is likely to be different from what the country really wants. In addition, under the adjustable-peg system, countries may avoid the discipline by using owned or borrowed reserves, by imposing direct controls on trade and payments (which interfere with economic efficiency), and, in the last resort, by devaluing their currencies, as the postwar record shows.

Moreover, the consequences of inflationary policies are more readily apparent to the general public under flexible exchange rates: The domestic currency would depreciate in the foreign exchange market, and the domestic price level would rise.

Finally, the proponents of flexible exchange rates make the valid point that a country must be free to choose that rate of domestic inflation its citizens desire. Flexible exchange rates make it possible for the authorities to pursue the public's choice of the right mixture of unemployment and inflation along a Phillips curve because they remove the balance-of-payments constraint.

21-6 SUMMARY

1   Under the flexible-exchange-rate system, the exchange rate adjusts instantaneously and maintains external balance constantly. To attain internal balance as well, the open economy may use fiscal and/or monetary policy.

2   When the net balance on international capital flows and unilateral transfers is zero, the flexible exchange rate guarantees that $\bar{X} - M(Y) = 0$ at all times and that the national-income equilibrium condition $Y = C(Y) + \bar{I} + \bar{X} - M(Y)$ reduces to $Y = C(Y) + \bar{I}$ (closed-economy equilibrium condition). The multiplier becomes equal to the closed-economy multiplier $(1/MPS)$ for all autonomous changes in C, I (and G); it becomes zero for changes in exports and imports (that is, shifts in domestic expenditure between domestic and foreign products).

3   The IS-LM model can be modified to incorporate flexible exchange

rates. General macroeconomic equilibrium occurs now at the point of intersection of three schedules: the *IS* and *LM* curves plus the external balance schedule.

4 Along the external balance schedule, the open economy may experience a balance-of-*trade* surplus or deficit, depending on whether the net capital flow is negative or positive. Thus, the balance of trade may now exert a direct influence on national income. Yet exogenous changes in exports and imports continue to leave the equilibrium level of income unchanged (in the absence of any indirect effects, such as the terms-of-trade effect).

5 Insofar as its effects on national income are concerned, monetary policy is more powerful under a flexible-exchange-rate system than under a fixed-exchange-rate system.

6 When the external balance schedule is steeper (flatter) than the *LM* curve—that is, when expansionary fiscal policy causes a depreciation (appreciation) of the domestic currency because of low (high) capital mobility—fiscal policy has a larger effect on national income under flexible (fixed) exchange rates.

7 In general, the flexible-exchange-rate system provides more stability to the open economy in relation to disturbances that originate in the foreign sector, such as autonomous changes in exports and imports. Countries that suffer from export instability can stabilize their domestic economies by adopting the flexible-exchange-rate system.

8 Internal monetary shocks, such as autonomous shifts in the liquidity preference and changes in the money supply, are more disruptive (or destabilizing) under flexible exchange rates than under fixed exchange rates. Thus, countries that suffer from such internal shocks can facilitate their stabilization policy by adopting fixed exchange rates.

9 Internal shocks in domestic spending (*C*, *I*, or *G*) are more disruptive under flexible (fixed) exchange rates when the degree of capital mobility is low (high). Thus, countries that suffer from such internal shocks in domestic spending and at the same time experience a low (high) degree of capital mobility can facilitate their stabilization policy by adopting fixed (flexible) exchange rates.

10 Countries that experience sudden inflows or outflows of funds should, when feasible, adopt the fixed-exchange-rate system and sterilize any payments imbalances.

11 The case for flexible exchange rates rests on their simplicity in maintaining external balance. In a classical world of price flexibility, it is simpler to change the exchange rate than millions of commodity and factor prices. In a Keynesian world of rigid prices, fixed exchange rates give rise to an extra policy target (external balance) and increase the difficulties of stabilization policy. Flexible exchange rates, on the other hand, reduce the tasks of monetary and fiscal policy, remove the balance-of-payments motive for restrictions on international trade and payments, and provide autonomy to individual countries with respect to their use of public policy (particularly monetary policy).

12 One argument against flexible exchange rates is that they would be highly unstable (because of low import-demand elasticities and/or destabilizing speculation), reducing seriously the flows of international trade and investment. The proponents counter that flexible exchange rates need not be unstable; fixed exchange rates are not free of risk and uncertainty; exchange risk on short-term transactions can be covered in the forward market; and the world economy tends to provide automatic hedging for long-term transactions.

13 Whether speculation under flexible exchange rates is stabilizing or destabilizing is at bottom an empirical question, even though there may be a presumption that it is stabilizing.

14 Another argument against flexible exchange rates concerns fears that they would generate excessive inflation because governments would not be subject to the price discipline imposed by fixed exchange rates and the balance-of-payments constraint. The proponents counter that fixed exchange rates do not guarantee price stability: A country must maintain at home that rate of inflation which prevails in the rest of the world, and under the adjustable-peg system countries may avoid the discipline by using reserves (owned or borrowed), by imposing direct controls, or finally by devaluing their currencies.

SUGGESTED READING

Chacholiades, M. (1978). *International Monetary Theory and Policy*. McGraw-Hill Book Company, New York, chaps. 5, 6, 11, 17, and 19.

Friedman, M. (1953). "The Case for Flexible Exchange Rates." In M. Friedman. *Essays in Positive Economics*. University of Chicago Press, Chicago. Reprinted in R. E. Caves and H. G. Johnson (eds.), AEA *Readings in International Economics*. Richard D. Irwin, Inc., Homewood, Ill., 1968.

Johnson, H. G. (1970). "The Case for Flexible Exchange Rates, 1969." In G. N. Halm (ed.). *Approaches to Greater Flexibility of Exchange Rates*. Princeton University Press, Princeton, N.J.

Laursen, S., and L. A. Metzler (1950). "Flexible Exchange Rates and the Theory of Employment." *Review of Economics and Statistics,* vol. 32, no. 4 (November), pp. 281–299.

Mundell, R. A. (1968). *International Economics*. The Macmillan Company, New York, chaps. 17 and 18.

Sohmen, E. (1969). *Flexible Exchange Rates*, 2d ed. University of Chicago Press, Chicago.

Chapter Twenty-Two

The International Monetary System

This final chapter deals with those special problems that arise in connection with the international monetary system, that is, the rules and conventions that govern the international financial conduct of nations.

The chapter is divided into eight sections. The first three deal with general principles. In particular, Section 22-1 classifies the various types of international monetary systems according to two important criteria: (1) the role of exchange rates and (2) the nature of the reserve asset(s). Section 22-2 discusses the general characteristics of a good international monetary system. The question here is: What criteria should we use to judge whether a certain system is good or bad? The discussion of general principles concludes in Section 22-3 with the clarification of three important concepts (adjustment, liquidity, and confidence) that economists use to judge the performance of the international monetary system.

The rest of the chapter deals with the actual systems that have existed over the last century or so, such as the gold standard (Section 22-4), the interwar attempts to restore the classical gold standard and the general instability of this period (Section 22-5), the Bretton Woods system (Section 22-6), the present system of managed flexibility (Section 22-7), and the new European Monetary System (Section 22-8).

22-1   TYPES OF INTERNATIONAL MONETARY SYSTEMS

The term *international monetary system*[1] refers to the framework of rules, regulations, and conventions that govern the financial relations among nations.
The foreign financial conduct of nations can be organized in many different
ways. Accordingly, the international monetary system can assume many different types. All international monetary systems (that is, types) have much in
common and differ only in certain respects. Economists usually use several alternative criteria for classifying the various possible international monetary
systems. For our purposes, it is sufficient to concentrate on only two of these
criteria (or dimensions): (1) the role of exchange rates and (2) the nature of the
reserve asset(s).

Exchange-Rate Regimes (or Systems)

From one point of view, international finance deals with the difficulties of international money changing—difficulties of turning one money into another. It is
for this reason that the exchange rates play a crucial role in all international
monetary systems. Indeed, we can classify the various possible international
monetary systems according to the degree of flexibility (or rigidity) of foreign
exchange rates.

We are already familiar with the two polar alternatives of permanently
fixed or absolutely flexible exchange rates. Between these two extremes, there
is a large array of possible compromises. The most widely discussed
compromises include: the *adjustable peg* (in which nations may alter their
"fixed" par values whenever necessary to correct a fundamental disequilibrium); the *wide band* (in which the exchange rate is flexible within wide
limits—known as the "wide band"—but is prevented from moving outside the
band); the *crawling peg* (in which the exchange rate changes continuously but
by very small amounts each time; that is, it is "crawling"); and *managed floating* (in which there are no fixed parities, but where the monetary authorities do
intervene in the foreign exchange market to limit the frequency and amplitude
of fluctuations of exchange rates around their long-term trend).

Monetary Standards

Another important dimension of international monetary systems is the nature
of the reserve asset(s). In general, international monetary reserves are divided
into two major categories: (1) commodity reserves and (2) fiduciary (or fiat)
reserves. Commodity reserves (such as gold) do have some intrinsic value quite
apart from their value as money. On the other hand, fiduciary reserves (such as
Special Drawing Rights and national currencies that are inconvertible into
commodity reserves) have no intrinsic value.

Based on the nature of the reserve asset(s), we can classify international
monetary systems into the following three categories:

[1]Some authors prefer the terms international monetary *order* or international monetary
regime to international monetary *system*.

1   *Pure commodity standards* (in which all reserves consist of commodity reserves, as in the case of the gold standard)

2   *Pure fiduciary standards* (in which all reserves are fiduciary reserves, as illustrated by the "inconvertible-paper standard")

3   *Mixed standards* (the reserves of which are a mixture of commodity reserves and fiduciary reserves, as illustrated by the gold-exchange standard)

Incidentally, note that during the course of time, the term *monetary standard* has undergone a fundamental change. Originally, when gold (or silver) was used as a standard, a certain quantity of the metal served as a unit of account. Thus, it was possible to express the exchange values of all goods and services in terms of the standard commodity (gold or silver), which in turn facilitated the comparison of different quantities of goods and services. Today the term *standard* refers to any monetary system, even though no "standard commodity" may be present.

Finally, note that the various exchange-rate regimes and monetary standards refer to the same population of international monetary systems. The difference lies in the fact that these two classifications use different criteria in grouping the total population of international monetary systems into different sets. This explains why economists may often use different names to refer to the same international monetary system. For instance, economists may refer to the gold standard as either a fixed-exchange-rate system (when they want to emphasize that under this system the exchange rates are fixed) or a pure commodity standard (when they want to emphasize that gold is a commodity-reserve asset).

22-2   THE CHARACTERISTICS OF A GOOD INTERNATIONAL MONETARY SYSTEM

Having surveyed the various possible types of international monetary systems and having shown how they may be classified by two important features [the role of the exchange rate and the nature of the reserve asset(s)], we now turn to the choice of an international monetary system.

The Ultimate Objectives of the International Monetary System

What is a good international monetary system? How can we tell whether a certain system is good or bad? What criteria should we use for this purpose? These are extremely important questions. To answer them, we must first identify what the international monetary system does, or what it is supposed to do.

It must be clear that the international monetary system is not an end in itself. Its main function is to enable the fundamental economic processes of production and distribution to operate as smoothly and efficiently as possible. It is mainly for this reason that Adam Smith called the international monetary system the "great wheel." When the wheel turns effortlessly, international monetary relations become inconspicuous, taken for granted, as the attention turns to the resultant large, constant flow of goods and services that go to satisfy human wants in every corner of the globe. But when the wheel turns badly, the international flow of goods and services is interrupted, with grave consequences for the economic welfare of nations. It is particularly during such crises that most people become aware of the existence and significance of the international monetary system (the wheel).

We therefore conclude that the ultimate objectives of the international monetary system are: (1) the maximization of total world output and employment and (2) the achievement of a desirable distribution of economic welfare among nations as well as among different groups within each nation.

A well-organized international monetary system can lead to the maximization of total world output (by permitting the fullest use of efficient division of labor among the nations of the world) and to an acceptable distribution of that output among the members of the world community. This, of course, presupposes the free flow of goods and services, capital, labor, and even ideas, among nations. Direct controls for balance-of-payments reasons have no place in a well-organized international monetary system.

Cooperation and Rivalry among Nations

Before going any further, we should draw attention to the elements of cooperation and rivalry that exist among nations. The element of cooperation emanates from the common policy objective of maximizing total world output and thus promoting the highest level of global welfare. The element of rivalry, on the other hand, emanates from the divergent policy objectives of nations concerning the distribution of economic welfare among nations.

The element of rivalry may lead to serious policy conflicts. Like selfish individuals, nations usually prefer a bigger slice of the pie, even though such preference may lead to a smaller overall pie with the result that all nations become worse off in absolute terms than they need be. We saw an example of this in Chapter 8 in relation to the optimal tariff. A large country imposes an optimal tariff in order to exploit its monopolistic position in international trade. However, such selfish policy may lead to a tariff war, as other countries retaliate in an attempt to maximize their own national welfare. The tariff war comes to an end only when no country can gain further through unilateral action. As we already know, such a tariff war may leave all countries worse off. Put differently, all countries may benefit by agreeing to remove all tariffs. Similar examples in the monetary realm are presented later on in this chapter.

It must be clear by now that a good international monetary system which minimizes the element of rivalry among nations can be beneficial to the entire world community, since it can preserve the joint gain that the world economy can achieve through an efficient international division of labor.

We therefore conclude that a good international monetary system is one that reconciles the elements of cooperation and rivalry which exist among nations. Some minimum degree of consistency among the policies of nations is absolutely necessary for the preservation of the joint gains that spring from an efficient division of labor among nations.

Autarky versus Anarchy

One possible way of minimizing the element of rivalry is to adopt the system of *autarky*. Each nation could seal off its borders and prohibit the inflow and outflow of goods and services, capital, and labor. Thus, each nation could become self-sufficient. The absurdity of this solution must be clear: It eliminates the element of rivalry by sacrificing all the benefits that emanate from international trade and investment. We reject it.

At the other extreme, there is the alternative of *anarchy*. Here there would be no rules or conventions at all, and each nation would be free to do what it thought best. We reject anarchy also. Such a system (if we could call it that) would allow large, powerful nations to exploit smaller, weaker nations. It would disorganize markets as various nations pursued inconsistent policy objectives. For instance, suppose that the Bank of Canada started buying U.S. dollars in order to force a depreciation of the Canadian dollar. Assume further that the United States did not like the idea and preferred the current exchange rate. It must be clear that the United States (the stronger country) could frustrate the Canadian plan by purchasing Canadian dollars at the same rate as Canada (the weaker country) issues them.

22-3 ADJUSTMENT, LIQUIDITY, AND CONFIDENCE

To appraise the actual performance of the international monetary system, economists have developed three important tests: *adjustment, liquidity,* and *confidence*. Adjustment refers to the capacity of nations to maintain or restore equilibrium in their international payments. Liquidity refers to the adequacy of international reserves. Confidence refers to the absence of destabilizing (panicky) shifts from one reserve asset to another when there are many reserve assets. The purpose of this section is to clarify the meaning and significance of these three concepts.

Adjustment

We are already familiar with the problem of balance-of-payments adjustment, which involves a marginal reallocation of resources prompted by changes in incomes, relative prices, and/or exchange rates (see especially Chapter 14). We also know that payments-adjustment policies are divided into expenditure-adjusting policies (mainly fiscal and monetary policies) and expenditure-switching policies (mainly exchange-rate adjustment and direct controls), depending on whether they rely primarily on income changes or price changes.

The essence of the adjustment problem is that every adjustment policy involves economic costs. For instance, to correct its external deficit, a country may have to deflate its economy and accept domestic unemployment. On the other hand, a surplus country may eliminate its unwanted surplus by having to accept inflation. If adjustment costs are inevitable and adjustment is unavoidable, the role of the international monetary system must surely be to enable countries to choose those policies (or combinations of policies) that (1) minimize the overall cost of adjustment and (2) distribute that minimum cost equitably among all nations.

Unfortunately, the designing of rules, regulations, and conventions (that is, the drafting of the constitution of the international monetary system) that meet the above objectives is not an easy matter, as the history of international monetary relations shows. There are several reasons for this pessimistic view. First, there is the real problem that the costs associated with each policy are not easily predictable—indeed, these costs may be high or low depending on circumstances (such as the state of economy). In addition, there is the fundamental difficulty that each nation, in the final analysis, is concerned with its own responsibilities and costs of adjustment, not the aggregate costs of the world community. It is mainly for this reason that nations do not adjust willingly. Deficit countries ordinarily refuse to accept the intolerable cost of domestic unemployment, while surplus countries refuse to accept the consequences of domestic inflation. Indeed, for prestige and political reasons, every nation ordinarily wants other nations to take the initiative in restoring external balance—usually governments interpret such initiative as failure on their part.

The adjustment process is further complicated by the fact that groups within each nation are apt to lobby vigorously against any policies that they perceive to be detrimental to their own interests. For instance, labor unions in deficit countries may oppose deflationary fiscal and monetary policies. Similarly, the foreign-trade sector of a nation may lobby against exchange-rate flexibility and direct controls.

Liquidity

International economists use the term *liquidity* to refer to the volume of gross international monetary reserves. A good international monetary system must provide an adequate supply (and growth) of reserves. (In our current international monetary system, reserves consist of total official holdings of gold, convertible foreign currencies, Special Drawing Rights, and net reserve positions in the International Monetary Fund.)

What is the main function of reserves (or liquidity)? We may recall from our earlier discussion that temporary external disequilibria call for financing—not adjustment. Only permanent (or fundamental) disequilibria require real adjustment. Nevertheless, even in the case of permanent disequilibria, the availability of financing gives the authorities some desirable leeway in choosing among the various policy options. Thus, the availabilty of financing often enables the authorities to adopt a slow-working policy whose adjustment costs are lower than the corresponding costs of other policy alternatives. The main purpose of reserves is to make financing of external disequilibria possible. Indeed, the optimal volume (and rate of growth) of reserves is that which ensures the most efficient mix of financing and adjustment.

Seigniorage

The creation of international liquidity generates benefits and costs. Nations often find themselves in conflict over the distribution of these benefits and costs. The main bone of contention in this connection is the profit from issuing money, known as *seigniorage*.

Seigniorage is a technical term in monetary economics. Originally seigniorage referred to the difference between the cost of producing money (that is, the cost of bullion plus the cost of minting) and the value of money in exchange. This difference represented a once-and-for-all gain to the issuer of money, the king or *seigneur*.

Today seigniorage means the profit from issuing any kind of money, including international money. Domestically, all governments (through their central banks) have a monopoly power in issuing currency and thus enjoy all seigniorage (monopoly profit). Internationally, governments similarly have a strong desire to benefit from any seigniorage arising from the issue of international money.

Whether the amount of seigniorage arising from the issue of international money is large or small depends crucially on the type of monetary standard that happens to be in operation. For instance, a pure commodity standard, such as the gold standard, implies a relatively small amount of seigniorage because of the high cost of producing and storing gold. On the other hand, under a pure fiduciary standard, such as the dollar standard, international money is costless to produce and there is a relatively large amount of seigniorage, which must be distributed in some way among nations. When the issuer of the fiduciary reserve asset pays no interest on reserve holdings, then all the seigniorage gains accrue to him (the issuer). On the other hand, when the issuer is obliged to pay interest on his liabilities, part (or all) of seigniorage gains accrue to the holders of reserves in the form of interest income.

Confidence

When several reserve assets coexist, there is always the danger of destabilizing shifts from one reserve asset to another, as predicted by Gresham's law: "Bad money drives out good."

The confidence needed for the smooth functioning of the international monetary system refers to the willingness of the holders of the various reserve assets to continue holding them. Confidence essentially means the absence of panicky shifts from one reserve asset to another.

A crisis of confidence arises when the holders of the various reserve assets become discontented with the composition of their portfolios and attempt to switch from one asset to another. A good international monetary system must have safeguards against the occurrence of crises of confidence or at least must be able to cope satisfactorily with such crises.

As we shall see in Section 22-6, the danger of crises of confidence was particularly serious under the Bretton Woods system.

22-4 THE GOLD STANDARD (1870–1914)

Under an international gold standard, each country ties its money to gold and allows the unrestricted import and export of gold. In particular, the central bank of each gold-standard country stands ready to buy and sell gold (and only gold) freely at a fixed price in terms of the domestic currency, while its private residents are entirely free to export or import gold. The essence of an international gold standard is that the rates of exchange are fixed.

Even though the use of gold coins dates back to antiquity, the international gold standard was a relatively brief episode in world history. It emerged during the 1870s and lasted until the outbreak of World War I in 1914. This period is often described as the Golden Age of the gold standard. During these four decades world trade and investment flourished, promoting international specialization and global welfare. The balance-of-payments mechanism appeared to be working smoothly. Conflicts of policy among nations were extremely rare. Consequently, after World War I, it was quite natural for nations and scholars to look back on the prewar gold standard with nostalgia.

At the center of the gold-standard stage was Great Britain because of her leading role in commercial and financial affairs. At that time, Britain was the supreme industrial nation, a significant importer of foodstuffs and raw materials, the biggest exporter of manufactured goods, and the largest source of long- and short-term capital. London was the financial center of the world. Britain had been on the gold standard since 1821, half a century before other major countries joined the bandwagon. As a result, sterling came to be identified with gold and was freely accepted and widely used. Indeed, a substantial proportion of world trade was financed with sterling, and as a consequence sizable sterling balances were held in London. Furthermore, Britain pursued a free-trade policy and also acted as lender of last resort in times of exchange crisis.

The pre-1914 gold standard did not really encompass the entire world. Only a core of major European countries were actually on the gold standard and maintained fixed exchange rates. The exchange rates of other, less developed, primary-producing countries outside of the British empire, particularly in Latin America, fluctuated widely during the 1870–1914 period in response to shifts of foreign demand for their exports as well as sudden interruptions of capital inflows.

What accounts for the apparent success of the pre-1914 gold standard? In retrospect, it is clear its success, the image of a Golden Age, was actually a myth. The fact is that during the 1870–1914 period, the world economy did not really experience any dramatic shocks (such as World Wars I and II, the Great Depression of the 1930s, or even the 1973–1974 OPEC oil price increase). On the contrary, during this period the major trading countries experienced a broad synchronization of fluctuations in their economic activity as well as a parallel movement of their exports and imports, both individually and as a group. Thus, the gold standard existed during a rather tranquil period and was not really put to test.

The myth of the Golden Age reflected two serious misconceptions: (1) that the price-specie-flow mechanism (see Chapter 15) worked smoothly and maintained external balance automatically and (2) that the monetary authorities of the gold-standard countries followed the "rules of the game," allowing gold flows to exert their full influence on the domestic money supplies and price levels. These misconceptions, in turn, generated the belief that the gold standard was an impersonal, automatic, and politically symmetrical system.

Historical data show that during the 1870–1914 period, prices in the major trading countries moved in a parallel fashion rather than in a divergent fashion as required by the price-specie-flow mechanism. This fact actually puzzled contemporary economists, who were unable to reconcile their observations with the predictions of the price-specie-flow mechanism. For instance, in the 1920s Frank Taussig and his Harvard students studied historical examples of balance-of-payments adjustment and expressed surprise at the observed smoothness and speed of adjustment in many countries before World War I. Essentially, they observed that small gold flows and relative price changes seemed to restore equilibrium in the balance of payments quite promptly. This result was too good to believe and led Taussig to suspect that some important economic forces were ignored by the classical theory. Indeed, the missing link was recognized after the publication of the *General Theory* to be the income-adjustment mechanism.

In addition, Bloomfield (1959) demonstrated convincingly that the pre-1914 central banks did not really follow the rules of the game. In the majority of cases, central banks did not administer the classical medicine. Rather, they sterilized payments imbalances, effectively shielding their money supplies from the balance of payments and thus short-circuiting the adjustment mechanism.

What, then, did maintain and restore external balance during the pre-1914 period? In the case of Great Britain, the main instrument was the *Bank Rate* (analogous to the discount rate of the Federal Reserve banks in the United States). In the presence of a deficit, the Bank of England raised its Bank Rate, rendering London a relatively more attractive place to lend and a relatively less attractive place to borrow. As a result, large amounts of funds flowed into London, strengthening sterling in the foreign exchange market and discouraging the outflow of gold. Similarly, in the presence of a surplus, the Bank of England lowered its Bank Rate. The lower Bank Rate, in turn, encouraged a capital outflow and suspended the need to import gold. Accordingly, in the case of Great Britain, stabilizing capital movements maintained external balance.

The other "core" countries did not have any major degree of monetary independence. They followed the lead of the Bank of England. To maintain external balance, the major central banks (for example, that of France) often used their reserves, and on many occasions they simply resorted to the manipulation of gold points, intervention in the foreign exchange market, borrowing from foreigners, and so on.

22-5 THE INTERWAR PERIOD

If the pre-1914 gold-standard era is viewed as the Golden Age of international monetary relations, the interwar period may be viewed as the Dark Age, a nightmare. With the outbreak of World War I, the Golden Age came to an end. Initially, the belligerent nations suspended convertibility of their currencies into gold and put an embargo on gold exports in order to protect their gold reserves. Soon after most other nations adopted the same policy. The classical gold standard was dead.

In the foreign exchange market, private individuals could still trade one paper currency against another but at prices determined by supply and demand conditions. Thus, a purely floating exchange-rate regime succeeded the fixed-exchange-rate system of the gold standard. In the ensuing years, exchange rates gyrated chaotically, particularly in response to two great disturbances: World War I and the Great Depression.

For a few years after World War I (1919–1923), currency values fluctuated violently in the foreign exchange market. However, most nations viewed the regime of fluctuating exchange rates as a temporary arrangement. Thus, they immediately turned their attention to the problem of reforming the international monetary system. Lulled by the myth of the Golden Age, nations were determined to restore the classical gold standard. However, gold was still valued at its old prewar parities; and in view of the rapid price inflations that almost all countries had experienced during and immediately after the war, there was an obvious shortage of gold.

To overcome this shortage, the Financial Committee of the Genoa Conference, which took place in 1922, recommended worldwide adoption of a gold-exchange standard. The major financial centers (for example, London) were to maintain convertibility of their currencies into gold, while the monetary authorities of the rest of the countries were to maintain convertibility of their currencies into "gold exchange" (that is, currencies convertible into gold, such as sterling). Gold was to be concentrated in the major financial centers as the monetary authorities of the rest of the countries proceeded to convert their unnecessary gold holdings into "gold exchange." In this way, the world would economize on the use of gold.

In 1925 Britain reestablished the convertibility of sterling into gold and removed all restrictions on the export of gold. Soon after the British action, country after country restored convertibility at the prewar parities. The gold-exchange standard was born. Unfortunately, the experiment did not last long. The system collapsed in 1931, when the British had to suspend convertibility once again because of a run on their reserves, and all the king's horses could not put it together again. From that moment on, the world was divided into three competing and hostile blocks: (1) the *sterling block* (organized around Great Britain), (2) the *dollar block* (organized around the United States), and (3) the *gold block* (organized around France). In addition, many other countries, such as Germany and Eastern European countries, abandoned convertibility altogether and imposed exchange control.

The decade of the Great Depression was a period of open economic warfare. As the Depression deepened, governments pursued in vain the game of competitive depreciations in the hope of eliminating their domestic unemployment and restoring external balance. During the 5-year period 1931–1935, international cooperation reached its nadir.

In 1936 there appeared some sign of cooperation as Britain, France, and the United States signed the Tripartite Agreement, which permitted France to devalue its overvalued franc without retaliation. But even this trace of cooperation was abruptly interrupted by World War II. Meaningful international monetary reform had to be postponed until the end of the war.

Why did the interwar experiment fail? Economic historians usually point out that not only was the Golden Age actually a myth but the world economy had experienced very significant changes as well. In particular, the prewar parities were totally inappropriate, particularly because various countries had experienced quite different degrees of inflation (see the discussion of the purchasing-power-parity theory in Chapter 15). Thus, most currencies were either overvalued or undervalued by significant amounts. The Great Depression further disrupted the world economy to a considerable degree. Prices and money wages were becoming increasingly rigid, especially in the downward direction. Concerned with domestic stability, countries also tended to sterilize their payments imbalances. Finally, London had ceased to be the single dominant financial center of the world. As other competitive financial centers (such as Paris and New York) came into existence, there emerged a growing tendency (after 1931) for short-term funds to move from one country to another ("hot money" movements) in search of security and in response to political alarms and rumors—the familiar confidence problem.

22-6 THE BRETTON WOODS SYSTEM (1944–1971)

In 1944, delegates of 44 non-Communist nations of the world held a conference at Bretton Woods, New Hampshire. The main objective of the conference was to reform the international monetary system. For this purpose, the delegates considered two rival plans: A British plan developed by Lord Keynes and an American plan developed by Harry Dexter White of the U.S. Treasury.

Keynes proposed the creation of a Clearing Union with overdraft facilities (virtually an automatic line of credit) and the ability to create reserves. In addition, he proposed the creation of a new international unit of account (to be called *bancor*), which was to be used only on the books of the Clearing Union. Another important feature of the Keynes plan was that not only bancor borrowers but also bancor creditors would pay interest on their balances—an attempt to place at least part of the adjustment responsibility on surplus countries.

The system the delegates finally endorsed, however, was akin to the White plan. It later became known as the *Bretton Woods system*. It served the world from 1944 to 1971, a period of 27 years that was known as the Bretton Woods era.

The most important principles of the Bretton Woods system were as follows:

1 *International institutions.* International monetary cooperation requires the creation of an international agency with defined functions and powers.

2 *The adjustable peg.* Exchange rates should be fixed in the short run but adjustable from time to time in the presence of "fundamental disequilibrium."

3 *International monetary reserves.* For the smooth functioning of the adjustable-peg system, countries (individually and as a group) require a large volume of reserves. Accordingly, there must be some augmentation of gold and currency reserves.

4 *Currency convertibility.* In the interests of political harmony and economic welfare, all countries must adhere to a system of unfettered multilateral trade and convertible currencies.

In this section, we review the above principles. In addition, we provide some insights into the inherent drawbacks of the system, as economic observers saw them unfold during the Bretton Woods era.

International Institutions

The Bretton Woods conferees agreed that international monetary cooperation required the creation of an international agency with defined functions and powers. They felt that a permanent institution was necessary to serve as a forum for international consultation and cooperation on monetary matters. For this purpose, they created the International Monetary Fund (IMF), which has provided the framework and determined the code of behavior for the postwar international monetary system.

The Adjustable-Peg System

The negotiators at Bretton Woods sought an exchange-rate system that would combine the advantages of both the fixed- and the flexible-exchange-rate systems. For this purpose, they adopted the system of the *adjustable peg,* which provides for exchange-rate stability in the short run (and in this respect is similar to the gold standard) but allows for the possibility of exchange-rate adjustment when a country's balance of payments is in fundamental disequilibrium (and in this respect is similar to the flexible-exchange-rate system under which external equilibrium is maintained by exchange-rate adjustments). Unfortunately, the adjustable-peg system lacked the stability, certainty, and automaticity of the gold standard and the flexibility of the flexible-exchange-rate system, a fact which led to its downfall.

The system of the adjustable peg is similar to the gold standard with respect to the determination and maintenance of the spot-exchange rates in the short run. According to the initial agreement, the dollar was pegged to gold at the fixed parity of $35 per ounce of gold, and dollars held by official monetary institutions were convertible freely into gold, as the United States was prepared to buy and sell unlimited amounts of gold at the official price. In this sense, the dollar became the *key currency.* Every other country was required to (1) declare the *par value* (or *parity*) of its currency in terms of gold or the U.S. dollar and (2) stand ready to defend the declared parity in the foreign exchange market by buying and selling dollars, at least in the short run. In this sense, the dollar became the primary *intervention currency*. (For practical reasons the operative standard for most countries was the dollar as such.) Exchange rates could vary only within the so-called *support points* or *intervention points*, which were initially set at 1 percent above or below parity.

Only the United States was not required to intervene in the foreign exchange market, as it was up to the other countries to maintain fixed dollar prices. Indeed, because in a world of n countries only $n-1$ external policies (be they adjustment or liquidity policies) can be independently formulated (a technical difficulty that is known as the *redundancy problem*), the United States followed a policy of "benign neglect" in order to ensure consistency among national policies. This policy came back to haunt the United States during the final years of the Bretton Woods era.

Incidentally, while the monetary authorities of member countries were required to intervene in the *spot market* and to maintain the *spot rates* within the support points, no such requirement was stipulated with respect to the *forward market* and the *forward rates*. Individual countries were free to choose whether or not to intervene in the forward market at their discretion. Accordingly, forward rates occasionally moved outside the limits ("band") set for the spot rates. This was mainly the result of heavy speculation.

Member countries retained the right to alter par values to correct a "fundamental disequilibrium." However, the negotiators at Bretton Woods did not spell out a precise definition of the concept of fundamental disequilibrium.

International Monetary Reserves

With the interwar experience still vivid in their memories, the negotiators at Bretton Woods were convinced that the adjustable-peg system required an adequate supply of international monetary reserves. For this purpose, they developed the IMF system of quotas and subscriptions.

Each member country was assigned a *quota*. (This quota was actually based on a complicated formula that was supposed to reflect each country's relative significance in world trade.) Then each member country had to make into the IMF a subscription equal to its quota. In particular, each member country had to contribute 25 percent of its quota in gold[2] or currency convertible into gold (mainly U.S. dollars) and 75 percent in the member's own currency.

In turn, a member's quota determined the maximum amount of loans that the member was eligible to receive from the Fund when short of reserves. In particular, each member's borrowing rights were limited to five *tranches* (or shares). Each tranche was equal to 25 percent of the member's quota. Thus, a member's maximum borrowing was restricted to 125 percent of its quota.

The first tranche was referred to as the *gold tranche*[3] (because it was equal to the member's gold subscription). With respect to its gold tranche, the

---

[2] Since 1978 convertible foreign currencies have been substituted for gold.
[3] The gold tranche is now called the *reserve tranche*.

member's drawing rights were unconditional (that is, the member could borrow within the gold tranche with no questions asked). The remaining four tranches were referred to as *credit tranches*. With respect to the credit tranches, the member's drawing rights were conditional (that is, required approval by the Fund).

From another point of view, a member could "purchase" (that is, borrow) from the Fund foreign exchange in return for equivalent amounts of its own currency. Such purchases could proceed up to the point where the Fund's holdings of the member's currency equalled 200 percent of its quota. Thus, maximum purchases of foreign exchange by a member were set equal to 125 percent of that member's quota, because of the member's initial 75 percent subscription of its own currency. However, in the event the Fund's holdings of a member's currency were less than 75 percent of that member's quota (presumably because other members had purchased that currency from the Fund), the member's borrowing capacity were correspondingly increased.[4] The resultant increase in the member's borrowing capacity was referred to as the *super-gold tranche*. With respect to the super-gold tranche, the member's drawing rights were unconditional, just as in the case of the gold tranche.

A member's *net reserve position* with the IMF equaled its gold tranche plus its super-gold tranche, if any (or minus any borrowings by the country from the Fund). In other words, a member's net reserve position with the IMF equaled its quota minus the Fund's holdings of the member's own currency. Countries now add their net reserve positions with the IMF to their official reserve assets.

As it turned out, the Fund's initial pool of international liquidity was totally inadequate. As a result, the United States became the main source of international liquidity growth through its balance-of-payments deficits. In this way, the dollar became the primary *reserve currency,* and observers soon began to refer to the postwar monetary system as a dollar standard.

Currency Convertibility and Multilateral Trade

In the interests of political harmony and economic welfare, all countries agreed to a system of unfettered multilateral trade and convertible currencies. Members agreed to refrain from imposing any restrictions on *current* international transactions. Members were not permitted to engage in any discriminatory currency arrangements or exchange control. All currencies were to be freely convertible into one another at official rates.

However, because most countries were simply devastated by the war (with huge import needs and exhausted monetary reserves), it was agreed that the dismantling of controls and the return to convertibility should be gradual. Indeed, Europe's currencies did not return to convertibility until 1958.

---

[4] In the event the Fund ran out of a currency altogether, it was supposed to declare that currency "scarce" and permit other countries to discriminate against it. This provision reflected the view of the negotiators that adjustment was the joint responsibility of both deficit and surplus countries.

The principle of multilateral trade and currency convertibility, however, carried with it the necessity of a real adjustment mechanism, something that the Bretton Woods system was lacking. On the one hand, because of the chaotic experience of the 1930s, the system exhibited a bias against frequent exchange-rate adjustments—governments had to demonstrate the existence of a fundamental disequilibrium before they could adjust their par values. On the other hand, nations became increasingly concerned with domestic employment and removed the link between the balance of payments and the money supply by sterilizing payments imbalances. Thus, deficit countries were left with the possibility of regulating capital account transactions only. (Such capital controls were even encouraged because of the experience of the 1930s.)

Speculation

One major drawback of the adjustable-peg system is that speculation becomes at times destabilizing because of the possibility of parity changes. The main reason for this phenomenon is the *one-way option* offered to speculators. When a currency is under suspicion, there is some doubt as to whether it will be devalued and to what extent; but there is practically no doubt about the direction of change.

For instance, assume that speculators observe that a country is persistently running huge deficits and that they come to expect the country to devalue its currency. To benefit from the expected devaluation, the speculators sell the currency in the hope of buying it later at a lower price. If the country actually devalues, the speculators make substantial profits. On the other hand, if the country does not devalue, their potential losses are minimal, since the narrow band around the par value prevents the currency from appreciating significantly.

Such destabilizing speculation can force the deficit country to devalue its currency by bleeding its reserves, even in cases in which the country could have weathered the storm in the absence of destabilizing speculation. The lower the reserves fall, the stronger the incentive for continued bear speculation becomes.

Defects in the Liquidity-Creation Mechanism

Triffin (1961) was first to notice that international monetary reserves under the Bretton Woods system were not growing fast enough. He even expressed doubts as to whether the system could indeed generate reserves in sufficient amounts without undermining its very foundations.

Triffin's reasoning was relatively simple. He argued that given the slow growth of the stock of monetary gold (less than 1 percent a year), world reserves could increase only if the key-currency countries (mainly the United States) ran huge balance-of-payments deficits in order to pump into the world monetary system sufficient amounts of reserve-currency deposits (the fiduciary element). But this, he continued, would undermine confidence in the dollar, because the stock of U.S. liabilities to the rest of the world would grow larger and larger relative to the U.S. stock of gold. Soon foreign central banks and private holders would become restless and find the dollar weak and redundant. A switch from dollars to gold would cause the system to collapse.

According to Triffin, the world faced a difficult dilemma: To avoid a liquidity shortage, the United States would have to run deficits, and this would undermine confidence in the dollar; on the other hand, to avoid speculation against the dollar, the U.S. deficits would have to cease—but this would create a liquidity shortage. Consequently, Triffin concluded, a way must be found to increase international reserves without breeding instability into the system.

During the 1960s a series of ad hoc measures were initiated in an effort to contain the mounting speculation against the dollar. These measures included currency "swaps" between the Federal Reserve and other central banks; enlargement of the potential lending authority of the IMF (through the General Agreements to Borrow); a gold pool among the major financial powers to stabilize the price of gold in private markets; a two-tier gold-price system (with one price for the private market determined by supply and demand and the official price of $35 for transactions between central banks), which actually replaced the gold pool in 1968; and, finally, the creation of Special Drawing Rights (SDRs).

Special Drawing Rights

Awareness of the Triffin diagnosis eventually led to the creation of Special Drawing Rights (SDRs). Often called "paper gold," SDRs are a new form of international reserve assets whose creation was authorized in 1968 by the First Amendment to the Articles of Agreement of the International Monetary Fund. Some $9.5 billion Special Drawing Rights were first distributed in 1970, 1971, and 1972, and further allocations were made in the 1979–1981 period.

How was the IMF to allocate the newly created SDRs among the member countries? This was a question of seigniorage. Many proposed to "link" the mechanisms of liquidity creation and development finance and thus deliberately direct all the benefits of SDR creation toward the less developed countries ("link" proposal). However, this proposal was rejected. The method the IMF finally adopted was to allocate the newly created SDRs among member countries in proportion to their quotas. The justification was that this method of distribution was neutral: It broadly conformed to the pattern of demand for reserves to hold rather than to the demand for reserves to spend.

Special Drawing Rights are transferable among member countries (and certain eligible international organizations), and they form a genuine supplement to the volume of international monetary reserves. SDRs constitute resources freely available to member countries and are thus added to the list of assets included in official monetary reserves. Consequently, since 1970 the list of reserve assets has included gold, convertible foreign currencies (that is, foreign exchange, such as dollars, pounds sterling, and marks), net reserve positions with the IMF, and SDRs.

Each unit of SDR was initially defined in terms of gold to equal one 1970 U.S. dollar. After the two devaluations of the dollar, one in 1971 and another in

1973 (see below), each SDR unit became equal to $1.20 (approximately). After the collapse of the Bretton Woods system and the widespread use of fluctuating exchange rates, the IMF adopted a new system of valuation for the SDRs. In particular, since 1974 the IMF has calculated daily the value of each SDR unit as a weighted average of a "basket" of 16 representative currencies.

The IMF changes periodically the composition of the SDR basket of currencies. The object is to maintain a standard basket that includes the currencies of the countries with the largest shares in world exports during the most recent 5-year period. The weight assigned to each currency is roughly equal to the country's relative share in world exports, with some extra weight given to currencies that have traditionally played major roles in world payments.

The original basket, which went into effect on July 1, 1974, reflected the relative importance of countries during the 5-year period 1968–1972. This original basket included the currencies of the following countries: United States (.33), Germany (.125), United Kingdom (.09), France (.075), Japan (.075), Canada (.06), Italy (.06), the Netherlands (.045), Belgium (.035), Sweden (.025), Australia (.015), Spain (.015), Norway (.015), Denmark (.015), Austria (.01), and South Africa (.01), with the numbers in parentheses showing the assigned weights.

The IMF revised the original basket on July 1, 1978. This revised basket reflected the relative importance of countries during the period 1972–1976. The IMF dropped the currencies of Denmark and South Africa and replaced them by the currencies of Saudi Arabia and Iran. The next basket adjustment is scheduled to go into effect on July 1, 1983.

The Road to Collapse

The Bretton Woods era can be conveniently divided into two periods: (1) the period of the "dollar shortage" (1944–1958) and (2) the period of the "dollar glut" (1959–1971).

The period of the dollar shortage, which was actually the heyday of the dollar standard, was characterized by mild U.S. deficits (beginning in 1950, following a round of devaluations of European currencies in 1949). Those early U.S. deficits were, on average, about $1 billion annually, and they served the useful purpose of providing the world with much needed liquidity.

However, in 1958 the annual U.S. deficit jumped to about $3.5 billion, followed by even larger deficits in the following years. At the same time the European economies felt saturated with dollars and began to convert a large portion of their dollar balances into gold. (Recall that the European currencies returned to convertibility in 1958.) The U.S. Congress responded by eliminating the federal gold-reserve requirement for all domestic currency (except notes) in order to free the U.S. stock of gold to meet the increasing world demand. In addition, the U.S. government adopted several other ad hoc measures, such as the interest equalization tax and export promotion. (In this respect, you may also recall our earlier reference to "swaps," the gold pool, and the two-tier gold-price system.)

In retrospect, it seems ironic that in the late 1960s the IMF created the

SDRs in response to an alleged "shortage" of international liquidity. As it turned out, the first allocations of SDRs occurred in those years (1970, 1971, and 1972) in which international liquidity was growing at an alarming rate.

The most serious adjustment problem during the period of the dollar glut was the persistent payments imbalance between the United States and the surplus countries of Europe (particularly Germany) and Japan. Germany and Japan were resisting the obvious solution to the problem, that is, revaluation of the mark and the yen, respectively, and they were arguing that it was the responsibility of the United States "to put its house in order" (that is, take appropriate steps to restore external balance). More important, the European countries and Japan felt that America was exploiting the rest of the world because of her privilege of financing her payments deficits by issuing dollars (the problem of seigniorage)—a privilege no other country had. President Charles de Gaulle of France called this privilege "exorbitant" and claimed that the dollar standard required France to finance the U.S. involvement in the Vietnam war. Indeed, it was felt that the dollar deposits held by foreigners were involuntary and thus any interest paid by the United States to official holders of dollar balances was like "meals served to a kidnap victim, hardly an offset to the loss of liberty."

On the other hand, the United States felt severely constrained, particularly in its use of exchange-rate policy, because of an inherent *asymmetry* in the dollar standard. In particular, because other nations were using the dollar as their primary intervention currency, the United States could not effectively change the prices of other currencies in terms of dollars; that is, the United States lacked exchange-rate autonomy. Accordingly, the United States argued that it was up to the surplus countries of Europe and Japan to revalue their currencies, since the United States simply could not devalue the dollar.

The European countries and Japan could, of course, put more pressure on the United States by converting their accumulated dollar balances into gold, or at least by threatening to do so. They did not (with the singular exception of France). The reason was simple: The dollar "overhang" was much larger than the U.S. gold stock, and any attempt at conversion would have caused the entire system to collapse—a fact that was not in their best interests.

The agony ended on August 15, 1971, when President Nixon announced his "new economic policy," which in effect suspended the link between the dollar and gold and withdrew the U.S. promise to exchange gold for dollars. Once the dollar was declared inconvertible and the U.S. gold window was firmly closed, America regained its exchange-rate autonomy and the Bretton Woods era came to a close.

22-7 THE PRESENT SYSTEM OF MANAGED FLEXIBILITY

Following the dramatic events on August 15, 1971, almost all major currencies began to float freely in the foreign exchange market. Nevertheless, the major financial nations of the world were not yet ready to accept the regime of freely floating exchange rates. On December 18, 1971, the Group of Ten (Belgium,

Canada, France, Germany, Italy, Japan, the Netherlands, Sweden, the United Kingdom, and the United States) reached an agreement at the Smithsonian Institution in Washington, D.C. This agreement became known as the Smithsonian Agreement.

The three major provisions of the Smithsonian Agreement were as follows:

1 The United States agreed to raise the official price of gold to $38 an ounce from the $35 price that had prevailed since 1934. However, the United States refused to restore the free convertibility of dollars into gold.

2 Other nations agreed to realign their exchange rates upward in an effort to cope with the problem of the overvalued dollar. This fundamental realignment effectively amounted to a devaluation of the dollar of about 12 percent (on the basis of a weighted average).

3 Exchange rates were permitted to fluctuate within a wider band—2.25 percent on either side of the new parities, instead of the initial 1 percent.

Even though President Nixon called it "the greatest monetary agreement in the history of the world," the Smithsonian Agreement did not really solve any of the fundamental defects of the Bretton Woods system. Within 6 months, the pound sterling had to return to floating. In February 1973, the United States raised the price of gold for a second time, to $42.22 an ounce, but again without restoring the free convertibility of dollars into gold. Finally, in March 1973, all the major currencies of the world started floating again. What emerged was a new exchange-rate regime: a system of "managed" floating.

Actually, the members of the European Economic Community (plus some non-EEC countries) pegged their currencies to each other and floated jointly against the dollar. This experiment of joint European float is referred to as the "snake" within the "tunnel," because the resulting movement of the jointly floating currencies within a narrow band (the tunnel, which is actually a spread of 2.25 percent between the dollar rates of the strongest and weakest currencies) produces a "snake-crawling-in-a-tunnel" pattern. This arrangement did not last for long, however, as Britain, Italy, and France soon allowed their currencies to drop well below the "tunnel."

The widespread floating that replaced the Bretton Woods par value system in 1973 was not actually legalized until the conference in Kingston, Jamaica, on January 7–9, 1976. At the Jamaica conference, the Interim Committee of the Board of Governors of the IMF formulated the Second Amendment to the Articles of Agreement (of the IMF), which actually established (or perhaps legalized) the current international monetary framework.

The Jamaica accord abolished the official price of gold and took several steps toward the demonetization of gold (such as eliminating the obligation of Fund members to use gold in certain transactions with the Fund and permitting the Fund to sell part of its stock of gold). Further, the Jamaica conference raised the Fund quotas by 33 percent. Nevertheless, the key feature of the conference was the agreement that countries were free to choose the type of exchange-rate system that best suited their own individual needs. Pegged and floating rates were given equal legal status. Countries were no longer compelled to maintain specific par values for their currencies. Instead, they were urged to pursue domestic economic policies that would be conducive to stability, in the belief that exchange-rate stability is a result of underlying economic and financial stability. In addition, countries were admonished to refrain from such practices as competitive depreciations in order "to gain an unfair competitive advantage over other members."

The new regime of managed floating reflected a compromise between France (which was seeking a return to the adjustable peg) and the United States (which was advocating for a totally unrestricted regime of floating exchange rates). This diplomatic compromise was achieved at an economic summit meeting among Britain, France, Germany, Italy, Japan, and the United States at Rambouillet, France, in November 1975.

The major problem of the Jamaica accord was how to ensure that countries would actually refrain from competitive depreciations and other similar practices, For this purpose, the Second Amendment empowered the Fund to "exercise firm surveillance over the exchange rate policies of members" and to "adopt specific principles for the guidance of all members with respect to those policies." Unfortunately, however, "unfair competitive advantage" was not defined, nor were specific functions for the Fund stipulated to give substance to the term "firm surveillance,"

In practice, the IMF member countries have adopted widely different exchange-rate regimes. For instance, according to the International Monetary Fund (*International Financial Statistics,* vol. 32, no. 8, August 1979, p. 11), the following exchange arrangements prevailed as of June 30, 1979:

1   Forty-one countries were pegging their currencies to the U.S. dollar.
2   Fourteen countries were pegging their currencies to the French franc.
3   Three countries were pegging their currencies to the pound sterling.
4   Thirteen countries were pegging their currencies to the SDR.
5   Four countries were pegging their currencies to other individual currencies (besides the U.S. dollar, the French franc, the pound sterling, and the SDR).
6   Eighteen countries were pegging their currencies to various "baskets" of currencies other than the SDR basket.
7   Four countries were adjusting their exchange rates "at relatively frequent intervals, on the basis of indicators determined by the respective member countries."
8   Eight European countries were keeping their currencies pegged together under the new European Monetary System (see Section 22-8).
9   Finally, the last 33 countries (including the main industrial countries outside the European snake) covered a heterogeneous group of exchange-rate arrangements. [In this group, we find countries whose currencies were floating independently as well as countries that were pursuing ad hoc exchange arrange-

ments ("managed flexibility") and could not be classified under other categories.]

22-8   THE NEW EUROPEAN MONETARY SYSTEM

In March 1979, the European Economic Community (EEC) put into operation the European Monetary System (EMS), which is based on the following principles:

1   The European snake should be enlarged. The three weak EEC currencies (British pound, French franc, and Italian lira) should join the club again.
(As it turned out, the French and the Italian did return to the "snake," but the British refused to do so. In addition, the Italian lira was allowed a special margin of plus or minus 6 percent, instead of the usual 2.25 percent.)
2   A large credit fund must be created to enable member countries to maintain the external values of their currencies within the permissible limits (band). For this purpose, it was agreed that member countries should contribute into a European reserve pool 20 percent of their gold and dollar reserves in exchange for European Currency Units (ECUs), a new reserve asset similar to the SDR. The initial size of this reserve pool was on the order of $25 billion.
3   The European Economic Community should create the European Currency Unit (ECU) to serve: (a) as a new reserve asset; (b) as a unit of account (in which role it is supposed to replace the existing European Unit of Account): (c) as an official means of payment between central banks; (d) as an indicator of divergence of national currencies; and (e) perhaps as an intervention medium.
4   The new ECU should be defined as a "basket" of all EEC currencies (as is the SDR).

It seems a little premature to judge how successful the new European Monetary System will be and whether it will seriously affect the status of the dollar.

22-9   SUMMARY

1   The term *international monetary system* refers to the framework of rules, regulations, and conventions that govern the financial relations among nations.
2   Economists often classify international monetary systems according to the degree of exchange-rate flexibility. Between the polar cases of permanently fixed and absolutely flexible exchange rates there are many compromises, such as the adjustable peg, the wide band, the crawling peg, and managed floating.
3   International monetary reserves are divided into commodity reserves (that is, those reserve assets, such as gold, that have intrinsic value) and fiduciary (or fiat) reserves (that is, those that have no intrinsic value, such as SDRs).
4   Based on the nature of the reserve asset(s), economists classify inter-

national monetary systems into (a) pure commodity standards, (b) pure fiduciary standards, and (c) mixed standards.

5 The two ultimate objectives of the international monetary system are: (a) the maximization of total world output and (b) the achievement of a desirable distribution of economic welfare among nations.

6 A good international monetary system is one that reconciles the elements of cooperation and rivalry that exist among nations. However, neither autarky nor anarchy are acceptable.

7 To appraise the actual performance of an international monetary system, economists use three tests: adjustment, liquidity, and confidence.

8 Every adjustment policy involves costs. The international monetary system must (a) enable countries to choose those policies that minimize the overall adjustment cost and (b) distribute that minimum cost equitably among nations. Unfortunately, designing rules that meet these objectives is very difficult.

9 A good international monetary system must provide an adequate supply (and growth) of reserves (that is, liquidity) in order to make the financing of external disequilibria possible. The availability of financing is necessary not only for temporary disequilibria but also for fundamental disequilibria, because it gives the authorities desirable leeway in choosing among the various policy options.

10 Originally, *seigniorage* referred to the difference between the cost of producing money and its value in exchange. Today seigniorage means the profit from issuing any kind of money, including international money. All nations want to benefit from seigniorage arising from the issue of international money, and they often find themselves in conflict.

11 Confidence means absence of panicky shifts from one reserve asset to another (when several reserve assets coexist). A good international monetary system must have safeguards against crises of confidence.

12 The international gold standard, with Great Britain at its center, emerged during the 1870s and lasted until 1914—a relatively tranquil period. The myth of the Golden Age reflected two misconceptions: (a) that the price-specie-flow mechanism worked smoothly and (b) that the gold-standard countries followed the "rules of the game."

13 The interwar attempts to restore the gold standard failed because (a) the image of the Golden Age was a myth, and (b) the world economy had experienced significant changes as a result of World War I and the Great Depression.

14 The Bretton Woods system (1944–1971) adopted the adjustable peg. Each country (except the United States) had to defend the declared parity of its currency in terms of gold or the U.S. dollar, adjusting it only in the presence of fundamental disequilibrium. In addition, the Bretton Woods conference created the International Monetary Fund (IMF) and the IMF system of quotas and subscriptions (which later proved to be a totally inadequate liquidity mechanism). Finally, all countries agreed to refrain from imposing restrictions on *current* international transactions.

15 The Bretton Woods system (a) lacked a real adjustment mechanism; (b) offered a one-way option to speculators, which meant that speculation was at times destabilizing; and (c) suffered from a defective liquidity-creation mechanism.

16   According to Triffin, the world faced a dilemma: To avoid a liquidity shortage, the United States would have to run deficits, undermining confidence in the dollar; but to maintain confidence in the dollar, the U.S. deficits would have to cease, creating a liquidity shortage. He concluded that a way must be found to increase reserves without breeding instability into the system. Awareness of the Triffin diagnosis led eventually to the creation of SDRs, which are a genuine supplement to the volume of international reserves.

17   Since 1974, the IMF calculates daily the value of each SDR unit as a weighted average of a "basket" of 16 currencies (of countries with the largest shares in world exports). The composition of the SDR basket changes periodically.

18   The Smithsonian Agreement reached by the Group of Ten on December 18, 1971, did not repair the fundamental defects of the Bretton Woods system. By March 1973 all major currencies were floating. What emerged was the new regime of managed flexibility, which was legalized in 1976 at the Jamaica conference.

19   In March 1979 the European Economic Community put into operation the European Monetary System (EMS), which enlarged the European "snake" and created a large credit fund plus the European Currency Unit (ECU), defined as a basket of all EEC currencies.

SUGGESTED READING

Adams, J. (ed.) (1979). *The Contemporary International Economy: A Reader.* St. Martin's Press, Inc., New York, part 4.

Aliber, R. Z. (1979). *The International Money Game,* 3d ed. Basic Books, Inc., Publishers, New York.

Bloomfield, A. I. (1959). *Monetary Policy under the International Gold Standard: 1880–1914.* Federal Reserve Bank of New York, New York.

Cohen, B. J. (1977). *Organizing the World's Money.* Basic Books, Inc., Publishers, New York.

Cooper, R. N. (1975). "Prolegomena to the Choice of an International Monetary System." *International Organization,* vol. 29, no. 1 (Winter), pp. 64–97.

Hawtrey, R. G. (1947). *The Gold Standard in Theory and Practice.* Longmans, Green & Co., Ltd., London.

Machlup, F. (1975). *International Monetary Systems.* General Learning Press, Morristown, N.J.

Mundell, R. A., and A. Swoboda (eds.) (1968). *Monetary Problems of the International Economy.* University of Chicago Press, Chicago.

Officer, L. H., and T. D. Willett (eds.) (1969). *The International Monetary System: Problems and Proposals.* Prentice-Hall, Inc., Englewood Cliffs, N.J.

Tew, B. (1977). *The Evolution of the International Monetary System, 1945–77.* John Wiley & Sons, New York.

Triffin, R. (1960). *Gold and the Dollar Crisis.* Yale University Press, New Haven, Conn.

———(1968). *Our International Monetary System: Yesterday, Today, and Tomorrow.* Random House, New York.

Name Index

Subject Index

Destabilizing speculation, 344, 353
  and adjustable peg, 557, 564
  and devaluation, 557
  and fiscal–monetary policy mix, 514, 515
  and flexible exchange rates, 537–539,
    541–542
  and fundamental disequilibrium, 457
Devaluation:
  and balance-of-payments deficit, 343, 356
  versus depreciation, 343, 355
  and destabilizing speculation, 557
  versus direct controls, 479, 492, 493
  of dollar, 561
  effects of, 344, 363–369, 384–388, 409,
    468–469
  versus export subsidy, 488
  and foreign-trade multiplier, 406
  and fundamental disequilibrium, 346, 353,
    375
  versus import tax, 484, 495
  and labor unions, 344, 353, 368–369
  and Marshall-Lerner condition, 368, 381
  and national prestige, 540
  and real income, 344
  as switching policy, 413, 497
  symmetry between import taxes plus export
    subsidies and, 479
  and unemployment, 413, 481
  and unexpected losses, 537
Diminishing returns to capital, 134, 137
  (See also Law of diminishing returns)
Direct controls, 8, 478–495, 497
  and adjustable peg, 540, 542
  classification of, 479
  desirability of, 492
  versus devaluation, 479, 492, 493
  effectiveness of, 480, 492, 493
  and expenditure-adjusting policy, 479, 485,
    494
  flexibility of, 480, 493, 494
  inefficiencies of, 536
  and international monetary system, 546
  welfare argument for, 493–495
Direct investment:
  and capital formation, 349
  and exchange risk, 538
  and foreign branches and subsidiaries, 314,
    315
  and managerial interest, 315
  and national income, 439
  versus portfolio investment, 315, 329
  and short-term capital flows, 324
Direction of trade (see Pattern of trade)

"Dirty" floating, 326, 327, 344
Discount rate, 420, 421, 446
  and Bank Rate, 551
Discriminating monopolist, 243
Discrimination, 248
  age, sex, or race, 210
  and allocation of resources, 248
  commodity, 259
  country, 259–260
  geographical, 259–260, 263
Discriminatory tax, 168, 260
"Dismal science," 133
Dissaving, 394
Distortion:
  in domestic consumption, 209, 220, 223, 249
  in domestic production, 202–209, 212,
    217–218, 220, 223
  in factor employment, 209, 217, 223
  and immiserizing growth, 152, 216–219
  and Leontief paradox, 121
  (See also Domestic distortions; Foreign
    distortion)
Distribution, theory of, 7
Distribution of income:
  and domestic prices, 177
  effect of tariff on, 167, 174–175, 228
  effect of transfer on, 349
  and Euler's theorem, 43
  and identical and homothetic tastes, 59
  internal, 157, 174
  international, 155, 201
  and movement along production frontier,
    73
  and terms of trade, 78
  and trade taxes and subsidies, 481
  and welfare, 57, 59
Disturbances (see Balance-of-payments
    disturbances; Economic disturbances)
Diversification in production, 332
Division of labor, 4, 26, 80
  (See also International division of labor)
Dollar block, 552
Dollar glut, 326, 559, 560
Dollar overhang, 326, 348, 560
Dollar shortage, 559
Dollar standard, 556
  asymmetry in, 560
  and dollar shortage, 559
  and seigniorage, 549, 560
Domestic distortions, 199–224, 481
  theory of, 7, 165, 199–200
  (See also Distortion)
Domestic goods (see Nontraded goods)